Microsoft® Excel 2007: Comprehensive

D1283376

Trisha Hakola
Poway Adult School

Sandra Rittman
Long Beach City College

LABYRINTH
L E A R N I N G ™

Microsoft Excel 2007: Comprehensive
by Trisha Hakola and Sandra Rittman

Copyright © 2007 by Labyrinth Learning

LABYRINTH
LEARNING™

Labyrinth Learning
PO Box 20820
El Sobrante, California 94803
800.522.9746
On the Web at labpub.com

President:
Brian Favro

Chief Operating Officer:
Ted Ricks

Series Editor:
Russel Stolins

Managing Editor:
Laura A. Lionello

Production Manager:
Rad Proctor

Editorial/Production Team:
DocumentJones, Karen Henry, ITC,
Tess Roach, and Julie Van Keuren

Indexing: Joanne Sprott

Cover Design:
Seventeenth Street Studios

ITEM: 1-59136-110-9
ISBN-13: 978-1-59136-110-7

Manufactured in the United States of America.

10 9 8 7

Microsoft Excel 2007: Comprehensive

Contents in Brief

UNIT 3 ADVANCED SKILLS

Table of Contents

UNIT 2 BEYOND THE BASICS

Keyboard Shortcut Summary

Document Commands

Help	F1
Name Manager dialog box	Ctrl + F3
Open	Ctrl + O
Print	Ctrl + P
Refresh all data sources	Ctrl + Alt + F5
Save	Ctrl + S
Select All	Ctrl + A
View macros	Alt + F8

Editing Commands

Clear cell contents	Delete
Copy	Ctrl + C
Cut	Ctrl + X
Insert a line break	Alt + Enter
Insert comment	Shift + F2
Insert hyperlink	Ctrl + K
Paste	Ctrl + V
Place a chart on its own sheet	F11
Redo	Ctrl + Y
Select a column	Ctrl + Spacebar
Select a row	Shift + Spacebar
Select all	Ctrl + A
Undo	Ctrl + Z

Find/Replace Commands

Find	Ctrl + F
Replace	Ctrl + H

Format Font Commands

Bold	Ctrl + B
Italic	Ctrl + I
Underline	Ctrl + U

Formula Commands

Autosum	Alt + =
Show formulas	Ctrl + `

Quick Reference Table Summary

List of New Features

Preface

What Is Covered: *Microsoft® Excel 2007: Comprehensive* is a complete survey of Microsoft Excel. In Unit 1, students are introduced to Excel and the new Ribbon interface. They also enter and edit data, select cells and ranges, print worksheets, create formulas and functions, and format cell contents. In Unit 2, students work with large worksheets; insert clip art, pictures, and SmartArt; use templates; manage multiple-sheet workbooks; and create tables and outlines. In Unit 3, students create PivotTables and macros, use financial functions and data analysis, create auditing and additional functions, use advanced formatting and analysis tools, collaborate with others, and integrate Excel with other Office 2007 applications.

What Is Different: For more than a decade, Labyrinth has been working to perfect our unique instructional design. The benefit of our approach is that learning is faster and easier for students. Instructors have found that our approach works well in self-paced, instructor-led, and "blended" learning environments. The Labyrinth approach has many key features, including the following:

- *Concise concept discussions* followed by Hands-On exercises that give students experience with those concepts right away.

- *Figures* are always in close context with the text so no figure numbers are necessary.

- *Quick Reference* sections summarize key tasks with generic steps that will work without repeating an exercise. These can be particularly useful during open-book tests.

- *Hands-On exercises* are carefully written and repeatedly tested to be absolutely reliable. Many exercise steps are illustrated with figures to make them easier to follow.

- *Skill Builder exercises* provide additional practice on key skills using less detailed exercise steps as the student progresses through the lesson.

We are now expanding our book list by adapting this approach to teaching other application programs, including Intuit® QuickBooks®, Adobe Photoshop Elements®, Macromedia® Dreamweaver®, digital photography, and more.

Comprehensive Support: This course is also supported on the Labyrinth website with a comprehensive instructor support package that includes detailed lesson plans, PowerPoint presentations, a course syllabus, extensive test banks, and more. Our unique WebSims allow students to perform realistic exercises with the web, email, and application program tasks that would be difficult to set up in a computer lab.

Microsoft Excel 2007: Comprehensive has a companion online course for this textbook that includes integrated multimedia content and is available for the Blackboard Learning System™. The same strengths of instructional design and carefully crafted hands-on exercises that work so well in the classroom also enable students to study effectively at home or in the office with minimal need to contact an instructor for assistance.

We are grateful to the many teachers who have used Labyrinth titles and suggested improvements to us during the 10 years we have been writing and publishing books. *Microsoft Excel 2007: Comprehensive* has benefited greatly from the reviewing and suggestions of Douglas Cross, Clackamas CC (Oregon City, OR); Bethany Faber, Asheville-Buncombe Technical CC (Asheville, NC); Jacquelyn Grehl, Woodbridge HS (Woodbridge, NJ); Sherry Heidkamp, Savannah Technical College (Savannah, GA); Judy Johnson, Crump Technical College (Crump, TN); Cindy Miller, Indiana Technical CC (Lafayette, IN); Gladys Ota, San Mateo ROP (San Mateo, CA); Leesa Pohl, Donnelly College (Kansas City, KS); Susanne Silk, Western Technical College (Sayre, OK); Sen Varda, Coastline CC (Huntington Beach, CA); and Marjory Wooten, Lanier Technical College, Dawson Campus (Dawsonville, GA).

How This Book Is Organized

The information in this book is presented so that you master the fundamental skills first, and then build on those skills as you work with the more comprehensive topics.

Visual Conventions

This book uses many visual and typographic cues to guide you through the lessons. This page provides examples and describes the function of each cue.

`Type this text`

Anything you should type at the keyboard is printed in this typeface.

Tips, Notes, and Warnings are used throughout the text to draw attention to certain topics.

Command→
Command→
Command, etc.

This convention indicates how to give a command from the Ribbon. The commands are written: Ribbon Tab→Command Group→Command→[subcommand].

FROM THE KEYBOARD

Ctrl + S to save

These margin notes indicate shortcut keys for executing a task described in the text.

This icon indicates features that have changed dramatically from Office 2003 to Office 2007.

Quick Reference tables provide generic instructions for key tasks. Only perform these tasks if you are instructed to do so in an exercise.

This icon indicates the availability of a web-based simulation for an exercise or other online content. You many need to use a WebSim if your computer lab is not set up to support particular exercises.

Hands-On exercises are introduced immediately after concept discussions. They provide detailed, step-by-step tutorials so you can master the skills presented.

The Concepts Review section includes both true/false and multiple choice questions designed to gauge your understanding of concepts.

Skill Builder exercises provide additional hands-on practice with moderate assistance.

Assessment exercises test your skills by describing the correct results without providing specific instructions on how to achieve them.

Critical Thinking exercises are the most challenging. They provide generic instructions, allowing you to use your skills and creativity to achieve the result you envision.

About the Authors

Trisha Hakola (BS, Biology) is an assistant principal for Poway Adult School in San Diego, CA. She has been using Excel since 1991 and teaching students to use the application since 1998. She earned her Bachelor of Science degree from Washington State University and has a Designated Subjects Vocational Education Teaching Credential from the state of California. In addition, she has a Certificate in Online Teaching from the University of California, San Diego (Extension). Currently, Trish is working on her Master's in Education Leadership at Point Loma Nazarene University. Trish serves as the President-Elect on the CAROCP (California Association of Regional Centers and Programs) Board for the counties of San Diego and Imperial. Trish is also the author of Labyrinth's *QuickBooks Pro 2004* and *2005: Comprehensive Course, QuickBooks Pro 2006: Essentials Course,* and the upcoming *QuickBooks Pro 2007: Essentials.*

Sandra Rittman (BA Business Administration, MA Business Education, Ed.D. Education) has more than thirty years of experience teaching computer applications and office technology to students at Long Beach City College in California, as well as at other community colleges and California State University. Using her experience working with students of all ages with diverse educational goals, Sandra designs distance learning courses and curricula for traditional and self-paced learners. She is Microsoft Office Specialist certified and has coauthored several other textbooks on desktop publishing and business communications.

Microsoft Excel 2007: Comprehensive

Unit 1

Basic Skills

In this unit, you will begin your exploration of Excel, a powerful electronic spreadsheet program. You will start by reviewing the new Ribbon interface and familiarizing yourself with the Excel program window. You will enter and edit entries, select cells and ranges, and clear cell contents. You will also learn how to print entire worksheets and worksheet selections. Excel is most powerful in its ability to "crunch" numbers, and so you will learn how to create and modify basic formulas and functions, reference cells in formulas, and use AutoSum. You will format your worksheets with styles, colors, fills, dates, and themes. You will also modify column widths and row heights, hide columns and rows, and change the alignment of text within cells. Finally, in this unit you will begin to work with multiple-sheet workbooks and learn how to create, size, move, and embed charts.

Lesson 1: Exploring Excel 2007

Lesson 2: Editing, Viewing, and Printing Worksheets

Lesson 3: Working with Formulas and Functions

Lesson 4: Formatting the Contents of Cells

Lesson 5: Changing the Appearance of Worksheets

Lesson 6: Discovering the Magic of Excel Charting

LESSON 1

Exploring Excel 2007

In this lesson, you will develop fundamental Excel 2007 skills. This lesson will provide you with a solid understanding of Excel so you are prepared to master the advanced features introduced in later lessons. You will learn how to navigate around a worksheet, enter various types of data, and select cells.

LESSON OBJECTIVES

After studying this lesson, you will be able to:

- Explain ways Excel can help your productivity
- Launch the Excel program
- Navigate around the Excel window
- Utilize the tabs and Ribbon to issue commands
- Enter text and numbers into cells
- Distinguish between a text and a number entry in a cell
- Save and "save as" your workbooks
- Close a workbook and exit from Excel

Case Study: Building a Basic Spreadsheet

Charlie Arnold is a volunteer coordinator at South Coast Hospital. Mendy Laubach, the human resources manager for the hospital, has asked Charlie to maintain a list of hours worked by his volunteers from Wednesday to Sunday (Charlie's workweek). Mendy asks Charlie to report the data on a daily basis. After analyzing Mendy's request, Charlie decides that Excel 2007 is the right tool for the job and proceeds to organize the data in a worksheet. Charlie's worksheet is shown in the following illustration.

	A	B	C	D	E	F	G
1	Hospital Volunteers-Hours Worked						
2							
3			Wednesd	Thursday	Friday	Saturday	Sunday
4	Gift Shop						
5		Evelyn	3	2	4	0	6
6		Gene	4	2	1	7	3
7		Karel	6	1	2	3	3
8		Bill	3	5	2	2	3
9		Total					
10	Candy Stripers						
11		Ginny	7	0	2	1	4
12		Karel	2	4	1	3	2
13		Ann	4	1	5	2	0
14		Total					
15	Bookmobile						
16		Mohamed	3	6	0	3	2
17		Leticia	1	7	2	2	3
18		Maria	5	2	4	2	0
19		Total					

Notice that Excel makes it easy for you to organize your data in columns and rows. The total rows have been included in the example, although you will not learn how to create formulas until Lesson 3.

Presenting Excel 2007

Microsoft Office Excel 2007 is an electronic spreadsheet program. It allows you to work with numbers and data much more efficiently than the pen-and-paper method. Excel is used in virtually all industries and many households for a variety of tasks such as:

- Creating and maintaining detailed budgets

- Keeping track of extensive customer lists

- Performing "what-if" scenarios and break-even analyses

- Determining the profitability of a business or sector

- Creating tables to organize information

- Tracking employee information

- Producing detailed charts to graphically display information

- Creating invoices or purchase orders

- Determining the future value of an investment, the present value of an annuity, or the payment for a loan

- Working with reports exported from small business accounting software programs such as Intuit's QuickBooks®

As you can see from this list, Excel is not just used to crunch numbers. It is a very powerful program that is used not only to work with numbers but also to maintain databases. If you have started a database in Excel, you can even import it into Microsoft Access (the program in the Microsoft Office Suite that is specialized for working with databases). Many people may use Excel to track their databases rather than Access because of its ease of use and because Access is not included in all of the Microsoft Office editions. If you are tracking multiple databases that you wish to include in reports and data queries, you will want to consider utilizing Access, though, as it really is designed to work with multiple tables of data.

!**NOTE!** *Throughout this book, we will look at different personal and business scenarios and how Excel is used to streamline the workflow.*

Starting Excel

The method you use to start Excel depends in large part on whether you intend to create a new workbook or open an existing workbook. A workbook is a file containing one or more worksheets. To create a new workbook, use one of the following methods. Once the Excel program has started, you can begin working in the new workbook that appears.

- Click the button and choose Microsoft Office Excel 2007 from the All Programs menu. (Depending on your installation of Microsoft Office, you may need to choose Microsoft Office from the All Programs menu and then choose Microsoft Office Excel 2007.)

- Click the Microsoft Office Excel 2007 button on the Quick Launch toolbar located to the right of the Start button. (This button may not appear on all computers.)

Use one of the following methods if you intend to open an existing Excel workbook. Once the Excel program has started, the desired workbook will open in an Excel window.

■ Navigate to the desired document using Windows Explorer or My Computer and double-click the workbook.

■ Click the ⚍ start button and point to My Recent Documents. You can choose the desired workbooks from the documents list, which displays the most-recently used documents.

 Hands-On 1.1   Start Excel

In this exercise, you will help Charlie start the Excel program.

1. Start your computer, and the Windows Desktop will appear.

2. Click the ⚍ start button and choose (All) Programs.

3. Choose the Microsoft Office folder, and then choose Microsoft Office Excel 2007.
   After a pause, the Excel program loads and the Excel window appears.

Exploring the Excel Program Window

When you launch Excel, you will see a blank workbook displayed. The window is filled with many objects and a space for you to create your spreadsheet. Using the figures that follow, you will have an opportunity to learn the names of some of the objects that you can see on your screen.

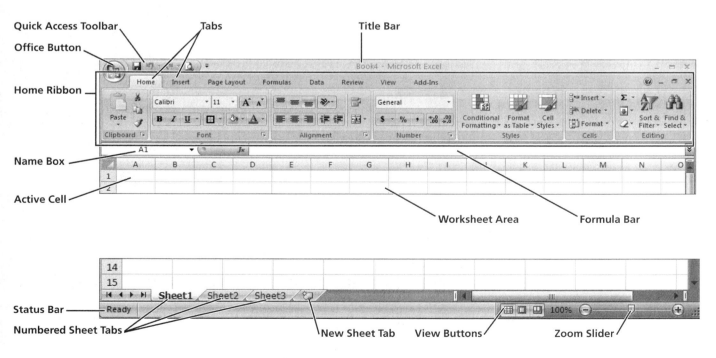

Using Worksheets and Workbooks

Excel displays a blank workbook the moment you start the program. A workbook is composed of worksheets. This is similar to a paper notebook with many sheets of paper. You enter text, numbers, formulas, charts, and other objects in worksheets. By default, Excel displays three worksheets in a new workbook, each accessible by a separate tab at the bottom of the screen. The maximum number of worksheets you can insert is limited only by the amount of memory available on your computer.

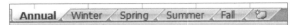

In this example, the sheet tabs are named so that you can organize data for each season as well as track annual information.

A worksheet has a grid structure with horizontal rows and vertical columns. A new worksheet has 16,384 columns and 1,048,576 rows! However, at any given time only a small number of the rows and columns are visible in the worksheet

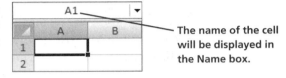

The name of the cell will be displayed in the Name box.

window. The intersection of each row and column is a cell. Each cell is identified by a reference. The reference is the column letter followed by the row number. For example, A1 is the reference of the cell in the top-left corner of the worksheet. So, we refer to this as cell A1.

Mousing Around in Excel

The shape of the mouse pointer will change as you move it around the Excel window. The shape of the pointer will let you know what will happen if you click over that spot.

Mouse Pointer Shape	Function
✛	Click to select a cell.
	Click and drag to select multiple cells.
➕	The fill handle pointer; you will learn what this tool can do for you in Lesson 2, Editing, Viewing, and Printing Worksheets.
▷	Allows you to perform a variety of tasks when clicked, such as issue a command from the Ribbon or select a new tab.
✛▷	The move pointer; if you drag with this, it will move cell contents from one location to another.
↔	The resize pointer; dragging this pointer will allow you to change the size of objects such as rows, pictures, and charts.
→ ↓	Select a row or column.
I	Click with the I-beam pointer to enter text, such as in the Formula Bar.

Scrolling Along in a Worksheet

There are two scroll bars visible in the Excel window, both vertical and horizontal. They allow you to see other areas of the worksheet without changing which cell is active. There are three ways to use the scroll bars to view other areas of your spreadsheet.

Click and drag the scroll box to control the scroll more precisely.

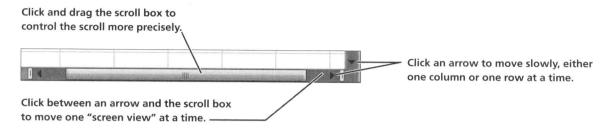

Click an arrow to move slowly, either one column or one row at a time.

Click between an arrow and the scroll box to move one "screen view" at a time.

Navigating in a Worksheet

When you have a cell selected, it is surrounded by a thick line, which indicates that it is the active cell. You can change the active cell by clicking in another cell or by using the keyboard. This is important because data is entered into the active cell. The vertical and horizontal scroll bars let you navigate through a worksheet; however, scrolling does not change which cell is active. After scrolling you will have to select which cell is to be active, either by clicking or using one of the keystrokes listed below.

Keystroke(s)	How the Highlight Moves
→ ← ↑ ↓	One cell right, left, up, or down
Home	Beginning of current row
Ctrl + →	End of current row
Ctrl + Home	Home cell, usually cell A1
Ctrl + End	Last cell in active part of worksheet
Page Down	Down one visible screen
Page Up	Up one visible screen
Alt + Page Down	One visible screen right
Alt + Page Up	One visible screen left
Ctrl + G	Displays Go To dialog box—enter cell reference and click OK

Hands-On 1.2　Move the Selection and Explore the Excel Window

In this exercise, you will practice selecting the active cell in a worksheet so that you can become comfortable enough with the program to help Charlie begin to create his spreadsheet.

Navigate with the Mouse

1. Slide the mouse over the screen and notice the thick cross shape ✚ when it is in the worksheet area.
   If you click with this pointer shape, you will select a cell.

2. Click the cross-shaped pointer on any cell and notice that the cell becomes active.

3. Move the selection five times by clicking in various cells.

Navigate with the Keyboard

Now that you have practiced using the mouse, it is time to learn how to use the keyboard in order to move about a worksheet. You should use the keys on your keyboard that are between the main part and the numeric keypad on the far right.

4. Use the →, ←, ↑, and ↓ keys to position the highlight in cell F10.

5. Tap the ⎡Home⎤ key and see that the highlight moves to cell A10.
   The ⎡Home⎤ key always makes the cell in column A of the current row active.

6. Press ⎡Ctrl⎤ + ⎡Home⎤ to make A1 the active cell.

7. Tap the ⎡Page Down⎤ key two or three times.
   Notice that Excel displays the next 30 or so rows (one "visible" screen's worth) each time you tap ⎡Page Down⎤.

8. Press and hold down the ↑ key until A1 is the active cell.

Use the Scroll Bars

The scroll bars allow you to see other areas of the Excel worksheet area without changing which cell is active.

9. Click the Scroll Right ▶ button on the horizontal scroll bar until columns AA and AB are visible.
   Excel labels the first 26 columns A–Z and the next 26 columns AA–AZ. A similar labeling scheme is used for the remaining columns out to the final column, XFD.

10. Click the Scroll Down ▼ button on the vertical scroll bar until row 100 is visible.
    Notice that the highlight has not moved. To move the highlight, you must click in a cell or use the keyboard.

11. Take a few minutes to practice scrolling and moving the selection.

Use the Go To Command

As you learned in the preceding Quick Reference table, you can use Ctrl + G *to display the Go To box, where you can go to a specific cell by entering the desired cell reference in the Reference box and clicking OK. You can use* Ctrl + Home *to select cell A1.*

12. Press Ctrl + G to display the Go To dialog box.

13. Type **g250** in the Reference box and click OK.
    Notice that cell references are not case sensitive.

14. Use the Go To command to move to two or three different cells.

15. Press Ctrl + Home to return to cell A1.

Explore the Excel Window

Now that you have learned how to select cells and move around in the window, it is time to explore the Excel window a bit further.

16. Follow these steps to explore the Excel window:

Ⓐ Notice the Name box.

Ⓑ Click the Sheet2 tab and notice that a blank worksheet appears. The number of worksheets you can have is limited only by the amount of available memory in the computer.

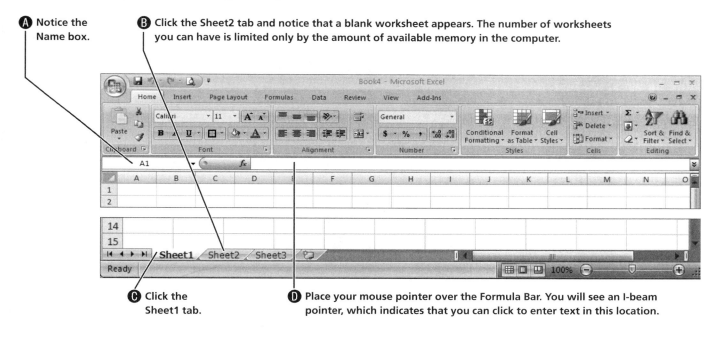

Ⓒ Click the Sheet1 tab.

Ⓓ Place your mouse pointer over the Formula Bar. You will see an I-beam pointer, which indicates that you can click to enter text in this location.

17. Press Ctrl + Home to move the highlight to cell A1.

Working with Tabs and Ribbons

In Microsoft Office 2007, Excel does not have the traditional menu and toolbars with which computer users are familiar. You are able to access the commands that will allow you to effectively utilize Excel through the tabs, ribbons, and Office button located at the top of window.

The Office Button

 The Office button, when clicked, accesses a menu that allows you to issue file management commands. File management simply means working with Excel on the level of the "file"—such as creating new files, opening existing files, saving the file you are working on, and printing your file.

The Quick Access Toolbar

Excel 2007 has one remaining toolbar (compared with previous versions), which is located at the top of the window. It is similar to the Quick Launch toolbar in Windows in that it contains commands that you use frequently. It is also customizable, unlike the Ribbon, which is set. The Quick Access toolbar, with the default buttons, is displayed in the following illustration.

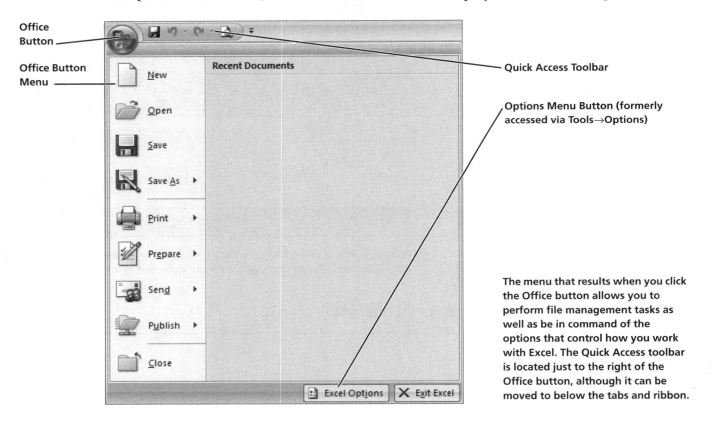

Office Button

Office Button Menu

Quick Access Toolbar

Options Menu Button (formerly accessed via Tools→Options)

The menu that results when you click the Office button allows you to perform file management tasks as well as be in command of the options that control how you work with Excel. The Quick Access toolbar is located just to the right of the Office button, although it can be moved to below the tabs and ribbon.

Customizing the Quick Access Toolbar

The Quick Access toolbar can be customized to include commands that you frequently use. If you regularly use the Open command, you may wish to add it to the Quick Access toolbar, as shown.

Displaying Tabs and Working with Ribbons

**2007
new!**

The tabs at the top of the Excel window organize the commands into eight categories. The commands appear on ribbons displayed across the screen. In order to view a new tab, you simply need to single-click it. The commands on the Ribbon can be chosen by a single-click as well.

Excel's Home Ribbon

The standard tabs along with the Ribbon are displayed in the preceding illustration. Additional contextual tabs will become visible as necessary. For instance, if you are working with a picture, a picture tab will appear.

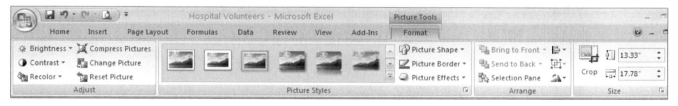

The Ribbon with a contextual tab displayed. When a picture is selected, a special Picture Tools Format tab appears. All of the commands on this ribbon deal with the formatting of the picture.

ScreenTips

A ScreenTip is a little window that appears to describe the function of the object at which you are pointing. ScreenTips appear when you rest your mouse pointer over an option on a ribbon, the Quick Access toolbar, or the Office button. In Excel 2007, there are also Enhanced ScreenTips that appear for some of the commands. An Enhanced ScreenTip is a larger window that is more descriptive than a ScreenTip and also provides a link to an Excel help topic.

When you place your mouse pointer over an object on the Ribbon, a ScreenTip appears.

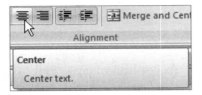

Sometimes you will see an Enhanced ScreenTip when you place your mouse pointer over an object. In this case, you receive an Enhanced ScreenTip explaining the function of the Office button with a link to a help topic.

Dialog Box Launchers

Many of the groups on the Ribbon have Dialog Box Launchers ▣. Clicking on the dialog box launcher will open a window that allows you to issue additional commands.

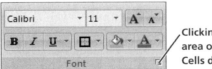

Clicking the Dialog Box Launcher in the font area of the Home ribbon will open the Format Cells dialog box with the Font tab displayed.

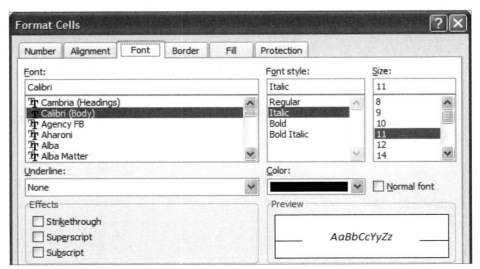

The Font tab of the Format Cells dialog box allows you to make changes to how the font appears in the selected cell(s).

Hiding the Ribbon

There may be times when you do not want the Ribbon displayed at the top of the window. In order to hide it, simply double-click on the tab that is currently displayed. To display the Ribbon once again, click on the tab you wish to view.

QUICK REFERENCE: USING TABS AND RIBBONS AND CUSTOMIZING THE QUICK ACCESS TOOLBAR

Task	Procedure
Hide the Ribbon	■ Double-click the tab of the Ribbon that is displayed.
Unhide the Ribbon	■ Double-click any of the tabs at the top of the window, or click the hidden tab.
Customize the Quick Access toolbar with a Ribbon command	■ Right-click the Ribbon command you wish to add. ■ Choose Add to Quick Access Toolbar.
Customize the Quick Access toolbar with a command not available on the Ribbon	■ Click the Office button. ■ Click the Excel Options button. ■ Click the Customize option in the list to the left. ■ Choose from where you wish the command to come. ■ Click the command you wish to add. ■ Click Add.
Remove a button from the Quick Access toolbar	■ Right-click the button you wish to remove. ■ Choose Remove from Quick Access Toolbar.

Hands-On 1.3   Explore the Tabs, Ribbons, and Quick Access Toolbar

In this exercise, you will have the opportunity to explore the tabs and Ribbon at the top of the Excel window. In addition, you will add a button to the Quick Access toolbar that you feel is important to always have readily available.

Display the Page Layout Ribbon

In this exercise, you will display the Page Layout tab of the Ribbon and open the Page Setup dialog box.

1. Click the Page Layout tab at the top of the window.

The Page Layout tab is displayed.

2. Click the Dialog Box Launcher at the bottom-right corner of the Page Setup section of the Ribbon.

The Page Setup dialog box appears.

3. Click the Cancel button at the bottom of the dialog box to close it.

4. Move your mouse pointer over various commands on the Page Layout tab of the Ribbon display their ScreenTips and explore what will occur if you choose to click them.

Add a Button to the Quick Access Toolbar

In this section, you will add a button to the Quick Access toolbar that will allow you to easily open another workbook.

5. Follow these steps to add Open to the Quick Access toolbar:

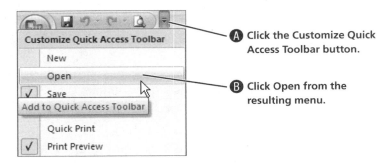

Notice the ScreenTip that displays below the mouse pointer when you point at a menu option, explaining what will occur if you choose that option. The Open button will appear on the Quick Access toolbar.

The new button appears on the Quick Access toolbar.

Remove a Button from the Quick Access Toolbar

In order to remove the Open button from the Quick Access toolbar, you will repeat the steps you took to add it.

6. Click the Customize Quick Access Toolbar button.

7. Choose Open from the resulting menu.
Excel will essentially "remove the checkmark" from the Open option and remove the button from the toolbar. Leave the Excel window open, as you will continue to work with it in the next exercise.

Entering Data in Excel

You can begin entering data the moment Excel is started. Data is entered into the active cell (the cell with the thick line around it). Text and numbers are used for different purposes in a worksheet. For instance, text entries cannot be used in calculations, whereas number entries can. Text is used for descriptive headings and entries that require alphabetic characters or a combination of alphabetic and numeric characters and spaces. Numbers can be entered directly or can be calculated using formulas. Excel recognizes the data you enter and decides whether the entry is text, a number, or a formula. You will learn about entering formulas in Lesson 3, Working with Formulas and Functions.

Data Types

Entries are defined as one of two main classifications: constant values or formulas. Constant values can be text, numeric, or a combination of both. The one thing that makes an entry constant is that the value does not change when other information changes. Conversely, formula entries display the results of calculations, and a result can change when a value in another cell changes.

This entry is a constant value; it will not change as other cells are updated.

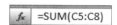

When a formula entry is used, it will refer to one or more cells and will change as the indicated cells are updated.

Completing Cell Entries

Text and numbers are entered by positioning the highlight in the desired cell, typing the desired text or number, and completing the entry. You can use Enter, Tab, or any of the arrow keys (→, ←, ↑, ↓) to complete an entry. The position of the active cell following a cell entry depends on the method by which you complete the entry.

Entry Completion Method	Where the Active Cell Will Appear
Enter	It will move down to the next cell.
Tab	It will move to the next cell to the right.
→ ↑ ↓ ←	It will move to the next cell in the direction of the arrow key.
Esc	The entry will be deleted and the current cell will remain active.

The Enter and Cancel Buttons

The Enter ✔ and Cancel ✘ buttons appear on the Formula Bar whenever you enter or edit an entry. The Enter button completes the entry and keeps the highlight in the current cell. The Cancel button cancels the entry, as does the Esc key.

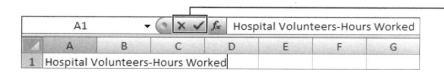

The Cancel and Enter buttons appear when an entry is being entered or edited.

Deleting and Replacing Entries

You can delete an entire entry after it has been completed by clicking in the cell and tapping Delete. Likewise, you can replace an entry by clicking in the cell and typing a new entry. The new entry will replace the original entry. You will learn all about editing entries in Lesson 2, Editing, Viewing, and Printing Worksheets.

Long Text Entries

Text entries often do not fit in a cell. These entries are known as long entries. Excel uses the following rules when deciding how to display long entries:

■ If the cell to the right of the long entry is empty, then the long entry displays over the adjacent cell.

■ If the cell to the right of the long entry contains an entry, then Excel shortens, or truncates, the display of the long entry.

Keep in mind that Excel does not actually change the long entry; it simply truncates the display of the entry. You can always widen a column to accommodate a long entry.

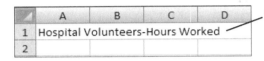 The entry, Hospital Volunteers-Hours Worked, is a long entry. The entire phrase is entered in cell A1 although it displays over cells A1-D1.

 Hands-On 1.4   Enter Text

In this exercise, you will enter text into your worksheet.

Type a Long Entry

First, you will have the opportunity to see how text can flow into empty cells to the right of its "home" cell.

1. Make cell A1 active by clicking the mouse pointer ✛ in it.

2. Type **Hospital Volunteers-Hours Worked** and tap Enter.
The text is entered in the cell and the highlight moves down to cell A2. Excel moves the highlight down when you tap Enter because most people enter data column by column. Notice that the entry displays over cells B1, C1, and D1. The long entry would not display over these cells if they contained data.

3. Click cell A1 and note the appearance of the Formula Bar.

Notice that the Formula Bar displays the name of the active cell (A1) as well as its content. In this example, the cell's content is the title, Hospital Volunteers-Hours Worked. The title is a long entry because it is wider than cell A1. Cells B1-D1 are empty so the long entry is displayed over them. Keep in mind, however, that the entire entry belongs to cell A1. This concept will be demonstrated in the next few steps.

Verify that the Entry Belongs to Cell A1

4. Tap the ⟶ key to make cell B1 active.

5. Look at the Formula Bar and notice that cell B1 is empty.
The long entry belongs to cell A1 even though it is displayed over cells A1–D1.

Type Additional Text Entries

6. Click in cell C3.

7. Type **Wednesday** and tap ⟶ once.
Notice that the entry is completed and the highlight moves to cell D3. You can always use the arrow keys to complete an entry and move the highlight in the desired direction.

8. Type **Thursday** in cell D3 and tap ⟶.
Notice that the display of Wednesday *is shortened, or truncated. However, the Wednesday entry is still contained in its entirety in cell C3. A long entry is always truncated when the cell to the right contains text or a number.*

9. Enter the remaining text entries shown in the following illustration:

	A	B	C	D	E	F	G
1	Hospital Volunteers-Hours Worked						
2							
3			Wednesd.	Thursday	Friday	Saturday	Sunday
4	Gift Shop						
5		Evelyn					
6		Gene					
7		Karel					
8		Bill					
9		Total					
10	Candy Stripers						
11		Ginny					
12		Karel					
13		Ann					
14		Total					
15	Bookmobile						
16		Mohamed					
17		Leticia					
18		Maria					
19		Total					

If Excel proposes any entries for you as you type, simply continue typing. You will learn more about the AutoFill feature in Lesson 2, Editing, Viewing, and Printing Worksheets.

Working with Numbers

Number entries can contain only the digits 0–9 and a few other characters. Excel initially right-aligns numbers in cells, although you can change this alignment. The following table lists characters that Excel accepts as part of a number entry.

 TIP! *Entering numbers using the numeric keypad is very quick. The keypad is designed like a calculator. It includes its own decimal point and an Enter key.*

> **Valid Characters in Number Entries**
>
> The digits 0–9
>
> The following characters: + – ( ) , / $ % . *

Number Formats

It isn't necessary to type commas, dollar signs, and other number formats when entering numbers. It's easier to simply enter the numbers and use Excel's formatting commands to add the desired number format(s). You will learn how to format numbers soon.

Decimals and Negative Numbers

You should always type a decimal point if the number you are entering requires one. Likewise, you should precede a negative number entry with a minus (–) sign or enclose it in parentheses ( ).

 ## Hands-On 1.5   Enter Numbers

In this exercise, you will practice entering numbers and canceling entries before completion.

Use the Enter Button

1. Position the highlight in cell C5.

2. Type **3** but don't complete the entry.

3. Look at the Formula Bar and notice the Cancel ⊠ and Enter ✔ buttons.
   These buttons appear whenever you begin entering or editing data in a cell.

4. Click the Enter ✔ button to complete the entry.
   Notice that the highlight remains in cell C5. You can use the Enter button to complete entries, though it is more efficient to use the keyboard when building a worksheet. This is because the highlight automatically moves to the next cell. The Enter button is most useful when editing entries.

Use the Cancel and the Esc Key

5. Position the highlight in cell C6 and type **4**, but don't complete the entry.

6. Click the Cancel ⊠ button on the Formula Bar to cancel the entry.

7. Type **4** again, but this time tap Esc on the keyboard.
   The Esc key has the same effect as the Cancel button.

8. Type **4** once again, and this time tap ⬇ .
   Notice that Excel right-aligns the number in the cell.

9. Enter the remaining numbers shown in the following illustration.

TIP! *To use the numeric keypad to enter numbers, the* [Num Lock] *light must be on. If it's not, press the* [Num Lock] *key on the keypad.*

	A	B	C	D	E	F	G
1	Hospital Volunteers-Hours Worked						
2							
3			Wednesd	Thursday	Friday	Saturday	Sunday
4	Gift Shop						
5		Evelyn	3	2	4	0	6
6		Gene	4	2	1	7	3
7		Karel	6	1	2	3	3
8		Bill	3	5	2	2	3
9		Total					
10	Candy Stripers						
11		Ginny	7	0	2	1	4
12		Karel	2	4	1	3	2
13		Ann	4	1	5	2	0
14		Total					
15	Bookmobile						
16		Mohamed	3	6	0	3	2
17		Leticia	1	7	2	2	3
18		Maria	5	2	4	2	0
19		Total					

10. Take a minute to verify that you have correctly entered all the numbers.
    It is so important for you to be accurate when you are entering data into Excel. Learning how to use complex formulas and functions will not do you any good if your original data is inaccurate!

Understanding Save Concepts

One important lesson to learn is to save your workbooks early and often! Power outages and careless accidents can result in lost data. The best protection is to save your workbooks every 10 or 15 minutes or after making significant changes. Workbooks are saved to storage locations such as a USB drive, the My Documents folder, a shared network drive, and websites on the Internet.

Storing Your Exercise Files

Throughout this book you will be referred to files in a folder that corresponds to the lesson number you are studying (for example, "the Lesson 02 folder"). You can store your exercise files on various media such as a USB flash drive, the My Documents folder, or a network drive at a school or company. While some figures may display files on a USB flash drive, it is assumed that you will substitute your own location for that shown in the figure. See Appendix A, Storing Your Exercise Files, for additional information on alternative file storage media.

The Save Command

The Save button on the Quick Access toolbar and →Save initiate the Save command. If a document has been saved previously, Excel replaces the original version with the new, edited version. If a document has never been saved, Excel displays the Save As dialog box. The Save As dialog box lets you specify the name and storage location of the document. You can also use the Save As dialog box to make a copy of a document by saving it under a new name or to a different location. Your filenames can have up to 255 characters, including spaces, giving you the flexibility to create descriptive names for your workbooks.

Save As Options

2007 new!

In Excel 2007, you are given multiple options as to how to save your workbook. How you save it depends on how it will be used and who will be using it. If you are collaborating with someone who has a previous version of Excel installed on his computer, you will need to save the file in the Excel 97-2003 Format. If you wish to publish your workbook and do not wish for others to make changes to it, you may wish to save it as a PDF file if you have Adobe Acrobat's program. The default format is the Excel 2007 format, which is great to use if everyone who will be utilizing the file has Excel 2007 installed on his computer.

If you click the Save As button, the Save As dialog box will be displayed.

If you place your mouse pointer over this menu button, you will see the menu displayed here that gives you additional options for saving your workbook.

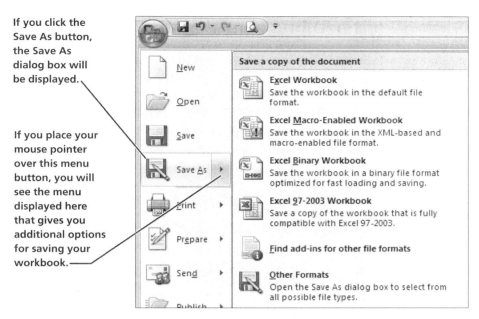

The Save As options available from the Office menu.

Locating Workbooks

Both the Save As and Open dialog boxes (discussed in Lesson 2, Editing, Viewing, and Printing Worksheets) let you locate workbooks on your local drives, in network locations, and on the web. The Places Bar appears on the left side of the Save As and Open dialog boxes. You can use the Places Bar or the Save In list to locate workbooks, as described in the following illustration.

Choose a storage location from the Save In list or click a button on the Places Bar.

This button takes you to the previously viewed storage location.

This button moves you up one level in the storage hierarchy.

This button changes the view of files and folders.

The My Recent Documents button on the Places Bar displays the last 20–50 documents and folders accessed.

These buttons allow you to quickly navigate to other parts of the computer system.

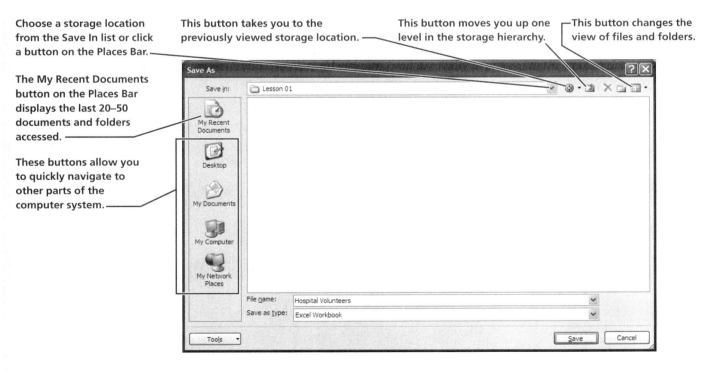

Issuing Commands from the Keyboard

FROM THE KEYBOARD

 Ctrl + S to save

There are many times when it is more convenient to issue a command from the keyboard than to chase it down with your mouse. These commands are termed keyboard shortcuts and can help you to be more efficient as you can enter them "on the fly" without removing your fingers from the keyboard. In this book, you will see keyboard shortcuts displayed in a special feature called From the Keyboard. Whenever you issue a keyboard command, you will first hold down the shortcut key (Ctrl, Alt, or Shift) and then tap the additional key to issue the command. This is similar to holding down the Shift key and then tapping a letter to make it capital. Throughout this book you will be asked to use Ctrl + S to save your worksheet.

QR> QUICK REFERENCE: SAVING A WORKBOOK

Task	Procedure
Save for the first time	■ Click the Save button on the Quick Access toolbar. ■ Name the workbook and choose the location in which to save it. ■ Click Save.
Save changes in the workbook	■ Click the Save button on the Quick Access toolbar.
Save in a new location or with a new name	■ Click the Office button and choose Save As. ■ Change the name of the workbook, the storage location, or both. ■ Click Save.
Save the workbook in the Excel 97-2003 Format	■ Click the Office button. ■ Place your mouse pointer over the arrow to the right of Save As. ■ Click Excel 97-2003 Format in the resulting menu displayed to the right.

Hands-On 1.6 Save the Workbook

In this exercise, you will save the workbook created in the previous exercises to your file storage location.

Before You Begin: If you have not done so already, please turn to Downloading the Student Exercise Files section of Appendix A, Storing Your Exercise files, for instructions on how to retrieve the student exercise files for this book from the Labyrinth website and for copying the files to your file storage location for use in this and future lessons.

1. Click the Save 🖫 button on the Quick Access toolbar.
   The Save As dialog box appears because this is the first time you are saving the workbook.

2. Follow these steps to save the workbook:
   Keep in mind that your My Documents folder or other storage location may contain different folders and files than those displayed here.

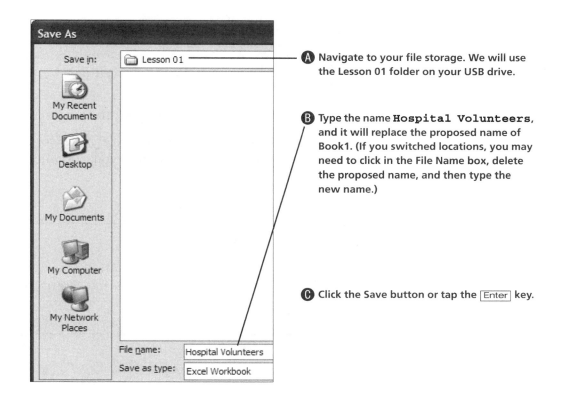

A Navigate to your file storage. We will use the Lesson 01 folder on your USB drive.

B Type the name **Hospital Volunteers**, and it will replace the proposed name of Book1. (If you switched locations, you may need to click in the File Name box, delete the proposed name, and then type the new name.)

C Click the Save button or tap the [Enter] key.

Notice that the workbook is saved (the name will appear in the Title Bar of the window) and remains on the screen. Leave it open as we will continue to use it for the remaining exercises.

Closing Workbooks

The →Close command is used to close an open workbook. When you close a workbook that has not been saved, Excel prompts you to save the changes. If you choose Yes at the prompt and the workbook has previously been saved, Excel simply saves the changes. If the workbook is new, Excel displays the Save As dialog box, allowing you to assign a name and storage location to the workbook.

Hands-On 1.7   Close the Workbook

In this exercise, you will close the workbook that you have been working on throughout this lesson.

1. Choose ⊞→Close.

2. Click the Yes button if Excel asks you if you want to save the changes.
   Notice that no workbook appears in the Excel window. The Excel window always has this appearance when all workbooks have been closed.

Exiting from Excel

You should close Excel and other programs if you are certain you won't be using them for some time. This will free up memory for other programs. When you close Excel, you will be prompted to save any workbooks that have unsaved edits.

- Click the Office button, and then click X Exit Excel to exit the program.
- Clicking the Close button X will close only your current Excel 2007 workbook; any other Excel workbooks that are being used will remain open until you close them.

 Hands-On 1.8   Exit from Excel

In this exercise, you will exit from the Excel program.

1. Click the Office button, and then click the X Exit Excel button.
   Excel will close without prompting you to save the workbook because you have not changed it since it was opened last.

Concepts Review

True/False Questions

1. Each workbook can have a maximum of one worksheet.   TRUE   FALSE

2. A worksheet is composed of horizontal rows and vertical columns.   TRUE   FALSE

3. You cannot customize the commands on the Ribbon.   TRUE   FALSE

4. Text entries can contain spaces.   TRUE   FALSE

5. Number entries can contain only the digits 0–9. No other characters are permitted.   TRUE   FALSE

6. A filename can contain spaces.   TRUE   FALSE

7. Text entries can be used in calculations.   TRUE   FALSE

8. The Save As command allows you to save your workbook with a different name.   TRUE   FALSE

9. You should wait to save your workbook until you are done entering all of your data.   TRUE   FALSE

10. When you click the Close button of the workbook you are working on, it will close all open Excel workbooks.   TRUE   FALSE

Multiple Choice Questions

1. Which of the following keystrokes moves the highlight to cell A1?
   a. End
   b. Ctrl + Tab
   c. Ctrl + Home
   d. Ctrl + Insert

2. What happens when you insert an entry in the cell to the right of a long text entry?
   a. The display of the long entry is truncated.
   b. The long entry is replaced by the entry in the cell to the right.
   c. It has no effect on the long entry.
   d. None of the above

3. How do you hide the Ribbon?
   a. Choose Home→Hide from the Ribbon
   b. Choose Office button→Hide Ribbon
   c. Double-click the tab that is displayed
   d. Double-click one of the sheet tabs of the workbook

4. What occurs when you tap Esc while entering data into a cell?
   a. The workbook will close.
   b. The entry will be entered and the cell to the right will become active.
   c. Nothing, you can continue entering the data into the cell.
   d. The cell entry will be canceled.

Skill Builders

Skill Builder 1.1   Create a Workbook

In this exercise, you will create a workbook. You will start Excel and then enter text and numbers that contain two decimal places.

Start Excel and Enter Text

1. Start Excel by selecting (All) Programs→Microsoft Office→Microsoft Office Excel 2007 from the Start menu.
   Notice that a blank workbook with three worksheets is displayed when you open Excel.

2. Enter text in rows 1 and 3 as shown in the following illustration.
   Try using the Tab *key to enter the data in row 3.*

	A	B	C	D	E	F	G	H
1	Order Tracking Sheet							
2								
3	Order #	Cust ID	Ord Stat	Item #	In Stock?	Ord Tot	Shipping Address	

3. In cells A4:E8 and G4:G8, enter the data shown in the following illustration.
   Make sure to type the entire shipping address in column G.

	A	B	C	D	E	F	G	H	I	J	K
1	Order Tracking Sheet										
2											
3	Order #	Cust ID	Ord Stat	Item #	In Stock?	Ord Tot	Shipping Address				
4	1	341	S	A423	Y		1603 Catalina Avenue, Redondo Beach, CA 90277				
5	2	234	S	A321	Y		Will Pick Up				
6	3	567	I	S345	N		450 Terrace Drive, Santa Clara, CA 95050				
7	4	879	H	D567	N		No address at this point				
8	5	233	I	B444	Y		23 Maple Lane, Crawfordsville, IN 47933				

Enter Numbers with Decimals

4. Click cell F4.

5. Type **100.91** and tap Enter.
   You should always type a decimal point if the number requires one.

6. Type **45.87** and tap Enter.

7. Enter the numbers shown in the following illustration into cells F6, F7, and F8.

	A	B	C	D	E	F	G	H	I	J	K
1	Order Tracking Sheet										
2											
3	Order #	Cust ID	Ord Stat	Item #	In Stock?	Ord Tot	Shipping Address				
4	1	341	S	A423	Y	100.91	1603 Catalina Avenue, Redondo Beach, CA 90277				
5	2	234	S	A321	Y	45.87	Will Pick Up				
6		567	I	S345	N	43.23	450 Terrace Drive, Santa Clara, CA 95050				
7		879	H	D567	N	78.92	No address at this point				
8		233	I	B444	Y	23.45	23 Maple Lane, Crawfordsville, IN 47933				

Leave the workbook open, as you will use it in the next exercise.

Skill Builder 1.2   Explore the Excel Window and Save and Close Your Workbook

In this exercise, you will take a look at the features of the Excel window before saving and closing your new workbook.

1. Click to display the data tab of the Ribbon.
Look at the types of commands available. Many of them will be covered in later lessons of this book.

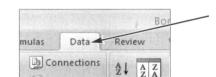

2. Click to display the View tab of the Ribbon.

3. Double-click the View tab to hide the Ribbon.

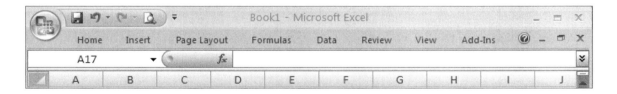

4. Double-click the Home tab to display the Ribbon once again.
Notice that the Home tab will be displayed because you chose it to redisplay the Ribbon.

5. Click cell H4, and then look at the Formula Bar.

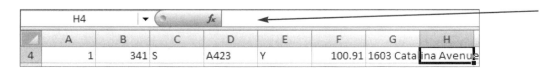

There is nothing displayed because the entire entry is contained in cell G4 and is simply spilling over into cell H4 because it is empty.

6. Type your name, and then click the Enter ✔ button.

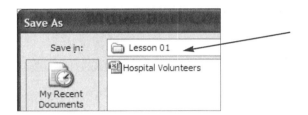

	A	B	C	D	E	F	G	H
4	1	341	S	A423	Y	100.91	1603 Cata	Trish

Your name will now appear in cell H4, and the address in cell G4 will be truncated.

7. Tap Delete.
Your name will be deleted, and the address from G4 will once again spill over into the cells to the right.

8. Click Save 🖫 on the Quick Access toolbar.

9. Choose to save the workbook in your file storage location (in this example, Lesson 01).

Save As

Save in: 📁 Lesson 01 ←

My Recent Documents

📊 Hospital Volunteers

10. Type **sb-Order Tracking**, and tap Enter.
The workbook will be saved in the location that you specified.

11. Click the Close ☒ button at the top right of the Excel window.
Your workbook will close. If you have any other workbooks open, they will remain so until you choose to exit from Excel or close them individually.

 **Assessments**

Assessment 1.1   Create a New Workbook

In this exercise, you will create a new worksheet and then save and close the workbook.

1. Start Excel by selecting (All) Programs from the Start menu.

2. Choose Office→New, and then tap Enter .
   This allows you to create a new workbook while leaving the current one open.

3. Create the worksheet shown in the following illustration. Make sure the numbers match.

	A	B	C	D	E
1	Big City Diner Q1 Expenses				
2					
3	Item		January	February	March
4	Building	Rent	800	800	800
5		Utilities	340	400	250
6		Phone	250	200	300
7		Insurance	350	0	0
8		Total			
9					
10	Food Cost	Produce	2500	2320	1700
11		Meat	4000	3400	3700
12		Grains	1000	1200	890
13		Total			
14					
15	Salaries	Simmons	800	780	800
16		Swanson	750	650	870
17		Martinez	900	780	680
18		Richardso	1200	1000	990
19		Total			
20					
21	Other	Advertisir	500	300	0
22		Uniforms	0	340	0
23		Janitorial	200	200	200
24		Misc	100	2000	0
25		Total			

You will learn to create formulas to calculate totals in Lesson 3, Working with Formulas and Functions.

4. Save the workbook as **as-Q1 Expenses**, and then close it.

Critical Thinking

Critical Thinking 1.1   Tracking Test Scores

Jeremy Diemer is a math teacher at Washington High School. Jeremy wants an Excel workbook that tracks students' test scores for his trigonometry class. Students receive a final letter grade for the course that is determined by the total number of points they accumulate throughout the course. Students are given four 1-hour tests, a midterm, a final, and four extra credit homework assignments. They can receive a maximum of 100 points for each of the four tests, 200 points for the midterm, 300 points for the final, and 25 points for each extra credit homework assignment. Thus, the total number of possible points for the course is 1,000. Letter grades are assigned as follows:

A	900 or more points
B	800–899 points
C	700–799 points
D	600–699 points
F	Less than 600 points

You have been assigned the task of setting up a worksheet for Jeremy. The worksheet should list the points received by each student for the tests, midterm, final, and homework assignments. Include scores for the following four students: Jack Simmons, Samantha Torres, Elaine Wilkins, and Tonya Robertson. Assign points to the students, as you deem appropriate. Save your workbook as **ct-Grades**.

Critical Thinking 1.2   Applicant Information

Big Slice Pizza is a rapidly growing pizza chain that serves the best deep-dish pizza in town. An important part of Big Slice's growth strategy is the development of a franchise network using independent franchise owners. Recently, Big Slice launched a West Coast advertising campaign to attract new franchise owners. You have been assigned the task of collecting the franchise applications and creating a worksheet that summarizes the application information. Your worksheet should include each prospective franchise owner's name, city and state, investment amount, telephone number, and whether or not the prospect has previous franchise experience. Include information for the following prospects: Ben Barksdale, Sylvia Ramirez, Bill Chin, Wanda Stone, and Terry Collins. You determine the remaining information for each prospective owner. Save your workbook as **ct-Pizza Franchises**.

Critical Thinking 1.3   Technology Purchase Research

Alexia Williams is the Information Systems Manager for Bellmont Health Care, a rapidly growing health care company with more than $1 billion in FY 2006 revenues. Alexia has mandated that, beginning in FY 2007, at least 50% of Bellmont's technology purchases will be made using online purchasing systems. Alexia believes this strategy will reduce costs and increase the efficiency of the procurement process. As an intern working under Alexia's direction, you have been assigned the task of locating five online vendors that sell personal computers and accessories. Alexia has asked you to construct a worksheet that includes each vendor's name and customer service telephone number. Use Internet Explorer and a search engine of your choice to conduct your research. Record your results in a worksheet saved as **ct-Computer Buys Online**.

Critical Thinking 1.4   Auto Sales Research

George Miller is the Operations Manager for Speedy Package Delivery Service, a same-day package delivery service. Speedy is located in the heart of Silicon Valley. George needs to purchase six new minivans to be used for package delivery. He has assigned you the task of locating three websites that have information on different minivans and where they can be purchased. Use Internet Explorer and a search engine of your choice to locate three websites that specialize in vehicle sales. Set up a worksheet that lists the names of three such websites. For each website, include the posted retail price for Toyota Sienna, Honda Odyssey, and Dodge Caravan minivans. Use a consistent vehicle configuration from each website so the pricing comparisons are valid. Include any additional vehicle information that you think would be useful to George. Save your workbook as **ct-Car Pricing**.

LESSON 2

Editing, Viewing, and Printing Worksheets

In this lesson, you will expand on the basic skills you learned in Lesson 1. You will learn various methods of editing worksheets: replacing and deleting entries, using Undo and Redo, working with AutoCorrect, and more. You will also learn about printing Excel worksheets and working with different views. When you have finished this lesson, you will have developed the skills necessary to produce carefully edited and proofed worksheets.

LESSON OBJECTIVES

After studying this lesson, you will be able to:

- Open and edit a workbook file
- Use a variety of techniques to select cells and ranges
- Move and copy cell entries
- Undo and redo commands
- Clear cell contents, including formatting
- Use AutoFill and AutoComplete
- Work with various Excel views and the zoom feature
- Preview your worksheet before printing
- Print your worksheet, including printing specific sections of your worksheet

Case Study: Creating a Basic List in Excel

Ken Hazell is the owner of Carmel Automotive Repair. He realizes that Excel would be the best tool to keep track of his employees' personal data. Excel can be used as a simple database to keep track of lists of employees, inventory, or other items. You will learn more about Excel's database features in Lesson 12, Creating PivotTables and Macros. Microsoft Excel is an important tool for any entrepreneur in today's highly competitive business world.

	A	B	C	D	E
1	Carmel Automotive Repair				
2	Employee Roster				
3					
4	Name	Phone	Position	Employment Date	Lock-up Day
5	Ken Hazell	619-555-3224	Owner		
6	Christina Chu	858-555-3098	Front Office	5/25/2004	Monday
7	Isabella Soprano-Birdsell	619-555-3309	Front Office	3/28/2003	Tuesday
8	Derek Navarro	951-555-0826	Front Office	8/3/2005	Wednesday
9	Jason Rogers	858-555-4987	Front Office	1/5/1999	Thursday
10	Matt Bernardo	858-555-0211	Front Office	4/13/2001	Friday
11	Meredith Baxter	858-555-1002	Mechanic	5/10/2003	
12	George Springhurst	858-555-0021	Mechanic	10/30/2002	
13	Preston Washington	760-555-3876	Mechanic	12/24/2003	
14	Steve Porter	619-555-4016	Mechanic	4/23/2002	
15	David Scott	760-555-0728	Mechanic	7/29/2000	
16	Charlie Simpson	858-555-3718	Mechanic	5/15/2007	
17	Leisa Malimali	619-555-4017	Manager	5/15/2007	

Ken will use this spreadsheet to organize his employees' phone numbers, dates of employment, and the day that each front office worker is responsible for locking up the shop.

Opening Workbooks

FROM THE KEYBOARD
[Ctrl]+[O] to open

The Office button →Open command displays the Open dialog box. The Open dialog box lets you navigate to any storage location and open previously saved workbooks. Once a workbook is open, you can browse it, print it, and make editing changes. The organization and layout of the Open dialog box are similar to those of the Save As dialog box.

Hands-On 2.1   Open the Workbook

In this exercise, you will open a workbook that lists the employees of Carmel Automotive Repair.

1. Start Excel.

2. Click the Office button, and then choose the Open command.
   The Open dialog box is displayed.

!NOTE!   *In future lessons this command will be written, Choose Office→Open.*

3. Follow these steps to open the CAR Employee Roster workbook:
   Keep in mind that your storage location (such as a USB drive) may contain different folders and files than those displayed here.

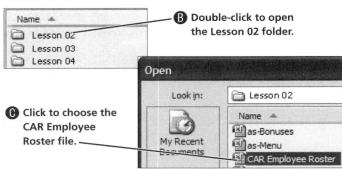

Ⓐ Navigate to your file storage location. This will likely be your USB flash drive.

Ⓑ Double-click to open the Lesson 02 folder.

Ⓒ Click to choose the CAR Employee Roster file.

Ⓓ Click the Open button.

!TIP!   *You can also double-click a document in the Open dialog box to open it.*

Editing Entries

You can edit the active cell by clicking in the Formula Bar and making the desired changes. You can also double-click a cell and edit the contents directly there. This technique is known as in-cell editing.

Replacing Entries

Editing an entry is efficient if the entry is so long that retyping it would be time-consuming. Editing can also be helpful when working with complex formulas and other functions that are difficult to re-create. If the entry requires little typing, however, it is usually easier to simply retype it. If you retype an entry, the new entry will be replace whatever is contained in the cell.

Deleting Characters

Use the Delete and Backspace keys to edit entries in the Formula Bar and within a cell. The Delete key removes the character to the right of the insertion point, while the Backspace key removes the character to the left of the insertion point.

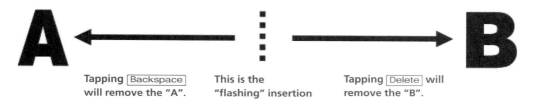

Tapping Backspace will remove the "A".

This is the "flashing" insertion

Tapping Delete will remove the "B".

 Hands-On 2.2   Edit Entries

In this exercise, you will use the Formula Bar to revise the contents of cell A2. You will also edit cells B3 and B15 directly in the cells.

Edit in the Formula Bar

1. Click cell A2 to select it.

2. Follow these steps to edit cell A2 using the Formula Bar:

Ⓐ Click in the Formula Bar just to the right of the word *List*.

Ⓒ Click the Enter button.

Ⓑ Tap Backspace four times to remove the word *List*, and then type **Roster**.

Replace an Entry

3. Click cell D4.

4. Type **Employment Date** and tap Enter.
   The entry Employment Date *replaces the entry* Starting Date. *Notice that the cell formatting (underlining the word) applied to the new entry as well. Also note that the new entry is cut off or truncated (as you learned about in the previous lesson) since the cell to the right contains an entry.*

Use In-Cell Editing

5. Double-click cell A7 (the cell with the name Isabella Soprano).

6. Use the mouse or the → key to position the flashing insertion point to the right of the last name, Soprano.

7. Type **-Birdsell**, and then tap Enter to complete the change.
   The entry should now read Isabella Soprano-Birdsell.

8. Click the Save 💾 button to update the changes.
   Clicking the Save button automatically saves changes to a workbook that has previously been saved.

Selecting Cells and Ranges

FROM THE KEYBOARD
Ctrl+A to select all
Ctrl+Spacebar to select a column
Shift+Spacebar to select a row

When you want to change something in a worksheet—for instance, move, copy, delete, format, or print specific data—you must first select the cell(s). The most efficient way to select cells is with the mouse, though you can also use the keyboard method. You can select one or many cells. A group of contiguous (adjacent) cells is called a range.

Excel Ranges

In the last lesson, you learned that each cell has a reference. For example, A1 refers to the first cell in a worksheet. Likewise, a range reference specifies the cells included within a range. The range reference includes the first and last cells in the range separated by a colon (:). For example, the range A4:E4 includes all cells between A4 and E4 inclusive. The following illustration highlights several ranges and their corresponding range references.

A6	▼	f_x	Christina Chu		
	A	B	C	D	E
1	Carmel Automotive Repair				
2	Employee Roster				
3					
4	Name	Phone	Position	Employment Dat	Lock-up Day
5	Ken Hazell	619-555-3224	Owner		
6	Christina Chu	858-555-3098	Front Office	5/25/2004	
7	Isabella Soprano-Birdsell	619-555-3309	Front Office	3/28/2003	
8	Derek Navarro	951-555-0826	Front Office	8/3/2005	
9	Jason Rogers	858-555-4987	Front Office	1/5/1999	
10	Matt Bernardo	858-555-0211	Front Office	4/13/2001	
11	Meredith Baxter	858-555-1002	Mechanic	5/10/2003	
12	George Springhurst	858-555-0021	Mechanic	10/30/2002	
13	Preston Washington	760-555-3876	Mechanic	12/24/2003	
14	Steve Porter	619-555-4016	Mechanic	4/23/2002	
15	David Scott	760-555-0728	Mechanic	7/29/2000	

Range A1:A2 — (rows 1–2)
Range A4:E4 — (row 4)
Range A6:D10 — (rows 6–10)

The selected ranges in the worksheet are shaded, as displayed above. In addition, the first cell in the last range selected, A6, shows no shading and has an outline around it. This indicates that it is the active cell, which is displayed in the Name box and Formula Bar.

The following Quick Reference table describes selection techniques in Excel.

QUICK REFERENCE: SELECTING CELLS AND RANGES

Techniques	How to Do It
Select a range	Drag the mouse pointer over the desired cells.
Select several ranges	Select a range, and then press Ctrl while selecting additional range(s).
Select an entire column	Click a column heading or press Ctrl+Spacebar.
Select an entire row	Click a row heading or press Shift+Spacebar.
Select multiple columns or rows	Drag the mouse pointer over the desired column or row headings.
Select an entire worksheet	Click the Select All button ◢ at the top-left corner of the worksheet or press Ctrl+A.
Select a range with Shift	Position the highlight in the first cell you wish to select, press Shift, and click the last cell in the range.
Extend or decrease a selection with Shift	Press Shift while tapping an arrow key.

 Hands-On 2.3   Practice Making Selections

In this exercise, you will practice selecting multiple ranges and entire rows and columns using the mouse. You will also use the Shift and Ctrl keys to practice selecting cell ranges.

Click and Drag to Select a Range

1. Position the mouse pointer ✚ over cell A4.

2. Press and hold down the left mouse button while dragging the mouse to the right until the range A4:E4 is selected, and then release the mouse button.
Notice that for each range that is selected, the corresponding row and column headers are displayed in orange.

3. Click once anywhere in the worksheet to deselect the cells.

Select Multiple Ranges

4. Follow these steps to select two ranges:

A Select the range A4:E4 as you did in steps 1 and 2 above.

B Press and hold down the Ctrl key while dragging to select the range A6:D10.

C Release the Ctrl key after the second range is selected.

	A	B	C	D	E
1	Carmel Automotive Repair				
2	Employee Roster				
3					
4	Name	Phone	Position	Employment Dat	Lock-up Day
5	Ken Hazell	619-555-3224	Owner		
6	Christina Chu	858-555-3098	Front Office	5/25/2004	
7	Isabella Soprano-Birdsell	619-555-3309	Front Office	3/28/2003	
8	Derek Navarro	951-555-0826	Front Office	8/3/2005	
9	Jason Rogers	858-555-4987	Front Office	1/5/1999	
10	Matt Bernardo	858-555-0211	Front Office	4/13/2001	

Both the A4:E4 and A6:D10 ranges are selected now. The Ctrl key lets you select more than one range at the same time.

5. Press and hold down the Ctrl key while you select another range, and then release the Ctrl key.
You should now have three ranges selected.

6. Make sure you have released the Ctrl key, and then click once anywhere on the worksheet to deselect the ranges.
The highlighting of the previous selections disappears.

Select Entire Rows and Columns

7. Follow these steps to select various rows and columns:

A Click the column A heading to select the entire column.

B Position the mouse pointer on the column C heading and drag to the right until columns C, D, and E are selected.

	A	B	C	D	E
1	Carmel Automotive Repair				
2	Employee Roster				
3					
4	Name	Phone	Position	Employment Dat	Lock-up Day
5	Ken Hazell	619-555-3224	Owner		
6	Christina Chu	858-555-3098	Front Office	5/25/2004	
7	Isabella Soprano-Birdsell	619-555-3309	Front Office	3/28/2003	
8	Derek Navarro	951-555-0826	Front Office	8/3/2005	

Column A will be deselected since you were not holding down the Ctrl *key.*

C Click the Select All button to select the entire worksheet.

D Click the row 1 heading to select the entire row.

E Drag the mouse pointer down over the headings from row 6 to row 10 to select them.

	A	B	C
1	Carmel Automotive Repair		
2	Employee Roster		
3			
4	Name	Phone	Position
5	Ken Hazell	619-555-3224	Owner
6	Christina Chu	858-555-3098	Front Office
7	Isabella Soprano-Birdsell	619-555-3309	Front Office
8	Derek Navarro	951-555-0826	Front Office
9	Jason Rogers	858-555-4987	Front Office
10	Matt Bernardo	858-555-0211	Front Office

Use Keyboard Techniques

8. Follow these steps to use keyboard techniques to select cells:

A Click cell A4.

	A	B	C	D	E
4	Name	Phone	Position	Employment Dat	Lock-up Day
5	Ken Hazell	619-555-3224	Owner		
6	Christina Chu	858-555-3098	Front Office	5/25/2004	
7	Isabella Soprano-Birdsell	619-555-3309	Front Office	3/28/2003	
8	Derek Navarro	951-555-0826	Front Office	8/3/2005	
9	Jason Rogers	858-555-4987	Front Office	1/5/1999	
10	Matt Bernardo	858-555-0211	Front Office	4/13/2001	
11	Meredith Baxter	858-555-1002	Mechanic	5/10/2003	
12	George Springhurst	858-555-0021	Mechanic	10/30/2002	
13	Preston Washington	760-555-3876	Mechanic	12/24/2003	
14	Steve Porter	619-555-4016	Mechanic	4/23/2002	
15	David Scott	760-555-0728	Mechanic	7/29/2000	

B Press and hold down the Shift key and click cell E15 to select the range A4:E15.

C Click cell A11.

	A	B	C	D
11	Meredith Baxter	858-555-1002	Mechanic	5/10/2003
12	George Springhurst	858-555-0021	Mechanic	10/30/2002
13	Preston Washington	760-555-3876	Mechanic	12/24/2003
14	Steve Porter	619-555-4016	Mechanic	4/23/2002
15	David Scott	760-555-0728	Mechanic	7/29/2000

D Press and hold down the Shift key, and then tap → three times and ↓ four times.

The range A11:D15 is selected. Notice that the Shift *key techniques give you precise control when selecting. You should use the* Shift *key techniques if you find selecting with the mouse difficult or if you have a large range to select that is not entirely visible on your screen.*

9. Take a few moments to practice selection techniques. See if you can select any portion of a worksheet you wish.

Working with Cut, Copy, and Paste

FROM THE KEYBOARD
Ctrl+C to copy
Ctrl+X to cut
Ctrl+V to paste

The Cut, Copy, and Paste commands are available in all Office 2007 applications. With Cut, Copy, and Paste, you can move or copy cells within a worksheet, between worksheets, or between different Office applications. For example, you could use the Copy command to copy a range from one worksheet and the Paste command to paste the range into another worksheet. Cut, Copy, and Paste are most efficient for moving or copying cells a long distance within a worksheet or between worksheets. Cut, Copy, and Paste are easy to use if you remember the following guidelines:

- You must select cells before issuing a Cut or Copy command.

- You must position the highlight at the desired location before issuing the Paste command. This is important because the range you paste will overwrite any cells in the paste area.

You can also right-click on a cell or range of cells in order to get a shortcut menu specific to the selection. The Cut, Copy, and Paste commands are available on this menu as well. There are many ways to issue commands; your job is to simply figure out which method works best for you!

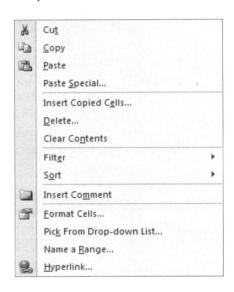

When you right-click a cell or range of cells, a shortcut menu appears that provides options specific to the selection. Notice that you can choose to Cut, Copy, and Paste from this menu.

The Office Clipboard

The Office Clipboard lets you collect items from any Office worksheet or program and paste them into any other Office document. For example, you can collect a paragraph from a Word document, data from an Excel worksheet, and a graphic from a PowerPoint slide and then paste them all into a new Word document. The Office Clipboard can also be used within a single application like Excel to collect several items and then paste them as desired. The Office Clipboard can hold up to 24 items.

How It Works

You can place items on the Office Clipboard using the standard Cut and Copy commands; however, the Office Clipboard task pane must first be displayed. It is displayed by clicking the Launcher button in the Clipboard area of the Home Ribbon.

Moving Cells via Drag and Drop

Drag and Drop produces the same results as Cut, Copy, and Paste. However, Drag and Drop is usually more efficient if you are moving or copying entries a short distance within the same worksheet. If the original location and new destination are both visible in the current window, then it is usually easier to use Drag and Drop. With Drag and Drop, you select the cells you wish to move or copy, and then you point to the edge of the selected range and drag the range to the desired destination. If you press the Ctrl key while dragging the selected area, the cells are copied to the destination. Drag and Drop does not place items on the Office Clipboard, however, so you will want to use either the Cut or the Copy command if you wish to work with the Clipboard.

Editing Cells via Right-Dragging

Right-dragging is a variation of the Drag and Drop technique. Many beginners find Drag and Drop difficult to use because they have difficulty controlling the mouse. This difficulty is compounded if they are trying to copy entries using Drag and Drop. This is because copying requires the Ctrl key to be held while the selected range is dragged. With the right-drag method, the right mouse button is used when dragging. When the right mouse button is released at the destination, a pop-up menu appears. The pop-up menu gives you several options including Move, Copy, and Cancel. This provides more control because there is no need to use the Ctrl key when copying, and you have the option of canceling the move or copy.

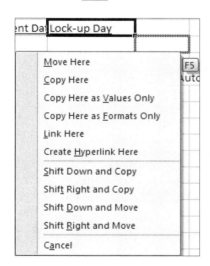

When you right-drag and drop, you will receive a pop-up menu at the destination so that you can choose whether to move or copy the data. Many of the rest of the options displayed will be covered in subsequent lessons.

QUICK REFERENCE: CUTTING, COPYING, AND PASTING

Command	Discussion	Procedure
Cut	The Cut command removes entries from selected cells and places them on the Office Clipboard.	■ Select what you wish to move or copy. ■ Click the Cut ✂ button, or press Ctrl+X.
Copy	The Copy command also places entries on the Office Clipboard, but it leaves a copy of the entries in the original cells.	■ Select what you wish to move or copy. ■ Click the Copy 📋 button, or press Ctrl+C.
Paste	The Paste command pastes entries from the Office Clipboard to worksheet cells beginning at the highlight location.	■ Click once where you wish the clipboard contents to be pasted. ■ Click the Paste 📋 button, or press Ctrl+V.

Hands-On 2.4   Move and Copy Selections

In this exercise, you will have the opportunity to use the Cut, Copy, and Paste commands as well as drag and drop to move and copy selections.

Copy and Paste

1. Click cell A1 to select it.

2. Make sure the Home tab is displayed, locate the Clipboard command group, and then click the Copy 📋 button on the Ribbon.
   A "marquee" will dance around the selection that you have copied and placed on the clipboard.

3. Click cell C2.

4. Choose Home→Clipboard→Paste 📋 from the Ribbon to paste the selection in cell C2.

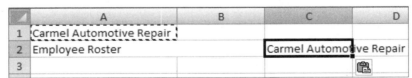

The contents of cell A1 will remain there as well as appear in cell C2 when you choose to copy the selection. Notice the dashed lines around the cell that is being copied and the Paste Options button that appears to the bottom right of the cell in which the selection was pasted.

Cut and Paste

5. Right-click cell C2.

When you right-click a cell, a shortcut menu appears with options specific to the cell, as well as the Mini Toolbar.

6. Choose Cut from the shortcut menu.

7. Right-click cell E2 and choose Paste from the shortcut menu.

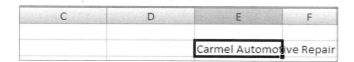

Cell C2 will now be empty since the contents were moved to cell E2.

Drag and Drop

8. Follow these steps to move the contents of cell E2 via drag and drop:

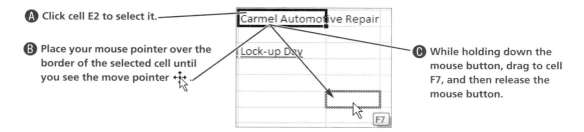

Ⓐ Click cell E2 to select it.

Ⓑ Place your mouse pointer over the border of the selected cell until you see the move pointer.

Ⓒ While holding down the mouse button, drag to cell F7, and then release the mouse button.

When you drag a cell with this method, Excel shows what cell the selection will be dropped into by displaying it on a ScreenTip as well as placing a highlight around the cell.

Right-Drag a Selection

9. Select cell E4, and then place your mouse pointer over the border of the selected cell until you see the move pointer as shown at right.

10. Start dragging with the right (not the left) mouse button. Keep the right mouse button held down until told to release it in the next step.

11. Drag down to cell F5, and then release the right mouse button.

A pop-up menu appears, listing your choices for the right-drag.

12. Choose Copy Here from the pop-up menu.

The contents of cell E4 remain in the cell and are copied to the destination cell, F5.

Using Undo and Redo

Excel's Undo button lets you reverse actions that have occurred in Excel. You can reverse simple actions such as accidentally deleting a cell's content or more complex actions such as deleting an entire row. Most actions can be undone, but those that cannot include printing and saving workbooks. The Undo command can become your best friend when you have to undo an action that you are not sure how you issued. Don't you wish life had an undo button at times!

The Redo button reverses an Undo command. Use Redo when you undo an action but then decide to go through with that action after all. The Redo button will be visible on the Quick Access toolbar only after you have undone an action.

Undoing Multiple Actions

FROM THE KEYBOARD
Ctrl + Z to undo
Ctrl + Y to redo

Clicking the arrow on the Undo button displays a list of actions that can be undone. You can undo multiple actions by dragging the mouse over the desired actions. However, you must undo actions in the order in which they appear on the drop-down list.

When you click the arrow on the Undo button, you will see a list of previous commands.

Limitations to "Undoing"

In Excel, there are some times when the Undo command will not work. If you click the Office button and choose any command, it cannot be undone (such as saving a workbook). When an action cannot be undone, Excel will change the Undo ScreenTip to "Can't Undo."

QR

QUICK REFERENCE: UNDOING AND REDOING ACTIONS	
Task	**Procedure**
Undo the last command	■ Click the Undo button on the Quick Access toolbar or tap Ctrl + Z.
Undo a series of commands	■ Click the drop-down arrow on the Undo button to display a list of previous commands. ■ Choose the last command that you wish to have undone.
Redo an undone command	■ Click the Redo button on the Quick Access toolbar.

In this exercise, you will delete the contents of a cell and then use Undo to reverse the deletion. When you do, the original data will display in the cell again. You will also use Redo to reverse an Undo command.

Delete the Entry and Use Undo and Redo

1. Click the column A heading to select the entire column.

2. Tap ⌑Delete⌐.
   All of the contents in column A have been deleted! There are many times that you will use Undo in order to reverse an action you did not wish to make.

3. Click Undo ⟲ to restore the entry.

4. Follow these steps to undo the last four commands from the previous section:

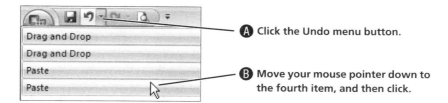

   Ⓐ Click the Undo menu button.

   Ⓑ Move your mouse pointer down to the fourth item, and then click.

   Excel undoes your last four commands.

5. Click the Redo ↻ button four times to restore the four actions that you "undid."

6. Use ⌑Ctrl⌐+⌑S⌐ to save the changes, but don't close the workbook.
   Remember, as you learned in the last lesson, you must hold down the ⌑Ctrl⌐ key first and then tap the ⌑S⌐ to issue the Save command.

Clearing Cell Contents and Formats

FROM THE KEYBOARD

`Delete` to clear cell contents

In Excel, you can format cell content by changing the font style, size, and color. You can also add enhancements such as bold, italics, and underline. Cells with numeric data can be formatted as currency, dates, times, percents, and more. In Lesson 4, Formatting the Contents of Cells you will learn how to format cells.

Clicking the Clear button displays a menu that lets you clear content, formats, and comments from cells. The submenu also contains an All option that clears all of these items from the selected cell(s).

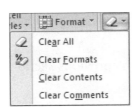

Clicking the Clear button in the Editing section of the Home Ribbon will display a menu that shows all of the options for clearing cell contents.

Excel's Options for Clearing Cells

Contents	Clearing the content has the same effect as tapping the `Delete` key. The cell contents are deleted, but any format applied to the cell remains and will be in effect when new data is entered in the cell.
Formats	The Formats option removes all text and number formats, leaving unformatted entries in the cell(s).
Comments	You can insert comments in cells to document your worksheet. The Comments option also removes comments from the selected cells.
All	This command will clear everything listed above.

One of the most useful functions of Excel's Clear command is removing numeric value formats. This is because once a cell is formatted as a particular numeric format, such as a date or currency, Excel remembers that formatting even if the cell contents are deleted.

QR ► QUICK REFERENCE: CLEARING CELL CONTENTS AND FORMATTING

Task	Procedure
Clear the contents of a cell	■ Select the cell or range that you wish to clear. ■ Choose Home→Editing→Clear on the Ribbon. ■ Choose Clear Contents from the resulting menu.
Clear the formatting from a cell	■ Select the cell or range that you wish to clear. ■ Choose Home→Editing→Clear on the Ribbon. ■ Choose Clear Formats from the resulting menu.
Clear contents and formatting from a cell	■ Select the cell or range that you wish to clear. ■ Choose Home→Editing→Clear on the Ribbon. ■ Choose Clear All from the resulting menu.

Hands-On 2.6   Clear Cell Contents and Formatting

In this exercise, you will use the Clear command to delete cell contents and cell formats.

1. Click cell F5.

2. Choose Home→Editing→Clear ⟨🧽⟩ from the Ribbon, choose Clear Formats, and then tap ⟨Enter⟩ twice.
   The contents of the cell were underlined, a type of formatting. When you choose to clear only the formats, the contents will remain and only the formatting is removed. Notice that the contents are no longer underlined.

3. Click the Undo ⟨↩⟩ button on the Quick Access toolbar.

4. Ensure that cell F5 is selected, and then click the Clear ⟨🧽⟩ button and choose Clear All.

5. Type your name and tap ⟨Enter⟩.
   Notice that the contents are no longer underlined in cell F5 since you cleared "all" (formatting and contents) from it.

6. Use ⟨Ctrl⟩+⟨Z⟩ to undo the typing of your name.

7. Click cell F7 and tap ⟨Delete⟩.
   The ⟨Delete⟩ key functions the same as if you had clicked the Clear button and chosen Clear Contents. Any formatting will remain in the cell.

8. Click the Save ⟨💾⟩ button.

Using Auto Features

Excel offers many "auto" features that help you to work more efficiently. AutoFill allows you to quickly fill a range of cells. AutoComplete makes it easy to enter long entries by typing an acronym or series of characters, which are "converted" to the desired entry. AutoCorrect can also assist in correcting commonly misspelled words.

Working with AutoFill

AutoFill allows you to quickly extend a series, copy data, or copy a formula into adjacent cells by selecting cells and dragging the fill handle. You will learn about using AutoFill to copy formulas in Lesson 3, Working with Formulas and Functions If the selected cell does not contain data that AutoFill recognizes as a series, the data will simply be copied into the adjacent cells. The fill handle is a small black square at the bottom-right corner of the active cell. A black cross appears when you position the mouse pointer on the fill handle. You can drag the fill handle to fill adjacent cells as described below.

■ Copy an entry—If the entry in the active cell is a number, a formula, or a text entry, the fill handle copies the entry to adjacent cells.

- Expand a repeating series of numbers—If you select two or more cells containing numbers, Excel assumes you want to expand a repeating series. For example, if you select two cells containing the numbers 5 and 10 and drag the fill handle, Excel will fill the adjacent cells with the numbers 15, 20, 25, etc.

- AutoFill of date entries—If the active cell contains any type of date entry, Excel will determine the increment of the date value and fill in the adjacent cells. For example, if the current cell contains the entry Q1 and you drag the fill handle, AutoFill will insert the entries Q2, Q3, and Q4 in the adjacent cells.

The following table and illustrations provide examples of series that AutoFill can extend.

Selected Cells	Extended Series
Mon	Tue, Wed, Thu
Monday	Tuesday, Wednesday, Thursday
Jan	Feb, Mar, Apr
January	February, March, April
Jan, Apr	Jul, Oct, Jan
1, 2	3, 4, 5, 6
100, 125	150, 175, 200
1/10/07	1/11/07, 1/12/07, 1/13/07
1/15/07, 2/15/07	3/15/07, 4/15/07, 5/15/07
1st Qtr	2nd Qtr, 3rd Qtr, 4th Qtr

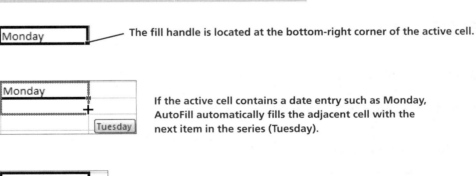

The fill handle is located at the bottom-right corner of the active cell.

If the active cell contains a date entry such as Monday, AutoFill automatically fills the adjacent cell with the next item in the series (Tuesday).

The completed series with the AutoFill Options button displayed

AutoFill Options

The AutoFill Options 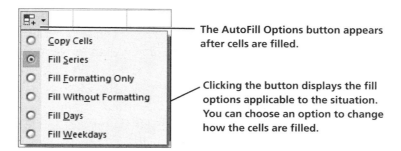 button appears below your filled selection after you fill cells in a worksheet. A menu of fill options appears when you click the button.

The AutoFill Options button appears after cells are filled.

Clicking the button displays the fill options applicable to the situation. You can choose an option to change how the cells are filled.

If you choose to Fill without Formatting, you can fill cells without copying the formatting from the original cell.

AutoComplete vs. AutoFill

The AutoComplete feature is useful when you want the same entry repeated more than once in a column. AutoFill allows you to select a cell and fill in entries either by completing a series or copying the source cell, whereas AutoComplete works within a cell as you type. If the first few characters you type match another entry in the column, then AutoComplete will offer to complete the entry for you. You accept the offer by tapping Enter or reject the offer by typing the remainder of the entry yourself.

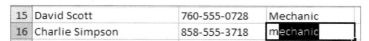

In this situation, an "m" was typed and the AutoComplete feature kicked into gear, suggesting that you may be interested in completing the entry as *Mechanic* since you have already typed that entry earlier in the column. In order to accept *Mechanic* as the entry, you would simply tap Enter.

 TIP! *AutoComplete will complete the entry "case sensitive."*

In this exercise, you will enter two new employees in the worksheet and use AutoComplete to aid in your entries. In addition, you will look at how to use AutoFill to complete a series of the days of the week.

Use AutoComplete

1. Click cell A16 and type **Charlie Simpson**, and then tap ⌈Tab⌉ to move to the next cell to the right.

2. Type **858-555-3718** and tap ⌈Tab⌉.

3. Type **m** and notice that Excel will suggest *Mechanic* as the entry. Tap ⌈Tab⌉ to accept the suggestion and move to the next cell to the right.
   Notice that the entry will be capitalized just as it is in the cells above.

4. Type today's date, and then type ⌈Enter⌉.
   Notice that when you tap ⌈Enter⌉, it will take you to cell A17 where you can begin typing the next entry of the list.

5. Type **Leisa Malimali** and tap ⌈Tab⌉.

6. Type **619-555-4017** and tap ⌈Tab⌉.

7. Type **M** in cell C17.
   Excel will suggest Mechanic *as it did in the previous row. In this case, Leisa is a manager, so you will need to continue typing your entry. Make sure that you have typed in a capital M as it will not pull from the previous entries.*

8. Continue typing **anager** and tap ⌈Tab⌉.
   Excel will replace the AutoCorrect suggestion with the entry that you type, Manager.

9. Type today's date and tap ⌈Enter⌉.

Use AutoFill to Expand a Series

In this section of the exercise, you will help Ken to fill in the column showing the front office employee responsible for locking up each day.

10. Click cell E6.

11. Type **Monday**, and then click the Enter ✓ button.
    Now that cell E6 contains Monday, Excel will recognize it as the beginning of the series including Tuesday, Wednesday, Thursday, and so forth. E6 will remain the active cell.

12. Follow these steps to fill the adjacent cells:

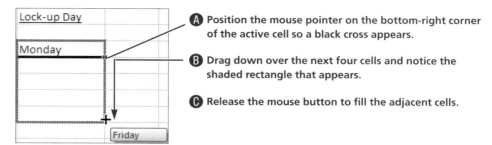

A Position the mouse pointer on the bottom-right corner of the active cell so a black cross appears.

B Drag down over the next four cells and notice the shaded rectangle that appears.

C Release the mouse button to fill the adjacent cells.

Excel recognizes days of the week (Monday), quarters (1st Qtr, Quarter 1, First Quarter), months (January), and other date values as the beginning of a series. You can expand any of these series with the fill handle.

13. Click the AutoFill Options button and note the various fill options.
If desired, you can choose an option to change how the cells are filled.

14. For now, just tap Esc to dismiss the menu.

Exploring the Many Views of Excel

When you change the view in Excel, it does not change how the worksheet will print. For instance, if you change the zoom to 300%, the worksheet will appear much larger on the screen but will still print normally. There are other views in Excel that will aid you in working with your file and assist you in making changes to the final printed worksheet. There is an additional view option that will be covered in Lesson 7, Working with Large Worksheets, Page Break Preview, that allows you to set where pages will break when printed.

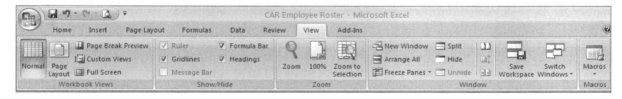

The View tab on the Ribbon provides options for how to view your workbook, which screen elements to show or hide, control of the zoom, and other window display options such as Freeze Panes and Split Window. This lesson will cover Page Layout view and Zoom. Remember that your Ribbon may appear differently, depending on the size of your Excel window.

Working in Page Layout View

Page Layout view allows you to see how your spreadsheet will appear when you print it, page by page. You can even add headers and footers and edit your worksheet in this view.

Zooming the View

2007 new!

The Zoom control lets you zoom in to get a close-up view of a worksheet and zoom out to see the full view. Zooming changes the size of the onscreen worksheet but has no effect on the printed worksheet. You can zoom from 10% to 400%.

You can move the slider to change the zoom.

You can also click the Zoom Out ⊖ and Zoom In ⊕ buttons to change the zoom.

Clicking the Zoom button will open the Zoom dialog box so that you can set the zoom more precisely.

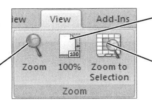

The 100% button allows you to quickly return the zoom to 100%.

The Zoom to Selection button on the Ribbon will customize the zoom to display the selected range of cells.

QUICK REFERENCE: WORKING WITH EXCEL'S VIEWS

Task	Procedure
Change the zoom of a worksheet	■ Click and drag the zoom slider at the bottom right of the worksheet window.
Zoom in to a selection	■ Select the range you wish to zoom in on. ■ Display the View Ribbon. ■ Click the Zoom to Selection button in the Zoom area.
View a worksheet in Page Layout view	■ Display the View Ribbon. ■ Click the Page Layout View button in the Workbook Views group of the Ribbon.

Hands-On 2.8   Change Views and Use the Zoom Control

In this exercise, you will practice using commands to change the zoom and switch between Page Layout and Normal views.

Change the Zoom

1. Follow these steps to adjust the zoom percentage:

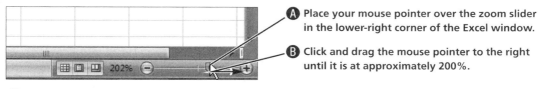

Ⓐ Place your mouse pointer over the zoom slider in the lower-right corner of the Excel window.

Ⓑ Click and drag the mouse pointer to the right until it is at approximately 200%.

Ⓒ Release the mouse button.

2. Click the Zoom Out ⊖ button several times until the zoom displays 100%.

3. Drag to select the range A1:E17.

4. Click the View tab to display the View Ribbon.

5. Click the Zoom to Selection button in the Zoom area of the Ribbon.

6. Choose View→Zoom→100% from the Ribbon.

Switch Between Page Layout and Normal Views

7. Choose View→Workbook Views→Page Layout View from the Ribbon.
   Notice that this view will allow you to see how the worksheet will print and allows you to simply click to add headers and footers.

8. Choose View→Workbook Views→Normal from the Ribbon.
   The worksheet will return to Normal view, and you are ready to proceed to the next section.

Printing Worksheets

Excel gives you many ways to print your work. The method you choose depends on what you want to print. The basic print command, for instance, offers you print options such as printing specified pages, a selected range, or the entire workbook. Additional choices include printing multiple copies and collating options.

The Quick Print button can be added to the Quick Access toolbar. When clicked, it will print one copy of the entire worksheet. For large workbooks in which you frequently want to print only a certain selection, you can print a selection or set a print area. Before printing, you can use Print Preview or Page Layout view to see what is going to be printed. In Lesson 7, Working with Large Worksheets, you will learn how to change page setup options such as changing the print orientation, printing column headings on every page, setting the print area, and many others.

Print Preview

The Print Preview command displays the Print Preview window. Print Preview lets you see exactly how a worksheet will look when printed. Print Preview can save time, paper, and wear and tear on your printer. It is especially useful when printing large worksheets and those with charts and intricate formatting. It is always wise to preview a large or complex worksheet before sending it to the printer. When you display the Print Preview window, the normal Ribbons are replaced by a Print Preview Ribbon. Print Preview is a very valuable tool in looking at how your worksheet will look when printed, but you are not able to edit your worksheet when you are in print preview mode (you will want to use Page Layout view for this purpose).

Choose Print to access the Print dialog box.

Choose Page Setup to access the Page Setup dialog box.

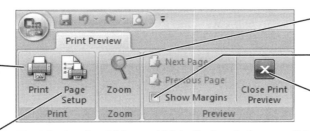

You can zoom in and out to check your worksheet to be printed more closely.

You can show margins and adjust them in the Print Preview window.

Use the Close Print Preview command to close the preview window and return to your worksheet.

The Print Preview Ribbon, which is displayed after you click the Print Preview button on the Quick Access toolbar.

Print the Worksheet

 You can customize your Quick Access toolbar to include the Quick Print button, which sends the entire worksheet to the current printer. You must display the Print dialog box if you want to change printers, adjust the number of copies to be  printed, or set other printing options such as printing only selected cells. The Print dialog box is displayed by clicking the Office button and choosing the Print command. The following illustration explains the most important options available in the Print dialog box.

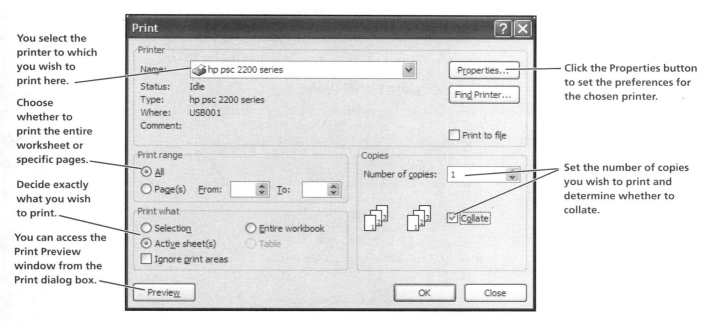

You select the printer to which you wish to print here.

Choose whether to print the entire worksheet or specific pages.

Decide exactly what you wish to print.

You can access the Print Preview window from the Print dialog box.

Click the Properties button to set the preferences for the chosen printer.

Set the number of copies you wish to print and determine whether to collate.

Printing Selections

Many times you will want to print only a range of cells. You can do this by selecting the desired cells, displaying the Print dialog box, choosing to print the selection, and clicking OK. You also use this technique to print nonadjacent selections within a worksheet or workbook. For example, use this technique to print two non-adjacent sections of a worksheet or two or more sections on different worksheets. Non-adjacent selections print on separate pages.

FROM THE KEYBOARD
Ctrl + P to print

TIP! *To print a selection, you must select the cell range before displaying the Print dialog box.*

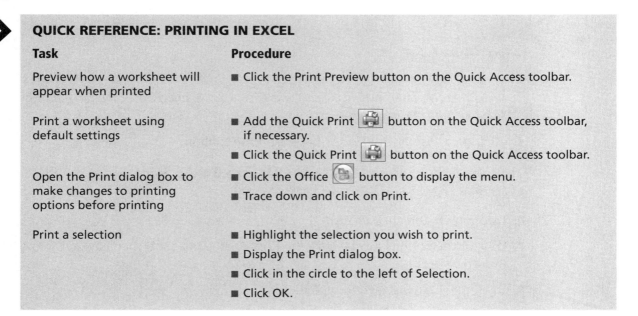

QR **QUICK REFERENCE: PRINTING IN EXCEL**

Task	Procedure
Preview how a worksheet will appear when printed	■ Click the Print Preview button on the Quick Access toolbar.
Print a worksheet using default settings	■ Add the Quick Print 🖨 button on the Quick Access toolbar, if necessary. ■ Click the Quick Print 🖨 button on the Quick Access toolbar.
Open the Print dialog box to make changes to printing options before printing	■ Click the Office 📖 button to display the menu. ■ Trace down and click on Print.
Print a selection	■ Highlight the selection you wish to print. ■ Display the Print dialog box. ■ Click in the circle to the left of Selection. ■ Click OK.

Hands-On 2.9   Preview and Print a Worksheet

In this exercise, you will preview the worksheet you have been working on and send it to the printer.

Preview How Your Worksheet Will Print

1. Follow these steps to preview the worksheet before printing:

Ⓐ Click the Office button.

Ⓑ Trace your mouse down to the arrow to the right of Print.

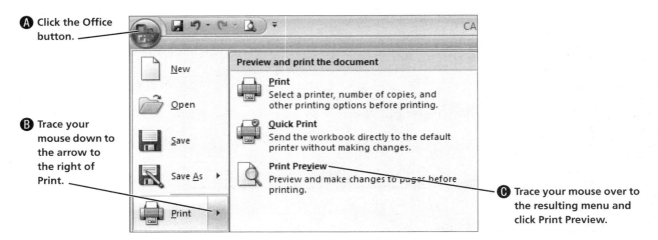

Ⓒ Trace your mouse over to the resulting menu and click Print Preview.

> **⚠ NOTE!** *In future lessons, this command will be written Choose Office →Print menu ▼ →Print Preview. The ▼ notation indicates that you will click the arrow on the button to access a menu of options.*

2. Click the Zoom button to zoom in on your worksheet and then again to zoom out.

3. Click in the box to the left of Show Margins.

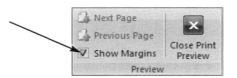

> *Notice that Excel will display the page margins as dotted lines, which you can adjust by clicking and dragging in the Print Preview window.*

4. Click the Close Print Preview button on the Ribbon.

Print Your Worksheet Using the Dialog Box

5. Click the Office button to display the menu.

6. Trace down and click Print.

7. Look at the options available in the Print Dialog box, and then click OK to print the worksheet.

8. Tap ⌨Ctrl⌨+⌨s⌨ to save your worksheet.

9. Click the Office button and choose Close.

Concepts Review

True/False Questions

1. Excel allows you to undo all commands issued.   TRUE **FALSE**

2. Double-clicking in a cell lets you revise the contents of the cell without replacing the entire contents.   **TRUE** FALSE

3. When you delete the contents of a cell using the [Delete] key on the keyboard, the formatting remains.   **TRUE** FALSE

4. If you drag and drop using the left mouse button, you will be able to choose the command to issue when the mouse button is released.   TRUE **FALSE**

5. You cannot delete the formats in a cell without deleting the contents as well.   **TRUE** FALSE

6. You select an entire row by clicking the row header.   **TRUE** FALSE

7. Page Layout view allows you to add headings and footers to your worksheet.   **TRUE** FALSE

8. You can print a group of cells without printing the entire worksheet.   **TRUE** FALSE

9. Changing the zoom in a worksheet will change the way it prints.   TRUE **FALSE**

10. AutoFill allows you to easily enter contents into cells that have been entered into another cell in the column.   **TRUE** FALSE

Multiple Choice Questions

1. What happens when you enter text in a cell that already contains an entry?
   a. The text replaces the original entry.
   b. Excel rejects the new entry, keeping the original entry intact.
   c. The cell contains both the original entry and the new entry.
   d. None of the above

2. Which command can be issued when you click the Clear button on the Ribbon?
   a. Clear the entire worksheet.
   b. Clear the formatting from a cell.
   c. Clear the formula from a cell.
   d. None of the above

3. What must you do before issuing a Cut or Copy command?
   a. Choose Home→Clipboard→Cut, or Home→ Clipboard→ Copy from the Ribbon.
   b. Double-click the cell from which you wish to cut or copy.
   c. Click the column header of the cell from which you wish to cut or copy.
   d. Select the cell(s) you wish to cut or copy.

4. What does the Print Preview view allow you to do?
   a. Add headers and footers to your worksheet.
   b. Observe how your spreadsheet will look when printed.
   c. Edit your worksheet.
   d. Both a and b

Skill Builders

Skill Builder 2.1   Edit a Worksheet

In this exercise, you will edit a worksheet. This exercise demonstrates that sometimes it is easier to replace entries while at other times it is easier to edit them.

Replace Several Entries

1. Start Excel and choose Office→Open.

2. Navigate to the Lesson 02 folder in your file storage location and open sb-Customers.

3. Click cell B4.

4. Type **Ralph** and tap ⎡Enter⎤.
   Notice that it is easy to replace the entry because the name Ralph is easy to type.

5. Replace the name *Calvin* in cell B6 with the name **Stephen**.

Edit Using the Formula Bar

6. Click cell D4.

7. Click in the Formula Bar just in front of the telephone prefix *333*.

8. Tap ⎡Delete⎤ three times to remove the prefix.

9. Type **222** and complete ☑ the entry.

10. Change the area code in cell D8 from *814* to **914**.
    In these entries, it was easier to edit than to retype entire phone numbers.

Use In-Cell and "Your Choice" Editing

11. Double-click cell E4.

12. Use ⎡→⎤ or ⎡←⎤ to position the insertion point in front of the word Lane.

13. Tap ⎡Delete⎤ four times to remove the word *Lane*.

14. Type **Reservoir** and complete the entry.

15. Edit the next five addresses using either the Formula Bar or in-cell editing. The required changes appear bold in the following table.

Cell	Make These Changes
E5	2900 **Carleton** Drive, San Mateo, CA 94401
E6	**2300** Palm Drive, Miami, FL 33147
E7	888 Wilson Street, **Concord**, CA 94565
E8	320 Main Street, **Pittsburgh**, PA 17951
E9	5120 132nd Street, Los Angeles, CA **90045**

Leave the workbook open as you will use it for Skill Builder 2.2

Skill Builder 2.2   Use AutoComplete and AutoFill

In this exercise, you will add data to the worksheet you created in Skill Builder 2.1 by using AutoComplete and AutoFill.

Use AutoComplete

1. Click cell B10, and type **ja**.
   Notice that AutoComplete does not suggest an entry when you only type a "j" as there are two "j" entries in the column.

2. Tap ⎡Enter⎤ to accept the suggested entry of Jack.

3. Using the following figure, complete the customer's information, using AutoComplete in column F.

	A	B	C	D	E	F
9		Judy	Alioto	(213) 222-3344	5120 132nd Street, Los Angeles, CA 90045	West
10		Jack	LaRue	(360) 444-0489	359 Peninsula Avenue, Port Angeles, WA 98363	West

Use AutoFill

4. Click cell A4.
   Before using AutoFill, you must first select the cell that you will be using as the basis for the fill information.

5. Place your mouse pointer over the fill handle at the bottom-right corner of the selected cell, drag down through cell A10, and then release the mouse button when the ScreenTip shows C-07.

	A	B
3	Customer #	Firstna
4	C-01	Ralph
5		Willie
6		Steph
7		Susan
8		Jack
9		Judy
10		Jack
11		
		C-07

	A
3	Customer #
4	C-01
5	C-02
6	C-03
7	C-04
8	C-05
9	C-06
10	C-07

Notice that Excel recognizes C-01 as the beginning of a series (C-02, C-03, C-04, …).

Enter Additional Customers

6. Enter the following three customers, in rows 11–13, into the list, using AutoFill and AutoComplete when possible.

	A	B	C	D	E	F
10	C-07	Jack	LaRue	(360) 444-0489	359 Peninsula Avenue, Port Angeles, WA 98363	West
11	C-08	Edgar	Martinez	(206) 111-1111	11 Mariners Way, Seattle, WA 98101	West
12	C-09	Trevor	Hoffman	(619) 555-1111	51 Camino de Padres, San Diego, CA 92101	West
13	C-10	Derek	Jeter	(212) 222-5555	2 Yankee Avenue, New York, NY 10002	East

7. Use Ctrl + S to save your workbook, then leave it open for the next exercise.

Skill Builder 2.3   Move and Copy Cell Contents

In this exercise, you will use the workbook from Skill Builder 2.2 and move and copy the contents of cells.

1. Click to select cell E1.

2. Choose Home→Clipboard→Cut from the Ribbon.

3. Click cell A1, and choose Home→Clipboard→Paste.

4. Select A11:F11, and copy the range using the keyboard command Ctrl + C.

5. Click cell A14, and paste the range using Ctrl + V.
   This can come in handy if you have a new entry that is very similar to an existing one!

6. Use Ctrl + Z to undo the Paste command.

7. Close × Excel, choosing to save your workbook.

 # Assessments

Assessment 2.1   Edit a Worksheet and Use Page Layout View

In this exercise, you will edit a worksheet in both Normal and Page Layout views. You will also use AutoFill to extend a series.

1. Open the workbook named as-Bonuses from the Lesson 02 folder in your file storage location.

2. Edit the title in cell A1 to read **Computer Depot Sales Bonuses**.

3. AutoFill the months February through June in cells C3:G3.

4. Edit the label in cell A4 to **Employee Name**.

5. Change the name Mary Johnson in cell A5 to **Sally Adams**.

6. View the worksheet in Page Layout view.

7. While in Page Layout view, edit the label in cell A9 to read **Grand Total** and complete the entry.

8. Add the following centered footer: **Computer Depot Bonuses, January–June 2007**. *You will need to scroll down to below row 51 to type in the footer.*

9. Save the changes and close the workbook.

Assessment 2.2   Select, Move, and Copy in a Worksheet

In this exercise, you will practice selecting various ranges and cells in order to move and copy them.

1. Open the workbook named as-Menu from the Lesson 02 folder in your file storage location.

2. Select A7:B27; try using the Shift technique.

3. Place your mouse pointer over the edge of the selection until you see the move pointer, and then click and drag up until the top left of the selection is in row 3. *The selection will now be contained in the range A3:B23.*

4. Copy the contents of cell A4 into cell A12.

5. Select A18:B23 and issue the Cut command.

6. Click cell A20 and issue the Paste command.

7. Save the worksheet and leave it open for the next exercise.

Assessment 2.3   Work with Undo, Clear, and AutoComplete

In this exercise, you will work with the workbook from Assessment 2.2 to clear formatting, undo commands, and use AutoComplete.

1. The as-Menu worksheet from Assessment 2.2 should still be open; if it is not, open it from your default storage location.

2. Select column B by clicking the column header.

3. Choose Home→Editing→Clear→Clear Formats from the Ribbon.
   Notice that the numbers remain in column B, but they are no longer formatted as currency.

4. Click the Undo button on the Quick Access toolbar to bring back the cleared formatting.

5. Click cell A9 and type **s**, observing the AutoComplete option that appears.

6. Tap [Enter] to accept the AutoComplete suggestion.

7. Click cell A9 and tap [Delete] to clear the contents of the cell.

8. Choose Office→Print menu ▾→Print Preview.
   Take a look at how the menu will print. Notice the simplified Ribbon that is displayed in this specialized setting.

9. Choose Print Preview→Print from the modified Ribbon.

10. Print the menu for your instructor.

11. Save the changes to the workbook and exit from Excel.

Critical Thinking

Critical Thinking 2.1 Fred's Job Log

Fred Watson is the owner of Fred's Quality Lawn Care service. Fred has provided high-quality lawn care and landscaping services for more than 25 years. Recently, Fred purchased a personal computer with Office 2007 preinstalled. He intends to use his new computer and Office 2007 to improve his customer service, conduct mailings, computerize his billing processes, and increase his profits. Fred recently took an Excel class at a local community college. He wants to use Excel to track his activities and help maximize his profits, so he asks you to clean up a job log that he has created. You will also be responsible for updating and maintaining it.

The worksheet assigns a number to each job. It includes the customer name, day of the week, type of work performed, number of hours required to complete the activity, and other important information. Using the ct-Fred's Job Log workbook, examine the worksheet that Fred has created and edit it to match the following illustration.

	A	B	C	D	E	F
1	Fred's Quality Lawn					
2						
3	Job #	Customer	Day	Work	Hrs Req	Amt Billed
4	100	Smythe	Monday	Mowing	2	40
5	101	Jonesby	Monday	General	4	75
6	102	Patrick	Tuesday	Irrigation	4	210
7	103	Benning	Tuesday	Tree Trim	3	140
8	104	Curtis	Wednesda	Irrigation	6	320
9	105	Hacker	Thursday	Mowing	2	40

When you are finished, save your changes and then close the workbook.

Critical Thinking 2.2   Test Results

Cindi Canning conducts tests of PC hard drives at Data Storage Incorporated. Cindi has created a worksheet, named ct-Test Results, and asks you to update it for her. Cindi provides you with her notes and asks you to enter the following additional data into the worksheet:

Unit Type	Produced	Passed	Repaired	Destroyed
CX256-256 GB	9500	9200	240	60
CX256-512 GB	8000	7450	350	200
CX512-512 GB	7000	6910	25	65

Cindi also hands you a printed copy of her original worksheet, which she has edited in purple ink. She would like you to make the following changes to her data:

■ Change the value in cell B5 to **8500**.

■ Change the value in cell C5 to **7950**.

■ Change the value in cell D5 to **125**.

■ Change the value in cell B6 to **7700**.

■ Change the value in cell C6 to **7510**.

■ Change the value in cell D6 to **125**.

When you finish editing the worksheet, print a copy of it for Cindi. Save the changes and close the workbook.

Critical Thinking 2.3   College Research

Dominique Aguyo is a senior at Bernardo Ranch High School. She is certain she wants to major in chemical engineering when she attends college in the fall. Your task is to help Dominique identify schools that offer chemical engineering as a major. Use Internet Explorer and a search engine of your choice to locate at least five universities that offer chemical engineering majors. Record your results in an Excel spreadsheet. Include the school, city and state, size of the student population, and other information you think would help Dominique make her decision. Save it as **ct-CE Colleges** and close it.

Critical Thinking 2.4   Software Use Research

Set up a worksheet to record whether people have used Windows, Outlook, Word, Excel, Access, PowerPoint, and Internet Explorer in a business environment. Survey five of your friends, relatives, or coworkers, and record the results of your survey in the worksheet. Use an X to indicate experience with a particular program and a 0 to indicate no experience. Examining the results should give you some idea of how much each program is used in business. Save your workbook as **ct-Survey**.

LESSON 3

Working with Formulas and Functions

The magic of the Excel spreadsheet lies in its ability to crunch numbers and make sense of data. The heart of this magic lies in the formulas and functions that are used for this number crunching. In this lesson, you will be introduced to creating and modifying basic formulas and functions in Excel. You will learn how to reference cells in formulas as well as how to use another automated feature of Excel, AutoSum. Sit back and relax as you begin to discover the true power of Excel.

LESSON OBJECTIVES

After studying this lesson, you will be able to:

- Create formulas to calculate values, utilizing the proper syntax and order of operations
- Use a variety of methods to create statistical functions to determine the sum, average, maximum, and minimum of a range of numbers
- Use relative and absolute cell references in formulas and functions
- Modify and copy formulas and functions
- Display the formulas contained within cells rather than the resulting value

Case Study: Creating a Spreadsheet with Formulas

The Big Bear Mountain Inn is a 200-room hotel located next to a ski resort. The manager of the hotel, Glen Livingston, has asked the accountant, Tammy McJagger, to prepare commission and monthly projected profit reports for the first quarter. Commissions are not paid for in-house bookings but are paid to outside agencies who book rooms for the inn.

Tammy has set up a workbook with two worksheets, one to track commissions and the other to help Glen view how the projected profit changes based on occupancy. Your job will be to help Tammy create the necessary formulas and functions for the workbook.

	A	B	C	D	E
1	Big Bear Mountain Inn				
2	First Quarter Commissions				
3					
4		Nights Booked			
5	Booking Agent	January	February	March	1st Qtr Total
6	Betty's Better Travel	250	486	274	1010
7	Mountain Travel Agency	342	276	299	917
8	Rent Online 4 Less	74	149	101	324
9	Sea to Mountain Travel	113	109	88	310
10	Skiingtrips.com	337	265	124	726
11	Total	1116	1285	886	3287
12	Average	223.2	257	177.2	657.4
13	Maximum	342	486	299	1010
14	Minimum	74	109	88	310

The Commissions worksheet will show the number of nights booked by each agency that is due a commission.

	A	B	C	D	E	F
1	Big Bear Mountain Inn					
2	Monthly Projected Profits					
3						
4	Projected Nights Booked	3,000	3,750	4,500	5,250	5,700
5	Occupancy Rate	50%	63%	75%	88%	95%
6	Revenue	$267,000	$333,750	$400,500	$ 467,250	$507,300
7	Operating Cost	260,000	275,000	290,000	305,000	314,000
8	Advertising	3,500	3,500	3,500	3,500	3,500
9	Commissions	14,632	14,632	14,632	14,632	14,632
10	Office Expenses	5,000	5,000	5,000	5,000	5,000
11						
12	Total Costs	283,132	298,132	313,132	328,132	337,132
13	Gross Profit	(16,132)	35,618	87,368	139,118	170,168
14	Net Profit	$ (12,099)	$ 26,714	$ 65,526	$ 104,339	$127,626
15	Gross Profit vs. Revenue	-6%	11%	22%	30%	34%
16						
17	Average Room Rate	$ 89		Commission Rate	15%	
18	Monthly Fixed Operating Cost	$200,000		Tax Rate	25%	
19	Nights Per Month	6,000		Variable Cost per Night	$ 20.00	

The Monthly Projected Profits worksheet will help Glen to understand how his bottom line changes in relation to occupancy rate.

Working with Formulas and Functions

A formula is simply a math problem done in Excel. You can add, subtract, multiply, divide, and group numbers and cell contents in order to make your data work for you. A function is a prewritten formula that helps to simplify complex procedures, both for numbers and for text. For instance, a function can be used to sum a group of numbers, to determine the payment amount on a loan, and to search for text.

Using AutoSum

FROM THE KEYBOARD

 for Autosum

The power of Excel becomes apparent when you begin using formulas and functions. The most common type of calculation is summing a column or row of numbers. In fact, this type of calculation is so common that Excel provides the AutoSum feature specifically for this purpose.

The **Σ AutoSum ▾** button on the Home tab automatically sums a column or row of numbers. When you click AutoSum, Excel proposes a range of cells. Excel will first look "up" for a range to sum, and if a range is not found there, it will next look left. You can accept the proposed range or drag in the worksheet to select a different range. When you complete the entry, Excel places a SUM function in the worksheet, which adds the numbers in the range.

You can include empty cells in the range that you wish to AutoSum, although if you are averaging a range of cells you will want to include only those cells with a value that should be included in the average.

!TIP! *If your Excel window is smaller, the button may be displayed like this:* **Σ ▾** .

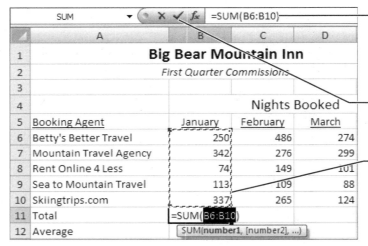

Excel will look "up" and propose to sum the range B6:B10 in cell B11 and display it in the Formula Bar. All formulas begin with an equals (=) sign. SUM is a built-in function that adds the numbers in a range (B6:B10 in this

When you click the Enter ✔ button on the Formula Bar to complete the entry, the total should be 1116.

A flashing marquee (marching ants) surrounds the range B6:B10. AutoSum assumes you want to add together all cells above B11 until the first empty cell (or cell not containing a number) is reached. The marquee identifies this range of cells.

Other Functions Available Through the AutoSum Button

The AutoSum button does not stop at simply summing a group of numbers. The following statistical functions are also available as automated features: average, count numbers, maximum, and minimum.

Auto Function	Description
Sum	Adds the cells indicated in the formula
Average	Averages the values in the cells indicated in the formula
Count	Counts the number of values in the cells indicated in the formula
Maximum	Returns the maximum value in the cells indicated in the formula
Minimum	Returns the minimum value in the cells indicated in the formula

 TIP! *Once you have entered a function in a cell, you can use AutoFill to copy it to adjacent cells.*

Status Bar Functions and Customization

The status bar, which is displayed at the bottom of the Excel window, allows you to view information about a range of numbers without actually inserting a function in the worksheet. You can customize the status bar to display the following functions: Average, Count, Numerical Count, Minimum, Maximum, and Sum. To customize the status bar, right-click anywhere on it and click to add or remove features. Other than functions, you can also customize additional features of the status bar such as zoom, signatures, overtype mode, and macros.

The range of B6:D10 has been selected in the worksheet.

When you right-click on the status bar, you will get a menu by which you can customize the status bar.

Notice that the sum in cell E11 matches the sum displayed on the status bar.

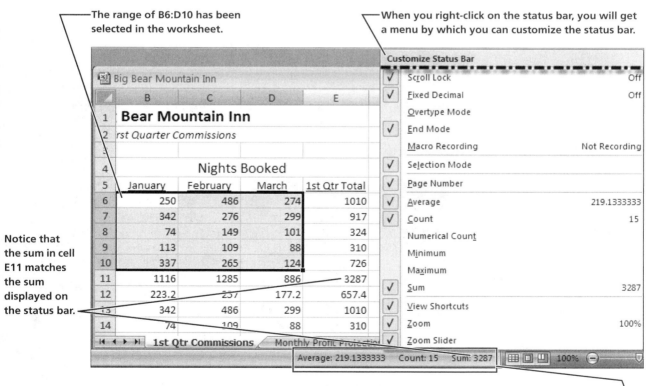

By default, Excel displays the sum, average, and count values of the selected range on the status bar.

QUICK REFERENCE: USING AUTOSUM AND THE STATUS BAR

Task	Procedure
AutoSum a range of cells	■ Click in the cell where you want the sum to appear. ■ Display the Home tab and click the AutoSum button on the Ribbon. ■ If the proposed range is correct, tap [Enter] to complete the function. ■ If the proposed range is incorrect, click and drag to select the correct range before tapping [Enter].
Use Status Bar Functions	■ Drag to select the range of cells to which you wish to apply the function. ■ Look at the Status bar at the bottom of your Excel window to view the sum, average, and count of the range of cells.

 ## Hands-On 3.1   Use AutoSum and Status Bar Functions

In this exercise, you will use AutoSum to calculate the number of rooms booked by each agency to whom you pay a commission, as well as the quarterly totals. You will also explore the functions on the status bar.

Open an Excel File

1. Start Excel.

2. Open the Big Bear Mountain Inn workbook from the Lesson 03 folder in your file storage location.
   Take a look at the workbook. There are two tabs at the bottom of the window: 1st Qtr Commissions and Monthly Profit Projection. On the Monthly Profit Projection worksheet, there are bookings entered; it will be up to you to calculate the total, average, maximum, and minimum values.

Use AutoSum

3. Click cell B11.

4. Choose Home→Editing→Sum **Σ** from the Ribbon.
   Excel displays a marquee (marching ants) around the part of the spreadsheet where it thinks the formula should be applied. You can change this selection as necessary.

5. Follow these steps to complete the AutoSum formula.

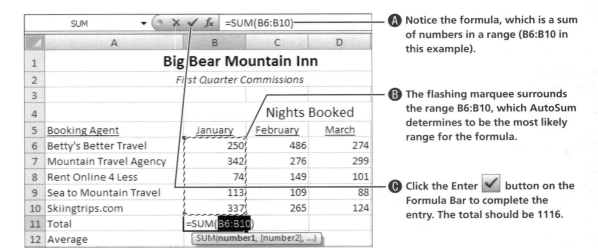

A Notice the formula, which is a sum of numbers in a range (B6:B10 in this example).

B The flashing marquee surrounds the range B6:B10, which AutoSum determines to be the most likely range for the formula.

C Click the Enter ✔ button on the Formula Bar to complete the entry. The total should be 1116.

6. Click in cell C11.

7. Choose Home→Editing→Sum Σ from the Ribbon and complete ✓ the entry.

8. Use the preceding technique to calculate the column total in cell D11.

Calculate the Quarterly Totals

9. Click in cell E6.

10. Choose Home→Editing→Sum Σ from the Ribbon.
    Notice that since there are no values above cell E6, Excel will look to the left to find a range to sum, B6:D6.

11. Tap [Enter] to complete the entry.

12. Use the preceding technique to calculate the row total in cell E7.

Override the Range AutoSum Proposes

13. Click in cell E8, and then choose Home→Editing→Sum Σ from the Ribbon.
    Excel will assume you want to sum the cells E6 and E7, above E8. This assumption is incorrect. Excel made this assumption because there were two cells above E8, which is enough to make a range.

14. Follow these steps to override the proposed range:

A Position the mouse pointer over cell B8, and then click and drag to the right until the range B8:D8 is selected.

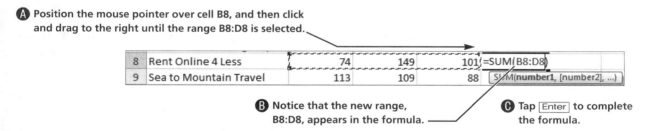

B Notice that the new range, B8:D8, appears in the formula.

C Tap [Enter] to complete the formula.

Use AutoFill to Extend a Formula

You can use AutoFill, which was introduced in the previous lesson, to extend a formula just as you used it to extend a series of days of the week.

15. Follow these steps to AutoFill the formula in cell E8 to the three cells below it:

A Click cell E8.

B Position your mouse pointer over the fill handle at the bottom-right corner of the cell until you see the thin cross, and then press the left mouse button and drag down through cell E11.

C Release the mouse button to fill the formula into the cells.

	A	B	C	D	E
5	Booking Agent	January	February	March	1st Qtr Total
6	Betty's Better Travel	250	486	274	1010
7	Mountain Travel Agency	342	276	299	917
8	Rent Online 4 Less	74	149	101	324
9	Sea to Mountain Travel	113	109	88	
10	Skiingtrips.com	337	265	124	
11	Total	1116	1285	886	
12	Average				

Use AutoCalculate

16. Drag to select the range B6:D10.

17. Look at the Status bar to see the sum value displayed by AutoCalculate.

18. Click the save 💾 button, but leave the spreadsheet open for the next exercise.

Creating Formulas

You have already learned how to compute totals with AutoSum. AutoSum provides a convenient method for summing a range of numbers. However, you will need to use many other types of formulas in Excel. In fact, many worksheets, such as financial models, require hundreds or even thousands of complex formulas.

Beginning Character in Formulas

As you saw in the AutoSum discussion in the previous section, functions begin with an equals (=) sign. If you are typing a formula in a cell, it is recommended that you also begin it with an equals (=) sign, even though you can begin it with a plus (+) or a minus (–) sign. It is best to adopt one method in order to create consistency.

Cell and Range References

Formulas derive their power from the use of cell and range references. For example, in the previous exercise, you used AutoSum to insert the formula =SUM(B6:B10) in cell B11. Because the range reference (B6:B11) was used in the formula, you were able to copy the formula across the row using the fill handle. There are two important benefits to using references in formulas.

■ When references are used, formulas can be copied to other cells.

■ Since a reference refers to a cell or a range of cells, the formula results are automatically recalculated when the data is changed in the referenced cell(s).

The Language of Excel Formulas

Formulas can include the standard arithmetic operators shown in the following table. You can also use spaces within formulas to improve their appearance and readability. Notice that each formula in the table begins with an equals (=) sign. Also, keep in mind that each formula is entered into the same cell that displays the resulting calculation.

QUICK REFERENCE: USING ARITHMETIC OPERATORS IN FORMULAS

Operator	Example	Comments
+ (addition)	=B7+B11	Adds the values in B7 and B11
– (subtraction)	=B7–B11	Subtracts the value in B11 from the value in B7
* (multiplication)	=B7*B11	Multiplies the values in B7 and B11
/ (division)	=B7/B11	Divides the value in B7 by the value in B11
^ (exponentiation)	=B7^3	Raises the value in B7 to the third power (B7*B7*B7)
% (percent)	=B7*10%	Multiplies the value in B7 by 10% (0.10)
( ) (grouping)	=B7/(C4–C2)	Subtracts the value in C2 from the value in C4 and then divides the result by the value in B7

 TIP! *When typing a cell reference in a formula, you can simply type the column letter in lowercase and Excel will capitalize it for you.*

Please Excuse My Dear Aunt Sally

Excel formulas follow the algebraic hierarchy you learned about way back in middle or high school. This means that the formula completes operations in a specific order. You may have learned to memorize this hierarchy with the mnemonic "Please Excuse My Dear Aunt Sally":

Please-	Parentheses (grouping symbols)
Excuse-	Exponents
My-	Multiplication
Dear-	Division
Aunt-	Addition
Sally-	Subtraction

In order to control the order of operations, you can use parentheses to cause Excel to add before multiplying or subtract before dividing. Take a look at the following examples to see how the order of operations works with and without parentheses and how the resulting value will be different.

=53+7*5=53+35=88   Multiplication then addition

=(53+7)*5=(60)*5=300   Parentheses then multiplication

Hands-On 3.2   Use the Keyboard to Create a Basic Formula

In this exercise, you will use the keyboard to enter formulas into the spreadsheet.

1. Click the Monthly Profit Projection sheet tab at the bottom of the Excel window.

2. Click cell B6.

3. Type **=B4*B17** in the cell, and then tap ⎕Enter to complete the formula.
   In order to calculate the revenue, you will need to multiply the number of nights booked (B4) by the average room rate (B17).

4. Click cell B5.

5. Type **=b4/b19** in the cell, and then tap ⎕Enter to complete the formula.
   Formulas are not case sensitive. Notice that regardless of whether you type the cell references as upper- or lowercase, the formula will work properly. In this example, the cell has been formatted to display a percentage for you. You will learn how to apply different number formats in Lesson 4, Formatting the Contents of Cells.

Using Cell References in Formulas

A cell reference identifies which cell or range of cells contains the values to use in a formula. Cell references are one of three types: relative, absolute, or mixed. All formulas use the relative cell reference unless you specifically instruct Excel to use another type. You used relative cell references in the formulas you created in the last exercise. As this lesson continues, you will learn about the other two types of cell references.

Relative Cell References

A relative cell reference means the cell is *relative* to the cell that contains the formula. For example, when you create a formula in cell C3 to subtract A3 minus B3 (=A3–B3), Excel finds that the first value is two cells to the left of the formula. The second value is one cell to the left of the formula.

When you copy a formula, the cell references update automatically and refer to new cells relative to the new formula cell. For example, if you copied the formula mentioned in the previous paragraph down to cell C4, the new formula would be A4 minus B4 (=A4–B4). The first and second values are still relative to the same number of cells to the left of the formula cell.

	A	B	C	D	E	F
12	Total Costs	=SUM(B7:B10)	=SUM(C7:C10)	=SUM(D7:D10)	=SUM(E7:E10)	=SUM(F7:F10)
13	Gross Profit	=B6-B12	=C6-C12	=D6-D12	=E6-E12	=F6-F12

Notice that when a formula utilizing relative cell references in column B is copied through to column F, the cells referenced in the copied formulas will refer to cells relative to where they are pasted.

Point Mode

One potential danger that can occur when typing formulas is accidentally typing the incorrect cell reference. This is easy to do, especially if the worksheet is complex. Point mode can help you avoid this problem. With point mode, you can insert a cell reference in a formula by clicking the desired cell as you are typing the formula. Likewise, you can insert a range reference in a formula by dragging over the desired cells. You will use point mode in the next exercise.

Absolute Cell References

You have been using relative references thus far in this course. Relative references are convenient because they update automatically when formulas are moved or copied. In some situations, you may not want references updated when a formula is moved or copied. You must use absolute or mixed references in these situations. Absolute references always refer to the same cell, regardless of which cell the formula is moved or copied to. You can refer to cells on other worksheets or in other workbooks as well. In Lesson 10, Managing Multiple-Sheet Workbooks, you will learn about referring to cells in other locations.

Creating Absolute References

You create absolute references by placing dollar signs in front of the column and row components of the reference: for example, $C$1. You can type the dollar signs as you enter a formula or add them later by editing the formula. The following illustration shows an example of how absolute references are used in formulas.

	A	B	C	D	E	F
12	Total Costs	=SUM(B7:B10)	=SUM(C7:C10)	=SUM(D7:D10)	=SUM(E7:E10)	=SUM(F7:F10)
13	Gross Profit	=B6-B12	=C6-C12	=D6-D12	=E6-E12	=F6-F12
14	Net Profit	=B13*(1-$F$18)	=C13*(1-$F$18)	=D13*(1-$F$18)	=E13*(1-$F$18)	=F13*(1-$F$18)
15	Gross Profit vs. Revenue	=B13/B6	=C13/C6	=D13/D6	=E13/E6	=F13/F6

Cell B14 displays a formula that has both a relative cell reference (B13) and an absolute cell reference ($F$18).

When copied to cell C14, the relative cell reference will refer to the cell relative to where it is pasted (C13), but the absolute cell reference will remain the same.

Mixed References

You can mix relative and absolute references within a reference. For example, the reference $C1 is a combination of an absolute reference to column C and a relative reference to row 1. Mixed references are useful when copying many types of formulas.

Using the [F4] Function Key

You make a reference absolute or mixed by typing dollar signs while entering the reference. You can also click in front of a reference in the Formula Bar and use the [F4] function key to insert the dollar signs. The first time you tap [F4], dollar signs are placed in front of both the column and row components of the reference. If you tap [F4] again, the dollar sign is removed from the column component, thus creating a mixed reference. If you tap [F4] a third time, a dollar sign is placed in front of just the column component and removed from the row component. One more tap of [F4] will return you to a relative cell reference.

What-If Analysis

Another great advantage to using cell references in formulas is that it allows you to perform what-if analyses. A what-if analysis is as simple as changing the value in a cell that is referenced in a formula and observing the overall change in the data. You can perform these simple analyses at any time by replacing the value(s) in referenced cells. The Undo command can come in very handy when performing a what-if analysis as it provides a quick way to return the worksheet to the original values. If you wish to perform an extensive what-if analysis and not worry about losing your original data, you may wish to save your workbook under a different name as a "practice" file.

 Hands-On 3.3   Create Formulas Using Cell References

In this exercise, you will use absolute cell references to create formulas that can be copied to other cells.

Enter a Formula Using Point Mode

1. Click cell B7, and type **=** to begin a formula.

2. Click cell B18, and then tap the ⌐F4⌐ function key.

NOTE! *If you have a keyboard that uses the function keys for other purposes, you may have to tap the ⌐F Lock⌐ key to be able to utilize ⌐F4⌐ for absolute or mixed references in Excel.*

Tapping ⌐F4⌐ will make the B18 cell reference an absolute by adding the $ symbol to both the column and row references. Take a look at the Formula Bar and you will see $B$18.

3. Type **+(** to continue the formula.

4. Click cell F19, and then tap ⌐F4⌐.

5. Type *****, and then click cell B4.

6. Type **)**, and then click the Enter ✓ button to complete the formula.
   You have created a formula using point mode consisting of both absolute and relative cell references. Notice how the formula appears in the Formula Bar: =$B$18+($F$19*B4). This means that no matter where you copy this formula to, it will always reference cells B18 and F19.

Enter Fixed Values and Calculate the Commissions

7. Click cell B8, type **3500**, and then tap ⌐Enter⌐ to complete the entry.

8. Click cell B10, type **5000**, and then tap ⌐Enter⌐.

9. Click the 1st Qtr Commissions tab.

10. Select the range B11:D11, and then look at the Status bar to determine the average number of commissionable nights booked per month.

Average: 1095.666667 Count: 3 Sum: 3287

Notice that the average number of nights you will be paying a commission on in the first quarter is 1,096 (rounded up). We will use this figure to calculate the commissions for the monthly profit projection sheet.

11. Click the Monthly Profit Projection tab to return to that worksheet.

12. Click cell B9, and enter the formula **=1096*$B$17*$F$17** to calculate the commissions. Tap ⌐Enter⌐ to complete the entry.

Now that you have learned how to use point mode as well as type formulas, you can choose which method to use for the rest of this exercise. Remember, though, that point mode is much more accurate, especially with large and complex worksheets.

Calculate the Total Costs and Profits

13. Click cell B12, and choose Home→Editing→Sum **Σ** from the Ribbon.

14. Click and drag to select B7:B10 as the range, and then tap ⌐Enter⌐.

15. Enter **=B6−B12** in cell B13, tapping ⌐Enter⌐ to complete the entry.
Now that you have calculated the gross profit, you can calculate the net profit since you know the tax rate.

16. Enter **=B13*(1−$F$18)** in cell B14, tapping ⌐Enter⌐ to complete the entry.

17. Enter **=B13/B6** in cell B15, tapping ⌐Enter⌐ to complete the entry.
You have now entered all of the formulas for column B. In the next exercise, you will learn how to edit the contents of cells B5 and B6 to reflect absolute cell references where necessary.

18. Take a look at the formulas displayed in the figure below to see how using absolute cell references differs from using relative cell references.

	A	B	C	D	E	F
4	Projected Nights Booked	=100*30	=125*30	=150*30	=175*30	=190*30
5	Occupancy Rate	=B4/$B$19	=C4/$B$19	=D4/$B$19	=E4/$B$19	=F4/$B$19
6	Revenue	=B4*$B$17	=C4*$B$17	=D4*$B$17	=E4*$B$17	=F4*$B$17
7	Operating Cost	=$B$18+($F$19*B4)	=$B$18+($F$19*C4)	=$B$18+($F$19*D4)	=$B$18+($F$19*E4)	=$B$18+($F$19*F4)
8	Advertising	3500	3500	3500	3500	3500
9	Commissions	=1096*$B$17*$F$17	=1096*$B$17*$F$17	=1096*$B$17*$F$17	=1096*$B$17*$F$17	=1096*$B$17*$F$17
10	Office Expenses	5000	5000	5000	5000	5000
11						
12	Total Costs	=SUM(B7:B10)	=SUM(C7:C10)	=SUM(D7:D10)	=SUM(E7:E10)	=SUM(F7:F10)
13	Gross Profit	=B6-B12	=C6-C12	=D6-D12	=E6-E12	=F6-F12
14	Net Profit	=B13*(1-$F$18)	=C13*(1-$F$18)	=D13*(1-$F$18)	=E13*(1-$F$18)	=F13*(1-$F$18)
15	Gross Profit vs. Revenue	=B13/B6	=C13/C6	=D13/D6	=E13/E6	=F13/F6
16						
17	Average Room Rate	89		Commission Rate		0.15
18	Monthly Fixed Operating Cost	200000		Tax Rate		0.25
19	Nights Per Month	=200*30		Variable Cost per Night		20

Modifying and Copying Formulas

You can modify and copy formulas in much the same way that you learned to edit and copy cells in the last lesson. We will use the tools learned previously and apply them to formulas in the next exercise.

Modifying Formulas

You can modify formulas in either the Formula Bar or the cell. If you select a cell and enter a new formula, it replaces the previous contents of the cell.

When you select a formula in order to edit it, you will see colored lines around all of the cells that are referenced by the formula. This can help you to visually determine if the formula is correct.

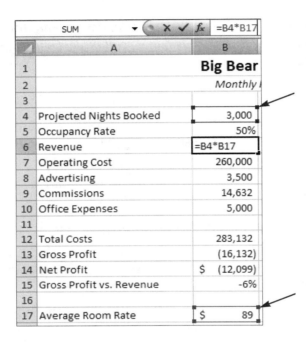

Notice that when the formula in B6 is selected for editing (as indicated by the insertion point in the Formula Bar), Excel will graphically display the cells that are being referenced by the formula, in this case cells B4 and B17.

Copying Formulas

You can use either the Copy and Paste commands with formulas or AutoFill in order to copy them to new cells. You can copy formulas to one cell at a time or to a range of cells using either method.

If you use AutoFill, the AutoFill Options button will appear once you have released the mouse button. Clicking this button will allow you to customize your fill.

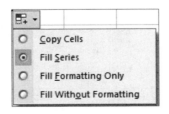

You can change what was copied in the cells through AutoFill by clicking the AutoFill Options button and choosing a different option.

Hands-On 3.4   Modify and Copy Formulas

In this exercise, you will use previously learned techniques to modify and copy formulas in order to complete your profit projection.

1. Click cell B5, and enter **=B4/$B$19** to replace the current formula.
    Make sure you tap Enter *to complete the entry of the formula or it will continue to build when you click the next cell!*

2. Click cell B6, and then follow these steps to edit the formula in the cell.

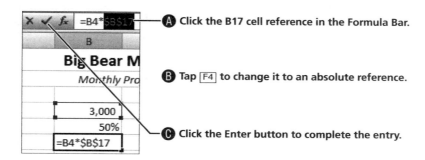

Ⓐ Click the B17 cell reference in the Formula Bar.

Ⓑ Tap F4 to change it to an absolute reference.

Ⓒ Click the Enter button to complete the entry.

Use Copy and Paste Commands to Copy a Formula

3. Click cell B5, and then use Ctrl+C to copy the formula.

4. Click cell C5, and then use Ctrl+V to paste the formula in the new cell.
    This method works great if you need to copy a formula to just one cell. You can use these commands to copy a formula to a range of cells as well.

5. Select the range D5:F5, and then use Ctrl+V.
    The formula that you copied in step 3 is now pasted to the range of cells selected.

6. Click in cell D5, and look at the formula in the Formula Bar.

D5	▾	f_x	=D4/$B$19	
	A	B	C	D
4	Projected Nights Booked	3,000	3,750	4,500
5	Occupancy Rate	50%	63%	75%

Notice that the relative cell reference now indicates cell D4, whereas the absolute cell reference is still looking to cell B19.

Use AutoFill to Copy Formulas

7. Follow these steps to copy the formula from cell B6 to the range C6:F6.

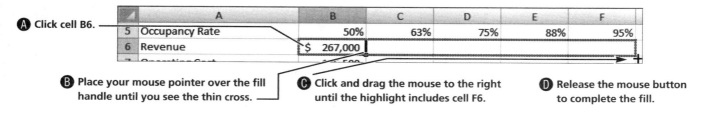

Ⓐ Click cell B6.

	A	B	C	D	E	F
5	Occupancy Rate	50%	63%	75%	88%	95%
6	Revenue	$ 267,000				

Ⓑ Place your mouse pointer over the fill handle until you see the thin cross.

Ⓒ Click and drag the mouse to the right until the highlight includes cell F6.

Ⓓ Release the mouse button to complete the fill.

Next, you will use AutoFill to copy formulas from B7:B15 all the way through F7:F15.

8. Select the range B7:B15.

9. Place your mouse pointer over the fill handle at the bottom right of the selected range.

10. When you see the thin cross **+**, drag to the right until the highlight includes the cells in column F.

260,000	275,000	290,000	305,000	314,000
3,500	3,501	3,502	3,503	3,504
14,632	14,632	14,632	14,632	14,632
5,000	5,001	5,002	5,003	5,004
283,132	298,134	313,136	328,138	337,140
(16,132)	35,616	87,364	139,112	170,160
$ (12,099)	$ 26,712	$ 65,523	$ 104,334	$ 127,620
-6%	11%	22%	30%	34%

Once you have AutoFilled the cells, the AutoFill Options button appears. Notice that the Advertising and Office Expenses rows have filled across as a series rather than copying the initial value. The AutoFill Options button will help you to solve this problem.

11. Click the AutoFill Options ![icon] button.

12. Click in the circle to the left of Copy Cells.
Excel revises the AutoFilled formula that filled in as a series (3,500; 3,501; 3,502; 3,503; and 3,504) rather than copying 3,500 all the way across.

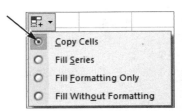

- ○ Copy Cells
- ○ Fill Series
- ○ Fill Formatting Only
- ○ Fill Without Formatting

Displaying Formulas

FROM THE KEYBOARD
Ctrl+` to show formulas

Excel normally displays the results of formulas in worksheet cells. However, you may need to display the actual formulas from time to time. Displaying the formulas can be helpful, especially in complex financial worksheets. Displaying formulas can help you understand how a worksheet functions. It can also be used to "debug" the worksheet and locate potential problems.

To display formulas, you will use the Show Formulas button on the Formulas tab of the Ribbon. You can edit a formula in this view, but you will need to show values again to see the result. In order to view the values once again, click the Show Formulas button again.

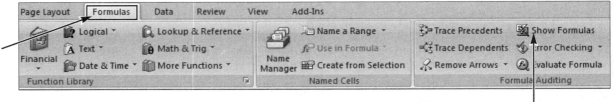

Depending on your monitor size, the buttons may appear as only icons, without the text descriptors, or as large buttons.

C	D	E
Big Bear Mountain Inn		
Monthly Projected Profits		
=125*30	=150*30	=175*30
=C4/$B$19	=D4/$B$19	=E4/$B$19
=C4*$B$17	=D4*$B$17	=E4*$B$17
=$B$18+($F$19*C4)	=$B$18+($F$19*D4)	=$B$18+($F$19*E4)
3500	3500	3500
=1096*$B$17*$F$17	=1096*$B$17*$F$17	=1096*$B$17*$F$17
5000	5000	5000
=SUM(C7:C10)	=SUM(D7:D10)	=SUM(E7:E10)
=C6-C12	=D6-D12	=E6-E12
=C13*(1-$F$18)	=D13*(1-$F$18)	=E13*(1-$F$18)
=C13/C6	=D13/D6	=E13/E6

When you choose to show formulas, you will see the formulas in the cells rather than the values as before. If a cell does not contain a formula, the contents will be visible in this view.

QUICK REFERENCE: VIEWING FORMULAS

Task	Procedure
Display or hide the formulas in a workbook	Choose Formulas→Formula Auditing→Show Formulas from the Ribbon.

 Hands-On 3.5   Display Formulas in a Worksheet

In this exercise, you will display the formulas in the profit projection worksheet to see how it is constructed and to be able to troubleshoot any potentially inaccurate formulas.

1. Choose Formulas→Formula Auditing→Show Formulas from the Ribbon.
   Take a look at the worksheet. You can use this feature to easily examine your formulas more closely.

2. Choose Formulas→Formula Auditing→Show Formulas from the Ribbon.
   The values will be displayed once again.

Using Formula AutoComplete

Excel 2007 includes a feature that serves to assist you in creating and editing formulas. Formula AutoComplete will jump into action once you have typed an equals (=) sign and the beginning letters of a function in a cell. It works by displaying a list of functions beginning with the typed letters below the active cell.

Functions Defined

A function is a predefined formula that performs calculations or returns a desired result. Excel has more than 400 built-in functions. You construct functions using a set of basic rules known as syntax. Fortunately, most functions use the same or similar syntax. This syntax also applies to the MIN, MAX, AVERAGE, and COUNT functions.

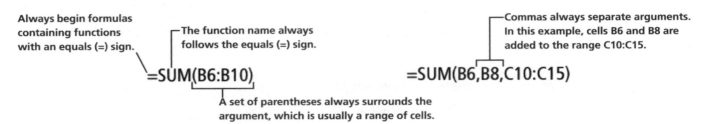

Always begin formulas containing functions with an equals (=) sign.

The function name always follows the equals (=) sign.

A set of parentheses always surrounds the argument, which is usually a range of cells.

Commas always separate arguments. In this example, cells B6 and B8 are added to the range C10:C15.

=SUM(B6:B10)

=SUM(B6,B8,C10:C15)

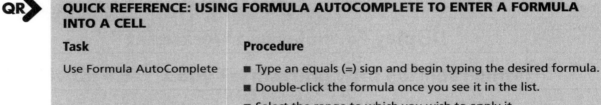

QUICK REFERENCE: USING FORMULA AUTOCOMPLETE TO ENTER A FORMULA INTO A CELL	
Task	**Procedure**
Use Formula AutoComplete	■ Type an equals (=) sign and begin typing the desired formula.
	■ Double-click the formula once you see it in the list.
	■ Select the range to which you wish to apply it.
	■ Type a closed parenthesis,), to finish the formula.
	■ Complete the entry.

Hands-On 3.6   Use Formula AutoComplete

In this exercise, you will have an opportunity to use the Formula AutoComplete feature to create a formula.

1. Display the 1st Qtr Commissions worksheet by clicking the sheet tab.

2. Click cell B12.

3. Type **=ave** and observe the list that results.

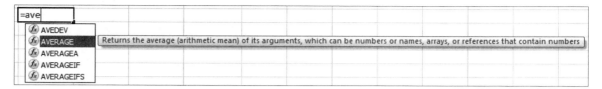

When you use Formula AutoComplete, Excel will show you a list of functions that begin with the letters you type in. If you click on a function in the list, a ScreenTip will display the results you will obtain if you select it.

4. Double-click AVERAGE in the list.
Excel will fill in the formula name for you. It will be up to you to select the range next.

5. Drag to select cells B6:B10 as the range for the formula.

NOTE! *You do not include total rows or columns when completing most functions.*

6. Type **)** to complete the function, and then tap Enter.

7. Click on cell B12, and use the fill handle to copy the function to the range of C12:E12.

11	Total	1116	1285	886	3287
12	Average	223.2	257	177.2	657.4
13	Maximum				

You now have the average number of bookings for each month and the entire quarter.

Using the Function Wizard

The Function Wizard ![fx] button displays the Insert Function dialog box. This dialog box provides access to all of Excel's built-in functions. It allows you to locate a function by typing a description or searching by category. When you locate the desired function and click OK, Excel displays the Function Arguments box. The Function Arguments box helps you enter arguments in functions. The Insert Function box and the Function Arguments box are shown in the following illustrations.

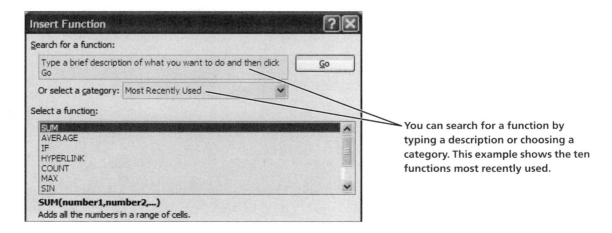

You can search for a function by typing a description or choosing a category. This example shows the ten functions most recently used.

The Function Arguments box appears when you choose a function and click OK. ——

You can type the argument (typically a range) in this box or select the desired range in the worksheet. ——

As you build the function, Excel displays it in the Formula Bar.

You can use the Collapse button to collapse (hide) the Function Arguments box while you select the desired range in the worksheet.

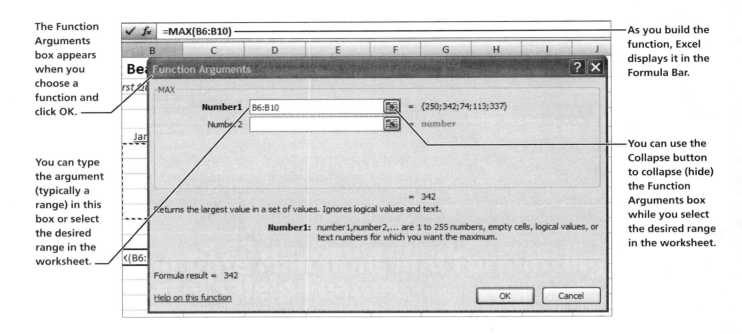

✓ fx   =MAX(B6:B10)

Function Arguments

MAX

Number1   B6:B10   = {250;342;74;113;337}
Number2   = number

= 342

Returns the largest value in a set of values. Ignores logical values and text.

Number1:   number1,number2,... are 1 to 255 numbers, empty cells, logical values, or text numbers for which you want the maximum.

Formula result = 342

Help on this function   OK   Cancel

 NOTE! *The ScreenTip for the Function Wizard* fx *is displayed as Insert Function.*

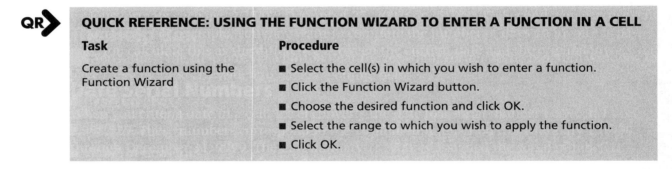

QR **QUICK REFERENCE: USING THE FUNCTION WIZARD TO ENTER A FUNCTION IN A CELL**

Task	Procedure
Create a function using the Function Wizard	■ Select the cell(s) in which you wish to enter a function. ■ Click the Function Wizard button. ■ Choose the desired function and click OK. ■ Select the range to which you wish to apply the function. ■ Click OK.

Hands-On 3.7   Use the Function Wizard

In this exercise, you will complete the commissions worksheet by using the Function Wizard to create both the maximum and minimum functions.

1. Click in cell B13.

2. Follow these steps to create the Maximum function.

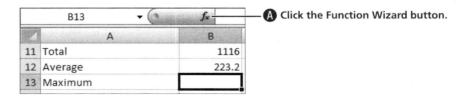

Ⓐ Click the Function Wizard button.

	A	B
11	Total	1116
12	Average	223.2
13	Maximum	

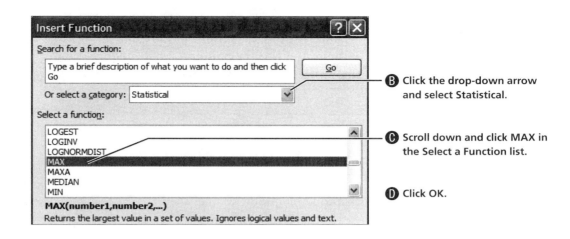

B Click the drop-down arrow and select Statistical.

C Scroll down and click MAX in the Select a Function list.

D Click OK.

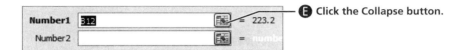

E Click the Collapse button.

F Click and drag to select the range B6:B10.

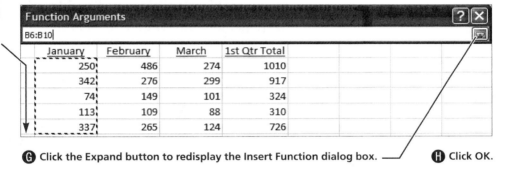

G Click the Expand button to redisplay the Insert Function dialog box. ⎯⎯⎯ **H** Click OK.

3. Use the fill handle to copy the formula to the range of C13:E13.

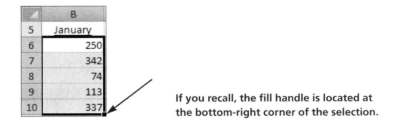

If you recall, the fill handle is located at the bottom-right corner of the selection.

4. Using the steps outlined in step 2, create the Minimum function in cell B14.

5. Copy the function in cell B14 to the range of C14:E14.

6. Save your workbook and close Excel.

Concepts Review

True/False Questions

1. All formulas begin with an equals (=) sign or a cell reference. **TRUE** FALSE
2. AutoSum can total a range of cells that contains blanks. **TRUE** FALSE
3. MIN and MAX are examples of functions. **TRUE** FALSE
4. Function arguments are always surrounded by quotation marks (" "). TRUE **FALSE**
5. You can use more than one arithmetic operator in a formula. **TRUE** FALSE
6. When you type a cell reference in a formula, you must type the column letter in uppercase. TRUE **FALSE**
7. You use F4 to make a cell reference absolute. **TRUE** FALSE
8. You can use AutoFill to copy a formula. **TRUE** FALSE
9. Formula AutoComplete is the only way to sum a range of cells. TRUE **FALSE**
10. "Please Excuse Sally My Dear Aunt" is a way to remember the arithmetic order of operations. **TRUE** FALSE

Multiple Choice Questions

1. Which button launches the Function Wizard?
   a. AutoSum
   b. Insert Function
   c. Create Function
   d. AutoFunction

2. Which function calculates the highest value in a selection?
   a. COUNT
   b. MIN
   c. MAX
   d. AVERAGE

3. Which of the following statements about using AutoSum is true?
   a. AutoSum automatically sums a non-adjacent column or row of numbers.
   b. AutoSum automatically sums an adjacent column or row of numbers.
   c. AutoSum can sum only a list of values in the column above.
   d. None of the above

4. Which cell reference contains dollar signs?
   a. Absolute
   b. Relative
   c. Mixed
   d. Both a and c

Skill Builders

Skill Builder 3.1   Use the AutoSum Function

In this exercise, you will use AutoSum to compute totals.

1. Open the sb-Benefit Plan workbook from the Lesson 03 folder in your file storage location.

2. Click cell C10, and then choose Home→Editing→Sum from the Ribbon.
   Notice that Excel proposes the formula =SUM(C8:C9). Excel proposes this incorrect formula because there are empty cells in the range you are to sum.

3. Drag the mouse pointer over the range C5:C9.
   The flashing marquee will surround the range C5:C9.

4. Complete the entry.
   The total should equal 650.

5. Use the techniques described in the preceding steps to compute the totals in cells E10, G10, and I10.

6. Save the changes to your workbook and close it.

Skill Builder 3.2   Create Simple Formulas

In this exercise, you will create formulas using the keyboard as well as the point-and-click method.

1. Open the sb-Orders and Returns workbook from the Lesson 03 folder in your file storage location.

2. Click cell B18.

3. Type =.

4. Click in cell B4, and type +.

5. Click in cell B9, and type +.

6. Click in cell B14, and tap Enter.

7. Use AutoFill to copy the formula to cells C18 and D18.

8. Using the techniques described in the preceding steps, create a formula in cell B19 that totals the exchanges from all three stores.

9. Create another formula in cell B20 that totals the returns from all three stores.

10. Use AutoFill to copy the formulas into the appropriate cells.

11. Take a few minutes to examine the formulas in the Formula Bar.

12. When finished, save and close the workbook.

Skill Builder 3.3   Use Formula AutoComplete and AutoFill

In this exercise, you will calculate averages by using the Formula AutoComplete feature.

1. Open the sb-Greeting Cards workbook from the Lesson 03 folder in your file storage location.

2. Click cell B8.

3. Begin typing the formula **=aver**, and then tap Tab to choose AVERAGE as the function.

4. Drag to select B3:B6, and then tap Enter.
   The result should equal 33.

5. Use the fill handle to copy the formula across row 8.

6. Click cell B17.

7. Use Formula AutoComplete to average the range B12:B15.
   The result should equal 23.5. Once again, you can type the function name and arguments in lowercase and Excel will convert them to uppercase.

8. Use the fill handle to copy the formula across row 17.

9. Click cell B20.

10. Use point mode to enter the formula =B7-B16, and complete the entry.
    The result should be 38.

11. Use the fill handle to copy the formula across row 20.

12. Save and close the workbook.

Skill Builder 3.4 Use Absolute References and Perform a What-If Analysis

In this exercise, you will create a worksheet that calculates commissions as total sales multiplied by the commission rate. You will change the commission rate to see the impact this change has on the total sales. You will use an absolute reference when referencing the commission rate.

1. Start a new workbook, and set up the following worksheet. Type all numbers as shown.

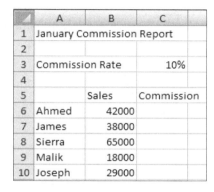

	A	B	C	
1	January Commission Report			
2				
3	Commission Rate		10%	
4				
5		Sales	Commission	
6	Ahmed	42000		
7	James	38000		
8	Sierra	65000		
9	Malik	18000		
10	Joseph	29000		

2. Click cell C6, and enter the formula **=B6*$C$3** in the cell.
   The result should be 4200. Cell C3 needs an absolute reference because you will copy the formula down the column and because the new formulas must also reference C3.

3. Use the fill handle to copy the formula down the column to cells C7 through C10.

4. Click cell C3, and change the percentage to **15%**.
   By this time, you should see the benefit of setting up values first (such as the commission rate) and referencing them in formulas. It allows you to perform what-if analyses. In most cases, you will need absolute references when referencing variables in this manner. Absolute references are necessary whenever you copy a formula that references a variable in a fixed location.

5. Change the commission percentage back to **10%**.

6. Save the workbook as **sb-January Commissions** in the Lesson 03 folder and close it.

 **Assessments**

Assessment 3.1   Create Simple Formulas

In this exercise, you will develop a worksheet with simple formulas.

1. Open the as-Credit Limits workbook from the Lesson 03 folder in your file storage location.

2. Follow these guidelines to create the following worksheet:

   ■ Enter all remaining text and number entries.

   ■ Use formulas in columns D and F to calculate subtotals and new balances. Calculate each subtotal as the previous balance plus new charges. Calculate each new balance as the subtotal minus the payment amount.

   ■ Use AutoSum to calculate totals for the range B11:F11.

	A	B	C	D	E	F
1	Joe's Place-Customer Credit Lines					
2						
3	Customer	Previous Balance	New Charges	Subtotal	Payment Amount	New Balance
4	Meredith Gray	100	50		150	
5	Derek Shepard	230	85		315	
6	Preston Burke	58	100		100	
7	Christina Yang	60	35		0	
8	Izzy Stephens	140	80		0	
9	Miranda Bailey	200	150		350	
10	George O'Malley	90	65		100	
11	Total Credit					

3. Use Print Preview to view your completed worksheet, and then print it.

4. Save your workbook and close it.

Assessment 3.2   Use AutoSum, MIN, and MAX

In this exercise, you will create a new worksheet that includes text and numbers. You will enter formulas and functions. Finally, you will save, print, and close the workbook.

1. Follow these guidelines to create the worksheet shown:

   ■ Enter the text and numbers as shown in the following table.

   ■ Use the formulas in the following table to calculate the interest charge in column E and the new balance in column F. Use parentheses in the Interest Charge formula to change the order of the calculation. You want Excel to subtract the payments from the beginning balance and then multiply the result by 1.5%. Don't type the words *Beginning Balance*, etc., in the formulas; use the appropriate cell references. Use AutoFill to extend the formulas from row 5 through row 9.

   Interest Charge = 1.5% * (Beginning Balance – Payments)

   New Balance = Beginning Balance + Purchases – Payments + Interest Charge

   ■ Use AutoSum to calculate the totals in row 10.

   ■ Use the MAX and MIN functions to calculate the highest and lowest numbers in rows 11 and 12.

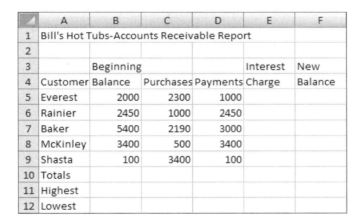

	A	B	C	D	E	F
1	Bill's Hot Tubs-Accounts Receivable Report					
2						
3		Beginning			Interest	New
4	Customer	Balance	Purchases	Payments	Charge	Balance
5	Everest	2000	2300	1000		
6	Rainier	2450	1000	2450		
7	Baker	5400	2190	3000		
8	McKinley	3400	500	3400		
9	Shasta	100	3400	100		
10	Totals					
11	Highest					
12	Lowest					

2. Print the worksheet when you have finished.

3. Save the workbook as **as-Accounts Receivable**, and then close it.

Assessment 3.3 Use Absolute References

In this exercise, you will create formulas using absolute references.

1. Open the as-Jan Price Change workbook.

2. Follow these guidelines to complete the following worksheet:
   - Enter the text entries as shown. Enter the numbers in column B and the percentage in cell B3.
   - Use a formula to calculate the discounted price in cell C7. Use an absolute reference when referring to the discount rate in cell B3. Remember that you are calculating the discounted price, so your formula must subtract the discount rate in B3 from 1. The generic formula is Discounted Price = Original Price * (1 − Discount Rate).
   - Copy the formula in cell C7 down the column.

3. Change the percentage in cell B3 to **10%**, and watch the worksheet recalculate.

4. Change the percentage in cell B3 back to **15%**, and watch the worksheet recalculate.

5. Save and close the workbook.

	A	B	C
1	January Price Change Worksheet		
2			
3	January Discount Rate	15%	
4			
5		Original	Discounted
6	Item	Price	Price
7	Track and Walk Footwear	34.50	
8	Action Aerobics Wear	19.00	
9	Designer Jeans	50.00	
10	Sherman Cowboy Boots	67.95	
11	Jensen Backpacks	34.55	
12	Rain or Shine Coats	45.00	
13	Diamond Black Socks	2.95	
14	Steck-Harman Shirts	19.95	
15	Back Country Jeans	24.95	

Assessment 3.4   Create a Financial Report

In this exercise, you will create a worksheet by entering data, creating formulas, and using absolute references. You will also save, print a section of, and close the workbook.

1. Open the as-2008 Projected Net Income workbook from the Lesson 03 folder in your file storage location.

2. Use these guidelines to create the following financial report:

   - Type the headings, labels, and numbers as shown in the following illustration. Use AutoFill whenever possible to copy cells or complete a series (for example, with the Q1, Q2, Q3, and Q4 headers).

   - Use formulas to calculate the numbers in rows 6–9. The formulas should multiply the revenue in row 4 by the variables in rows 15–19. For example, the employee costs in cell B6 are calculated as the revenue in cell B4 multiplied by the percentage in cell B15. Use absolute references in these formulas when referring to the variables so you can copy the formulas across the rows. You must use absolute references to get full credit for this assessment!

   - Use AutoSum to calculate the total costs in row 10.

   - Calculate the gross profit in row 12 as Revenue – Total Costs.

   - Calculate the net profit in row 13 as Gross Profit * (1 – Tax Rate). Once again, use absolute references when referring to the tax rate in cell B19.

3. Perform a what-if analysis on your worksheet by changing the percentages in rows 15–19. Make sure the report recalculates correctly when the values are changed.

4. Print the worksheet.

5. Select the range A1:E13, and print just that area.

6. Issue the command to show the formulas in the worksheet.

7. Print the range A1:E13.
   Notice that the column widths are automatically increased to accommodate the width of the formulas. This will cause it to print on two pages.

8. Save the workbook, and then close it.

	A	B	C	D	E
1	2008 Projected Income				
2					
3		Q1	Q2	Q3	Q4
4	Revenue	345000	390000	480000	500000
5					
6	Employee Costs				
7	Capital Expenditures				
8	Manufacturing				
9	Marketing & Sales				
10	Total Costs				
11					
12	Gross Profit				
13	Net Profit				
14					
15	Employee Costs	18%			
16	Capital Expenditures	22%			
17	Manufacturing	17%			
18	Marketing & Sales	16%			
19	Tax Rate	40%			

Critical Thinking

Critical Thinking 3.1   Customer Base Analysis

Stacey Prius is a freelance graphic designer and website developer. She specializes in helping small businesses establish corporate identities. Stacey's computer skills allow her to transform creative ideas into stunning visual designs that win over customers and earn her lucrative contracts. She wants to focus her energies on customers who produce the highest rates of return. Stacey asks you to set up a worksheet to help her analyze her customer base. She provides you with the following initial data:

Company Type	Number of Projects	Total Billings	Total Hours
Consulting	14	$25,900	235
Technology	23	$81,420	679
Manufacturing	6	$16,200	171
Food Service	8	$15,200	179
Retail Sales	12	$30,480	311

■ Calculate the total number of projects, total billings, and total hours.

■ Calculate the average billings per project for each company type.

■ Create a formula to calculate the average hourly billing rate for each company type. Use the AVERAGE function to calculate the average total billings and the average hourly rate for all company types combined.

■ Save the workbook as **ct-Customer Analysis**.

Critical Thinking 3.2   Customer Habits

Marina Berkman is a manager in the research department of CTA, Inc. CTA prepares studies on consumer buying habits for companies and organizations throughout the United States. Marina asks you to prepare a worksheet to record the food-buying habits of consumers. The worksheet must record on a daily basis the amount of money spent on groceries, breakfast out, lunch out, dinner out, and snacks out. The worksheet should record the information for one person over an entire week. Enter the data you desire, and include totals of all expenditures for each day of the week and expenditure type. Use the AVERAGE function to calculate the average daily expenditures for each expenditure type. Save your workbook as **ct-Buying Habits**.

Critical Thinking 3.3   Income and Expense Worksheet

John Jennings is the founder and owner of Crispy Crust Pizza. He started Crispy Crust in a stall in his local shopping mall and has had so much success that he wants to expand by opening three more stores over the next 18 months. John thinks he can increase the profit margin of Crispy Crust by opening these stores. He figures that the combined sales volume of the four stores will allow him to lower his food and packaging costs. In addition, he will be able to allocate his advertising, management, and overhead costs over the four stores. John hires you to prepare an income and expense worksheet.

Use Excel to set up a financial worksheet for Crispy Crust Pizza using the following information for the original (first) store. In addition, calculate the pretax profit and the profit versus revenue for the original store. The pretax profit is simply the revenue minus total costs and expenses.

First store forecasted revenue	$200,000
Food costs as a percentage of revenue	12%
Packaging costs as a percentage of revenue	2%
Advertising expenses as a percentage of revenue	14%
Management expenses as a percentage of revenue	13%
Overhead costs as a percentage of revenue	22%

Set up a variable section in the worksheet with the following initial percentages:

Per-store sales increase: 10%	Advertising savings: 38%
Food cost savings: 4%	Management cost savings: 23%
Packaging savings: 16%	Overhead savings: 12%

Calculate the revenue, expenses, pretax profit, and pretax profit versus revenue for the additional stores. Assume that the revenue and expenses are equal to the original store revenue and expenses multiplied by the number of stores. Adjust the revenue and expenses using percentages in the variable section. For example, the revenue for the second store would be equal to the revenue of the original store plus an additional 10%. The revenue for the third store would be the revenue of the second store plus an additional 10%. John assumes the additional revenue will result from crossover traffic between stores. Use absolute references in formulas that refer to the variable section of the worksheet. Copy formulas whenever possible, and use absolute references where necessary so you can copy formulas. Save your completed worksheet as **ct-Pizza Report**.

Critical Thinking 3.4   Harvard Costs

David is a junior in high school with a 4.0 GPA and a bright future. David's parents want him to attend Harvard University. They ask you to set up an expense worksheet for a four-year stay at Harvard. Use Internet Explorer and a search engine of your choice to locate Harvard University's website. Determine the approximate tuition, fees, room, board, and personal expenses for a full-time undergraduate student. The purpose of your worksheet is to determine the out-of-pocket expenses for which David's parents must plan. Use the following payment sources for the first year of attendance:

- David's contribution (first year): $3,500

- Scholarship contribution (first year): $12,500

- Student loans (first year): $5,700

Use formulas to calculate the amount that David's parents will need to contribute for each of the next four years. Begin by determining the costs per year, and then use formulas to adjust the expenses and payment sources for David's sophomore, junior, and senior years as shown below.

- Tuition, fees, room, board, and personal expenses: 5% annual increase

- David's contribution: 15% annual increase

- Scholarships: No change ($12,500 each year)

- Student loans: 10% annual increase

When you have finished, save your workbook as **ct-Harvard Costs**.

LESSON 4

Formatting the Contents of Cells

In this lesson, you will learn how to use several of Excel's formatting features to enhance your worksheets. You will also learn powerful tools and techniques such as AutoFormat and the Format Painter. By the end of this lesson, you will have developed the skills necessary to produce professional-looking worksheets.

LESSON OBJECTIVES

After studying this lesson, you will be able to:

- Format worksheets using a variety of methods: Ribbon, Mini Toolbar, Format Cells Dialog Box
- Horizontally align and indent cell entries
- Apply and cancel text control options: merge, wrap text, and shrink to fit
- Format cell borders and fill colors
- Use the Format Painter tool to copy formatting
- Apply a theme to your worksheet
- Work with dates and create date and time functions

Case Study: Formatting with Excel

Mendy Dobranski runs a computer and QuickBooks consulting business. She is working on her 3rd Quarter Income Statement for 2008. So far she has entered all of the data, but the report looks very drab and boring. She is now ready to spruce it up by using many of Excel's formatting features. Mendy will work to enhance the look of the text and numbers as well as cell characteristics such as the color displayed in the cells and the lines surrounding them.

	A	B	C	D	E
1	Mendy's Computer Services				
2	Income Statement				
3	3rd Quarter 2008				
4					
5		July	August	September	Quarter Total
6	INCOME				
7	Computer Tutoring	1750	1900	1550	5200
8	Contract Teaching	1300	1250	1650	4200
9	QuickBooks Consulting	4350	4125	3900	12375
10	Total Income	7400	7275	7100	21775

	A	B	C	D	E
1		Mendy's Computer Services			
2		Income Statement			
3		3rd Quarter 2008			
4					
5		July	August	September	Quarter Total
6	INCOME				
7	Computer Tutoring	$ 1,750	$ 1,900	$ 1,550	$ 5,200
8	Contract Teaching	1,300	1,250	1,650	4,200
9	QuickBooks Consulting	4,350	4,125	3,900	12,375
10	Total Income	$ 7,400	$ 7,275	$ 7,100	$ 21,775

The top figure represents the income portion of the Income Statement before you work your formatting magic. The bottom figure shows how the worksheet will appear at the end of the lesson.

Formatting Worksheets

Formatting deals with changing how the data in your worksheet looks, not with changing the data itself. In Excel and other Office programs, you can format text by changing the font, font size, and font color. You can also apply various font enhancements, including bold, italic, and underline. To format cells, select the desired cell(s) and apply formats using buttons on the Home tab of the Ribbon, by using the Format Cells dialog box, or by using the mini toolbar that appears when you right-click a cell or select text.

Formatting Entries with the Ribbon

The Font group on the Home tab of the Ribbon provides you with many popular formatting commands.

The Font group on the Home tab of the Ribbon makes finding formatting options easy.

Using the Mini Toolbar

The mini toolbar, a new feature in the Office 2007 Suite, will appear when text is selected. It will appear transparent until you move the mouse pointer over it. If you right-click a cell, the mini toolbar will appear non-transparent, ready to use. The mini toolbar will allow you to format the selected text without having to have the Home tab of the Ribbon displayed. This can be extremely convenient when you are primarily working with another tab of the Ribbon.

If you select text, the mini toolbar will appear transparent.

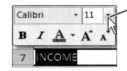
Once the mouse pointer is placed over a cell or you right-click it, the mini toolbar will appear "solid."

The mini toolbar will appear when text is selected, such as when "INCOME" is selected above.

Live Preview

In Office 2007, you will have the opportunity to preview how many formatting changes will look before actually issuing the command. Where this feature is available, you will see how the selected area will look when you place your mouse pointer over the formatting option.

FROM THE KEYBOARD
Ctrl+B for bold
Ctrl+I for italicize
Ctrl+U for underline

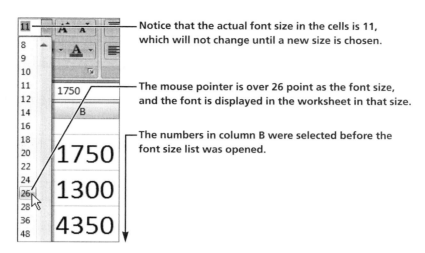

Notice that the actual font size in the cells is 11, which will not change until a new size is chosen.

The mouse pointer is over 26 point as the font size, and the font is displayed in the worksheet in that size.

The numbers in column B were selected before the font size list was opened.

Hands-On 4.1   Format Cells with the Ribbon and Mini Toolbar

In this exercise, you will begin to format the worksheet by using both the Ribbon and the mini toolbar.

Open an Excel File

1. Start Excel.

2. Open the Mendy's Computer Services workbook in the Lesson 04 folder in your file storage location.
   You will see a worksheet displayed that contains all of the data and formulas but that is very much in need of some "beautification"! We will begin by changing the font size of the entire worksheet.

Use the Ribbon to Format

In this section, you will first select the entire worksheet. This means that any formatting that is applied will affect the contents of the whole worksheet.

3. Follow these steps to change the font size for the entire worksheet:

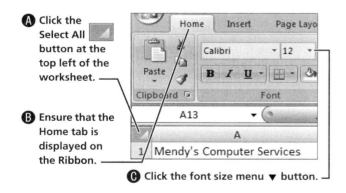

Ⓐ Click the Select All button at the top left of the worksheet.

Ⓑ Ensure that the Home tab is displayed on the Ribbon.

Ⓒ Click the font size menu ▼ button.

Ⓓ Choose 12.

Notice that as you move the mouse pointer over the font size list, Excel will allow you to preview how the worksheet would appear if each font size were selected.

Use the Mini Toolbar to Format

4. Click cell A6.

5. Double-click the word *INCOME* in cell A6 two times—once to select the word, and once to open the mini toolbar.
The first time you double-click, the cell will be available for editing; the second time, INCOME will be selected and a translucent mini toolbar will appear above the selection.

6. Move the mouse pointer over the mini toolbar and click the Bold **B** button.
When you move your mouse pointer over the transparent mini toolbar, it will become visible and you can choose the Bold option.

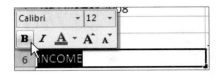

7. Right-click cell A12.
Right-clicking a cell will also display the mini toolbar.

8. Click the Bold **B** button on the mini toolbar.

9. Use Ctrl + S to save your work before you move to the next topic.

Using Excel's Alignment and Indent Features

Excel allows you to alter how the text is aligned within cells. In addition to the standard left, center, right, and justify horizontal alignments, you can indent the contents within a cell from either edge.

Aligning Entries

The Align Left ☰, Center ☰, and Align Right ☰ buttons on the Home tab of the Ribbon let you align entries within cells. By default, text entries are left aligned and number entries are right aligned. To change alignment, select the cell(s) and click the desired alignment button.

Indenting Cell Entries

The Increase Indent ☰ button and Decrease Indent ☰ button in the Alignment group on the Home tab of the Ribbon let you offset entries from the edges of cells. If a cell entry is left aligned, it will indent from the left edge, and if it is right aligned, it will indent from the right edge. Indenting is useful for conveying the hierarchy of entries. The following illustration shows indented cells:

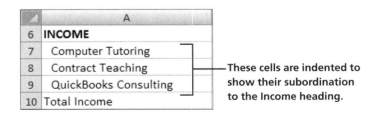

These cells are indented to show their subordination to the Income heading.

QUICK REFERENCE: WORKING WITH ALIGNMENTS AND INDENTS

Task	Procedure
Change the alignment in cells	■ Select the cells in which you wish to change the alignment. ■ Click the appropriate button in the Alignment group on the Home tab of the Ribbon.
Indent a cell or range of cells	■ Select the cells that you wish to indent. ■ Click the appropriate button in the Alignment group on the Home tab of the Ribbon.

Hands-On 4.2   Work with Alignment and Indent

In this exercise, you will set the alignment in cells as well as indent entries.

Change the Alignment in Cells

1. Select the range B5:E5.

2. Choose Home→Alignment→Align Text Right ▤ from the Ribbon.

3. Click cell A28.

4. Choose Home→Alignment→Align Text Right ▤ from the Ribbon.

Indent Cell Entries

5. Follow these steps to indent entries in a range of cells:

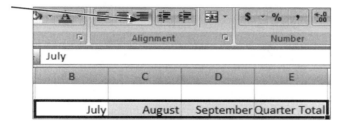

A Select the range A7:A9.

B Choose Home→Alignment→Increase Indent from the Ribbon.

6. Select the range A13:23.

7. Choose Home→Alignment→Increase Indent ▤ from the Ribbon.
Now both the types of income and the expenses have been "set off" from the left edge of the cell.

Using Excel's Text Control Options

The Alignment tab of the Format Cells dialog box provides options that allow you to merge, wrap, and shrink cell entries. You can add multiple lines to a cell by inserting a line break or setting the Wrap Text option in the Format Cells dialog box.

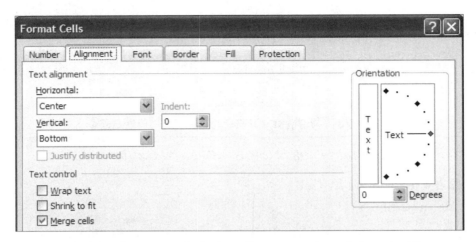

You can control the alignment and whether cells are merged or split from the Alignment tab of the Format Cells dialog box.

Merging and Splitting Cells

Excel's Merge Cells option allows you to combine cells. Merged cells behave as one large cell, and you can merge cells vertically and horizontally. The merged cell takes on the name of the top left cell in the merged range. For example, if you merge cells A1:E1, the resulting merged cell will be named A1.

Merging Cells

The Merge Cells option is useful if you want to place a large block of text like a paragraph in the worksheet. You can merge cells by selecting the desired cells, clicking the Dialog Box Launcher button (as shown in the following figure) in the Alignment group on the Home tab of the Ribbon, and checking the Merge Cells box on the Alignment tab. Likewise, you can split a merged cell into the original cell configuration by removing the checkmark from the Merge Cells box.

Notice that the merged range is now named A1; essentially cells B1 to E1 do not exist as long as they are merged into A1.

Notice that the options that apply to the selected cell are displayed in orange on the Ribbon.

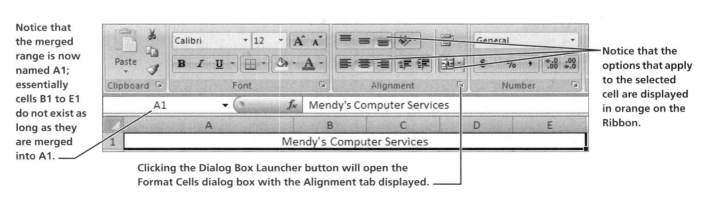

Clicking the Dialog Box Launcher button will open the Format Cells dialog box with the Alignment tab displayed.

Merge & Center Command

The Merge & Center ⊞ button merges selected cells and changes the alignment of the merged cell to center. This technique is often used to center a heading across columns. You split a merged and centered cell by clicking the Merge & Center button again. The Merge & Center menu button (see the following illustration) displays a menu with additional merge options.

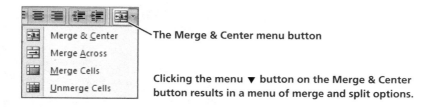

The Merge & Center menu button

Clicking the menu ▼ button on the Merge & Center button results in a menu of merge and split options.

	A	B	C	D	E
1	Mendy's Computer Services				
2	Income Statement				
3	3rd Quarter 2008				

Cells A1:E1 are merged, and the Mendy's Computer Services heading is centered above columns A–E. The entire heading is contained within cell A1.

Wrapping Text

The Wrap Text option forces text to wrap within a cell as it would in a word processing document. You can turn the Wrap Text option on and off by selecting the desired cell(s), displaying the Alignment tab of the Format Cells dialog box, and checking or unchecking the Wrap Text box. You can also select the cells in which to wrap text and choose the Wrap Text button from the Home tab of the Ribbon.

Entering a Line Break

You can add multiple lines to a cell by inserting a line break or setting the Wrap Text option in the Format Cells dialog box. Use the keystroke command [Alt] + [Enter] to insert a line break. To delete a line break, click to the right of the last word on the first line and tap [Delete].

FROM THE KEYBOARD

[Alt]+[Enter] to insert a line break

Shrinking Text to Fit Within a Cell

There may be times when changing the width of a column or wrapping text is not appropriate, yet you still want all of the text within the cell to be displayed. Excel has a feature on the Alignment tab of the Format Cells dialog box that allows you to shrink the cell entry to fit the cell "as is." This option is termed Shrink to Fit.

QUICK REFERENCE: MERGING CELLS AND WRAPPING TEXT

Task	Procedure
Merge and center a range of cells	■ Select the cells you wish to merge together. ■ Display the Home tab of the Ribbon. ■ Choose Home →Alignment→Merge & Center 🔲.
Wrap text within a cell	■ Select the cell(s) in which you wish to have text wrapped. ■ Display the Home tab of the Ribbon. ■ Choose Home →Alignment→Wrap Text 🔲.
Shrink text to fit the column width	■ Select the cell(s) in which you wish to shrink the contents to fit. ■ Place your mouse pointer over the selection and right-click. ■ Choose Format Cells from the pop-up menu. ■ Display the Alignment tab. ■ Click in the box to the left of Shrink to Fit. ■ Click OK.

 ## Hands-On 4.3   Control Text in Cells

In this exercise, you will have the opportunity to merge and center cells as well as wrap text within a cell.

Merge and Center a Range of Cells

1. Select the range A1:E1.

2. Choose Home→Alignment→Merge & Center 🔲 from the Ribbon.
   The entry from cell A1 is now centered over columns A through E.

3. Click cell C1.
   Notice that A1 is displayed in the Name box. While cell C1 is merged with A1, B1, D1, and E1, it essentially no longer exists!

4. Select A2:E2.

5. Choose Home→Alignment→Merge & Center 🔲 from the Ribbon.

6. Repeat steps 4 and 5 for the range A3:E3.

Wrap Text within a Cell

7. Click cell E5.

8. Choose Home→Alignment→Wrap Text 🔲 from the Ribbon.

9. use Ctrl + Z to undo the last command.

10. Follow these steps to manually enter a line break in the cell:

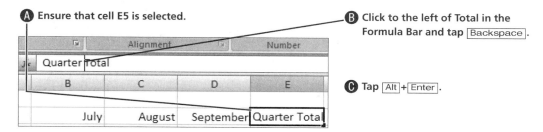

Ⓐ **Ensure that cell E5 is selected.**

Ⓑ **Click to the left of Total in the Formula Bar and tap** `Backspace`.

Ⓒ **Tap** `Alt`+`Enter`.

11. Tap `Enter` to complete the entry.
    Excel applies wrapped text formatting to the cell and applies the line break where you tapped `Alt`+`Enter`.

12. Use `Ctrl`+`S` to save your work.

Formatting Numbers

Excel lets you format numbers in a variety of ways. Number formats change the way numbers are displayed, though they do not change the actual numbers. Once a number formatting has been applied to a cell, it remains with the cell—even if the contents are deleted. The following table describes the most common number formats.

Number Format	Description
General	Numbers are formatted with the General Style format by default. It does not apply any special formats to the numbers.
Comma	The Comma Style format inserts a comma after every third digit in the number. It also inserts a decimal point and two decimal places, which can be removed if desired.
Currency	The Currency Style format is the same as the Comma format except that it adds a dollar ($) sign in front of the number.
Percent	A percent (%) sign is inserted to the right of the number in the Percent Style. The percentage is calculated by multiplying the number by 100.

!TIP! *If you begin an entry with a dollar sign, the Currency format will automatically be applied.*

The following table provides several examples of formatted numbers.

Number Entered	Format	How the Number Is Displayed
5347.82	General	5347.82
5347.82	Comma with 0 decimal places	5,348
5347.82	Comma with 2 decimal places	5,347.82
5347.82	Currency with 0 decimal places	$5,347
5347.82	Currency with 2 decimal places	$5,347.82
.5347	Percentage with 0 decimal places	53%
.5347	Percentage with 2 decimal places	53.47%

Using the Number Command Group

The Number Command group on the Home tab of the Ribbon allows you to format your numbers in a variety of ways, with the most common styles displayed as buttons. The top area of the group displays the number formatting of the selected cell(s). Clicking the menu button to the right of the current number formatting displays a menu of additional number format options.

If you click the Dialog Box Launcher button in the Number group, the Format Cells dialog box will appear with the Number tab displayed.

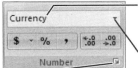

Notice that the number style of the selected cell(s) is displayed at the top of the group (in this example it is Currency).

This menu button displays additional formatting styles.

Clicking the Dialog Box Launcher button will open the Format Cells dialog box with the Number tab selected.

Using Accounting and Currency Styles

There are two number styles that apply currency symbols (such as dollar signs) to numbers. You will notice a difference in where the dollar sign is placed based on the style you select. If you choose the accounting style, currency symbols will appear fixed at the left of the cells. The currency style, on the other hand, will display the currency symbol next to the number in the cell.

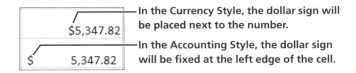

In the Currency Style, the dollar sign will be placed next to the number.

In the Accounting Style, the dollar sign will be fixed at the left edge of the cell.

Applying the Percent Style

In the Hands-On exercise from the previous lesson, cells were formatted with the Percent Style for you. This should reinforce the idea that once you apply formatting to a cell, it will remain until you change or clear it, regardless of whether there is any data contained in the cell. In order to apply the Percent Style yourself, you have two options.

- Select the cells that you wish to format as Percent Style and apply the formatting. If you format the cells first, you can type 25 and it will be formatted as 25%.

- Type the value in the cell first, and then apply the Percent Style formatting. If you type in the value first, you will need to type it in as a decimal. For instance, you will need to type in .25 in order for it to format properly as 25%. If you type in 25 and then apply Percent Style formatting, it will appear as 2500%.

Displaying Negative Numbers

Negative number displays can be either preceded by a minus sign or surrounded by parentheses. You can also display negative numbers in red. The Currency option and Number option in the Format Cells dialog box let you choose the format for negative numbers.

The negative number format you choose affects the alignment of numbers in the cells. If the format displays negative numbers in parentheses, a small space equal to the width of a closing parenthesis appears on the right edge of cells containing positive numbers. Excel does this so the decimal points are aligned in columns containing both positive and negative numbers.

16	Internet	45	45
17	Professional Dues	0	500
18	Rent	1500	1500
19	Software	-50	0
20	Subscriptions	25	0

When the numbers are formatted as General Style, the negative numbers will be displayed with a minus sign in front of them.

16	Internet	45.00	45.00
17	Professional Dues	-	500.00
18	Rent	1,500.00	1,500.00
19	Software	(50.00)	-
20	Subscriptions	25.00	-

When you choose the Comma Style format, you can accept the default negative number format with parentheses or change it to display a minus sign in the Format Cells dialog box. If you choose to format negative numbers with parentheses, the positive numbers will be set a bit further from the right edge of the cell in order for the decimal points to be aligned. Notice also that the cells containing the number 0 are displayed with dashes.

Hands-On 4.4   Format Numbers

In this exercise, you will apply various number formatting options to the worksheet.

1. Follow these steps to apply Currency Style format to a range of cells:

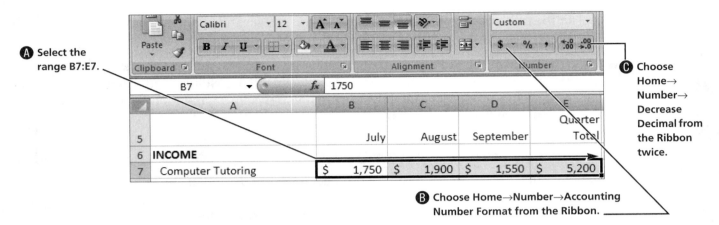

Ⓐ Select the range B7:E7.

Ⓒ Choose Home→ Number→ Decrease Decimal from the Ribbon twice.

Ⓑ Choose Home→Number→Accounting Number Format from the Ribbon.

Notice that the Accounting Number Format will display the dollar sign as fixed at the left edge of the cells. "Custom" will be displayed as the number format since you changed the number of decimal places of the Currency Style.

2. Select the range B8:E9.

3. Choose Home→Number→Comma Style [,] from the Ribbon.

4. Choose Home→ Number→Decrease Decimal [.00] from the Ribbon twice.

5. Select the range B10:E10, hold down [Ctrl], and select the range B24:E25.
   Remember that by using [Ctrl], you can select multiple ranges to which you can apply formatting.

6. Choose Home→Accounting Number Format [$] from the Ribbon.

7. Choose Home→Decrease Decimal [.00] from the Ribbon twice.

8. Select the range B13:E23.

9. Apply Comma Style formatting with no decimals to the selection.

10. Use [Ctrl]+[S] to save your work.
    Notice that all of the 0 entries are now displayed as dashes with comma formatting applied.

Using the Format Cells Dialog Box

We have discussed the Number and Alignment tabs of the Format Cells dialog box; now we will examine in more depth how to truly utilize this important dialog box. There are six tabs in the Format Cells dialog box that allow you to format different aspects of your worksheet: Number, Alignment, Font, Border, Fill, and Protection.

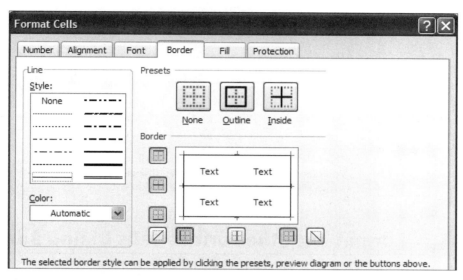

The Border tab of the Format Cells dialog box allows you to set the borders for the selected cells. In this example, a line will appear around the entire selection as well as between each row that is selected.

Borders and Fill Color

The Borders ⊞▾ button on the Home tab of the Ribbon lets you add borders to cell edges. When you click the Borders menu ▾ button, a list of options appears. You can apply a border style to all selected cells by choosing it from the list. You can also choose More Borders from the bottom of the list to display the Borders tab of the Format Cells dialog box.

The image displayed on the Borders button on the Ribbon will change based on the last border applied. This feature makes it easy to apply the same border formatting throughout the workbook.

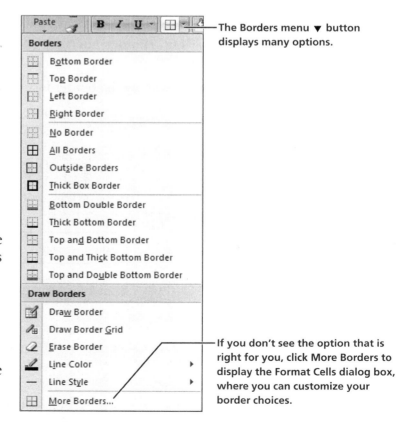

The Borders menu ▾ button displays many options.

If you don't see the option that is right for you, click More Borders to display the Format Cells dialog box, where you can customize your border choices.

Applying Fill Colors and Patterns

The Fill Color button on the Home tab of the Ribbon lets you fill the background of selected cells with color. When you click the Fill Color menu button, a palette of colors appears. You can apply a color to all selected cells by choosing it from the palette. The fill color is independent of the font color used to format text and numbers. The Format Cells dialog box has a Fill tab that lets you apply fill colors and a variety of patterns and effects.

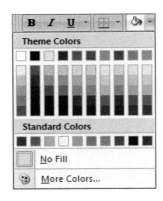

This palette of colors results when you click the Fill Color menu ▼ button. The color you choose will fill the cell but will not affect the color of the font.

Hands-On 4.5   Format with the Format Cells Dialog Box

In this exercise, you will apply borders and fill coloring to the worksheet.

Apply Borders to a Selection

1. Select the range A1:E25.
   When you choose A1, you will actually be choosing the entire merged cell that spans across column E.

2. Choose Home→Font→Borders menu ▼→More Borders from the Ribbon.

3. Follow these steps to apply the border formatting:

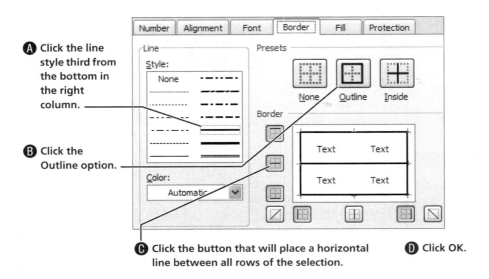

Ⓐ Click the line style third from the bottom in the right column.

Ⓑ Click the Outline option.

Ⓒ Click the button that will place a horizontal line between all rows of the selection.

Ⓓ Click OK.

Notice that the Borders button now displays the icon ⊞▼, which represents the More Borders option on the Borders menu. It will always display the last option selected from the Borders menu.

4. Use $\boxed{\text{Ctrl}}$ + $\boxed{\text{Z}}$ to undo the borders.

5. Select the range B9:E9, hold down the $\boxed{\text{Ctrl}}$ key, and select the range B23:E23. Then release the $\boxed{\text{Ctrl}}$ key.

6. Click the Borders menu ▼ button.

7. Choose the Bottom Border option to place a border along the bottom of the selected cells.

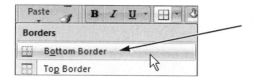

A border will appear along the bottom of both of the selected ranges. The Borders button will now display the Bottom Border icon.

8. Select the range B25:E25.

9. Click the Borders button drop-down arrow, and choose Top and Double Bottom Border.

Apply Fill Color to a Range

10. Select the range A6:E6, hold down the $\boxed{\text{Ctrl}}$ key, and select A12:E12. Then release the $\boxed{\text{Ctrl}}$ key.

11. Follow these steps to apply a fill color to the selected ranges:

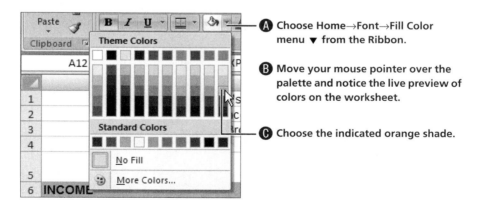

Ⓐ Choose Home→Font→Fill Color menu ▼ from the Ribbon.

Ⓑ Move your mouse pointer over the palette and notice the live preview of colors on the worksheet.

Ⓒ Choose the indicated orange shade.

12. Click away from the selection to view the color in the selected ranges.
    Notice that the cells are now orange, but the text has remained black.

13. Use $\boxed{\text{Ctrl}}$ + $\boxed{\text{S}}$ to save your work.

Using the Format Painter Tool

 There may be times when you want to copy the formatting from one cell to another without copying the contents. The Format Painter lets you copy text formats and number formats from one cell to another. This tool can be extremely helpful if you have a cell to which many formatting options have been applied and you do not wish to apply each option individually to another cell or range of cells.

QR **QUICK REFERENCE: USING THE FORMAT PAINTER**

Task	Procedure
Copy formats to one other cell or range	■ Click the cell that has the format(s) you wish to copy.
	■ Choose Home →Clipboard→Format Painter from the Ribbon.
	■ Select the cell or range to which you want to copy the format(s).
Copy formats to multiple locations	■ Click the cell that has the format(s) you wish to copy.
	■ Double-click the Home →Clipboard→Format Painter button.
	■ Select the cells or ranges to which you want to copy the format(s).
	■ When you are finished, click the Format Painter button to turn it off.

!TIP! *When you double-click Format Painter, you can scroll through the worksheet to reach the desired location(s). You can even click a sheet tab to copy formatting to a different worksheet in the workbook.*

 Hands-On 4.6   Copy Formatting with Format Painter

In this exercise, you will copy the formatting from one cell to a range of cells.

1. Click cell A12.
   You must first select the cell from which you wish to copy the formatting.

2. Choose Home→Clipboard→Format Painter button from the Ribbon.

3. Select the range A25:E25.
   The formatting from A12 will be applied to the entire range of A25:E25. Notice that the general number formatting is also copied.

4. Choose Home→Number→Accounting Number Format $ from the Ribbon.

5. Choose Home→Number→Decrease Decimal from the Ribbon twice.

Formatting with Themes

Themes allow you to easily apply formatting to your entire worksheet. The themes provided in Excel have been developed by designers at Microsoft and help you to choose fonts, styles, and colors that match nicely.

There is good advice that you should heed when using different font styles—do not use too many of them on one worksheet. You can "overformat" your worksheet! Themes allow you to choose matching fonts and styles if you are design-challenged.

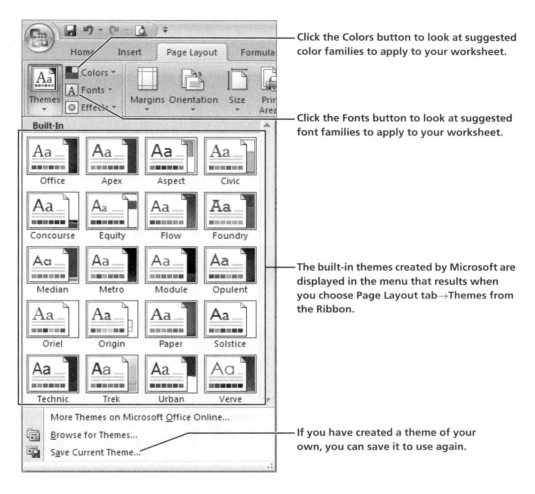

Click the Colors button to look at suggested color families to apply to your worksheet.

Click the Fonts button to look at suggested font families to apply to your worksheet.

The built-in themes created by Microsoft are displayed in the menu that results when you choose Page Layout tab→Themes from the Ribbon.

If you have created a theme of your own, you can save it to use again.

QUICK REFERENCE: APPLYING A THEME

Task	Procedure
Apply a theme to a range	■ Select the range to which you wish to apply the theme. ■ Choose Page Layout →Themes→Themes from the Ribbon. ■ Choose a theme to apply.

Hands-On 4.7 **Apply a Theme to a Worksheet**

In this exercise, you will apply a theme to Mendy's worksheet.

1. Select the range A1:E25.

2. Choose Page Layout →Themes→Themes from the Ribbon.

3. Choose the Apex theme.
   Notice the color and font in the worksheet now corresponds to those indicated in the theme.

4. Practice applying themes until you find one that suits you.

Inserting Date Functions and Formatting

In the previous lesson, we explored a variety of statistical functions. Now we will insert a function that will always display today's date. Excel will determine the date to display according to your computer's clock feature.

Working with Dates

Dates are used in workbooks in two ways. First, you can simply display dates in cells using various formats such as 12/25/07; December 25, 2007; or 25-Dec-07. Second, you can use dates in formulas. For example, you may want to compute the number of days an invoice is past due. You calculate this as the difference between the current date and the original invoice date.

Date Serial Numbers

When you enter a date in a cell, Excel converts the date to a serial number between 1 and 2,958,525. These numbers correspond to the 10-millennium period from January 1, 1900, through December 31, 9999. The date January 1, 1900, is assigned the serial number 1; January 2, 1900, is assigned the serial number 2; and December 31, 9999, is assigned the serial number 2,958,525. When dates are converted to numbers, you can use the numbers/dates in calculations. Best of all, it's done for you automatically!

Entering Dates

Excel performs the following steps when you enter a date in a cell:

■ It recognizes the entry as a date if you enter it using a standard date format such as 12/25/07; December 25, 2007; or 25-Dec-07.

■ It converts the date to a serial number between 1 and 2,958,525.

■ It formats the serial number entry with the same date format you used when you entered the date.

This roundabout process occurs behind the scenes so you never see it happening. The benefit of converting dates to numbers and then formatting them with a date format is that the dates can be used in calculations.

Inserting Date and Time Functions

In Lesson 3, Working with Formulas and Functions, you learned about some of Excel's powerful statistical functions. In Lesson 13, Using Financial Functions and Data Analysis and Lesson 14, Auditing and Additional Functions, you will learn about financial and database functions. In this lesson, you will see the value of using date and time functions in Excel.

About Date Functions

The current date is often required in worksheets. You may also want to show the date the worksheet was created or printed. The following details apply in general to dates you insert with date functions:

- You can insert a date function rather than typing the date in a worksheet.

- Date functions produce the current date and, depending on the specific function, can update automatically.

- You insert date functions with the Insert Function dialog box or by typing the function in the result cell.

- Date functions are not case sensitive so you can type the formula in lowercase.

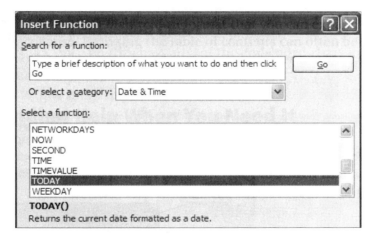

In the Date & Time function category, Excel provides a variety of functions. Notice that there is a description of the selected function displayed below the list.

The following table discusses three of the most common date and time functions.

Function	Description
TODAY( )	This function displays the current system date and calculates the serial number. The date updates automatically when the worksheet is recalculated or reopened.
NOW( )	This function displays the current system date and time and calculates the serial number. The date updates automatically when the worksheet is recalculated or reopened.
DATE(year,month,day)	This function returns the date entered in the default date format and calculates the serial number. The date does not update when the worksheet is recalculated or reopened.

QUICK REFERENCE: CREATING DATE AND TIME FUNCTIONS

Task	Procedure
Insert a Date or Time Function	■ Click the cell in which you wish to place the function result.
	■ Click the Insert Function f_x button.
	■ Choose the Date & Time category.
	■ Select the function you wish to create, and then click OK.
	■ Enter the appropriate function arguments.
	■ Click OK.

 Hands-On 4.8   Use the TODAY Function and Format a Date

In this exercise, you will create a formula that will calculate the current date and you will learn how to format dates.

Type a Date

1. Click cell B28.

2. Type **9/1/07** in the cell, and then click Enter ✓ on the Formula Bar.
   Look at the Number group on the Home tab of the Ribbon. The number format style displayed is Date, which Excel formatted for you when you typed the number in the date format.

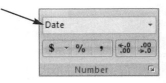

3. Display the Home tab of the Ribbon.

4. Click the Dialog Box Launcher 🔲 in the Number group of the Home tab.
   The Format Cells dialog box will open with the Number tab displayed.

5. Follow these steps to change the date format:

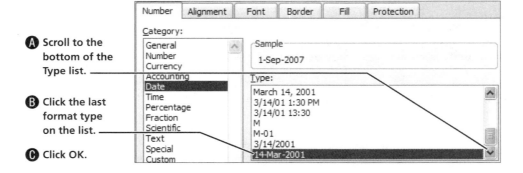

Ⓐ Scroll to the bottom of the Type list.

Ⓑ Click the last format type on the list.

Ⓒ Click OK.

6. Ensure that cell B28 is still selected, and then tap ⌷Delete⌷.
   Look at the Number group on the Home tab of the Ribbon and notice that even when you remove the contents of the cell (the date you typed in), the number format for the cell will remain as Date.

Enter a Date Function

7. Follow these steps to enter the TODAY function:

Ⓐ Click the Insert Function button.

Ⓑ Choose Date & Time as the category.

Ⓒ Scroll down until TODAY is visible.

Ⓓ Double-click TODAY.

Ⓔ Click OK in the Function Argument dialog box.

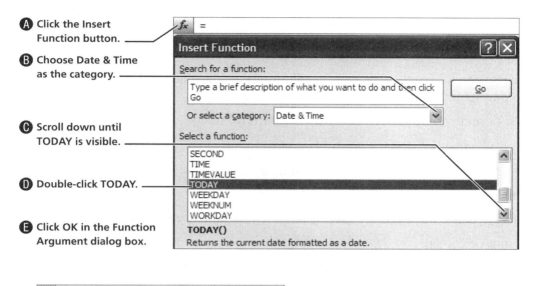

| 28 | Date Printed: | 28-Aug-2007 |

The date will appear with the number formatting you set for the cell.

8. Use [Ctrl]+[S] to save your work.

9. Close [×] Excel.

Concepts Review

True/False Questions

1. When you choose to fill a cell with color, it will automatically change the font color to one that complements it.   TRUE   FALSE

2. The Merge & Center command can be used only with numbers.   TRUE   FALSE

3. The Comma Style inserts a dollar sign in front of numbers.   TRUE   FALSE

4. The Format Painter copies text formats but not number formats.   TRUE   FALSE

5. You can change a font's style and size but not its color.   TRUE   FALSE

6. You can use a keyboard command to force a line break and text wrapping in a cell.   TRUE   FALSE

7. Formats cannot be copied.   TRUE   FALSE

8. By double-clicking the Format Painter button, you can copy formats into multiple locations.   TRUE   FALSE

9. Titles can be centered across multiple columns.   TRUE   FALSE

10. Dates are not able to be used in formulas and functions.   TRUE   FALSE

Multiple Choice Questions

1. Which feature allows you to easily apply formatting when the Home tab of the Ribbon is not displayed?
   a. Mini toolbar
   b. Quick Access toolbar
   c. Live Preview
   d. None of the above

2. What must you do before clicking the Merge & Center button?
   a. Click the cell that contains the entry you wish to center.
   b. Select the cells you wish to center the entry across, making sure the entry is included in the selection.
   c. Select the entire row that contains the entry you wish to merge.
   d. None of the above

3. What keyboard command creates a line break within a cell?
   a. Alt + Enter
   b. Ctrl + Shift
   c. Alt + Shift
   d. Ctrl + Enter

4. Which function displays the current system date and time and calculates the serial number?
   a. =TODAY ( )
   b. =TODAY'S DATE ( )
   c. =DATE ( )
   d. =NOW ( )

Skill Builders

Skill Builder 4.1   Format a Worksheet with the Ribbon

In this exercise, you will format a worksheet using commands available on the Home tab of the Ribbon.

1. Open the sb-PTA Budget Formatting workbook in the Lesson 04 folder from your file storage location.

2. Change the font for the entire worksheet to Arial Narrow.

3. Select A1, A7, A16, and A31 using the Ctrl key.

4. Choose Home→Font→Bold **B** from the Ribbon.

5. Select B8:D8, B14:D14, B17:D17, and B30:D30 using the Ctrl key.

6. Choose Home→Number→Accounting Number Format **$** from the Ribbon.

7. Select B9:D13 and B18:D29 using the Ctrl key.

8. Choose Home→Number→Comma Style **,** from the Ribbon.

9. Select D5.

10. Ensuring the Home tab is displayed, click the Number Format menu ▼ button and choose Currency from the list.
    If you click the Accounting Number Format **$** *button, the cell will be formatted differently, so make sure to choose Currency from the Number Format list as displayed. Notice that it is formatted with a different number format option and therefore appears different from cells B8, C8, etc.*

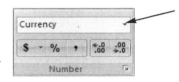

11. Save your workbook and leave it open as you will use it for the next exercise.

Skill Builder 4.2   Align Data and Copy Formats

In this exercise, you will change the alignment within cells and copy formatting from one cell to another. You can use the same file you used in Skill Builder 4.1, or you can open a file from the Lesson 04 folder if you did not complete the previous exercise.

1. Open the sb-PTA Budget Alignment workbook if you are not continuing from the previous exercise. (If you are continuing, your file should already be open.)

2. Select cell A5 and choose to right-align the entry.

3. Select cell B30.

4. Choose Home→Clipboard→Format Painter 🖌 from the Ribbon.

5. Select the range B31:D31.
   The formatting from cell B30 will be applied to the range B31:D31.

6. Save your workbook and leave it open as you will use it for the next exercise.

Skill Builder 4.3　Work with Text Control Options

In this exercise, you will merge and center entries as well as use the Shrink to Fit feature. You can use the same file you used in Skill Builder 4.2, or you can open a file from the Lesson 04 folder if you did not complete the previous exercise.

1. Open the sb-PTA Budget Text Control workbook if you are not continuing from the previous exercise. (If you are continuing, your file should already be open.)

2. Select the range A1:D1.

3. Choose Home→Alignment→Merge & Center ⊞ from the Ribbon.

4. Repeat the above command for the ranges A2:D2 and A3:D3.

5. Select the range B6:D6.

6. Choose Home→Alignment→Dialog Box Launcher ⬚ from the Ribbon.

7. Place a checkmark in the Shrink to Fit box under Text Control as shown at right, and then click OK.
   The contents of the cells will shrink to fit into the cells with the current width.

   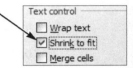

8. Save your workbook and leave it open as you will use it for the next exercise.

Skill Builder 4.4   Create a Date Function and Format a Date

In this exercise, you will enter a date function that will calculate the current date for you. You will be using the same file you used in the previous exercise, Skill Builder 4.3, or you can open a file from the Lesson 04 folder if you did not complete the previous exercise.

1. Open the sb-PTA Budget Date Function workbook, if it is not still open from the previous exercise.

2. Select cell B5.

3. Click the Insert Function f_x button.

4. Choose the Date & Time category.

5. Scroll down, and then click to select the TODAY function.

6. Click OK.

7. Click OK again in the Function Arguments window.
   The date will be returned in the default MM/DD/YYYY format.

8. Choose Home→Number→Dialog Box Launcher ⬚ from the Ribbon.

9. Scroll down if necessary, and then choose the format that will display the date as "1-Jan-07"
   Excel uses March 14, 2001, as its "example date" in the Format Cells dialog box. Rest assured that the date displayed will not be March 14, 2001, unless that is the date entered in the cell or the date resulting from a formula you may have created.

10. Add any additional formatting you wish to the worksheet, and then save your work.

11. Close the workbook.

# Assessments

Assessment 4.1   Format Text and Numbers

In this exercise, you will format and add enhancements to text and numbers.

1. Open the workbook named as-Atlantic Pools Formatting in the Lesson 04 folder on your file storage location.

2. Format B5:F5, B10:F10, and B11:F11 in Currency Style with 0 decimals using the Ribbon.

3. Format rows B6:F9 in Comma Style with 0 decimals.

4. Apply bold formatting to the entries in rows 10 and 11.

5. Format the title with bold, and change the font size to 14.

6. Format the column and row headings with bold.

7. Save your worksheet and leave it open for the next exercise.

Assessment 4.2   Control Your Text, Add a Border, and Use Format Painter

In this exercise, you will indent cell entries, center the title across worksheet columns, apply a border to cells, and use the Format Painter feature. You will be using the same file you used in the previous exercise, Assessment 4.1, or you can open a file from the Lesson 04 folder if you did not complete the previous exercise.

1. Open the as-Atlantic Pools Text Control workbook, if it is not still open from the previous exercise.

2. Indent the customer names in A5:A9.

3. Merge and center the title in cell A1 across columns A through F.

4. Right-align the entries in B3:F4.

5. Place a single border along the top of the range B10:F10 and a double line along the bottom.

6. Select cell B11.

7. Use the Format Painter feature to apply the formatting from cell B11 to the range B12:F12.

8. Save your worksheet and leave it open for the next exercise.

Assessment 4.3   Use Fill and Font Colors, and Apply a Theme

In this exercise, you will apply a theme to your worksheet. You will be using the same file you used in the previous exercise, Assessment 4.2, or you can open a file from the Lesson 04 folder if you did not complete the previous exercise.

1. Open the as-Atlantic Pools Colors workbook, if it is not still open from the previous exercise.

2. Add the fill color of your choice to A5:F9.

3. Change the font color of A1:F4 and A10:F12.

4. Choose to apply the Flow theme to the worksheet.

5. Save your work and close your workbook.

Critical Thinking

Critical Thinking 4.1   Customer Returns

Mary Perkins is the Customer Service Manager at a large retail store that sells everything from potato chips to television sets. Mary asks you to set up a worksheet to track customer returns. The worksheet should include customer name, item name, SKU code, purchase price, purchase date, return date, and reason for return. Enter five items into your worksheet, using your imagination to determine the product names, SKU codes, prices, dates, etc. Add your choice of formatting and enhancements. Save your workbook in the Lesson 04 folder as **ct-Customer Returns**.

Critical Thinking 4.2   Music Research

Use Internet Explorer and a search engine of your choice to locate three websites that sell music CDs. Choose five of your favorite CDs and set up a worksheet to categorize and analyze the information you find. In particular, include the name of the website, the CD title, the artist, and the price of the CD. Gather this information for all five CDs from the three websites. Use formats and enhancements to make your worksheet look professional. Use formulas to calculate the total cost of each CD from each website. Use the MIN and MAX functions to determine the least and most expensive CDs. Format your worksheet as desired. Save your workbook in the Lesson 04 folder as **ct-CD Titles**.

Critical Thinking 4.3   Stock Analysis Research

You have been assigned the task of setting up a worksheet that tracks and analyzes an investment portfolio of publicly traded stocks. You are given the following information as a starting point:

Symbol	Purchase Price	Shares Purchased
MSFT	27	500
ORCL	16	100
LU	2	200
DELL	21	300
SBUX	33	250

Use Internet Explorer and a search engine of your choice to locate a website that offers free stock quotes. Use the site you locate and the symbols shown in the preceding table to determine the current price at which the stocks are trading and the company names associated with the symbols.

Set up a worksheet that contains the information shown in the preceding table. Also include the company name and current price of each stock. Use formulas to calculate the initial value of each investment and the current value based on the quotes you receive. Calculate the gain or loss of each stock in dollars as well as percentage. Use the SUM function to calculate the total value of the initial portfolio and the total current portfolio value. Calculate the total gain or loss for the portfolio. Calculate the average gain or loss percentage of the entire portfolio. Format the worksheet using the theme of your choice. You know you will need to track this every month, so go ahead and copy the data and formulas you've created and paste them on separate sheets. Save your workbook in the Lesson 04 folder as **ct-Stock Info**.

LESSON 5

Changing the Appearance of Worksheets

In this lesson, you will learn techniques for changing the structure of worksheets as it relates to rows, columns, and additional cell alignment options. In addition, you will learn about a variety of Excel's tools such as the Spelling tool and features such as Find and Replace. After you complete this lesson, you will have all of the basics you need to work with Excel.

LESSON OBJECTIVES

After studying this lesson, you will be able to:

- Modify column width and row height
- Insert as well as delete columns, rows, and cells
- Hide and unhide rows and columns
- Set the vertical alignment and rotate the text
- Find data in a worksheet and replace both data and formatting
- Effectively utilize AutoCorrect
- Search Help to learn how to complete a task
- Work with Excel tools: Spelling, Research, Thesaurus, and Translation

Case Study: Creating Mr. Fitzpatrick's Test Blueprint

Mr. Fitzpatrick is creating a test blueprint in order to ensure that the test he is about to create for Lesson 3, Working with Formulas and Functions, is aligned to the learning objectives in the lesson. The blueprint includes a content outline that lists the learning objectives, Bloom's Taxonomy categories (which delineate the levels of complexity of the questions), an area where the number of test items is recorded, and Total and Percentage columns. You will be working with the structure of the worksheet, finding and replacing text and formats, working with vertical alignment and rotation, and utilizing Excel's proofing tools such as the spelling checker to finalize the worksheet.

	A	B	C	D	E	F	G	H
1		Mr. Fitzpatrick's Class						
2		Test Blueprint						
3					Categories			
4		Content Outline	Knowledge	Comprehension	Application	Analysis	Total	Percentage
5					(Number of Items)			
6	1.	*Create formulas to calculate values, utilizing the proper syntax and order of operations*						
7	a.	The learner can create a formula using the proper mathematical operators.			2		2	6%
8	b.	The learner will demonstrate an understanding of order of operation rules by creating formulas utilizing proper syntax.		1	2		3	9%
9	c.	The learner will use point mode to enter cell references into a formula.			3		3	9%
10	d.	The learner will demonstrate how to use functions on the status bar in order to determine the minimum and maximum values in a range of cells.			2		2	6%
11	2.	*Use a variety of methods to create statistical functions to determine the sum, average, max and min of a range of numbers*						
12	a.	The learner will be able to explain the difference between the following statistical functions: SUM, AVE, MIN, and MAX.	1				1	3%
13	b.	The learner will demonstrate how to use AutoSum to create a statistical function.			2		2	6%

Modifying Columns and Rows

As you have seen, many entries do not fit within the default column size. Worksheets can also appear overcrowded with the standard row heights, which may tempt you to insert blank rows to make the worksheet more readable. The problem with this "fix," though, is that it can cause problems down the road when you begin to use some of Excel's more powerful features. In this lesson, you will use more time-saving techniques to fix column width and row height issues, such as changing multiple columns and rows at the same time and using AutoFit to let Excel figure out the best width or height. Both of these commands simply require you to select multiple columns or rows before issuing the command.

	A	B	C	D	E	F
1	Test Bluepr	Content Outline	Categories			
2			Knowledg	Comprehe	Applicatic	Analysis
3			(Number of Items)			
4	1.	Create formulas to calculate values, utilizng the proper syntax and order of operations				

You can see that we have a lot of work to do here in resizing rows and columns!

Column Widths and Row Heights

There are a variety of methods for changing widths of columns and heights of rows. They can be performed on either one or multiple columns or rows. Probably the most efficient way to adjust widths and heights is to simply drag the heading lines of the column(s) or row(s).

Standard Column Widths and Row Heights

Each column in a new worksheet has a standard width of 8.43 characters, where the default character is Calibri 11 point. Each row has a standard height of 15 points, which is approximately one-fifth of an inch.

AutoFit

You can adjust both column widths and row heights with the AutoFit command. AutoFit adjusts column widths to fit the widest entry in a column. Likewise, AutoFit adjusts row heights to accommodate the tallest entry in a row. The following Quick Reference table discusses AutoFit options and other commands for setting column widths and row heights.

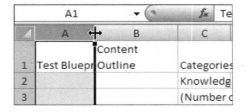

When you point to the border between columns or rows, a double-pointed arrow lets you know you can manually drag to change its size or double-click to issue the AutoFit command.

QUICK REFERENCE: CHANGING COLUMN WIDTHS AND ROW HEIGHTS

Technique	Procedure
Set a precise column width	▪ Select the column for which you wish to change the width. ▪ Choose Home→Cells→Format→Column Width from the Ribbon. ▪ Type in the column width you desire. ▪ Click OK.
Set column widths with AutoFit using the Ribbon	▪ Select the column(s) for which you wish to change the width. ▪ Choose Home→Cells→Format→AutoFit Column Width from the Ribbon.
Set column widths with AutoFit by double-clicking	▪ Select a single or multiple columns for which you wish to change the width. ▪ Double-click between any two selected headings or to the right of the selected single column heading. Make sure you double-click only when you see the double arrow mouse pointer. ▪ This will AutoFit all selected columns.
Set a precise row height	▪ Select the row for which you wish to change the height. ▪ Choose Home→Cells→Format→Row Height from the Ribbon. ▪ Type in the row height you desire. ▪ Click OK.
Set row heights with AutoFit	▪ Select the row for which you wish to change the height. ▪ Choose Home→Cells→Format→AutoFit Row Height from the Ribbon. You can also select multiple rows and double-click between any two selected headings. This will AutoFit all selected rows.
Manually adjust column widths and row heights	▪ Select the desired columns or rows and drag the column or row heading lines.

In this exercise, you will change the column width and row height to ensure that the cell entries fit properly.

1. Open the Mr. Fitzpatrick's Content Outline file from the Lesson 05 folder in your file storage location.

Adjust Column Widths

2. Follow these steps to resize column A:

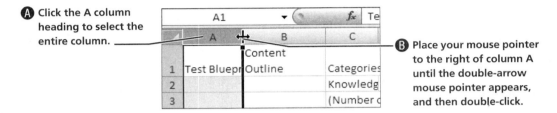

(A) Click the A column heading to select the entire column.

(B) Place your mouse pointer to the right of column A until the double-arrow mouse pointer appears, and then double-click.

Notice that the column is resized to fit the widest entry, which is in row 1. We will be merging and centering the title in row 1, so this column is too wide for our use.

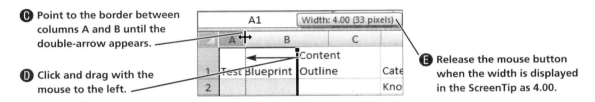

(C) Point to the border between columns A and B until the double-arrow appears.

(D) Click and drag with the mouse to the left.

(E) Release the mouse button when the width is displayed in the ScreenTip as 4.00.

Set a Precise Column Width

3. Click the column B header to select the entire column.

4. Follow these steps to precisely set the column width:

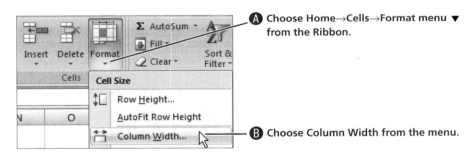

(A) Choose Home→Cells→Format menu ▼ from the Ribbon.

(B) Choose Column Width from the menu.

(C) Type 60, and then tap Enter.

The column has been sized much larger to accommodate the larger cell entries, which have "spread out" since the cells are formatted to wrap text.

Use AutoFit to Adjust the Row Height

5. Click the header for row 4, and then drag down through row 23.
Rows 4 through 23 should now be selected. Any command issued will apply to all selected rows.

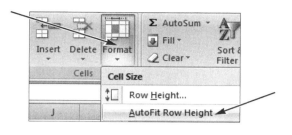

6. Choose Home→Cells→Format menu ▼→AutoFit Row Height from the Ribbon as shown.
All of the selected rows will shrink to fit the tallest entry.

7. Use Ctrl + S to save your work.

Inserting and Deleting Columns, Rows, and Cells

You can insert and delete columns, rows, and cells as needed in your worksheets. You probably figure that you will have plenty of rows and columns since you start out with more than 1,000,000 and 16,000 of them, respectively. The ability to insert and delete will come in handy when you want to restructure your worksheet after it has been created.

Inserting and Deleting Rows and Columns

Excel lets you insert and delete rows and columns. This gives you the flexibility to restructure your worksheets after they have been set up. The Quick Reference table in this section discusses the various procedures used to insert and delete rows and columns.

Inserting and Deleting Cells

If you want to insert or delete only cells, not entire rows or columns, you need to issue a command to insert or delete cells. This will allow you to add or remove a "chunk" or range of cells from your worksheet. This may cause problems because it alters the structure of your entire worksheet. For this reason, use this feature cautiously.

Shift Cells Option

When you add or remove a range of cells from your worksheet, you will need to tell Excel how to shift the surrounding cells to either make room for the addition or fill the space from the deletion.

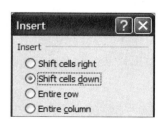

There are four Shift Cells options for you to choose from when you insert cells.

The Appearance of the Cells Group Commands

The buttons in the Cells group of the Home tab of the Ribbon will appear differently depending on the size of your Excel window (which may be determined by the size of your monitor).

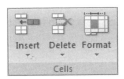

The figure on the left displays how the Cells group buttons will be displayed in a larger window, whereas the figure on the right displays the buttons as displayed in a smaller window. In the exercise steps, you will see the illustrations depicting the larger Ribbon buttons.

QUICK REFERENCE: INSERTING AND DELETING ROWS, COLUMNS, AND CELLS

Task	Procedure
Insert rows	■ Select the number of rows you wish to insert (the same number of new rows will be inserted above the selected rows). ■ Choose Home→Cells→Insert from the Ribbon.
Insert columns	■ Select the number of columns you wish to insert (the same number of new columns will be inserted to the left of the selected columns). ■ Choose Home→Cells→Insert from the Ribbon.
Delete rows	■ Select the rows you wish to delete. ■ Right-click the selection and choose Delete.
Delete columns	■ Select the columns you wish to delete. ■ Right-click the selection and choose Delete.
Insert cells	■ Select the cells in the worksheet where you want the inserted cells to appear. ■ Choose Home→Cells→Insert from the Ribbon. ■ Choose the desired Shift Cells option.
Delete cells	■ Select the cells you wish to delete. ■ Choose Home→Cells→Delete from the Ribbon. ■ Choose the desired Shift Cells option.

In this exercise, you will insert and delete rows, as well as insert cells into the worksheet.

Delete Unnecessary Rows

1. Select rows 15 and 23, using the [Ctrl] key to select nonadjacent rows.
    The rows in which there are no objectives listed are now selected.

2. Choose Home→Cells→Delete menu ▼→Delete Sheet Rows from the Ribbon.

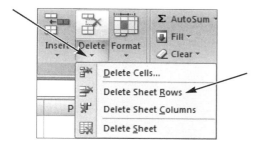

Add Another Row to the Sheet

3. Select row 8.
    When you choose to insert a row, it will be placed above the row you have selected.

4. Point (don't click) over the Home→Cells→Insert ▦ button on the Ribbon as shown.
    Notice that when you place your mouse pointer over the Insert button, there is a line that divides it into two halves. If you click above or to the left of the line (depending on how large the Ribbon appears on your computer), a new cell, row, or column will be inserted above or to the left of your selection. If you click below or to the right of the line, a menu appears from which you can select a command.

5. Click the Insert ▦ button (not the menu ▼ button).

6. Enter the text in the following illustration into the appropriate cells.

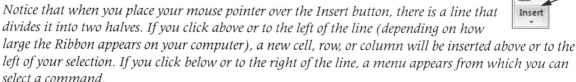

	A	B	C	D	E
8	d.	The student will demonstrate how to use functions on the status bar in order to determine the minimum and maximum values in a range of cells.			2

7. Follow these steps to copy the necessary formulas:

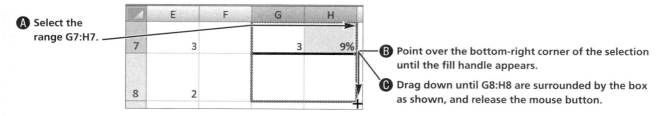

Ⓐ Select the range G7:H7.

Ⓑ Point over the bottom-right corner of the selection until the fill handle appears.

Ⓒ Drag down until G8:H8 are surrounded by the box as shown, and release the mouse button.

All of the formulas and functions have automatically been updated since cell references were used in creating the worksheet.

Insert Cells into the Worksheet

You have discovered that you want to merge and center the contents of cell A1 over the entire worksheet. You will need to "bump" everything in columns B through H down one row.

8. Select the range B1:H1.

9. Follow these steps to insert the cells and shift your existing data down:

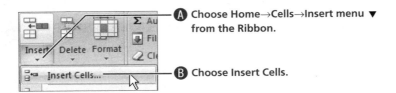

Ⓐ Choose Home→Cells→Insert menu ▼ from the Ribbon.

Ⓑ Choose Insert Cells.

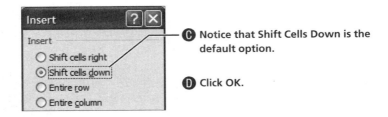

Ⓒ Notice that Shift Cells Down is the default option.

Ⓓ Click OK.

10. Select cell A3.

11. Choose Home→Cells→Insert from the Ribbon.
    Everything in column A, below cell A3, will be shifted down one cell.

12. Select row 1.

13. Choose Home→Cells→Insert from the Ribbon again.
    Since you selected an entire row first, a new row will be inserted.

Time to Format!

Now that we have shaken up the structure of the worksheet a bit, we will do some formatting to make it more presentable.

14. Follow these steps to merge and center a range:
    - Select the range A1:H1.
    - Choose Home→Alignment→Merge & Center from the Ribbon.
    There is nothing in this cell at this time, but it will be ready for later!

15. Merge & Center A2:H2, and then change the font size to 20.

16. Move (cut and paste) the contents of B3 to A3, and then merge and center A3:B3.

17. Select B3:B4, and then click the Merge & Center button twice.
    Notice that the Merge & Center command works for both horizontal and vertical ranges.

18. Merge and center C3:H3, and then place a border along the bottom of the cells.

19. Merge and center C5:G5.

20. Right-align B25:B26.

Once you are done formatting, your worksheet should resemble the following figure.

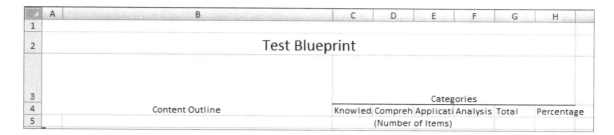

21. Use Ctrl + S to save your work.

Hiding Columns and Rows

There may be times when you wish to hide certain rows or columns from view. The hidden rows and columns will not be visible, nor will they print. However, the hidden rows and columns will still be part of the worksheet, and their values and formulas could still be referenced by other formulas in the visible rows and columns. Hiding rows and columns can be useful when you want to focus attention on other parts of the worksheet.

Notice that column F and row 1 are not visible once the Hide command is issued.

Unhiding Columns and Rows

After rows or columns have been hidden, you must issue an Unhide command to make them visible once again. Before the command to unhide rows is issued, you must select at least one row above and one row below the hidden ones. Likewise, you must select at least one column to the left and one to the right of the hidden ones before issuing the Unhide command. If you have hidden column A or row 1, you will need to drag to select from row 2 up to the column headers or from column B left through the row headers.

QR ▶ **QUICK REFERENCE: HIDING AND UNHIDING ROWS AND COLUMNS**

Task	Procedure
Hide columns or rows	▪ Select the column(s) or row(s) you wish to hide.
	▪ Choose Home→Cells→Format→Hide & Unhide→Hide Columns or Hide Rows from the Ribbon.
Unhide columns or rows	▪ Select the columns to the left and right or the rows above and below the column(s) or row(s) you wish to unhide.
	▪ Choose Home→Cells→Format→Hide & Unhide→Unhide Columns or Unhide Rows from the Ribbon.

In this exercise, you will have the opportunity to hide and unhide rows and columns.

Hide a Column and a Row

Mr. Fitzpatrick realized that he will not be assessing the students with items from the analysis category, so he has decided to hide column F. You will also hide row 1 since you have yet to enter anything in it.

1. Follow these steps to hide column F:

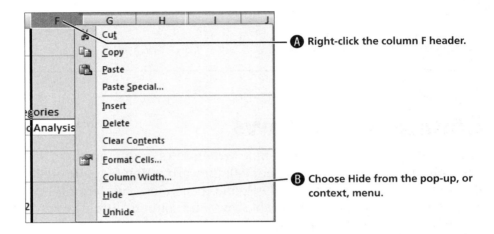

A Right-click the column F header.

B Choose Hide from the pop-up, or context, menu.

Column F will no longer be visible. It is still a part of the worksheet and can be revealed again with a simple Unhide command.

2. Right-click the row 1 header, and then choose Hide from the context menu.

Unhide the Hidden Column and Row

3. Follow these steps to unhide column F:

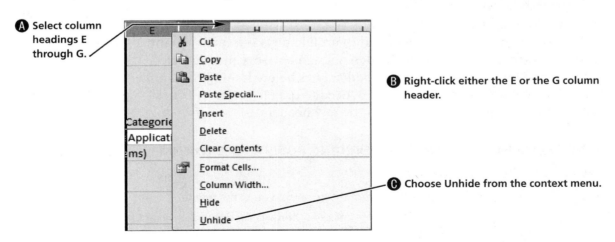

A Select column headings E through G.

B Right-click either the E or the G column header.

C Choose Unhide from the context menu.

Remember that to unhide a column you must first select the columns to the left and right of the hidden column (or the rows above and below a hidden row).

4. Follow these steps to unhide row 1:

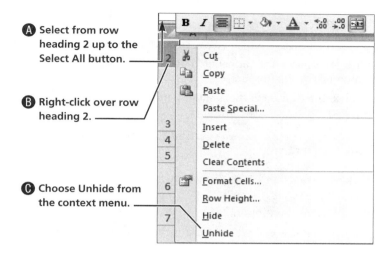

A Select from row heading 2 up to the Select All button.

B Right-click over row heading 2.

C Choose Unhide from the context menu.

Row 1 will once again be visible.

5. Use [Ctrl]+[S] to save your work.

Changing Vertical Alignment and Rotating Text

You have already learned many techniques for arranging data. Now you will be expanding on that knowledge and learning how to change the vertical alignment and rotate the contents of cells.

Setting Vertical Alignment

In the previous lesson, you learned how to align the contents of cells horizontally. This lesson will focus on vertical alignment within cells. Vertical alignment options include top, bottom, center, and justify. The default alignment is bottom. The Justify option is useful with multiple-line entries. For example, the Justify option evenly distributes unused space between lines in a multiple-line entry. Vertical alignment is set by choosing the Dialog Box Launcher button in the Alignment group on the Home tab of the Ribbon. You can also set top, bottom, and middle vertical alignment via buttons on the Ribbon.

Rotating Text

Text can be rotated from 0 to 90 degrees using the Orientation option on the Alignment tab in the Format Cells dialog box. Excel automatically increases the row height to accommodate the rotated text. When column headings are extra wide, making the worksheet spread out too far horizontally, you might consider rotating the text to save room. It can also be used for aesthetic purposes as it can spice up the appearance of a worksheet.

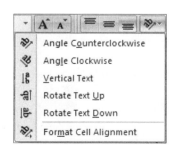

Excel has several preset rotations available on the Ribbon that you can apply to text in a cell.

QUICK REFERENCE: SETTING VERTICAL ALIGNMENT AND TEXT ROTATION

Task	Procedure
Set the vertical alignment in a cell	■ Select the cell(s) in which you wish to change the vertical alignment. ■ Click the Dialog Box Launcher ⬚ button in the Alignment group of the Home tab of the Ribbon. ■ Choose the desired vertical alignment in the Format Cells dialog box. ■ Click OK. ■ In addition, you can use the vertical alignment buttons located on the Home tab of the Ribbon.
Rotate text within a cell	■ Select the cell(s) in which you wish to rotate text. ■ Click the Dialog Box Launcher ⬚ button in the Alignment group of the Home tab of the Ribbon. ■ Choose the desired text rotation in the Format Cells dialog box. ■ Click OK. ■ In addition, you can use the Rotate ⬚ button located on the Home tab of the Ribbon.

 Hands-On 5.4   Change Text's Vertical Alignment and Rotation

In this exercise, you will rotate the categories at the top of the worksheet as well as change the vertical alignment in a cell.

Rotate Text

1. Follow these steps to rotate text:

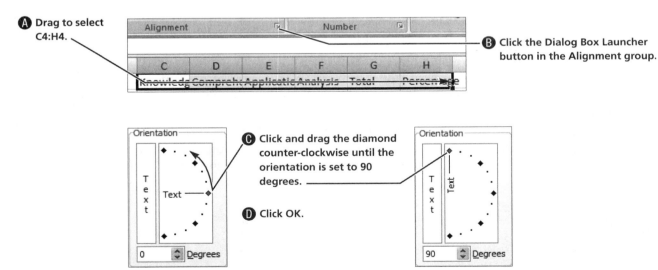

Ⓐ Drag to select C4:H4.

Ⓑ Click the Dialog Box Launcher button in the Alignment group.

Ⓒ Click and drag the diamond counter-clockwise until the orientation is set to 90 degrees.

Ⓓ Click OK.

2. Follow these steps to AutoFit columns C through H:

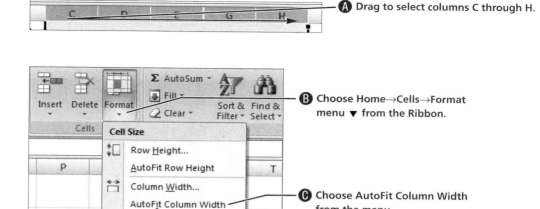

A Drag to select columns C through H.

B Choose Home→Cells→Format menu ▼ from the Ribbon.

C Choose AutoFit Column Width from the menu.

3. Select the row headings for rows 3 and 4.

4. Choose Home→Cells→Format menu ▼→AutoFit Row Height from the Ribbon.

5. Follow these steps to finish adjusting the row height for row 4:

A Place your mouse pointer below row header 4 until you see the double arrow.

B Drag until the height is 84.00.

Change Vertical Alignment

6. Select cell A3.
Remember, this is a vertically and horizontally merged cell so it is quite large.

7. Choose Home→Alignment→Middle Align ≡ from the Ribbon.

8. Set the font size of cell A3 to 16.

9. Use ⌨Ctrl + ⌨S to save your work.

Using Excel's Find and Replace Command

Excel's Find command performs searches on a worksheet or an entire workbook. It can search for a particular word, number, cell reference, formula, or format. Find is often the quickest way to locate an item in a workbook. The Replace feature helps you to find an item and replace it with a specified item.

Replacing Cell Formats

FROM THE KEYBOARD
Ctrl+F to find
Ctrl+H to replace

Excel lets you find and replace not just text but also cell formats. For example, you may want to search all worksheets and workbooks for cells formatted with Currency Style with no decimals and replace that format with Currency Style with two decimals. Finding and replacing cell formats can be a big time-saver, especially with large worksheets and multiple-sheet workbooks.

You can limit the Find and Replace command to specific areas of a workbook.

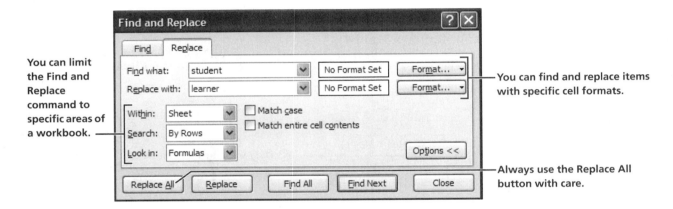

You can find and replace items with specific cell formats.

Always use the Replace All button with care.

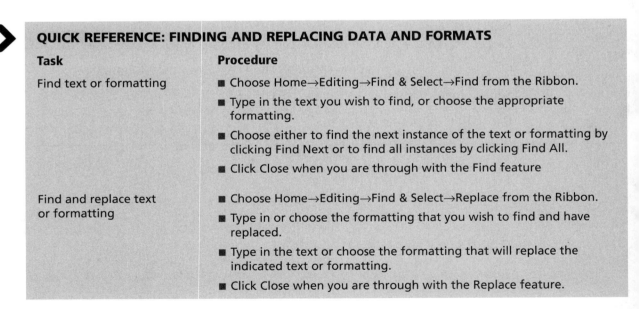

QUICK REFERENCE: FINDING AND REPLACING DATA AND FORMATS

Task	Procedure
Find text or formatting	■ Choose Home→Editing→Find & Select→Find from the Ribbon. ■ Type in the text you wish to find, or choose the appropriate formatting. ■ Choose either to find the next instance of the text or formatting by clicking Find Next or to find all instances by clicking Find All. ■ Click Close when you are through with the Find feature
Find and replace text or formatting	■ Choose Home→Editing→Find & Select→Replace from the Ribbon. ■ Type in or choose the formatting that you wish to find and have replaced. ■ Type in the text or choose the formatting that will replace the indicated text or formatting. ■ Click Close when you are through with the Replace feature.

In this exercise, you will find and replace text as well as formatting.

Find and Replace Text

1. Choose Home→Editing→Find & Select  →Replace from the Ribbon.

The Find and Replace dialog box will open.

2. Follow these steps to prepare to replace all instances of *student* with *learner*:

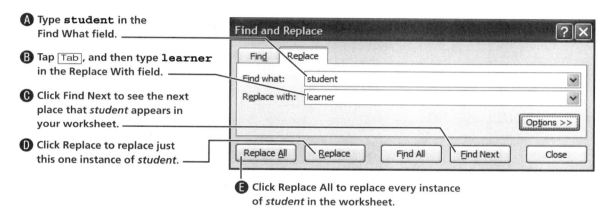

Ⓐ Type **student** in the Find What field.

Ⓑ Tap [Tab], and then type **learner** in the Replace With field.

Ⓒ Click Find Next to see the next place that *student* appears in your worksheet.

Ⓓ Click Replace to replace just this one instance of *student*.

Ⓔ Click Replace All to replace every instance of *student* in the worksheet.

3. Click OK to acknowledge the total number of replacements.

After replacing all, Excel will let you know the total number of replacements. Leave the Find and Replace dialog box open for the next step.

Find and Replace Formatting

4. Click the Options button in the Find and Replace dialog box.
Excel displays a dialog box with additional Find and Replace settings.

5. Follow these steps to set the formatting to find:

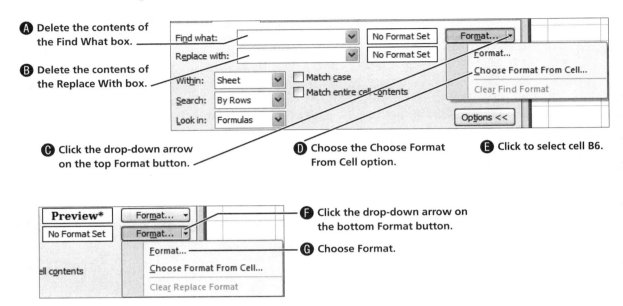

A Delete the contents of the Find What box.

B Delete the contents of the Replace With box.

C Click the drop-down arrow on the top Format button.

D Choose the Choose Format From Cell option.

E Click to select cell B6.

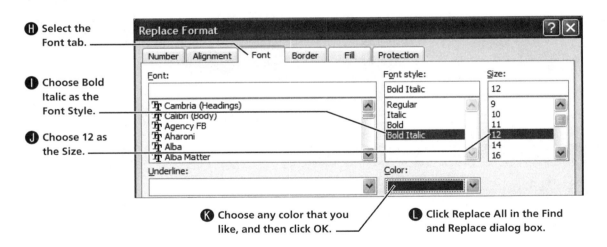

F Click the drop-down arrow on the bottom Format button.

G Choose Format.

H Select the Font tab.

I Choose Bold Italic as the Font Style.

J Choose 12 as the Size.

K Choose any color that you like, and then click OK.

L Click Replace All in the Find and Replace dialog box.

All instances of formatting that are the same as that in cell B6 will be replaced with the new formatting that you have chosen.

 TIP! *Be aware that the format searched for here may still be in the Find and Replace dialog box the next time you wish to use it. If so, you will need to delete the formatting options you just set before continuing to find and replace.*

6. Click OK, and then click Close to close the Find and Replace dialog box.

Using AutoCorrect

Excel's AutoCorrect feature can improve the speed and accuracy of entering text. AutoCorrect is most useful for replacing abbreviations with a full phrase of up to 255 characters. For example, you could set up AutoCorrect to substitute *Mr. Fitzpatrick's Class* whenever you type *mfc*. AutoCorrect also automatically corrects common misspellings and typographical errors. For example, the word *the* is often misspelled as *teh*, and the word *and* is often misspelled as *adn*. These and other common spelling mistakes are fixed automatically. AutoCorrect also automatically capitalizes the first letter of a day if you type it in lowercase. For example, if you type *sunday* and complete the entry, AutoCorrect will enter *Sunday* in the cell. Finally, AutoCorrect fixes words that have two initial capital letters by switching the second letter to lowercase.

The AutoCorrect dialog box allows you to customize how the AutoCorrect feature will work for you.

 TIP! *AutoCorrect entries are shared by all programs in the Microsoft Office Suite, so if you've already added some in Word, they are available for you to use in Excel as well.*

Expanding AutoCorrect Entries

AutoCorrect goes into action when you type a word in a text entry and tap [Spacebar] or when you complete a text entry. The word or entry is compared with all entries in the AutoCorrect table. The AutoCorrect table contains a list of words and their replacement phrases. If the word you type matches an entry in the AutoCorrect table, a phrase from the table is substituted for the word. This is known as expanding the AutoCorrect entry.

Undoing AutoCorrect Entries

There may be times that AutoCorrect replaces an entry against your wishes. AutoCorrect is treated as a single "character," meaning that it is viewed by the Undo feature the same as if you typed an "a" or tapped [Delete]. Therefore, you can use the Undo feature you learned about in Lesson 2, Editing, Viewing, and Printing Worksheets, to reverse an AutoCorrect entry.

Creating and Editing AutoCorrect Entries

The AutoCorrect dialog box allows you to add entries to the AutoCorrect table, delete entries from the table, and set other AutoCorrect options. To add an entry, type the desired abbreviation in the Replace box and the desired expansion for the abbreviation in the With box.

 TIP! *If you create the abbreviation using uppercase letters, it will not work if you type it in lowercase letters later. Type all abbreviations in lowercase so you don't have to remember to type them in upper- or lowercase in the worksheet.*

QUICK REFERENCE: USING AUTOCORRECT	
Task	**Procedure**
Modify AutoCorrect options	■ Choose Office→Excel Options.
	■ Click the Proofing option from the left-side menu.
	■ Click AutoCorrect Options.
	■ Make any desired changes to the AutoCorrect feature.
	■ Click OK.
	■ Click OK to close the Excel Options window.

 ## Hands-On 5.6   Use AutoCorrect

In this exercise, you will train AutoCorrect to replace an abbreviation with a phrase and learn how to override AutoCorrect.

Observe How AutoCorrect Works

1. Select cell A1.

2. Type **teh cat adn dog ran fast**, and then tap ⌷Enter⌷.
   Notice that both of the spelling errors have been corrected for you by AutoCorrect.

Override an AutoCorrect Command

3. Click cell A1.

4. Type **adn** and tap ⌷Spacebar⌷.
   AutoCorrect has corrected the misspelling.

5. Use ⌷Ctrl⌷+⌷Z⌷ to undo the last command.
   Undo will reverse the last command, in this case AutoCorrect.

6. Tap ⌷Esc⌷ to cancel the entry.

Create an AutoCorrect Entry

7. Choose Office [icon]→Excel Options.

8. Follow these steps to display the AutoCorrect dialog box:

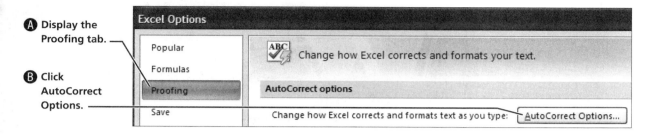

A Display the Proofing tab.

B Click AutoCorrect Options.

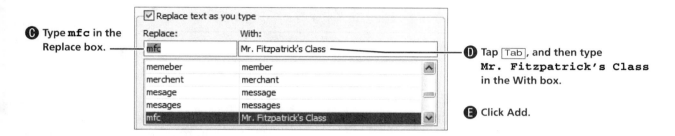

C Type **mfc** in the Replace box.

D Tap ⌈Tab⌉, and then type **Mr. Fitzpatrick's Class** in the With box.

E Click Add.

Your entry will be added to the list.

9. Click OK in the AutoCorrect dialog box.

10. Click OK in the Excel Options dialog box.

Use an AutoCorrect Entry

11. Ensure that cell A1 is still selected.

12. Type **mfc**, and then tap ⌈Enter⌉.
   The AutoCorrect entry that you created is entered into the cell.

13. Change the font size of cell A1 to 24.

Delete an AutoCorrect Entry

It is important for you to delete the AutoCorrect entry you just created. Otherwise it will still be there when the next student uses the computer.

14. Choose Office 🔳→Excel Options.

15. Display the Proofing tab.

16. Click AutoCorrect Options.

17. Follow these steps to delete the AutoCorrect entry you have created:

A Type **mfc** in the Replace box.

B Click Delete, and then tap [Enter].

C Click OK.

18. Use [Ctrl] + [S] to save your work.

Using Excel's Help Feature

Excel's online Help feature puts a complete reference book at your fingertips. You can get the help you need for just about any topic you can imagine. Plus, if you have an Internet connection, additional help is available directly from the Microsoft website. When you are connected to the Internet and search for a help topic, Help automatically searches for the requested topics at Microsoft.com and displays a results list from which you can choose the desired topic.

The Help Box

You launch the Help box via a button near the top-right corner of the program window. You have three methods by which to navigate online help:

- Question Box
- Browse Topics
- Table of Contents

Question Box

This method uses powerful natural-language processing to interpret your question and display several items that are likely to contain the answer. Simply type your question in the box and tap [Enter]. The Help box displays a list of items related to your question.

Browse Help

Categorized lists display commonly performed tasks. Each category features a list of subcategories and individual items that give instructions to perform specific tasks.

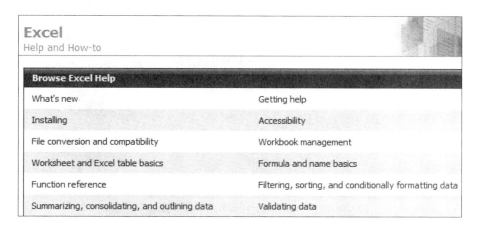

Search the Table of Contents

The Table of Contents panel displays the complete online help content in a hierarchical format that you can expand and collapse. Browsing the table of contents can often be a good way to search when you're not quite certain of a feature's name.

Finding Help When You Need It

In order to access Help in Excel 2007, you will need to click on the Help ⓘ button to the far right of the Ribbon tabs. In addition, you can tap the F1 key to search Help.

The Help Window Toolbar

The toolbar in the Excel Help window looks very similar to the toolbar seen in Internet Explorer. It allows you to navigate Excel's help topics much the same way as you navigate through the Internet.

FROM THE KEYBOARD
F1 to find help

The buttons on the Help window toolbar look very similar to buttons you may be used to seeing on your Internet browser.

Hands-On 5.7   Use Help

In this exercise, you will use Help to learn more about Excel's Spelling tool.

1. Click the Help 🔘 button.
   The Excel Help window will launch.

2. Type **spell check** as the keywords and tap ⌷Enter⌷.

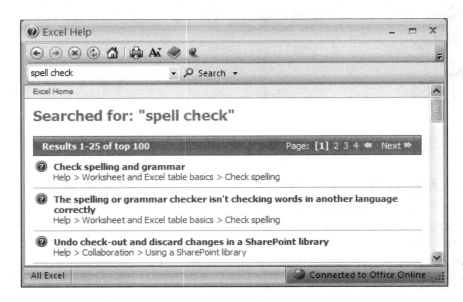

Excel will display all of the results relating to your keyword search.

3. Click the result titled "Check spelling and grammar."

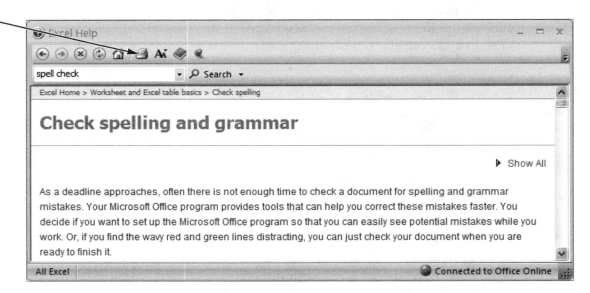

Excel will display the topic you have chosen. You can now print it if you wish by clicking the Print button on the Help toolbar.

4. Think of a task that you would like to be able to perform in Excel.

5. Use Excel's Help window to search for instructions on how to complete the task.

6. Close the Excel Help window.

Using Excel's Proofing Tools

Excel comes with powerful proofing tools to aid you in your work. These tools appear in the Proofing group on the Review tab of the Ribbon.

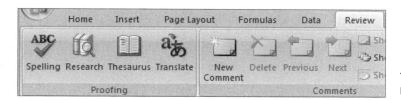

The Proofing group on the Review tab of the Ribbon

Spelling Checker

Excel's spelling checker helps you to locate spelling errors in your worksheet. The Spelling feature checks the spelling of all text entries in the current worksheet. Excel's spelling checker functions much like the one in Microsoft Word, with which it shares the same main and custom dictionaries. The following Quick Reference table describes the options available.

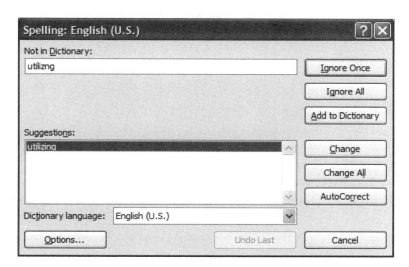

When you issue the spelling checker command, Excel will display the Spelling box that allows you to choose how to deal with words not in the dictionary.

QUICK REFERENCE: SPELLING CHECKER OPTIONS

Button	Function
Ignore Once	This button ignores the misspelled word one time only and prompts you the next time it encounters the same misspelling.
Ignore All	This button ignores the misspelled word now and for all spelling checks during the current Excel session.
Add to Dictionary	This button adds the misspelled word to a custom dictionary.
Change	This button replaces the misspelled word with the word highlighted on the Suggestions list.
Change All	This button replaces all occurrences of the misspelled word in this worksheet with the word highlighted on the Suggestions list.
AutoCorrect	This button corrects and then adds the misspelled (and corrected) word to the list of entries in AutoCorrect.

 TIP! *There are many instances where a word will be incorrect but will not be caught by the Spelling tool. For instance, if you type* work *instead of* word, *it will not be flagged since* work *is also a word that is spelled correctly. The spelling checker is no replacement for good, solid proofreading!*

Research References

 Excel's Research task pane gives access to various useful reference sources and research sites. Most of this information arrives via an Internet connection. The following are examples of these resources:

■ Dictionary and thesaurus

■ Encyclopedia

■ Stock quote services

Research Options

Choosing the Research Options button at the bottom of the Research pane displays a dialog box of research sources that Excel will search for answers to your queries. The categories from which you may choose are Reference Books, Research Sites, Business and Financial Sites, and Other Services.

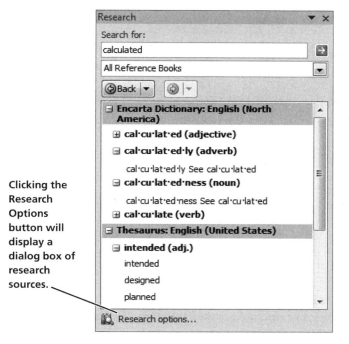

Clicking the Research Options button will display a dialog box of research sources.

Research services, "books," and websites are displayed in the dialog box.

The Research Options button displays various reference and research sources.

Thesaurus

Have you ever experienced the feeling that the word you want to use is "just on the tip of your tongue"? Excel has a built-in thesaurus that can help you to find just that right word. If a cell contains the word for which you wish to find a replacement, simply click on it and then choose Thesaurus from the Proofing group on the Review tab of the Ribbon. If the word is contained within a cell with multiple words, double-click the word to select it before choosing Thesaurus.

Translation

In addition to the tools about which we have already learned, Excel also provides a tool that allows you to translate words and phrases into another language. The figure at right shows the languages into which you can translate your English word or phrase.

Hands-On 5.8   Work with Proofing Tools

In this exercise, you will use Excel's four proofing tools.

Spellcheck Your Worksheet

1. Choose Review→Proofing→Spelling 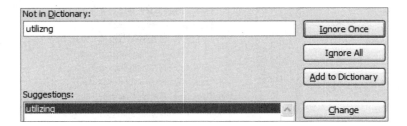 from the Ribbon.
   The Spelling tool immediately finds the first misspelled word in the worksheet, utilizng*.*

2. Click the Change button to accept the suggested spelling.
   Notice that Excel makes suggestions for misspelled words based on its dictionary.

3. Continue with the spelling check, accepting the suggestions for the last four misspellings.

4. Click OK to close the window indicating that the spelling check is complete for the entire sheet.

5. Use Ctrl + S to save your work.

Research a Topic

Mr. Fitzpatrick has decided to research the analysis category a bit further.

6. Select cell F4.

7. Choose Review→Proofing→Research from the Ribbon.
   A Research pane opens with the word Analysis *displayed in the search field.*

8. Click the Start Searching button on the Research pane.
   Research displays its results. Read through them briefly, paying attention to item number 4, which deals with assessment.

9. Choose Review→Proofing→Research from the Ribbon to close the Research pane.

Use the Thesaurus

10. Scroll down and select cell B24.

11. Double-click the word *understand* in the Formula Bar.

12. Choose Review→Proofing→Thesaurus from the Ribbon.
    The Research pane opens again to display thesaurus entries.

13. Tap [Enter] to close the cell for editing and issue the search command.

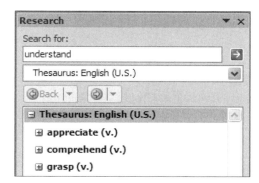

Excel will display additional meanings for the word understand. *If you click the plus + sign to the left of one of the entries, you will see a list of synonyms displayed.*

Translate a Phrase into Italian

Your computer may not have the necessary translation tools installed. If this exercise does not work for you, you would need to install the translation component of Office before you can complete it.

14. Select cell A2.

15. Choose Review→Proofing→Translate ![icon] from the Ribbon.
If your computer does not have the dictionary installed, click Cancel to finish this exercise.

16. Choose Italian as the language to which to translate.

17. Take a look at the translation in the Research pane, and then Close ![X] the task pane.

18. Use [Ctrl]+[S] to save your file.

19. Close ![X] the Excel window.

Concepts Review

True/False Questions

1. After you rotate text within a cell, you must manually resize the row to fit the rotated text.　　TRUE　FALSE

2. The AutoFit command changes the column width to fit the narrowest entry in the column.　　TRUE　FALSE

3. Row heights cannot be adjusted using AutoFit.　　TRUE　FALSE

4. New columns are inserted to the left of selected columns.　　TRUE　FALSE

5. Using the Research task pane, you can download current stock quotes from the Internet.　　TRUE　FALSE

6. Hidden columns and rows will not print.　　TRUE　FALSE

7. Excel's Spelling tool shares its dictionary with Word and other Office applications.　　TRUE　FALSE

8. You can search Excel Help by using keywords.　　TRUE　FALSE

9. You must program an AutoCorrect entry in each Office application in which you wish to use it.　　TRUE　FALSE

10. You can find and replace cell formatting as well as text entries.　　TRUE　FALSE

Multiple Choice Questions

1. How many rows are inserted if you select three rows and choose the Home→Cells→Insert command from the Ribbon?
   a. One, above the selection
   b. Three, below the selection
   c. Three, above the selection
   d. None; that is not the correct command

2. How can you reverse an AutoCorrect entry?
   a. Tap Delete
   b. Choose Edit→Reverse→Undo from the Ribbon
   c. Click the Undo button on the Quick Access toolbar
   d. Tap Backspace

3. Which of the following is not a method by which you can search for help in Excel?
   a. Indexed Topic List
   b. Browse Help Topics
   c. Table of Contents
   d. Question Box

4. Which Excel tool would you use to help you find just the right word?
   a. Encyclopedia
   b. Thesaurus
   c. Translation
   d. Research

Skill Builders

Skill Builder 5.1   Insert and Delete Rows

In this exercise, you will modify an order entry worksheet by removing and inserting line items.

1. Open the sb-Andrew's Office Supplies file from the Lesson 05 folder in your file storage location.

Create Formulas

2. Click cell D7, and enter a formula that calculates the Extended Price as the Quantity multiplied by the Unit Price.
   The result should be 239.7.

3. Copy the Extended Price formula down through rows 8–11.

4. Use AutoSum to compute the subtotal for the extended prices in column D.

5. Calculate the Sales Tax as the Subtotal multiplied by 7.75%.

6. Calculate the Total as the Subtotal plus the Sales Tax.

7. Select all of the numbers in columns C–D and change the decimals to 2.

Delete a Row and Insert New Rows

The customer has decided to cancel the electric pencil sharpeners from his order and add toner cartridges.

8. Select row 8 by clicking the row heading.

9. Choose Home→Cells→Delete 🗍 (taking care not to click the menu ▼ button) from the Ribbon.
   The Subtotal, Sales Tax, and Total should be automatically recalculated.

10. Click anywhere in row 10, and choose Home→Cells→Insert 🗍 menu ▼→Insert Sheet Rows from the Ribbon.

11. Add the following item, and be sure to use a formula in cell D10, which can be copied via the fill handle from D9:

	A	B	C	D
10	Toner cartridge	10	119.00	1190.00

12. Select row 12, and choose Home→Cells→Insert 🗍 from the Ribbon.
    Notice that if you select the entire row below where you wish to insert a row, you can simply click the Insert button without having to choose the menu button and the Insert Sheet Rows command on the menu.

13. Add the following item to the new row, tapping ⎣Tab⎤ after typing 145 in cell C12, as Excel will automatically calculate the value in cell D12:

	A	B	C	D
12	Two-line phone	5	145.00	725.00

14. Click in cell D13 and notice that the SUM function has been updated automatically to include the value in cell D12 that was added when you inserted the row.
Excel adjusted the formula reference because the rows inserted were within the range referenced in the formula.

15. Use the TODAY function to insert the current date in D3.

16. Format the date with the date format of your choice.

17. Select columns A, C, and D, and use the AutoFit command to adjust the column widths.

18. Manually size column B so that the word *Quantity* in B6 is visible.
You will not want to AutoFit column B as it will fit to Baltimore Petroleum *in B4, which is much too wide.*

19. Save and close the workbook.

Skill Builder 5.2   Adjust Column and Row Properties

In this exercise, you will change the column width as well as hide a row that is not needed but that you do not wish to delete.

1. Open the sb-Benefits Plan Adjust Properties file from the Lesson 05 folder.

2. Merge and center the contents of cell A1 over columns A through I, and do the same with the contents of cell A15 over columns A through I.

Change Column Widths

3. Select columns A through I.

4. Place your mouse pointer between any of the selected column headers, and when you see a double-arrow, double-click.
All of the columns will be sized to fit the widest entry. Notice that the cells that have been merged and centered over multiple columns are not factored in to the AutoFit command.

Hide a Row

5. Select row 12.

6. Choose Home→Cells→Format →Hide & Unhide→Hide Rows from the Ribbon.
Row 12 is now hidden from view.

7. Select A4:I11.

8. Copy the selected range, and paste it to A18:I25.

Delete a Row

Brian Asbury is no longer with the company, so you will delete him from the 2008 data.

9. Select row 22.

10. Choose Home→Cells→Delete ⊞ from the Ribbon.

11. Save your workbook and keep it open for the next exercise.

Skill Builder 5.3   Use AutoCorrect

In this exercise, you will edit a worksheet by creating, using, and deleting AutoCorrect entries.

1. If you did not complete Skill Builder 5.2 and therefore do not have the resulting file displayed, open sb-Benefits Plan AutoCorrect from the Lesson 05 folder.

Create AutoCorrect Entries

2. Choose Office 🔘 →Excel Options.

3. Click the Proofing option along the left-side menu, and then click AutoCorrect Options.

4. In the Replace box, type **q1** and then tap Tab.
   Remember to type the abbreviation in lowercase.

5. In the With box, type **First Quarter**.

6. Click the Add button.
   Do not click the OK button right now as you are going to create a few more AutoCorrect entries.

7. Create the following three entries. Click OK when you are finished.

   q2   Second Quarter

   q3   Third Quarter

   q4   Fourth Quarter

8. Click OK to close the Excel Options window.

Use AutoCorrect Entries

9. Click cell B3.

10. Type **q1** and tap Spacebar.
    First Quarter *will appear in the cell.*

11. Tap Tab twice to move the highlight to cell D3.

12. Type **q2**, and tap Tab twice.

13. Using AutoCorrect, enter the last two quarters in F3 and H3.

14. Using the method of your choice, either AutoCorrect or Copy and Paste, enter the same First through Fourth Quarter headings in cells B17, D17, F17, and H17.

Delete AutoCorrect Entries

Remember that the AutoCorrect entries that you create can be used in all Office applications. You may find that you do not want First Quarter *to appear each time you type* **q1**. *We will now delete the AutoCorrect entries that were created.*

15. Choose Office ⬛ →Excel Options.

16. Click the Proofing option along the left-side menu, and then click AutoCorrect Options.

17. In the Replace box, type **q1**.
    The First Quarter *AutoCorrect entry appears in the With box next to the* q1 *abbreviation in the Replace box.*

18. Click the Delete button under the AutoCorrect entry list.

19. Delete the AutoCorrect entries for q2, q3, and q4.
    In order to have the correct "With" entry appear, you will need to delete the previously deleted entry from the field first.

20. When you finish deleting all four entries, click OK.

21. Click OK to close the Excel Options window.

22. Save the changes and close the workbook.

Skill Builder 5.4   Check Spelling in a Worksheet

In this exercise, you will open a workbook and run the spelling checker, making the necessary corrections.

1. Open the workbook named sb-Database Spelling from the Lesson 05 folder.

2. Choose Review→Proofing→Spelling 🔤 from the Ribbon.

3. The first problem that the spelling checker encounters is in cell A3, which contains the entry *Firstname*.
   It is a good practice to avoid using spaces in database fields (Excel can be used as a database, and column headings are used as the fields). However, since this spelling is not in the Spelling tool's dictionary, it doesn't like it. We want to leave it like it is.

4. Click the Ignore Once button in the dialog box.

5. Continue spellchecking the entire worksheet, using your best judgment on corrections (whether to ignore or change).
   If you are in a classroom setting, do not use the Add or AutoCorrect buttons. If you are using the book on your own, feel free to add items to your dictionary or AutoCorrect list.

6. Once the spelling check is complete, click OK to acknowledge the prompt.

7. Save and close the workbook.

Skill Builder 5.5   Use Find and Replace

In this exercise, you will experiment with finding and replacing contents and formats.

1. Open the workbook named sb-Misawa Quarterly Sales from the Lesson 05 folder.

Find and Replace Contents

2. Choose Home→Editing→Find & Select 🔍→Replace from the Ribbon.

3. Replace *California* with **Southwest**.
   You do not have to use a capital "C" in the Find What box. If you want the replacement text to be capitalized, though, you must type it that way in the Replace With box.

4. Make the following additional replacements:
   - Replace *Washington* with **Pacific Northwest**.
   - Replace *Florida* with **Southeast**.

   You can choose to Find Next and then Replace to address each entry individually or, if you know that you want to change every instance in a worksheet, you can choose to Replace All. Notice that one of the sales reps' names is Washington, so you will need to be careful when replacing it with Pacific Northwest.

5. Close the Find and Replace dialog box, and then AutoFit any columns that are too narrow to fit the widest entry.

Find and Replace Formats

6. Use Ctrl + H to display the Find and Replace dialog box.

7. Delete the entries in the Find What and Replace With fields.

8. Click the Options button to expand the dialog box.

9. Click the drop-down arrow on the Format button in the Find What row, and then click the Choose Format From Cell command on the menu.

10. Click cell A6.

11. Click the Format button for the Replace With box (not the drop-down button) to display the Replace Format box.

12. Display the Font tab, choose to make the Font style Regular and the color black, and then click OK.

13. Choose to Replace All.

14. Click OK to acknowledge the number of replacements made.

15. Close the Find and Replace dialog box, and then save and close your workbook.

# Assessments

Assessment 5.1   Restructure an Accounts Receivable Report

In this exercise, you will insert and move columns and rows, create a formula, and apply a theme to the report.

1. Open the as-Warner Springs Accounts Receivable workbook from the Lesson 05 folder in your file storage location.

2. Use the TODAY function to insert the current date in cell E4.

3. Insert and move rows as necessary to alphabetize rows 7–12.
   Yes, there is an easier way to alphabetize rows, which you will learn, but this exercise is meant to help you practice how to work with moving and inserting rows.

4. Insert a column between columns A and B, and enter the invoice numbers shown in the illustration at the end of the exercise. Also, enter the heading shown in cell B6, and wrap the text within the cell.

5. Use formulas in column E to calculate the number of days since the invoices were issued as the current date minus the invoice date (in cell E7, you will enter **=$F$4-C7**). Make sure to use an absolute cell reference as indicated. Use AutoFill to extend the formula.

6. Format the entries in column E with the General Style number format.

7. Format the entries in column D in Currency Style with no decimal.

8. Use formulas in column F to calculate the number of days the invoices are past due. Assume the terms are net 30 days. Your formulas should subtract 30 from the number of days since the invoice was issued.

9. Change the fill color so that every other row is shaded.

10. Apply the theme of your choice to change the formatting of the worksheet. Resize any rows or columns so all text and numbers appear.

11. Your completed worksheet should look similar to the following illustration. However, the data in columns E and F will be different based on your report date (differences may also occur based on the theme you chose).

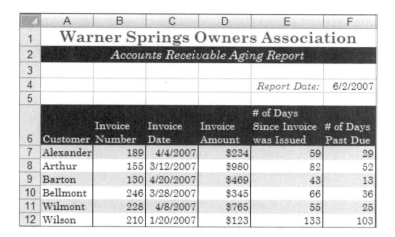

12. Print the worksheet, save the changes, and close the workbook.

Assessment 5.2   Work with Vertical Alignment and Text Rotation

In this exercise, you will create a worksheet, practice creating formulas, and change the vertical alignment and text rotation.

1. Open a new Excel file and enter all text, numbers, and dates as shown in the illustration at the end of this exercise. Follow these guidelines to create the large paragraph shown near the top of the worksheet:

- Use the Merge & Center command to merge cells A2:H2.
- Set the height of row 2 to 75.00 points.
- Turn on the Wrap Text option.
- Type the text in the large merged cell.
- Change the vertical alignment to center and the horizontal alignment to left.

2. Rotate the text in B5:H5 to 90 degrees. Use ⎡Alt⎤ + ⎡Enter⎤ to force line breaks in F4:H4.

3. Apply the borders as shown. You will want to merge and center the contents of A5, F5, G5, and H5 with the empty row 4 cells above. Merge and center B4:C4 and D4:E4.

4. Use formulas in column F to calculate the number of days between the two tests.

5. Format the entries in column F with the General Style number format.

6. Use formulas in column G to calculate the point increase between the two test scores.

7. Use formulas to calculate the percentage increase in column H. The percentage increase is calculated as the point increase in column G divided by the first test score in column C.

8. Use the AVERAGE function to calculate the averages in cells F12 and H13.

9. Add a border around cells A12–H13.

10. Format all numbers, dates, and text as desired. Adjust row heights and column widths as shown. Format the percentage increases in column H as Percent Style with no decimals.

11. Print the worksheet when you have finished.

12. Save the workbook as **as-Performance Evaluations** and close it.

	A	B	C	D	E	Number of Days Between Tests	Point Increase	Percentage Increase
1	Grade 10 Performance Evaluations							
2	This worksheet computes the percentage increase in test scores for students who have been receiving special assistance. The average number of days required to achieve the results is also shown.							
3								
4		First Test		Second Test				
5	Student	Date	Score	Date	Score			
6	Helen Chang	2/3/2008	78	3/30/2008	87			
7	Clara Levy	2/5/2008	77	3/28/2008	82			
8	Miranda Simek	2/5/2008	65	4/5/2008	80			
9	Tariq Aziz	3/10/2008	64	4/1/2008	72			
10	Elizabeth Crawford	3/12/2008	68	4/2/2008	78			
11	Bernice Barton	2/1/2008	72	3/10/2008	88			
12	Average Days							
13	Average Increase							

Assessment 5.3   Find and Replace

In this exercise, you will find and replace both a word (text) and formatting in the worksheet you created for one of the Hands-On exercises in this lesson.

1. Open the as-Test Blueprint workbook from the Lesson 05 folder in your file storage location.

2. Find every instance of the word *demonstrate* and replace it with *show*.

3. Using Find and Replace, change the formatting in B6 and every other cell with the same formatting so that they are no longer italicized and are blue (you choose the exact shade of blue) rather than a dark shade of red.

4. Save and close your workbook.

5. Exit from Excel.

Critical Thinking

Critical Thinking 5.1   PTA Fundraiser

Open the ct-PTA Fundraiser workbook from the Lesson 05 folder in your default storage location. Use the following guidelines to complete the worksheet:

■ Insert the following class information, ensuring that the teachers' names remain in alphabetic order:

Teacher	Total Buyout	Total Sales	Net Sales Profit	Net to PTA	Buyout Count	Number in Class	Class Average
Madden	160.00	982.00			4	20	
Bradshaw	230.00	864.00			7	19	
Swan	120.00	1,639.50			3	30	
Zorn	400.00	1,274.00			10	32	
Largent	305.00	775.00			6	18	

■ Change the text rotation in the cells in row 1 so that they are at 45 degrees. Change the row heights and column widths as necessary.

■ Insert a row at the top of the worksheet and merge and center the following title over the active columns: **Creekview PTA 2008 Fundraiser**. Change the font size to 16.

■ Create a formula in column D to calculate the Net Sales Profit by multiplying the Total Sales by 50%. Copy the formula down to all teachers.

■ Create a formula in the Net to PTA column that sums the Total Buyout and Net Sales Profit. Copy the formula down to all teachers.

■ Calculate the average sales per child for each class in column H, copying the formula down to all teachers.

■ Create a formula in cell H43 to calculate the school's average per class. Place a box around the cell.

■ Copy the entire worksheet and paste it into Sheet1 and Sheet2.

■ On Sheet1, delete the Total Buyout, Net to PTA, and Buyout Count columns. Adjust any formulas as necessary.

■ On Sheet2, delete the Total Sales, Net Sales Profit, Net to PTA, and Class Average columns. Adjust any formulas as necessary.

Save your workbook and close Excel.

Critical Thinking 5.2   Store Returns

Open the ct-Big Time Stores Returns workbook from the Lesson 05 folder in your default storage location. Insert a column immediately to the right of the Return Date column. Use a formula to calculate the number of days between the Return Date and the Purchase Date. Format the cells in the Number of Days column so that numbers are displayed with no decimal places. Reorganize the columns so that the Purchase Price column is to the right of the Number of Days column. Calculate the total value of the returns in cell G9. Adjust all column widths to fit the widest entries in the columns. Merge and center the title over the worksheet. Apply any other formatting you desire, and then save the changes and close the workbook.

Critical Thinking 5.3   Stock Portfolio

Open the ct-Personal Portfolio workbook from the Lesson 05 folder in your default storage location. Assume the stocks in the portfolio were purchased on the following dates:

Stock Symbol	Date Purchased
GLC	3/5/05
HD	11/5/04
LU	11/6/06
MSFT	8/5/05
ORCL	9/1/06
SBUX	4/25/04

Insert a column to the left of the Purchase Price column, and enter the Date Purchased information. Be sure you associate the correct purchase date with the correct stock symbol. Format the dates in the Date Purchased column with a date format of your choice. Add another column to the worksheet that calculates the number of days the investment has been held as of today's date. The formula should automatically recalculate the number of days whenever the workbook is opened. Format all cells in the Number of Days column to display a number with no decimals. AutoFit all columns to fit the widest entry. Apply a theme of your choice to the worksheet. Save the changes and close the workbook.

Critical Thinking 5.4   Stock Research

Open the ct-Stock Research workbook, located in the Lesson 05 folder. Use the Research pane to get quotes on stocks with the symbols CSCO, INTC, and PAYX. Add the stock symbols, company names, and dates purchased to the worksheet. Insert this new information so that the rows are in alphabetical order by stock symbol. Assume you are buying 100 shares of each company's stock and that the purchase price and current price are the same. If necessary, copy formulas from other cells to the empty cells in the new rows. Format all cells as necessary. Save and close the workbook.

LESSON 6

Discovering the Magic of Excel Charting

In this lesson, you will use Excel's charting features to create various types of charts. Charting is an important skill to have when using worksheets because comparisons, trends, and other relationships are often conveyed more effectively with charts. You will use Excel to create column charts, line charts, and pie charts. In addition, you will learn how to edit and format chart objects using the visual chart element pickers. When a theme is applied to a worksheet, it includes special effects for charts as well.

LESSON OBJECTIVES

After studying this lesson, you will be able to:

- Manage multiple worksheets in a workbook
- Create a variety of different types of charts
- Move and size embedded charts
- Preview and print charts
- Modify existing charts
- Format charts
- Apply styles to charts

Case Study: Charting with Autosoft Software Company

Christie Giamo is the founder and CEO of Autosoft, a rapidly growing software development company. Christie has asked her sales manager, Steve Broderick, to prepare several charts depicting revenue for the 2007 fiscal year. Christie wants charts that compare sales in the various quarters, the growth trend throughout the year, and the contributions of each sales rep to the company sales. Steve uses Excel's charting tools to produce impressive charts to meet Christie's high standards.

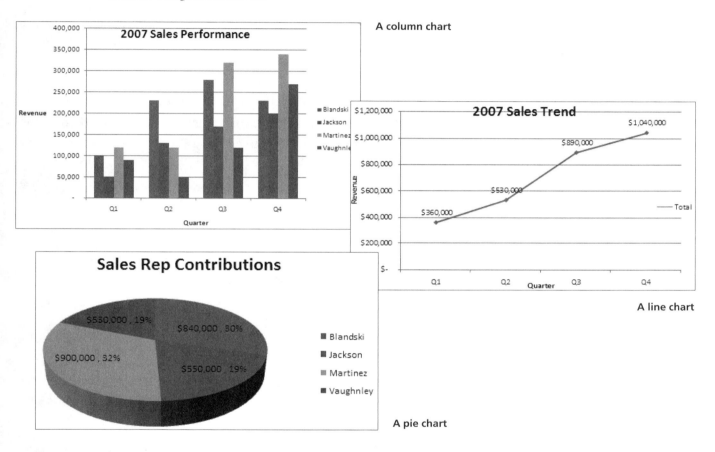

A column chart

A line chart

A pie chart

Managing Worksheets

As you begin to work with more advanced topics like charts and create more in-depth workbooks, you will need to be comfortable with workbook management and maneuvering around multiple worksheets. In Lesson 10, Managing Multiple-Sheet Workbooks, you will learn more about working with multiple worksheets.

Inserting and Deleting Worksheets

Although Excel displays three worksheets in a new workbook by default, you can insert as many new worksheets as your available computer memory allows. Excel 2007 makes it very easy to insert a new worksheet with the Insert Worksheet button located at the far right of the worksheet tabs. In order to clean up the appearance of your workbook, you may wish to delete unused worksheets. Realize, though, that if you delete a worksheet it cannot be undone!

Rearranging, Renaming, and Formatting Worksheets

Sheet tabs can be placed in any order simply by dragging. You can also rename a worksheet tab in order to give it a more descriptive name. If you desire to spruce up your workbook a bit, you can also change the color of the tabs. The active worksheet tab name will be displayed in bold. Take a look at the following figure to learn more about worksheet tabs.

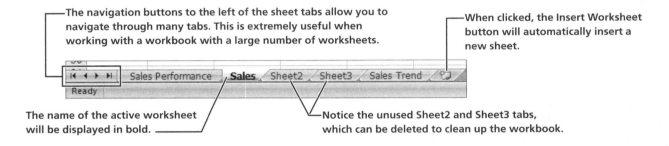

The navigation buttons to the left of the sheet tabs allow you to navigate through many tabs. This is extremely useful when working with a workbook with a large number of worksheets.

When clicked, the Insert Worksheet button will automatically insert a new sheet.

The name of the active worksheet will be displayed in bold.

Notice the unused Sheet2 and Sheet3 tabs, which can be deleted to clean up the workbook.

 WARNING! *You cannot undo the Delete Worksheet command. However, if you issue the command by mistake, you can close the workbook without saving it and then reopen it to recover the lost worksheet.*

QR **QUICK REFERENCE: MANAGING WORKSHEETS**

Task	Procedure
Activate a worksheet	■ Click the desired worksheet tab.
Rename a worksheet	■ Double-click the worksheet tab to be renamed. ■ Type a new name and tap Enter.
Change the worksheet tab color	■ Right-click the desired sheet tab. ■ Choose Tab Color, and then trace your mouse over and click the desired color.
Insert a worksheet	■ Click the Insert Worksheet button to the right of the last tab displayed.

QUICK REFERENCE: MANAGING WORKSHEETS (CONTINUED)

Task	Procedure
Delete a worksheet	■ Right-click the tab of the worksheet you wish to delete.
	■ Choose Delete.
	■ Remember, once a sheet is deleted, it cannot be undone.
Move a worksheet	■ Drag the worksheet tab to the desired position in the worksheet order.
Copy a worksheet	■ Hold down Ctrl while dragging the tab of the sheet you wish to copy.
	■ Release Ctrl and the mouse button when the new tab is in the desired position.

 Hands-On 6.1   Modify Workbooks and Sheet Tabs

In this exercise, you will change the color of and rename a worksheet tab, insert and move a new sheet, and delete a worksheet.

1. Open the workbook named Autosoft Quarterly Sales from the Lesson 06 folder in your default storage location.

2. Follow these steps to rename Sheet1:

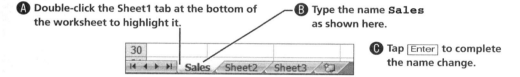

Ⓐ Double-click the Sheet1 tab at the bottom of the worksheet to highlight it.

Ⓑ Type the name `Sales` as shown here.

Ⓒ Tap Enter to complete the name change.

3. Right-click the Sales worksheet tab, choose Tab Color, and then choose a color for the tab. *The color you chose appears at the bottom of the tab.*

4. Click any other worksheet tab. *The newly colored worksheet tab is now fully visible.*

5. Follow these steps to move the worksheet:

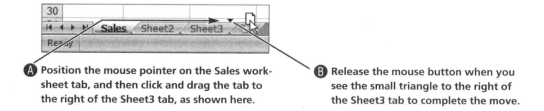

Ⓐ Position the mouse pointer on the Sales worksheet tab, and then click and drag the tab to the right of the Sheet3 tab, as shown here.

Ⓑ Release the mouse button when you see the small triangle to the right of the Sheet3 tab to complete the move.

Excel moves the Sales worksheet to the new location.

6. Drag the Sales sheet back to the first position in the sheet order.

7. Right-click the Sheet3 tab, and then choose Delete from the menu.

8. Click Undo on the Quick Access toolbar.
Notice that the Sheet3 worksheet cannot be restored, and all that has been undone is the tab color.

⚠️ **TIP!** *The only way to recover a deleted sheet is to close the workbook without saving and then reopen it. All other changes since your most recent Save command will be lost, but the worksheet will be recovered.*

9. Choose Home→Cells→Insert menu ▾→Insert Sheet from the Ribbon.
Excel inserts a new worksheet to the left of the currently displayed worksheet.

10. Drag the new sheet to the right of Sheet2, and rename it **2008 Sales**.

11. Apply the tab color of your choice to the sheet tabs.

12. Display the Sales sheet, and then continue with the next topic.

Creating Charts in Excel

Numerical data is often easier to interpret when presented in a chart. You can embed a chart in a worksheet so that it appears alongside the worksheet data, or you can place the chart on a separate worksheet. Putting the chart on a separate worksheet prevents the chart from cluttering the data worksheet. Regardless of their placement, charts are always linked to the data from which they are created. Thus, charts are automatically updated when worksheet data changes. Charts are made up of individual objects including the chart title, legend, plot area, value axis, category axis, and data series. You can apply many options and enhancements to each object.

Integrated Chart Engine

New to Office 2007, a chart engine is integrated throughout the suite of programs. It is now easy to create a chart in Microsoft Word or PowerPoint as well as in Excel. Once you have mastered the topics in this lesson, you will be able to understand how to create charts in the other Microsoft Office applications as well! When a chart is created in another application, it is actually saved and stored as an Excel chart.

Introducing OfficeArt

OfficeArt is a new feature in Office 2007 that allows you to draw and format shapes. Charts are drawn with OfficeArt so you can format them with effects available to all OfficeArt shapes, such as realistic 3-D effects, shadow and glow effects, and gradient or texture fill effects. You will learn much more about OfficeArt in Lesson 8, Adding Graphics to Worksheets.

Creating New Charts

Charts can be created by choosing the chart type from the Insert tab of the Ribbon. If you want to see the entire list of chart types displayed before you make your choice, you can open the Insert Chart dialog box. When you create a chart, you have the option of either embedding it into the current worksheet where the data is or placing it on a separate sheet of its own. To place a chart on its own sheet, simply select it and then tap the [F11] key. A new chart will be created on a separate sheet, and the embedded chart will remain as well. When you use the [F11] key, the chart on the new sheet will be based on the default chart type, not the type that is embedded in the worksheet. An advantage of creating charts based on data within a workbook is that the chart data will automatically be updated when changes are made to the source data.

FROM THE KEYBOARD

[F11] to place a chart on its own sheet

Choosing the Proper Source Data

It is important to select the proper data on which to base your chart. In addition to selecting the raw data for the chart, you will also want to ensure that you select any "total" rows that should be included in the chart. You should make sure that you select the proper row and column headings for your column and bar charts. If you notice that any of these important pieces are missing, you will need to reselect your source data.

Chart Types

Excel provides 11 major chart types. Each chart type also has several subtypes from which you can choose. Excel has a chart for every occasion.

Built-In Chart Types

Each chart type represents data in a different manner. You can present the same data in completely different ways by changing the chart type. For this reason, you should always use the chart type that most effectively represents your data. The three most common chart types are column, pie, and line. You will be creating all three types in this lesson.

User-Defined Charts

Excel lets you create and save customized charts to meet your particular needs. For example, you can create a customized chart that contains the name of your company and its color(s) in the background and use it as the basis for all new charts of that type.

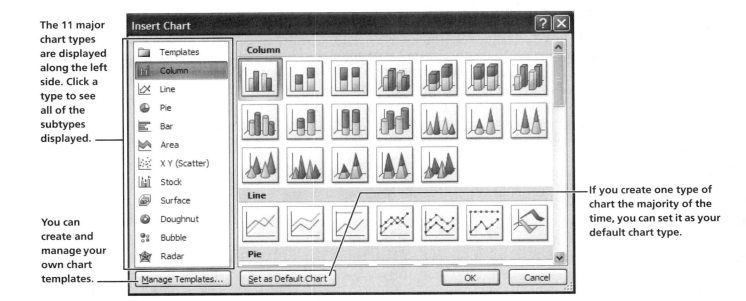

The 11 major chart types are displayed along the left side. Click a type to see all of the subtypes displayed.

You can create and manage your own chart templates.

If you create one type of chart the majority of the time, you can set it as your default chart type.

Column Charts and Bar Charts

Column charts compare values (numbers) using vertical bars. Bar charts compare values using horizontal bars. Each column or bar represents a value from the worksheet. Column charts and bar charts are most useful for comparing sets of values (called data series). Column and bar charts can be created in 2-D or 3-D formats.

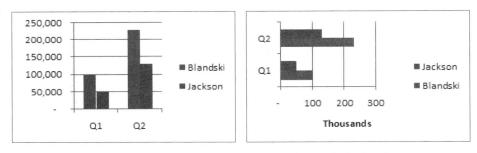

The column chart on the left and the bar chart on the right are displaying the exact same data, but the chart types are different. In this situation, the charts are showing a comparison of the quarterly sales for two employees, Blandski and Jackson.

Category Axis and Value Axis

The horizontal line that forms the base of a column chart is the category axis. The category axis typically measures units of time such as days, months, and quarters, although it can also measure products, people, tests, and other categories. The vertical line on the left side of a column chart is the value axis. The value axis typically measures values such as dollars. Most chart types (including column and bar charts) have a category and a value axis. The following illustrations show the worksheet data and one of the two column charts you will create in the next exercise. The illustrations show the objects included on most column charts and the corresponding data used to create the chart. Take a few minutes to study the following illustrations carefully.

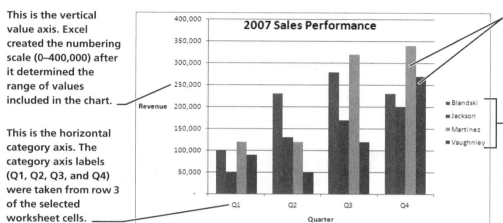

	A	B	C	D	E
1	Autosoft 2007 Quarterly Sales				
2					
3		Q1	Q2	Q3	Q4
4	Blandski	100,000	230,000	280,000	230,000
5	Jackson	50,000	130,000	170,000	200,000
6	Martinez	120,000	120,000	320,000	340,000
7	Vaughnley	90,000	50,000	120,000	270,000
8					
9	Total	$ 360,000	$ 530,000	$ 890,000	$ 1,040,000

The following chart was created using the selected data shown here. Notice that the Total row was not included in the selection. The column chart compares the sales numbers for the individual quarters, but it does not include the total sales from row 9.

This is the vertical value axis. Excel created the numbering scale (0–400,000) after it determined the range of values included in the chart.

This is the horizontal category axis. The category axis labels (Q1, Q2, Q3, and Q4) were taken from row 3 of the selected worksheet cells.

Notice the chart columns. The columns represent values from the various data series. The first data series are the Blandski numbers in row 4. The first column in each quarter represents the Blandski numbers.

This is a legend that identifies the various columns. The legend text (Blandski, Jackson, Martinez, and Vaughnley) was taken from the first column of the selected worksheet cells.

Notice that the chart includes a chart title (2007 Sales Performance), a value axis title (Revenue), and a category axis title (Quarter).

Chart and Axis Titles

Excel allows you to create titles for your charts as well as the value and category axes. If you choose a range of information that includes what appears to Excel to be a title, Excel will include it in the new chart. You can always edit this title if it is not correct.

 TIP! *These additional Ribbon tabs are called contextual tabs.*

The Chart Tools

When a chart is selected, various Chart Tools will be displayed as additional tabs on the Ribbon. These tabs allow you to make changes to the design, layout, and formatting of the chart.

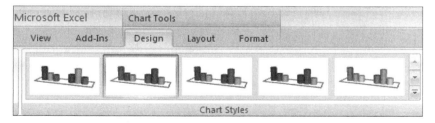

When a chart is selected, the Chart Tools will be displayed, adding the Design, Layout, and Format tabs to the Ribbon.

QUICK REFERENCE: CREATING A CHART

Task	Procedure
Create a chart	■ Enter the data you wish to chart into Excel. ■ Select the data range for the chart. ■ Display the Insert tab of the Ribbon. ■ Choose the type of chart from the Charts group.
Add a title to a chart	■ Select the chart to which you wish to add a title. ■ Choose Layout→Labels→Chart Title from the Ribbon to display the title options. ■ Choose how you wish the title to appear. ■ Select the default title "Chart Title," and type in the title you wish for your chart.
Add axis titles to a chart	■ Select the chart to which you wish to add an axis title. ■ Choose Layout→Labels→Axis Titles from the Ribbon to display the axis options. ■ Choose whether you wish to apply a horizontal or vertical axis title. ■ Choose how you wish the title to appear. ■ Select the default title "Axis Title," and type in the title you wish for your axis. ■ Repeat these steps for the other axis.

 Hands-On 6.2 Create a Chart

In this exercise, you will create two column charts, one in 2-D format and one in 3-D format. One chart will be embedded in the worksheet, and the other will be on a separate sheet.

Create an Embedded 2-D Column Chart

1. Select the range A3:E7.

2. Follow these steps to create a clustered column chart:

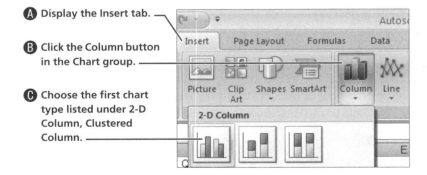

Ⓐ Display the Insert tab.

Ⓑ Click the Column button in the Chart group.

Ⓒ Choose the first chart type listed under 2-D Column, Clustered Column.

The chart will appear embedded in the Sales worksheet with the default properties for the clustered column chart type displayed. The data in the chart is based on the range of cells you preselected.

3. Look at the Ribbon and notice that the Chart Tools are now displayed.

Notice that the chart is covering part of the data. You will learn how to move charts around a sheet in the next exercise.

Create a 3-D Cylinder Column Chart on a New Sheet

4. Select A3:E7.
Even though the chart is partially covering your data, you can still drag to select the range.

5. Choose Insert→Chart→Column →All Chart Types from the Ribbon.
The Insert Chart dialog box will be displayed.

6. Click the Clustered Cylinder Column chart type and tap ⏎ Enter.
The new chart will appear embedded on the Sales worksheet. We will place it on a separate sheet in the next step.

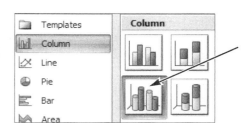

7. Tap F11.
Tapping F11 places the selected chart on a separate sheet, and it will be based on the default chart type of Clustered Column. You will see the Chart Tools displayed, which can be used to modify the chart.

Edit the Chart and Axis Titles

8. Choose Chart Tools→Layout→Labels→Chart Title →Centered Overlay Title from the Ribbon.

9. Follow these steps to title the chart:

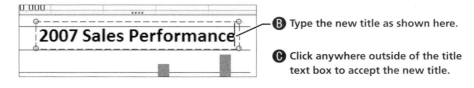

Ⓐ Select the default title, *Chart Title.*

Ⓑ Type the new title as shown here.

Ⓒ Click anywhere outside of the title text box to accept the new title.

10. Choose Layout→Labels→Axis Titles →Primary Horizontal Axis Title→Title Below Axis from the Ribbon.

11. Drag to select the default title, *Axis Title.*

12. Type in the new horizontal axis title, **Quarter**, and then click away to accept the new title.

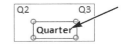

13. Choose Layout→Labels→Axis Titles →Primary Vertical Axis Title→Horizontal Title from the Ribbon.

14. Select the default title, *Axis Title.*

15. Type in the new vertical axis title, **Revenue**, and then click away to accept the new title.

Rename the Worksheets

16. Double-click the Chart1 sheet tab.

17. Type **Sales Performance** to rename the tab, and then tap Enter.

18. Click the Sales sheet tab.

Notice that the clustered column chart is still embedded on the Sales sheet. You can either leave a chart in both places or delete one, which you will do in the next exercise.

19. Save the workbook, and leave it open for the next exercise.

Moving and Sizing Embedded Charts

When a chart is selected, it is surrounded by a light blue border with sizing handles displayed. A selected chart can be both moved and resized when it is selected.

Moving Embedded Charts

Charts that are embedded in a worksheet can be easily moved to a new location. This can be accomplished by a simple drag, but you need to ensure that you click the chart area and not a separate element. Regardless of whether a chart is embedded within a worksheet or moved to a separate tab, the chart data will automatically update when values are changed in the source data.

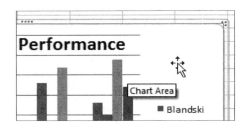

A four-pointed arrow indicates that you can drag to move this selected chart.

Sizing Embedded Charts

In order to size a chart, it must first be selected. You simply need to drag a sizing handle when the double-arrow mouse pointer is displayed. In order to change a chart size proportionately, hold Shift while dragging a corner handle.

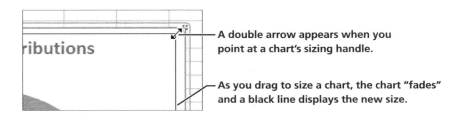

A double arrow appears when you point at a chart's sizing handle.

As you drag to size a chart, the chart "fades" and a black line displays the new size.

Deleting Charts

It is a very simple process to delete an embedded chart—just select the chart area and tap Delete. You can always use the Undo command if you delete an embedded chart by mistake. You delete a chart that is on its own tab by deleting the worksheet. This action cannot be undone, so Excel warns you with a prompt to confirm the deletion.

QUICK REFERENCE: MOVING AND SIZING EMBEDDED CHARTS	
Task	**Procedure**
Move an embedded chart	Drag the selected chart to a new location with the move pointer while it is positioned over the chart area.
Change the chart size	Drag any sizing handle.
Delete a chart	Embedded Chart: Select the chart, and then tap the Delete key.
	Worksheet Chart: Delete the worksheet.

 Hands-On 6.3   Move and Size a Chart

In this exercise, you will move and resize the column chart that you created in the previous exercise.

Move an Embedded Chart

1. Click once on the chart area of the embedded chart in the Sales sheet to select it.
   Sizing handles appear around the border of the chart.

2. Follow these steps to move the chart:

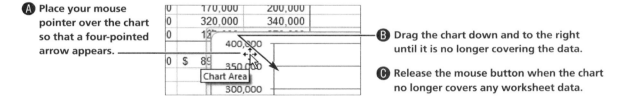

Ⓐ Place your mouse pointer over the chart so that a four-pointed arrow appears.

Ⓑ Drag the chart down and to the right until it is no longer covering the data.

Ⓒ Release the mouse button when the chart no longer covers any worksheet data.

You will see a rectangle "ghost" as you drag, showing you where the chart will land if you release the mouse button at that location.

Size a Chart

3. Follow these steps to resize the chart to be smaller:

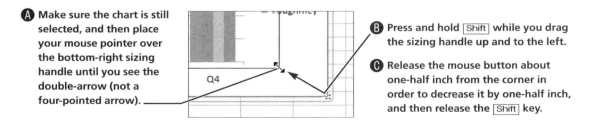

Ⓐ Make sure the chart is still selected, and then place your mouse pointer over the bottom-right sizing handle until you see the double-arrow (not a four-pointed arrow).

Ⓑ Press and hold Shift while you drag the sizing handle up and to the left.

Ⓒ Release the mouse button about one-half inch from the corner in order to decrease it by one-half inch, and then release the Shift key.

Notice that Excel resized the width and height proportionately. This is because you held down the Shift key as you resized the chart.

Delete an Embedded Chart

4. Click once to select the column chart, and then tap ⌷Delete⌷.
Excel deletes the embedded chart.

5. Use ⌷Ctrl⌷+⌷Z⌷ to undo the Delete command.
The embedded chart reappears on the worksheet.

6. Use ⌷Ctrl⌷+⌷Y⌷ to redo the Delete command.
The chart is once again deleted. (You will create a pie chart here in a later exercise.)

7. Use ⌷Ctrl⌷+⌷S⌷ to save your workbook, and leave it open for the next exercise.

Exploring Other Chart Types

In the last section, you learned about column and bar charts. Now we will explore line and pie charts and how they can make your data work for you.

Line Charts

Line charts are most useful for comparing trends over a period of time. For example, line charts are often used to show stock market activity where the upward or downward trend is important. Like column charts, line charts have category and value axes. Line charts also use the same or similar objects as column charts. The following illustration shows a line chart that depicts the trend in quarter sales throughout the year. Take a moment to study the following figures.

	A	B	C	D	E
1	Autosoft 2007 Quarterly Sales				
2					
3		Q1	Q2	Q3	Q4
4	Blandski	100,000	230,000	280,000	230,000
5	Jackson	50,000	130,000	170,000	200,000
6	Martinez	120,000	120,000	320,000	340,000
7	Vaughnley	90,000	50,000	120,000	270,000
8					
9	Total	$ 360,000	$ 530,000	$ 890,000	$ 1,040,000

The following chart was created using the selected data shown here. Notice that the data is in two separate ranges. You use the ⌷Ctrl⌷ key to select these nonadjacent ranges so that you can chart just the totals and the Q1–Q4 labels.

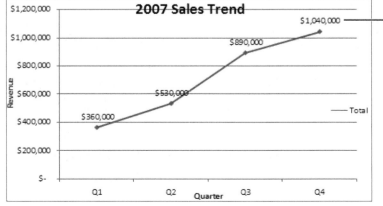

This is a data label. Data labels show the precise value of the various data points. You can use data labels with any chart type.

The line chart clearly depicts the upward trend in sales volume.

Hands-On 6.4 **Create a Line Chart**

In this exercise, you will create a line chart that displays the total sales.

Before you Begin: The Sales worksheet should be displayed.

Create a Line Chart

1. Follow these steps to select the data for the line chart:

Ⓐ Select the range A3:E3.

Ⓑ Press and hold down Ctrl while selecting the range A9:E9. Both ranges should be selected.

	A	B	C	D	E
1	Autosoft 2007 Quarterly Sales				
2					
3		Q1	Q2	Q3	Q4
4	Blandski	100,000	230,000	280,000	230,000
5	Jackson	50,000	130,000	170,000	200,000
6	Martinez	120,000	120,000	320,000	340,000
7	Vaughnley	90,000	50,000	120,000	270,000
8					
9	Total	$ 360,000	$ 530,000	$ 890,000	$ 1,040,000

2. Choose Insert→Charts→Line 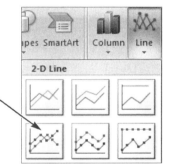→Line with Markers from the Ribbon, as shown.
Excel creates an embedded line chart in the current worksheet. Notice the light blue border and sizing handles, indicating the chart is selected. The Chart Tools contextual tabs are also visible on the Ribbon.

Move the Chart

Now you will move the chart to its own worksheet.

3. Follow these steps to move the chart:

   ■ Make sure the chart is selected (displays handles), which also makes the Chart Tools contextual tabs visible.

   ■ Choose Design→Location→Move Chart 🖼 from the Ribbon.

   The Move Chart dialog box appears. In this dialog box, you can choose where to place the chart as well as provide a name for a new sheet if you wish to create one.

4. Follow these steps to move the chart to its own sheet:

Ⓐ Click in the circle to the left of New Sheet.

Ⓑ Type **Sales Trend** as the name for the new sheet.

Ⓒ Click OK.

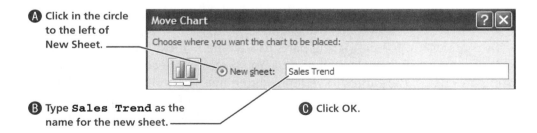

The chart will now appear on its own worksheet.

Edit the Chart

5. Click the Title text box once to select it, and then double-click the word *Total*.
The default title Total *will be selected and ready for you to type in the title of your choice.*

6. Type **2007 Sales Trend**, and then click another area of the chart.

7. Choose Layout→Labels→Axis Titles 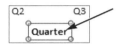→Primary Horizontal Axis Title→Title Below Axis from the Ribbon.
Excel provides a text box below the horizontal axis with a default name of Axis Title *displayed.*

8. Drag to select the default horizontal axis title.

9. Type in the new horizontal axis title, **Quarter**, and then click away to accept the new title.

10. Choose Layout→Labels→Axis Titles →Primary Vertical Axis Title→Rotated Title from the Ribbon.

11. Drag to select the default vertical axis title.

12. Type **Revenue** as the new vertical axis title, and then click away to accept the new title.

13. Choose Layout→Labels→Data Labels →Above from the Ribbon.
Excel displays the values above the data points on the chart.

14. Use Ctrl+S to save your worksheet, and leave it open for the next exercise.

Pie Charts

Pie charts are useful for comparing parts of a whole. For example, pie charts are often used in budgets to show how funds are allocated. You typically select only two sets of data when creating pie charts: the values to be represented by the pie slices and the labels to identify the slices. The following illustration shows a worksheet and an accompanying 3-D pie chart. Notice that the worksheet has a Total column. You will create a pie chart based on the Total column in the next exercise.

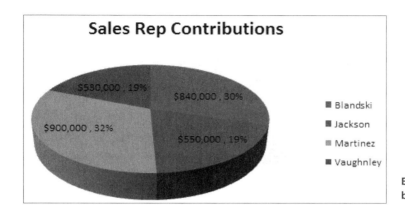

	A	B	C	D	E	F
3		Q1	Q2	Q3	Q4	Totals
4	Blandski	100,000	230,000	280,000	230,000	$840,000
5	Jackson	50,000	130,000	170,000	200,000	$550,000
6	Martinez	120,000	120,000	320,000	340,000	$900,000
7	Vaughnley	90,000	50,000	120,000	270,000	$530,000

The names in column A will become labels in the legend. The numbers in column F will determine the sizes of the slices.

Sales Rep Contributions

$530,000 , 19%

$840,000 , 30%

$900,000 , 32%

$550,000 , 19%

- Blandski
- Jackson
- Martinez
- Vaughnley

Excel calculates the percentages based on the numbers you select.

Exploding Pie Slices

There are times when you may want to draw attention to a particular slice of the pie chart. You can make one slice explode from the chart simply by dragging it out.

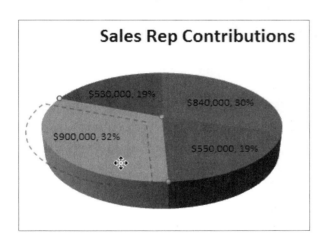

Sales Rep Contributions

$530,000, 19%

$840,000, 30%

$900,000, 32%

$550,000, 19%

Notice that as you drag a slice out to give it an exploded effect, Excel will show where it will land with a dashed line.

Rotating and Elevating Pie Charts

You have the option to change the rotation and elevation of pie charts in order to display data in a different position or change the angle at which it is viewed. The 3-D Rotation button on the Layout tab of the Ribbon will open a dialog box that allows changes to the rotation and elevation to take place.

Hands-On 6.5   Create a Pie Chart

In this exercise, you will create a pie chart with the same data used for the line chart and leave it embedded in the Sales worksheet.

Before You Begin: The Sales worksheet should be displayed.

Insert the Pie Chart

1. Select cell F3, and type the word **Totals**.

2. Select the range F4:F7.

3. Choose Home→Editing→Sum Σ from the Ribbon to compute the totals for column F.
   Excel calculates the total annual sales for each sales rep. Your totals should match those displayed in the figure for step 5.

4. Format the range of F4:F7 as Currency Style with no decimals.

5. Follow these steps to select the range for the chart:

A Drag to select A4:A7.

B While holding `Ctrl`, drag to select F4:F7.

◢	A	B	C	D	E	F
3		Q1	Q2	Q3	Q4	Totals
4	Blandski	100,000	230,000	280,000	230,000	$840,000
5	Jackson	50,000	130,000	170,000	200,000	$550,000
6	Martinez	120,000	120,000	320,000	340,000	$900,000
7	Vaughnley	90,000	50,000	120,000	270,000	$530,000

6. Choose Insert→Charts→Pie  →Pie in 3-D from the Ribbon as shown to the right.

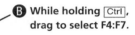

Edit the Chart

7. Place the mouse pointer over the chart area so that the four-pointed arrow appears, and then drag it down and to the right until it no longer covers the data.

8. Choose Layout→Labels→Chart Title ⊞→Above Chart from the Ribbon.

9. Select the default title and type **Sales Rep Contributions**, clicking outside of the Title box to accept the new title.

10. Choose Layout→Labels→Data Labels ⊞→More Data Label Options from the Ribbon.
    The Format Data Labels dialog box appears.

11. Follow these steps to format the data labels:

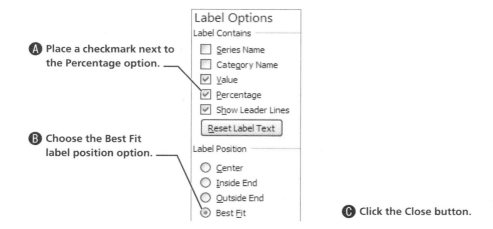

A Place a checkmark next to the Percentage option.

B Choose the Best Fit label position option.

C Click the Close button.

Excel will display both the value and the percentages in each pie slice wherever they "best fit."

Explode a Pie Slice

12. Click the slice representing Martinez's sales, and then pause and click it again.
The first click will select all slices, and the second click will select just the slice for Martinez.

13. Place your mouse pointer over the Martinez slice until you see a move pointer, and then drag out away from the pie chart slightly and release.

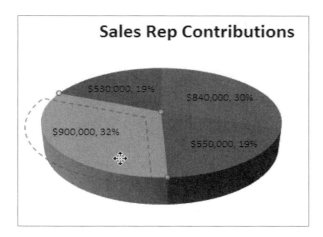

Sales Rep Contributions

$530,000, 19%
$840,000, 30%
$900,000, 32%
$550,000, 19%

Notice that as you drag the pie slice away from the main chart, a dashed line will display where it will land if you release the mouse button.

14. Use Ctrl + S to save your worksheet, and leave it open for the next exercise.

Previewing and Printing Charts

You can use the Print Preview and Print commands that you learned about in Lesson 2, Editing, Viewing, and Printing Worksheets to preview and print charts. If a chart is on a separate worksheet, you must first activate it by clicking the sheet tab. If a chart is embedded, you must first select the chart before issuing the Print Preview or Print commands. In Print Preview, the chart will display in black and white or in color, depending on the type of printer to which your computer is connected.

QUICK REFERENCE: PRINTING CHARTS	
Task	**Procedure**
Preview how a chart will look when printed	■ Select the chart by either clicking it if it is embedded or clicking the tab on which it is placed.
	■ Choose Office→Print menu ▶ →Print Preview.
Print a chart	■ Ensure that the chart you wish to print is selected.
	■ Choose Office→Print.

 Hands-On 6.6   Preview and Print a Chart

In this exercise, you will preview the pie chart you created in the last exercise and print the column chart.

Before You Begin: The Sales worksheet should be displayed.

1. Click once to select the pie chart on the Sales worksheet.

2. Choose Office→Print menu ▶ →Print Preview.
   The pie chart appears in the Print Preview window.

3. Choose Print Preview→Preview→Close Print Preview 🗙 from the Ribbon.

4. Click in a cell away from the pie chart to deselect the chart.

5. Choose Office→Print menu ▶ →Print Preview.
   Notice that when the chart is not selected, Excel will print the worksheet along with the embedded chart.

6. Choose Print Preview→Preview→Close Print Preview 🗙 from the Ribbon.

7. Display the Sales Performance worksheet.

8. Choose Office 🔘 →Print, click OK, and then retrieve the printout.
   Excel will print one copy of your chart to the default printer.

Modifying Existing Charts

You can modify any chart object after the chart has been created. You can change the size, font, color, and placement of titles; format the numbers on the value axis; change the background color of the chart area; and more. You can also add or remove objects such as legends and data labels. You can even move an embedded chart to a separate worksheet and vice versa. These changes are made with the Chart Tools, which are grouped onto three contextual Ribbon tabs that appear when a chart is selected: Design, Layout, and Format. The following table describes the various Chart Tools at your disposal to modify your charts.

QUICK REFERENCE: USING CHART TOOLS ON THE RIBBON

Contextual Tab	Command Groups on the Tab
Design	■ *Type* allows you to change the type of chart, set the default chart type, and save a chart as a template.
	■ *Data* allows you to switch the data displayed on rows and columns and to reselect the data for the chart.
	■ *Chart Layouts* allows you to change the overall layout of the chart.
	■ *Chart Styles* allows you to choose a preset style for your chart.
	■ *Location* allows you to switch a chart from being embedded to being placed on a sheet and vice versa.
Layout	■ *Current Selection* allows you to select a specific chart element and apply formatting to it.
	■ *Insert* allows you to insert objects into your chart.
	■ *Labels* allows you to make changes to various labels on your chart such as the title and data labels.
	■ *Axes* allows you to choose whether to display axes and gridlines, as well as to set the properties for them.
	■ *Background* allows you to change the background formatting, such as fill color, for the chart.
	■ *Analysis* allows you to analyze the data displayed within the chart.
	■ *Properties* allows you to change the name of the chart.
Format	■ *Current Selection* allows you to select a specific chart element and apply formatting to it.
	■ *Shape Styles* allows you to visually make changes to the selected chart element.
	■ *WordArt Styles* allows you to apply WordArt to text labels in your chart.
	■ *Arrange* allows you to change how your chart is arranged in relation to other objects in your worksheet.
	■ Size allows you to change the size of your chart by typing in exact values.

Changing the Chart Type

There are so many chart types available that you may wish to explore other options before making a final decision. It is easy to change the type of an existing chart by using the Chart Tools available in Excel. You will need to display the Change Chart Type dialog box in order to make this change. This dialog box is similar to the Insert Chart dialog box you saw earlier in this lesson.

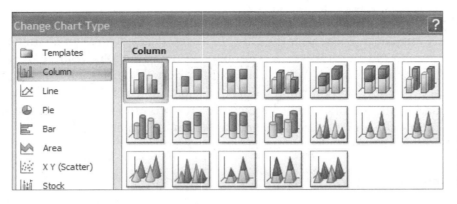

In the Change Chart Type dialog box, you can choose from many preset chart types if you wish to change the type of an existing chart.

Modifying Chart Elements

Charts are made up of various elements. For example, the legends, titles, and columns are all types of elements. You must select an element before you can perform an action on it. You can select an element by clicking it with the mouse. Once selected, you can delete, move, size, and format the element. You delete a selected element by tapping the $\boxed{\text{Delete}}$ key, move a selected element by dragging it with the mouse when you see the move pointer, and change the size by dragging a sizing handle.

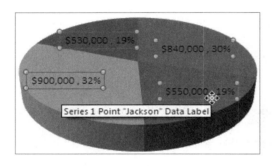

In this illustration, the data labels are the selected element, and the mouse is pointing at the data label for Jackson (which is evidenced by the ScreenTip that is displayed).

Formatting Charts

You can modify any chart element after the chart has been created by using the visual Chart Tools on the Ribbon. These are termed the visual chart element pickers due to the ease with which you can quickly change the formatting of any element.

Previewing Formatting Before Applying

If you recall in Lesson 4, Formatting the Contents of Cells, you were able to preview how a formatting change would appear before actually issuing the command to apply it. The same is true with the Chart Tools in Excel. If you place your mouse pointer over a button on one of the Chart Tools Ribbon tabs, it will display a preview of how the change will look in your chart.

QUICK REFERENCE: MODIFYING EXISTING CHARTS

Task	Procedure
Change the chart type	■ Select the chart you wish to change to a different type.
	■ Choose Design→Change Chart Type from the Ribbon.
	■ Browse the types available and double-click the type you wish.
Format an existing chart	■ Select the chart that you wish to format.
	■ Choose the Format tab of the Ribbon.
	■ Apply formatting as appropriate.

Hands-On 6.7   Apply Formatting to a Chart

In this exercise, you will change a chart type and then apply various formatting features to it.

Before You Begin: The Sales Performance worksheet should be displayed.

Change a Chart Type

1. Click anywhere within the column chart on the Sales Performance sheet to select the chart and display the Chart Tools Ribbon tabs.

2. Choose Design→Type→Change Chart Type ![icon] from the Ribbon.
   The Change Chart Type dialog box appears.

3. Follow these steps to change the chart type:

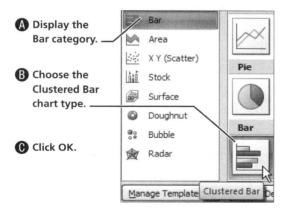

Ⓐ Display the Bar category.

Ⓑ Choose the Clustered Bar chart type.

Ⓒ Click OK.

Format a Chart Using the Ribbon

4. Click anywhere within the top bar in the chart, which represents the Vaughnley data series.

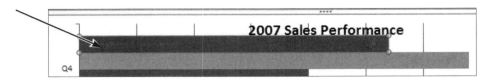

Make sure that you single-click because that will select the data series for all four quarters and leave the current tab displayed. If you double-click, it will display the Design tab with the current style displayed on the Ribbon. In this case, it won't matter as you are already viewing the Design tab, but it could cause you to take extra steps if you are already working on the Format tab.

5. Follow these steps to apply formatting to the Vaughnley data series:

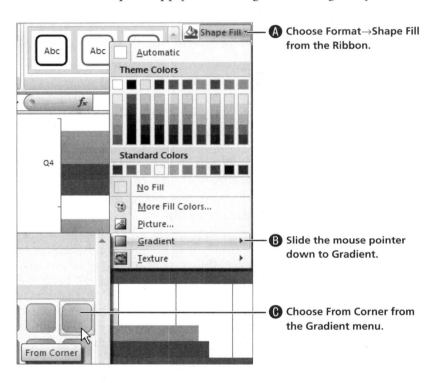

Ⓐ Choose Format→Shape Fill from the Ribbon.

Ⓑ Slide the mouse pointer down to Gradient.

Ⓒ Choose From Corner from the Gradient menu.

6. Click anywhere within the chart area to select it.
Remember that any formatting you choose will apply only to the chart element you have selected.

7. Choose Format→Shape Styles→Shape Outline 🖉→Weight→6 pt from the Ribbon.

8. Choose Format→Shape Styles→Shape Outline 🖉 from the Ribbon, and then apply the color of your choice.
There will now be a heavy line around the entire chart area. In the next few steps, you will be changing the font of the legend.

9. Click to select the legend.

   When you place your mouse pointer over the legend, a ScreenTip will let you know you are in the right place. Notice that when the legend is selected, sizing handles will appear around it.

10. Choose Home→Font ▾ →Arial Narrow from the Ribbon.

    As you can see, commands on the Ribbon can also adjust chart formatting.

11. Save your workbook.

Applying Styles to Charts

In an earlier lesson, you learned about themes in Excel. Chart styles are similar to themes in that they are based on the theme of your worksheet. There are many preset styles that you can apply to charts. The styles that will be displayed on the Design tab of the Ribbon are based on the type of chart that you currently have selected. In the figures displayed below, you can see that the styles available for column charts are different from those available for pie charts.

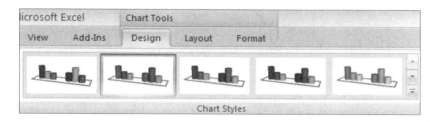

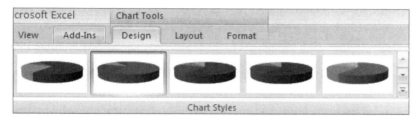

The chart styles available through Excel's Chart Tools will change based on the type of chart you have selected.

Formatting Attributes Controlled by the Selected Style

When you choose a style for your chart, it will change the colors, fonts, and effects (such as fill effects) to match the theme selected. Excel does not allow you to create your own styles, but you can create a template that includes formatting and use it as the basis for future charts.

Viewing All Available Styles for a Type

The Ribbon will display just a few of the styles that are available for the selected type. In order to view all of the styles, you need to click the More button in order to expand the Chart Styles group of the Ribbon.

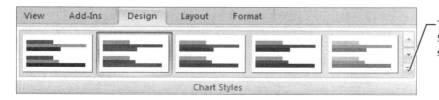

The More button in the Chart Styles group displays all available styles for the selected chart type.

Hands-On 6.8   Apply a Style to a Chart

In this exercise, you will apply a style to the bar chart you created in the last exercise.

Before You Begin: The Sales Performance worksheet should be displayed.

1. Ensure that the Sales Performance chart is selected.

2. Choose Design→Chart Styles→More ⬙ from the Ribbon.
   Excel displays all of the available chart styles for this type of chart.

3. Click once to apply a chart style you find attractive.
   Notice that choosing a style changes the formatting of the chart (such as the fonts, color scheme, fill effects, lines, etc.) to match the new style, which is based on a theme. However, if there were data on this worksheet, the data would not be affected by the new chart style. The application of a worksheet theme also does not affect a chart.

4. Repeat steps 2 and 3 if you wish to apply a different chart style.

5. Save 🖫 and close the workbook.

Concepts Review

True/False Questions

1. If you delete a worksheet, you can use Excel's Undo feature to retrieve it.   TRUE   FALSE

2. Embedded charts are updated when the worksheet data changes.   TRUE   FALSE

3. Charts on separate sheets are not updated when the worksheet data changes.   TRUE   FALSE

4. Column charts are most useful for comparing the parts of a whole.   TRUE   FALSE

5. You must select an embedded chart before you can move or resize it.   TRUE   FALSE

6. Print Preview will always display your chart in the full array of colors you have displayed.   TRUE   FALSE

7. You can preview formatting changes in a chart without actually applying them via Live Preview.   TRUE   FALSE

8. The horizontal line that forms the base of a column chart is the category axis.   TRUE   FALSE

9. Chart styles are based on the theme of the worksheet.   TRUE   FALSE

10. Bar charts compare data using vertical bars.   TRUE   FALSE

Multiple Choice Questions

1. How can you determine which worksheet is currently active?
   a. The sheet tab will be displayed in bold type.
   b. The sheet tab will appear beveled.
   c. It is the first sheet tab listed.
   d. Choose Home→Worksheet→Active Sheet from the Ribbon.

2. Which chart is better for showing a trend over a period of time?
   a. Bar
   b. Column
   c. Line
   d. Pie

3. Which command cannot be reversed with Excel's Undo feature?
   a. Deletion of an embedded chart
   b. Insertion of a chart
   c. Changing the type of a chart
   d. Worksheet deletion

4. Which chart type would you use to compare sales figures for a variety of departments over a period of time?
   a. Column
   b. Pie
   c. Doughnut
   d. Bubble

Skill Builders

Skill Builder 6.1   Manipulate Worksheets

In this exercise, you will insert and rename new worksheets and rearrange them.

1. Open the workbook named sb-Worksheet Manipulation from the Lesson 06 folder in your default storage location.

2. Drag the Sales worksheet tab to the far left so that it appears first, as in the figure at the end of the exercise.

3. Right-click the Sheet2 tab and choose Delete.

4. Click the Sheet3 tab to make the worksheet active.

5. Choose Home→Cells→Delete menu ▼ button→Delete Sheet from the Ribbon.
   Notice that there are two ways to delete a sheet. You can use whichever you prefer.

6. Right-click the Sales Performance tab.

7. Choose Tab Color, and then select the color of your choice.

8. Change the color of the Sales Trend tab to the color of your choice.

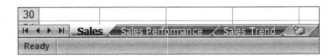

Notice how the worksheet tabs have been rearranged, unneeded tabs have been deleted, and each has been given a color.

9. Save and close your worksheet.

Skill Builder 6.2   Create a Column Chart

In this exercise, you will create a column chart to display student enrollment at a university.

Expand a Series

1. Open the workbook named sb-Enrollments from the Lesson 06 folder in your default storage location.

   Notice that the enrollment data has been completed in column B but that the years have not been completed in column A. In column A, the first two years (1991 and 1992) form the beginning of the series 1991–2007. The best way to expand this series is with the fill handle.

2. Select cells A4 and A5.

3. Drag the fill handle down to row 20 to expand the series.

4. Choose Home→Alignment→Align Text Left ![align left icon] from the Ribbon.

Create the Chart

5. Select the range A3:B20.

   This range includes the enrollment data and the Year *and* Total Enrollment *headings.*

6. Choose Insert→Charts→Column ![column icon] →Clustered Column from the Ribbon.

   Take a moment to study the chart and notice the problem. Excel is interpreting the years 1991–2007 as numbers. The numbers appear as a data series in the chart. The years are the short columns to the left of the tall, thin enrollment data columns. The years should actually be displayed as labels on the horizontal category axis. You will correct this next.

7. Choose Design→Data→Select Data ![select data icon] from the Ribbon.

   This will allow you to modify the data series plotted in the chart.

8. Follow these steps to remove the years from the series and to add them as horizontal (category) axis labels:

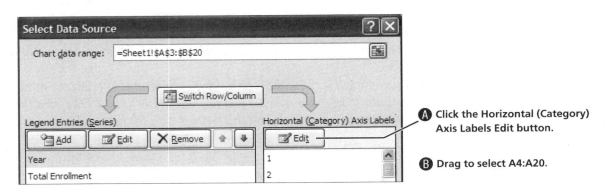

A — Click the Horizontal (Category) Axis Labels Edit button.

B — Drag to select A4:A20.

Excel will display the axis label range you proposed in the Axis Labels dialog box.

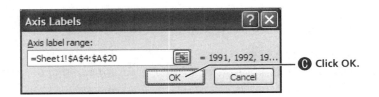

C — Click OK.

Take a careful look at the Select Data Source dialog box now. Notice that the chart data range is no longer displayed because it is too complex. In addition, the years from cells A4:A20 will now be displayed as the horizontal (category) axis labels.

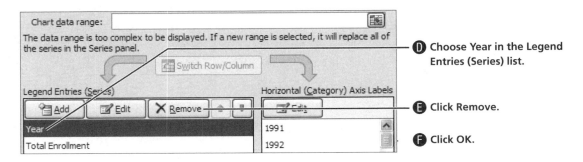

D — Choose Year in the Legend Entries (Series) list.

E — Click Remove.

F — Click OK.

Take a few moments to study your worksheet and chart. Be sure you understand the relationship between the worksheet data and the chart. Notice that with only one data series, Excel automatically uses the column header for that data as the chart title.

Create a Horizontal Axis Title for the Chart

9. Choose Layout→Labels→Axis Titles ⬛→Primary Horizontal Axis Title→Title Below Axis from the Ribbon.

10. Select the default title and replace it with **Year**.

11. Select B4:B20.

12. Apply Comma Style ⬛ formatting with no decimals ⬛.
Notice that when you format the source data, it will also translate to the chart data.

13. Save and close your workbook.

Skill Builder 6.3   Create a Doughnut Chart

In this exercise, you will create a chart for Holy Doughnuts. The chart will show the contributions of various types of doughnuts to the total sales volume for two different years. What type of chart will you use? Why, a doughnut chart! Like pie charts, doughnut charts are useful for comparing parts of a whole. However, doughnut charts can contain more than one data series. Each ring in a doughnut chart represents a data series.

Set Up the Worksheet

1. Choose Office→New, and then tap ⌐Enter⌐ to start a new worksheet.

2. Create the following worksheet. Format the numbers in columns B and C as Comma Style with no decimals. In A1:C4, change the font to 12 point and bold. Also, merge and center the Units Sold heading over cells B3 and C3, size column A to fit the contents of cell A4, and AutoFit columns B and C.

	A	B	C
1	**Holy Doughnuts Volume Comparison**		
2			
3		**Units Sold**	
4	**Type of Doughnut**	**2007**	**2008**
5	Creme Filled	12,000	14,500
6	Frosted	10,500	9,000
7	Nut Covered	2,300	2,500
8	Glazed	7,000	8,200
9	Old Fashioned	4,500	4,300

Create the Chart

Doughnut charts function much like pie charts because they compare parts of a whole. Therefore, you select the data in a manner similar to the way you select for pie charts.

3. Select A5:C9.

4. Choose Insert→Charts→Other Charts ⬤ →Exploded Doughnut from the Ribbon.

5. Choose Layout→Labels→Chart Title 📊 →Above Chart from the Ribbon.

6. Select the default title and replace it with **Doughnuts Sold: 2007 vs. 2008.**

Add Value Labels

7. Choose Layout→Labels→Data Labels 📊 →Show from the Ribbon.
   The outer exploded ring of the doughnut will display the 2008 values, and the inner ring will display the 2007 values.

8. Save the workbook as **sb-Doughnut Chart** and close it.

Skill Builder 6.4   Create Pie Charts

In this exercise, you will create two pie charts to illustrate employee expenses for Hollywood Productions, a motion picture production company. The pie charts will show how employee costs are divided among departments and how one department's employee costs are allocated. You will create each chart on a separate chart sheet.

Create the Company Chart

1. Open the workbook named sb-Hollywood Productions Expenses from the Lesson 06 folder in your default storage location.

2. Use the ⌨Ctrl key to select B3:D3 and B7:D7.

3. Choose Insert→Charts→Pie ⬤ →Pie in 3-D from the Ribbon, and create the pie chart shown on a separate chart sheet named **Hollywood Payroll Expenses**.
   Make sure the chart title and data labels match the chart shown here. Also, notice that the chart does not include a legend.

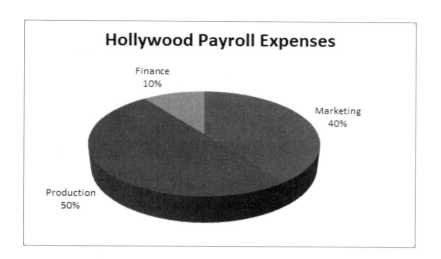

Hollywood Payroll Expenses

Finance 10%

Marketing 40%

Production 50%

Create a Pie Chart for the Marketing Department

4. Ensure that the Payroll Data worksheet tab is displayed.

5. Select A4:B6.

6. Choose Insert→Charts→Pie 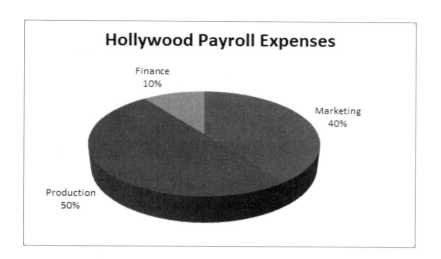→Pie in 3-D from the Ribbon.

7. Title the chart **Marketing Payroll Costs**.

8. Create data labels for the pieces of the pie, showing both the category name and percentage, outside at the end of each slice.

9. Delete the legend.

10. Place the chart on a separate sheet named **Marketing Chart**.

11. Save and close your workbook.

Skill Builder 6.5   Change the Chart Type

In this exercise, you will have the opportunity to convert a column chart to a line chart.

Convert the Chart to a Line Chart

Suppose you are interested in seeing only the trend in enrollments as opposed to the enrollments in individual years. You can easily convert the chart created in Skill Builder 6.2 to a line chart.

1. Open the workbook named sb-Chart Conversion from the Lesson 06 folder in your default storage location.
2. Click to select the chart.
3. Choose Design→Type→Change Chart Type from the Ribbon.
4. Double-click to choose the Line with Markers type from the Change Chart Type dialog box.

Format the Chart Title

5. Click the chart title.
6. Choose Home→Font→Font Color menu ▾ button from the Ribbon.
7. Select a color that will complement the line connecting data points on the chart.
8. Print the chart for your instructor.
9. Save and close your worksheet.

Assessments

Assessment 6.1   Create a Line Chart

In this exercise, you will create a line chart on a separate sheet, rename the sheet tabs, and print a chart.

1. Start a new workbook and create the following worksheet, using AutoFill to expand the date series and resizing the column widths:

	A	B	C	D
1	SysTech Stock Performance			
2	March 2007 through February 2008			
3				
4	Date	Stock Price		
5	3/1/2007	78		
6	4/1/2007	82.6		
7	5/1/2007	83		
8	6/1/2007	78.6		
9	7/1/2007	72		
10	8/1/2007	62		
11	9/1/2007	65.8		
12	10/1/2007	72.6		
13	11/1/2007	85		
14	12/1/2007	86		
15	1/1/2008	90		
16	2/1/2008	92		

2. Format the dates so that they are displayed as *Mar-07*.

3. Use the worksheet data to create the following chart.
   - Make sure you set up the axis labels and title as shown.
   - Do not include a legend.

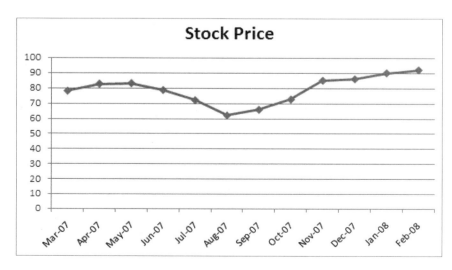

4. Place the chart on a separate sheet, naming it **Stock Performance**.

5. Rename the Sheet1 tab **Supporting Data**.

6. Print the chart.

7. Save the workbook as **as-SysTech Performance**, and then close it. ∎

Assessment 6.2   Create a Worksheet and Pie Chart

In this exercise, you will create a worksheet and a pie chart based on the data in the worksheet. You will also apply a style to the worksheet, insert formulas in the worksheet, and move, resize, and explode a piece of the pie chart.

1. Use the guidelines to create the worksheet and chart shown in the following illustration:

   ■ Type all numbers and text entries as shown, but use formulas to calculate the New Balance in column E and the Totals, Highest, and Lowest values in rows 9–11. The formula for New Balance is New Balance = Beginning Balance + Purchases – Payments. Calculate the Totals in row 9 with AutoSum, and use the MIN and MAX functions for the Highest and Lowest calculations in rows 10 and 11.

   ■ Use the font size of your choice for the title cell A1, merge and center the title across the worksheet, and then format the remainder of the worksheet with the theme of your choice.

   ■ Create the embedded 3-D pie chart shown in the illustration. The pie chart slices represent the new balance percentages of each customer. The pie chart does not represent any of the data in rows 9–11.

   ■ Adjust the position and size of the embedded chart as shown in the illustration.

   ■ Explode the Bishop slice, and adjust the chart rotation and elevation.

   ■ Bold all pie slice labels, and format the chart title with bold and italic by using commands on the Home tab of the Ribbon.

2. Print the worksheet and embedded chart on the same page.

3. Save the workbook as **as-Accounts Receivable Report** in your Lesson 06 folder, and then close it.

	A	B	C	D	E
1	Mary's Imported Rugs: Accounts Receivable Report				
2					
3	Customer	Beginning Balance	Purchases	Payments	New Balance
4	Allison	$ 4,000	$ 2,300	$ 2,000	$ 4,300
5	Washington	3,450	1,000	2,450	2,000
6	Bishop	6,500	2,190	3,000	5,690
7	Worthington	3,400	500	3,400	500
8	Cosby	3,000	3,400	5,000	1,400
9	Totals	$ 20,350	$ 9,390	$ 15,850	$ 13,890
10	Highest	$ 6,500	$ 3,400	$ 5,000	$ 5,690
11	Lowest	$ 3,000	$ 500	$ 2,000	$ 500
12					

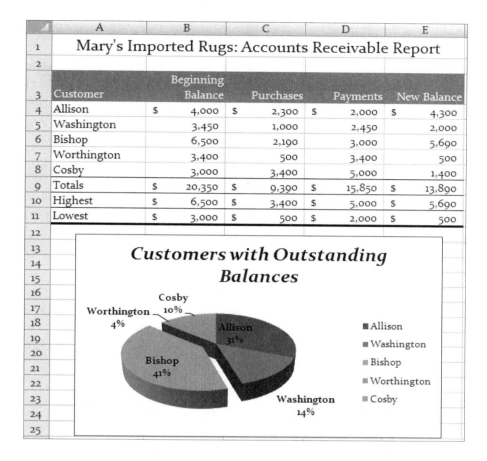

Assessment 6.3   Create a Column Chart and Edit Worksheets

In this exercise, you will create a column chart embedded in the worksheet and then move, resize, and print the chart.

1. Create the worksheet and embedded column chart shown in the following illustration. Use the font size of your choice for the title in cell A1. Notice that the column chart is 2-D. The differences in row 6 are simply the Budget numbers minus the Spent numbers. Notice that the negative numbers dip below the category axis in the chart. Adjust the position and size of the embedded chart as shown.

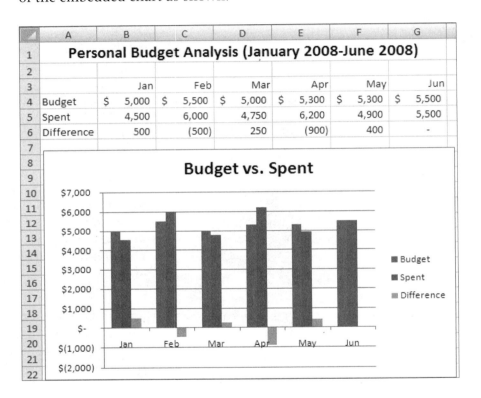

2. Rename the worksheet tab **Budget Analysis**.

3. Delete the unused sheet tabs, Sheet2 and Sheet3.

4. Add the color of your choice to the Budget Analysis sheet tab.

5. Print the worksheet and chart on a single page.

6. Save the workbook as **as-Budget Analysis**, and then close it.

Critical Thinking

Critical Thinking 6.1   Mileage Analysis

Open the workbook named ct-Delivery Expenses. Create an embedded column chart that displays the miles driven by each driver. Title the chart **Miles Driven**. The name of each driver should be displayed at the base of the columns. Use data labels to display the precise number of miles driven at the top of each column.

Create another embedded column chart that displays the total expenses for each driver. Use the chart title **Total Expenses**. The name of each driver should be displayed at the base of the columns. Use data labels to display the total expenses at the top of each column.

Adjust the size and position of the column charts so they are side by side and positioned below the worksheet data. Format the worksheet to print on a single page. Save the changes and close the workbook.

Critical Thinking 6.2   Analyzing Test Results

Open the workbook named ct-Test Results. Create a 3-D pie chart on a separate chart sheet showing the percentage that each unit type contributes to the total units produced. Include data labels that show the percentage and unit type label for each unit type. Do not display a legend. Title the chart **Percent of Unit Types Produced**. Rotate the chart so the largest slice is in the front of the chart. Increase the elevation of the chart, and explode the largest slice. Add the style of your choice to the chart. Change the sheet name to **Pie Chart**.

Insert a new column to the right of the Passed Test column. Use a formula in the new column to calculate the number of units that did not pass the test. Create a column chart on a separate chart sheet that compares the units produced to the units that did not pass the test. Use the Stacked Column chart subtype, which is simply a variation of the regular side-by-side columns. Display a chart legend but no data labels. Use the title **Total Produced vs. Did Not Pass**. Change the sheet name to **Stacked Column Chart**. Reorganize the sheets so that Test Results is first in the sheet order, Pie Chart second, and Stacked Column Chart third. Save the changes and close the workbook.

Critical Thinking 6.3   Billing Chart

Open the workbook named ct-Billings. Create an embedded pie chart that shows the contribution of each company type to the total billings. Include data labels that show only the company types. Do not display a legend. Title the chart **Billing Breakdown**. Position the chart below the data. Save the changes and close the workbook.

Critical Thinking 6.4   Stock Trends Chart

Use Internet Explorer and a search engine of your choice to locate a website that offers free stock quotes and charts. Search for the symbols CSCO, IBM, and ORCL, and display charts for each of the stocks. Set up an Excel workbook that includes a row for each stock and columns for each of the past 12 months. View the chart for one of the stocks, and enter the approximate value of the stock into your worksheet for each of the past 12 months. Create a line chart on a separate chart sheet that includes all three stocks on the same chart. The chart should show the stock trends over the past 12 months. Title the chart **12-Month Stock Trends**. Change the name of the chart sheet to **12-Month Trends Chart**. Save the workbook as **ct-Stock Trends**.

Critical Thinking 6.5   International GDP Chart

Use Internet Explorer and a search engine of your choice to find the gross domestic product of the G7 industrial nations in any given year. The G7 nations include the United States, Germany, Japan, Great Britain, France, Italy, and China. Set up a worksheet that lists the nations in order by largest GDP. The GDP numbers will be measured in trillions of dollars. You can eliminate the 12 zeros from the numbers and just include the multiples. For example, if a nation has a GDP of 1.4 trillion dollars, then use the number **1.4** in the worksheet. Create an embedded column chart to compare the various GDPs. Include data labels in the chart and a descriptive title. Save the workbook as **ct-Comparative GDPs**.

Unit 2

Beyond the Basics

In this unit, you will begin by sorting worksheet rows, freezing headings, and splitting a worksheet window. You will set print options, including margins, scaling, headers and footers, and page breaks. You will locate and insert photos and clip art on worksheets; draw, move, size, rotate, and add styles to images; and use SmartArt to create text charts. You will use Office templates and create custom templates to expedite your work. To protect formulas and other sensitive data, you will lock and unlock cells, apply worksheet protection, set a password, and attach a digital signature. You will copy and move worksheets, copy formatting between worksheets, and use linked formulas. You will create hyperlinks to navigate to areas within the workbook and to other documents. You will create and format tables, add calculation formulas, and sort and filter table data. Finally, you will hide detail data using the outline and grouping commands.

Lesson 7: Working with Large Worksheets

Lesson 8: Adding Graphics to Worksheets

Lesson 9: Using Templates and Protecting Workbooks

Lesson 10: Managing Multiple-Sheet Workbooks

Lesson 11: Creating Tables and Outlines

LESSON 7

Working with Large Worksheets

I n this lesson, you will learn several techniques for working with large worksheets. You will sort the worksheet rows in alphabetic or numeric order. You will freeze headings and split the worksheet window to compare data from separate areas of the worksheet. You will set print options, including margins, scaling, headers, and footers. For worksheets that cannot print on one page, you will set headings to print on each page and adjust page breaks.

LESSON OBJECTIVES

After studying this lesson, you will be able to:

- Sort worksheet rows in alphabetic and numeric order
- View nonadjacent areas of large worksheets
- Set printing options to center and fit the worksheet on one page
- Set options to print a worksheet on multiple pages

Case Study: Managing Large Worksheets

After teaching grades 7–12 for several years and completing business classes, Jesse Figueroa felt ready to start his own small business. He opened the Enrichment Academy three months ago and employs part-time tutors to help students after school. Now he wants to use workbook data to evaluate the attendance rate, fee structure, and potential cost of using a fee-billing service.

You will set worksheet views to help Jesse compare data in his large worksheet more easily. One of these views, a split window, is shown in the illustration below. You will sort the student records alphabetically by name.

To prepare for printing this large worksheet, you will set several options to help Jesse read the data across multiple pages. Your enhancements will enable Jesse to enter and analyze information in large worksheets more efficiently as he expands his Enrichment Academy business.

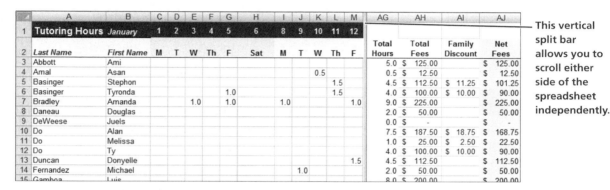

This vertical split bar allows you to scroll either side of the spreadsheet independently.

The worksheet window is split into two sections, which you may scroll in separately to bring totals into view.

Sorting Worksheet Data

When your worksheet must be organized in alphabetic or numeric order, Excel can easily sort the list. Rather than adding new records by inserting blank rows one by one within the list, you may enter the records at the end of the list and then sort the entire list. Excel can order the list based on the data in any single column that you select. For example, you may sort by name, date, item number, or dollar amount. By using the Sort command on the Ribbon, you may sort by multiple columns. In the following example, records with the same last name are then sorted by first name.

An unsorted list

Last Name	First Name
Tejani	Tabriz
Melendez	Eduardo
Do	Melissa
Abbott	Ami
Gavins-Moore	Gabrielle
Solomon	Molly
Do	Alan
Malinski	Ashton

Last Name	First Name
Abbott	Ami
Do	Alan
Do	Melissa
Gavins-Moore	Gabrielle
Malinski	Ashton
Melendez	Eduardo
Solomon	Molly
Tejani	Tabriz

The list after sorting on two columns with names in alphabetic order

A sort is performed on all adjacent rows. If your worksheet contains totals below the data rows, insert a blank row between the two sections to avoid including the total row in the sort. You may, however, select only certain rows to sort when necessary.

 TIP! *If a sorting problem arises and Undo is unavailable, just close the workbook without saving it. Reopen the workbook to restore its original appearance.*

Sorting by a Single Column

The Sort A to Z ![A-Z] and Sort Z to A ![Z-A] buttons let you sort quickly by one column. Sort A to Z will sort records in ascending order from lowest to highest, and Sort Z to A sorts in descending order from highest to lowest. Excel sorts all rows in the contiguous list unless it determines that the list has a header row. A header row is the row at the top of a list that contains column headings.

 TIP! *If you often perform sorts, remember that you may add the Sort A to Z and Sort Z to A buttons to the Quick Access toolbar.*

Sorting Selected Rows

If the list contains rows you do not want included in the sort, you must select the rows you *do* want sorted before selecting one of the sort buttons. Excel will use column A as the sort key by default.

 WARNING! *To keep the data together for each record, always select one cell in a column or entire rows prior to sorting. Do not attempt to sort by highlighting several cells in one column, such as the last names. The names would be in sequence, but the other cells belonging to each record would not move—a data disaster.*

QUICK REFERENCE: SORTING WORKSHEET DATA

Task	Procedure
Sort by a single column	■ Select one cell in the desired column on or under the header row. ■ Choose Data→Sort & Filter and choose one of the following from the Ribbon: ◆ Sort A to Z ◆ Sort Z to A
Sort selected rows by a single column	■ Select a cell in the sort key column. ■ Select the rows to be sorted. ■ Choose Data→Sort & Filter and choose one of the following from the Ribbon: ◆ Sort A to Z ◆ Sort Z to A
Sort by multiple columns	■ Choose Data→Sort & Filter→Sort from the Ribbon. ■ Choose the first column to be sorted from the Sort By list and change the Sort On and Order settings, if necessary. ■ Click the Add Level button to add a second sort category and change its settings, if necessary. ■ If desired, add a third sort category. ■ If the list to be sorted has a header row, place a checkmark next to My Data Has Headers. ■ Click OK.

Hands-On 7.1   Sort by One Column

In this exercise, you will use the sort buttons to sort a list in a workbook.

Sort Entire Lists

1. Open the Enrichment Academy workbook from the Lesson 07 folder in your file storage location.

2. If necessary, maximize ▭ the window.

3. Take a few moments to browse through this worksheet.
   Notice that this worksheet is very large and contains tutoring data for each day in January. You will use this worksheet throughout this lesson.

4. Scroll to the top of the worksheet and select cell A3.
   Notice that the rows are not in alphabetical order. In the next few steps, you will sort rows 3–41. The rows will be sorted by last name in column A because you selected a cell in this column. Keep in mind, however, that all the data in each row will stay together. Before you begin, notice that row 3 (Thomas Lang) has the values 1.0 in cell I3 and 2.0 in cell L3.

5. Choose Data→Sort & Filter→Sort A to Z ⬇ from the Ribbon. (Take care not to confuse this button with the Sort button on the Ribbon. Cancel the Sort dialog box if you opened it by mistake.)
   The Ami Abbott row is now on top because it is the first row in alphabetic order. Also notice that the entire rows have been rearranged. For example, the Thomas Lang row is now in the middle of the list and the values 1.0 and 2.0 are still part of that row. Notice that the header rows 1 and 2 were not included in the sort. Finally, notice that the total rows 43–45 were not included because a blank row separates the totals from the data rows.

6. Choose Data→Sort & Filter→Sort Z to A ⬇ from the Ribbon to reverse the sort order.

7. Scroll to the right until the totals on the right side of the spreadsheet are visible.

8. Select cell AG3.

9. Choose Data→Sort & Filter→Sort A to Z ⬇ from the Ribbon to sort the rows based on the total hours in column AG.
   The Sort A to Z and Sort Z to A buttons always sort rows based on the column that contains the pointer.

10. Choose Data→Sort & Filter→Sort Z to A ⬇ from the Ribbon to sort in descending order based on total hours.

11. Scroll to the left until column A is visible.

12. Select cell A3 and then choose the Sort A to Z ⬇ button.

13. Save 🖫 the changes.

Inadvertently Include Totals in a Sort

A blank line separates the list from the totals rows. Let's see what happens without a blank line.

14. Scroll down, as shown in the following illustration, until the weekly totals are visible.

40	Tejani	Tabriz											2.0			
41	Zorn	Paul													1.0	
42																
43	**Daily Hours**		0.0	0.0	4.0	4.0	2.0	2.0	5.0	5.0	3.5	8.5	3.5	6.0	7.0	14.0 1
44	**Weekly Hours**							12.0						31.5		
45	**Weekly Fees**						$ 300.00							$ 787.50		
46																

January

15. Point to the row selector for row 42, right-click, and choose Delete from the pop-up (or context) menu.

The blank row is deleted, and the rows containing totals now are a part of the list.

16. Select cell A39, and then choose Data→Sort & Filter→Sort A to Z ⬇ from the Ribbon. *Notice that Excel included the totals rows in the sort with one total row now in row 8.*

17. Undo ↩ the sort.
Next you will select rows 3–41 and sort. Because the first and last rows do not display on the same screen, dragging to select rows would be difficult.

Sort Selected Rows

When no blank line separates the list from the totals, select only the rows to be sorted.

18. Select cell A3 to set column A as the sort key.

19. Follow these steps to select rows 3–41:

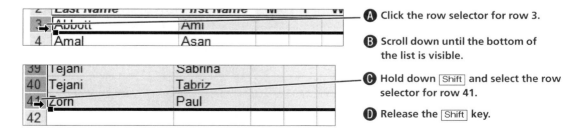

Ⓐ Click the row selector for row 3.

Ⓑ Scroll down until the bottom of the list is visible.

Ⓒ Hold down Shift and select the row selector for row 41.

Ⓓ Release the Shift key.

Rows 3–41 should appear highlighted. Make certain that entire rows are selected. If you select only certain cells in the rows, such as the names in the range A3:A41, Excel will sort only those cells. The data would not match the names and would be useless.

20. Choose Data→Sort & Filter→Sort A to Z $\begin{smallmatrix}A\\Z\end{smallmatrix}↓$ from the Ribbon.
Only the selected student data rows are sorted. You did not include the totals in your selection.

21. Insert a blank row at row 42 to separate the data from the totals rows.
Inserting the blank row will ensure that totals are not included in future sorts. The student data should appear sorted alphabetically by last name. If you had a problem with sorting, close the workbook without saving and reopen it.

Sorting by Multiple Columns

 The Sort dialog box is used to specify multiple sort keys for multiple column sorts. For example, Jesse's worksheet displays last names in column A and first names in column B. Using the Sort dialog box, you may instruct Excel to sort the rows by last name and then by first name. This way, all rows with the same last name, such as Do, will be grouped together. Then those rows would be sorted by first name within each group (Do, Alan, followed by Do, Melissa, and then Do, Ty). You may sort by more than two columns when necessary. You display the Sort dialog box with the Data→Sort & Filter→Sort command.

Hands-On 7.2   Sort by Multiple Columns

In this exercise, you will use the Sort dialog box to perform a two-column sort.

1. Select any cell in the data list.

2. Choose Data→Sort & Filter→Sort $\begin{smallmatrix}A&Z\\Z&A\end{smallmatrix}$ from the Ribbon.
The Sort dialog box appears.

3. Follow these steps to sort the list by last name and then by first name:

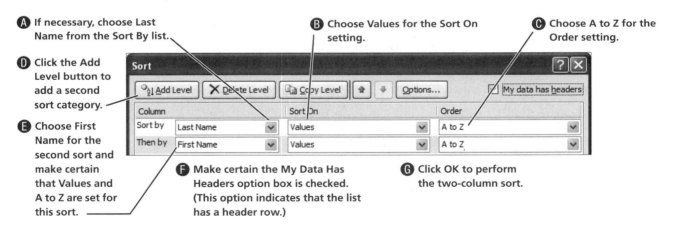

Ⓐ If necessary, choose Last Name from the Sort By list.

Ⓑ Choose Values for the Sort On setting.

Ⓒ Choose A to Z for the Order setting.

Ⓓ Click the Add Level button to add a second sort category.

Ⓔ Choose First Name for the second sort and make certain that Values and A to Z are set for this sort.

Ⓕ Make certain the My Data Has Headers option box is checked. (This option indicates that the list has a header row.)

Ⓖ Click OK to perform the two-column sort.

Notice that the records with last name Do are sorted alphabetically by first name. Check that other records with the same last name are then sorted by first name.

4. Save 🖫 the changes but leave the workbook open.

Using Flexible Worksheet Views

Excel allows you to view two areas of a large worksheet that normally could not display together. When done, you may restore the worksheet to its original view. The Freeze Panes and Split commands affect only how the worksheet displays. The worksheet prints as usual. When a workbook is opened, each worksheet displays the view that was in effect when the workbook was last saved.

Freezing Rows or Columns

 When you scroll to the right on a wide worksheet, the headings in column A are no longer visible as you bring the next columns into view. As you scroll down, the row containing the column headings disappears. Without the headings, you cannot identify the person or category to which the data belong. Freezing the headings helps you keep your place as you scroll to the right or down the worksheet. When you give the Freeze Panes command, Excel freezes all rows above the selected cell and all columns to the left of the selected cell. You may freeze rows, columns, or both. The following illustration shows a cell selected before freezing headings in both rows and columns.

> **!TIP!** *Use the Freeze Panes* ⊞ *command to lock the headings in all worksheets that have more rows or columns than can fit on one screen.*

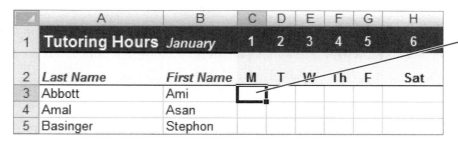

Before freezing

Selecting a cell before giving the Freeze Panes command tells Excel where you want the panes frozen.

After freezing: As you scroll, rows above and columns to the left of the selected cell are frozen.

Hands-On 7.3   Freeze Rows and Columns

In this exercise, you will freeze both rows and columns, rows only, and columns only.

Freeze Rows and Columns

1. Scroll to the right until the totals columns on the right side of the spreadsheet are visible.

AG	AH	AI	AJ
Total Hours	**Total Fees**	**Family Discount**	**Net Fees**
2.0	$ 50.00		$ 50
2.0	$ 50.00	$ 5.00	$ 45
6.0	$ 150.00	$ 15.00	$ 135

Columns A and B, which contain the students' names, dropped off the window. Without those headings, you cannot identify the student belonging to the data.

2. Use Ctrl + Home to move the highlight to cell A1.
   This keystroke combination is quite useful when working with large worksheets.

3. Select cell C3.
   This cell is below the headings in rows 1 and 2 and to the right of the headings in columns A and B.

4. Choose View→Window→Freeze Panes ⊞ menu ▾, and then choose Freeze Panes from the Ribbon.
   The area above and to the left of cell C3 is frozen, indicated by a horizontal and a vertical separation line.

5. Scroll to the right until the totals on the right side of the spreadsheet are in view.
   The frozen columns A and B remain visible to identify the students belonging to the totals.

6. Use Ctrl + Home from the keyboard to jump back to the home cell, and notice that the highlight moves to cell C3 instead of A1.
   Cell C3 is now the home cell because you froze the window panes at that location.

7. Select cell B1.
   Notice that you could edit this cell if desired. Frozen columns and rows still are available for editing.

8. Scroll down until the weekly totals are visible as shown below.

39	Tejani	Sabrina											7.0	
40	Tejani	Tabriz											2.0	
41	Zorn	Paul												1.0
42														
43	**Daily Hours**		0.0	0.0	4.0	4.0	2.0	2.0	5.0	5.0	3.5	8.5	3.5	6.0 7.0 14.0 1
44	**Weekly Hours**							12.0						31.5
45	**Weekly Fees**							$ 300.00						$ 787.50
46														

◄ ◄ ► ►◄   January

The frozen rows 1 and 2 remain visible to identify the dates belonging to the totals.

Let's say Jesse asks, "What is the total income from January tutoring?" The frozen panes will make it easier to locate this information.

9. Scroll to the right until the totals on the right side of the spreadsheet are visible.

	A	B	AE	AF	AG	AH	AI	AJ
1	**Tutoring Hours** *January*							
2	*Last Name*	*First Name*	*F*	*Sat*	**Total Hours**	**Total Fees**	**Family Discount**	**Net Fees**
39	Tejani	Sabrina			2.0	$ 50.00	$ 5.00	$ 45.00
40	Tejani	Tabriz			6.0	$ 150.00	$ 15.00	$ 135.00
41	Zorn	Paul			2.0	$ 50.00		$ 50.00
42								
43	**Daily Hours**		0.0	0.0	189.0	**$4,725.00**	**$ 115.00**	**$4,610.00**
44	**Weekly Hours**			27.0	⇑			
45	**Weekly Fees**			$ 675.00		**$4,725.00**		

The Net Fees total is $4,610.00, computed as Total Fees minus the Family Discount.

10. Choose Office [icon] →Print ▸ menu→Print Preview [icon].
The frozen panes do not affect printing. The entire worksheet would print. You will learn to repeat row and column headings on each printed page of large worksheets later in this lesson.

11. Choose Close Print Preview [icon] to exit the view without printing.

12. Choose View→Window→Freeze Panes [icon] menu ▾, and then choose Unfreeze Panes from the Ribbon.
Excel unfreezes the heading rows and columns and restores the worksheet to its original view.

Freeze Rows Only

Now you will select a cell that has no columns to the left of it. This tells Excel to freeze only rows.

13. Select cell A3, and then choose View→Window→Freeze Panes [icon] menu ▾→Freeze Panes from the Ribbon.
Rows 1 and 2 are frozen, but no columns are frozen.

14. Scroll down and right to verify that only rows are frozen.
When all columns of a worksheet fit in the window, you may freeze rows only.

15. Unfreeze the panes.

Freeze Columns Only

16. Select cell C1, and then choose View→Window→Freeze Panes [icon] menu ▾→Freeze Panes from the Ribbon.
Columns A and B are frozen, but no rows are frozen.

17. Scroll down and right to verify that only columns are frozen.
When all rows of a worksheet fit in the window, you may freeze columns only.

18. Unfreeze the panes.

19. Choose Office [icon] →Close to close the Enrichment Academy workbook. Choose No if Excel asks if you wish to save the workbook.

Using Flexible Worksheet Views   **223**

Splitting the Worksheet Window

At times, you will want to split the window to scroll within two areas of a worksheet. For example, a manager may want to compare data in rows 3–15 with rows 203–215. Use the Split command for this purpose. As with the Freeze Panes command, you should select the appropriate cell before choosing Split. To divide the window into two panes, select the first cell in a row or column. You may display four panes by selecting any other cell, but displaying two panes usually is sufficient. Using the same Split command, which now displays a highlight, removes the split. This type of command is called a *toggle*. Click it once to switch the command on and again to switch it off.

Splitting Compared to Freezing

Freezing is useful to keep headings always visible. However, you may not easily view two nonadjacent groups of data. Splitting the window allows you to view two or four nonadjacent groups. Each pane has its own set of scroll bars. You may drag the split bar to adjust the number of rows or columns displayed in each pane. The following illustrations contrast a split window with a frozen window.

A split window

Split bar

9	DeWeese	Juels
10	Do	Alan
37	Solomon	Molly
38	Sufi	Seri

The panes may be scrolled to view nonadjacent areas of the worksheet.

A frozen window

1	**Tutoring Hours** *January*		1
2	*Last Name*	*First Name*	M
9	DeWeese	Juels	
10	Do	Alan	

Headings remain visible, but the ability to view nonadjacent areas is limited.

!TIP! *Use only Split or Freeze, not both together. One does not operate correctly when the other is in effect.*

QUICK REFERENCE: CONTROLLING WORKSHEET VIEWS

Task	Procedure
Freeze columns and rows	■ Select the cell below and to the right of the area to be frozen.
	■ Choose View→Window→Freeze Panes menu ▼→Freeze Panes from the Ribbon.
Freeze columns	■ Select the first cell in the column to the right of the column(s) to be frozen.
	■ Choose View→Window→Freeze Panes menu ▼→Freeze Panes from the Ribbon.
Freeze rows	■ Select the first cell in the row below the row(s) to be frozen.
	■ Choose View→Window→Freeze Panes menu ▼→Freeze Panes from the Ribbon.
Unfreeze all	■ Choose View→Window→Freeze Panes menu ▼→Unfreeze Panes from the Ribbon.

Task	Procedure
Split window between columns or rows	■ Select the first cell in the column or row in which the split is to occur. ■ Choose View→Window→Split ⬚ from the Ribbon.
Adjust split	■ Drag the split bar that divides the window panes.
Remove split	■ Choose View→Window→Split ⬚ from the Ribbon.
Enlarge or shrink worksheet view	■ Drag the Zoom slider at the bottom right of the worksheet window.

 Hands-On 7.4   Split the Worksheet Window

In this exercise, you will split a worksheet window into two panes to scroll and compare data in two areas.

Split between Columns

1. Open the workbook named Enrichment Academy that you saved in Hands-On 7.2. (You did not save any changes in Hands-On 7.3.)
   The list should appear sorted by last name, and records with the same last name are then sorted by first name.

2. Follow these steps to split the window between columns:

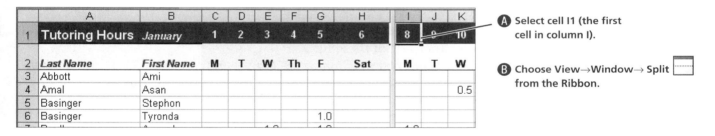

A Select cell I1 (the first cell in column I).

B Choose View→Window→ Split ⬚ from the Ribbon.

The window displays two panes with a gray split bar between them.

3. In the pane on the right, drag the scroll box in the horizontal scroll bar to the right until the columns for January 15–20 are in view, as shown in the following illustration.

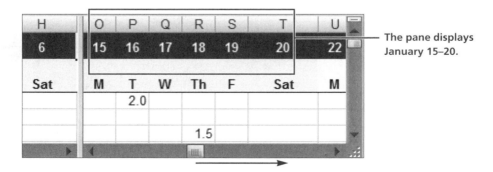

The pane displays January 15–20.

Compare the tutoring attendance pattern for the first week, January 1–6, with that of January 15–20. Fewer students attended during the first week.

4. In the left pane, scroll right until column I is the first column visible.

	I	J	K
1	8	9	10
2	M	T	W
3			
4			0.5

Notice that the headings in columns A and B are no longer visible. They cannot be frozen while the window is split. You are comparing attendance patterns for the entire group, so viewing the student names is not necessary.

5. In the right pane, scroll right until January 22–31 is visible.

6. Follow these steps to move the split bar:

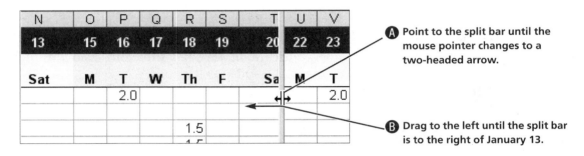

Ⓐ Point to the split bar until the mouse pointer changes to a two-headed arrow.

Ⓑ Drag to the left until the split bar is to the right of January 13.

7. If necessary, scroll the two panes to the left or right until January 8–13 and January 22–31 are close together on either side of the split.
Compare the tutoring attendance pattern of January 8–13 with that of January 22–31. The totals in columns AG–AJ also are visible because you moved the split bar to display fewer columns in the left pane and more columns in the right pane.

8. Choose View→Window→Split ⊞ from the Ribbon to remove the split and restore the worksheet to its original view.
Unlike Freeze Panes, the Split command toggles on and off when you click the same button.

Split between Rows

9. Experiment further by splitting the window to compare various *rows* of the worksheet.

10. Remove the split.

Printing Multipage Worksheets

Excel provides a number of options for improving the format of large printed worksheets. For example, you may adjust settings such as:

- Decreasing the page margins to include more rows and columns
- Centering the worksheet on the page
- Printing pages horizontally (landscape) or vertically (portrait)
- Printing only a selected range of worksheet cells

Setting Print Format in Page Layout View

Previously, you edited a worksheet in Normal view and used Print Preview to see how the worksheet would look as printed. Print Preview allows you to view one page at a time. As an alternative, display Page Layout view, which previews all printed pages and was introduced in Lesson 2, Editing, Viewing, and Printing Worksheets. As you choose a printing option from the Ribbon, you can view the result immediately. You also may edit the worksheet in Page Layout view. You may change the view by using the View Ribbon or the view buttons in the status bar at the lower-right corner of the window.

The view buttons displayed in the lower-right corner of the worksheet window

Hands-On 7.5   Display Page Layout View

In this exercise, you will preview the worksheet in Page Layout view.

1. Use Ctrl + Home to move the pointer to cell A1.

2. Choose View→Workbook Views→Page Layout [ ] from the Ribbon.
   The worksheet displays as it would print on paper. The status bar at the lower left of the window displays Pages: 1 of 3 to show that the cell pointer is in page 1 of three pages total.

3. Drag the scroll box in the horizontal scroll bar to the right to view pages 2 and 3.

4. Drag the scroll box in the vertical scroll bar down to view the bottom of the pages.

5. Drag the slider in the Zoom control in the lower-right corner of the window to about 25%.

The worksheet shrinks dramatically. Dimmed pages will not print, as those columns and rows are empty in the worksheet. The zoom level affects only how you are viewing the worksheet, not its printed appearance.

6. Drag the Zoom slider to about 40%.

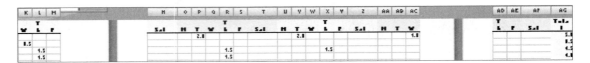

The three pages should almost fill the view. If necessary, use a different zoom percentage to adjust for your computer monitor.

7. Choose View→Worksheet Views→Normal ▦ from the Ribbon to return to Normal view.

8. Click the Page Layout view button in the status bar at the lower-right corner of the window.

The view returns to the zoom percentage that you set previously. Notice how the columns fall on the pages. Page breaks split up the weekly data, and pages 2 and 3 are without headings to identify the student belonging to each row. You will resolve these problems in the next exercises.

9. Save 💾 the changes to your workbook.

Page Layout Ribbon

The print options are accessed on the Page Layout Ribbon in the Page Setup, Scale to Fit, and Sheet Options command groups. You may change the page orientation, adjust margins, and scale the worksheet size. As an alternative, the Page Setup dialog box available in prior Excel versions is launched by clicking the button in the lower-right corner of the command group. You will use the Page Setup dialog box occasionally for commands not located on the Ribbon.

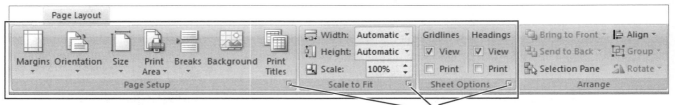

The Page Layout Ribbon with printing options in the Page Setup, Scale to Fit, and Sheet Options command groups.

Excel users who prefer changing settings in the Page Setup dialog box may click here.

Sizing Options

The Page Setup and Scale to Fit command groups on the Page Layout Ribbon contain several options to help fit large worksheets on printed pages. Four useful sizing options are shown in the following illustration.

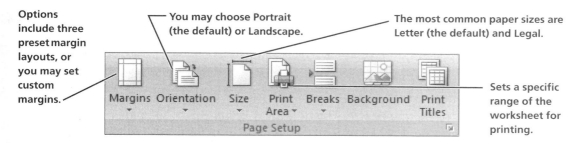

Options include three preset margin layouts, or you may set custom margins.

You may choose Portrait (the default) or Landscape.

The most common paper sizes are Letter (the default) and Legal.

Sets a specific range of the worksheet for printing.

Margins

The margins determine the space between the edge of the paper and the worksheet. You may choose from three preset margin layouts—Normal, Wide, and Narrow—as well as a Custom Margins option. Choose Narrow to fit more columns and rows on the printed page. Choose Custom Margins to launch the Page Setup dialog box with the Margins tab displayed. On this tab you may set specific worksheet margins and center the worksheet horizontally and vertically on the paper. Header and footer margins are covered later in this lesson. The illustration below describes the dialog box options.

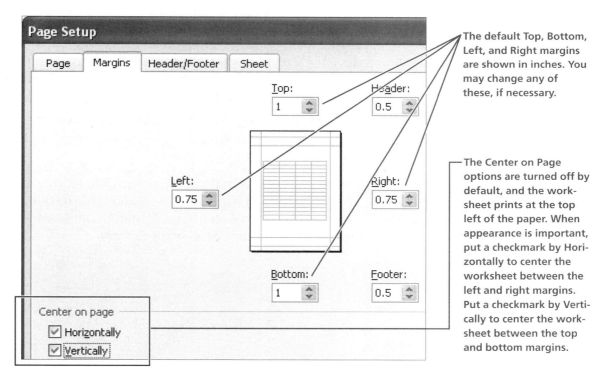

The default Top, Bottom, Left, and Right margins are shown in inches. You may change any of these, if necessary.

The Center on Page options are turned off by default, and the worksheet prints at the top left of the paper. When appearance is important, put a checkmark by Horizontally to center the worksheet between the left and right margins. Put a checkmark by Vertically to center the worksheet between the top and bottom margins.

Orientation

 The orientation indicates the direction of printing. Portrait is the default and prints across the narrow edge of the paper. Landscape orientation prints across the wide edge of the paper and is useful with wide worksheets like January in the Enrichment Academy workbook.

Portrait orientation   **Landscape orientation**

Size

The Size option refers to the paper size. The default is Letter 8.5" × 11" paper. You can fit more columns on the page using Legal 8.5" × 14" paper, but keep in mind that the larger size paper may be more difficult to store.

Print Area

You may set any range of cells in the worksheet as the print area to reduce the number of printed pages or leave out nonessential cells containing comments. The Set Print Area command makes the range permanent until you set a different range or choose Clear Print Area to restore the entire worksheet for printing. Use Set Print Area if you plan to print a specific range most of the time.

Scale to Fit

The Scale to Fit command group on the Page Layout Ribbon provides automated scaling options to shrink the worksheet for printing.

- **Width**—You may reduce the size of a worksheet containing many columns to fit its width on one, two, or more pages as appropriate. When a few worksheet columns spill onto the next printed page, set the Width to one page less.

- **Height**—You may set the Height for one page less when a few rows spill onto another page. Reduce the size of a worksheet containing many rows to fit its height on one, two, or more pages as appropriate.

- **Scale**—To shrink the width and height in the same proportion, set the Scale to less than 100%. Note that you may scale a small worksheet to greater than 100% for legibility. To use Scale, Width and Height must be set to Automatic. Keep in mind that a scaled worksheet may fit on fewer pages, but the text may be too small to read.

!**TIP!** *To reset the Height and Width to normal size, choose Automatic from each drop-down list. Make certain to change Scale to 100%, as the percentage does not reset automatically.*

QUICK REFERENCE: SETTING PRINT OPTIONS

Task	Procedure
Display Page Layout view	■ Choose View→Workbook Views→Page Layout ⬚ from the Ribbon or click the Page Layout view button in the lower-right corner of the window.
Change to preset margins	■ Choose Page Layout→Page Setup→Margins ⬚ menu ▼ and choose Normal, Narrow, or Wide from the Ribbon.
Change specific margins	■ Choose Page Layout→Page Setup→Margins ⬚ menu ▼ and choose Custom Margins from the Ribbon. ■ Change the Top, Bottom, Left, or Right margin in the Page Setup dialog box.
Center the worksheet on printed page(s)	■ Click the dialog box launcher ⬚ button in the bottom-right corner of the Page Setup command group of the Page Layout Ribbon. ■ Choose the Margins tab in the Page Layout dialog box. ■ Under Center on Page, place a checkmark next to Horizontally to center between the left and right margins. ■ Under Center on Page, place a checkmark next to Vertically to center between the top and bottom margins.
Change the orientation	■ Choose Page Layout→Page Setup→Orientation ⬚ menu ▼ and choose Portrait or Landscape from the Ribbon.
Change paper size	■ Choose Page Layout→Page Setup→Size ⬚ menu ▼ and choose a paper size from the Ribbon.
Scale the worksheet to fit on fewer pages	■ Choose Page Layout→Scale to Fit, select 100% in the Scale box, type the desired percentage, and tap ⌷Enter⌷.
Scale the worksheet width or height	■ Choose Page Layout→Scale to Fit→Width menu ▼ or Height menu ▼ and set the desired number of pages.
Set a print range	■ Select the desired cells. ■ Choose Page Layout→Page Setup→Print Area ⬚ menu ▼→Set Print Area from the Ribbon.
Remove the print range	■ Choose Page Layout→Page Setup→Print Area ⬚ menu ▼→Clear Print Area from the Ribbon. The entire worksheet area containing data is restored as the print area.

Hands-On 7.6   Use Sizing Options

In this exercise, you will change the orientation and margins. You also will scale the worksheet to print on fewer pages. You will use commands on the Ribbon as well as in the Page Setup dialog box.

Switch to Landscape Orientation

1. Verify that the Enrichment Academy workbook is open from the previous exercise. The January worksheet should be displayed in Page Layout view at about 40% zoom.

Notice that the pages appear in portrait orientation with the narrow edge of the paper on top.

 NOTE! *If the worksheet does not display the page edges, the current view might be set to Normal. Switch to Page Layout view. You may choose printing options in Normal view, but you cannot see the results.*

2. Choose Page Layout→Page Setup→Orientation 🔲 menu ▾→Landscape from the Ribbon. *By printing along the wide edge of the page, you have reduced the worksheet width to two pages. A few rows, however, still spill down onto additional pages.*

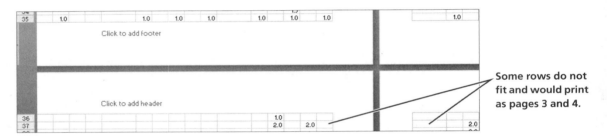

Some rows do not fit and would print as pages 3 and 4.

3. Save 🔲 the change to your workbook.

Change Margins and Center the Worksheet

4. Choose Page Layout→Page Setup→Margins 🔲 menu ▾→Narrow from the Ribbon.

5. Experiment with the choices in the Margins 🔲 menu ▾ by choosing Wide, then Normal, and then returning to Narrow.
Decreasing the margins allows more columns and rows to fit on a page, but the rows still do not fit onto one page in height. You will fix this in a moment, but let's look at one more option grouped with the margin commands.

6. Choose Page Layout→Page Setup→Margins ⬜ menu ▼, and choose Custom Margins from the Ribbon.

The Page Setup dialog box opens with the Margins tab displayed. The narrow margin settings in inches for Top, Bottom, Left, and Right may be different in your dialog box depending on the printer that you use.

Because you opened the dialog box from the Margins menu of the Page Setup command group, the Margins tab is displayed.

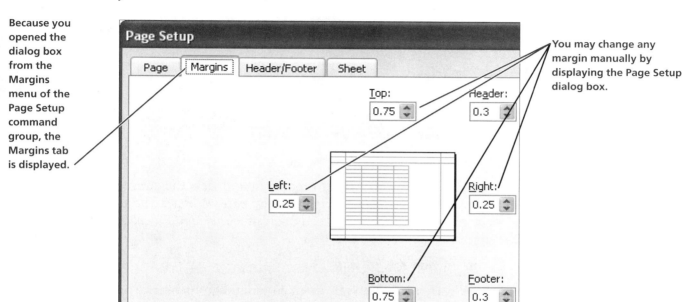

You may change any margin manually by displaying the Page Setup dialog box.

If you needed to fit one or two more rows onto one page, you could reduce the Top and Bottom margins a bit more, such as to 0.5. You will not adjust these margins.

Notice the options under Center on Page in the dialog box.

7. To center the printed worksheet on the paper, place a checkmark by Vertically and then click OK.

You will not see the effect in Page Layout view but would see the worksheet centered between the top and bottom margins in Print Preview. You did not center horizontally because the worksheet is wider than one page. The first column on page 2 should align with the left margin.

8. Save 💾 the changes to your workbook.

Use the Scale to Fit Options

Recall that your worksheet still does not fit on one page in height. Notice that the worksheet is significantly wider than it is tall.

9. Choose 100% in the Scale box in the Scale to Fit command group of the Page Layout Ribbon, type **54**, and tap [Enter].

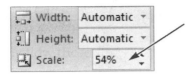

Both the width and height were scaled to almost half size to fit on one page.

10. Choose Office [🏢]→Print ▶→Print Preview [🔍].

11. If necessary, click anywhere on the page to zoom out and view the entire page.
As you can see, it wasn't such a good idea to compress a two-page worksheet onto one page. The printed worksheet would be unreadable. The Scale option works best when only a few columns and rows spill over to an extra page.

12. Choose Close Print Preview [✖].

13. Choose 54% in the Scale box in the Scale to Fit command group of the Page Layout Ribbon, type **100**, and tap [Enter].
Next, you will instruct Excel to shrink the rows to fit on one page in height without affecting the width.

14. Choose Page Layout→Scale to Fit→Height menu ▼→1 page from the Ribbon.

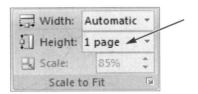

Your worksheet now fits on two pages. The status bar should display Pages: 1 of 2. If you change the Width or Height, the Scale option becomes unavailable, and the opposite also is true.

Set the Print Area

Assume that you want to print only part of the worksheet.

15. Click the Normal view button in the lower-right corner of the window.

16. Select cells A1:H13.

17. Choose Page Layout→Page Setup→Print Area [📄] menu ▼→Set Print Area from the Ribbon.
The print area appears surrounded by a fence border.

Preview the Printout

18. Choose Office 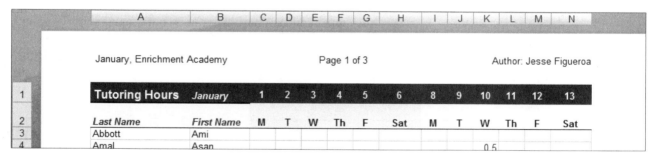→Print ▸→Print Preview 🔍.
Excel would print only the cells that you set as the print area.

19. Choose Close Print Preview ⊠.

20. Choose Page Layout→Page Setup→Print Area 🖨 menu ▾→Clear Print Area from the Ribbon.
The fence border disappears because the print area is reset to include all cells containing data in the entire worksheet.

21. Select any cell to deselect the highlighted cells.

22. Save 💾 the changes to your workbook.

23. Print the worksheet.
Examine your printed worksheet for the settings you performed. Now you have learned a sequence of techniques you may use to size a large worksheet for printing.

Headers and Footers

Headers print at the top of every page, and footers print at the bottom of every page. They identify the worksheet name, page number, and so on. Excel provides a variety of predesigned headers and footers from which you may choose. You may even create customized headers and footers to suit your particular needs. The following illustration contains a header.

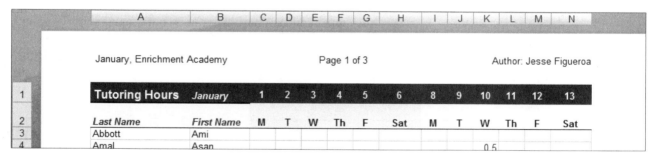

The three sections of this header print on every page and include the worksheet tab name, workbook name, page number, and text.

⚠**NOTE!** *Use Page Layout view or Print Preview to see headers and footers. They do not display in Normal view.*

Creating and Formatting Headers and Footers

Headers and footers are created most conveniently in Page Layout view. Excel divides headers and footers into left, center, and right sections of the page. You need not fill in all three sections. To activate a section, just click in it to display the Design Ribbon filled with header and footer options. Once you activate a section, there are three ways to add content to it:

- Choose a predesigned item from the Header or Footer drop-down lists in the Header & Footer command group.

- Insert an element from the Ribbon.

The Header & Footer Elements command group in the Header & Footer Tools Design tab on the Ribbon

Options include the workbook filename, worksheet tab name, current date, time, and page number. When you choose an option from the Header & Footer Elements command group, Excel displays a code to represent the item. For example, the code *&[Date]* rather than the actual date displays because the current date will change. When you click outside the header section, Excel converts *&[Date]* to the actual date.

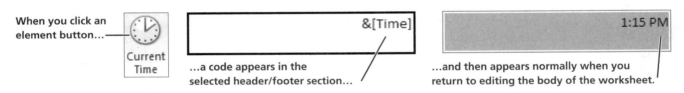

When you click an element button... ...a code appears in the selected header/footer section... ...and then appears normally when you return to editing the body of the worksheet.

- Type your own custom text.

Excel allows you to use a combination of these methods to create header/footer content. You may also format headers and footers. For example, you may change the font, size, and color.

QUICK REFERENCE: CREATING HEADERS AND FOOTERS

Task	Procedure
Display Page Layout view	■ Choose View→Workbook Views→Page Layout ▯ from the Ribbon or click the Page Layout view button from the status bar at the lower-right corner of the window.
Select a predesigned page header or footer	■ Display Page Layout view ▯ from the status bar. ■ Select Click to Add Header above the worksheet or Click to Add Footer below the worksheet. ■ Choose Design→Header & Footer→Header menu ▼ or Footer menu ▼, and then choose a predesigned item in the Ribbon.
Create a custom page header or footer	■ Display Page Layout view ▯ from the status bar. ■ Select the left, center, or right header section above the worksheet or footer section below the worksheet. ■ Type text and set options from the Header & Footer Elements command group on the Ribbon.
Set header and footer margins	■ Click the dialog box launcher ▣ button in the bottom-right corner of the Page Setup command group of the Page Layout Ribbon. ■ Choose the Margins tab in the Page Setup dialog box. ■ Change the Header or Footer margin.
Remove a header or footer	■ Select any section of the header or footer, choose Design→Header & Footer→Header menu ▼ or Footer menu ▼, and choose (None) from the Ribbon.

Hands-On 7.7   Set the Headers and Footers

In this exercise, you will select predefined headers and footers, remove a footer, create custom headers and footers, and change the margins for these items.

Use Predefined Headers and Footers

1. Verify that the Enrichment Academy workbook is open from the previous exercise.

2. Choose Page Layout view from the status bar at the lower-right corner of the window.

3. Change the zoom level to about 75%.

4. Scroll up to view the top of the page, if necessary, and choose Click to Add Header.

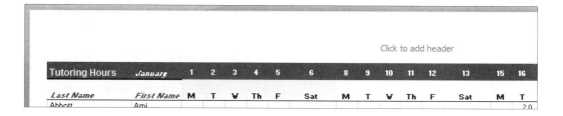

The center header section is activated, and the Design Ribbon displays.

5. Choose Design→Header & Footer→Header menu ▼, browse the available predefined header choices, and then choose Page 1 of ? in the Ribbon.

The predefined header consists of one center section and displays as Page 1 of 2. *The page number is updated on every page. For example, the header displays* Page 2 of 2 *on the second page.*

6. Follow these steps to select a predefined footer:

Ⓐ Scroll to the bottom of the page.

Ⓑ Select any footer section (left, center, or right).

Ⓒ Choose Design→Header & Footer→Footer menu ▼ and choose any predefined footer from the Ribbon.

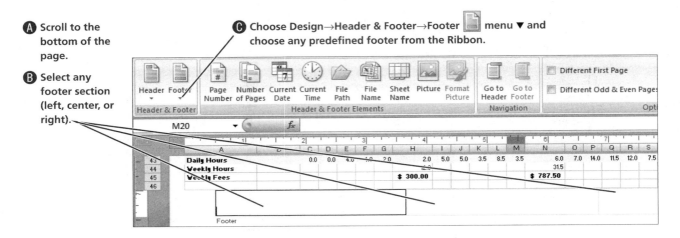

You may select any of the three sections before choosing a predefined header or footer.

7. Display the worksheet in Print Preview, check the header and footer, and then choose Close Print Preview.

Remove a Footer

8. Select any section of the footer.

9. Choose Design→Header & Footer→Footer menu ▼, and select (None) at the beginning of the menu in the Ribbon.

The previous footer was removed because you chose (None). The footer area displays Click to Add Footer.

Create a Custom Header and Footer

10. Scroll up in the worksheet to display the header.

Next, you will insert items in the header by clicking buttons on the Header & Footer Elements command group.

11. Select the left header section, click the Sheet Name button, type a comma, tap ⌨Spacebar, and then click the File Name button.

The footer section displays &[Tab], &[File]. *When you click outside the section, the display changes to* January, Enrichment Academy. *You may add text, punctuation, and spaces between elements. You may tap* ⌨Enter *and add to the header section, but unexpected results may occur. Always check the header and footer in Print Preview before printing.*

12. Select the right header section, type your name, and click outside the header.

13. Add the current time and current date to any section of the footer. Separate the two elements with punctuation or spaces so that you can read each element easily.
You may have noticed that some total cells display #### because the current zoom level is less than 100%. Be assured that the totals will print correctly.

Change the Header and Footer Margins

14. Click the dialog box launcher ⊡ button in the bottom-right corner of the Page Setup command group of the Page Layout Ribbon.
If the commands on the Ribbon appear dimmed, make certain that the pointer is in a cell outside the header and footer.

15. Follow these steps to change the header and footer margins:

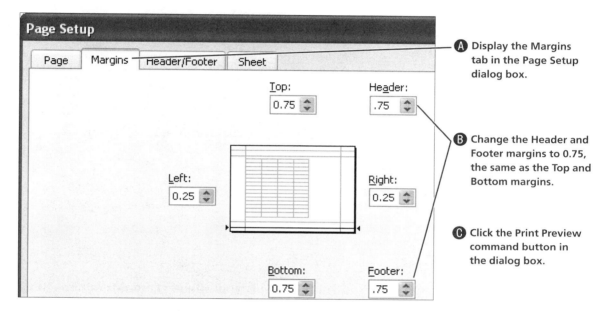

Ⓐ Display the Margins tab in the Page Setup dialog box.

Ⓑ Change the Header and Footer margins to 0.75, the same as the Top and Bottom margins.

Ⓒ Click the Print Preview command button in the dialog box.

16. Examine the header and footer positions.
Your header should look like the following illustration.

Now the header and footer are positioned farther from the top of the page but overlap the worksheet. You should always make the header and footer margins smaller than the top and bottom margins so that the header and footer print in the margin area.

17. Click the Page Setup ⊞ button in Print Preview.
This is another way to display the Page Setup dialog box.

18. Change the Header and Footer margins to an appropriate position of your choice and check the position in Print Preview.
While typing the position, such as .3, in a text box, make certain to include the decimal point.

19. Choose Close Print Preview ⊠.

20. Save ⊟ the changes to your workbook.

Setting Title Rows and Columns

 You may specify one or more rows as title rows and one or more columns as title columns. Title rows and columns are printed on every page of a worksheet. For example, recall that the Enrichment Academy worksheet prints on multiple pages. Rows 1 and 2 contain the dates, and columns A and B contain the student names that describe the content of the various rows. Without that information, the data on the second page may be difficult to understand. This can be resolved by specifying rows 1 and 2 as title rows and columns A and B as title columns so that they appear on all pages. You will set title rows or columns in the Page Setup dialog box.

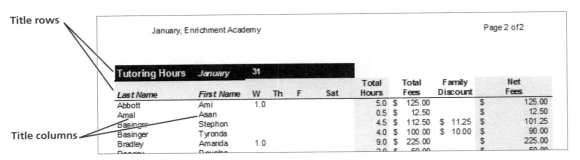

Page 2 of the printed worksheet with title rows and title columns repeating on every page

> **!TIP!** *The Title Rows and Title Columns options are not available if you display the Page Setup dialog box from within Print Preview. To use these options, you must launch the Page Setup dialog box from the Page Layout Ribbon.*

Sheet Options

The Sheet command group of the Page Layout Ribbon contains options that affect the worksheet view and all printed pages of the worksheet. You may choose some options separately for viewing the worksheet and for printing.

Gridlines

By default, light gray gridlines surround every cell in the worksheet view. Normally you should leave that option on, but you may view the worksheet without gridlines. By default, gridlines do not print. You may find it useful to print with gridlines to help the eyes track data across rows and down columns in large worksheets.

Gavins-Moore	Gabrielle		
Grisson	Madison		1.0
Harris	Patti		2.0

The printed worksheet without gridlines (the default setting)

Gavins-Moore	Gabrielle		
Grisson	Madison		1.0
Harris	Patti	2.0	

The printed worksheet with gridlines that appear as dotted lines in Print Preview but actually print as solid lines

Headings

By default, column headings (letters A, B, and so on) and row headings (numbers 1, 2, and so on) display in the worksheet view. You rarely would need to turn the display off. By default, these headings do not print. Including the headings may be useful for worksheet design, training, and group discussions.

Column headings ————

Row headings ————

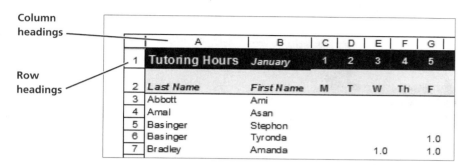

The printed worksheet with column and row headings

QUICK REFERENCE: SETTING TITLES, GRIDLINES, AND HEADINGS

Task	Procedure
Print title rows on every page	■ Choose Page Layout→Page Setup→Print Titles from the Ribbon. ■ Click in the Rows to Repeat at Top box. ■ Drag to select the desired rows in the worksheet. ■ Click Print Preview or OK.
Print title columns on every page	■ Choose Page Layout→Page Setup→Print Titles from the Ribbon. ■ Click in the Columns to Repeat at Left box. ■ Drag to select the desired columns in the worksheet. ■ Click Print Preview or OK.
Print gridlines	■ Choose Page Layout→Sheet Options→Gridlines→Print from the Ribbon.
Print Excel column and row headings	■ Choose Page Layout→Sheet Options→Headings→Print from the Ribbon.

Hands-On 7.8   Set Sheet Options

In this exercise, you will set options to print repeating title rows and title columns, gridlines, and row and column headings on a multipage worksheet.

Set Title Rows and Columns

1. Display the January worksheet in Page Layout view at a zoom percentage that is comfortable for you.

2. Use Ctrl + Home to jump to cell A1.

3. Choose Page Layout→Page Setup→Print Titles from the Ribbon.
The Page Setup dialog box displays with the Sheet tab active.

4. Follow these steps to set title rows and title columns:

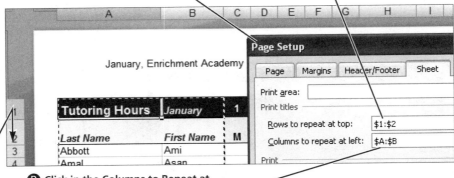

Ⓐ If necessary, drag the Page Setup dialog box by its title bar to make columns A and B and rows 1 and 2 visible.

Ⓑ Click in the Rows to Repeat at Top box, which is currently empty.

Ⓒ Drag to select rows 1 and 2. A flashing marquee appears around the rows. The Rows to Repeat at Top box should display $1:$2.

Ⓓ Click in the Columns to Repeat at Left box, which is currently empty.

Ⓔ Point to the column selector for column A and drag right to include column B. A flashing marquee appears around the columns. The Columns to Repeat at Left box should display $A:$B.

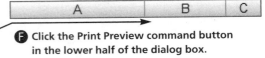

Ⓕ Click the Print Preview command button in the lower half of the dialog box.

5. Click the Next Page 🔽 button in Print Preview.
Examine the results for page 2 in the Print Preview window. The title rows and columns repeat on every page of the printed worksheet. Now it is easier to identify the student and dates that belong to each row of data on page 2.

6. Click the Page Setup 🔲 button in Print Preview; notice that the Print Titles section is unavailable.
The Page Setup dialog box must be displayed through the Page Layout Ribbon if you want to set print titles.

7. Click Cancel to exit the Page Setup dialog box.

8. Choose Close Print Preview ⊠.

Turn Gridlines and Headings On and Off

9. Click the Normal view button in the lower-right corner of the window.

10. Choose Page Layout→Sheet Options→Gridlines→View from the Ribbon to turn off the option.
The lines around the cells disappear. Occasionally you might want to turn off gridlines to help proofread or identify borders you applied manually around cells.

Gridlines
☐ View

11. Follow these steps to turn gridlines back on and to display gridlines and headings when you print:

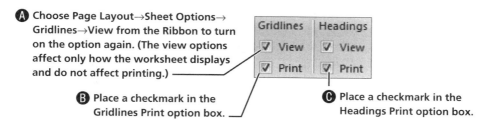

A Choose Page Layout→Sheet Options→ Gridlines→View from the Ribbon to turn on the option again. (The view options affect only how the worksheet displays and do not affect printing.)

B Place a checkmark in the Gridlines Print option box.

C Place a checkmark in the Headings Print option box.

You do not see the effect of these last two settings in either Normal or Page Layout views.

12. Choose Office 🗃→Print ▶ menu→Print Preview 🔍 and click the upper-left area of the worksheet to zoom in.
   Gridlines appear as dotted lines but will print as solid lines. The column headings (A, B, and so on) and row headings (1, 2, and so on) also display above and to the left of the worksheet. You must use Print Preview to see these effects.

13. Choose Close Print Preview ⊠.

14. Save 💾 the changes to your workbook.

Working with Page Breaks

You may use Page Break Preview to see where Excel's automatic page breaks occur in a worksheet and which part of the worksheet will be printed. This view also allows you to insert additional page breaks manually when they are needed. In Page Break Preview, the print area of the worksheet appears in white and nonprinting areas appear in gray.

The Page Break Preview button

Adjusting Automatic Page Breaks

Excel formats most printed worksheets by inserting automatic page breaks when pages are full. An automatic page break appears as a dashed line.

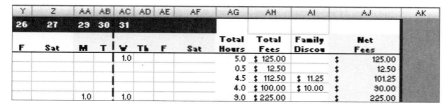

Excel inserts an automatic page break, which appears as a dashed line.

You may want to force a page break in a different place at times. For example, in the tutoring hours worksheet, Excel splits a week by printing the Tuesday column on the first page and the

Wednesday column on the second page. All columns for a given week should be printed on the same page. You may adjust the location of a page break by clicking and dragging it in Page Break Preview. The page break then displays as a solid line, indicating that it is a manual page break.

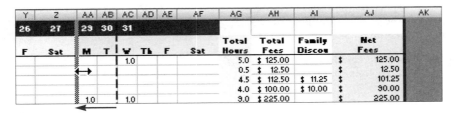

The two-headed arrow indicates that the page break is being dragged to the left.
A page break that you move or add appears as a solid line.

 NOTE! *An automatic page break indicates that the page is filled, so you must move a vertical page break to the left to shift columns to the next page. Move a horizontal page break up to shift rows to the next page. You cannot increase columns or rows on a full page without adjusting other print options.*

Inserting and Removing Page Breaks

Even if the worksheet fits on one page, you may need to add a page break at times. For example, you might want the data for each week to print on separate pages. You must select a cell in an appropriate column or row before issuing the Insert Page Break command. The page break appears as a solid line in the column to the left of the selected cell or the row above the selected cell. You may remove any page break that you set manually. If necessary, Excel will insert automatic page breaks after you remove manual page breaks.

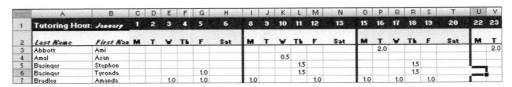

The worksheet with page breaks added manually, shown as solid lines

QUICK REFERENCE: SETTING PAGE BREAKS

Task	Procedure
Adjust an automatic page break	■ Choose the Page Break Preview button from the status bar at the bottom right of the window. ■ Drag a vertical dashed automatic page break line to the left or a horizontal page break line up. ■ Observe the page break change to a solid line to indicate a manual page break.
Add a manual page break	■ Choose the Page Break Preview button from the status bar at the bottom right of the window. ■ Select a cell below or to the right of the desired page break location. ■ Choose Page Layout→Page Setup→Breaks →Insert Page Break from the Ribbon, or right-click the cell and choose Insert Page Break from the context menu.
Remove a manual page break	■ Choose the Page Break Preview button from the status bar at the bottom right of the window. ■ Select the cell to the right of the desired vertical page break line or below a horizontal page break line. ■ Choose Page Layout→Page Setup→Breaks →Remove Page Break from the Ribbon, or right-click the cell and choose Remove Page Break from the context menu.

Hands-On 7.9   Work with Page Breaks

In this exercise, you will move, add, and remove a page break in Page Break Preview.

Display Page Break Preview

1. Use Ctrl + Home to display cell A1.

2. Choose the Page Break Preview button from the status bar at the bottom right of the window.

3. If the Welcome to Page Break Preview dialog box appears, click OK to close the dialog box. *The words* Page 1 *and* Page 2 *on the worksheet indicate the area to be printed on each page. You should see a dark blue, dashed automatic page break line between columns AB and AC. The columns for the week of Monday, January 29, are split between two pages. You will adjust the page break to force the Monday column to the next page.*

Adjust a Page Break

4. Click anywhere on the blue automatic page break line and drag to the left until it is to the left of column AA.

Y	Z	AA	AB	AC	AD	AE	AF	AG	AH	AI	AJ	AK
26	27	29	30	31								
F	Sat	M	T	W	Th	F	Sat	Total Hours	Total Fees	Family Discou	Net Fees	
				1.0				5.0	$ 125.00		$ 125.00	
		↔						0.5	$ 12.50		$ 12.50	
								4.5	$ 112.50	$ 11.25	$ 101.25	
								4.0	$ 100.00	$ 10.00	$ 90.00	
		1.0		1.0				3.0	$ 225.00		$ 225.00	

The data for Monday and Tuesday now will print on page 2 along with the data for the rest of that week. The worksheet still fits on two pages.

5. Select a cell anywhere on page 1.

6. Choose Office ⊞→Print ▸ menu→Print Preview ▢.

7. In Print Preview, click anywhere on page 1 to zoom out and then click near column Z to zoom in.
   Page 1 ends with column Z, a Saturday.

8. Click anywhere on page 1 to zoom out.

9. Click the Next Page ▢ button in Print Preview.
   Page 2 contains the names in columns A and B and then displays column AA, a Monday.

10. Close ▣ the Print Preview window.

Insert and Remove a Page Break

11. In Page Break Preview, select any cell in column I, a Monday.

12. Choose Page Layout→Page Setup→Breaks ▢→Insert Page Break from the Ribbon.

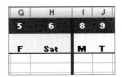

A solid blue, manual page break line now appears to the left of column I.

13. Point to any cell in column O, right-click, and choose Insert Page Break on the context menu.
    Do not move the pointer off column O as you right-click.

    You may add or remove page breaks by choosing a command either on the Ribbon or in the context menu.

14. Use either method you have just learned to add a page break to the left of column U.
    The worksheet now would print on five pages. Next you will remove all but one page break.

15. Select any cell in column I.

16. Choose Page Layout→Page Setup→Breaks ▢→Remove Page Break from the Ribbon.

17. Point to any cell in column O, right-click, and choose Remove Page Break in the context menu.

18. Use either method you have just learned to remove the page break to the left of column U.
    The worksheet now should contain only one page break to the left of column AA.

19. Save ▢ your changes and print ▢ the worksheet.

20. Close ▢ the workbook.

Concepts Review

True/False Questions

1. Before performing a sort, you should select all the cells in one column.   TRUE   FALSE

2. The Sort dialog box is used to sort on more than one sort key.   TRUE   FALSE

3. The Freeze Panes 🔲 command can keep the contents of column A visible as you scroll to the end of the worksheet.   TRUE   FALSE

4. The Split 🔲 command is used to move two areas of the worksheet into a separate workbook.   TRUE   FALSE

5. Page Layout view displays all printed pages, and Print Preview displays one page at a time.   TRUE   FALSE

6. You must use the Print Area 🔲 command every time you print.   TRUE   FALSE

7. The Scale option changes both the width and height of the printed worksheet.   TRUE   FALSE

8. A header or footer has three sections.   TRUE   FALSE

9. You may type text in a header or footer.   TRUE   FALSE

10. You may adjust or add page breaks in Normal view.   TRUE   FALSE

Multiple Choice Questions

1. Which of the following may you freeze before scrolling the worksheet?
   a. The Print Preview window
   b. Multiple columns and rows
   c. One cell
   d. All formulas

2. Which columns and rows are frozen when you issue the Freeze Panes 🔲 command?
   a. Columns to the left of and rows above the selected cell
   b. Columns to the left of and rows below the selected cell
   c. Columns to the right of and rows below the selected cell
   d. Columns to the right of and rows above the selected cell

3. Which orientation prints along the wider edge of the paper?
   a. Header
   b. Footer
   c. Portrait
   d. Landscape

4. How does Page Layout view display page breaks that you add manually?
   a. As gridlines
   b. As dashed lines (- - -)
   c. As solid lines (—)
   d. None of the above

Skill Builders

Skill Builder 7.1   Insert Formulas and Sort Rows

In this exercise, you will open a workbook that contains an accounts receivable aging report. You will create a formula to calculate the number of days the accounts are past due. You will also sort the rows.

Create the Formulas

1. Open the sb-Aging Report workbook from the Lesson 07 folder in your file storage location.

2. If necessary, maximize ▫ the window.

3. Type **7/1** in cell B2.
   The date displays with the current year because the cell was formatted previously.

4. Enter the following invoice dates in column C:

Customer	Invoice Date	Customer	Invoice Date
Soeur	1/25	Cheng	4/27
Arias	3/6	Washington	5/6
Jones	3/14	Smith	5/9
Alexander	4/17	Alcaraz	5/18
Suzuki	4/23	Bellmont	5/24

5. Select cell E5 and enter the formula **=$B$2-C5**.
   This formula calculates the number of days between July 1 and the invoice date. Cell B2 must be an absolute cell reference in the formula.

6. Use the fill handle to copy the formula down the column.

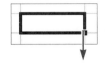

7. Select cell F5 and enter the formula **=E5-30**.
   An invoice is considered past due if not paid within 30 days.

8. Use the fill handle to copy the formula down the column.

Sort the Rows

Notice that the rows currently are sorted by invoice number in column B.

9. Select cell A5 and choose Data→Sort & Filter→Sort A to Z ⬇ from the Ribbon.
   The rows are sorted by the names in column A.

10. Sort the rows in descending order by the invoice amount.
    The largest invoice amount should appear at the top of the list.

11. Select cell F5 and choose Data→Sort & Filter→Sort Z to A 🔼 from the Ribbon.
    The rows now are sorted by the number of days past due from highest to lowest.

12. Save 💾 the changes and close ❎ the workbook.

Skill Builder 7.2   Use Multiple Sort Keys

In this exercise, you will use the Sort dialog box to sort worksheet rows using two sort keys.

1. Open the sb-Balance Due Report workbook from the Lesson 07 folder.
    Notice that the list is currently sorted by the Outstanding Balance column.

2. Select any cell in the Lastname column.

3. Choose Data→Sort & Filter→Sort 🔼 from the Ribbon.
    Excel will identify the list and select the correct rows. The header row will not be selected.

4. Set the first Sort By box to Lastname and sort values in A to Z order.

5. Add a second level, set the Then By key to Firstname and sort values in A to Z order, and click OK.
    Take a moment to study the results. Notice that rows with the same last names are grouped together. Those groups are then sorted by the first names.

6. Choose Data→Sort & Filter→Sort 🔼 from the Ribbon.
    Now you will change the sort order. First you will sort the list by the Lastname column. Then you will sort those groups by the Customer ID Number column.

7. Use the Lastname column for the Sort By box and sort in A to Z order.

8. Use the Customer ID Number column for the first Then By box and sort by smallest to largest.

9. Click OK.
    Notice that the rows with the same last names are still grouped together. Notice also that the groups are sorted by the Customer ID Number column. You will perform one more sort in the next step.

10. Sort the rows in descending order using only the Outstanding Balance column.
    You don't have to use the Sort dialog box because you are using only one sort key. Select any item in column D and click the Sort Z to A button. All rows with an Outstanding Balance code of Y should move to the top of the list.

11. Save 💾 the changes and close ❎ the workbook.

Skill Builder 7.3　Create a Custom Footer

In this exercise, you will remove a footer and create a custom footer. You will also preview and print the worksheet.

1. Open the sb-Customer ID List from the Lesson 07 folder.

2. Display Page Layout view by clicking its button in the lower right of the window.

3. Select any section of the footer.
   Next you will remove the existing footer.

4. Choose Design→Header & Footer→Footer 📄 menu ▼, and choose (None) from the top of the list.

5. Follow these steps to create a custom footer and format the footer:

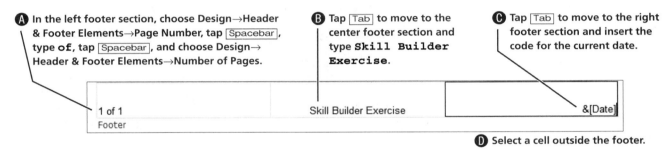

Ⓐ In the left footer section, choose Design→Header & Footer Elements→Page Number, tap Spacebar, type **of**, tap Spacebar, and choose Design→ Header & Footer Elements→Number of Pages.

Ⓑ Tap Tab to move to the center footer section and type **Skill Builder Exercise**.

Ⓒ Tap Tab to move to the right footer section and insert the code for the current date.

| 1 of 1 | Skill Builder Exercise | &[Date] |
| Footer | | |

Ⓓ Select a cell outside the footer.

The custom footer displays below the worksheet in Page Layout view.

6. Choose Office 🔘 →Print ▸ menu→Print Preview 🔍.

7. Use the Zoom button to examine the footer at the bottom of the page.

8. Choose Close Print Preview ❎.

9. Save 💾 the changes and close ✖ the workbook.

Skill Builder 7.4　Print a Large Worksheet on One Page

In this exercise, you will set a worksheet to print on a single page. You will accomplish this by using landscape orientation and the Scale to Fit option. You also will add a header and experiment with paper size options.

1. Open the sb-Volume Comparison workbook from the Lesson 07 folder.

2. Display Page Layout view by clicking its button in the lower right of the window.
   Notice that the worksheet currently is in portrait orientation with the narrow edge of the page on top.

3. Drag the Zoom slider in the lower-right corner of the window to a percentage that allows you to see all the pages.
   The worksheet is three pages wide and one page high. In the remainder of this exercise, you will adjust settings in the Page Layout Ribbon to fit this worksheet on a single page.

   During the remainder of this exercise, change the zoom level as needed.

4. Choose Page Layout→Page Setup→Orientation [icon] menu ▼→Landscape from the Ribbon.

Change the Paper Size

5. Choose Page Layout→Page Setup→Size [icon] menu ▼→Legal 8.5" × 14" from the Ribbon.
   More columns fit on page 1. Printing on wider paper and making a few other adjustments may fit a worksheet on fewer pages. Assume, however, that you want to use only letter-size paper because you find it inconvenient to switch paper in your printer and store wide printouts in notebooks and file folders.

6. Change the paper size back to Letter 8.5" × 11".

Launch the Page Setup Dialog Box

7. Click the dialog box launcher [icon] button in the bottom-right corner of the Page Setup command group of the Page Layout Ribbon.
   The Page Setup dialog box appears with the Page tab displayed. If a different tab is active, click the Page tab. Notice that the Orientation and Paper Size options are available in the dialog box as well as on the Ribbon. Also notice that the dialog box contains command buttons to jump to the Print dialog box and Print Preview.

8. Click Cancel to exit the dialog box without making any changes.

Scale the Worksheet and Add a Header

9. Choose Page Layout→Scale to Fit→Width menu ▼→1 Page from the Ribbon.
   Now the worksheet fits on one page. The worksheet originally was one page high, so it is not necessary to change the Height option.

10. Select any section of the header.

11. Choose the predefined header Page 1 of ?.

12. Save [icon] the changes and close [icon] the workbook.

Assessments

Assessment 7.1   Use Multiple Sort Keys

In this exercise, you will sort the rows in a worksheet using three sort keys.

1. Open the as-Orders workbook from the Lesson 07 folder in your file storage location.

2. If necessary, maximize ⬚ the window.

3. Format the numbers in column D as Comma style with no decimal places.

4. AutoFit all column widths.
   Notice that the rows are currently sorted by Sales Volume in column D.

5. Use the Sort dialog box to sort the rows using three sort keys: key 1, Customer in A to Z order; key 2, Division in A to Z order; and key 3, Key Contact in A to Z order.
   Key Contact will be sorted within groups by first name, as each cell entry begins with the first name.

   Your completed worksheet should match the following example.

	A	B	C	D
1	**Orders**			
2				
3	Customer	Division	Key Contact	Sales Volume
4	Alexis	Battery Division	Frank Jordan	3,303,336
5	Alexis	Battery Division	Richard Warren	1,605,476
6	Alexis	Battery Division	Susan Christopher	1,775,262
7	Alexis	Battery Division	William J. Pinckerton	4,831,410
8	Dimension Systems	Automotive	Michael Chricton	2,624,192
9	Dimension Systems	Automotive	Michael Wilson	3,473,122
10	Dimension Systems	Automotive	Stephen Crane	2,963,764
11	Dimension Systems	Large Vehicle	Bill Clayton	2,114,834
12	Dimension Systems	Large Vehicle	Carl Bartholomew	4,152,266
13	Dimension Systems	Large Vehicle	Larry Alexander	4,661,624
14	Qualtron	Computer Technology	Bill Thompson	2,454,406
15	Qualtron	Computer Technology	Dick Morris	1,435,690
16	Qualtron	Computer Technology	Sandy Princeton	2,793,978
17	Qualtron	Medical Technologies	Joe Gecko	3,133,550
18	Qualtron	Space Systems	Bill Rogers	1,945,048
19	Qualtron	Space Systems	Stacey Crawford	4,322,052
20	Qualtron	Space Systems	Stan Barnes	1,265,904
21	Qualtron	Space Systems	Wanda Wilson	3,812,694
22	Zenex	CAD	Alice Senton	4,491,838
23	Zenex	CAD	Joseph Harding	3,982,480
24	Zenex	Semiconductor	Ben Warren	3,642,908
25	Zenex	Semiconductor	Lois Lane	2,284,620

6. Save 🖫 the changes, print the worksheet, and close ✖ the workbook.

Assessment 7.2   Print a Large Worksheet on One Page

In this exercise, you will use the Page Layout Ribbon to format the worksheet so that it prints on one page. You also will include a header and footer.

1. Open the as-Maria Fernandez Expenses workbook from the Lesson 07 folder.

2. Choose Page Layout from the Ribbon and change the orientation.

3. Change the margins or use the Scale to Fit options so that the worksheet will print on one page.

4. Add the header and footer shown in the following illustration. Use the current date.

5. Type your name in the footer.

6. Use Print Preview to review the worksheet prior to printing.
   Your printed worksheet should fit on one page as in the following example showing the top and bottom of the page.

							as-Maria Fernandez Expenses					
Expenses for Maria Fernandez												
	January	February	March	April	May	June	July	August	September	October	November	December
Cell Phone	245	270	295	320	345	370	205	220	235	250	265	280
Automobile	325	345	365	385	405	425	205	240	275	310	345	380

Page 1 of 1	4/17/2011	Student Name

7. Save 🖫 the changes, print 🖶 the worksheet, and close ⊠ the workbook.

Assessment 7.3   Print a Title Column and Gridlines

In this exercise, you will use the Page Layout Ribbon to format the worksheet so that it prints a title column and gridlines.

1. Open the as-David Sutton Expenses workbook from the Lesson 07 folder.

2. Choose Page Layout from the Ribbon and turn on gridlines for printing.

3. Set column A as a title column on every page.
   Do not change the orientation from portrait.

4. Use Print Preview to review the worksheet prior to printing.

5. Save 🖫 the changes, print 🖨 the worksheet, and close ⊠ the workbook.
   Your two-page printout should match the following example.

	January	February	March	April	May	June	July	August
Cell Phone	245	270	295	320	345	370	205	220
Automobile	325	345	365	385	405	425	205	240
Entertainment	150	170	190	210	230	250	15	70
Miscellaneous	105	115	125	135	145	160	165	170

	September	October	November	December
Cell Phone	235	250	265	280
Automobile	275	310	345	380
Entertainment	125	180	235	290
Miscellaneous	175	180	185	190

Critical Thinking

Critical Thinking 7.1   Create an Order Tracking Worksheet

Carmen Brandow is an administrative assistant at Fremont Pet Supplies, a wholesale distributor of pet supplies to companies in Northern California. Carmen asks you to set up a worksheet to track the number of orders and their total dollar value for Fremont's six largest customers. She tells you to record the information on a monthly basis for each month of the year. Carmen provides you with the following data for January orders.

Customer	# of Orders	Total Dollar Value
Northern California Pet Care	12	$ 2,568
My Pet Stores	16	$ 4,568
John Adams Pet Stores	23	$ 6,870
Pinnacle Pet Care	10	$ 1,250
West Side Pet Care	6	$ 5,900
Perfect Pets	52	$19,900

- Set up a worksheet using this data.
- Center the month headings above the # of Orders and Total Dollar Value columns.
- Center the values in the # of Orders column, and use Currency style with no decimal places for the dollar values.
- Bold the column headings, and align them with the data in their columns.
- Set up the worksheet for all 12 months of the year but enter only the numeric data for January, February, and March (you determine the numbers used for February and March).
- Freeze the worksheet so that row and column headings always will be visible as the worksheet is used the rest of the year.
- Save as **ct-Customer Orders** in the Lesson 07 folder in your file storage location and continue with the next exercise.

Critical Thinking 7.2   Set Up a Worksheet for Printing

Before You Begin: You must have completed Critical Thinking 7.1, and the ct-Customer Orders workbook should be open.

- Save the workbook as **ct-Quarterly Orders** in the Lesson 07 folder.
- Insert a row above the row containing the months.
- Use the Merge & Center command to center the headings Quarter 1, Quarter 2, Quarter 3, and Quarter 4 above the corresponding months. For example, Quarter 1 should be centered above the January–March headings.
- Copy the Quarter 1 data and paste the duplicate data into the new quarters (columns H–Y).
- Add a totals row that calculates the total number of orders and total dollar value of orders for each month.
- Make the worksheet print on four pages in portrait orientation. Each page should include the headings and data for one quarter. For example, all of the Quarter 1 information will print on the first page, Quarter 2 will print on the second page, and so on.
- Set the customer names in column A to print on every page.
- Format the worksheet as desired and save the workbook. You will use this workbook in Critical Thinking 7.4.

Critical Thinking 7.3   Create a Customer Account Worksheet

Brittany Barton is the manager of the accounting department of Kids in Cloth, a provider of reusable cloth baby diapers. Some aspects of Kids in Cloth's business can be quite messy, but not Brittany's accounting department. Brittany asks you to prepare a worksheet that lists each customer account and the number of diapers used on a weekly basis.

- Set up a worksheet to track this information.

- Use customer numbers beginning with the number 100 and continuing sequentially through 200.

- Enter the headings Week 1 through Week 52, which you can do very rapidly by using the fill handle.

- Enter a number in the first cell requiring a number and copy the number to all other cells in the worksheet. Each cell will have the same number, but this is a quick way to fill the sheet with sample data.

- Set the week number row and the customer number column always to display during scrolling.

- Set up the worksheet to print in portrait orientation two pages high and five pages wide. Make certain that the customer numbers and the weeks would print on every page.

- Do *not* print the worksheet but use Print Preview to review your work.

- Save the workbook as **ct-Diaper Usage** in the Lesson 07 folder.

Critical Thinking 7.4   Present Pet Supply Research

Before You Begin: You must have completed Critical Thinking 7.1 and Critical Thinking 7.2.

- Open the ct-Quarterly Orders workbook, which you saved in Critical Thinking 7.2, from the Lesson 07 folder.

- Save the workbook as **ct-Potential Customers** in the Lesson 07 folder.

- Use Internet Explorer and a search engine of your choice to locate potential customers for Fremont Pet Supplies in Northern California.

- Enter the customer names, location (city), website URLs, and telephone numbers in Sheet2 of the workbook. Also include any information that may be useful to the sales force at Fremont Pet Supplies, such as the company size and the types of pets to which it caters. Include as many potential customers as you can find.

- Format the worksheet to print on a single page. You may use either portrait or landscape orientation.

- Save the workbook when you are finished.

Critical Thinking 7.5   Present Bookstore Research

Martha Aziz is the owner of Martha's Books. In recent years, Martha's business has come under intense competitive pressure from online booksellers. Martha hires you to conduct a research project to help her analyze the threat posed by her deep-pocketed competitors.

- Locate three online booksellers and visit their websites to get pricing information on six different book titles. You choose the book titles or use titles you find on the sites.

- Set up a worksheet with the three online booksellers' names and URLs, the six titles you have chosen, suggested retail prices, actual selling prices, shipping charges, and Martha's price for the same titles (you determine Martha's prices).

- Set the book title column always to display during scrolling.

- Create formulas to calculate the total price of each online seller's book, which includes the selling price plus shipping. Format all total cells with a blue color. For each title, use a formula to calculate the difference between Martha's price and the average price of the three online booksellers.

- Set up the worksheet to print on a single page in landscape orientation.

- Save the workbook as **ct-Competition Research** in the Lesson 07 folder.

LESSON 8

Adding Graphics to Worksheets

Enhancing your workbooks with graphics may help you illustrate the worksheet theme and call attention to important details. In this lesson, you will locate picture sources and then insert photos and clip art on worksheets. You will draw shapes using Excel's large gallery of drawing tools and move, size, rotate, and add styles to images. With SmartArt, you will create text charts that visually demonstrate a process or relationship.

LESSON OBJECTIVES

After studying this lesson, you will be able to:

■ Use keywords to locate clip art in picture collections

■ Insert and modify pictures and clip art on worksheets

■ Draw, modify, and add text to shapes

■ Customize SmartArt to convey ideas, processes, and data relationships

Case Study: Analyzing Sales Performance

Recently promoted to an administrative marketing position, David Nguyen is eager to begin his first project. His company, Sports World, sells sports equipment and clothing in retail stores in several large U.S. cities. The marketing vice president is concerned that the current year's sales are not as strong as the previous year's. David has been asked to present several sales performance worksheets at a management strategy meeting. The data and charts already have been entered into the workbook. David thinks that adding some graphics will highlight and connect the key points of his presentation. You will add graphics to several worksheets while applying some principles of good design. You will work with the graphics shown in the following illustration, including a picture file and a shape containing text.

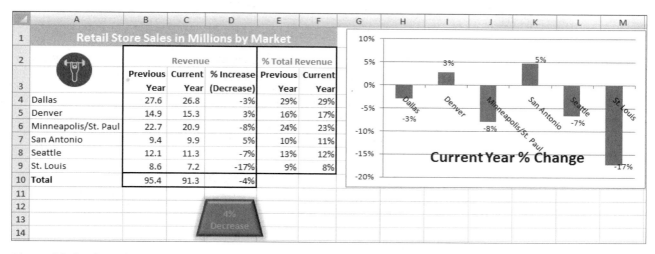

Along with the chart, this worksheet displays a picture and a shape with text.

Using Illustrations with Excel

You can dress up your worksheets using the professionally designed clip art provided with Office 2007. You may also insert your own pictures, such as a company logo or a scanned picture.

Design Principles

Graphics are fun to create, but that should not be the reason that you add them to a workbook. Before you add art, review the following generally accepted design rules:

- Each graphic should have a purpose, such as to call attention to an important number, summarize data, or contribute to the worksheet theme.

- Graphics should enhance and not distract or clutter the worksheet.

- The image colors, size, alignment, and other formatting should contribute toward a balanced appearance with other worksheet objects.

- Copyright law prohibits the use of many images for commercial use without permission. However, there are also websites featuring copyright-free art. The clip art that comes with Excel is also free to use as long as you don't try to resell the clip art itself.

The Illustrations Group on the Ribbon

To place a graphic on the worksheet, start with one of the tools in the Illustrations group on the Insert Ribbon.

Inserting Pictures and Clip Art

The Picture command adds an image saved as a file. Sources may include a digital camera, scanner, and purchased images. The Clip Art command adds a drawing or photo from a gallery of images available in Office 2007. You may adjust several image characteristics, including the location, colors, and brightness. You may apply effects, such as a picture frame or blurred edges. Immediately after it is inserted, the picture or clip art image displays with sizing handles and a rotation lever, as shown in the following illustration.

An inserted clip art image or picture displays sizing handles and a rotation lever.

Inserting a Picture from a File

After you choose the Picture command from the Ribbon, Excel displays the Insert Picture dialog box, similar to the Open dialog box for workbooks. Navigate to the folder containing the desired picture and select its file. A variety of image file formats, including JPEG and TIFF, are compatible with Excel.

 Hands-On 8.1   **Insert a Picture**

In this exercise, you will add a picture to a worksheet.

1. Open the Sports World Sales workbook from the Lesson 08 folder in your file storage location.

2. Maximize ▭ the window.

3. Display the By Dept worksheet.
   Take a few moments to browse the three worksheets in this workbook. You will add a picture to the By Market worksheet.

4. Display the By Market worksheet.

5. Select cell B14, and choose Insert→Illustrations→Picture 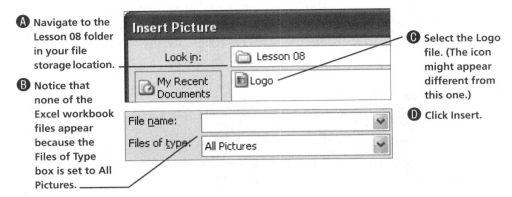 from the Ribbon.

Ⓐ Navigate to the Lesson 08 folder in your file storage location.

Ⓑ Notice that none of the Excel workbook files appear because the Files of Type box is set to All Pictures.

Ⓒ Select the Logo file. (The icon might appear different from this one.)

Ⓓ Click Insert.

The picture appears on cell B14, which you selected, but it is not attached to the cell.

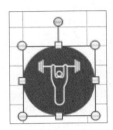

6. Save 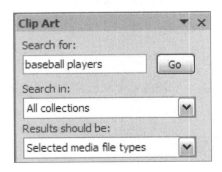 the changes to your workbook.

Inserting Clip Art

The Clip Art ▦ command on the Insert Ribbon displays the Clip Art task pane. This pane lets you search for clip art using keywords. Every clip art image provided with Office 2007 has a number of keywords associated with it that describe the image. For example, a baseball player image may be located using keywords such as *baseball players, sports,* and *athletes.*

The Clip Art task pane lets you search Excel's large clip art collections.

Clip Art Collections

The clip art that comes with Excel is from essentially two different sources. You may limit the search to only the Office Collections on disk or the Web Collections on the Microsoft website.

- **My Collections & Office Collections**—These are clip art images stored on your hard drive. These collections are quite limited.

- **Web Collections**—Almost all of the available clip art is stored on the Internet and only available when you have an Internet connection.

Clip Art Types

Clip art comes in four different media types. However, only two of these types actually work with Excel. You may limit a clip art search to specific media types.

- **Clip Art**—These are drawings in a variety of designs and colors.

- **Photographs**—These are images from a camera.

- **Movies**—These are simple animations. They do not work in Excel, looking like clip art pictures instead. (These movies do work in other Office applications such as PowerPoint.)

- **Sounds**—These are brief audio clips. Sound clips do not work in Excel but do work in some other Office applications.

Hands-On 8.2   Insert Clip Art

In this exercise, you will search for clip art images and add one to a worksheet.

1. Display the Analysis worksheet in the Sports World Sales workbook, and select cell C6.

2. Choose Insert→Illustrations→Clip Art ⊞ from the Ribbon.
   The Clip Art task pane appears on the right of the Excel window. The selections from a previous search may display.

3. Follow these steps to conduct a search:

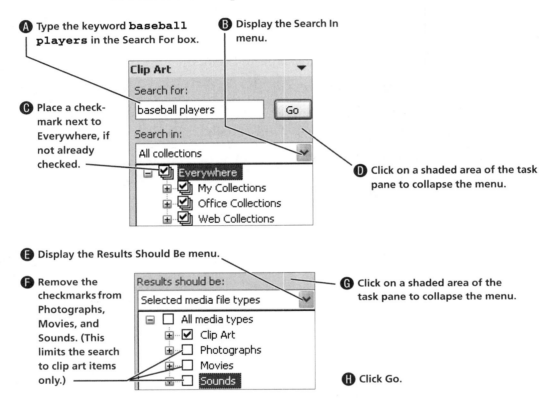

Ⓐ Type the keyword **baseball players** in the Search For box.

Ⓑ Display the Search In menu.

Ⓒ Place a check-mark next to Everywhere, if not already checked.

Ⓓ Click on a shaded area of the task pane to collapse the menu.

Ⓔ Display the Results Should Be menu.

Ⓕ Remove the checkmarks from Photographs, Movies, and Sounds. (This limits the search to clip art items only.)

Ⓖ Click on a shaded area of the task pane to collapse the menu.

Ⓗ Click Go.

After a pause, results of the search appear in the body of the Clip Art task pane.

NOTE! *If you are not connected to the Internet, very few images will show in your search results. Choose any image if the one below is not available.*

4. Scroll through the clips that appear and click the one shown at right.
   The image displays at cell C6. As an alternative to clicking, drag the image from the Clip Art task pane to the desired location.

5. Close the Clip Art task pane when you are finished.

6. Save 🖫 the changes to your workbook.

Moving, Sizing, and Rotating Images

When you select a picture or clip art image, sizing handles and a rotation handle appear. You can size, move, and rotate a selected object as described in the following illustration.

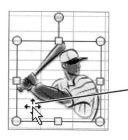

Handles on the outside of the selected image allow you to change its size and shape.

This move pointer appears when you drag from the middle of the image.

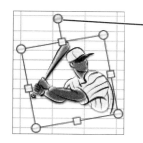

The Rotation handle allows you to rotate the image.

 TIP! *To delete a graphic, select it and tap* Delete .

 Hands-On 8.3   **Move, Rotate, and Size Images**

In this exercise, you will modify the appearance of the picture and clip art image you inserted in previous exercises.

Adjust Clip Art

1. Follow these steps to move, rotate, and size the baseball player clip art image in the Analysis worksheet of the Sports World Sales workbook:
   Your image may be different from the one shown.

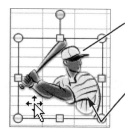

A If the resizing handles do not display, click the object to select it.

B Drag the lower-right corner handle diagonally up and to the left to shrink the image.

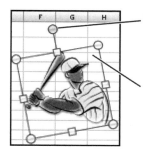

C To rotate, drag the circle in the rotation handle to the left. (If your image is different, you may need to rotate to the right.)

D Point anywhere in the image except on a resizing handle and drag to move so that the top of the image is near the top of cell F3. Then tap the arrow keys several times to nudge the image in small increments.

Delete and Restore an Image

2. Select the baseball player image and tap Delete .
   The image is removed.

3. Undo ⤺ the delete.

Adjust and Duplicate an Image

4. Display the By Market worksheet.

5. Follow these steps to size, move, and duplicate the image:

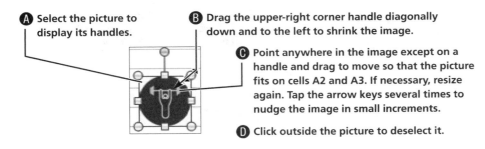

Ⓐ Select the picture to display its handles.

Ⓑ Drag the upper-right corner handle diagonally down and to the left to shrink the image.

Ⓒ Point anywhere in the image except on a handle and drag to move so that the picture fits on cells A2 and A3. If necessary, resize again. Tap the arrow keys several times to nudge the image in small increments.

Ⓓ Click outside the picture to deselect it.

The image should look similar to the following example.

6. Select the picture, use Ctrl + C to copy, and then deselect the picture.

7. Display the By Dept worksheet, select cell A2, and use Ctrl + V to paste.

8. Move the picture, if necessary, so that it fits attractively on cells A2 and A3.

9. Deselect the picture.

10. Save 💾 the changes to your workbook.

Scaling and Cropping Images

When you select an image, various Picture Tools become available on the Ribbon. To adjust most characteristics, you will use the Format Ribbon.

Scaling

Scaling a picture reduces its overall size to a percentage of its original size. The effect is equal to having dragged a corner handle on the object. You can scale more precisely, however, by typing a number of inches in the Ribbon or using the spinner arrows to increase or decrease the scale in increments.

A picture at its original size

The picture scaled to 50 percent of its original size

Changing the height or width also changes the other dimension in the same proportion.

This button launches the Size and Properties dialog box.

The cropping and scaling options in the Format Ribbon

Cropping

If you want to use part of a picture or clip art image, you may use the Crop command. The object remains the same size, and you drag the handles inward to cut off one or more edges of the image.

The mouse pointer displays as the cropping tool.

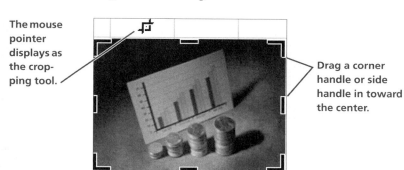

Drag a corner handle or side handle in toward the center.

The picture ready to be cropped

The picture after cropping each of its four sides

The Size and Properties Dialog Box

You may launch the Size and Properties dialog box from the Format Ribbon to set a number of options precisely when you need the same measurements for multiple objects or prefer not to use the mouse. You may set the height, width, rotation, scale percentage, and crop dimensions. The object's original size also is listed.

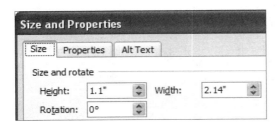

The Size tab of the Size and Properties dialog box

Resetting an Image

 If you want to start over, you may reset the image to its original characteristics by choosing Reset Picture on the Format Ribbon or the Reset command in the Size and Properties dialog box. Use Undo to reverse only the previous change.

 TIP! *The Reset Picture command removes* all *changes to the image. If you are satisfied with the size and cropping, you may want to copy and paste a duplicate image before experimenting with additional effects.*

Hands-On 8.4   Scale and Crop an Image

In this exercise, you will scale a clip art image to smaller than its original size and crop the image.

Scale Using the Ribbon

1. Display the Analysis worksheet in the Sports World Sales workbook.
2. Choose Insert→Illustrations→Clip Art ⊞ from the Ribbon.
3. In the Clip Art task pane, type **profit** as the keyword. Under Search In, set Everywhere. Set the Results Should Be option so that only Clip Art has a checkmark, and click Go.
4. Scroll through the results and drag the image shown to the right from the Clip Art task pane to cell B12. If this image is not available, select an appropriate image for the worksheet.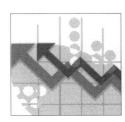
5. Close ✕ the Clip Art task pane.
6. If the profit image does not display sizing handles, select the image.
7. Choose the Format Ribbon if it is not already displayed.
8. Follow these steps to scale the image using the Ribbon:

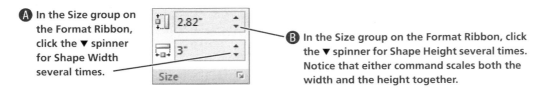

Ⓐ In the Size group on the Format Ribbon, click the ▼ spinner for Shape Width several times.

Ⓑ In the Size group on the Format Ribbon, click the ▼ spinner for Shape Height several times. Notice that either command scales both the width and the height together.

Scale Using the Size and Properties Dialog Box

9. In the Size group on the Format Ribbon, click the dialog box launcher 🔲 button.

10. Follow these steps to scale the profit image using the Size and Properties dialog box:

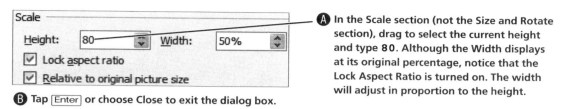

Ⓐ In the Scale section (not the Size and Rotate section), drag to select the current height and type **80**. Although the Width displays at its original percentage, notice that the Lock Aspect Ratio is turned on. The width will adjust in proportion to the height.

Ⓑ Tap Enter or choose Close to exit the dialog box.

The image displays at 80 percent of its original size.

11. Right-click the profit image and choose Size and Properties from the pop-up (or context) menu.

12. In the Size and Properties dialog box, edit the scale width to **50** and tap Enter. If you are using a different image than the one shown, use an appropriate percentage.

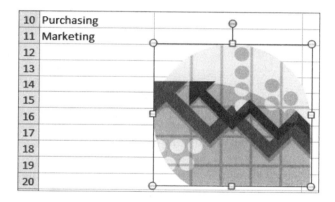

The image is half its original size. The height scales in proportion to the width that you set.

Crop Using the Cropping Tool on the Ribbon

13. If the profit image does not display sizing handles, select the image.

14. Choose Format→Size→Crop ⬚ from the Ribbon.

15. Follow these steps to crop the image:

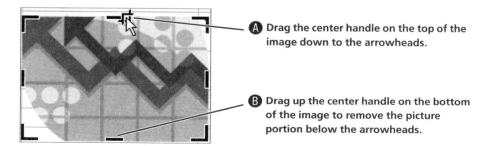

Ⓐ Drag the center handle on the top of the image down to the arrowheads.

Ⓑ Drag up the center handle on the bottom of the image to remove the picture portion below the arrowheads.

Your cropped image may look similar to the following illustration.

16. Experiment with the cropping handles until you are satisfied with the image. If needed, scale the image larger or smaller so that it balances well with other objects on the worksheet.

Reset the Image to the Original Characteristics

17. With the profit image selected, choose Format→Adjust→Reset Picture from the Ribbon.
    All changes are removed, and the original image is restored.

18. Undo ↺ the reset.

19. Click outside the image to deselect it.

20. Save 💾 the changes to your workbook.

Adjusting Images and Special Effects

2007 new!
The Format menu for Picture Tools contains some options new to Office 2007. The brightness, contrast, and recolor options change the image differently than in previous Excel versions. The Picture Styles group includes options to frame an image or apply a reflection. With the Picture Effects you may angle, bevel, shadow, or reflect the image for a 3-D appearance. You may preview the effect of any option to the selected image by passing the mouse pointer over the choices on the Ribbon.

The Adjust group and Picture Styles group on the Format menu display when a clip art or picture image is selected.

The dialog box launcher in the Picture Styles group of the Format Ribbon displays the Format Picture dialog box, where you may set some options more precisely than you can with the options available on the menus. For example, you may set a contrast of 12%.

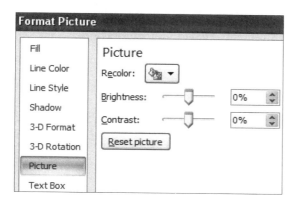

QUICK REFERENCE: EDITING IMAGES

Task	Procedure
Scale an image	■ Select the image and do one of the following: ♦ Choose Format→Size→Shape Height or Shape Width from the Ribbon and edit the size or use the spinner arrows. or ♦ Launch 🔲 the Size and Properties dialog box from the Format Ribbon, choose Height or Width under Scaling, and change the percentage.
Rotate an image	■ Select the image and drag its rotation handle.
Crop an image	■ Select the image and choose Format→Size→Crop ⌗ from the Ribbon and drag a cropping handle on the image.
Adjust image brightness	■ Select the image, choose Format→Adjust→Brightness ☼ menu ▼ from the Ribbon, and select a brightness level.
Adjust image contrast	■ Select the image, choose Format→Adjust→Contrast ◑ menu ▼ from the Ribbon, and select a contrast level.
Recolor an image	■ Select the image, choose Format→Adjust→Recolor ▧ menu ▼ from the Ribbon, and select a color option.
Apply a picture style to an image	■ Select the image, choose Format→Picture Styles, and choose a style from the Ribbon.
Apply a picture effect to an image	■ Choose Format→Picture Styles→Picture Effects ▱ menu ▼ from the Ribbon and choose a preset or other effect while the image is selected.
Reset an image to its original properties	■ Choose Format→Adjust→Reset Picture ▧ from the Ribbon while the image is selected.

Hands-On 8.5   Adjust Images and Apply Special Effects

In this exercise, you will change the brightness and contrast of the profit image and then recolor it with a color theme. You will apply a picture style and picture effects to images.

1. Display the Analysis worksheet of the Sports World Sales workbook.

2. Select the profit picture.

Adjust the Brightness and Contrast

3. Choose Format→Adjust→Brightness ⚙ menu ▼ from the Ribbon, trace down to each menu item to preview the effect on the image, and then choose +10%.

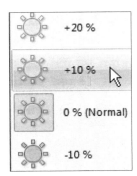

4. Choose Format→Adjust→Contrast ◑ menu ▼ from the Ribbon, trace down to each menu item to preview its effect, and then choose −10%.

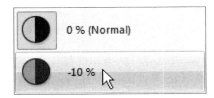

Recolor an Image

5. Choose Format→Adjust→Recolor  menu ▼ from the Ribbon, point to each menu item to preview its effect, and then choose Accent Color 6 Light, the last option under Light Variations.

The adjusted image is more muted than the original. Your image may be different from the following example.

6. Drag the profit image to a position near cell F13 so that it looks centered under the baseball player image.
David Nguyen now has these two images available for additional worksheets that he may create.

7. Feel free to copy and paste the profit image, drag the duplicate to row 26, and experiment with the other options in the Brightness, Contrast, and Recolor menus.

Add a Picture Style to an Image

8. Select the profit image in row 13.

9. Choose Format→Picture Styles→Drop Shadow Rectangle (the fourth choice from the left) from the Ribbon.

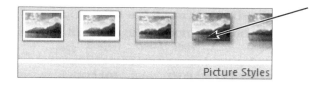

The image displays a drop shadow effect, as shown in the following illustration.

10. Choose Format→Picture Styles→ More ▼ menu ▼ from the Ribbon, point to some of the menu items to preview their effects, and then tap [Esc] to cancel without making a selection.

Apply a Picture Effect to an Image

11. Select the baseball player image on cell F3.

12. Drag the scroll box in the horizontal scroll bar to the right so that the image will be visible as you display a menu.

13. Choose Format→Picture Styles→Picture Effects 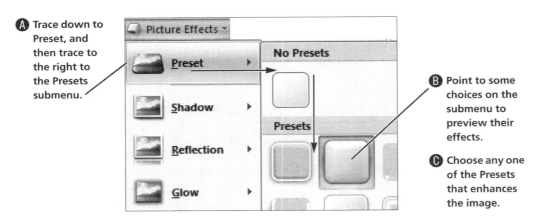 menu ▾ from the Ribbon, and then follow these steps to choose a preset:

Ⓐ Trace down to Preset, and then trace to the right to the Presets submenu.

Ⓑ Point to some choices on the submenu to preview their effects.

Ⓒ Choose any one of the Presets that enhances the image.

The preset picture effect that you chose may be different from the one shown here. While you may apply individual effects on the Picture Effects menu, such as a reflection or glow, the presets are quick and easy to use.

A preset Charcoal Drawing picture effect

14. Save 🖫 the changes to your workbook.

Getting into Shapes

With the Office 2007 shape tools, you may draw lines, ovals, rectangles, arrows, and many other shapes. Lines and callouts containing text are particularly useful to emphasize areas of interest on worksheets and charts. The Shapes command is used to add these objects, and you may type text into any shape except lines, brackets, and braces. The following illustration highlights some categories on the Shapes menu.

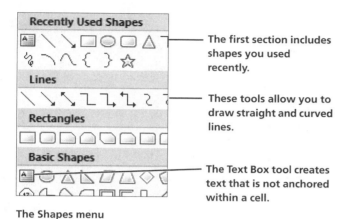

The Shapes menu

The first section includes shapes you used recently.

These tools allow you to draw straight and curved lines.

The Text Box tool creates text that is not anchored within a cell.

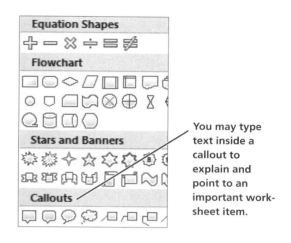

You may type text inside a callout to explain and point to an important worksheet item.

Inserting Shapes

To draw a shape, choose the desired tool on the Shapes menu and then either click or drag in the worksheet. Clicking creates a shape of a predefined size, and dragging allows you to customize the width and

Arrows drawn using the dragging method

height. You may use resizing handles on the shape or the Sizing commands on the Format Ribbon to change the size after drawing. You may type text within the shape after drawing or selecting it. After you create or select a shape, the Drawing Tools appear on the Ribbon. The Format Ribbon contains options to change the size, fill, and outline; add an effect; and insert more shapes.

Constraining Objects

You may hold down the Shift key to draw shapes that remain in equal proportion of width to height. A rectangle is constrained to a square, and an oval is constrained to a circle. You also may constrain lines to 90- or 45-degree angles.

Text Boxes

The Text Box command creates a very useful object. Text boxes are slightly different from rectangle shapes, which display centered text. As you type in a text box, text is left aligned by default, and the text box lengthens automatically to display all the text. You may

Sports World Sales Summary

A text box may be layered over a cell, picture, clip art, or shape.

position a text box anywhere on a worksheet, even over worksheet entries, pictures, and other graphics.

Applying Shape Styles and Effects

While a shape is selected, you may apply options from the Shape Styles group on the Format Ribbon. You may apply a predesigned outline and fill, or you may create a custom outline or fill. The Shape Effects menu contains options to angle, bevel, shadow, or reflect the image for a 3-D appearance.

QUICK REFERENCE: INSERTING AND EDITING SHAPES

Task	Procedure
Insert a shape	■ Choose Insert→Illustrations→Shapes ⬚ menu ▼, and choose a shape tool from the Ribbon.
	■ Click on the worksheet to create the shape or drag to control the shape's size.
	■ Hold down Shift while dragging to constrain the shape to a perfect square, circle, or 90- or 45-degree line.
Insert a text box	■ Choose Insert→Text→Text Box ⬚ from the Ribbon.
	■ Click in the worksheet and type the text.
Apply an outline or fill to a shape	■ Select the image, choose Format→Shape Styles, and choose a predesigned style from the Ribbon or choose Shape Fill or Shape Outline for custom settings.
Apply a shape effect	■ Choose Format→Shape Styles→Shape Effects ⬚ menu ▼ from the Ribbon and choose a Preset or other effect while the shape is selected.

 ## Hands-On 8.6   Insert and Edit Shapes

In this exercise, you will draw various shapes, including a callout and a text box. You will change the appearance of shapes, and you will apply a glow effect to one of the shapes.

Draw and Format an Oval

1. Display the By Dept worksheet in the Sports World Sales workbook.

2. Choose Insert→Illustrations→Shapes menu ▼→Basic Shapes→Oval ⬚ from the Ribbon.

3. Follow these steps to draw an oval on cell D6:

Ⓐ Position the mouse pointer slightly above and to the left of the number −55% and then drag down and right.

Ⓑ Release the mouse button to end the oval.

The oval hides the number because the oval contains a fill.

4. With the oval selected, choose Format→Shape Styles→Shape Fill ⬚ menu ▼→No Fill from the Ribbon.
The number now appears through the oval.

5. With the oval selected, choose Format→Shape Styles→Shape Outline menu ▼ from the Ribbon, pause the mouse over various orange shades, and choose one that will call attention to the circled number.

6. Move and resize the oval to center it over the number.

Draw and Format a Callout Shape

7. Choose Insert→Illustrations→Shapes→Callouts→Line Callout 1 ⬛ from the Ribbon.
   As an alternative, with the oval graphic still selected, you may choose Format→Insert Shapes→More menu ▼ from the Ribbon and select the tool. That method is faster.

8. Follow these steps to draw a callout on cell G15 in the By Dept worksheet:

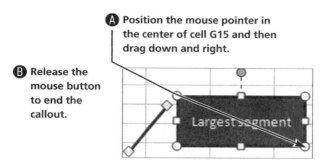

Ⓐ Position the mouse pointer in the center of cell G15 and then drag down and right.

Ⓑ Release the mouse button to end the callout.

Ⓒ While the shape is still selected, right-click on the shape and choose Italic from the context menu. Type **Largest segment** but do *not* tap [Enter].

9. Drag a handle to resize the box so that the text fits on one line. If necessary, drag the callout box to move it slightly.

10. Choose Format→Shape Styles→More ▾ menu ▼, trace down, and select Moderate Effect – Accent 6 (row 5, column 7).
    Your callout should contain italicized text, a graduated orange fill, and a thin shadow. Using the preset effects saves time. Next you will move the callout line so that it points to the largest pie wedge in the chart.

11. Follow these steps to rotate and lengthen the callout line:

Ⓐ Point to the lower connector (yellow diamond).

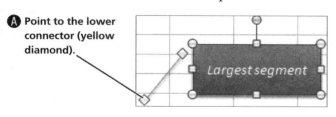

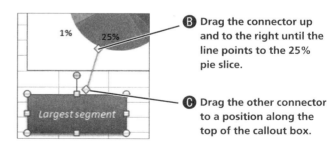

Ⓑ Drag the connector up and to the right until the line points to the 25% pie slice.

Ⓒ Drag the other connector to a position along the top of the callout box.

Draw a Text Box

12. Display the Analysis worksheet in the workbook.

13. Choose Insert→Illustrations→Shapes→Basic Shapes→Text Box ⬛ from the Ribbon.
    The tool also is available by choosing Insert→Text→Text Box from the Ribbon.

14. Follow these steps to draw a text box on the baseball player image:

Ⓐ Position the mouse pointer on the baseball player image and then drag down and right.

Ⓑ Release the mouse button to end the shape.

Ⓒ With the shape still selected, type **Sports World Sales Summary** but do *not* tap Enter.

Ⓓ If necessary, move and resize the shape so most of the baseball player is visible.

Sports World Sales Summary

To move a text box, point to its border rather than inside the shape.

Draw a Trapezoid

15. Click the By Market worksheet tab in the workbook.

16. Choose Insert→Illustrations→Shapes→Basic Shapes→Trapezoid ⬜ from the Ribbon.

17. Follow these steps to draw a trapezoid on cell D12:

Ⓐ Position the mouse pointer slightly above and to the left of cell D12 and then drag down and right.

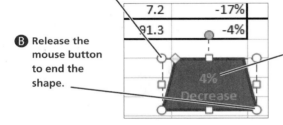

Ⓑ Release the mouse button to end the shape.

Ⓒ Right-click the shape and choose Bold from the Mini toolbar. Drop down the Font Color list and choose Orange, Accent 6 in the first row of Theme Colors. Type **4%**, tap Enter, and type **Decrease**.

Ⓓ If necessary, move and resize the shape so that it is centered on column D.

Apply a Shape Effect

18. With the trapezoid selected, choose Format→Shape Styles→Shape Effects ⬜ menu ▾→ Glow from the Ribbon, trace right and down, preview each of the orange glow choices, and choose one.
Because the shape has a glow effect, some other effects now are unavailable. The shape will not preview a change when you point to those effects on the menu.

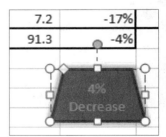

19. Feel free to preview other Shape Effects. Copy and paste the trapezoid, move the duplicate to row 26, and choose Format→ Shape Effects menu ▾→ No Glow from the Ribbon. Preview various effects from the Shape Effects menu.

20. Save ⬜ the changes to your workbook.

Introducing SmartArt

Office 2007 supplies a new illustration category named SmartArt 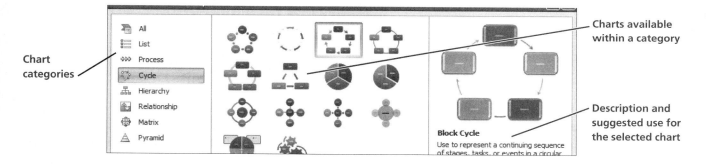. While you use line, column, and pie charts to summarize worksheet data, you will use SmartArt to present ideas. For example, David Nguyen will show several worksheets and charts to his executive team to outline areas of decreasing sales, but more important is the team's decision-making process to solve the problem. With SmartArt, David can illustrate a procedure, process, or decision tree. SmartArt includes charts to show relationships between ideas, an information cycle, and project workflow steps.

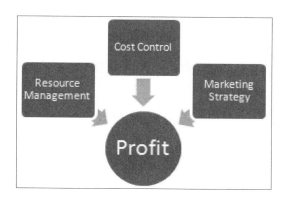

SmartArt conveys ideas using brief text phrases.

Using SmartArt

The Choose a SmartArt Graphic dialog box displays charts within categories. When you select a chart, its description displays to the right so that you may decide if it meets your presentation needs.

Chart categories

Charts available within a category

Description and suggested use for the selected chart

Adding Text to SmartArt

After a SmartArt chart is inserted on the worksheet, you may select one of its graphics and begin typing text into it. Depending on the chart type, you may prefer to display the Text pane and enter all text as an outline. You are not restricted to the number of levels that display in the initial chart. You may add or delete levels and type as many items within a level as needed.

The expand button to display the Text pane

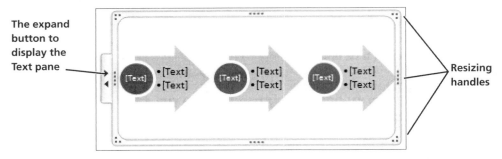

Resizing handles

A SmartArt chart

You may use the Text pane to type text more easily as an outline.

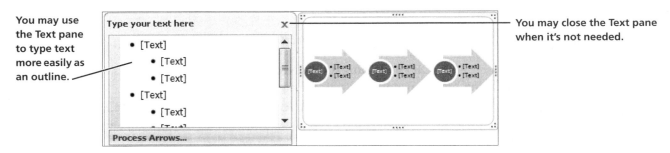

You may close the Text pane when it's not needed.

The Text pane open on a SmartArt chart

 TIP! *Keep text brief in SmartArt. Use short, descriptive phrases rather than complete sentences.*

Formatting SmartArt

The SmartArt Tools display when a SmartArt graphic is selected. You may change the chart's layout, colors, and number of shapes on the Design Ribbon. There you also will find SmartArt Styles, which add shape fills, shadows, and 3-D effects with the click of a button. As with other options, you may preview by pausing the mouse pointer over the choices on the Ribbon.

 TIP! *To delete an object in a SmartArt chart, select the object and tap* Delete *. To delete an entire chart, select its frame and tap* Delete *.*

QUICK REFERENCE: WORKING WITH SMARTART

Task	Procedure
Insert a SmartArt chart	■ Choose Insert→Illustrations→SmartArt from the Ribbon. ■ In the Choose a SmartArt Graphic dialog box, choose a chart category, choose a specific chart type, and click OK.
Edit a SmartArt chart	■ Select a graphic in the chart and type text. ■ To type text for all chart graphics at one time, click the expand button on the left of the chart frame to display the text pane, select all text, tap Delete, and then type the new text. ■ Use Tab to demote text to the next lower level and Shift+Tab to promote text to the next higher level.

Hands-On 8.7   Insert SmartArt

In this exercise, you will create a SmartArt graphic to convey a relationship. You will move, resize, and change colors on the graphic. You also will apply a style.

1. Display the Analysis worksheet in the Sports World Sales workbook.
   You will convert the labels National and Sector to SmartArt to show a dynamic relationship.

2. Select any cell and tap Home to display column A.

3. Select cells B2:C2 and tap Delete to remove the labels.

Insert an Arrow Ribbon and Add Text

4. Choose Insert→Illustrations→SmartArt 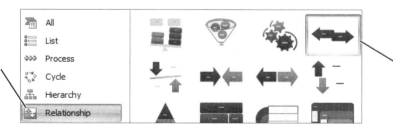 from the Ribbon.
   The Choose a SmartArt Graphic dialog box displays.

5. Follow these steps to insert an arrow ribbon chart from the Choose a SmartArt Graphic dialog box:

Ⓐ Trace down and choose the Relationship category.

Ⓑ Choose the Arrow Ribbon graphic (row 1, column 4). Read the description of the graphic.

Ⓒ Click OK.

The arrow ribbon appears on the worksheet surrounded by a nonprinting frame. The SmartArt Tools appear on the Ribbon.

Format, Resize, and Move the Arrow Ribbon

Make certain that the arrow ribbon graphic is still selected.

6. Choose Design→SmartArt Styles→Change Colors 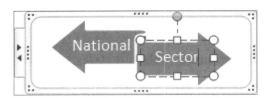 menu ▼ from the Ribbon. Scroll down to Accent 6, preview several shades by pausing the mouse over them, and then select a shade appropriate for the worksheet.

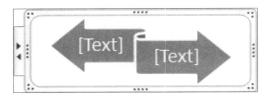

The graphic changes to the shade you chose.

7. Select the text box on the left if not already selected, type **National**, and do not tap Enter. Select the text box on the right, type **Sector**, and do not tap Enter.

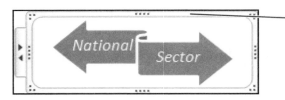

8. Follow these steps to change the text to italic:

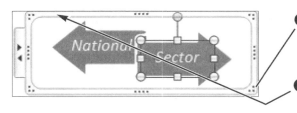

Ⓐ Click on the frame to select the entire graphic. Make certain that none of the arrow text boxes appear selected.

Ⓑ Choose Home→Font→Italic *I* from the Ribbon.

9. Follow these steps to shrink the graphic and move it into position:
An arrow graphic is selected in the illustration to demonstrate the difference between the frame resizing handles and an object's resizing handles.

Ⓐ Point to the lower-right corner resizing handle on the frame and drag up and left to make the entire graphic smaller. Make certain that you do not select the resizing handle of an object inside the frame.

Ⓑ Drag the frame until the SmartArt is centered under the word *Analysis*.

Your graphic may look slightly different from the following illustration.

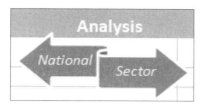

Apply a SmartArt Style

10. If the SmartArt arrow ribbon does not display its frame, click anywhere in the graphic to select it.

11. Choose Design→SmartArt Styles→More ⬚ menu ▼ from the Ribbon. Preview by pausing the mouse on each choice under Best Match for Document, and then select one.
Your choice may be different from the following one.

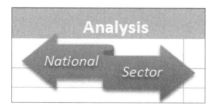

You decide that the original effect looked better.

12. Undo ⬚ the style change.

13. Save ⬚ the changes and close ⬚ the workbook.

Concepts Review

True/False Questions

1. You should follow copyright law when choosing images to insert in documents. TRUE FALSE

2. The Picture command is used to insert clip art from the Office gallery. TRUE FALSE

3. You may change the size of clip art images after they have been inserted. TRUE FALSE

4. Scaling an object means to apply a special effect, such as a drop shadow. TRUE FALSE

5. The Reset command will undo only the most recent change to an image. TRUE FALSE

6. You may type text in a shape, such as a callout. TRUE FALSE

7. A callout is created with one of the Shapes tools. TRUE FALSE

8. A text box lengthens automatically as you type more text. TRUE FALSE

9. SmartArt is used to add motion to a graphic. TRUE FALSE

10. You may type text in SmartArt. TRUE FALSE

Multiple Choice Questions

1. Which term indicates the text that you type while searching for clip art?
   a. Pictures
   b. Images
   c. Categories
   d. Keywords

2. Which handle maintains the proportion of height to width while you resize a graphic?
   a. Corner
   b. Top
   c. Side
   d. Bottom

3. Which term means cutting off one or more unnecessary edges of an image?
   a. Scaling
   b. Cropping
   c. Resizing
   d. Resetting

4. Which command allows you to draw lines and triangles?
   a. Clip Art
   b. Picture
   c. Shapes
   d. SmartArt

Skill Builders

Skill Builder 8.1 Insert Clip Art and Shapes

In this exercise, you will search a specific category for clip art and then insert and flip the image. You will draw an arrow constrained to a horizontal line and apply a shape style. You will also create a text box and a rectangle and then move objects together.

Insert and Flip Clip Art

1. If a blank workbook is not displayed, choose Office ⊞→New ⬜ to start a new workbook.

2. Maximize ⬜ the window.

3. Select cell D10.
   When you insert clip art in the next steps, it will be positioned on cell D10.

4. Choose Insert→Illustrations→Clip Art ⊞ from the Ribbon to display the Clip Art task pane.

5. Follow these steps to conduct a search for bird clips in only one category of the Web Collections:

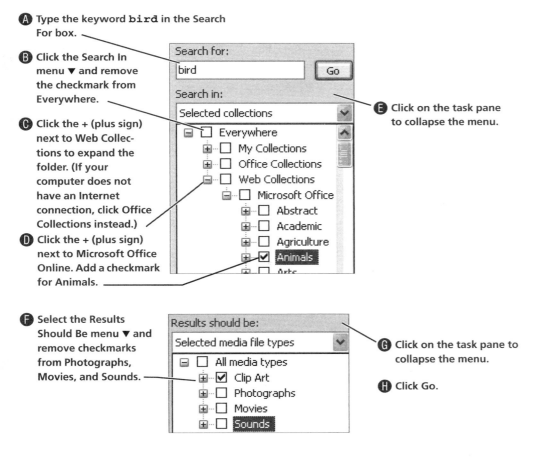

Ⓐ Type the keyword **bird** in the Search For box.

Ⓑ Click the Search In menu ▼ and remove the checkmark from Everywhere.

Ⓒ Click the + (plus sign) next to Web Collections to expand the folder. (If your computer does not have an Internet connection, click Office Collections instead.)

Ⓓ Click the + (plus sign) next to Microsoft Office Online. Add a checkmark for Animals.

Ⓔ Click on the task pane to collapse the menu.

Ⓕ Select the Results Should Be menu ▼ and remove checkmarks from Photographs, Movies, and Sounds.

Ⓖ Click on the task pane to collapse the menu.

Ⓗ Click Go.

6. Insert any bird clip by selecting it from the results list. (If no birds are available, delete the keyword **bird** to leave the Search For box empty, click Go to search for all animals, and choose one.)

7. Resize the image smaller by dragging one of the corner sizing handles.

8. Choose Format→Arrange→Rotate  menu ▼, pause the mouse to preview the effect of each menu choice, and choose Flip Horizontal. (Make certain the animal image is still selected if this Ribbon command does not appear.)
The animal will face the opposite direction. If the animal's eyes now are looking to the left, choose Undo.

The animal should face toward the right.

Draw a Text Box

9. Follow these steps to create a text box:

Ⓐ Choose Insert→Text →Text Box from the Ribbon and click on cell F10.

Ⓑ Type **Fly to Florida with me this winter!** and do *not* tap Enter.

Ⓒ Drag the lower-right corner handle until the text displays on two lines.

Fly to Florida with me this winter!

Next you will draw an arrow shape.

Draw a Horizontal Arrow

10. Choose Insert→Illustrations→Shapes 🔲 menu ▼, and under Lines, choose Arrow (the second item).

11. Place the mouse pointer in cell E12, hold down Shift, and drag to the left about an inch or less. Release the mouse and then release Shift.
The arrow should be perfectly horizontal because you constrained it with Shift.

Add a Shape Style to the Arrow

12. With the arrow still selected, choose Format→Shape Styles→More ⬔ menu ▼ from the Ribbon. Preview by pausing the mouse on various choices, and then select a style color that harmonizes with the colors in the clip art.

13. Move or resize any of the objects to align them attractively.
    For example, move the text box by pointing anywhere on its border except a handle and then dragging, as shown in the following illustration.

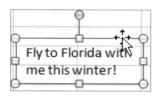

The graphics should look similar to the following illustration. Your clip art may be different.

14. Select the arrow or text box and choose the Format Ribbon.
    Notice the Insert Shapes group on the Ribbon. If a shape is selected, you may choose another shape tool to draw a new shape without having to choose Insert→Shapes.

15. Choose Format→Insert Shapes→Rectangle ☐ from the Ribbon.

16. Follow these steps to draw a rectangle around the objects:

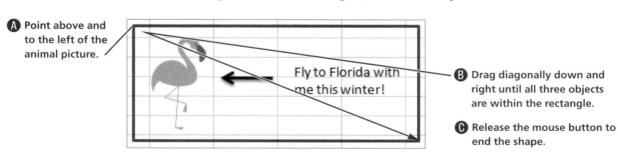

Ⓐ Point above and to the left of the animal picture.

Ⓑ Drag diagonally down and right until all three objects are within the rectangle.

Ⓒ Release the mouse button to end the shape.

The filled rectangle is layered on top of the other graphics. Make certain that the rectangle is still selected.

17. Choose Format→Shape Styles→Shape Fill 🎨→No Fill from the Ribbon.

18. If necessary, move and resize the rectangle until all three objects appear centered within the rectangle.

19. Feel free to experiment with other drawing techniques, such as the following:

- Choose a rectangle tool and hold down Shift to draw a perfect square.
- Choose the oval tool and hold down Shift to draw a perfect circle.
- Choose a line or arrow tool and hold down Shift to draw lines constrained to a 90- or 45-degree angle.
- Right-click a line or arrow tool in the Shapes menu and choose Lock Drawing Mode. Draw multiple lines. When done, tap Esc to unlock the drawing mode. You may lock the drawing mode for any tool.
- Choose any tool on the Shapes menu and draw a shape. Resize, rotate, or flip the shape.
- Drag objects so that they overlap one another. Use the Bring to Front and Send to Back commands in the Arrange group on the Format Ribbon and observe the effects.

20. Save 💾 as **sb-Animal** in the Lesson 08 folder in your file storage location and close the workbook.

Skill Builder 8.2   Insert SmartArt and Change the Layout

In this exercise, you will insert a SmartArt chart, type text into an outline that automatically pours the text into the graphics, and change to a different chart type.

1. Open the sb-Sports World workbook from the Lesson 08 folder.

2. Maximize ☐ the window.

Insert a List Graphic and Add Text

You will group the labels from column A into a more dynamic list.

3. Choose Insert→Illustrations→SmartArt from the Ribbon. In the Choose a SmartArt Graphic dialog box, trace down to Relationship and click Picture Accent List (fourth row, fourth column), and then click OK.
This chart contains placeholders for adding pictures, but you will not use them now.

4. Click the expand button as shown to display the Text pane.

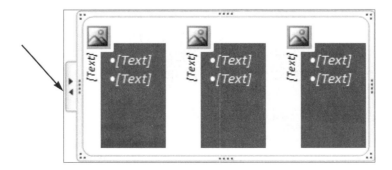

You could type text directly in the graphics, but you probably will find it easier to enter all text in the outline.

5. Follow these steps to type the text:

⚠️ **NOTE!** *First you will delete the sample text. The graphics disappear from the frame, but do not worry. As you type text, the graphics will reappear with the text in them.*

Ⓐ Select the item at the top of the list, use Ctrl+A to select all sample text, and tap Delete. Type **Revenue and Expenses** as a main topic and tap Enter.

Ⓑ Tap Tab to demote to a subtopic level, type **Gross Sales** and tap Enter.

Ⓒ Type the next three text items, tapping Enter once after the last item.

Ⓓ With the cursor on the blank line under Damage and Loss, use Shift+Tab to promote to the main topic level, type **Human Resources** and tap Enter.

Ⓔ Type the remaining text items using Enter, Tab, and Shift+Tab when necessary.

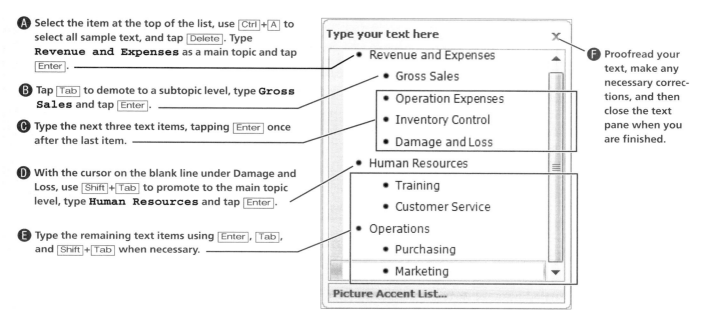

Ⓕ Proofread your text, make any necessary corrections, and then close the text pane when you are finished.

The SmartArt graphic should look like the following illustration.

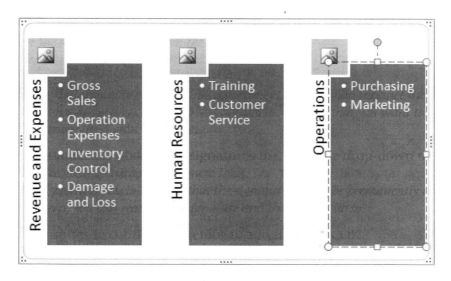

Change the Layout

6. If the SmartArt chart does not display its frame, click anywhere in the graphic to select it.

7. Choose Design→Layouts→ More ▾ →More Layouts from the Ribbon. In the Choose a SmartArt Graphic dialog box, click the Hierarchy category and then Hierarchy List (last choice in the group), and click OK.

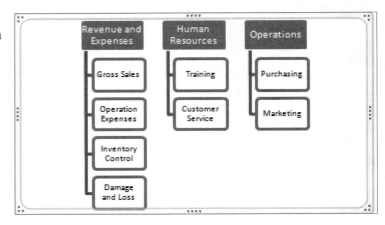

The chart now looks like the one shown. You may change layouts easily, but keep in mind that some layouts will not display all the items. You may also use the Ribbon to change colors, styles, and the number of shapes in the chart. For example, you may decide to add a fourth main topic box in this chart.

8. Delete the labels in column A of the worksheet.

9. Select the SmartArt chart, point to the frame, and drag the chart so that it is centered under the arrow ribbon.
Your graphics may look slightly different from the following illustration.

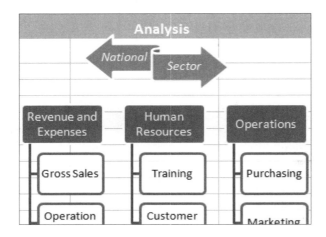

10. Feel free to insert a different SmartArt chart in a blank area of the worksheet. Explore options to add shapes, change colors, and change styles on the Design Ribbon.
Depending on the chart type, some options will be dimmed (unavailable) on the Ribbon.

11. Save 💾 the changes and close ⊠ the workbook.

Assessments

Assessment 8.1　　Use Shapes Tools

In this exercise, you will create a worksheet that includes a chart, a text box, and an arrow.

1. If a blank workbook is not displayed, choose Office →New to start a new workbook.

2. Maximize the window.

3. Enter and format the worksheet data as shown.

4. Create the chart as shown. Include the chart title and data labels over the chart columns.

5. Create the text box and apply a shape style.

6. Draw the arrow as a perfect horizontal line and apply a shape style.

7. Add a header with page numbering, the current date, and your name.

8. Print the worksheet, chart, and shapes on a single page.

9. Save with the name **as-Q1 Sales** in the Lesson 08 folder and close the workbook.

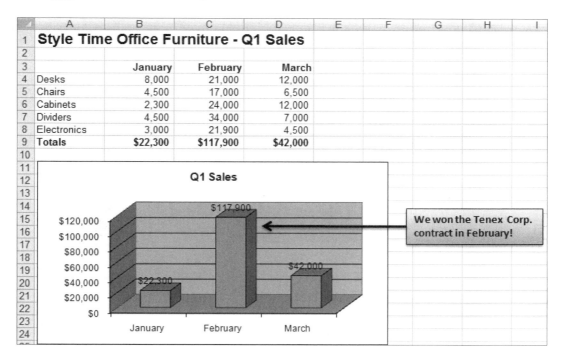

Assessment 8.2   Format Clip Art and a Shape

In this exercise, you will insert a clip art image and draw a star that contains text. You will crop, resize, and move objects. You also will apply shape styles and colors.

1. Open the as-Sales Star workbook from the Lesson 08 folder.

2. Maximize ▭ the window.

3. Insert four blank rows above row 3.

4. Add a clip art image to the worksheet. Modify the Search In box to look Everywhere and search for office furniture in the Clip Art task pane. Choose any image that illustrates the worksheet theme.

5. Crop away some of the edges around the clip art image.

6. Scale the clip art image smaller and move it into position.

7. Increase the brightness.

8. Delete the existing text box containing **Sales improved!**

9. Choose the 16-point star shape tool, hold down [Shift] to draw a perfect circle, and type **Wow! What a Month!**

10. Apply a shape style to match a color in the clip art or chart.

11. Change the font to 12pt Bold and a font color that matches the other art.

12. If necessary, resize the star so that its text displays completely.

13. Add a header with page numbering, the current date, and your name.

14. Save ▣ the changes and close ☒ the workbook.

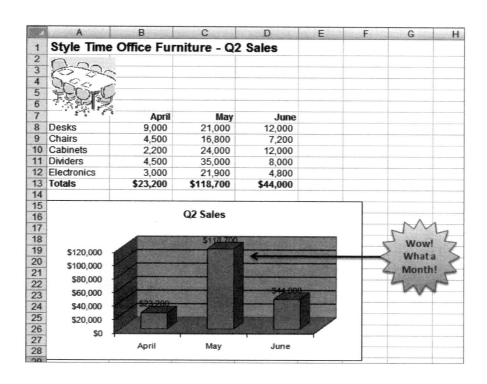

Assessment 8.3   Create SmartArt

In this exercise, you will insert and customize a SmartArt chart.

1. Open as-Accounting Formula workbook from the Lesson 08 folder.
2. Maximize ☐ the window.
3. Insert a column before column A.
4. In cell C7, create a formula that calculates the profit (not shown in the illustration below).
5. Copy cell C7 to D7.
6. Add a SmartArt chart to the worksheet. In the Relationships category, use the Equation chart (row 5, column 1).
7. Type the text as shown into the graphics.
8. Right-click the Plus (+) shape and choose Change Shape→Equation Shapes→ Minus (−) from the context menu.
9. Click the chart frame to select the entire chart and apply a bevel effect. (Your bevel effect may be different from that shown.)
10. Resize and move the chart so that it appears centered under the worksheet data.
11. Save 🖫 the changes and close ☒ the workbook.

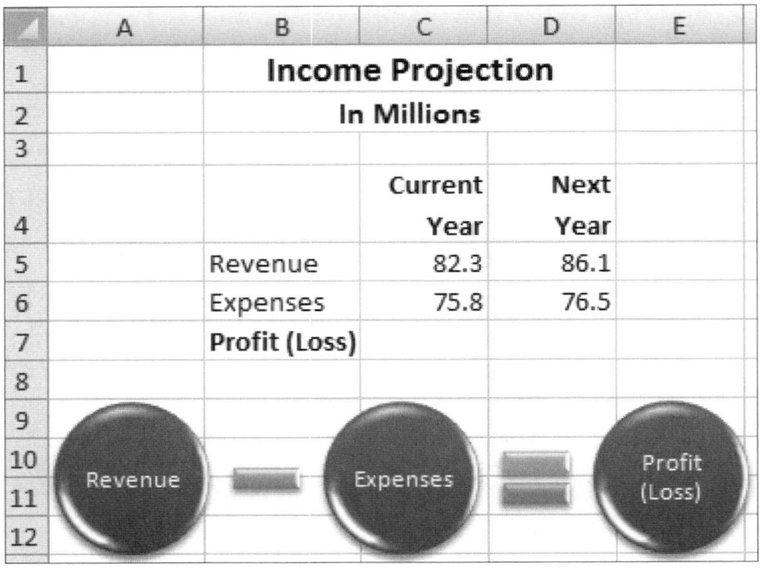

Critical Thinking

Critical Thinking 8.1   Create a Worksheet with a Chart and Callout

Jerri Copeland is the founder and CEO of Web Research Services, which conducts research for companies on a contract basis. Recently, Jerri signed a contract with Jack Norton of Norton Travel Alternatives. Jack wants to add a bidding software component to his website. Before making such a move, however, he wants to know the growth potential of this service in the online travel services industry for each of the next five years. This information will help Jack determine his budget and give him insight about his competition. After conducting the necessary research, Jerri crunched the numbers and came up with the following data:

Year	Estimated Revenue for Bidding Component
Fiscal Year 1	$1.1 million
Fiscal Year 2	$2.5 million
Fiscal Year 3	$3.7 million
Fiscal Year 4	$6.2 million
Fiscal Year 5	$7.9 million

- Using this data, set up a worksheet and an embedded column chart that shows the growth potential of the online bidding service. Use the years as the x-axis labels and the dollar amounts as the y-axis labels. Indicate in the chart title that the numbers are in millions of dollars. Remove the legend from the chart. Apply a chart style to the chart.

- Insert a callout shape that points to the last column in the chart. Use the following text in the callout: **`Growth is projected to increase nearly 700% over a five-year period`**. Format the callout text with an attractive color, apply a fill color, and set a shape effect.

- If necessary, adjust the page layout so that the data, chart, and callout will print on one page.

- Save 🖫 as **`ct-Estimated Revenue`** in the Lesson 08 folder in your file storage location and close the workbook.

Critical Thinking 8.2   Create a Worksheet with a Chart and Text Box

Roberta Maguire owns Hermosa Landscaping, which provides gardening and replacement landscaping to apartment owners in a suburban city. She wants to calculate the cost of various types of plants that she purchased for her clients during the past month. Roberta plans to track this information every month to negotiate large orders with a few reliable wholesale vendors. The following summarizes last month's purchases:

Product	Wholesale Cost
Trees	$4,628
Bushes and shrubs	$8,980
Ground cover	$3,223
Perennial flowers	$2,659
Seasonal flowers	$1,576
Sod	$6,327

■ Using this data, set up a worksheet and an embedded pie chart that shows each product as a portion of the total cost. Use the product names as the labels and the dollar amounts as the values to be charted. You decide how the pie chart should be formatted and whether any additional titles or labels should be included.

■ Add a text box on the largest pie slice with the text **One-third of purchases**. If necessary, adjust the page layout so that the data and chart will print on one page.

■ Save 💾 as **ct-Landscaping Costs** in the Lesson 08 folder and close the workbook.

Critical Thinking 8.3   Display Office Suite Research with SmartArt

Office 2007 is available in several versions. In this exercise, you will create a worksheet and SmartArt chart to compare some of the versions.

- Create a new workbook.

- Use Internet Explorer and a search engine of your choice to display the www.microsoft.com website. Search on the website to compare Office 2007 suite products.

- Choose three of the products except Office 2007 Basic. One of these three should be the version you are using, such as Office 2007 Professional. To check your suite version, choose Office→Excel Options→Resources→About.

- For each product, note the applications that are included. For each product, also conduct a web search for three retail prices, including any shipping charge. Look for the upgrade price for versions that may be upgraded from prior versions.

- Create a worksheet that includes the name of each product and its three prices in separate rows or columns. Enter a formula that averages the prices. Add titles and column labels to identify the data.

- Create a SmartArt chart to list the three product names in order from most applications to fewest applications. Resize and move the chart as necessary.

- Add a clip art image to the worksheet that complements the worksheet theme. Use your judgment in modifying the image. For example, you may resize, crop, recolor, or add an effect.

- Draw a shape to call attention to the lowest price.

- Save ▣ as **ct-Suite Research** in the Lesson 08 folder and close the workbook.

LESSON 9

Using Templates and Protecting Workbooks

As Excel becomes an integral part of your business toolkit, you may find a need to use certain workbooks repeatedly. For example, many salespeople need to fill out monthly expense reports, sales forecasts, and call reports. In this lesson, you will use predesigned Office templates and create custom templates as the basis for these and other frequently used workbook designs. Some projects require several people to work together on a workbook. To prevent others from changing important information such as formulas, you will learn how to lock and unlock certain cells, turn on worksheet protection, and set a password. You will also attach a digital signature to certify that your file has not been altered since you last saved it.

LESSON OBJECTIVES

After studying this lesson, you will be able to:

- Use existing workbooks and Office templates as the basis for new workbooks
- Create and modify custom templates
- Protect workbooks and worksheet contents
- Set a password to limit workbook access
- Add a digital signature to a workbook

Case Study: Sailing Event Template

Megan Shepherd is a manager for Trade Winds Sailing Club. The sailing club sponsors frequent sailing events for club members, and Megan is responsible for organizing these events. Race results are typically one of the reports the club publishes. Because these reports usually look the same, Megan creates a template that contains the skeleton of a sailing club race result. Part of the template design is protection for specific cells, which prevents inadvertent modification. In this lesson, you will create a template as the basis for future event workbooks and protect certain cells from being changed by others who use the workbook. You will set a password for worksheet access and create a digital signature to assure club members that the file is authentic. With these features in every workbook, Megan will "sail" through her reporting tasks.

8			Race Results		
9			[Type event name here]		
10			[Enter month and day here]		
11					
12	Place	Name	Owner	Score	
13	1				
14	2				[Type a message or select the graphic and press Delete.]
15	3				
16	4				
17	5				
18		Average		#DIV/0!	

Megan's template contains all the basic headings and formulas used for a typical race results report. Each template gives a fresh start with the same design.

8			Race Results		
9			Silver Cup Fall Regatta		
10			10/28		
11					
12	Place	Name	Owner	Score	
13	1	Lucky Lady	Linda Burke	38	
14	2	Night Watch	Donna Billings	41	A seven-point improvement over last year!
15	3	Sandpiper	Jay Walton	45	
16	4	Donna Marie	Ben Prince	45	
17	5	Second Wind	Lisa Levine	53	
18		Average		44.4	
19					
20					3/27/
21					
22					
23				X Megan Shepherd	
24				Megan Shepherd	
25				Manager	

After the sailing club officers use the template to fill in the data for a specific race, Megan includes a digital signature to authenticate the file.

Using Templates

You may use Excel's predesigned templates or create your own templates as the basis for new workbooks.

Template Features

Any Excel workbook may be saved as a template. Templates, therefore, may include any type of cell entries, formatting, pictures, shapes, charts, and formatting available in Excel that you wish to reuse for a new workbook. A workbook filename includes the extension .xlsx, as in Fall Gold Results.xlsx, although the operating system may be set to hide extensions from view. When you save a workbook as a template, the filename contains the extension .xltx. That extension tells Excel to open a *copy* of the template so that the original remains unchanged and available for reuse as many times as you like. The template file does not change when you edit workbooks based on that template. You may, however, open the template to make revisions. Those revisions will appear only in new workbooks based on the revised template.

The New Workbook Dialog Box

The New command in the Office menu displays the New Workbook dialog box, which you may use to create a new blank workbook, open a workbook recently used, or create a new workbook based on a template.

 TIP! *You may use the New from Existing command to create a new workbook based on an existing workbook that was not saved as a template.*

Choosing a Template

You may choose from among three types of templates: Installed Templates, custom templates in My Templates or another location, and Microsoft Office Online Templates. They are shown on the left in the following illustration.

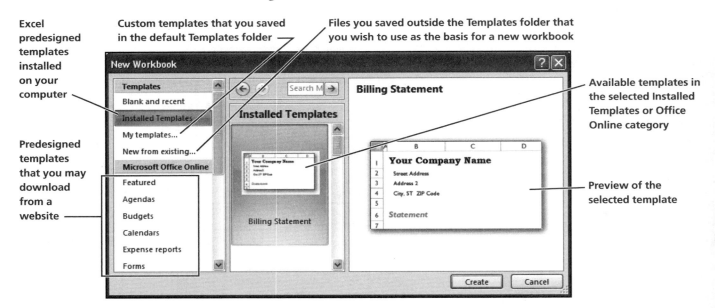

Office Online Templates

If connected to the Internet, you may choose from a variety of templates located on the Microsoft website, including calendars, budgets, calculators, and accounting worksheets. As you download one of these, Microsoft may verify that your Office program is legitimate.

Template Storage Locations

Excel's installed templates reside on the computer's hard drive or on a network drive, depending on the Office installation. Office Online templates are placed in your computer's Templates folder after downloading, and you may reuse them by choosing My Templates.

Custom templates that you create are saved by default to the Templates folder on your computer. To avoid hunting for your custom templates, save them in this folder. You may not have user privileges to save on some computers or networks. In that case, save to another file storage location. To use the template, you must navigate to that location.

 TIP! *Want to know where that Templates folder is on your computer? Check the last Quick Reference task in the following table.*

 QUICK REFERENCE: CREATING AND USING TEMPLATES

Task	Procedure
Create a workbook based on an existing workbook	■ Choose Office →New . ■ Choose New from Existing, navigate to the template's location, select the template, and click Create New.
Create a workbook based on an Excel installed template	■ Choose Office →New . ■ Choose Installed Templates, select a template, and click Create.
Create a workbook based on an Office Online template	■ Choose Office →New . ■ Choose a category under Microsoft Office Online, select a template, and click Download. ■ Respond to any message requiring verification of Office.
Reuse a downloaded Office Online template	■ Choose Office →New . ■ Choose My Templates and select a template.
View the path to the Templates folder	■ Choose Office →Save As . ■ Change the Save as Type option to Excel Template. ■ Now you can drop down the Look In list in the Save As dialog box. This displays the path to the Templates folder. ■ Cancel the Save As command.

Hands-On 9.1   Create a New Workbook from an Excel Template

In this exercise, you will use an installed template to create a new workbook.

Open a New Workbook Based on a Template

1. Choose Office 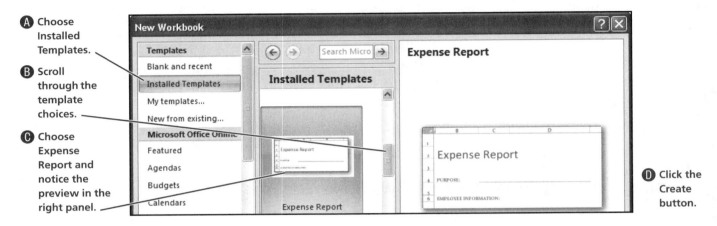→New to display the New Workbook dialog box.

2. Follow these steps to select the installed template named Expense Report:
   If Expense Report is not available, choose another template.

A Choose Installed Templates.

B Scroll through the template choices.

C Choose Expense Report and notice the preview in the right panel.

D Click the Create button.

Excel opens a new workbook containing an expense report form. Notice that the Excel title bar displays ExpenseReport1, indicating that you are working in a copy of the template rather than the original file. (ExpenseReport1 is a temporary document name for display only.)

3. Scroll through the worksheet and click cells containing a dollar sign ($) to view their formulas in the Formula Bar.

Revise and Save the Workbook

4. Fill in part of the form by typing text and numbers into some of the cells.

5. Save ⊟ the workbook as **Expense Report** in the Lesson 09 folder in your file storage location.
   Notice that the Save As dialog box opens so that you may type a filename and that the Save as Type shows Excel Workbook, the normal workbook file format.

6. Close × the workbook.

Customizing Templates

If a predesigned template does not suit your needs, you may create a workbook and save it as a template. You may revise your custom template, but workbooks based on the previous template version do not update.

Creating Your Own Templates

To create a template, first create a workbook as usual with the cell entries, formatting, graphics, and other settings that you want to reuse. You then choose the Save As command to change the file format to a template.

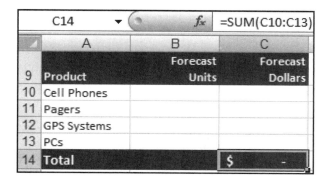

The formula in this routine report is ready to calculate data entered.

QUICK REFERENCE: USING CUSTOM TEMPLATES	
Task	**Procedure**
Create a custom template	■ Create the workbook as usual. ■ Choose Office ⬚→Save or Save As to display the Save As dialog box. ■ Type the filename, choose Excel Template in the Save as Type list, and click Save to store the template in the Templates folder. If you do not have user privileges to save in that folder, use a file storage location of your choice.
Create a new workbook based on a custom template saved in the Templates folder	■ Choose Office ⬚→New ⬚. ■ Choose My Templates and select a template.
Create a new workbook based on a custom template saved outside the Templates folder	■ Choose Office ⬚→New ⬚. ■ In the New Workbook dialog box, select New from Existing, navigate to the template's location, select the template, and click Create New.
Modify a custom template	■ Choose Office ⬚→New ⬚. ■ Choose My Templates and select a template. ■ Make the desired changes in the template. ■ Choose Office ⬚→Save or Save As. ■ Choose Excel Template in the Save as Type list, select the original filename, click Save, and click Yes to confirm.

Hands-On 9.2   Create a New Template

In this exercise, you will save your workbook as a template to your file storage location. You will not save templates to the hard drive or network drive because many computer classrooms prevent students from accessing those drives. See the preceding Quick Reference table for procedures to save and reuse templates from the Templates folder of a computer's hard drive.

1. Open the Fall Gold Results workbook from the Lesson 09 folder.

2. Maximize ☐ the window.

Make the Worksheet Generic

Megan Shepherd wants to make the Trade Winds Sailing Club workbook available to club officers. First you will make the workbook generic by removing data specific to the Gold Cup race. Then you will save the workbook as a template so that it may be used by the club officers.

3. Select cell B9 and replace Gold Cup Fall Regatta with the generic heading **[Type event name here]**.

4. Select the text in the callout graphic and replace with the generic text **[Type a message or select the graphic and press Delete.]**.

5. Delete the race results from the range B12:D16.
   The club officers will fill in the names and scores for a particular race each time they use the template as the basis for a new workbook. Notice that the D17 formula cell displays an error message because you deleted the data. Do not worry. When the officers enter their race results, the formula will calculate correctly.

Save the Workbook as a Template

6. Select cell B9.
   It is a good practice to leave a specific cell selected before saving. When you start a new workbook, the pointer will be in that cell ready for typing the event name.

7. Choose Office 🔵→Save As 🖫 and follow these steps to save the workbook as a template:

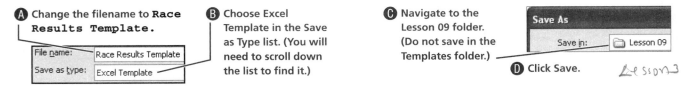

The Excel title bar now displays Race Results Template as the filename. The original Fall Gold Race file remains unchanged.

8. Close ☒ the template workbook.

Base a New Workbook on the Template

Use the following steps to access templates stored in locations such as a USB drive that prevent them from appearing in My Templates. Do not use the Open command to use such templates because you would be editing the template file rather than creating a new workbook based on the template.

9. Choose Office 🔵→New 🗋.

10. In the New Workbook dialog box, select New from Existing and navigate to the Lesson 09 folder, if necessary.

11. Select Race Results Template, and click Create New.
   A new generic workbook based on the template appears, and the temporary document name Race Results1 appears in the title bar.

Customize and Save the New Workbook

12. Follow these steps to enter the data for the Silver Cup race:

Ⓐ Type **Silver Cup Fall Regatta** in cell B9.

Ⓑ Type the data in cells B12:D16.

	A	B	C	D	E
8		Race Results			
9		Silver Cup Fall Regatta			
10					
11	Place	Name	Owner	Score	
12	1	Lucky Lady	Linda Burke	38	
13	2	Night Watch	Donna Billings	41	
14	3	Sandpiper	Jay Walton	45	
15	4	Donna Marie	Ben Prince	45	
16	5	Second Wind	Lisa Levine	53	
17		Average		44.4	

A seven-point improvement over last year!

Ⓒ Click in the callout text, use Ctrl+A to select all the text, and type **A seven-point improvement over last year!**

Ⓓ Click outside the callout.

13. Click the Save 💾 button on the Quick Access toolbar to display the Save As dialog box.
   Notice that the Save as Type setting is set to Excel Workbook. You are working with a new workbook based on the Race Results template. Your changes will be saved in the new workbook, leaving the underlying template unchanged.

14. Type **Fall Silver Results** as the filename, verify that the Lesson 09 folder is selected in your file storage location, and click Save.

15. Close ⊠ the workbook.

Modifying Custom Templates

You may modify a custom template after it has been created.

NOTE! *To modify a template, you must open it from within Excel. If you open the template from a folder window, you will simply create a new workbook.*

Browsing for a Template

You have learned to use the My Templates command to base a new workbook on a template in the default Templates folder and the New from Existing command for a template outside that folder. As an alternative, you may use a computer or folder window to navigate to a custom template and issue the Open command. Note that double-clicking a template file does not open the original template for editing but rather creates a new workbook based on the template.

Hands-On 9.3   Modify the Template

In this exercise, you will open the custom template, make a change, and resave.

Open the Template

1. Choose Office ⬛→Open 📂.

2. Navigate to the Lesson 09 folder.

3. Choose Race Results Template and click Open.
   Look at the Excel title bar and notice the name Race Results Template. You are now working with the original template—not a workbook based on the template.

Modify the Template and Save the Changes

Next you will add a row and format a cell for the date.

4. Insert a blank row at row 10.

5. Select cells B10:D10 and choose Home→Alignment→Merge & Center 🔳 from the Ribbon.

6. Select cell B10 and choose Home→Cells→Format→Format Cells 📇 from the Ribbon.

7. Follow these steps in the Format Cells dialog box to set a date format that displays the month and day in figures:

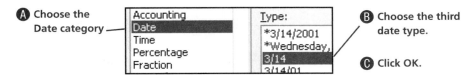

Ⓐ Choose the Date category

Ⓑ Choose the third date type.

Ⓒ Click OK.

8. In cell B10, type **[Enter month and day here]**.

Race Results
[Type event name here]
[Enter month and day here]

9. Select cell B9 to position the pointer for data entry when a new workbook is created.

10. Save 🖫 the changes and close ☒ the template.

Test the Modified Template
11. Choose Office 🔳→New 🗋.

12. In the New Workbook dialog box, select New from Existing and navigate to your file storage location containing the template, if necessary.

13. Select the Race Results Template, and click Create New.
    A new workbook based on the modified template appears.

14. Select cell B10 and enter **October 28**.
    The date formatted as 10/28 replaces the generic instruction.

15. Close ☒ the new workbook without saving it.

Protecting Workbooks and Worksheets

The protection options prevent your workbooks and worksheets from being accidentally or intentionally modified. Use protection to prevent inexperienced users from damaging workbooks. Excel offers three levels of protection:

- **Workbook Level Protection**—Protects the structure of the entire workbook, preventing changes to the way worksheets are displayed

- **Worksheet Level Protection**—Restricts changes to certain objects on worksheets

- **Cell Level Protection**—Limits access to certain cells on worksheets

Protecting the Workbook Structure

Protecting a workbook prevents structural changes from being made to the workbook. For example, you cannot delete, rename, copy, or move worksheets while the structure is protected. You may also protect a workbook window to prevent users from changing the window size and position. With Windows protection on, worksheets display consistently every time the workbook is opened. You may turn off workbook protection to make changes and then turn it on again.

Structure Protection Settings

The Protect Workbook command displays the dialog box shown in the following illustration. There are two types of protection you can choose. You may use both types simultaneously if desired. Using an optional password allows you to control who can switch this protection on and off.

- **Structure**—Protects worksheets from being reordered, copied, or deleted within the workbook

- **Windows**—Prevents users from changing the workbook window size and position

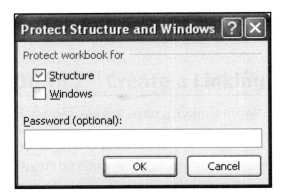

The Protect Workbook command allows you to create a password
so no one else can delete worksheets or alter their order.

Hands-On 9.4   Protect a Workbook

In this exercise, you will protect a workbook template. Megan Shepherd added a worksheet to the Race Results template and deleted the callout on the Results worksheet. You will open her file and protect the workbook structure and window.

Open a Template

1. Choose Office →Open .

2. Navigate to the Lesson 09 folder.

3. Choose the Protected Template file and click Open.
   Look at the Excel title bar and notice the name Protected Template. You are now working with Megan's original template—not a workbook based on the template.

Protect the Entire Workbook

Megan wants to standardize the look of the worksheet window each time the workbook is opened and prevent inexperienced users from deleting the worksheet.

Notice the two sets of quick-sizing buttons at the top-right corner of the Excel window. The top buttons size the program window and the bottom buttons size the worksheet within the program window. The bottom buttons will disappear once you protect the windows on the worksheet.

4. Choose Review→Changes→Protect Workbook  from the Ribbon.

5. Place a checkmark in both the Structure and Windows boxes and click OK.
   Notice that the bottom set of quick-sizing buttons has been removed from the window. The Windows protection option prevents you from sizing and moving the worksheet windows within the program window. If desired, you can still size and move the program window.

6. Try dragging the Results worksheet tab to another location in the workbook order.
   An icon indicates the action cannot be performed because the workbook is protected.

7. Double-click the Results worksheet tab to try changing its name.
   A message indicates that the workbook is protected.

8. Click OK to close the message box.
   At this point you are prevented from modifying the workbook structure. You still may work normally within the worksheet, however.

Unprotect and Protect the Workbook

9. Choose Review→Changes→Unprotect Workbook  from the Ribbon.

10. Double-click the Results worksheet tab and notice that now you could change the name if desired.

11. Click anywhere in the worksheet to cancel the renaming action.

12. Choose the Protect Workbook command, place a checkmark in both the Structure and Windows boxes, and click OK.

13. Save  the template workbook and leave it open.

Protecting Worksheet Elements

You may turn on protection for individual worksheets within a workbook. The Protect Sheet command even allows you to restrict activity on the worksheet to specific actions, such as selecting cells, formatting rows and columns, inserting or deleting rows and columns, etc.

The Protect Sheet dialog box allows you to restrict specific activities when protection is switched on.

Turning Protection On and Off

Although it might appear that you would turn worksheet protection on and off by using the Protect Worksheet and Contents of Locked Cells option, that is not the case. That option always should have a checkmark. Clicking OK actually turns on worksheet protection.

Allowing User Changes

By default only two user options are selected in the Protect Sheet dialog box, giving users permission only to click on cells. If you remove those checkmarks, users may scroll through the worksheet but may not select any cell. You may specify certain items that users still are allowed to change in a protected worksheet, such as editing graphics, deleting rows, and formatting columns.

Password Protection

For the highest level of protection, type a password in the Protect Sheet dialog box. Users must enter the password to unprotect the worksheet and make further changes. The Protect Structure and Windows dialog box also contains a password option.

 WARNING! *If you forget your workbook protection password, you must re-create the workbook, as you cannot get into the file. You will not assign workbook protection passwords in this lesson.*

Task	Procedure
QUICK REFERENCE: PROTECTING WORKBOOKS, WORKSHEET ELEMENTS, AND CELLS	
Set workbook level protection	■ Choose Review→Changes→Protect Workbook [icon] from the Ribbon.
	■ In the Protect Structure and Windows dialog box, place a checkmark in the Structure box and/or Windows box.
	■ (Optional) Enter a password if you wish to password-protect the protection settings. Then type the password again when prompted.
Unprotect a workbook	■ Choose Review→Changes→Unprotect Workbook [icon] from the Ribbon.
	■ Enter the workbook protection password if prompted.
Protect a worksheet	■ Choose Home→Cells→Format→Protect Sheet [icon] from the Ribbon.
	■ Place a checkmark by any items that users should have permission to change.
	■ (Optional) Type a password in the Password box. Retype the password when prompted.
Unprotect a worksheet	■ Choose Home→Cells→Format→Unprotect Sheet [icon] from the Ribbon.
	■ Enter the workbook protection password if prompted.

QUICK REFERENCE: PROTECTING WORKBOOKS, WORKSHEET ELEMENTS, AND CELLS (CONTINUED)

Task	Procedure
Unlock ranges of cells in a worksheet and protect all other cells	■ Select the desired cell range(s) in the worksheet to be unprotected/unlocked. ■ Choose Home→Cells→Format→Lock Cell 🔒 from the Ribbon to toggle the lock setting to off. ■ Choose Home→Cells→Format→Protect Sheet from the Ribbon.
Unlock one or more graphics in a worksheet and protect all other graphics	■ Select the graphic(s) in the worksheet to be unlocked. ■ Choose Format→Size dialog box launcher from the Ribbon. 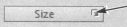 ■ Display the Properties tab. ■ Remove the checkmark from the Locked box and Lock Text box, if applicable. ■ Choose Home→Cells→Format→Protect Sheet from the Ribbon.

 ## Hands-On 9.5   Protect a Worksheet

In this exercise, you will explore worksheet protection with and without a password.

Protect a Worksheet

Megan added the Scoring worksheet in the workbook to explain how race participants are rated. She prefers that other users not be able to change any information in this worksheet.

1. Display the Scoring worksheet in the Protected Template.

2. Choose Home→Cells→Format→Protect Sheet from the Ribbon.

3. Take a moment to browse the protection options and then click OK.

4. Click any cell in the worksheet and try entering new text or numbers.
   Excel displays a message box indicating that the cell cannot be changed.

5. Click OK to close the message box.

Unprotect the Sheet

The Scoring worksheet still should be active. Assume that you need to edit the worksheet.

6. Choose Home→Cells→Format→Unprotect Sheet from the Ribbon.
   The command toggles between Protect Sheet and Unprotect Sheet. The Protect Sheet and Unprotect Sheet commands also are available on the Review Ribbon.

7. Click any empty cell in the worksheet and enter any number or text.
   With worksheet protection off, you may make any changes.

8. Undo ↶ the change.

Set a Worksheet Password

The Scoring worksheet still should be active. Megan wants to set a password for this worksheet because without that higher level of protection, users could unprotect the sheet and inadvertently make changes.

9. Choose the Protect Sheet command from the Ribbon.

10. In the Protect Sheet dialog box, type **abc123** in the Password to Unprotect Sheet box and click OK.

11. In the confirm dialog box, retype the password and click OK.
    You turned on worksheet protection and set a password to prevent users from unprotecting the sheet without authorization.

12. Click any cell in the worksheet and try entering new text or numbers.
    Excel displays a message box indicating that the cell cannot be changed because worksheet protection is turned on.

13. Click OK to close the message box.

Type the Password

You will use the password to unprotect the worksheet.

14. Choose the Unprotect Sheet command from the Ribbon.

15. Type **abc123** in the Password box and click OK.
    The password is no longer in effect. If you want to password-protect the worksheet again, you must repeat the steps.

Protect the Worksheet Without a Password

16. Choose the Protect Sheet command from the Ribbon and click OK without setting a password.
    At this point only the Scoring worksheet is protected.

17. Save the template workbook and leave it open.

Protecting Cells

You may protect the contents and formatting of certain cells from being changed. You also may hide formulas so that they do not display in the Formula Bar or when you use Ctrl+` to display formulas. All cells in a worksheet are locked by default until you unlock them. Why, then, have you been able to edit all locked cells in lessons up to this point? The cells' locked or unlocked condition has no effect until *worksheet protection* is turned on. *With protection on, you cannot change locked cells.*

The Protection Tab

You use the Protection tab of the Format Cells dialog box to change options for selected cells. There are two cell protection options you may set:

- **Locked**—Check or uncheck this option to lock/unlock currently selected cells on the worksheet.

- **Hidden**—This option affects only the display of formulas and does not hide labels, values, or formula results.

The Locked option causes the selected cells to be protected.

The Hidden option affects only the display of formulas within the selected cells.

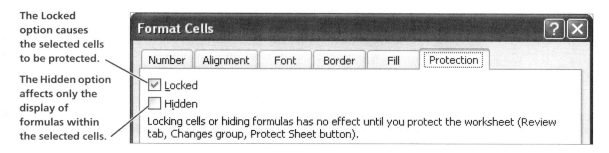

Unlocking Cells in a Protected Worksheet

When the Locked option is unchecked, selected cells are unlocked. Unlocked cells may be edited even though the overall worksheet is protected. This way, you can protect formulas and labels while allowing data entry in specific parts of the worksheet. You must unlock the cells before protecting the worksheet.

The Changes Area

For rapid data entry into unlocked cells, you may press ⊺ab after entering data in each cell. When you reach the end of a row within the changes area and press ⊺ab, the pointer wraps to the next row.

To Lock or Not to Lock

Because cells may be locked or unlocked, you may be wondering which option to use. If your worksheet contains only a few cell ranges that users are allowed to change, unlock those cells. The rest of the worksheet remains locked when you turn on worksheet protection. If most of the worksheet needs to be accessible for updating, you may want to choose Select All, select Unlock, and then lock just the cells that you want to protect.

 TIP! *Use the* Ctrl *key to select multiple cell ranges and then select Unlock, Lock, or Hidden to apply the option to multiple ranges at once.*

Hands-On 9.6   Unlock Cells in a Worksheet

In this exercise, you will unlock a range of cells in the Results worksheet of the Protected Template. You will then turn on protection to prevent labels and the formula from being changed.

Before You Begin: *The Protected Template workbook should be open in Excel. If it is not, repeat steps 1–3 of Hands-On 9.5*

Unlock Cells in the Results Worksheet

You will set a changes area for data entry in the Results worksheet.

1. In the Results worksheet of the Protected Template workbook, select the range B13:D17. *This range includes all cells that will change for each sailing event.*

2. Choose Home→Cells→Format from the Ribbon and notice the Lock Cell 🔒 button on the menu.

The shaded button indicates that the selected cells are currently locked.

3. Complete the command by choosing Lock Cell 🔒 to toggle the lock setting to off.

4. With the range still selected, choose Home→Cells→Format and notice the Lock Cell button. (Do not click the Lock Cell command.)

The button is not shaded, indicating that the selected cells are unlocked.

5. Click on a worksheet cell to exit the Format menu without choosing a command.

6. Issue the command to unlock cells B9:B10.
Remember that these actions have no effect on unlocked and locked cells until you protect the worksheet in the next step.

Protect the Sheet and Test Cell Attributes

7. Choose Home→Cells→Format→Protect Sheet 📋 from the Ribbon and click OK.

8. Select cell A13 and try entering data in the cell.
A message box appears to indicate that the cell is protected.

9. Click OK to close the message box.

10. Select cell B13, type **800**, and press ⌨Tab.
Excel lets you enter the number because you unlocked the cell prior to protecting the sheet. Using Tab speeds cell data entry in the changes area.

11. Undo the cell entry.

12. Select cell B9 to position the pointer for data entry when a new workbook is created.

13. Save 💾 the changes.

14. Choose Office →Close to close the workbook without exiting Excel.
Because the workbook window is protected, the window's Close *button is unavailable.*

Create a New Workbook

After designing a template, you will find it a good practice to test its use.

15. Choose Office →New.

16. In the New Workbook dialog box, select New from Existing and navigate to the Lesson 09 folder, if necessary.

17. Choose Protected Template, and click Create New.
A new generic workbook based on the template appears.

Enter Sample Data

The pointer is in cell B9 ready for data entry.

18. Type **Spring Invitational Regatta** in cell B9.

19. Type **April 17** in cell B10.
The date formatted as 4/17 displays.

20. Enter the following data:

Place	Name	Owner	Score
1	Donna Marie	Ben Prince	37
2	Night Watch	Donna Billings	39
3	Lucky Lady	Linda Burke	40
4	Sandpiper	Jay Walton	47
5	Second Wind	Lisa Levine	49

21. Verify that other cells are locked by trying to enter data in a few cells.

22. Save the workbook as **Spring Invitational Results** in the Lesson 09 folder.

23. Choose Office →Close to close the workbook.

Creating Digital Signatures

A digital signature authenticates that your workbook originated from you, came from a reliable source, and was not altered—possibly by a virus—after the digital signature was applied. Digital signatures are sometimes called digital IDs.

If anyone (or a computer virus) modifies the worksheet in any way, the digital signature is removed when the changes are saved, and the digital signature must be reapplied.

When to Use a Digital Signature

You may use a digital signature when giving workbooks or templates to others as email attachments, as a downloadable file on your organization's intranet, from a website, or on a disk. In addition, you may send a document to someone for an electronic signature as you would a paper document.

Creating a Digital Certificate

You add a digital signature to a file by attaching a digital certificate. If no certificate is installed when you use the Add a Digital Signature command, a dialog box appears to allow you to get a certificate. You may obtain a digital signature using one of the following methods:

- **Via Self Signature**—You may create your own digital certificate, although its use is limited. The authenticity of the digital signature can be verified only on your own computer.

- **Via Digital Certificate**—Digital certificates may be obtained from third-party vendors, which check identification before issuing a certificate. If you post workbooks on an intranet or the Internet, your network administrator usually will provide you with an authentic digital certificate.

This dialog box displays if a digital certificate (digital ID) is not installed.

 NOTE! *Your network security administrator may provide the digital certificates for your organization, so check with that person before creating your own. You will not obtain or install a third-party digital certificate in this lesson. You may not have user permission to create a digital certificate on your classroom computer.*

Hands-On 9.7   Create a Digital Certificate

In this exercise, you will create a temporary digital certificate on your local computer.

Create a Digital Certificate on the Local Computer

Although you will not install a digital certificate from a third party in this lesson, you would use most of the following steps in doing so.

1. Open the Fall Silver Results workbook from the Lesson 09 folder.
   You created this workbook in Hands-On 9.2.

2. Choose Office →Prepare→Add a Digital Signature.
   If a digital signature already exists on your computer, the dialog boxes may differ from those described in the next steps.

3. In the Microsoft Office Excel dialog box, click OK.
   If a digital ID is already installed on the computer, the Sign dialog box appears. Otherwise, the Get a Digital ID dialog box appears.

4. If the Sign dialog box is visible, skip to step 8; otherwise continue with step 5.

5. Read the descriptions for the two options in the Get a Digital ID dialog box.
   It's not necessary to purchase a digital ID in order to sign a document. In this case, you will simply create your own self-signature.

6. Choose Create Your Own Digital ID and click OK.
   The Create a Digital ID dialog box appears. Here you can add descriptive information for your self-signature.

7. Follow these steps to fill in the digital ID information for Karen Choi:

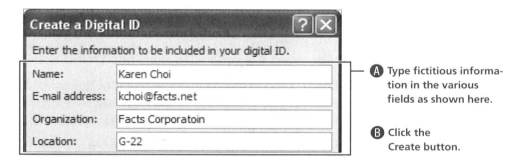

A Type fictitious information in the various fields as shown here.

B Click the Create button.

Excel creates the digital ID, which is stored in your computer. The Sign dialog box displays.

8. Leave the Sign dialog box open for the next exercise.

Creating a Digital Signature

Your digital signature may be embedded in the workbook with or without a signature line visible on a worksheet.

Electronic vs. Written Signature Lines

Paper forms and other documents often contain signature lines. You may add similar signature lines electronically to Excel workbooks and templates by using the Signature Line menu on the Insert Ribbon. The recipient adds an electronic signature next to the X by typing the name or adding a picture of a handwritten signature. A digital signature is added automatically to the file to authenticate the recipient's identity.

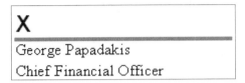

An electronic signature line added to a document

Invisible Signatures

If a signature line is not necessary, you may add just the digital signature, which does not display on any worksheet. However, the signature is visible in the Signatures task pane (see the next topic). So this signature is not literally invisible, it's just not openly displayed like the formal signature line described in the previous topic.

Checking Signature Details

The status bar displays the Signatures button whenever you open a digitally signed workbook. Clicking this button displays the Signatures task pane, where you may view the signature details to verify that there is no problem with the signature. When a signed document is attached to email, the recipient should look in the email message for the Signatures button and a Signed By line.

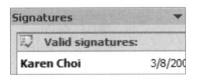

The Signatures task pane displays the digital signature name and certificate expiration date. View other details from the name's drop-down menu.

Removing Digital Signatures

You display the Signatures task pane to view signatures that have been created. A digital signature may be removed at any time by using the drop-down menu on each signature name. Note, however, that you would remove a digital *certificate* in Internet Explorer, not in Excel.

QUICK REFERENCE: CREATING A DIGITAL CERTIFICATE AND DIGITAL SIGNATURES

Task	Procedure
Create a self-signature certificate on the local computer and create an invisible digital signature	■ Choose Office →Prepare→Add a Digital Signature. ■ If the Microsoft Office Excel dialog box displays, click OK. ■ If the Get a Digital ID dialog box displays, choose Create Your Own Digital ID and click OK. ■ Type your information in the Create a Digital ID dialog box and click OK. ■ Fill in the Purpose for Signing This Document box, if desired, and click Sign.
Remove a digital certificate	■ Launch Internet Explorer. (Depending on your browser version, you may need to modify the next steps.) ■ Choose Tools→Internet Options, and display the Content tab. ■ Under Certificates, click the Certificates button. ■ Display the Personal tab, choose the certificate, click Remove, click Yes, and then click Close.
Apply an invisible digital signature (digital certificate installed)	■ Choose Office →Prepare→Add a Digital Signature. ■ Fill in the Purpose for Signing This Document box, if desired, and click Sign.
Remove a digital signature	■ Choose Office →Prepare→View Digital Signatures if the Signatures task pane is not already displayed. ■ Drop down the menu on the signature name and choose Remove Signature.
Add a visible signature line to a worksheet	■ Choose Insert→Text→Signature Line menu ▼→Microsoft Office Signature Line from the Ribbon. ■ In the Signature Setup dialog box, type the text to appear under the signature line, and select any desired options.
Sign a signature line	■ Double-click the signature line in the worksheet. ■ In the Sign dialog box, do one of the following: ◆ Type your name next to the X. ◆ Click Select Image, navigate to the folder containing the image file, select the file, and click Select. ◆ Write a handwritten signature next to the X using a tablet PC.

In this exercise, you will add a digital signature to the Fall Silver Results file and view details about the digital signature.

Now that you have created a digital certificate, you may add a digital signature to the workbook.

1. If the Sign dialog box is not open from the last exercise, choose Office→Prepare→Add a Digital Signature from the Ribbon and click OK.

2. Read the information in the Sign dialog box, type **Confidential data** in the Purpose for Signing This Document box, and click Sign.
   Typing the purpose is optional for a digital signature.

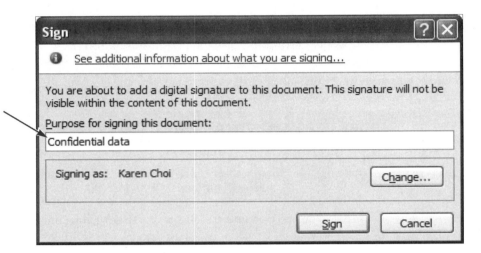

3. Click OK to confirm.
   The Signatures task pane displays with Karen's name as a valid signature and the digital certificate's expiration date.

4. Follow these steps to display signature details:

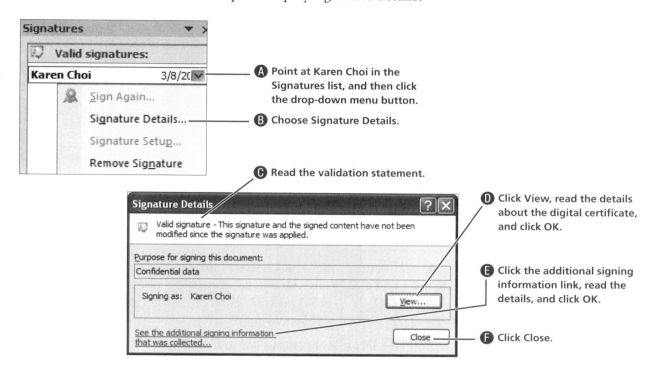

A **Point at Karen Choi in the Signatures list, and then click the drop-down menu button.**

B **Choose Signature Details.**

C **Read the validation statement.**

D **Click View, read the details about the digital certificate, and click OK.**

E **Click the additional signing information link, read the details, and click OK.**

F **Click Close.**

Notice that the Excel title bar displays [Read-Only]. Also notice that the Save button is dimmed in the Quick Access toolbar.

 ## Hands-On 9.9   Remove a Digital Signature

In this exercise, you will remove the digital signature from the Excel workbook file, reapply it, and then remove the digital certificate from the computer.

Remove the Digital Signature

Because a digital signature verifies that a document has not changed since the digital signature was applied, Excel does not allow any changes to this document. Assume that you want to change the document, so you need to remove the digital signature.

1. Point at Karen Choi in the signatures list, click the drop-down menu button, and choose Remove Signature.
   Excel prompts you to confirm that the signature should be permanently removed from the document. However, you can reapply the signature and shortly will do so.

2. Choose Yes to confirm the removal, and then click OK.
   The document is now available for changes.

Reapply the Digital Signature

Assume that you changed some data. You will reapply the digital signature.

3. Choose Office [icon] →Prepare→Add a Digital Signature from the Ribbon, click OK, click Sign, and click OK.
   Adding a digital signature was quicker this time because the digital certificate already exists.

4. Close the task pane.

5. Close [x] the workbook.
   You are not prompted to save.

Remove the Digital Certificate from the Local Computer

You will remove the digital certificate to restore the local computer to its original condition.

6. Launch Internet Explorer.
   Depending on your browser version, you may need to modify the next steps.

7. Choose Tools→Internet Options, and display the Content tab.

8. In the Certificates section, click the Certificates button.

9. In the Certificates dialog box, display the Personal tab, if necessary.

10. Select the Karen Choi certificate, and then click the Remove button.
    Internet Explorer displays a prompt that you cannot decrypt data that was encrypted with the certificate and asks you to confirm the removal.

11. Choose Yes to confirm removal of the certificate.

12. Click the Close button to close the Certificates dialog box.

13. Click OK to close the Internet Options dialog box.
    You have removed the digital certificate to restore the setup for other users.

14. Exit Internet Explorer.

Concepts Review

True/False Questions

1. A template may contain graphics and charts. TRUE FALSE

2. Excel saves a workbook based on a template also in a template format. TRUE FALSE

3. A custom template is updated each time you save a workbook based on the template. TRUE FALSE

4. To access the original template file for editing, you must open it from within Excel. TRUE FALSE

5. You may protect a workbook so that users are prevented from changing the worksheet order. TRUE FALSE

6. You may protect just one worksheet in a multiple-worksheet workbook. TRUE FALSE

7. A worksheet password prevents unauthorized users from making any changes to the worksheet. TRUE FALSE

8. When worksheet protection is off, you may edit locked and unlocked cells. TRUE FALSE

9. A valid digital signature shows that a file has not been altered. TRUE FALSE

10. A digital certificate must exist before you may create a digital signature. TRUE FALSE

Multiple Choice Questions

1. Which of the following is the default storage location for Excel templates?
   a. Custom folder
   b. Download folder
   c. Templates folder
   d. Workbook folder

2. What happens after you use the Office → New command to navigate to a template and then choose the template?
   a. Excel creates a new workbook based on the template.
   b. The template opens for editing.
   c. An error message displays.
   d. The Protect Workbook dialog box displays.

3. Which attribute is assigned to all cells in a worksheet until you change the attribute?
   a. Hidden
   b. Locked
   c. Protected
   d. Unlocked

4. What must be done so that locking and unlocking cells takes effect?
   a. Save the workbook
   b. Create a workbook based on a template
   c. Protect the worksheet
   d. Type a password

 # Skill Builders

Skill Builder 9.1   Use a Workbook as a Template

In this exercise, you will use the Fall Gold Results workbook as the basis for a new workbook. To accomplish this, you will use the New from Existing option in the New Workbook dialog box.

Create the New Workbook

1. Choose Office ⬛ →New ▭ to display the New Workbook dialog box.

2. Click New from Existing.
   The New from Existing Workbook box appears. This box lets you locate an existing workbook to be used as the basis of a new workbook.

3. Navigate to the Lesson 09 folder.

4. Choose the Fall Gold Results workbook and click the Create New button.
   A new workbook identical to the Fall Gold Results workbook appears. Notice that the Excel title bar displays the temporary display name Fall Gold Results1, indicating that this is a copy of the original file.

5. Maximize ▭ the window.

Modify the Workbook

6. Click in cell B9 and change the word *Gold* to **Bronze**.

7. Change the scores in column D as follows: **38, 41, 45, 50, 53**
   The Average function in cell D17 will recalculate the average based on the new numbers.

8. Click in the callout and edit the phrase to **two-point**.

9. Apply a different shape style to the callout.
   Choose a style with a color that blends with other colors in the worksheet.

Save the Workbook

10. Click Save 💾 in the Quick Access toolbar.
    The Save As dialog box appears, allowing you to save the workbook with a new name. The New from Existing command in the New Workbook dialog box allows you to use an existing workbook just like you would use a template.

11. Save the workbook as **sb-Fall Bronze Results** in the Lesson 09 folder.
    Make certain to delete the number 1 from the filename before completing the save.

12. Close ✗ the workbook.

Skill Builder 9.2   Unlock a Graphic in a Template

You have learned how to unlock certain cells to allow changes when worksheet protection is turned on. In this exercise, you will unlock a graphic so that it may be changed.

1. Use the Open command to open sb-Sailing Event Template in the Lesson 09 folder. Verify that the Excel title bar displays the template filename and does not include a number.
   You are working in the original template file rather than a workbook copy.

2. Maximize ▭ the window.

3. Display the Results worksheet.

4. Choose Home→Cells→Format→Unprotect Sheet 🔓 from the Ribbon.
   You must unprotect the sheet to unlock a graphic.

5. Select the callout.

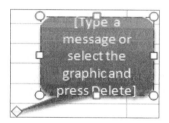

6. With the callout selected, choose the Format Ribbon and click the dialog box launcher button in the Size group on the Ribbon.
   The Size and Properties dialog box displays. You will unlock this graphic so that users may change its text or delete the graphic when it is not needed.

7. Click the Properties tab, uncheck Locked and Lock Text, and click Close.

☑ Print object
☐ Locked
☐ Lock text

8. Choose Home→Cells→Format→Protect Sheet 🔒 from the Ribbon and click OK in the Protect Sheet dialog box.
   New workbooks based on this template will allow users to edit the callout, but the other worksheet graphics are still locked.

9. Select cell B9 to position the pointer for data entry when a new workbook is created.

10. Save 💾 and close ✖ the template.

Skill Builder 9.3   Create a Template

In this exercise, you will create a template that will be used for quarterly forecasts at Zephron Industries. All Zephron sales reps will use the template as a basis for quarterly sales forecasts. The template includes three worksheets: a data sheet, a column chart sheet, and a pie chart sheet. You will format the data worksheet, remove the sample data, and save the workbook as a template. This way, the sales reps need only enter their data, and the charts already are created for them.

Set Up the Worksheet Using Sample Data

You will set up the worksheet in the next few steps. You will include sample data to test the template. The data will be deleted prior to saving the template.

1. Open 📂 the **sb-Sales Forecast** workbook from the Lesson 09 folder and maximize the window.

2. Display the Revenue Forecast worksheet to view the bar chart and then display the Revenue Breakdown worksheet to view the pie chart.

3. In the Data Sheet worksheet, click the Select All ◢ button.

4. Choose Home→Cells→Format→Column Width and set the column widths to 12.

Design the Worksheet

5. Use the Merge & Center 🔘 button on the Ribbon to center the title and subtitle in rows 2 and 4 across columns A–G.

6. Use a SUM formula in cell C14.

7. Apply a fill color and font color to the cells in rows 1–5, 9, and 14. The example uses a dark fill color and a white font color.

8. Format the numbers with Comma Style and Accounting number format as shown.

	A	B	C	D	E	F	G
1							
2			Zephron Quarterly Sales Forecast				
3							
4			Sales Rep - Donna Wilson				
5							
6							
7							
8							
9	Product	Forecast Units	Forecast Dollars				
10	Cell Phones	230	21,900				
11	Pagers	560	24,000				
12	GPS Systems	725	65,000				
13	PCs	120	190,000				
14	Total		$ 300,900				

Delete the Sample Data and Save the Workbook as a Template

9. Select the numbers in the range B10:C13 in the Data Sheet worksheet.

10. Tap [Delete] to delete the data.
    The total in cell C14 displays as a dash (zero). The formula is still intact, however, so the total will recalculate when new data are entered in the cells. The charts will be meaningless until data are entered into the Data Sheet.

11. Select cell B10 to set the pointer in the data entry area when a workbook is opened.

12. Choose Office→Save As and set the Save as Type to Excel Template.

13. Change the filename to **sb-Sales Forecast Template** and save it to the Lesson 09 folder (not the Templates folder).

14. Leave the template open for the next exercise.
    You will set protection options in the next exercise.

Skill Builder 9.4   Use and Modify a Template

The Sales Forecast Template that you created in Skill Builder 9.3 contains text, formatting, formulas, and charts. Creating a template with such items is especially useful for inexperienced users who may have learned only how to enter data. In this exercise, you will protect chart sheets and worksheet cells to prevent users from inadvertently altering the design.

Before You Begin: *You must have completed Skill Builder 9.3, and the sb-Sales Forecast Template workbook should be open.*

Protect a Template

1. If necessary, open sb-Sales Forecast Template from the Lesson 09 folder.

2. Verify that the Excel title bar displays the template filename and does not include a number.
   You are working in the original template file rather than a workbook copy.

3. Maximize 🗖 the window.

4. Display the Revenue Forecast worksheet.

5. Choose Home→Cells→Format→Protect Sheet 🔒 from the Ribbon and click OK in the Protect Sheet dialog box.

6. Choose the command to protect the Revenue Breakdown worksheet also.
   Next you will set a changes area by unlocking cells and turning on worksheet protection.

7. Display the Data Sheet worksheet.

8. Select the range B10:C13.

9. Choose Home→Cells→Format→ Lock Cell 🔒 from the Ribbon to unlock the selected cells.

10. Choose the command to protect the Data Sheet worksheet.

11. Select cell B10 to position the pointer for data entry when a new workbook is created.

12. Save 💾 and close ☒ the template.
    You will use the template to create a new workbook in the next exercise.

Skill Builder 9.5   Use a Template

In this exercise, you will create a new workbook based on the sb-Sales Forecast Template, and then enter data.

Before You Begin: *You must have completed Skill Builder 9.3 and Skill Builder 9.4.*

Create a New Workbook Based on the Template

1. Choose Office 🄱 →New→New from Existing.

2. Navigate to the Lesson 09 folder, select sb-Sales Forecast Template, and click Create New.
   A new workbook based on the Sales Forecast Template file appears. Notice that no data currently exists in cells B10:C13.

3. Maximize 🗖 the window.

4. Display the Revenue Forecast worksheet to view the bar chart and then display the Revenue Breakdown worksheet to view the pie chart.
   Notice that these chart sheets currently do not display charts because the Data Sheet cells are empty. The charts will be generated as you enter data in the next step.

5. Enter the numbers shown to the right into columns B and C of the Data Sheet. After typing each number, tap Tab.
   The pointer will wrap to the next row of the changes area for rapid data entry.

   The Total for Forecast Dollars should equal $457,500. The data are formatted with the Comma Style and Accounting number format that you already set in the template.

	A	B	C
		Forecast	Forecast
9	Product	Units	Dollars
10	Cell Phones	100	12,500
11	Pagers	200	10,000
12	GPS Systems	450	85,000
13	PCs	250	350,000

6. Display the Revenue Forecast worksheet and then display the Revenue Breakdown worksheet.
   Notice that the charts have been generated.

7. Click Save 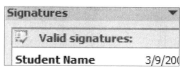 in the Quick Access toolbar to display the Save As dialog box.

8. Change the filename to **sb-Wilson Forecast** and save to the Lesson 09 folder.
   The workbook has been saved and the template is ready to be used for future forecasts.

9. Close ⊠ the workbook.

Skill Builder 9.6   Create a Digital Signature

In this exercise, you will create a digital certificate and apply a digital signature to a workbook.

Create a Digital Certificate on the Local Computer

You will create a temporary digital certificate rather than install a digital certificate from a third party.

1. Open 📂 the sb-Sales workbook from the Lesson 09 folder.

2. Choose Office 🔘→Prepare→Add a Digital Signature.
   If a digital signature already exists on your computer, the dialog boxes may differ from those described in the next steps.

3. In the Microsoft Office Excel dialog box, click OK.

4. Choose Create Your Own Digital ID and click OK.
   You are creating a self-signature digital certificate on your local computer.

5. In the Create a Digital ID dialog box, type your information (make up details as necessary) and click Create.
   The Sign dialog box displays.

Add a Digital Signature to a Workbook

Now that you have created a digital certificate, you may use the Sign dialog box to add a digital signature to the workbook.

6. Type **Confidential data** in the Purpose for Signing This Document box, and click Sign.

7. Click OK to confirm.
   The Signatures task pane displays as shown with your name as a valid signature and the digital certificate's expiration date.

   Notice that the Excel title bar displays [Read-Only]. Also notice that the Save button is dimmed in the Quick Access toolbar. The digital signature ensures recipients that the file was not altered, possibly by a computer virus.

   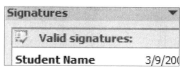

8. Close ⊠ the task pane.

9. Choose Office 🔘→Exit Excel.
   You are not prompted to save. (Excel saved the workbook when you added the digital signature.)

Remove the Digital Certificate from the Local Computer

You will remove the digital certificate to restore the local computer to its original condition.

10. Launch Internet Explorer.
Depending on your browser version, you may need to modify the next steps.

11. Choose Tools→Internet Options, and display the Content tab.

12. Under Certificates, click the Certificates button.

13. In the Certificates dialog box, display the Personal tab, if necessary.

14. Select your certificate, click Remove, click Yes, click Close, and then click OK.
You have removed the digital certificate to restore the setup for other users.

Assessments

Assessment 9.1　Create and Use a Template

In this exercise, you will create a template for the Redmont School District. Each school within the district will use the template to create a budget workbook and an accompanying chart. They will use the New from Existing command in the New Workbook dialog box to base their new workbooks on the template you create.

Create the Template

1. Start Excel and open the as-Budget Allocation workbook from the Lesson 09 folder.

2. Maximize ⬜ the window.
   The worksheet contains sample data and an embedded pie chart.

3. Delete the sample data in the range B4:B8.

4. Choose Office 🔵→Print ▸ menu→Print Preview 🔍 and verify that the workbook and chart would print on one page.
   Notice that a footer displays the filename in the center section.

5. Choose Close Print Preview ❎ to exit the view without printing.

6. Save 💾 as a template named **as-Budget Allocation Template**. Make certain to save your template in the Lesson 09 folder, not the Templates folder.

7. Close ✖ the template.

Create a New Workbook Based on the Template

8. Use the New from Existing command in the New Workbook dialog box to create a new workbook based on the as-Budget Allocation Template file.

9. Rename the Sheet1 tab to **Barrett**.

10. Type **Barrett School** in cell C1.

11. Enter the data shown into the range B4:B8. The chart in your new workbook should display the new percentages.

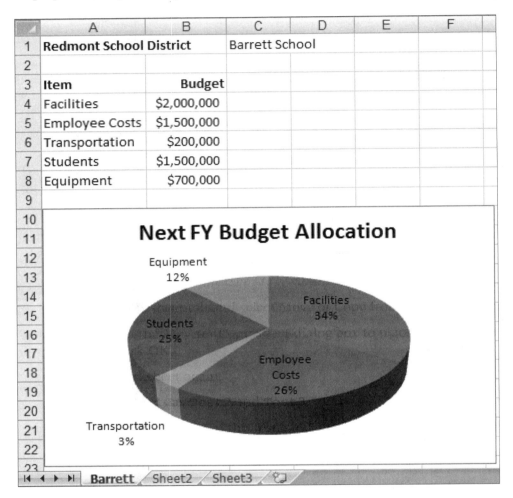

	A	B	C	D	E	F
1	**Redmont School District**		Barrett School			
2						
3	**Item**	**Budget**				
4	Facilities	$2,000,000				
5	Employee Costs	$1,500,000				
6	Transportation	$200,000				
7	Students	$1,500,000				
8	Equipment	$700,000				
9						

Next FY Budget Allocation

Equipment 12%
Facilities 34%
Students 25%
Employee Costs 26%
Transportation 3%

Barrett / Sheet2 / Sheet3

12. Save 💾 with the name **as-Barrett Budget** in the Lesson 09 folder and close the workbook.

Assessment 9.2   Protect a Template

In this exercise, you will protect specific cells in a worksheet and protect a workbook template.

1. Open the as-Budget Template from the Lesson 09 folder.
   You should be working in the original template file rather than a workbook copy.

2. Maximize ☐ the window.

3. Create a header that displays the date in the left section, the filename in the center section, and your name in the right section.

Protect the Template

4. Protect cells B4:B8 and cell C1 so that the user may enter data only in those cells. The user should not be allowed to change any other cells.

5. Protect the Budget worksheet.

6. Protect the template so that users may not delete or insert any sheet tabs.

7. Save ☐ the template.

8. Have your instructor or a teaching assistant initial that you successfully applied cell protection, worksheet protection, and workbook protection to the template. _____

9. Leave the template open.
   You will apply a digital signature to the template in the next exercise.

Assessment 9.3   Apply a Digital Signature

In this exercise, you will create a digital ID and use it to apply a digital signature to a workbook.

1. Open the as-Budget Template from the Lesson 09 folder if it is not already open.
   You should be working in the original template file rather than a workbook copy.

2. Maximize ☐ the window.

Create a Digital ID

3. Create a digital ID on your computer with your name, a made-up email address, and the name of your class.

Apply a Digital Signature

4. Apply a digital signature to the template.

5. Have your instructor or a teaching assistant initial that you successfully applied a digital signature to the document. _____

6. Close ☒ the template.

Assessment 9.4   Remove a Digital Signature

In this exercise, you will remove a digital signature from a workbook and remove the digital ID from the computer.

Before You Begin: *You must have completed* Assessment 9.3 *and the as-Budget Template workbook should be open.*

Remove the Digital Signature

1. Remove the digital signature from the as-Budget Template workbook.

2. Have your instructor or a teaching assistant initial that you successfully removed the digital signature. _____

3. Close ⊠ the template and exit Excel.

Remove the Digital ID

4. Remove the digital ID from the computer.

5. Have your instructor or a teaching assistant initial that you successfully removed the digital ID. _____

Critical Thinking

Critical Thinking 9.1   Create a Template from an Existing Workbook

Julie Roberts is the owner of Julie's Rental Equipment. She has three stores in the local area. Julie already has created a workbook to track her best customers' rental activities. She asks you to convert the workbook to a template, add protection, and apply a digital signature. She will email the template to each store manager to put on their computers.

- Open the ct-Frequent Renters workbook from the Lesson 09 folder.

- Save it as a template named **ct-Frequent Renters Template** in the Lesson 09 folder (not the Templates folder).

- Delete the information relating to specific customers. Julie wants all her store managers to use the same generic layout to track their frequent renters.

- Protect the headings, formulas, and table but allow store managers to enter their customer names and points earned.

- Save the template.

- Create a digital certificate and digital signature to authenticate the file.

Critical Thinking 9.2   Create a Protected Workbook

Jeff Adams is the sales manager for Performance Office Systems, a company that distributes high-end computer systems, monitors, printers, and copy machines. Jeff manages three salespeople, each with a monthly quota of $100,000. He asks you to set up a workbook that can be distributed to each salesperson.

- Create a workbook that includes a row for each item (computers, monitors, printers, and copy machines), the model, the number of units sold for the current month, the dollar value of the units sold, the number of units forecasted for the next month, and the dollar value of the forecasted units to be sold.

- Add sample data and a Totals row with formulas. Then delete all sample data but leave the formulas in the Totals row intact.

- Add worksheet protection by unlocking or locking cells and turning on worksheet protection.

- Save as a template named **ct-Sales Template** in the Lesson 09 folder.

LESSON 10

Managing Multiple-Sheet Workbooks

As you continue to work with Excel, you may find your workbooks growing in size and complexity. In this lesson, you will manage workbooks by copying and moving worksheets, as well as copying formatting from one worksheet to another. Workbooks may be organized with a summary worksheet and two or more detail worksheets, each containing data for one month, quarter, region, or other category. By using linked formulas on the summary worksheet, you will summarize information from the detail worksheets. You will use the power of defined names to identify cells, navigate worksheets more efficiently, and produce formulas that are easier to understand. You will create hyperlinks to navigate to areas within the workbook and to other documents. After selecting multiple worksheets, you will choose print options and print all the worksheets using a single command.

LESSON OBJECTIVES

After studying this lesson, you will be able to:

- Change the default number of sheets for new workbooks
- Create formulas that summarize data from multiple worksheets
- Copy worksheets and their formats
- Create cell names for navigation and formulas
- Construct hyperlinks to worksheet cells and external documents
- Print multiple worksheets of a workbook

Case Study: Tracking Grant Expenditures

Folsom Technical College has just received its annual funding grant. Anthony Ngo, the finance department director, has allocated the grant money to various budget categories. Anthony needs a workbook that tracks the year-to-date expenditures and consolidates the information on a summary worksheet. The summary worksheet will give Anthony an instant overview of the amounts spent compared to the budget allocations. The workbook will be dynamic. Formulas in the summary worksheet will be linked to cells in the detail sheets, where all the necessary detail information will be stored. The following illustrations show the summary worksheet and three of the detail sheets that you will create in this lesson.

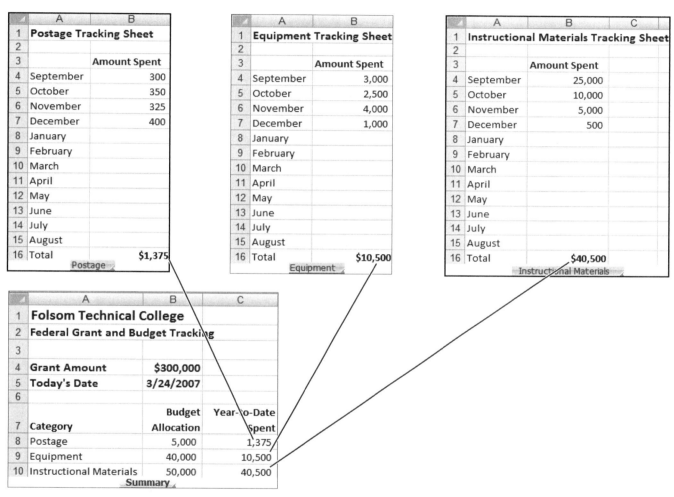

The summary worksheet tracks the totals from the detail sheets.

Using Multiple Worksheets

You may add worksheets in a workbook, limited only to the amount of available memory on your computer. Worksheets may also be deleted as necessary. Much like pages in a word processor document, multiple worksheets are a convenient way to organize your data logically into more manageable sections. Any worksheet can contain formulas that perform calculations on data contained in other worksheets. For example, you may set up a summary worksheet that totals data from multiple detail worksheets.

Modifying the Default Number of Sheets

Each new workbook contains three worksheets. You may change the default number of sheets for new workbooks using the Excel Options dialog box. Changing the default number can save time if your workbooks typically contain only one worksheet or more than three sheets.

 Hands-On 10.1   Change the Default for Sheets in Workbooks

In this exercise, you will change the number of sheets in new workbooks, test the change, and restore the default to three.

1. Open Excel.

2. Choose Office [image]→Excel Options to display the Popular options in the Excel Options dialog box.

3. Follow these steps to change the default number of sheets in a workbook:

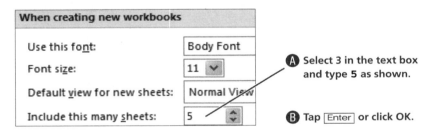

4. Use ⌐Ctrl⌐+⌐N⌐ to start a new workbook.
   Notice the five sheet tabs at the bottom of the worksheet window.

5. Display the Excel Options dialog box again.

6. Change the default number of sheets back to **3** and click OK.

7. Use ⌐Ctrl⌐+⌐N⌐ to verify that the number of sheets is three.

8. Taking care not to close the Excel program window, close ⌐x⌐ the open workbooks. Choose No if you are prompted to save either workbook.

Linking Cells and Formulas

Excel lets you link cells from different worksheets in the same workbook or in other workbooks. Linking lets you place values from a source worksheet into a destination worksheet. This powerful capability is the glue that binds worksheets together.

Why Link Cells?

Linking often is used to create totals in summary worksheets from values in detail worksheets. This lets you keep detailed information in the detail sheets and see the totals in the summary worksheet. This capability reflects the needs of many organizations. For example, top-level managers usually are interested in seeing the big picture, while detailed information is needed at the departmental level. Because the original data are entered only once, linking ensures that all references to the data are accurate. If the contents of the original cells are changed, the appropriate cell in the summary worksheet updates automatically.

Linking Formulas

You link cells by creating a linking formula in the summary worksheet. Linking formulas specify cells from the detail worksheets. You must use specific syntax—or language—when creating a linking formula.

Creating Linking Formulas

As with normal formulas, before you create a linking formula, you must select the cell in the summary worksheet where you want the result to appear. Also as with all other formulas, a linking formula begins with the equals (=) sign. You may type a linking formula, but using the mouse to select cells is more accurate and highly recommended.

Linking Cells from Other Worksheets in Formulas

The formulas shown will link the contents of one cell from a detail worksheet to a cell in the summary worksheet. The sheet name and cell reference are separated by an exclamation point (!). If the sheet name contains spaces or other nonalphabetic characters, the sheet name must be surrounded by single quotes ('), as in the second example.

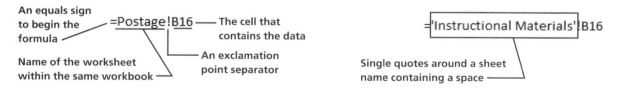

You may create calculation formulas on a summary worksheet using data from one or more detail worksheets. The following example sums the sales from four quarterly sheets to result in the yearly total. Notice that you may use commas to separate the four cell references. You will learn how to use 3-D cell references in Lesson 14, Auditing and Additional Functions to create a more powerful formula for this type of calculation.

=SUM(Quarter1!D18, Quarter2!D18, Quarter3!D18, Quarter4!D18)

Linking Cells from Other Workbooks in Formulas

If the source cell is in a different workbook, you must include the full workbook name in square brackets. Because the example workbook name contains a space, single quotes (') are included before the workbook name and after the worksheet name. Selecting the cell with the mouse will add all of this syntax for you.

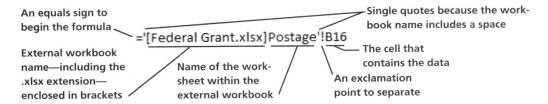

An equals sign to begin the formula

Single quotes because the workbook name includes a space

External workbook name—including the .xlsx extension—enclosed in brackets

Name of the worksheet within the external workbook

The cell that contains the data

An exclamation point to separate

 Hands-On 10.2   Create a Linking Formula

In this exercise, you will create a formula to link a cell in the Postage worksheet to the Summary worksheet.

Browse the Workbook

1. Open the Federal Grant workbook from the Lesson 10 folder in your file storage location.

2. Maximize the window.

3. Select cell B4 in the Summary worksheet and notice that the cell contains the number $300,000.
    This is the grant amount awarded to Folsom Technical College for the current school year.

4. Select cell B5 and notice that the cell contains the TODAY function.
    This cell will always display the current date.

5. Review the categories in column A and the budget allocations in column B.
    The budget allocations add up to $300,000, as shown in cell B19. As you can see, the total budgeted is equal to the total grant of $300,000.

6. Review column C and notice that these cells will contain the Year-to-Date Spent numbers.
    The cells in column C will be linked to the year-to-date expenditure totals in the detail sheets, such as Postage and others you will add.

7. Review column D.
    The Available Balance in column D will be the difference between the Budget Allocation in column B and the Year-to-Date Spent total in column C. Column D will show the remaining budgeted amount for each category.

Create a Total Formula in a Detail Worksheet

8. Display the Postage worksheet.
    The amount spent on postage is entered for each month to date. You will link the total in cell B16 to cell C8 in the Summary worksheet.

9. Select cell B16 and use Home→Editing→AutoSum Σ to calculate the column total.
    The total should equal $975. Notice that AutoSum summed the entire range B4:B15. This is desirable because AutoSum will keep a running total as you enter data throughout the year.

    The text in cells A1 and B3 is smaller than that of other cells; you will apply formatting in a later exercise.

Create Linking Formulas Using Point Mode

You may use point mode to create linking formulas as you do with other formulas.

10. Display the Summary worksheet.

11. Select cell C8 and type an equals (**=**) sign.
    Excel displays the equals sign in the Formula Bar.

12. Display the Postage worksheet.
    Excel displays the Postage worksheet. The sheet name Postage appears in the Formula Bar followed by an exclamation point.

13. Select cell B16.
    The linking formula =Postage!B16 displays in the Formula Bar.

14. Complete the formula by clicking the Enter ☑ button on the Formula Bar or tapping
    Enter.
    Excel displays the Summary worksheet with the completed link in cell C8. The number 975 appears in cell C8. Notice that the formula instructs Excel to link to cell B16 in the Postage worksheet. The exclamation point separates the two arguments (parts of the formula).

15. Display the Postage worksheet.

16. Select cell B7 and type **400**.
    The total in cell B16 displays $1,375.

17. Display the Summary worksheet.
    Cell C8 now displays $1,375. The link is dynamic, always reflecting the current value in the source cell.

18. Save 🖫 the changes.

Calculate the Available Balance

19. In the Summary worksheet, select cell D8 and use point mode to subtract cell C8 from cell B8.
    If your result does not equal 3,625, make certain that the cell references in the formula are in the correct order for subtraction. You will complete the remaining formulas for columns C and D in a later exercise.

20. Save 🖫 the changes and leave the workbook open.

Copying Worksheets

The Folsom grant and budget workbook eventually will contain more expenditure worksheets with the same structure as the Postage worksheet. Rather than inserting new blank sheets, you may use the Move or Copy Sheet command to copy an existing worksheet and then edit the duplicate. You learned how to move worksheets within the same workbook in Lesson 6, Discovering the Magic of Excel Charting.

The Move or Copy Dialog Box

A *copied* worksheet created with the Move or Copy Sheet command is an exact duplicate of the original worksheet. The data, structure, print settings, and page setup settings are identical to the original worksheet. To move or copy a worksheet to another workbook, both workbooks must be open. Placing a checkmark in the Create a Copy box creates a *copy*. Leaving the box blank *moves* the selected worksheet. A worksheet moved to another workbook no longer exists in the original workbook.

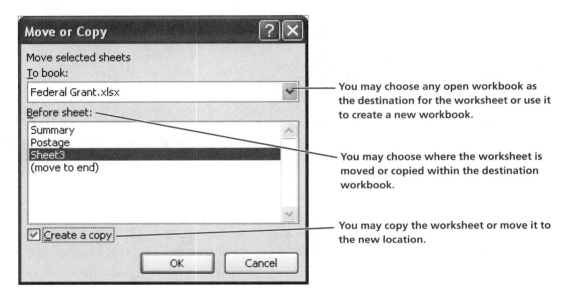

You may choose any open workbook as the destination for the worksheet or use it to create a new workbook.

You may choose where the worksheet is moved or copied within the destination workbook.

You may copy the worksheet or move it to the new location.

QUICK REFERENCE: COPYING AND MOVING WORKSHEETS

Task	Procedure
Copy or move a worksheet using the Ribbon	■ Select the desired sheet tab to be copied or moved. ■ Choose Home→Cells→Format →Move or Copy Sheet from the Ribbon. or ■ Right-click the sheet tab and choose Move or Copy from the pop-up (or context) menu. ■ Choose the destination workbook or (New Book) for a new blank workbook from the To Book list. ■ Select the worksheet position from the Before Sheet list. ■ To copy, place a checkmark in the Create a Copy box. To move, leave the box empty.
Copy or move a worksheet in the same workbook using the mouse	■ To move, drag the sheet tab to the desired location within the tabs. ■ To copy, hold down Ctrl and drag the sheet tab.

 Hands-On 10.3   Create a Copy of a Worksheet

In this exercise, you will make two copies of the Postage worksheet to create new sheets named Equipment and Instructional Materials.

NOTE! *Scroll through the sheet tabs using the ◄ and ► buttons if any tab is not visible during the exercise.*

Create the Equipment Worksheet

1. Display the Postage worksheet in the Federal Grant workbook.
   The active worksheet always is the worksheet that is copied.

2. Choose Home→Cells→Format ▦→Move or Copy Sheet from the Ribbon.

3. Follow these steps to create a copy of the Postage worksheet.

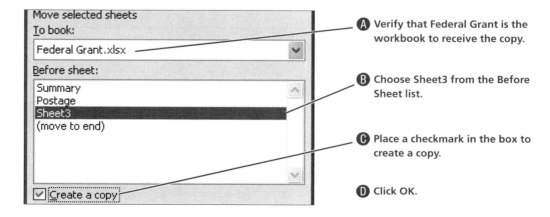

Ⓐ Verify that Federal Grant is the workbook to receive the copy.

Ⓑ Choose Sheet3 from the Before Sheet list.

Ⓒ Place a checkmark in the box to create a copy.

Ⓓ Click OK.

Excel positions the duplicate worksheet before Sheet3 and names it Postage (2).

4. Double-click the Postage (2) sheet tab, type the new name **Equipment**, and tap Enter to rename the sheet.

Edit the Title and Number Entries in the Equipment Worksheet

5. Double-click cell A1 to position the insertion point in the cell.

6. Double-click again on the word Postage to select it.

7. Type the word **Equipment** and complete the entry.
The title now should read Equipment Tracking Sheet.

8. Change the numbers in the range B4:B7 as shown in the following illustration:

	A	B
1	Equipment Tracking Sheet	
2		
3		Amount Spent
4	September	3,000
5	October	2,500
6	November	4,000
7	December	1,000

Notice that cell B16 contains a sum formula. Copying a worksheet includes all cell contents and formatting from the original worksheet.

9. Save [💾] the changes.

Create the Instructional Materials Worksheet

You will use the context menu to select the Move or Copy Sheet command.

10. Display the Postage worksheet.

11. Right-click the Postage sheet tab and choose Move or Copy from the context menu.

12. As you did previously in the Move or Copy dialog box, choose Sheet3 from the Before Sheet list, place a checkmark in the Create a Copy box, and click OK.

13. Change the name of the new sheet to **Instructional Materials**.
The sheet tabs should look like those shown. If necessary, drag a sheet tab to the correct position in the worksheet order.

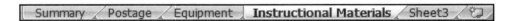

Summary / Postage / Equipment / **Instructional Materials** / Sheet3

14. Edit the title in cell A1 of the Instructional Materials worksheet and change the numbers in the range B4:B7 as shown in the following illustration:

	A	B	C
1	Instructional Materials Tracking Sheet		
2			
3		Amount Spent	
4	September	25,000	
5	October	10,000	
6	November	2,500	
7	December	500	

Create the Mileage Worksheet

15. Display the Postage worksheet.

16. Right-click the Postage sheet tab and choose Move or Copy from the context menu.

17. Choose options in the Move or Copy dialog box to create a copy to be positioned before Sheet3, and click OK.

18. Change the name of the new sheet to **Mileage**.

19. Edit the title in cell A1 of the Mileage worksheet and change the numbers in the range B4:B7 as shown in the following illustration:

	A	B
1	Mileage Tracking Sheet	
2		
3		Amount Spent
4	September	2,000
5	October	1,700
6	November	1,280
7	December	1,000

Delete the Sheet3 Worksheet

Recall that the default number of worksheets for a new workbook is three. You will delete Sheet3, as it is not needed.

20. Display the Sheet3 worksheet.

21. Right-click the Sheet3 tab and choose Delete from the context menu. Choose Delete in the Microsoft Office Excel dialog box to confirm.

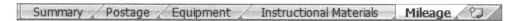

Summary Postage Equipment Instructional Materials Mileage

Copy the Salaries Worksheet from a Different Workbook

When you move or copy a worksheet to a different workbook, both files must be open.

22. Open the Salaries workbook from the Lesson 10 folder.

23. Right-click the Salaries sheet tab and choose Move or Copy from the context menu.

24. Follow these steps to copy the Salaries worksheet:

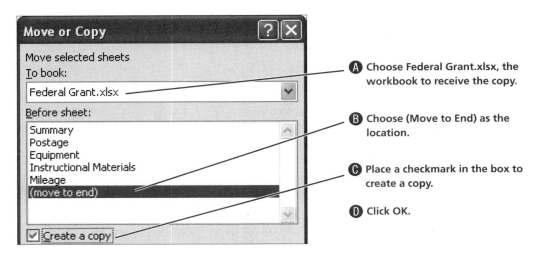

Excel positions the Salaries worksheet after the Mileage worksheet in the Federal Grant workbook.

25. Close ⊠ the Salaries workbook.

26. Save 🖫 the changes to the Federal Grant workbook and leave it open.

Copying Formats between Worksheets

Excel provides two ways to copy just the cell formatting from one worksheet to another without copying the text or numbers in the cells:

- The Format Painter

- The Paste Special command

You may want to copy the format of titles, headings, and numbers from one worksheet to other sheets to give them a unified appearance. You also may want to copy formatting into new worksheets in which the data will be entered later.

Format Painter

FROM THE KEYBOARD

`Ctrl`+`A` to select all

Use the Format Painter 🖌 tool on the Home Ribbon to copy formatting to cells in the target worksheet. The Format Painter was introduced in Lesson 4, Formatting the Contents of Cells. You may select any of the following before using the Format Painter button: one or more cells, columns, or rows, or the entire worksheet. The column width or row height is not applied unless you select an entire column or row before using Format Painter.

> **!TIP!** *Use the Select All ◢ button above the top-left corner of the worksheet to select the entire worksheet.*

Paste Special

You may use the Copy and Paste Special commands to limit the type of formatting that is applied to the target cells. Use this method when it is not desirable to copy all the formatting from selected cells. For example, you may apply just the column width from a selected cell. The following illustration shows the Paste Special dialog box.

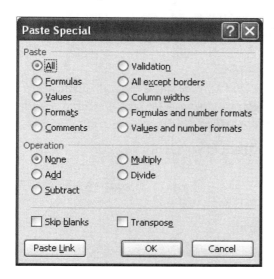

By using the Paste options in the Paste Special dialog box, you may limit the types of formatting and content that are transferred to the target cells.

 ## Hands-On 10.4 Copy Formats

In this exercise, you will use the Format Painter to copy formatting from the Summary worksheet to the Postage worksheet. You also will apply formatting from the Postage worksheet to the three worksheets you created in Hands-On 10.3.

Copy Formatting from the Summary Worksheet to the Postage Worksheet

1. Display the Summary worksheet in the Federal Grant workbook and select cell A2.
   You will copy the text format from this subheading to the heading in the Postage worksheet.

2. Choose Home→Clipboard→Format Painter ![icon] from the Ribbon.
   Cell A2 displays a marquee, and the mouse pointer changes to a block cross with a paintbrush.

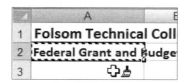

3. Display the Postage worksheet.

4. Select cell A1, and the format is copied to that cell.
   The font in cell A1 now has the same dark blue color and size as the subheading in the Summary worksheet. Notice that you may switch to any worksheet after the Format Painter has been activated.

5. Display the Summary worksheet and select cell A4.

6. Choose Format Painter ![Format Painter icon] from the Ribbon.

7. Display the Postage worksheet and select cell B3 to copy the format to that cell.

8. Display the Summary worksheet and select cells A19 and B19 (the cells in the Total row).

9. Choose Format Painter ![Format Painter icon] from the Ribbon.

10. Display the Postage worksheet and select cell A16 (the first cell in the Total row).
    Bold and the Currency Style number format are copied to cells A16:B16.

Copy All Formats to Another Worksheet

The Postage, Equipment, Instructional Materials, and Mileage sheets have an identical structure and format. You will use the Format Painter to copy all formatting—for text, numbers, column widths, and row heights—from the Postage worksheet to the other sheets.

11. Display the Postage worksheet, if not already displayed.

12. Click the Select All ![Select All button] button.

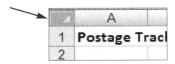

    The entire Postage worksheet is selected.

13. Choose Format Painter ![Format Painter icon] from the Ribbon.

14. Display the Equipment worksheet, and then click the Select All ![Select All button] button.
    Excel applies the Format Painter command to the entire selection.

15. Click anywhere in the worksheet to deselect the cells.
    The entire worksheet has the same formatting as the Postage worksheet. Notice that this technique creates consistent formatting between worksheets (provided they have an identical structure).

16. In the Equipment worksheet, click the Select All ![Select All button] button.

17. Double-click Format Painter ![Format Painter icon] on the Ribbon.
    Double-clicking the Format Painter button lets you apply the format as many times as needed.

18. Display the Instructional Materials worksheet and click the Select All ![Select All button] button.
    Notice that the Format Painter is still active.

19. Display the Mileage worksheet and click the Select All ![Select All button] button.

20. Click Format Painter ![Format Painter icon] on the Ribbon to deactivate it.

21. Click anywhere in the worksheet to deselect the highlighted cells.

Deselect Cells

22. Take a few moments to review the various sheets and deselect highlighted cells.
    Entire ranges may still appear selected from a previous use of Format Painter. Clearing the selections prevents cell contents from being changed or deleted accidentally.

23. Save ![Save icon] the changes.

Edit the Mileage Worksheet

24. Display the Mileage worksheet.

25. Change the cell B3 heading to **Mileage**, and click the Align Text Right ▤ button on the Ribbon.
The numbers in column B are the number of miles driven in a given month. You will add another column to calculate the actual mileage expense. The mileage expense is calculated as the number of miles multiplied by a cost of 32 cents per mile.

26. Select cell C3 and enter the heading **Mileage Expense**.

27. Select cell C4 and enter the formula **=B4*.32**.
The result should equal 640.00 or 640. You will standardize the cell formatting in a moment.

28. Use the fill handle to copy the formula down the column to row 15.
Some of the cells will display zeros or dashes (depending on the default settings on your computer) because some values have not yet been entered into column B.

29. Use the AutoSum Σ button to calculate the total mileage expense in cell C16.

Format the Mileage Worksheet

30. Use Format Painter 🖌 to copy the format from range B3:B16 to C3.
You need select only the first cell of the destination range. The formatting is applied to the other cells in the same direction as the source cells.

31. Use Format Painter 🖌 to copy the Comma Style format from cell B4 to cell B16.
The Total should not display a dollar sign.

Use the Paste Special Command

The label in cell C3 now is right aligned and does not display entirely. In the next steps, you will apply just a column width from the Summary worksheet to column C.

32. Display the Summary worksheet.

33. Select cell A7 and choose the Copy 📋 command from the Ribbon.

34. Display the Mileage worksheet, select cell C3, and choose Home→Clipboard→Paste menu ▾→Paste Special.
The Paste Special dialog box displays.

35. Under Paste, choose Column Widths, and click OK.
Column C widens slightly, but no other formatting is applied from cell A7 in the Summary worksheet.

36. Display each worksheet in the workbook, and make certain that only one cell is selected in each and that the marquee around cell A7 is deactivated in the Summary worksheet.

37. Save 💾 the changes and leave the workbook open.

Naming Cells and Ranges

You may use a descriptive name instead of cell references in formulas and for worksheet navigation. Range names are easier to type, recognize, and remember. Excel refers to these as *defined names*. You may create a name for one cell or a range of cells.

Naming Rules

Excel has a few rules for naming cells. Defined names:

- Must begin with a letter.

- Cannot resemble a cell reference, as in A3 or BC14.

- Cannot consist of the single letters C or R, which Excel interprets as column or row.

- Cannot contain spaces, hyphens, or symbols.

- May contain an underscore, period, or capital letter to connect words. Examples are Total_Sales, Total.Sales, and TotalSales.

Creating Defined Names

Defined names are available throughout a workbook by default. You may define a name in one worksheet and use the name to navigate to its cell reference(s) from within any other worksheet. You may create names using any of the following methods.

Name Box

You may create a name quickly by selecting the range and typing a name in the Name box of the Formula Bar above the upper-left corner of the worksheet. You must tap Enter after typing the name. If you simply click outside the Name box, the name will not be created.

The Name box

 TIP! *The Name box may be widened to view an entire name by dragging the curved border between the Name box and the Formula box.*

New Name Dialog Box

 The Define Name command displays the New Name dialog box, in which you may name a range and set its scope—or availability—to all worksheets in the workbook or just one worksheet. Usually you should leave Scope set to Workbook.

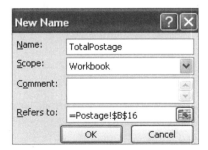

The New Name dialog box

Creating Cell Names from Row or Column Titles

 You may use existing row or column titles to name individual cells. These cells usually are adjacent to the title cells. You select both the titles and the cells to which you wish to assign the names and then use the Create from Selection command to create the names.

Using Defined Names

Defined names are used mainly to navigate workbooks and create linking formulas or calculation formulas.

Using Names to Navigate

Create defined names to move quickly to areas of the worksheet that you view or update frequently, such as a total, the first data cell at the top of a column, or a range of cells. To navigate to a named cell or range, you select its name from the Name list on the Formula Bar.

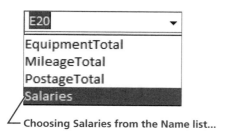

Choosing Salaries from the Name list...

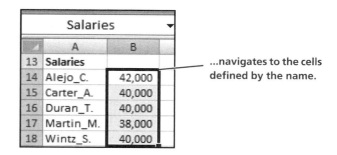

...navigates to the cells defined by the name.

Using Names in Formulas

Formulas containing defined names help others to understand what the formulas are calculating. For example, the formula =SUM(JuneExpenses) is easier to understand than =SUM(AJ4:AJ23). Workbook users might prefer the linking formula =TotalPostage, which uses a defined name, rather than =Postage!B16. You may substitute a defined name for cell references in any formula. You may type the defined name or select it from the Use in Formula list on the Ribbon.

> **!TIP!** *If the error message #NAME? displays in a cell instead of the formula result, compare the spelling of the name in the formula with the name in the Name list and make certain the name was not deleted.*

Modifying and Deleting Defined Names

2007 new!

Use the Name Manager dialog box to view all defined names and edit their properties. The dialog box was redesigned from the previous Excel version and includes property columns and filtering. You may add and delete names in Name Manager. Formulas will not work, however, after names have been deleted. You will need to re-create formulas that used any deleted name. You may select an existing name and edit the name or the cell(s) to which it refers by using the Collapse button.

FROM THE KEYBOARD
[Ctrl]+[F3] to open the Name Manager dialog box

> **!NOTE!** *If you copy a worksheet, Excel creates duplicate defined names with only a Worksheet scope. Neither the Name list on the Formula bar nor the Use in Formula list displays these names. You should re-create unique defined names with a Workbook scope and delete the previous names in the Name Manager.*

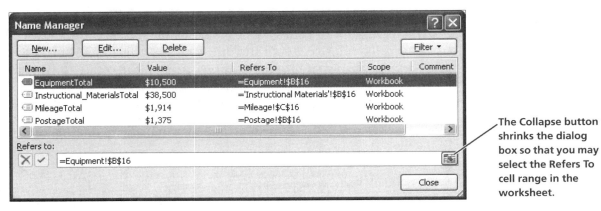

The Collapse button shrinks the dialog box so that you may select the Refers To cell range in the worksheet.

The Name Manager dialog box

⚠️ **WARNING!** *To change the Refers To entry, use the Collapse button and point mode to select cells in the worksheet. Do not use arrow keys to edit the entry, as Excel would insert cell references rather than move the cursor.*

QUICK REFERENCE: USING NAMED CELLS AND RANGES

Task	Procedure
Name cells	■ Select the range of cells, type a name in the Name box on the Formula Bar, and tap Enter.
Create names from existing row or column titles	■ Select the labels and the cells to which they will refer. ■ Choose Formulas→Defined Names→Create from Selection 🖼 from the Ribbon. ■ Place a checkmark to indicate the location of the labels.
Change a defined name	■ Choose Formulas→Defined Names→Name Manager 🗂 from the Ribbon. ■ In the Name Manager dialog box, choose an existing name and click Edit. ■ Edit the name.
Change the range to which a name refers	■ Choose Formulas→Defined Names→Name Manager 🗂 from the Ribbon. ■ In the Name Manager dialog box, choose an existing name. ■ Click the Collapse 🖼 button next to Refers To, select the new range in the worksheet, and click the Expand button. ■ Close ⊠ the Name Manager dialog box, and click Yes to confirm the change.
Delete a defined name	■ Choose Formulas→Defined Names→Name Manager 🗂 from the Ribbon. ■ Choose an existing name, click Delete, and click OK to confirm the change.
Navigate to a defined range	■ Choose the name from the Name list in the Formula Bar.

QUICK REFERENCE: USING NAMED CELLS AND RANGES (CONTINUED)

Task	Procedure
Use a defined name in a linking formula	■ Select the cell to contain the summary formula. ■ Choose Formulas→Defined Names→Use in Formula f_x from the Ribbon, choose the defined name, and tap Enter to complete the formula.
Use one or more defined names in a calculation formula	■ Select the cell to contain the formula. ■ Type the function beginning, such as =SUM(. ■ Choose Formulas→Defined Names→Use in Formula f_x from the Ribbon, choose the defined name, continue typing the formula and choosing defined names as needed, and tap Enter to complete the formula.

 Hands-On 10.5 Create and Use Cell Names

Navigating large workbooks becomes easier with defined names. In this exercise, you will create names for single cells and a cell range and then navigate to important areas of the workbook. You also will use defined names to create linking formulas.

!NOTE! *Scroll through the sheet tabs using the ◄ and ► buttons if any tab is not visible during the exercise.*

Create Names in the Name Box

1. Display the Equipment worksheet in the Federal Grant workbook and select cell B16.

2. Follow these steps to name the cell:

Ⓐ Click in the Name box at the left of the Formula Bar, which selects the B16 cell reference.

Ⓑ Type **EquipmentTotal** (do not include a space) and tap Enter.

Remember that range names may include capital letters, underscores, or periods, but no spaces.

You must tap Enter after typing the name. If you simply click outside the Name box, the name will not be created.

3. Select any cell other than B16.

4. Select cell B16 again.
   The Name box displays EquipmentTotal. The Name box displays the defined name or reference for the active cell.

5. Display the Instructional Materials worksheet and select cell B16.

6. Click in the Name box.

7. Type **Instructional_Materials_Total** (do not include a space) and tap Enter.
   The underscore character is inserted by holding down Shift and tapping the hyphen - key.

8. To view the entire name, drag the curved border between the Name box and the Formula box to the right.

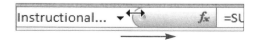

Create a Name in the New Name Dialog Box

9. Display the Mileage worksheet and select cell C16.

10. Choose Formulas→Defined Names→Define Name ⬚ from the Ribbon.

11. In the New Name dialog box, type the name **MileageTotal**.
    Notice that the Scope option is set to Workbook, allowing the defined name to be selected from within any worksheet in this workbook.

12. Click OK.

13. Save ⬚ the changes.

Use Names to Navigate

14. Choose EquipmentTotal from the Name list in the Formula Bar.
    The cell pointer moves to cell B16 in the Equipment worksheet.

15. Navigate to MileageTotal.
    Navigation is quick, and you do not need to memorize cell addresses.

Use Names to Create Linking Formulas

You will complete linking formulas on the Summary worksheet by using defined names.

16. Display the Summary worksheet.

17. Select cell C9, choose Formulas→Defined Names→Use in Formula ⬚ from the Ribbon, choose the defined name EquipmentTotal, and complete the formula.

18. Use the appropriate defined names to create linking formulas in cells C10 and C11.

19. Use the fill handle to copy the formula in D8 down to D11.
    Your totals should equal those shown.

	A	B	C	D
		Budget Allocation	Year-to-Date Spent	Available Balance
7	Category			
8	Postage	5,000	1,375	3,625
9	Equipment	40,000	10,500	29,500
10	Instructional Materials	50,000	38,000	12,000
11	Mileage	5,000	1,914	3,086

20. Save ⬚ the changes and leave the workbook open.

Create Names from Titles in a Column

Using a single command, you will assign names to each of the budgeted salary amounts in column B of the Summary worksheet.

21. Display the Summary worksheet if not already displayed.

22. Select the range A14:B18, as shown to the right.
    Notice that each employee name in column A contains an underscore (_) because you will use these names as the basis for defined names. Remember that defined names may not include spaces.

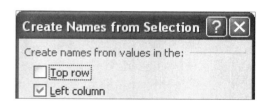

	A	B
13	Salaries	
14	Alejo_C.	42,000
15	Carter_A.	40,000
16	Duran_T.	40,000
17	Martin_M.	38,000
18	Wintz_S.	40,000

23. Choose Formulas→Defined Names→Create from Selection ⊞ from the Ribbon.

24. In the Create Names from Selection dialog box, make certain a checkmark is in the Left Column box and click OK.
    Your choice specifies which cells should be used for the names. In this step, the cells in the left column (column A) are used to name the cells in column B.

25. Select cell B14 and notice that Alejo_C. appears in the Name box.
    The defined name Alejo_C. was assigned to this cell.

26. Select cell B15 and notice that this cell has been assigned the name Carter_A.

27. Click the Name box drop-down arrow ▾ button and read the list of names.

Alejo_C.

Notice that the defined names for each employee's salary now appear in the list. Defined names are sorted in alphabetic order.

28. Tab [Esc] to collapse the Name list without making a selection.

Insert Linking Formulas in the Salaries Worksheet

You will use the names you just created to construct linking formulas in the Salaries worksheet. The linking formulas will reflect the budgeted amounts from column B of the Summary worksheet.

29. Display the Salaries worksheet.

30. Type **Budget** in cell A18.

31. Select cell B18.
    Next you will use a command that quickly creates a linking formula.

32. Choose Formulas→Defined Names→Use in Formula fx from the Ribbon, choose the defined name Alejo_C., and complete the formula.
   The number $42,000 appears. This is the budgeted salary amount for employee Alejo_C. from the Summary worksheet.

   Notice the linking formula in the Formula Bar. Excel added the equals (=) sign to the formula for you.

33. Select cell C18, choose Formulas→Defined Names→Use in Formula fx from the Ribbon, choose the defined name Carter_A., and complete the formula.

34. Create linking formulas in cells D18, E18, and F18.

35. Save the changes and leave the workbook open.

Creating Hyperlinks

FROM THE KEYBOARD
Ctrl+K to insert a hyperlink

A hyperlink is a piece of text or a graphic that takes the user to another location when clicked. Web pages use hyperlinks to navigate from one web page to another. You may create hyperlinks in Excel worksheets that work just like the ones on web pages. Hyperlinks help others to navigate to important items of data or to documents outside the workbook. You create links with the Hyperlink command on the Ribbon.

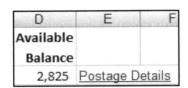

When a user clicks the Postage Details hyperlink, the pointer jumps to a cell in a different worksheet.

Types of Hyperlinks

You may create several types of links on a worksheet, including items inside or outside the workbook.

Internal Hyperlinks

■ **To cells in a workbook**—A hyperlink may point to a cell address or defined name in the workbook. You add hyperlink text or a graphic to a cell. The user may click the hyperlink on the worksheet rather than use the Name box to navigate.

Hyperlinks to External Sources

■ **To another file**—A hyperlink can open a Word document containing information related to a workbook. Another hyperlink can open a different Excel workbook and point to a cell.

■ **To a web page**—A hyperlink can point to a page on the web or on a corporate intranet. You may launch Internet Explorer and navigate to the desired web page from within the Insert Hyperlink dialog box. Excel then places the web page URL into the dialog box to save you the complexity of typing the URL or pasting it from the address bar.

■ **To an email address**—A hyperlink can open an Office Outlook window to send an email message.

Insert Hyperlink Dialog Box

You choose the link type in the Insert Hyperlink dialog box. The dialog box options change for each type of link except for two options that are always available: Text to Display is the text description that the user clicks to activate the hyperlink, and the optional ScreenTip displays an instruction or other text when the user points to the hyperlink. The following illustration shows the dialog box entries for jumping to a worksheet cell.

Hyperlinks may link to various locations, such as cells in workbooks, web pages, non-Excel files, and email addresses.

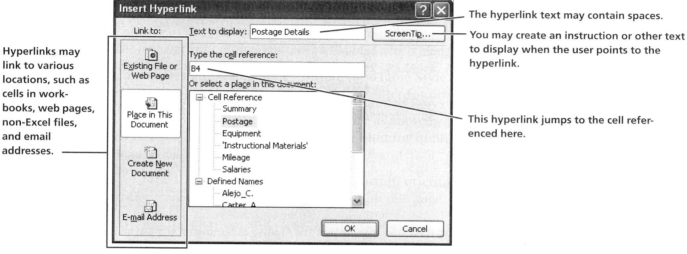

The hyperlink text may contain spaces.

You may create an instruction or other text to display when the user points to the hyperlink.

This hyperlink jumps to the cell referenced here.

Creating a hyperlink to jump to a cell in a different worksheet of the same workbook

Editing and Removing Hyperlinks

You may edit a hyperlink to change the type of destination and specific location to which it points. For example, you may edit a hyperlink that points to a web page so that it points to a Word document (or some other type of file) instead. Although you may use the Remove Hyperlink command, you probably will find it more efficient to use Delete to erase the hyperlink contents from a cell.

QUICK REFERENCE: CREATING, EDITING, AND REMOVING HYPERLINKS

Task	Procedure
Insert a hyperlink to a cell reference in the same workbook	■ Select the cell or graphic to contain the hyperlink. ■ Choose Insert→Links→Hyperlink ⬛ from the Ribbon or use Ctrl+K from the keyboard. ■ Choose the Place in This Document option. ■ Type a brief description in the Text to Display box. ■ Type the desired target cell in the Type the Cell Reference box. ■ Choose the desired worksheet from the Cell Reference list.
Insert a hyperlink to a named cell or range in the same workbook	■ Select the cell or graphic to contain the hyperlink. ■ Choose Insert→Links→Hyperlink ⬛ from the Ribbon or use Ctrl+K from the keyboard. ■ Choose the Place in This Document option. ■ Type a brief description in the Text to Display box. ■ Choose the desired name from the Defined Names list.

QUICK REFERENCE: CREATING, EDITING, AND REMOVING HYPERLINKS (CONTINUED)

Task	Procedure
Insert a hyperlink to a cell reference in a different workbook	■ Select the cell or graphic to contain the hyperlink. ■ Choose Insert→Links→Hyperlink from the Ribbon or use [Ctrl]+[K] from the keyboard. ■ Choose the Existing File or Web Page option. ■ Type a brief description in the Text to Display box. ■ Navigate to the desired file storage location and choose the desired file. ■ Click Bookmark to display the Select Place in Document dialog box. ■ Type the desired target cell in the Type in the Cell Reference box. ■ Choose the desired worksheet from the Cell Reference list and click OK.
Insert a hyperlink to a non-Excel file	■ Select the cell or graphic to contain the hyperlink. ■ Choose Insert→Links→Hyperlink from the Ribbon or use [Ctrl]+[K] from the keyboard. ■ Choose the Existing File or Web Page option. ■ Type a brief description in the Text to Display box. ■ Navigate to the desired file storage location and choose the desired file.
Insert a hyperlink to a web page	■ Select the cell or graphic to contain the hyperlink. ■ Choose Insert→Links→Hyperlink from the Ribbon or use [Ctrl]+[K] from the keyboard. ■ Choose the Existing File or Web Page option. ■ Type a brief description in the Text to Display box. ■ Click the Browse the Web button. ■ Navigate to the desired web page for the link. ■ Activate the Excel window, and the URL appears automatically in the Address text box of the Insert Hyperlink dialog box.
Edit an existing hyperlink	■ Right-click the hyperlink you wish to edit and choose Edit Hyperlink from the context menu. ■ Make the desired changes in the Edit Hyperlink dialog box and click OK.
Delete a hyperlink	■ Select the cell or graphic containing the hyperlink. ■ Right-click, and then choose Remove Hyperlink from the context menu.

Hands-On 10.6   Create Hyperlinks

In this exercise, you will create one link to a cell on a worksheet and another link to a Word document. You will edit one of the hyperlinks by adding a ScreenTip.

Create a Hyperlink to a Worksheet Cell

1. Display the Summary worksheet in the Federal Grant workbook.

2. Select cell E8 and choose Insert→Links→Hyperlink 🌐 from the Ribbon.
   You will create a link that points to the first detail cell in the Postage worksheet.

3. Follow these steps to create the hyperlink:

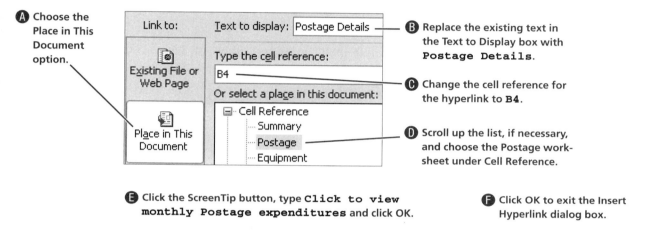

Ⓐ Choose the Place in This Document option.

Ⓑ Replace the existing text in the Text to Display box with **Postage Details**.

Ⓒ Change the cell reference for the hyperlink to **B4**.

Ⓓ Scroll up the list, if necessary, and choose the Postage worksheet under Cell Reference.

Ⓔ Click the ScreenTip button, type **Click to view monthly Postage expenditures** and click OK.

Ⓕ Click OK to exit the Insert Hyperlink dialog box.

A color change and underscore indicate that cell E8 contains a hyperlink.

Create a Hyperlink to a File

4. Display the Salaries worksheet.

5. Select cell G18 and choose Insert→Links→Hyperlink 🌐 from the Ribbon.

6. Follow these steps to create the hyperlink:

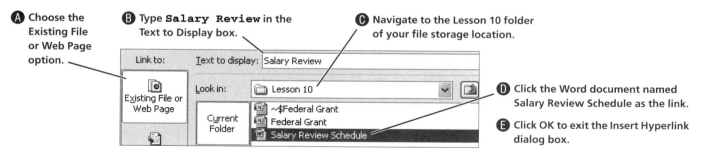

Ⓐ Choose the Existing File or Web Page option.

Ⓑ Type **Salary Review** in the Text to Display box.

Ⓒ Navigate to the Lesson 10 folder of your file storage location.

Ⓓ Click the Word document named Salary Review Schedule as the link.

Ⓔ Click OK to exit the Insert Hyperlink dialog box.

The text to display appears with an underscore to indicate its hyperlink status.

Edit a Hyperlink

7. Point the mouse on cell G18 (but do not click) to display its ScreenTip.
   If you do not enter your own ScreenTip text, Excel displays the path to the hyperlink item, such as file:///F:\ Lesson 10\ Salary Review Schedule.docx.

8. Right-click on the hyperlink display text in cell G18 and choose Edit Hyperlink from the context menu.

9. In the Edit Hyperlink dialog box, click the ScreenTip button, type **Click to view schedule** and click OK.

10. Click OK to exit the Edit Hyperlink dialog box.

11. Point the mouse on cell G18 (but do not click) to display your ScreenTip.

Navigate with the Hyperlinks

12. Display the Summary worksheet and click the hyperlink in cell E8.
    Excel jumps to cell B4 on the Postage worksheet.

13. Display the Salaries worksheet and click the hyperlink in cell G18.
    Word launches and displays the linked document. Hyperlinks also may be created to other Excel workbooks or any other type of document file.

14. Close ☒ the Word window.

15. Save 🖫 the changes and leave the workbook open.

Printing Multiple-Sheet Workbooks

Excel prints the active worksheet when you choose the Quick Print 🖨 command. If you are working with a multiple-sheet workbook, you may use various techniques to set options and print multiple sheets at one time.

Applying Page Setup Options to Multiple Sheets

In Lesson 7, Working with Large Worksheets, you learned how to adjust the margins, page orientation, headers and footers, and a variety of other settings that affect the printed worksheet. You may apply these settings to multiple worksheets by first using Ctrl to select nonadjacent sheet tabs or Shift to select adjacent sheet tabs.

Printing All Sheets in a Workbook

You may print all sheets in a workbook by using Shift to select the sheet tabs and choosing the Quick Print command. As an alternative, you may print all sheets without selecting their tabs by choosing the Entire Workbook option in the Print dialog box.

Printing Selected Sheets

You may print only certain sheets by using Ctrl to select the desired sheet tabs and choosing Print or Quick Print.

Hands-On 10.7   Preview and Print Selected Sheets

In this exercise, you will select multiple sheets, change their orientation, and preview them all at once.

Select Multiple Adjacent Sheets

1. Display the Summary worksheet in the Federal Grant workbook.

2. With the Summary worksheet active, hold down [Shift] and click the Instructional Materials sheet tab.

Four sheets appear selected. Using [Shift] selected the continuous range of sheets from the active sheet tab through the sheet tab that you clicked.

3. Choose Page Layout→Page Setup→Orientation→Landscape.
The Mileage and Salaries sheets remain in portrait orientation because you did not include them in the selected sheets.

4. Choose Office→ 🗐 Print ▸→Print 🖨 from the Ribbon.
Notice that the Active Sheet(s) option is selected. The four sheets are active and would print if you were to click OK. Do not print.

5. Click the Preview button in the Print dialog box.
Print Preview displays.

6. Use the Next Page 🗐 command to browse through the worksheets.
Notice that four sheets are available because you selected them prior to choosing Print Preview. Their orientation is landscape.

7. Click Close Print Preview ⊠.

Deselect Sheet Tabs

8. Click on any unselected sheet tab or right-click any sheet tab and choose Ungroup Sheets from the context menu.
Now only one sheet tab appears selected.

Select Multiple Nonadjacent Sheets

9. Display the Postage worksheet.

10. Hold down [Ctrl], click the Mileage sheet tab, click the Equipment sheet tab, and then release [Ctrl].
Three sheets are selected. Using [Ctrl] allows you to select certain sheets in any order.

11. Ungroup the sheets.
Now only one worksheet is active.

Select All Sheets in the Workbook for Printing

12. Choose Office 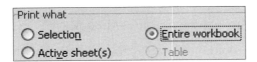 →Print ⬛ from the Ribbon.

13. In the Print dialog box, select the Entire Workbook option.

Print what
- ○ Selection   ● Entire workbook
- ○ Active sheet(s)   ○ Table

You may use this option to print the entire workbook without first selecting the sheets. Do not print.

14. Click Cancel to exit from the Print dialog box without printing.

15. Save 💾 and close ⊠ the workbook.

Concepts Review

True/False Questions

1. You may change the default number of worksheets for new workbooks. TRUE FALSE

2. While creating a linking formula, you may type the entire formula or point to the target cell with the mouse. TRUE FALSE

3. Worksheets may be moved or copied only within the same workbook. TRUE FALSE

4. The Hyperlink command may be used to copy formats between worksheets. TRUE FALSE

5. The Select All [ ] button may be used to select all worksheets in the workbook. TRUE FALSE

6. The defined name June_Sales follows Excel's rules for naming ranges. TRUE FALSE

7. Spaces are allowed in a defined name. TRUE FALSE

8. After you delete a defined name, the cells that used the name in a formula will display an error message. TRUE FALSE

9. By default, defined names may be used only within the worksheet in which they were created. TRUE FALSE

10. You may select multiple sheet tabs for printing even if they are not adjacent. TRUE FALSE

Multiple Choice Questions

1. Which of the following best describes the formula =January!M5?
   a. Indicates that cell M5 contains an error
   b. Links the active cell to cell M5 in the January worksheet of the same workbook
   c. Links the active cell to a cell named M5 in the January workbook
   d. Sums the cells named January and displays the total in cell M5

2. Which command is used to apply specific formatting rather than all formatting from the selected cells?
   a. Paste Special
   b. Tab
   c. Format Painter
   d. Font Copy

3. Which of the following allows you to edit and delete defined names in the workbook?
   a. Paste Special dialog box
   b. Insert Hyperlink dialog box
   c. Name box in the Formula Bar
   d. Name Manager dialog box

4. To which of the following items may you jump by creating a hyperlink?
   a. Only a cell in the active worksheet
   b. Only a cell in an Excel workbook
   c. Only a page on the web or a corporate intranet
   d. A cell, another file, or a page on the web or a corporate intranet

Skill Builders

Skill Builder 10.1 Copy and Format Worksheets

In this exercise, you will copy a worksheet twice to create three identical worksheets. You will then use the Format Painter to ensure consistent formatting among the sheets. Finally, you will name a range and use the name in a formula.

1. Open the sb-Testing workbook from the Lesson 10 folder on your file storage location.

2. Maximize ☐ the window.

3. Select cell B10 and choose Home→AutoSum Σ ▾ menu ▾→Average from the Ribbon. *Excel will propose the formula =Average(B6:B9).*

4. Click the AutoSum Σ button on the Ribbon to accept the proposed formula. *The formula result is 18.5.*

5. Copy the formula to cells C10 and D10.

6. Deselect the highlighted cells.

Copy a Worksheet

You will make two copies of the Test1 worksheet to be named Test2 and Test3.

7. Right-click the Test1 sheet tab and select Move or Copy from the context menu.

8. Make selections in the Move or Copy Sheet dialog box to place a copy after the Test1 worksheet and then click OK.

9. Copy the Test1 worksheet again.

10. Rename the new sheets as **Test2** and **Test3**.

11. Change the headings in row 3 of the Test2 and Test3 sheets to **Test 2** and **Test 3**.

12. Change a few of the numbers in the Test2 and Test3 sheets so the sheets contain different data.

Format the Test1 Worksheet

13. Display the Test1 worksheet, and then select cell A1.

14. Increase the font size to 14 and apply a font color **A** ▾ to the text.

15. Select cell A3 and increase the size to 12. Click the Font Color **A** button (not its menu arrow) to apply the same color that you used in the previous step.

16. Format the Average row in any way that you want.

Copy the Worksheet Formatting

17. Click the Select All ▨ button to select the entire worksheet.

18. Double-click the Format Painter ✎ button on the Ribbon.

19. Display the Test2 worksheet.

20. Click the Select All ▨ button to copy the formats to that worksheet.
    The Format Painter should still be active, so you may apply formatting again.

21. Display the Test3 worksheet and copy the formats to that worksheet.
    You were able to copy the formats in this manner because the sheets have an identical structure.

22. Click the Format Painter ✎ button on the Ribbon to deactivate it.

23. Display each worksheet and deselect the highlighted cells.

Create Defined Names and Construct Formulas

24. Display the Test1 worksheet.

25. Select the range B10:D10 and tap Delete to erase the average formulas.

26. Select the Ozone data in the range B6:B9.

27. Click in the Name box, type **Ozone**, and tap Enter.

28. Assign the name **Carbon_Monoxide** to the range C6:C9.

29. Assign the name **Particulate_Matter** to the range D6:D9.

30. Select cell B10, type the formula **=average(ozone)** and tap Enter to complete the formula.
    *After you type **=av** Excel may propose the AVERAGE function, and you may double-click Average. After you type a few letters of the defined name, Excel may propose Ozone, and you may double-click Ozone. The correct average, 18.5, should be displayed when you finish.*

31. Select cell C10 and type **=average(** and then choose Formulas→Defined Names→Use in Formula, choose Carbon_Monoxide, and tap Enter.

32. Enter an average formula in cell D10 using the name Particulate_Matter.

33. Save 🖫 the changes to the workbook then close ✕ it.

Skill Builder 10.2   Use Defined Names in Formulas

Several of your co-workers have collaborated on the Regional Sales workbook. In this exercise, you will create the remaining linking formulas to link the regional sheets with the National summary worksheet. You will create calculation formulas using defined names and correct the cell references for an important defined name.

Create Linking Formulas in the National Worksheet

1. Open the sb-Regional Sales workbook from the Lesson 10 folder.
   Take a few moments to browse the National summary worksheet and the three regional detail sheets, Eastern, Central, and Western. The detail sheets include sales figures for each of the four quarters in the year.

2. Choose Formulas→Defined Names→Name Manager 🖉 from the Ribbon to view all defined names and their properties.

3. Double-click the Refers To column border to autofit the contents.

Name	Value	Refers To	Scope
Central_Q1	$2,410,000	='Central Region'!$B$8	Workbook
Central_Q2	$1,875,000	='Central Region'!$C$8	Workbook
Central_Q3	$1,430,000	='Central Region'!$D$8	Workbook

Notice the defined names for Quarters 1–4. The National worksheet contains linking formulas to each of the defined cells for Quarters 1, 2, and 3. You will create linking formulas for Quarter 4.

4. Click the Close button to exit the Name Manager dialog box.

5. Display the National worksheet and select cell E4.
   This cell will contain a linked formula to the total for Q4 on the Eastern worksheet.

6. Choose Formulas→Defined Names→Use in Formula 🔎 from the Ribbon, choose Eastern_Q4, and click the Enter button on the Formula Bar or tap ⎣Enter⎦ to complete the formula.

7. Create linking formulas in cell E5 for the Central region and cell E6 for the Western region.

Q4
2,580,000
2,080,000
2,380,000
$ 7,040,000

Create Calculation Formulas in the National Worksheet

To help workbook users understand summing formulas more easily, you will use defined names rather than cell references to create totals formulas.

8. Select cell F4 in the National worksheet.

9. Choose Formulas→Defined Names→Use in Formula ![fx] →Eastern_Q1 from the Ribbon. *The command automatically starts the formula with an equals (=) sign.*

10. Tap the plus (+) sign on the keypad.

11. Use Eastern_Q2 in the formula and tap the plus (+) sign on the keypad.

12. Use Eastern_Q3 in the formula and tap the plus (+) sign on the keypad.

13. Use Eastern_Q4 in the formula.

14. Click the Enter button on the Formula Bar or tap (Enter) to complete the formula.

    =Eastern_Q1+ Eastern_Q2+Eastern_Q3+Eastern_Q4

    The total is $9,795,000.

15. Use the procedure from the previous steps to create a total formula in cell F5 for the Central region and cell F6 for the Western region.

Correct the Cell References for a Defined Name

16. Select cell F7 in the National worksheet.

Notice the formula in the Formula Bar. =SUM(Yearly_Sales) includes a defined name, but the result displays as a dash (—) or 0. Something clearly is not correct.

17. Choose Formulas→Defined Names→Name Manager 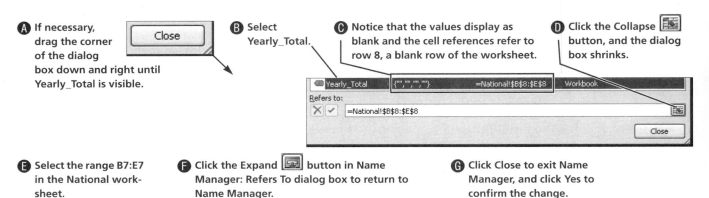 from the Ribbon and follow these steps to correct the error:

Ⓐ If necessary, drag the corner of the dialog box down and right until Yearly_Total is visible.

Ⓑ Select Yearly_Total.

Ⓒ Notice that the values display as blank and the cell references refer to row 8, a blank row of the worksheet.

Ⓓ Click the Collapse button, and the dialog box shrinks.

Ⓔ Select the range B7:E7 in the National worksheet.

Ⓕ Click the Expand button in Name Manager: Refers To dialog box to return to Name Manager.

Ⓖ Click Close to exit Name Manager, and click Yes to confirm the change.

The defined name now points to the correct cells, and the total displays as $26,585,000.

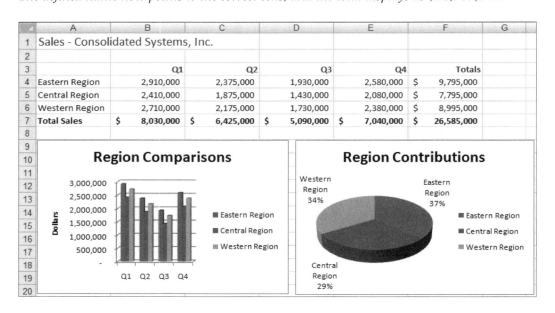

18. Save 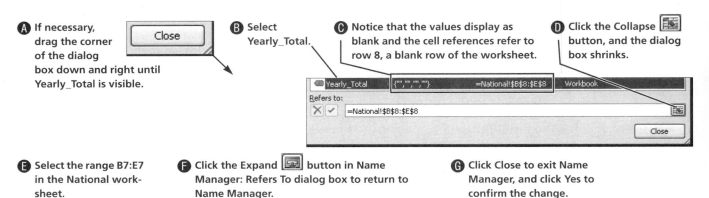 the changes to the workbook and continue with the next exercise.

Skill Builder 10.3   Create Hyperlinks

You will continue working on the sb-Regional Sales workbook. In this exercise, you will create a text hyperlink and graphic hyperlinks for workbook navigation.

Before You Begin: You must have completed Skill Builder 10.2, and the sb-Regional Sales workbook should be open.

Create a Text Hyperlink

1. Select cell D1 in the National worksheet.

2. Use ⌈Ctrl⌉+⌈K⌉ to open the Insert Hyperlink dialog box.

3. Follow these steps to create a text hyperlink to the Eastern worksheet:

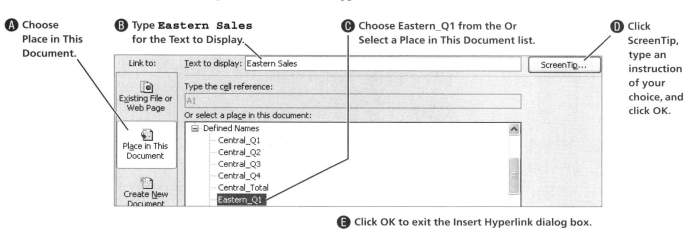

Ⓐ Choose Place in This Document.

Ⓑ Type **Eastern Sales** for the Text to Display.

Ⓒ Choose Eastern_Q1 from the Or Select a Place in This Document list.

Ⓓ Click ScreenTip, type an instruction of your choice, and click OK.

Ⓔ Click OK to exit the Insert Hyperlink dialog box.

4. Test the hyperlink by clicking the display text in cell D1.
   The pointer moves to the Q1 total on the Eastern worksheet.

Create Graphic Hyperlinks

You may link cells to buttons that you draw with the Shapes tools.

5. Display the National worksheet and select cell E1.

6. Choose Insert→Illustrations→Shapes→Rectangles→Rectangle ☐ shape tool from the Ribbon and drag to draw a rectangle in cell E1.
   While the shape is selected, you may type text in it. The cursor does not display until you begin typing.

7. Type **Central Sales** and do not tap ⌈Enter⌉.

8. Choose Format→Shape Styles→More ⏷ menu and select an effect that complements the workbook colors.
   Your button may look similar to the one shown.

   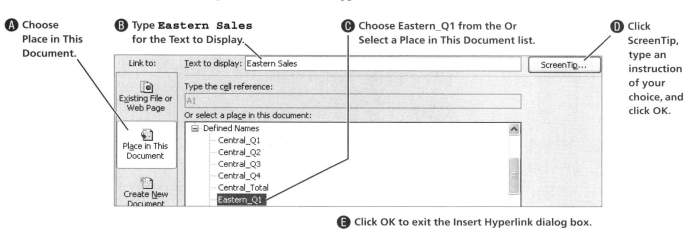
   Central Sales

9. Right-click the button you just created and choose Hyperlink from the context menu.

10. In the Insert Hyperlink dialog box, choose Central_Q1 from the Or Select a Place in This Document list.

11. Click ScreenTip, type an instruction of your choice, and click OK.

12. Click OK to exit the Insert Hyperlink dialog box.

13. Click in another cell to deselect the button.

14. Test the hyperlink by clicking the button in cell E1.
The pointer moves to the Q1 total on the Central worksheet.

15. Display the National worksheet.

16. Use the previous steps to create a hyperlink button in cell F1 to the defined name Western_Q1 and then test the button.

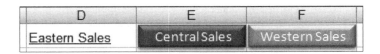

Buttons give a professional look to your hyperlinks. They may be copied and pasted to various sheets to make navigation easier for beginning Excel users.

17. Save ▣ the changes to the workbook and continue with the next exercise.

Skill Builder 10.4 Format Multiple Worksheets for Printing

You will continue working on the sb-Regional Sales workbook. In this exercise, you will create a header on all four sheets.

Before You Begin: *You must have completed Skill Builder 10.2 and Skill Builder 10.3, and the sb-Regional Sales workbook should be open.*

1. Right-click any sheet tab and choose Select All Sheets from the context menu.
   The four sheet tabs are selected.

2. Click the Page Layout button on the status bar at the lower-right corner of the window and drag the Zoom lever to the left until both the left and right edges of the page are visible.

3. Use the scroll bar to scroll to the top of the page.

Add a Header to All Sheets

Although it will appear that you are creating a header in the National worksheet, all selected sheets will contain the header.

4. Click the left header section and type **Consolidated Systems, Inc.**

5. Click the center header section and choose Design→Header & Footer Elements→Sheet Name.
   The & [Tab] code places the worksheet name in the header.

6. Click the right header section and choose Design→Header & Footer Elements→ Current Date.
   The & [Date] code places the current date in the header.

7. Select a worksheet cell, and the current date displays in the header.

8. Display the Eastern worksheet, and then display the Central worksheet and the Western worksheet.
   The header displays in each worksheet.

Print Headings on the Detail Sheets

9. Display the Eastern worksheet.

10. Hold down Shift and click the Western worksheet.
The three detail sheets are selected.

11. Choose Page Layout→Sheet Options→Headings and place a checkmark in the Print box.

12. Select all four sheet tabs and choose Office →Print ▶→Print Preview from the Ribbon.

13. Use the Next Page command to browse through the pages.
The National worksheet does not display column and row headings because you did not include that worksheet in the selection.

14. Click Close Print Preview.

15. Save the changes and close the workbook.

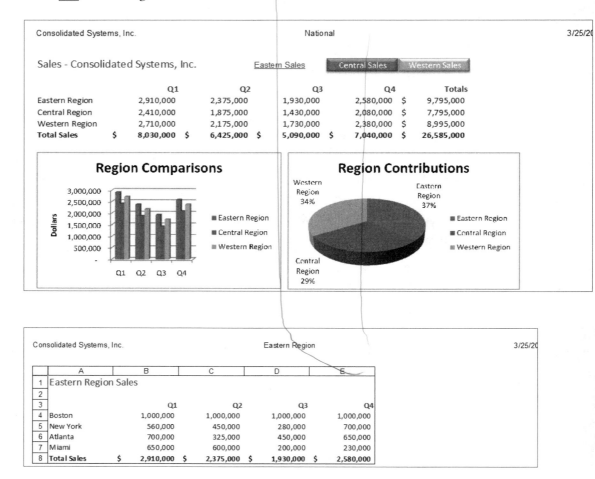

Assessments

Assessment 10.1 Move and Copy Worksheets

In this exercise, you will move a yearly budget worksheet, copy the worksheet, and apply formatting from one worksheet to another.

1. Open the as-Triad Budget workbook from the Lesson 10 folder in your file storage location.

2. Move the Budget worksheet so that it appears as the first worksheet.

3. Rename the Budget sheet tab to include the current year.

4. Copy the current year budget worksheet and rename it for the next year.

5. Copy the current year budget again and rename it for two years from now.

6. Arrange the sheet tabs in order.

7. Add the year as a label on each budget worksheet.

8. Add the current year as a label in the Expenses worksheet.

9. Copy the format from any budget worksheet to the Expenses worksheet for the worksheet title in cells A1:B1 and all formatting from columns L–N of the Budget worksheet to columns C–E of the Expenses worksheet.

10. Save 🖫 the changes and close the workbook.

	A	B	C	D	E
1	*Year 1*	*Expenses*		Triad Construction	
2	**Category**	**Jan**	**Feb**	**Mar**	**Total**
3	Salaries—Partners				-
4	Salaries—Sales				-
5	Salaries—Techn				-
20	Fuel				-
21	Supplies				-
22	**Total**	-	-	-	-

Assessment 10.2   Create a Linked Workbook

In this exercise, you will create a new workbook that contains three worksheets. You will also create cell names and then use those names in linking formulas.

1. Create a new workbook with the three worksheets shown in the illustrations at the end of this exercise. Name the summary worksheet **Both Stores** and name the detail sheets **Eastside Store** and **Westside Store**.

2. Enter the numbers and text shown into the three sheets.

3. Use AutoSum to calculate the totals in all three sheets. The SUM functions in the Totals row of the summary worksheet should sum the cells in rows 6 and 7 even though the cells are currently empty.

4. Create defined names for each total in row 11 of the detail sheets. Name the totals in the Eastside worksheet **Eastside_January**, **Eastside_February**, and **Eastside_March**. Use similar names for the totals in the Westside worksheet.

5. Use linking formulas to create links in rows 6 and 7 of the summary worksheet to the totals in the detail sheets.

6. Format the titles, headings, and numbers as shown. Use the Accounting number format with no decimal places for the totals in all Totals rows. Set font colors of your choice. Ensure consistent formatting across the worksheets by using Format Painter.

7. Save 💾 with the name **as-Collectibles Jan-Mar Sales** in the Lesson 10 folder, and then close the workbook.

	A	B	C	D
1	**Jane's Collectibles**			
2				
3	**January - March Sales**			
4				
5		January	February	March
6	Eastside Store	18,250	16,050	16,800
7	Westside Store	23,450	19,000	21,900
8	Totals	$ 41,700	$ 35,050	$ 38,700

	A	B	C	D
1	**Jane's Collectibles - Eastside Store**			
2				
3	**January - March Sales**			
4				
5		January	February	March
6	Dolls	5,000	3,450	4,500
7	Spoons	1,500	3,400	3,700
8	Figurines	2,750	2,000	2,300
9	Antiques	5,600	4,500	3,400
10	Crystal	3,400	2,700	2,900
11	Totals	$ 18,250	$ 16,050	$ 16,800

	A	B	C	D
1	**Jane's Collectibles - Westside Store**			
2				
3	**January - March Sales**			
4				
5		January	February	March
6	Dolls	7,500	4,000	6,000
7	Spoons	2,000	4,000	5,000
8	Figurines	2,950	3,000	3,700
9	Antiques	6,000	5,000	4,000
10	Crystal	5,000	3,000	3,200
11	Totals	$ 23,450	$ 19,000	$ 21,900

Assessment 10.3 Create Links and Print Settings for Multiple Sheets

In this exercise, you will create a new workbook and insert a new worksheet. You will create defined names for totals in the sheets and then use those names to create linking formulas. You also will create hyperlinks for navigation and prepare the workbook for printing.

1. Create a new workbook and enter the data into four separate sheets as shown in the illustrations at the end of this exercise. You will need to insert one new worksheet. Enter dates using the current year, which will vary from the year shown in the illustrations. Type the values shown for Finance Charge and Payment on the summary worksheet.

2. Use AutoSum to calculate the totals in all four sheets.

3. Name the summary worksheet **Transaction Summary** and name the detail worksheets **January**, **February**, and **March.**

4. Create defined names for the total in cell C10 of each detail worksheet. Name the total in cell C10 of the January worksheet **January_Total**. Likewise, name the totals in the February and March sheets **February_Total** and **March_Total**.

5. Create links in column D of the Transaction Summary worksheet to the totals in the detail sheets. Use the defined names from the detail sheets in the linking formulas.

6. Format the titles, headings, and numbers as shown. Use the Currency Style format with two decimal places for the totals. Set font colors of your choice. Ensure consistent formatting across the worksheets by using Format Painter.

7. Create three text hyperlinks on the summary worksheet that link to the total cell in each detail worksheet.

8. Create a hyperlink that links to the as-Credit Union Policy file (a Word document) in the Lesson 10 folder in your storage location. You may create either a text or graphic hyperlink.

9. Select the January, February, and March sheet tabs and choose 150% scale. The Transaction Summary worksheet should remain at 100% scale.

10. Use Print Preview to verify that the Transaction Summary worksheet would print at 100% size and the three detail sheets would print at 150% size.

11. Save 💾 with the name **as-Credit Card Summary** in the Lesson 10 folder, and then close the workbook.

Credit Card Transaction Summary

	A	B	C	D
1	Credit Card Transaction Summary			
2				
3	Month	Finance Charge	Payment	Transactions
4	January	75.73	900.00	315.55
5	February	103.51	100.00	431.30
6	March	66.22	100.00	275.90
7	April			
8	May			
9	June			
10	July			
11	August			
12	September			
13	October			
14	November			
15	December			
16	Total	$245.46	$1,100.00	$1,022.75

January Transactions

	A	B	C
1	January Transactions		
2			
3	Date	Description	Amount
4	1/2/2007	BayView Health Club	35.00
5	1/7/2007	Bob's Pizza	14.90
6	1/9/2007	Jamestown Books	34.90
7	1/14/2007	William's AutoCare	230.75
8			
9			
10	Total		$315.55

February Transactions

	A	B	C
1	February Transactions		
2			
3	Date	Description	Amount
4	2/2/2007	BayView Health Club	35.00
5	2/4/2007	Southeast Airlines	230.00
6	2/8/2007	Western Dental	120.50
7	2/16/2007	Mel's Diner	45.80
8			
9			
10	Total		$431.30

March Transactions

	A	B	C
1	March Transactions		
2			
3	Date	Description	Amount
4	3/2/2007	BayView Health Club	35.00
5	3/6/2007	Home Hardware	40.90
6	3/24/2007	Allied Insurance	200.00
7			
8			
9			
10	Total		$275.90

Critical Thinking

Critical Thinking 10.1   Create Names for Navigation and Formulas

Stefanie Martin is the owner of Stefanie's Used Computer Stores, which has three locations in various parts of the city. Stefanie emails each store manager an Excel worksheet to use as the basis for the worksheets they submit. Each of the store detail worksheets has an identical format so that Stefanie may easily summarize the data from the three stores. She wants the capability to navigate to various areas of the workbook.

- Open ct-Store Inventory from the Lesson 10 folder in your file storage location.

- Name cells for each total in the store detail sheets. Test navigation to the named cells.

- Use linking formulas to summarize the totals from the various sheets on the summary worksheet. Create formulas for the grand totals.

- Save 🖫 the changes and close the workbook.

Critical Thinking 10.2   Create Linking Formulas to Calculate Totals

Set up a revenue and expense workbook for Berkeley Bicycles, a retailer of racing and mountain bicycles.

- Include four sheets in the workbook that have an identical structure. The first worksheet should be a summary worksheet. Sheets 2–4 should contain revenue and expense data for Store 1, Store 2, and Store 3.

- Include revenue and expense data for four quarters (Q1, Q2, Q3, and Q4). The expenses should include employee costs, lease costs, inventory, and overhead. Use whatever revenue and expense numbers you think would be appropriate for a small bicycle retailer.

- Calculate the profit or loss of each store for each quarter by subtracting the expenses from the revenue.

- Use a linking formula in the summary worksheet to calculate the sum of combined revenue for Q1 for the three stores. Duplicate the formula, which should be easy to do if the structure of your summary worksheet is identical to the three source sheets.

- Format the numbers with either the Accounting number format or Comma Style format. Use other formatting to make the worksheet visually attractive.

- Save 🖫 the workbook as **ct-Bike Rev Exp** in the Lesson 10 folder, and then close the workbook.

Critical Thinking 10.3   Present College Cost Research

David's parents want to compare the costs of attending Yale and Princeton to the cost of attending Harvard.

- Open the ct-College Costs workbook from the Lesson 10 folder.

- Copy the Harvard worksheet twice. Name the duplicate sheets **Yale** and **Princeton**.

- Use Internet Explorer and a search engine of your choice to locate the websites of Yale University and Princeton University. Determine the approximate tuition, fees, room, board, and personal expenses for a full-time undergraduate student.

- Enter the expense numbers into the appropriate cell in column B of both the Yale and Princeton sheets. The estimated expenses for the remaining years will be calculated automatically by the formulas that were set up in the original Harvard worksheet.

- Create a hyperlink to the university website on each of the three worksheets.

- Save ![save icon] the changes and close the workbook.

LESSON 11

Creating Tables and Outlines

Excel is often used to store lists of information. Excel tables provide a good structure for organizing such data and provide several tools to help you enter, view, and analyze information based on specific characteristics of the data. In this lesson, you will enter data into a table, format with a table style, and quickly create calculation formulas. Some formulas will include structured references that point to specific areas within the table. You will sort and filter the table contents to view data in various ways. You will also hide detail data using the outline and grouping commands to view just the summary data.

LESSON OBJECTIVES

After studying this lesson, you will be able to:

■ Create and format tables from worksheet data
■ Display totals and use other functions to perform calculations
■ Sort data using various specifications
■ Display specific data records by filtering
■ Outline and group to summarize data

Case Study: Creating a Sales Performance Table

Ryan Lang understands that his clients need to track and analyze their data easily. His company, National Computing Solutions, creates customized hardware and software solutions for businesses. As the executive sales manager, Ryan needs to track and analyze the performance of his sales staff. You will develop a table so that Ryan may sort and filter employee data on specific criteria. He also wants to count, sum sales totals, and calculate an average for the entire group. The table that you will create is shown below.

	A	B	C	D	E	F	G	H	I	J
1	National Computing Solutions									
2	Sales Performance Table									
3										
4	Last Name	First Name	Years	Review Date	Position	Region	State	SW Sales	HW Sales	Total Sales
5	Alvizo	Alex	7	1-Mar	Senior Sales Rep	Western	CA	900,000	780,000	1,680,000
6	Clayton	Taneisha	2	1-Mar	Sales Rep	Central	IL	230,000	120,000	350,000
7	Cray	Karen	6	1-Sep	Telemarketer	Western	WA	162,000	251,000	413,000
8	Hasan	Taz	3	15-Jul	Telemarketer	Western	CA	546,000	120,000	666,000
9	Hill	Patricia	1	1-Jun	Sales Rep	Central	IL	120,000	170,000	290,000
10	Huy	Lin	3	15-Sep	Sales Rep	Western	CA	200,000	180,000	380,000
11	Knapp	Mai	2	15-Nov	Telemarketer	Eastern	FL	340,000	230,000	570,000
12	Martinez	Carlos	4	15-Sep	Senior Sales Rep	Eastern	FL	450,000	450,000	900,000
13	Mathis	Gerhardt	5	1-Aug	Senior Sales Rep	Central	IL	234,000	560,000	794,000
14	McGee	Olivia	8	1-Jun	Sales Rep	Eastern	MA	317,000	513,000	830,000
15	Richards	Paul	1	15-Jun	Telemarketer	Central	CO	128,000	216,000	344,000
16	Smith	Jacqui	1	15-Apr	Telemarketer	Eastern	MA	123,000	230,000	353,000
17	Williams	LaShaun	3	1-Sep	Sales Rep	Central	CO	120,000	340,000	460,000
18	Zain	Elizabeth	7	1-Feb	Senior Sales Rep	Western	CA	340,000	800,000	1,140,000
19	Total		4		14			4,210,000	4,960,000	9,170,000
20			Avg Yrs		Total Sales Staff			Total SW	Total HW	

This table may be sorted or filtered by any column.

What Happened to Excel Databases?

The database and list interface from prior Excel versions has changed in Excel 2007. Now you'll work with tables that look very similar to databases, and users of prior versions will notice a number of improved features.

Why Use a Table?

You may still create worksheet lists in the usual way, but at times you will want to convert data into a table on the worksheet. Features specific to tables include the following:

- **Automatic expansion**—As you type more data rows at the bottom of the table or columns to the right, the table expands to include them.

- **Calculated columns**—Entering a formula in one cell automatically copies the formula to all cells in the table column. You need not autofill or copy.

- **Table styles**—The previous AutoFormat command has been replaced with a style library only for tables. You must manually format cells not included in a table.

- **Filtering**—Filtering (displaying only those rows that meet certain criteria) is available immediately after you create a table, but you must turn on filtering in columns not included in a table.

- **Functions**—You may display a total row and create summary formulas instantly by choosing from a list of frequently used functions such as SUM and AVERAGE. All Excel functions may be used in tables. A wide variety of filtering options and the convenience of the total row avoid the use of somewhat complex database functions such as DSUM—familiar to users of previous Excel versions and still available in Excel 2007.

Working with Tables

An Excel table manages related data. For example, in this lesson you will create a table that holds sales performance data for each sales employee. The table data may be sorted, filtered, and calculated in various ways. Data are organized consistently throughout the table in rows and columns.

Table Rows

In Excel, each row in a table (called a record in a database) holds a collection of facts about a certain person, event, or other item. For example, your sales performance table will have one row for each sales employee.

Table Columns

Each column in a table (called a field in a database) contains one piece of information, such as last name or total sales achieved by the employee. For example, your sales performance table will have columns for each sales employee's last name, first name, position, and sales performance.

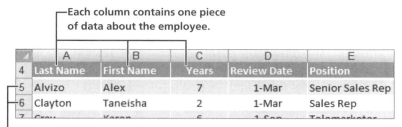

Each column contains one piece of data about the employee.

	A	B	C	D	E
4	Last Name	First Name	Years	Review Date	Position
5	Alvizo	Alex	7	1-Mar	Senior Sales Rep
6	Clayton	Taneisha	2	1-Mar	Sales Rep
7	Crow	Karen	6	1-Sep	Telemarketer

Each table row contains data about one person, event, or transaction—one row per employee in this example.

Creating a Table

You start a table by entering data in worksheet cells as you normally do. Do not use blank rows or columns to separate areas within the list because Excel does not include areas after blanks in a table. You may apply number formats and other formatting as desired. A worksheet may include more than one table and worksheet data outside of tables.

	A	B	C
4	Company	Order Number	Amt
5	Blue Chip	3056	$ 56.97
6	Razor Motors	3057	$ 30.16
7	US Fuel	3058	$168.43
8	Panda Foods	3059	$498.72

Worksheet cells ready to be converted to a table

Converting a Range to a Table

You may convert a worksheet list to a table by selecting any cell in the list and choosing the Format As Table command from the Ribbon. Excel includes all adjacent cells in the table until a blank row and column are encountered. You may change the suggested table range if it is not correct. The table appears in place of the original cells. During the conversion process, you choose a table style. Many styles will format the table rows with alternating color bands.

FROM THE KEYBOARD

Ctrl+T to create a table

You may change the table range if Excel guesses incorrectly.

The first row, containing column headings, will be used as the header row.

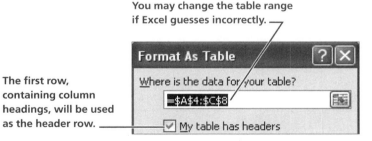

Format As Table [?] [X]

Where is the data for your table?

=$A$4:$C$8

☑ My table has headers

Setting the range to be converted to a table

	A	B	C
4	Company ▾	Order Num ▾	Amt ▾
5	Blue Chip	3056	$ 56.97
6	Razor Motors	3057	$ 30.16
7	US Fuel	3058	$168.43
8	Panda Foods	3059	$498.72

The table that results

 TIP! *Use Insert→Tables→Table from the Ribbon if you prefer to create a table and apply the default table style automatically.*

Creating a New Blank Table

As an alternative, you may start with blank cells in a table. After you select a range and choose the Format As Table command, the new table displays. Replace the generic column headings by typing your column labels and then enter the table data.

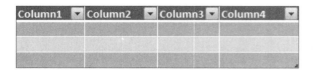

Renaming a Table

Excel names tables as Table1, Table2, and so on. Although you may use the generic names, renaming with a more descriptive title is a good practice because table names often are used in formulas. Recall the rules you applied in creating defined names for cells in Lesson 10, Managing Multiple-Sheet Workbooks. As with defined names, table names may not include spaces but may include multiple capital letters and underscores, as in OrderTable and Order_Table.

Table Name:
Order_Table

QUICK REFERENCE: CREATING AND RENAMING TABLES

Task	Procedure
Create a table from an existing range	■ Select the desired range in the worksheet.
	■ Choose Home→Styles→Format As Table ▦ from the Ribbon or use Ctrl + T from the keyboard.
	■ Choose a table style from the list.
	■ Change the suggested table range in the dialog box, if necessary.
	■ Edit column headings in the first table row as necessary and type data if not already entered.
Rename a table	■ Choose Design→Properties, click in the Table Name box to select the existing generic table name, type the new name (spaces are not allowed), and tap Enter.

Hands-On 11.1   Create a Table

In this exercise, you will create a table for National Computing Solutions' sales force. You will work with this table throughout the lesson.

1. Start Excel and open the Sales Performance workbook from the Lesson 11 folder in your file storage location.

2. Maximize ▭ the window.

Format an Existing Range as a Table

3. Select cell A4 in the Sales Performance Table worksheet.

Notice that the data in the range A4:I17 contain no blank rows or columns. You will convert this list from regular cells to a table.

4. Choose Home→Styles→Format As Table  from the Ribbon.

The table style palette appears.

5. Choose Table Style Light 9 under the Light category.

The table will be formatted in blue with thin lines separating the rows.

6. Make certain that the Format As Table dialog box options match the ones shown below, and click OK.

Although you selected only one cell in the range A4:I17, Excel suggests the entire range.

Rename the Table

7. Choose Design→Properties and click in the Table Name box to select the existing generic table name. Taking care to type an underscore using ⎡Shift⎤+⎡-⎤ between the two words, type **Sales_Performance** and tap ⎡Enter⎤.

You should rename a table to provide a clear description of any table names used in formulas. Table names may include underscores and multiple capital letters, as in SalesPerformance, but may not include spaces.

8. Deselect the highlighted table cells.

9. Save 🖫 the changes and leave the workbook open.

Header Row

Always enter column headings as the first row of a table. Excel uses this as the header row. Excel uses the following rules for column headings.

- **One Item per Column**—Each column must contain one piece of information to enable full sorting and filtering. For example, create seven separate columns for last name, first name, middle initial, street address, city, state, and postal code.

- **Unique Headings**—Each heading should be different. For example, you cannot type Name as the same heading for two columns. Last Name and First Name are acceptable because the labels contain at least one different character.

- **Special Characters**—You may use spaces and multiple capital letters in column headings. Special characters such as underscore (_), comma (,), period (.), and dollar sign ($) also are allowed. Avoid using pound signs (#), brackets ([and]), and single quotes ('), as those have special meanings in formulas.

With any table cell selected, the header row labels operate like frozen titles. They display in place of the column headings (A, B, C, and so on) as you scroll down the table.

The header row is frozen as you scroll so that column names remain visible.

	Last Name	First Name	Years	Review Date
10	Huy	Lin	3	15-Sep
11	Knapp	Mai	2	15-Nov

Total Row

After you create a table, you may display the total row below the last table row. You may turn off its display, if desired. If the last table column contains numbers, a total is calculated automatically. If the last column contains text or dates, the nonblank entries in the column are counted (the total would display 3 in the following table).

Company ▼	Order Num ▼	Amt ▼
Blue Chip	3056	$ 56.97
Razor Motors	3057	$ 30.16
US Fuel	3058	$ 168.43
Total		$ 255.56

The total row displays below the last table row with an automatic sum in the last column.

Creating Summary Formulas

A summary formula is a calculation displayed in the total row and based on the contents of its table column. You may create summary formulas very easily. Just choose from the total cell's list of commonly used functions such as SUM, AVERAGE, MIN, MAX, and COUNT. Excel performs the calculation on the entries in the table column, and you need not type anything or select any cells. By choosing More Functions in the list, you may access any other Excel function to create a custom formula or you may type the formula.

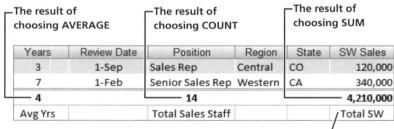

None
Average
Count
Count Numbers
Max
Min
Sum
StdDev
Var
More Functions…

The result of choosing AVERAGE

The result of choosing COUNT

The result of choosing SUM

Years	Review Date	Position	Region	State	SW Sales
3	1-Sep	Sales Rep	Central	CO	120,000
7	1-Feb	Senior Sales Rep	Western	CA	340,000
4		14			4,210,000
Avg Yrs		Total Sales Staff			Total SW

An optional label typed below the table to explain the total

Formatting a Table

The Design Ribbon activates while any table cell is selected. You may change the table style, create a custom style and set it as the default, or clear the table style from the selected table. You also may turn on or remove the display of the header row, total row, and banded rows and columns, and you may set the first or last column to display differently than the others. Apply other desired formatting such as bold, alignment, and number formats to selected cells as usual.

Table Styles   Table Style Options

Table formatting options on the Design tab of the Ribbon

QUICK REFERENCE: CHOOSING TOTAL ROW FORMULAS AND TABLE STYLE

Task	Procedure
Display/hide the header row or total row	■ Select any cell in the table. ■ Choose Design→Table Style Options→Header Row or Total Row from the Ribbon.
Create a formula in the total row	■ Select the desired cell in the total row. ■ Type a formula or choose the formula name or More Functions from the cell's formula list.
Change a table style	■ Select any cell in the table. ■ Choose Design→Table Styles→More ⯆ menu and choose a table style from the Ribbon. ■ Choose Design→Table Style Options and turn on/off First Column, Last Column, Banded Rows, and Banded Columns as desired.

Hands-On 11.2   Create Totals and Format a Table

In this exercise, you will view the header row and total row. You will create totals for some of the table columns. You also will change the table style.

1. Select any cell in the table on the Sales Performance Table worksheet.

Edit the Header Row

2. Review the column headings in row 4. Choose Design→Table Style Options→Header Row from the Ribbon if the header row is not displayed.

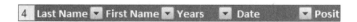

Excel formatted the first row of column headings as the header row. Column headings may contain spaces. Each heading displays a list button. You will learn how to filter using these buttons in a later topic of this lesson.

3. Double-click the Date column heading and edit to **Review Date**.

Scroll with the Header Row Frozen

4. With any table cell selected, scroll down until the table column headings replace the work-sheet column headings—A, B, C, and so on. Make certain that a table cell is selected if this does not occur.

	Last Name	First Name	Years	Review D...
7	Clayton	Taneisha	2	1-Mar
8	Smith	Jacqui	1	15-Apr
9	McGee	Olivia	8	1-Jun

The column headings freeze automatically as you scroll so they are always visible.

5. Scroll up until row 1 is visible.

6. Save the changes.

Create Formulas in the Total Row

7. Choose Design→Table Style Options→Total Row from the Ribbon if the total row is not displayed in row 18.

8. Notice the total row in row 18.

18	Total							4,730,000

Excel added a total in the last column automatically because the column contains numbers. A total may be deleted just like the contents of any other cell if you do not want it to display.

9. Select cell C18 and follow these steps to create a formula:

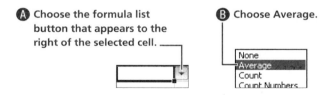

A Choose the formula list button that appears to the right of the selected cell.

B Choose Average.

None
Average
Count
Count Numbers

The average years employed displays as 4. Notice that you were not required to type an equals (=) sign or select cells to create the formula.

10. Select cell E18 and choose Count from the formula list.
The employees total 13. The COUNT function counts the number of nonblank entries in the table column.

11. Center the contents of cell E18.

12. Select cell H18 and choose Sum from the formula list.

13. Type the following labels in row 19.

18	Total		4		13		3,870,000	4,730,000
19			Avg Yrs		Total Sales Staff		Total SW	Total HW

These labels describe the calculations in row 18. The labels are optional and are not actually part of the table because they are below the total row.

14. Center the labels in row 19.

15. Save 💾 the changes.

Change the Table Style

16. Select any table cell and choose Design→Table Styles→More ⬇→Table Style Medium 16 from the Ribbon.
Excel formats the table in blue with gray shaded bands on alternating rows.

17. Choose Design→Table Style Options and place checkmarks next to First Column and Last Column in the Ribbon.
The first and last columns now are highlighted with a blue fill color to draw attention.

18. Choose Design→Table Styles→More ⬇→Table Style Medium 7 from the Ribbon.

19. Choose Design→Table Style Options→Banded Rows in the Ribbon to turn off alternating banded rows. Verify that the settings are as shown.

The table is formatted in orange without shaded bands on alternating rows. The text in the first and last columns changed to bold. The table styles are designed to contrast text clearly against its background.

20. Save 💾 the changes and leave the workbook open.

Adding and Deleting Rows and Columns

Tables are designed to help you add and delete records easily.

Table Rows

You may insert a row anywhere in the table by selecting a cell below the desired location and choosing the Insert command from the Ribbon or pop-up (or context) menu. Often it is easier to add records to the end of the table and then sort the list. After selecting the right-most cell in the last data row, you tap Tab to wrap to a new blank table row and continue using Tab after typing each cell entry. You use the Delete command from the Ribbon or context menu to remove rows after selecting a cell in the desired row(s).

	450,000	
	180,000	──More records may be entered by selecting
	4,730,000	the last data cell and tapping Tab.
	Total HW	

Table Columns

You may insert a column anywhere in the table by first selecting a cell to the right of the desired location. To insert a column between other columns, you must display the Insert menu from the Ribbon or context menu and choose a command. You may simply type in the blank column to the right of the last column to add it to the table. To delete a column, you must display the Delete menu from the Ribbon or context menu and choose a command.

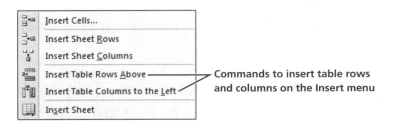

Commands to insert table rows and columns on the Insert menu

Automatic Extension

The table extends to include new rows and column(s), calculations are updated, and consistent formatting is applied automatically.

⚠ **WARNING!** *The table will not extend to add the items shown in the illustration if you just select a cell and type.*

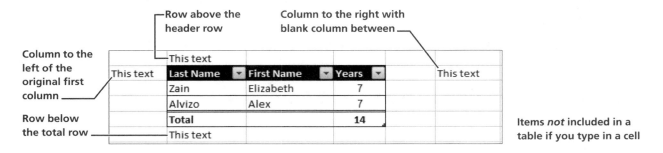

Selecting Table Rows and Columns

At times you may need to select all cells in a table row or column. For example, cells must be selected before changing their text color. Selecting cells by dragging may be difficult in tables with many rows or columns. Selecting a table row or column is different from selecting a row or column in the worksheet, as follows:

■ Selecting the row number selects the entire row through the end of the worksheet.

■ Selecting with the arrow pointer in the first cell of a table row selects just the cells in the table row.

■ Selecting the column letter selects the entire column through the end of the worksheet.

■ Selecting with the arrow pointer in a table column heading selects just the cells in the table column.

Examine the pointer position in the following illustrations.

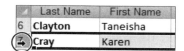

Placing the pointer on the 7 and clicking selects all row 7 cells through the end of the worksheet.

Placing the pointer inside the first cell in the row and clicking selects only cells in the table.

 Hands-On 11.3   Add and Delete Table Rows and Columns

In this exercise, you will add a record to the table and explore commands to insert and delete rows and columns. You will select a row and a column in the table without including cells outside the table.

Add a Record to the Table

1. Select cell I17 in the Sales Performance Table worksheet.
   This is the last data cell in the table.

2. Tap ⎣Tab⎦, and the pointer wraps to a newly inserted row.

3. Enter the following record, tapping ⎣Tab⎦ after each cell except the last. Tap ⎣Enter⎦ to complete the last entry, 230000.
   As you begin typing an entry, AutoComplete may fill in the remainder. Tap ⎣Tab⎦ to accept the entry and move to the next cell.

⚠**TIP!** *Click Undo* 🔄 *if you accidentally tap* ⎣Tab⎦ *after the last cell in the row.*

| 18 | Knapp | Mai | 2 | 15-Nov | Telemarketer | Eastern | FL | 340,000 | 230,000 |

Notice that the table expanded to include the new row, and formulas in the total row automatically recalculated to include the new numbers.

4. Save the changes.

Insert Rows and a Column Using the Ribbon

5. Select cell E14.

6. Choose Home→Cells→Insert from the Ribbon.

13	Mathis	Gerhardt	5	1-Aug	Senior Sales Rep	Centr.
14						
15	Williams	LaShaun	3	1-Sep	Sales Rep	Centr.

Excel inserts a blank table row above the selected cell. You may choose Insert without choosing its menu arrow ▼ when inserting one row.

7. Select cell K9 and type **Revised**. Type **Tuesday** in cell K10. (Do not enter this text in row 14.)

8. Select the range E9:E10 and choose Home→Cells→Insert menu ▾→Insert Table Rows Above from the Ribbon. (Make certain to choose the menu arrow ▾ rather than Insert.)

Telemarketer	Eastern	MA	123,000	230,000		
						Revised
						Tuesday
Sales Rep	Eastern	MA	317,000	513,000		

Two rows are inserted above row 9. Notice that the text in cells K9 and K10 did not move. Rows and columns inserted in a table do not affect the cells outside the table.

9. Select cell D7 and choose Home→Cells→Insert menu ▾→Insert Table Columns to the Left from the Ribbon.

10. Select cell D4 and replace the generic Column1 heading with **Phone**.

Years ▾	Phone ▾	Review Date ▾
7		1-Feb
7		1-Mar

Delete Rows and a Column Using the Context Menu

11. Point to any cell in table row 16, right-click, and choose Delete→Table Rows from the context menu.
Table row 16 (a blank row) is deleted. You may insert or delete rows or columns using the context menu.

12. Select the range D9:D10, right-click, and choose Delete→Table Rows from the context menu.
Table rows 9 and 10 (blank rows) are deleted. The text in cells L9 and L10 is not affected by the deletion because those cells are outside the table.

13. With the range D9:D10 still selected, right-click and choose Delete→Table Columns from the context menu to delete column D.
Now the table contains no blank rows or columns.

14. Save 🖫 the changes.

Select a Row

15. Point inside cell A9 near its left border as shown at right until the pointer displays as an arrow and then click. (Do not click the 9 to the left of cell A9, which would select the entire row.)
Excel selects the range A9:I9 within the table. Notice that cell K9 outside the table (containing Revised) is not selected.

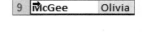

16. With the range A9:I9 still selected, choose Home→Font→Font Color 🅰▾→Red under Standard Colors.

Select Columns

17. In cell D4, point near the top of the Review Date column heading until the pointer displays an arrow, and drag to select both the Review Date and the Position table columns.

Notice that the cells below the table are not included in the selection.

18. Select any table cell to deselect the columns.

19. Save  the changes.

Calculated Columns

Any blank table column may become a calculated column. You create a formula in one cell, and Excel copies the formula to all of the other cells in the column automatically. If you do not want a calculated column, type text or a number in at least one cell before creating any formulas in the column.

Converting a Table to a Range

You may convert a table to a normal range in the worksheet. Be aware that some table formatting may be lost if you convert the list back into a table at a later time.

Printing a Table

The Table option in the Print dialog box may be used to print a table without including the other cells on the worksheet. The option is available only when you select a cell in the table before displaying the Print dialog box.

Deleting a Table

You may delete a table by selecting all table cells, including the total row if visible, and tapping ⌐Delete¬ or choosing the Delete Table Rows command.

QUICK REFERENCE: EDITING, PRINTING, AND DELETING TABLES

Task	Procedure
Add records to a table	■ Select the last cell in the last data row and tap Tab. ■ Type a cell entry, tap Tab, and continue this process until all records are added.
Insert one or more rows in a table	■ Select one cell or multiple cells below the desired location. ■ Choose Home→Cells→Insert from the Ribbon to insert one row. or ■ Choose Home→Cells→Insert menu ▼→Insert Table Rows Above from the Ribbon to insert multiple rows.
Delete one or more rows from a table	■ Select one cell in each row to be deleted. ■ Choose Home→Cells→Delete from the Ribbon to delete one row. or ■ Choose Home→Cells→Delete menu ▼→Delete Table Rows from the Ribbon to delete multiple rows.
Insert one or more columns in a table	■ Type data or a formula in the column to the right of the last column. or ■ Select one cell or multiple cells to the right of the desired location. ■ Choose Home→Cells→menu ▼→Insert Table Columns to the Left from the Ribbon.
Delete one or more columns from a table	■ Select one cell in each column to be deleted. ■ Choose Home→Cells→Delete menu ▼→Delete Table Columns from the Ribbon.
Select a table row	■ Place the mouse inside the first cell of the row to display the arrow pointer and click.
Select a table column	■ Place the mouse at the top of the table column heading to display the arrow pointer and click.
Create a calculated column	■ Create a formula in any cell of a blank table column, and the formula copies to all other column cells automatically.
Convert a table to a normal range	■ Select any cell in the table. ■ Choose Design→Tools→Convert to Range from the Ribbon.
Print a table only	■ Select any cell in the table. ■ Choose Office→Print from the Ribbon and choose Table in the Print dialog box.
Delete a table	■ Select all table cells, including the header row and table row. ■ Tap Delete.

Hands-On 11.4 Create a Calculated Column

In this exercise, you will create a Total Sales column as a calculated column to sum the software sales and hardware sales for each employee.

1. Select cell J10.
   Column J is the blank column immediately to the right of the last table column. The table will expand to include this column after you enter something in it.

2. Type **=** to begin the formula, and select cell H10.

   ```
   =Sales_Performance[[#This Row],[SW Sales]]
   ```

   Notice the cell reference in the Formula Bar. Excel uses a different type of reference for table cells. You will learn more about structured references in the next lesson topic.

3. Tap ⊞ on the keypad, select cell I10, and select Enter ✔ to complete the formula.
   The formula sums the software sales and hardware sales.

   Notice that the formula copied automatically for all other employees. This calculated column is now the last column in the table, so bolding transferred from column I to column J. A generic column heading displays.

Format the Calculated Column

4. Select cell J19 and choose Sum from the cell's formula list to display the column total.

5. Select the range J5:J19 and format as Comma Style with no decimal places.

6. Select cell J4 and replace the generic column heading with **Total Sales**.

7. Widen column J slightly to display the column heading completely.

8. Save 💾 the changes.

Print Preview the Table

9. Select any cell in the table, choose Office→Print, choose Table under Print What in the Print dialog box, and click Preview. Make certain that a table cell is selected if the Table print option is dimmed.
   Only the table would print on one page. The text in cells A1:A2 and K9:K10 do not print.

10. Close ✖ Print Preview.

11. Delete the contents of cells K9 and K10.

12. Save 💾 the change.

Understanding Structured References

Formulas in normal worksheet lists use cell references such as E7, but Excel uses structured references to refer to cells used in table formulas. Structured references allow formulas to adjust results automatically as rows and columns are added to or deleted from the table. They also adjust as you rename tables, edit column headings, and move or copy formulas. The generic syntax (language) of structured references allows you to create one formula in a calculated column so that the formula need not be copied to specific cells in the column as you must do in a normal worksheet range.

Formulas with Structured References

To understand how structured references differ from cell references, compare the two formulas shown. They both contain references to total SW Sales and HW Sales for one employee. The first formula would be used in a normal worksheet range, and the second is used in the Total Sales calculated column of the Sales Performance table.

=H5+I5

A worksheet formula containing relative cell references

=Sales_Performance[[#This Row],[SW Sales]]+Sales_Performance[[#This Row],[HW Sales]]

A table formula containing structured references

The cell reference H5 in the first formula is converted to a structured reference in a table as follows:

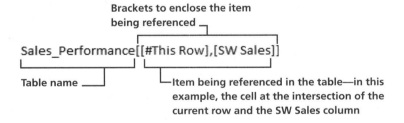

Brackets to enclose the item being referenced

Sales_Performance[[#This Row],[SW Sales]]

Table name

Item being referenced in the table—in this example, the cell at the intersection of the current row and the SW Sales column

QUICK REFERENCE: CREATING STRUCTURED REFERENCES IN TABLE FORMULAS

Task	Procedure
Create a structured reference	Use point mode to select a cell or a cell range while you create the table formulas. Excel creates the necessary structured references for you.

 TIP! *See Using Structured References with Excel Tables in Excel Help for more information about syntax in structured references to create complex formulas.*

 ## Hands-On 11.5   View Structured References

In this exercise, you will review formulas in the Total Sales column that you created as a calculated column in the previous exercise. You also will view formulas in the table's total row.

1. Select cell J5.

2. Review the addition formula containing two structured references for the values in the SW Sales and HW Sales columns.

   =Sales_Performance[[#This Row],[SW Sales]]+Sales_Performance[[#This Row],[HW Sales]]

3. Select cell J6.
   The same formula displays for every cell in the calculated column. Any records added to the table would automatically include the formula.

4. Select cell H19 in the total row.

   =SUBTOTAL(109,[SW Sales])

   This formula uses Excel's SUBTOTAL function, which consists of two arguments. The number 109 indicates the SUM function, and [SW Sales] is a structured reference to the cells in the SW Sales column.

5. Select cell C19 in the total row.
   The number 101 in the SUBTOTAL function indicates the AVERAGE function, and [Years] refers to the cells in the Years column.

   Now you have learned to recognize some structured references that Excel created for you in formulas.

Using Enhanced Sorting and Filtering

A table displays a list button ![ ] in each column heading to indicate that filtering is available. These column heading list buttons provide additional sorting and filtering options not available on the Ribbon. You also may display these buttons in a normal worksheet list. Excel 2007 provides the capability to sort by color and a wide variety of options to filter by color, text, number, and date. These options help you analyze the data to spot trends and potential problems.

!TIP! *The Data→Sort & Filter→Filter* ![Y] *command on the Ribbon turns on/off the display of the column heading list buttons for the selected table or list.*

Sorts

You learned how to sort a worksheet list into A to Z ![A/Z↓] or Z to A ![Z/A↓] order and to perform multicolumn sorts in Lesson 7, Working with Large Worksheets. Table rows may be sorted using these same commands on the Ribbon. The column heading list button changes to indicate that the table is sorted based on that column. An up arrow indicates the sort is from lowest to highest, and a down arrow indicates highest to lowest. Table rows also may be sorted by font color, fill color, or icons created through conditional formatting (see Conditional Formatting in Lesson 15, Using Advanced Formatting and Analysis Tools).

The sort and filter options for a text column

The arrow pointing up on the list button indicates that the table is sorted by last name from lowest to highest.

A sorted table

Hands-On 11.6　Sort a Table

In this exercise, you will sort the table rows in alphabetic, numeric, and color order.

NOTE!　*If the column heading buttons do not display during the following exercise, select any table cell and choose Data→Sort & Filter→Filter.*

1. Follow these steps to sort by last name in the table on the Sales Performance Table worksheet.

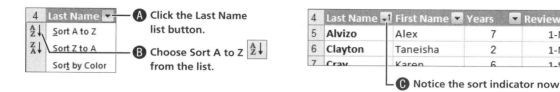

   The table rows are sorted in alphabetical order by last name. You could have used the identical sort command on the Data Ribbon.

2. Click the Position list button ▾ as shown at right, and then choose Sort by Color→red color box from the list.
   The table rows are sorted by color with a single row of red text displayed first.

3. Choose Total Sales list button ▾→Sort Largest to Smallest ↓ from the list.
   The table rows are sorted by total sales from highest to lowest.

4. Save 🖫 the change.

Filters

Filtering allows you to display only those rows that meet certain specifications that you choose. For example, you may display just the records for which the sales total is greater than $500,000 or display only records for employees with three years' experience. The records not meeting your specifications are hidden temporarily until you clear the filter. You may filter by color or with a text, number, or date option. The column heading list button displays a filter icon to alert you that the table is filtered and does not currently display all rows. You may filter on multiple columns using the list buttons.

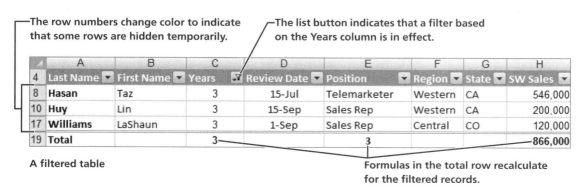

The row numbers change color to indicate that some rows are hidden temporarily.

The list button indicates that a filter based on the Years column is in effect.

	A	B	C	D	E	F	G	H
4	Last Name ▾	First Name ▾	Years ⌄	Review Date ▾	Position ▾	Region ▾	State ▾	SW Sales ▾
8	Hasan	Taz	3	15-Jul	Telemarketer	Western	CA	546,000
10	Huy	Lin	3	15-Sep	Sales Rep	Western	CA	200,000
17	Williams	LaShaun	3	1-Sep	Sales Rep	Central	CO	120,000
19	Total		3		3			866,000

A filtered table

Formulas in the total row recalculate for the filtered records.

Custom Filters

The Custom Filter command on the column heading list displays a dialog box that may be used to filter by two criteria in the same column. For example, you may filter for records with a Review Date between April 15 and June 15, using the And option as shown. The Or option displays every record that meets

either one of the two criteria—the record need not meet both criteria. The dialog box also displays after you choose any text filter option or some of the number and date filter options from the column heading list. You may choose one or both specifications in the dialog box as needed. For example, specifying a beginning date of April 15 and leaving the ending date blank would locate all Review Dates from April 15 through the most recent date.

QUICK REFERENCE: SORTING AND FILTERING TABLES AND LISTS

Task	Procedure
Sort a table	■ Select a table cell and choose Data→Sort & Filter→Filter 🔽 to display column heading list buttons, if necessary.
	■ Choose the column heading list button 🔽 and one of the following from the list:
	◆ Sort A to Z or Smallest to Largest or Newest to Oldest ↕
	◆ Sort Z to A or Largest to Smallest or Oldest to Newest ↕
	◆ Sort by Color and the desired color
Filter by selection in a table or list	■ Right-click the desired item in the column you want to filter.
	■ Choose Filter→Filter by Selected Cell's Value from the context menu.
Filter by values in a table or list	■ Choose the column heading list button 🔽 and do one of the following from the list:
	◆ Check and uncheck boxes for the desired values.
	◆ Choose Text Values, Number Values, or Date Values; the desired criteria command; and options in the Custom AutoFilter dialog box, if displayed.
Clear filter criteria from one column	■ Choose the column heading filter list button 🔽→Clear Filter From "[column name]" from the list.
Clear filter criteria from all columns	■ Choose Data→Sort & Filter→Clear 🔽 from the Ribbon.

Hands-On 11.7 Filter a Table

Ryan Lang, Executive Sales Manager of National Computing Solutions, wants to analyze his company's sales performance by filtering the table records. In this exercise, you will perform single-column and multi-column filters using text, numbers, and dates.

Filter by Selection

1. Right-click any Eastern cell in the Region column and choose Filter→Filter by Selected Cell's Value from the context menu.
   Four records containing Eastern in the Region column display, and the calculations in the total row change to reflect those records.

2. Select any table cell and choose Data→Sort & Filter→Clear 🏷 from the Ribbon.
   The table redisplays all 14 records.

Filter by Text Values

3. Follow these steps to filter for two job titles:

Only the records for Sales Rep and Senior Sales Rep display, the calculations in the total row are based on them, and the sort order is still largest to smallest Total Sales.

Filter by Values in Multiple Columns

Ryan wants to filter the previous results further. He wants to view the data for only the Sales Reps and Senior Sales Reps in Illinois.

4. Follow these steps to filter the previous results further:

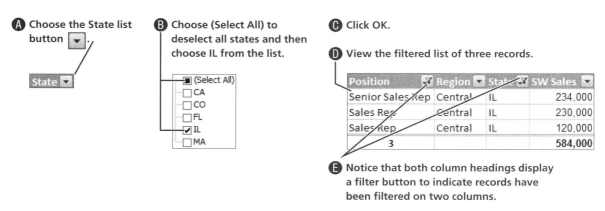

Clear the Filters

5. Choose the Position list button 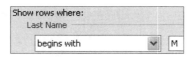→Clear Filter From "Position" from the list.

6. Clear the filter from the State column.
The list is restored to all 14 records.

Filter by Text Criteria

7. Sort the table by Last Name in A to Z order.
Note that if two or more records contained identical last names, you would use Data→Sort & Filter→ Sort on the Ribbon to perform a two-level sort on Last Name and First Name. You sorted using this command in Lesson 7, Working with Large Worksheets.

8. Save 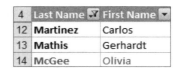 the change.
Next you will filter for records in which the last name begins with the letter M.

9. Choose Last Name list button 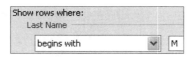→Text Filters→Begins With from the list.

10. In the AutoFilter dialog box, type **M** in the text box to the right of Begins With and click OK.
Criteria are not case-sensitive—you may type M or m. Three last names begin with M.

Show rows where:		
Last Name		
begins with	M	

4	Last Name	First Name
12	**Martinez**	Carlos
13	**Mathis**	Gerhardt
14	McGee	Olivia

11. Choose the Last Name list button 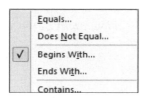→Text Filters from the list.

	Equals...
	Does Not Equal...
✓	Begins With...
	Ends With...
	Contains...

Notice that checkmarks display next to Text Filters and Begins With to indicate the current filter criteria. Read the other criteria options in the menu.

12. Choose the Clear Filter From "Last Name" command from the list.

Filter by Number Criteria

Ryan wants to reward California employees who made software sales of $450,000 or higher.

13. Choose the SW Sales list button 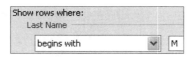→ Number Filters→Greater Than or Equal To. In the Custom AutoFilter dialog box, choose 450,000 from the list and click OK.
The filter displays three employees. You may choose from a list or type the criteria in the Custom AutoFilter dialog box.

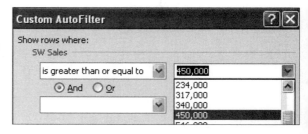

14. Also filter the State column for California (CA).

Two employees in CA have SW sales of $450,000 or greater.

15. Save 💾 the changes.

Copy and Paste Filter Results

Copying and pasting filtered rows allows you to save the results in the workbook for reference. The pasted cells are simply a worksheet list, although they could be converted to a table. These cells retain formatting from the table, but formulas are lost and those cells display the formula result as numbers or text.

16. In cell A22, type **California Employees with >$450,000 Software Sales** and format this label in italics.

The greater than symbol (>) is created by holding down ⌷Shift⌷ and tapping ⌷.⌷ (period).

17. Select the range A4:J19. (Do not select the labels in row 20 because cells below the total row are not part of the table.) Copy and paste to cell A23 as shown.

4	Last Name ▼	First Name ▼	Years ▼	Review Date ▼	Position ▼	Region ▼	State ⌄	SW Sales ⌄	HW Sales ▼	Total Sales ▼
5	**Alvizo**	Alex	7	1-Mar	Senior Sales Rep	Western	CA	900,000	780,000	**1,680,000**
8	**Hasan**	Taz	3	15-Jul	Telemarketer	Western	CA	546,000	120,000	**666,000**
19	**Total**		5			2		1,446,000	900,000	2,346,000
20			Avg Yrs		Total Sales Staff			Total SW	Total HW	
21										
22	*California Employees with >$450,000 Software Sales*									
23	Last Name	First Name	Years	Review Date	Position	Region	State	SW Sales	HW Sales	Total Sales
24	**Alvizo**	Alex	7	1-Mar	Senior Sales Rep	Western	CA	900,000	780,000	**1,680,000**
25	**Hasan**	Taz	3	15-Jul	Telemarketer	Western	CA	546,000	120,000	**666,000**
26	**Total**		5			2		1,446,000	900,000	2,346,000

18. Select any table cell in rows 4-19 and choose Data→ Sort & Filter→Clear 🔽 from the Ribbon.

The Ribbon command clears all filters from multiple columns at one time.

Explore Number and Date Criteria Options

19. Choose SW Sales list button 🔽→Number Filters and take a few moments to explore the other number criteria options.

20. Choose Review Date list button 🔽→Date Filters and take a few moments to explore the date criteria options and choose at least one option.

21. Select any table cell and choose Data→Sort & Filter→Clear 🔽 from the Ribbon when you are done.

The workbook should display 14 records sorted by last name.

22. Save 💾 the changes.

Using the Outline Feature

Excel's Outline feature helps you to control the display of detail data in worksheets. You may see the big picture while still being able to view the details when necessary. Outlining works best in normal worksheet ranges. The structure of tables limits the outlining options that you may use.

How Outlines Work

When you create an outline for a worksheet list, Excel organizes the data into detail groups. This structure is displayed visually along the top border for columns and along the left border for rows. You may click the level number buttons to display various levels of detail, with 1 being the least detail and each higher number displaying more detail. The outline area also contains expand (+) and collapse (–) buttons you may click to display and hide individual groups of data. The following example shows an outlined worksheet.

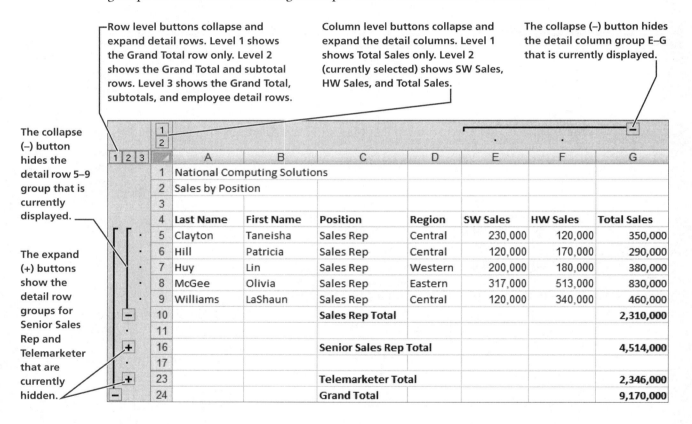

Row level buttons collapse and expand detail rows. Level 1 shows the Grand Total row only. Level 2 shows the Grand Total and subtotal rows. Level 3 shows the Grand Total, subtotals, and employee detail rows.

Column level buttons collapse and expand the detail columns. Level 1 shows Total Sales only. Level 2 (currently selected) shows SW Sales, HW Sales, and Total Sales.

The collapse (–) button hides the detail column group E–G that is currently displayed.

The collapse (–) button hides the detail row 5–9 group that is currently displayed.

The expand (+) buttons show the detail row groups for Senior Sales Rep and Telemarketer that are currently hidden.

	Last Name	First Name	Position	Region	SW Sales	HW Sales	Total Sales
1	National Computing Solutions						
2	Sales by Position						
3							
4	**Last Name**	**First Name**	**Position**	**Region**	**SW Sales**	**HW Sales**	**Total Sales**
5	Clayton	Taneisha	Sales Rep	Central	230,000	120,000	350,000
6	Hill	Patricia	Sales Rep	Central	120,000	170,000	290,000
7	Huy	Lin	Sales Rep	Western	200,000	180,000	380,000
8	McGee	Olivia	Sales Rep	Eastern	317,000	513,000	830,000
9	Williams	LaShaun	Sales Rep	Central	120,000	340,000	460,000
10			**Sales Rep Total**				**2,310,000**
11							
16			**Senior Sales Rep Total**				**4,514,000**
17							
23			**Telemarketer Total**				**2,346,000**
24			**Grand Total**				**9,170,000**

Auto Outline

Excel can apply an outline to most worksheet lists automatically. The key to smooth automatic outlining is to arrange the detail and summary data consistently according to the following rules:

- **Detail Columns**—Detail data in columns must appear all to the right or left of the summary formulas.

- **Detail Rows**—If you want the outline to group detail rows, sort the list by category and insert a subtotal formula after each change within the category.

The more hierarchical your layout is, the more effective the resulting outline will be. Excel will try to outline all data related to summary formulas in the worksheet. If you are not satisfied with the results of the Auto Outline command, you may group rows and columns manually.

Hands-On 11.8   Outline a Worksheet Automatically

In this exercise, you will use the Auto Outline command to outline a worksheet that contains summary formulas. Then you will collapse and expand the outline.

1. Display the Sales by Position worksheet of the Sales Performance workbook.
   This worksheet is a normal worksheet list, not a table. The five Sales Rep rows appear first in the list, followed by four Senior Sales Reps and then five Telemarketers. For outlining to be helpful, the data for each position should be together.

Create an Outline Automatically

Excel can group the detail rows in an outline because a total row follows the detail rows for each position.

2. Choose Data→Outline→Group 🔲 menu ▾→Auto Outline from the Ribbon. (The Group menu button may display as 🔲.)
   Excel automatically groups the rows and columns of the table, indicated by brackets to the left of and above the worksheet. Notice that the rows are divided into three bracketed groups at Level 2 and one larger group at Level 1. There is just one group bracketed for the columns. Excel reviewed the formulas on the worksheet to create these groupings.

3. Use ⌈Ctrl⌉+⌈Home⌉ to move to cell A1.

4. Scroll down until row 4 displays just below the Excel column heading letters.

5. Follow these steps to collapse and expand the display of all detail data:

Ⓐ Click the Level 1 button for columns. Notice that the SW Sales and HW Sales columns collapse, leaving only the Total Sales summary column visible.

Ⓑ Click the Level 1 button for the rows. This leaves only the grand total row visible.

Ⓒ Click the Level 2 button for the rows. This shows the grand total and subtotal rows.

Ⓓ Click the Level 3 button for the rows. This expands the view to show all detail rows.

6. Display Level 2 for the rows.
   Notice the expand (+) and collapse (−) buttons in the outline area. An outline level with a collapse button currently displays its detail data. An outline with an expand button has details that are not displayed.

7. Follow these steps to expand individual groups of row detail data:

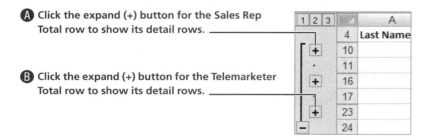

A Click the expand (+) button for the Sales Rep Total row to show its detail rows.

B Click the expand (+) button for the Telemarketer Total row to show its detail rows.

8. Click the Level 3 button for the row groups.
   This command reveals all detail row groups in the outline. You may use the expand and collapse buttons to display and hide individual groups. The Level 1, 2, and 3 buttons expand or collapse all groups in the level at once.

9. Save the changes.

Creating Groups Manually

When the detail rows do not include summary formulas or Excel simply does not outline the worksheet as you expected, you may group rows and columns manually. Row groups must be separated by a blank row, or Excel will combine all into one group. You select the rows or columns to be grouped and choose the Group command from the Ribbon. The selection is grouped in the outline or added to an existing adjacent group. You use a similar procedure to ungroup rows and columns manually. If desired, you may even ungroup rows and columns originally grouped by Excel's Auto Outline command.

QR

QUICK REFERENCE: GROUPING AND UNGROUPING IN LISTS AND TABLES

Task	Procedure
Automatically outline rows and columns	■ Move columns of detail data all to the right or left of the summary formulas. ■ Sort the list by category and insert a subtotal formula after each change within the category if you want the outline to group detail rows. ■ Choose Data→Outline→Group menu ▼→Auto Outline from the Ribbon.
Manually group rows or columns	■ Insert a blank row between each section of rows to be grouped, if necessary. ■ Select the detail row(s) or column(s) to be grouped. ■ Choose Data→Outline→Group from the Ribbon and choose Rows or Columns.
Manually ungroup rows or columns	■ Select the detail row(s) or column(s) to be ungrouped. ■ Choose Data→Outline→Ungroup from the Ribbon and choose Rows or Columns.
Remove an entire outline	■ Select any single worksheet cell. ■ Choose Data→Outline→Ungroup menu ▼→Clear Outline from the Ribbon.

Hands-On 11.9   Outline a Worksheet Manually

In this exercise, you will create groups manually in a table that has no summary formulas for the rows.

Sort a List by Years and Last Name

1. Display the Sales by Years worksheet of the Sales Performance workbook.

2. Select any cell in the list, choose Data→Sort & Filter→Sort ![sort icon], and set options to sort first by years of experience (largest to smallest) and then by last name as shown.
   Make certain a cell is selected in the list if an error message displays after you click OK in the Sort dialog box.

The list is sorted by Years from 8 to 1. Records containing the same number of years are further sorted by last name.

Create an Outline Automatically

3. Choose Data→Outline→Group ![group icon] menu ▼→Auto Outline from the Ribbon.
   Auto Outline grouped only columns H–I because Excel found total formulas in column J. The rows were not grouped because Excel found no summary formulas for them.

4. Insert a blank row at row 10.

Create Groups

You will create one group for 1–4 years of experience and another group for 5–8 years. The blank row separates the two groups. Excel cannot create groups unless you insert blank rows between them.

5. Select the range C5:C9.

6. Choose Data→Outline→Group, choose Rows from the Group dialog box, and click OK.

7. Select the range C11:C19 and group the rows.

8. Experiment by clicking each outline level button, expand button, and collapse button to view the effects.
   Outlining and grouping are alternatives to filtering. If you repeatedly filter for individual items, you may want to create groups rather than a table containing filter list buttons.

Ungroup Rows

9. Select the range E5:E9, choose Data→Outline→Ungroup ⊞ from the Ribbon, and click OK in the Ungroup dialog box. (The Ungroup button may display as ⬀.)

   When you select a cell range, the Ungroup command affects only outline levels that lie within the selected cells. Any cells outside the selection remain grouped.

Clear the Entire Outline

10. Select cell E5 and choose Data→Outline→Ungroup menu ▾→Clear Outline from the Ribbon.

    When you select only one cell, all outline groups in the worksheet are cleared, including groups you created manually. You cannot undo after clearing the outline.

11. Repeat steps 5–7 to regroup the rows, and then deselect cells.

12. Save 🖫 the changes.

Displaying Subtotals

The Subtotal ⊞ command creates subtotals and a grand total for numeric columns in a list. (The command is not available in tables.) You may specify the columns in which to display a subtotal. Excel automatically outlines rows of a list containing subtotals. The illustration shows the Sales by Region worksheet with subtotals displayed.

Excel automatically outlines the list after you create subtotals so that you may collapse or expand the details for each subtotaled group.

	F	G	H	I	J
4	**Region**	**State**	**SW Sales**	**HW Sales**	**Total Sales**
5	Central	CO	128,000	216,000	344,000
6	Central	CO	120,000	340,000	460,000
7	Central	IL	230,000	120,000	350,000
8	Central	IL	120,000	170,000	290,000
9	Central	IL	234,000	560,000	794,000
10	**Central Total**				2,238,000
11	Eastern	FL	340,000	230,000	570,000
12	Eastern	FL	450,000	450,000	900,000
13	Eastern	MA	317,000	513,000	830,000
14	Eastern	MA	123,000	230,000	353,000
15	**Eastern Total**				2,653,000
16	Western	CA	900,000	780,000	1,680,000
17	Western	CA	546,000	120,000	666,000
18	Western	CA	200,000	180,000	380,000
19	Western	CA	340,000	800,000	1,140,000
20	Western	WA	162,000	251,000	413,000
21	**Western Total**				4,279,000
22	**Grand Total**				9,170,000

Subtotals were created in the Total Sales column for each region.

The grand total sums all detail cells in the column.

Sorting the List

The first step in the subtotaling process is to sort the list on the column for which subtotals will be based. For example, sort on the State column if you want subtotals to appear each time the state changes. When you issue the Subtotal command, Excel groups all rows with the same state and calculates a subtotal for each group.

The Subtotal Dialog Box

The Subtotal command on the Ribbon displays the Subtotal dialog box. The options in the dialog box determine the column for which subtotals are calculated and the function used in the calculations. The following illustration describes the options in the Subtotal dialog box.

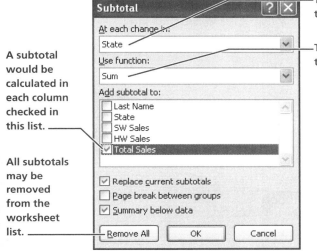

A subtotal would be calculated in each column checked in this list.

All subtotals may be removed from the worksheet list.

This setting must be the same column that you used when sorting the list.

The functions in this list are available to calculate the subtotals.

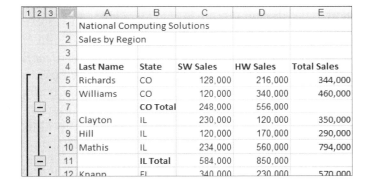

QUICK REFERENCE: DISPLAYING AND REMOVING SUBTOTALS FROM WORKSHEET LISTS	
Task	**Procedure**
Display subtotals	■ Sort the list by the column on which you want subtotals to be based.
	■ Choose Data→Outline→Subtotal ⊞ from the Ribbon.
	■ Set At Each Change In to the same column the sort is based on.
	■ Choose the desired function from the Use Function box.
	■ Choose the numeric columns you want subtotaled in the Add Subtotal To box.
Remove subtotals	■ Choose Data→Outline→Subtotal ⊞ from the Ribbon.
	■ Click Remove All.

In this exercise, you will sort a worksheet list and display subtotals for each state. You also will use the Outline Bar to control the amount of detail displayed in the worksheet.

Sort a List by Region and State

1. Display the Sales by Region worksheet of the Sales Performance workbook.

2. Select any cell in the list, choose Data→Sort & Filter→ , and set options to sort first by region and then by state as shown below.

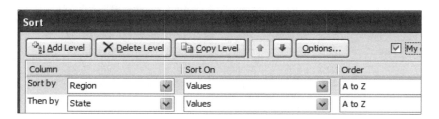

The five Central rows are listed in state order, followed by four Eastern and then five Western rows. For subtotals to calculate correctly, the data for each state must be together. You could have sorted just by state without putting the states in region order.

Display Subtotals

3. Choose Data→Outline→Subtotal from the Ribbon.
   If an error message displays, make certain a cell is selected in the list.

4. Follow these steps to set the subtotal options:

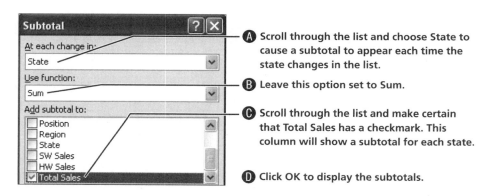

Ⓐ Scroll through the list and choose State to cause a subtotal to appear each time the state changes in the list.

Ⓑ Leave this option set to Sum.

Ⓒ Scroll through the list and make certain that Total Sales has a checkmark. This column will show a subtotal for each state.

Ⓓ Click OK to display the subtotals.

5. Autofit the State column.

6. Bold the six subtotal amounts and the grand total amount in column J to make them stand out.
   Take a few moments to review the subtotals and grand total before continuing.

Use the Outline Bar

7. Follow these steps to experiment with the Outline Bar for rows on the left side of the worksheet:

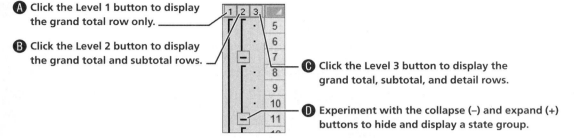

A Click the Level 1 button to display the grand total row only.

B Click the Level 2 button to display the grand total and subtotal rows.

C Click the Level 3 button to display the grand total, subtotal, and detail rows.

D Experiment with the collapse (–) and expand (+) buttons to hide and display a state group.

If you wanted to remove the subtotals from the list, you would use the Remove All button in the Subtotal dialog box. You will not remove subtotals in this exercise.

8. Save ▣ the changes and close the workbook.

Concepts Review

True/False Questions

1. You must insert blank rows in a table before adding more records. TRUE FALSE
2. The first name and last name should be typed in the same table column. TRUE FALSE
3. The total row of a table may contain functions such as SUM, AVERAGE, or any other Excel function. TRUE FALSE
4. Deleting a table row also deletes cells on the same row outside the table. TRUE FALSE
5. A table may be filtered by more than one column. TRUE FALSE
6. Filters may be performed using text, date, number, or color criteria. TRUE FALSE
7. You may outline a worksheet automatically and then add or delete groups manually. TRUE FALSE
8. Rows or columns defined with the Group command may be displayed or hidden by clicking a button. TRUE FALSE
9. Subtotals should be applied to an unsorted list. TRUE FALSE
10. You may calculate subtotals in more than one numeric column. TRUE FALSE

Multiple Choice Questions

1. Where are structured references located?
   a. Filter criteria
   b. Outlines
   c. Tables
   d. Sorts

2. What happens when you enter a formula in a blank table column?
   a. The formula is copied to all cells in that column.
   b. The formula is copied to all cells in the same row.
   c. The table is converted to a worksheet range.
   d. The table is converted to an outline.

3. What is the purpose of the column heading list button in a table?
   a. Creates a formula
   b. Creates an outline group
   c. Performs sorts and filters
   d. Converts the column to a row

4. What happens when you give the Auto Outline command?
   a. Only rows and columns using summary formulas are grouped.
   b. Excel creates groups for all types of detail data in the worksheet.
   c. You must select the rows or columns to be grouped and then give the Group command.
   d. Excel creates an outline based on your entries in a dialog box.

Skill Builders

Skill Builder 11.1   Convert to a Table and Create Formulas

In this exercise, you will convert a worksheet that tracks supporter information for a political campaign to a table. You will enter build total formulas, create a calculated column, and enter additional records.

1. Open the sb-Reynolds Supporters workbook from the Lesson 11 folder in your file storage location. Maximize the window.

Convert a Range to a Table

2. Select cell A4, choose Home→Styles→Format As Table ⊞ from the Ribbon, choose a table style, and click OK to confirm the table range.
Your table style may be different from the one shown in the illustrations that follow.

3. Choose Design→Properties→Table Name and change the existing name to **Contributions**.

4. Select the column headings in row 4 and left-align ≣ the text.
Left-aligning ensures that column headings are visible with their list buttons displayed.

5. Autofit the table column widths so that all text is visible in the table.

Create Formulas in the Total Row

6. Choose Design→Table Style Options→Total Row to display the total row in row 20.

7. Select cell E20 and choose Count from the total cell's list.

8. Select cell F20 and choose Average from the total cell's list.

9. Format the range F20:G20 in Accounting number format with no decimal places. (Do not select cell E20 because the calculation counts records rather than sums dollar amounts.)

| None |
| Average |
| Count |
| Count Numbers |
| Max |
| Min |
| Sum |
| StdDev |
| Var |
| More Functions… |
| 15 |

	750		450		1,000
	15	$	404	$	9,075

Create a Calculated Column

You will build a formula that finds the difference between contributions for the current election and those for the last election.

10. Select cell H4, type **Difference** as the column heading, and autofit the column width.

11. In cell H5, type an equals (**=**) sign.

12. Select cell E5 and type a plus (**+**) sign.

13. Select cell F5 and type a minus (**−**) sign.

14. Select cell G5 and complete the formula.

15. With cell H5 selected, tap F2 to display the formula in edit mode.

    Notice the three structured references in the formula. Excel copied this formula to all cells in the column except the total row.

16. Tap Esc to exit edit mode without making any changes.

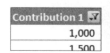

Add Two Records

17. Select cell H19 and tap Tab to create a new blank row.

18. Follow these steps to enter two records in rows 20–21:

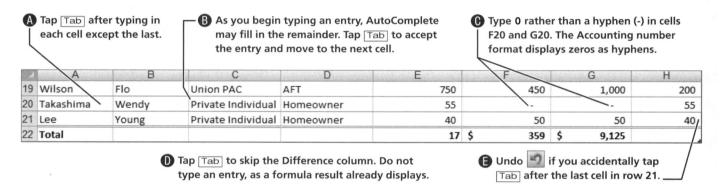

A Tap Tab after typing in each cell except the last.

B As you begin typing an entry, AutoComplete may fill in the remainder. Tap Tab to accept the entry and move to the next cell.

C Type 0 rather than a hyphen (-) in cells F20 and G20. The Accounting number format displays zeros as hyphens.

	A	B	C	D	E	F	G	H
19	Wilson	Flo	Union PAC	AFT	750	450	1,000	200
20	Takashima	Wendy	Private Individual	Homeowner	55	-	-	55
21	Lee	Young	Private Individual	Homeowner	40	50	50	40
22	**Total**				17 $	359 $	9,125	

D Tap Tab to skip the Difference column. Do not type an entry, as a formula result already displays.

E Undo ↺ if you accidentally tap Tab after the last cell in row 21.

19. Save 💾 the changes and leave the workbook open for the next exercise.

Skill Builder 11.2   Sort and Filter a Table

In this exercise, you will sort table records and filter by number.

Before You Begin: You must have completed Skill Builder 11.1 and the sb-Reynolds Supporters workbook should be open. Your table style may look different from the one shown in the illustrations that follow.

Sort the Table

1. Choose Difference list button ▾→Sort Largest to Smallest ↓ from the list.
   The table rows are sorted from highest to lowest.

Filter by Number

2. Choose Contribution 1 list button ▾→Number Filters→Above Average from the list.
   The filter displays seven records higher than the average contribution amount.

Contribution 1
1,000
1,500

3. Choose Contribution 1 list button ▾→Number Filters→Top 10 from the list, and click OK in the Top 10 AutoFilter dialog box.
   The filter displays the 10 highest difference amounts sorted from largest to smallest.

4. Choose Contribution 1 list button 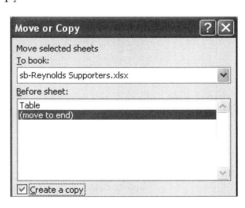→Clear Filter From "Contribution 1."
   The table view is restored to all 17 records.

5. Sort the Difference column from highest to lowest if its column heading filter button does not display the sort icon.

6. Save 💾 the changes and leave the workbook open for the next exercise.

Skill Builder 11.3   Create Subtotals and Use Outlining Tools

In this exercise, you will duplicate the worksheet and convert the table to a worksheet range. Then you will create subtotals for the contribution amounts by each type of contact.

Before You Begin: *You must have completed Skill Builder 11.1 and Skill Builder 11.2 and the sb-Reynolds Supporters workbook should be open. Your table style may look different from the one shown in the illustrations that follow.*

Copy the Table Worksheet

1. Rename Sheet1 of the sb-Reynolds Supporters workbook as **Table**.

2. Right-click the Table sheet tab and choose Move or Copy from the context menu.

3. Set the dialog box options as shown and click OK.

4. Rename the copied sheet as **Subtotals**.

Convert the Table to a Worksheet Range

5. Turn off the display of the total row.

6. Select the table range (including the header row), choose Design→Tools→Convert to Range, and click Yes to confirm.

Create Subtotals

7. Sort A to Z ↓ by contact type.

8. Choose Data→Outline→Subtotal 📊 and set options as shown.
   You will find the maximum contribution for each contact type in three columns of the worksheet list.

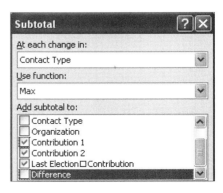

9. Click the collapse (−) button for Private Individual Max and Union PAC Max in the outline area.

1 2 3			A	B	C	
		4	**Last Name**	**First Name**	**Contact Type**	**Org**
	·	5	Gardner	Aaron	Business Owner	Sym
	·	6	Watkins	Edward	Business Owner	Ron
	·	7	Post	Wanda	Business Owner	Café
	·	8	Lopez	Jesse	Business Owner	PC S
	·	9	Pretinger	Deneice	Business Owner	Cab
	·	10	Rogers	Thomasina	Business Owner	Stev
	−	11			**Business Owner Max**	
	+	18			**Private Individual Max**	
	+	24			**Union PAC Max**	
	−	25			**Grand Max**	

Only the Business Owner detail rows display. Records are still in order by Difference from highest to lowest. You sorted the list in Skill Builder 11.2.

10. Click the Level 3 button to expand all detail rows.

11. Use an outline button to collapse the list to display just the subtotals and grand total.

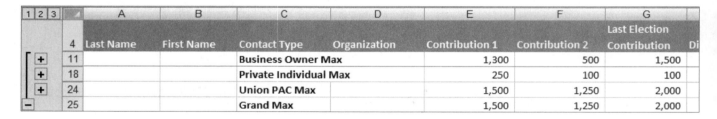

1 2 3		A	B	C	D	E	F	G	
	4	**Last Name**	**First Name**	**Contact Type**	**Organization**	**Contribution 1**	**Contribution 2**	**Last Election Contribution**	**Di**
+	11			**Business Owner Max**		1,300	500	1,500	
+	18			**Private Individual Max**		250	100	100	
+	24			**Union PAC Max**		1,500	1,250	2,000	
−	25			**Grand Max**		1,500	1,250	2,000	

Notice that the calculated formula in the Difference column was lost when you converted the table to a normal worksheet range. You could, however, re-create any lost formulas as normal Excel formulas.

12. Save 💾 the changes and close the workbook.

 **Assessments**

Assessment 11.1 Convert to a Table and Create Formulas

In this exercise, you will convert a worksheet range to a table. You will change a formula in the total row, create a calculated column, and add a record. You will also sort the table.

1. Open the as-Westside Employee Compensation workbook from the Lesson 11 folder in your file storage location. Maximize the window.

2. Convert the worksheet range to a table using a table style of your choice.

3. Rename the table as **Retirement Plan** following Excel's rules for naming tables.

4. Edit column heading names as necessary and adjust column widths.

5. Format the numbers in columns D and E with Comma Style. You determine the number of decimal places.

6. Change the formula in the total row to one that averages the retirement plan contributions. Change the label in cell A19 to **Average**.

7. Create a calculated column that computes Retirement Plan Contributions divided by Compensation. Format the results with Percent Style. Use **% of Compensation** as the column heading.

8. Add the record for Uyen shown in the illustration.

9. Sort by % of Compensation from highest to lowest.

	A	B	C	D	E	F
1	Westside Electric Supplies					
2	*Employee Compensation Table*					
3						
4	Last Name	First Name	Category	Compensation	Retirement Plan Contributions	% of Compensation
5	Wilson	Larry	Salaried	89,000	21,890	25%
6	Monroe	James	Hourly	34,000	4,250	13%
7	Erickson	Bryan	Hourly	38,000	4,500	12%
8	Barton	Lisa	Salaried	51,000	6,000	12%
9	Zurlow	Jacob	Hourly	30,000	3,450	12%
10	Jackson	Samuel	Salaried	45,000	4,700	10%
11	Uyen	Ty	Salaried	56,000	4,700	8%
12	Thomas	Lyn	Salaried	34,000	2,700	8%
13	Ellison	Linda	Salaried	32,000	2,500	8%
14	Parades	Lisa	Hourly	31,000	2,300	7%
15	Chin	Raymond	Salaried	56,000	3,450	6%
16	Watson	Guillermo	Hourly	27,000	1,600	6%
17	Plavan	Jaime	Salaried	45,000	1,900	4%
18	Hughes	Jason	Hourly	23,000	-	0%
19	Average				4,567	

The completed Employee Compensation table

10. Save 💾 the changes.

Assessment 11.2   Sort and Filter a Table

In this exercise, you will sort table records and filter by text and number.

1. Open the as-Monrovia Media Sales workbook from the Lesson 11 folder. Maximize the window.

2. Sort by Sales from highest to lowest as shown in the illustration.

3. Filter by New York in the Market column.

4. Copy and paste the filter results to cell A21.

5. In cell A20, type an appropriate title to describe the filter results.

6. Clear the filter.
   Now you will complete another filter.

7. Filter for units sold between 44 and 55 units.

8. Copy and paste the filter results below the New York market filter results.

9. Type an appropriate title to describe the filter.

10. Clear the filter.

11. Make certain that the table and two sets of pasted results will print on one page.

	A	B	C	D	E	F	G
1	Monrovia Media						
2	*Media Sales Table*						
3							
4	Last Name	First Name	Units Sold	Week	Promotion	Market	Sales
5	Mathis	Gerhardt	93	1-Aug	Senior Sales Rep	Cincinnati	76,200
6	Huy	Lin	81	15-Sep	Sales Rep	Dallas	65,200
7	Zain	Elizabeth	64	1-Feb	Senior Sales Rep	New York	57,800
8	Clayton	Taneisha	79	1-Mar	Sales Rep	New York	55,100
9	Knapp	Mai	62	15-Nov	Telemarketer	Dallas	42,100
10	McGee	Olivia	62	1-Jun	Sales Rep	Phoenix	31,700
11	Smith	Jacqui	55	15-Apr	Telemarketer	Phoenix	31,200
12	Alvizo	Alex	47	1-Mar	Senior Sales Rep	Phoenix	28,700
13	Hasan	Taz	47	15-Jul	Telemarketer	Las Vegas	25,100
14	Martinez	Carlos	45	15-Sep	Senior Sales Rep	Las Vegas	23,700
15	Williams	LaShaun	43	1-Sep	Las Vegas	Las Vegas	20,200
16	Richards	Paul	43	15-Jun	Telemarketer	Las Vegas	12,800
17	Cray	Karen	39	1-Sep	Telemarketer	New York	11,590
18	Hill	Patricia	27	1-Jun	Sales Rep	Cincinnati	9,000
19							
20	*New York Market*						
21	Last Name	First Name	Units Sold	Week	Promotion	Market	Sales
22	Zain	Elizabeth	64	1-Feb	Senior Sales Rep	New York	57,800

The completed Media Sales table

12. Save 🖫 the changes and close the workbook.

Assessment 11.3   Outline a Worksheet and Use Subtotals

In this exercise, you will sort records in a list that tracks monthly animal care expenses by cost, age, and health of the animals. You will outline the worksheet and display subtotals that calculate averages.

1. Open the as-March Expenses workbook from the Lesson 11 folder.

2. Perform a multicolumn sort by Age and Health.
   Now you will display subtotals as shown in the illustration at the end of this exercise.

3. Base subtotals on the animals' health.

4. Make subtotals average each of the cost columns.

5. Bold the subtotal and grand total amounts.
   Now you will outline the worksheet.

6. Group Shelter Cost and Veterinary Cost, but do not group the Date Arrived column.

	A	B	C	D	Shelter Cost	Veterinary Cost	Total Costs
4	Animal	Age	Health	Date Arrived			
5	Cat	Adult	Healthy	1-Mar	$ 82.50	$ 10.00	$ 92.50
6	Dog	Adult	Healthy	2-Mar	$ 79.75	$ 10.00	$ 89.75
7	Dog	Adult	Healthy	8-Mar	$ 63.25	$ 10.00	$ 73.25
8	Dog	Adult	Healthy	9-Mar	$ 60.50	$ 10.00	$ 70.50
9	Cat	Adult	Healthy	9-Mar	$ 60.50	$ 10.00	$ 70.50
10	Dog	Adult	Healthy	11-Mar	$ 55.00	$ 10.00	$ 65.00
11	Dog	Adult	Healthy	20-Mar	$ 30.25	$ 10.00	$ 40.25
12	Cat	Adult	Healthy	24-Mar	$ 19.25	$ 10.00	$ 29.25
13	Dog	Adult	Healthy	28-Mar	$ 8.25	$ 10.00	$ 18.25
14	Cat	Adult	Healthy	30-Mar	$ 2.75	$ 10.00	$ 12.75
15	Dog	Adult	Healthy	30-Mar	$ 2.75	$ 10.00	$ 12.75
16			**Healthy Average**		$ 42.25	$ 10.00	$ 52.25
17	Dog	Adult	Sick	20-Mar	$ 30.25	$ 25.00	$ 55.25
18			**Sick Average**		$ 30.25	$ 25.00	$ 55.25
19	Dog	Pup/Kitten	Healthy	3-Mar	$ 77.00	$ 10.00	$ 87.00
20	Cat	Pup/Kitten	Healthy	10-Mar	$ 57.75	$ 10.00	$ 67.75
21	Dog	Pup/Kitten	Healthy	13-Mar	$ 49.50	$ 10.00	$ 59.50
22			**Healthy Average**		$ 61.42	$ 10.00	$ 71.42
23	Dog	Pup/Kitten	Sick	3-Mar	$ 77.00	$ 75.00	$ 152.00
24	Cat	Pup/Kitten	Sick	3-Mar	$ 77.00	$ 25.00	$ 102.00
25	Dog	Pup/Kitten	Sick	15-Mar	$ 44.00	$ 25.00	$ 69.00
26	Dog	Pup/Kitten	Sick	27-Mar	$ 11.00	$ 50.00	$ 61.00
27			**Sick Average**		$ 52.25	$ 43.75	$ 96.00
28			**Grand Average**		$ 46.75	$ 17.89	$ 64.64

The outline after grouping

7. Use outline buttons to hide details for the two Pup/Kitten groups (not shown in the illustration).

8. Use outline buttons to hide the Shelter Cost and Veterinary Cost columns (not shown in the illustration).

9. Save 🖫 the changes and close the workbook.

Critical Thinking

Critical Thinking 11.1   Create a Supplier Deliveries Table

Linda Ochoa owns Ochoa Nursery, which sells garden tools and plants. Linda's suppliers deliver products to her every Friday. She wants to convert a worksheet to a table and then sort and filter the records.

- Open the ct-Supplier Deliveries workbook from the Lesson 11 folder in your file storage location.

- Convert the worksheet list to a table named Deliveries. (Do not rename the sheet tab.)

- Turn off the display of the total row, if it is displayed.

- Create a column for retail price, which is calculated as the wholesale price multiplied by 1.5. Use [Alt]+[Enter] to place the column heading on two lines within the cell to conserve column width.

NOTE! *The entire formula may not display in the Formula Bar. You may increase the height of the Formula Bar by dragging its bottom border.*

- Add the following records:

| Garden Warehouse | Stones | Building | 2.35 |
| Bright Flower Supply | Pails | Tools | 2.10 |

- Insert a Quantity column in the table between Category ID and Wholesale Price. Enter the following quantities down the column:

  12, 4, 144, 12, 144, 48, 12, 200, 6, 48, 36, 24, 48, 48, 72, 72, 24, 12, 24, 18

- Create a column at the end of the table for Wholesale Value, which is calculated as the quantity multiplied by the wholesale price.

- Select the range F4:F24 (Retail Price column), and cut and paste those cells to H4 to become the last column. If a blank column remains in column F, select and delete that table column.

- Include a formula in the total row that counts the product rows. Determine which other cell(s) in the total row should have a SUM formula based on the type of data in the column. Add or remove SUM formulas as necessary.

- Format the table attractively.

- Set landscape orientation for printing and adjust other options, if necessary, to print the worksheet on one page.

- Save 🖫 the changes and leave the workbook open for the next exercise.

Critical Thinking 11.2   Filter the Supplier Deliveries Table

Before You Begin: You must have completed Critical Thinking 11.1 and the ct-Supplier Deliveries workbook should be open.

Linda Ochoa wants the supply delivery data subtotaled and filtered in several ways.

■ Make two copies of the Table worksheet in the ct-Supplier Deliveries workbook. Name the new sheets **Product Filter** and **Multi Filter**. Also rename the tables.

■ Display the Product Filter worksheet and filter for products beginning with the letter S. Sort the results in alphabetic order by product.

■ Display the Multi Filter worksheet and filter for Building and Tools items with a wholesale value of $100 or less.

■ Select the three sheet tabs and choose portrait orientation and narrow margins. Preview to ensure that each worksheet would print on one page.

■ Save 🖫 the changes and close the workbook.

Critical Thinking 11.3   Create Subtotals in a Book Return List

Les Armstrong is the returns manager for Parker Book Publishers, Inc. He asks you to modify a worksheet list and create a column with a formula and subtotals to analyze customer returns.

■ Open the ct-Customer Returns workbook from the Lesson 11 folder.

■ Create a Refund Amount column in the worksheet list and determine the appropriate formula to use.

■ Subtotal the list with a SUM function to show subtotals in the Refund Amount column for each change in the Category column.

■ Use outline buttons to display only the subtotals, grand total, and Fitness detail rows.

■ Save 🖫 the changes and close the workbook.

Unit 3

Advanced Skills

In this unit, you will work with Excel's advanced features. You will use PivotTables and PivotCharts to perform sophisticated data analyses and create macros to automate repetitive tasks. In dealing with what-if analyses, you will use the PMT and FV functions, Goal Seek, Solver, the Analysis ToolPak, and the Scenario Manager. You will create 3-D cell references and use the HLOOKUP and VLOOKUP functions. You will also use formula auditing tools to help you locate errors in formulas. You will group worksheets, allowing you to enter data into multiple worksheets simultaneously. You will also work with Excel's Data Validation and Conditional Formatting tools, data tables, and trendlines. Knowing how to collaborate effectively is important. You will set up project folders, insert comments in a workbook, and attach a workbook to an email. You will create shared workbooks, track changes, and merge reviewer edits. You will also learn how to make Excel 2007 files compatible with prior Excel versions. Finally, you will integrate Excel with other Office programs.

Lesson 12: Creating PivotTables and Macros

Lesson 13: Using Financial Functions and Data Analysis

Lesson 14: Auditing and Additional Functions

Lesson 15: Using Advanced Formatting and Analysis Tools

Lesson 16: Collaborating in Excel

Lesson 17: Integrating Excel with Other Programs

LESSON 12

Creating PivotTables and Macros

Excel has many features to help you perform sophisticated data analyses, including the PivotTable and the PivotChart. PivotTables let you summarize worksheet data dynamically to view them in various ways. In this lesson, you will arrange your data with simple drag-and-drop commands and have Excel automatically create summary formulas in the rows and columns. You also will create PivotCharts to achieve the same power and flexibility for charting data. Many Excel workbooks are used on a recurring basis. Examples include monthly expense accounts, sales forecasts, and lists of various types. Often, the same tasks are performed in these workbooks over and over. Excel allows you to create macros to automate repetitive tasks. In addition, Excel lets you assign macros to shortcut keys, buttons on the Quick Access toolbar, and custom buttons or other graphics in a worksheet. In this lesson, you will create macros and custom buttons in an Excel workbook.

LESSON OBJECTIVES

After studying this lesson, you will be able to:

- Create PivotTables and change their fields
- Create PivotCharts from PivotTable data
- Set macro security to protect workbook data
- Record and run macros to automate tasks
- Add custom task buttons to worksheets

Case Study: Simplifying Repetitive Tasks

Allen Tuifamo is the assistant to the national sales manager at Media Marketing Group. As part of his monthly routine, Allen presents sales data to his sales manager. Allen is expected to create various views of data that help the sales manager analyze trends and track the efficiency of the sales staff.

When he began this job, Allen would create workbooks with several views of the sales data, but this rather static view didn't allow him to analyze the data very efficiently. Allen recently heard about Excel's PivotTable feature at a one-day training seminar. He learned that Pivot-Tables let you look at data in a variety of ways without requiring you to sort and lay out the data manually. The following is just one example of how a PivotTable may be designed.

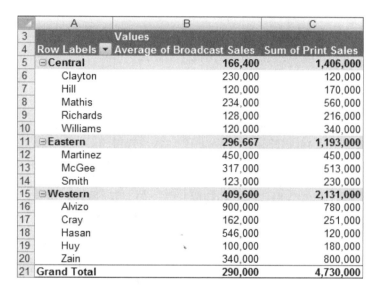

| Row Labels | Values | |
	Average of Broadcast Sales	Sum of Print Sales
Central	166,400	1,406,000
Clayton	230,000	120,000
Hill	120,000	170,000
Mathis	234,000	560,000
Richards	128,000	216,000
Williams	120,000	340,000
Eastern	296,667	1,193,000
Martinez	450,000	450,000
McGee	317,000	513,000
Smith	123,000	230,000
Western	409,600	2,131,000
Alvizo	900,000	780,000
Cray	162,000	251,000
Hasan	546,000	120,000
Huy	100,000	180,000
Zain	340,000	800,000
Grand Total	290,000	4,730,000

Allen also is responsible for maintaining a training roster for sales personnel, which he has set up in Excel. He uses macros to sort the roster in various ways. In addition, Allen adds buttons to the worksheet and attaches his macros to the buttons. Now with the click of a button, he can add new students and sort the roster.

	Instructor	Student	Level	Score			
1	Excel Training Student Roster						
3	Instructor	Student	Level	Score			
9	Allison	Yee, Donese	3	100			
10	Allison	Zobe, Wayne	1	85			
11	Dawes	Almore, Brian	3	97		Insert Student	
12	Dawes	Brown, Lisa	1	99			
13	Dawes	Carlson, Michael	2	82		Sort by Instructor	
14	Dawes	Davis, Ted	2	92			
15	Dawes	Jackson, Mary	1	87			

Creating PivotTables

PivotTables are powerful data analysis tools. They let you summarize data in various ways and instantly change the view you use. You created tables to sort and filter data and produced subtotals in Lesson 11, Creating Tables and Outlines. A PivotTable not only subtotals groups of related data, but also goes a step further and compares one group to another. Compared with performing similar data analyses on a standard worksheet, PivotTables offer tremendous speed and flexibility. You create PivotTables from columns or a table in an Excel worksheet. The following examples explain two PivotTables based on the same table.

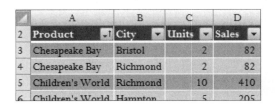

The worksheet table on which the sample PivotTables are based

PivotTable Example 1

You could sort the preceding table by product or city; however, you could not easily compare sales for the same product in each city. This is where the PivotTable comes into use. A PivotTable can summarize some or all of the data in any number of ways, and it creates grand totals for you. Examine the PivotTable and notice that the Product field from the table is used for the row labels, the City field for the column labels, and the Sales field for the data area and grand totals. Each row displays the sales for one product in the various cities.

This PivotTable summarizes sales for all products sold.

Sales of each product are displayed by city.

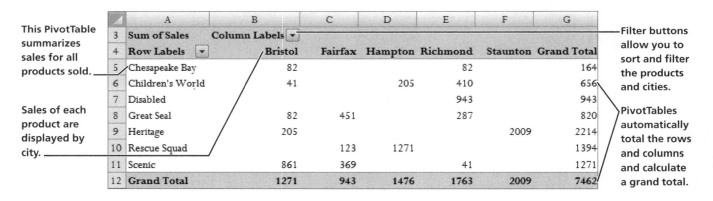

Filter buttons allow you to sort and filter the products and cities.

PivotTables automatically total the rows and columns and calculate a grand total.

PivotTable Example 2

Using the same table data, you may view the data differently—in this case, summarized first by city and then by product. To create this type of view, the PivotTable layout contains the City and Product fields for row labels, no column labels, and the Sales field for the data area and totals.

This PivotTable layout summarizes product sales for each city.

Buttons allow you to collapse and expand the level of detail.

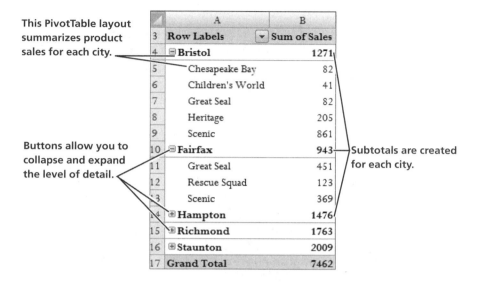

	A	B
3	**Row Labels** ▾	**Sum of Sales**
4	⊟ **Bristol**	1271
5	Chesapeake Bay	82
6	Children's World	41
7	Great Seal	82
8	Heritage	205
9	Scenic	861
10	⊟ **Fairfax**	943
11	Great Seal	451
12	Rescue Squad	123
13	Scenic	369
14	⊞ **Hampton**	1476
15	⊞ **Richmond**	1763
16	⊞ **Staunton**	2009
17	**Grand Total**	7462

Subtotals are created for each city.

In this lesson, you will learn how to lay out both of these types of PivotTables and much more.

How PivotTables Work

Each area of the PivotTable plays a role in data organization. The PivotTable Field List task pane displays after you define the worksheet range to be used. The areas of the task pane are explained in the following illustration showing the settings for the preceding PivotTable Example 1.

You may choose some or all columns from the worksheet data to appear in the PivotTable.

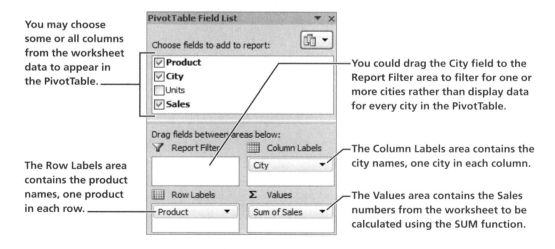

You could drag the City field to the Report Filter area to filter for one or more cities rather than display data for every city in the PivotTable.

The Row Labels area contains the product names, one product in each row.

The Column Labels area contains the city names, one city in each column.

The Values area contains the Sales numbers from the worksheet to be calculated using the SUM function.

!NOTE! *You must select a cell in the PivotTable to display the PivotTable Field List task pane.*

You design a PivotTable by choosing the columns (fields) to be included from the worksheet. Excel initially places all text columns in the Row Labels area and all number columns in the Values area for summing. If this is not your desired layout, you can drag and drop various fields into the correct areas of the task pane. Where you place fields determines how the PivotTable summarizes the data. You may choose from several functions—such as SUM, COUNT, and AVERAGE—to calculate fields containing values.

QUICK REFERENCE: CREATING A PIVOTTABLE

Task	Procedure
Create a PivotTable from a worksheet range or table	■ Select a cell in the worksheet range or table. ■ Choose Insert→Tables→PivotTable from the Ribbon. ■ Verify the worksheet range or table name in the Create PivotTable dialog box and click OK to place the PivotTable on a new worksheet. ■ In the PivotTable Field List task pane, place a checkmark by each worksheet field to be included in the design, selecting the fields in the order they should appear as row labels and values columns. ■ If necessary, drag and drop a field name to the correct area: Report Filter, Row Labels, Column Labels, or Values.
Name a PivotTable	■ Choose Options→PivotTable, type the name in the PivotTable name text box (spaces are allowed), and tap Enter.
Display the PivotTable Field List task pane	■ Select any cell within the PivotTable. ■ If the task pane is turned off, choose Options→Show/Hide→Field List from the Ribbon.

The best way to understand the dynamic capabilities of a PivotTable is to create one. In this exercise, you will create PivotTables from a worksheet range and a table.

Review the Worksheet Data

1. Start Excel and open the Media Sales workbook from the Lesson 12 folder on your file storage location.

2. Maximize ⬜ the window.

The Sales Summary worksheet contains the data you will use to create two PivotTables. Look at the column headings and the various records in the rows. Each record contains data for a specific salesperson. Notice the numeric data contained in the Broadcast Sales and Print Sales columns.

Create a PivotTable from a Worksheet Range

You will create a PivotTable that summarizes Broadcast Sales by salesperson with subtotals for each region.

3. Select cell D6.

You should select a cell within the worksheet range or table before you create the PivotTable. The range should contain no blank rows or columns.

4. Choose Insert→Tables→PivotTable 🖼 from the Ribbon.

The Create PivotTable dialog box appears.

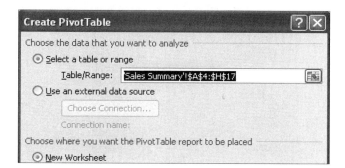

5. Verify the suggested range as shown, notice that the default is to place the PivotTable on a new worksheet, and click OK.

A new worksheet appears and contains an empty PivotTable placeholder. The PivotTable Field List task pane also displays. If the task pane is turned off, choose Options→Show/Hide→Field List from the Ribbon.

6. Rename Sheet1 as **PivotTable by Salesperson**.

7. Select cell E6, which is outside the boundary of the PivotTable outline.

Notice that the PivotTable Field List task pane disappears. You must select a cell within the PivotTable placeholder to display the task pane.

8. Select cell A3 within the PivotTable placeholder to restore the task pane.
   Notice that the PivotTable Field List task pane contains a list of all the data fields in the worksheet range. You will choose only some of them.

9. Follow these steps to define the PivotTable in the task pane:

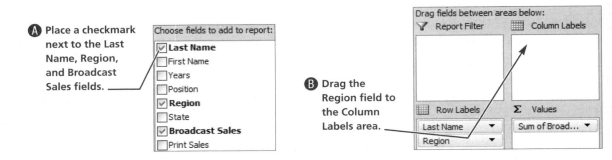

A Place a checkmark next to the Last Name, Region, and Broadcast Sales fields.

B Drag the Region field to the Column Labels area.

In the resulting PivotTable, notice that the salespeople's last names are displayed one per row, the three regions are displayed one per column, and the broadcast sales data is summarized with totals for each last name in column E and each region in row 18. The Central label is not aligned over its numbers, and you will fix this in a later exercise.

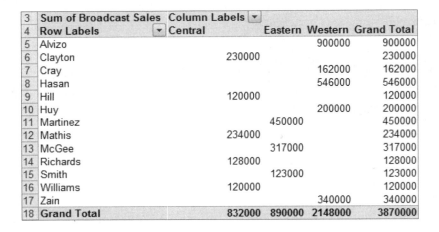

3	Sum of Broadcast Sales	Column Labels			
4	Row Labels	Central	Eastern	Western	Grand Total
5	Alvizo			900000	900000
6	Clayton	230000			230000
7	Cray			162000	162000
8	Hasan			546000	546000
9	Hill	120000			120000
10	Huy			200000	200000
11	Martinez		450000		450000
12	Mathis	234000			234000
13	McGee		317000		317000
14	Richards	128000			128000
15	Smith		123000		123000
16	Williams	120000			120000
17	Zain			340000	340000
18	Grand Total	832000	890000	2148000	3870000

Name the PivotTable

10. Choose Options→PivotTable from the Ribbon, type **BySalesperson** in the PivotTable name text box, and tap [Enter].

Convert the Worksheet Range to a Table

11. Display the Sales Summary worksheet.

12. Select cell A4.

13. Choose Insert→Tables→Table from the Ribbon to convert the list to a table. Accept the default options in the Create Table dialog box and click OK.

14. On the Design Ribbon, name the table **SalesSummary**.

Create a PivotTable from a Worksheet Table

The steps for creating a PivotTable from a worksheet table are the same as for a worksheet range. This time your PivotTable will group the data by region and then by salesperson within the region.

15. With any table cell selected, choose Insert→Tables→PivotTable from the Ribbon.

16. Verify that the suggested range is the SalesSummary table and click OK.

17. Rename the new sheet as **PivotTable by Region**.

18. In the PivotTable Field List task pane, place a checkmark next to field names *in this order:* Region, Last Name, Print Sales.

The task pane and the PivotTable results should display as shown. The records are grouped by region with the salespeople's last names in alphabetical order within each region. The Print Sales subtotal displays for each region, and a grand total appears at the bottom of the column. With this layout, you did not need to create any column labels.

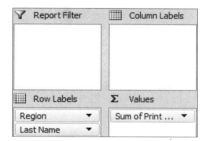
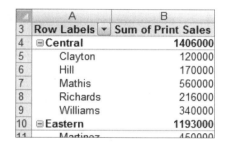

Name the PivotTable

19. Choose Options→PivotTable from the Ribbon, type **ByRegion** in the PivotTable name text box, and tap ⎡Enter⎤.

20. Save 💾 the changes to your workbook.

Formatting a PivotTable

Values and subtotals in the PivotTable do not automatically display the formatting from the original worksheet cells. You may set number formatting for a value field. You also may select and format one or more specific cells in the PivotTable. For example, you may align the column labels from the Home tab on the Ribbon. The Chart Tools' Design contextual tab contains a large selection of PivotTable styles to apply color, shading, and gridlines with one mouse click. The report layout displays in Compact Form by default, or you may choose from two other layouts. The field headers may be turned off to display just the column headings, which looks better during a presentation.

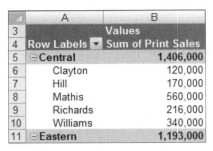

	A	B
3		Values
4	Row Labels ▼	Sum of Print Sales
5	⊟Central	1,406,000
6	Clayton	120,000
7	Hill	170,000
8	Mathis	560,000
9	Richards	216,000
10	Williams	340,000
11	⊟Eastern	1,193,000

The Compact Form report layout with a PivotTable style applied

	A	B	C
3			Values
4	Region ▼	Last Name ▼	Sum of Print Sales
5	⊟Central	Clayton	120,000
6		Hill	170,000
7		Mathis	560,000
8		Richards	216,000
9		Williams	340,000
10	Central Total		1,406,000

The Tabular Form report layout with filter buttons for each row label field

QUICK REFERENCE: FORMATTING A PIVOTTABLE

Task	Procedure
Apply number formatting to a column	Right-click a column cell in the PivotTable, choose Number Format from the pop-up (context) menu, and choose options from the Format Cells dialog box.
Change the subtotals or grand totals display	Choose Design→Layout→Subtotals ▦ or Grand Totals ▦ and choose an option from the Ribbon.
Apply a PivotTable style	Choose Design→PivotTable Styles and choose a style from the Ribbon.
Apply a report layout	Choose Design→Layout→Report Layout ▤ and choose the Compact (default), Outline, or Tabular layout from the Ribbon.
Turn off field headers to present a PivotTable	Choose Options→Show/Hide→Field Headers ▦ from the Ribbon.

Hands-On 12.2   Format a PivotTable

In this exercise, you will format the PivotTables that you created in the previous exercise. You will format selected cells, apply number formatting to values columns, choose a PivotTable style, and explore the report layout choices.

Format PivotTable Data

1. Display the PivotTable by Salesperson worksheet in the Media Sales workbook.

2. Select cells B4:D4 and right-align the labels to match the number alignment in their columns.
   Notice that row 18 contains totals for each of the three regions. The Grand Total column, however, is unnecessary because the totals merely repeat each salesperson's amount.

3. Right-click the Grand Total label in cell E4 and choose Remove Grand Total from the context menu.

4. Select any cell in the PivotTable to redisplay the PivotTable Field List task pane.

5. Follow these steps to format the Broadcast Sales numbers in the PivotTable:

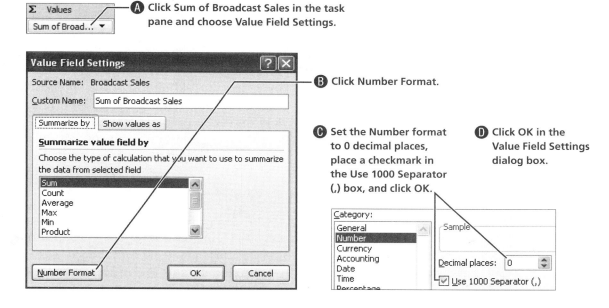

The numbers in all three columns display with the formatting that you chose because these columns all are based on Sum of Broadcast Sales.

Apply a PivotTable Style

6. Display the PivotTable by Region worksheet.

7. Choose the Design→PivotTable Styles→More [▾] button, scroll through the available styles, and choose PivotStyle Medium 9.
This style shades the subtotal rows.

Explore Report Layouts

8. Choose Design→Layout→Report Layout→Show in Outline Form from the Ribbon.
This layout divides the Region and Last Name fields into separate columns. Both column headings display a filter button.

9. Choose Design→Layout→Report Layout→Show in Tabular Form from the Ribbon.
This layout displays a subtotal row below its detail rows.

10. Choose Design→Layout→Report Layout→Show in Compact Form to return to the original layout.

11. Save [💾] the changes to your workbook.

Changing PivotTable Fields

You may add or remove fields on a PivotTable simply by adding or removing the checkmark next to the field name in the PivotTable Field List task pane. The PivotTable will automatically reconfigure to display the new data. You also may change the order of fields within the row and column areas. One of the most powerful ways of manipulating data is to move a field from the row area to the column area or vice versa. This is called *pivoting the field* (thus the name PivotTable). The display of the data field rotates to give you an entirely different view of your data, as illustrated in the two PivotTables you created in the previous exercise. There, you positioned the Region field to display as columns in the first PivotTable and as rows in the second.

Filtering the Display of Data Items

You may set the PivotTable to filter (exclude) specific items from the data summaries. The Row Labels and Column Labels areas on the PivotTable have drop-down list buttons that display sorting and filtering options very similar to those you used for tables in Lesson 11, Creating Tables and Outlines. You may uncheck individual items in the drop-down lists to suppress their display in the PivotTable.

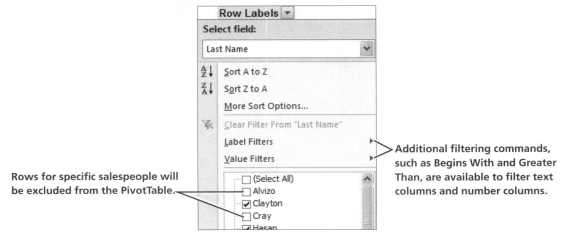

Rows for specific salespeople will be excluded from the PivotTable.

Additional filtering commands, such as Begins With and Greater Than, are available to filter text columns and number columns.

Filtering a PivotTable Report

The Report Filter area of the PivotTable Field List task pane lets you control the display of data, but the field used as the filtering criterion does not display as a column in the PivotTable. The field name displays with a filter drop-down list button above the PivotTable after you drag the field into the Report Filter area. You may choose to display all, some, or just one of the items from this field, such as a specific type of sales position. More than one field may be placed in the Report Filter area. You may filter multiple times for different types of data, but only the results of the most recent filter display in the PivotTable.

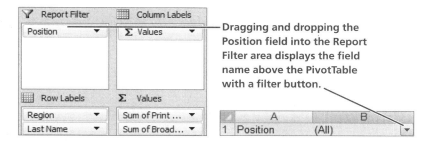

Dragging and dropping the Position field into the Report Filter area displays the field name above the PivotTable with a filter button.

Here, the Position field is used as the filtering criterion. The rows for each Sales Rep and Senior Sales Rep will be included in the PivotTable along with their values in any Sum columns. The position names need not display in the PivotTable for the filtering to occur.

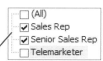

QUICK REFERENCE: CHANGING FIELDS AND FILTERING A PIVOTTABLE

Task	Procedure
Change the field order in rows or columns	■ Drag a field name above or below another field in an area list at the bottom of the PivotTable Field List task pane.
Remove a field	■ Uncheck the field name from the PivotTable Field List task pane.
Remove the display of specific data items	■ Click the filter button next to Row Labels, Column Labels, or a specific column label, if available, in the PivotTable. ■ Choose a field from the fields available in the filtering list. ■ Remove the checkmark from the desired item(s) or choose Label Filters or Value Filters, depending on the type of data in the column.
Filter based on a column not displayed in the PivotTable	■ Drag one or more field names into the Report Filter area at the bottom of the PivotTable Field List task pane. ■ Click the field's filter button next to (All) above the PivotTable. ■ Place a checkmark next to Select Multiple Items in the filter list. ■ Add or remove a checkmark from the desired item(s). ■ Optionally, to display the source data for each selected filter category in new worksheets, choose Options→PivotTable→Options menu ▼→Show Report Filter Pages from the Ribbon, choose the desired field, and click OK.

Hands-On 12.3   Change PivotTable Fields

In this exercise, you will add fields to the PivotTable and reorder the display of fields.

Add a Values Field

1. Display the PivotTable by Region worksheet.
   The ByRegion PivotTable contains data only for Print Sales. Now you will add Broadcast Sales.

2. Place a checkmark next to Broadcast Sales in the task pane to add this field to the PivotTable.
   Excel guesses correctly that this field should sum the values with subtotals and a grand total.

Reorder Fields

3. Drag Sum of Print Sales below Sum of Broadcast Sales in the list.

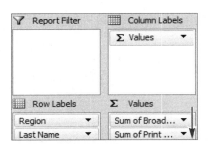 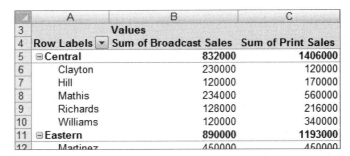

The PivotTable now includes columns for both sales categories in the order listed in the Values area of the task pane. Notice that Excel automatically added a Σ Values entry in the task pane Column Labels area because the PivotTable now contains two Sum columns.

Format PivotTable Data

4. Right-click any cell in the Sum of Broadcast Sales column of the PivotTable and choose Value Field Settings.

5. Click the Number Format button in the dialog box, set Number format to 0 decimal places, place a checkmark in the Use 1000 Separator(,) box, and click OK.

6. Click OK in the Value Field Settings dialog box.

7. Repeat the above steps in the Sum of Print Sales column.

Add and Then Remove a Labels Field

8. Place a checkmark by the State field in the top section of the PivotTable Field List task pane.

9. Drag the State field up one level in the Row Labels area of the task pane so it is between Region and Last Name.

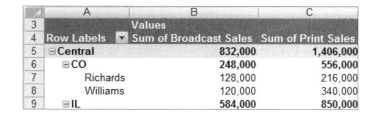

The records now are grouped by region, then state within the region, then last name within the state. Subtotals were added automatically for each state.

10. Remove the checkmark by the State field in the top section of the PivotTable Field List task pane.
    The states and their subtotals are removed from the PivotTable, and the Row Labels area in the task pane displays only Region and Last Name.

11. Save [💾] the changes to your workbook.

Editing PivotTable Calculations

You are not limited to summing values in a PivotTable, and you may create additional formulas.

Changing the Function for a Values Area Item

By default, the subtotals and grand totals in a PivotTable sum the values in a field. You may use the Summarize Data By command to change the SUM function to a different function, such as AVERAGE, MAX, or COUNT. Not all Excel functions are available by using this command.

 NOTE! *If the Values area of the PivotTable Field List task pane contains only one entry, all Sum columns will change to the function you selected. If multiple entries exist in the Values area, you may change the function for one entry at a time.*

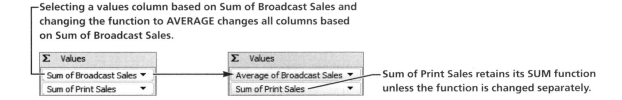

Selecting a values column based on Sum of Broadcast Sales and changing the function to AVERAGE changes all columns based on Sum of Broadcast Sales.

Sum of Print Sales retains its SUM function unless the function is changed separately.

Creating a Calculated Field

Some functions not available with the Summarize Data By command described previously may be typed in the Insert Calculated Field dialog box. A calculated field is a column that you create manually in the PivotTable. This field contains a formula using values from one or more existing fields. For example, the formula could subtract the value in one field from another to find the difference, as shown in the following illustration. You enter the formula once, and Excel displays the formula result in every record of the PivotTable. For accuracy, you should select field names from the list rather than type their names in creating the formula for a calculated field.

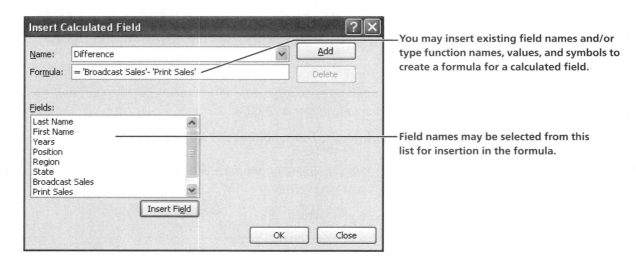

You may insert existing field names and/or type function names, values, and symbols to create a formula for a calculated field.

Field names may be selected from this list for insertion in the formula.

Refreshing PivotTable Data

!WARNING! *PivotTables do not automatically update after the source data is changed.*

FROM THE KEYBOARD
Ctrl + Alt + F5 to refresh all data sources

PivotTables often are created with data from sources external to the Excel workbook containing the PivotTables. For example, the source data may be in another Excel workbook or an Access database. After you change the source data—even if in a worksheet range or table within the same workbook—you must refresh the PivotTables manually. Using the Ribbon, you may refresh just the active PivotTable or all PivotTables in the workbook. You also may set a PivotTable option to refresh data from external sources when the workbook is opened.

QUICK REFERENCE: EDITING PIVOTTABLE CALCULATIONS AND REFRESHING DATA

Task	Procedure
Change the function used to calculate subtotals and grand total(s)	■ Right-click a number cell in any column of the PivotTable containing the existing calculation, choose Summarize Data By from the context menu, and choose a different function. ■ If desired, repeat for any other calculation listed separately in the Values list of the PivotTable Field List task pane.
Create a calculated field to the right of existing PivotTable columns	■ Select any cell within the PivotTable. ■ Choose Options→Tools→Formulas→Calculated Field from the Ribbon. ■ Type a name in the Name box of the Insert Calculated Field dialog box. ■ Edit the formula =0 to the desired formula by double-clicking field names and typing other parts of the formula, including math symbols (such as + or *).
Modify a formula in a calculated field	■ Choose Options→Tools→Formulas→Calculated Field from the Ribbon. ■ Choose the calculated field name in the Name list of the Insert Calculated Field dialog box. ■ Edit the formula and click Modify.
Delete a calculated field	■ Choose Options→Tools→Formulas→Calculated Field from the Ribbon. ■ Choose the calculated field name in the Name list of the Insert Calculated Field dialog box. ■ Click Delete.
Refresh PivotTables after changing source data	■ Choose Options→Data→Refresh menu ▼ from the Ribbon and choose one of the following: ◆ Refresh to update the active PivotTable. ◆ Refresh All (or use Ctrl + Alt + F5) to update all PivotTables in the workbook.

Hands-On 12.4   Change PivotTable Calculations

In this exercise, you will change the default SUM to a different function. You will create a calculated field to set a 110 percent print sales goal for each salesperson. You also will change a value in the original source table and observe the effect upon PivotTables.

1. Verify that the PivotTable by Region worksheet is displayed.

Change a Function

2. Right-click any cell in the Sum of Broadcast Sales column of the PivotTable, choose Summarize Data By in the context menu, and choose Average.
   The column heading changes to Average of Broadcast Sales in the PivotTable and the Values area of the task pane. The subtotals and grand total now calculate averages. Notice that the Sum of Print Sales column did not change. You must edit the function separately for each calculation listed in the Values area of the task pane. You will leave Sum of Print Sales as is.

Create a Calculated Field

Allen's manager set a goal for all salespeople to increase print sales by 110 percent within three months.

3. Choose Options→Tools→Formulas→Calculated Field from the Ribbon.

4. Follow these steps to create a calculated field in the Insert Calculated Field dialog box:

A Type **Goal 110% Print Sales** in the Name box.

B Press Tab to highlight =0 in the Formula box. Type an equals (**=**) sign to begin the formula.

C Double-click Print Sales and type *****110%** (make certain to type the asterisk) to finish the formula.

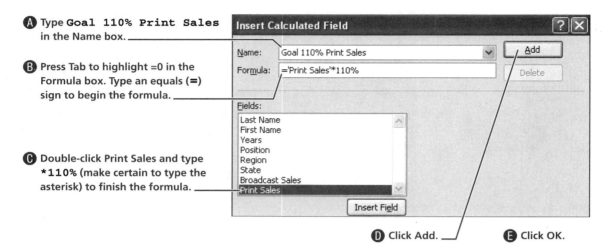

D Click Add.   **E** Click OK.

The calculated field displays as the last column of the PivotTable.

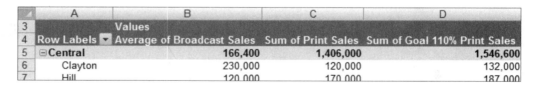

	A	B	C	D
3		Values		
4	Row Labels ▼	Average of Broadcast Sales	Sum of Print Sales	Sum of Goal 110% Print Sales
5	⊟Central	166,400	1,406,000	1,546,600
6	Clayton	230,000	120,000	132,000
7	Hill	120,000	170,000	187,000

Change Worksheet Data

5. Display the Sales Summary worksheet.

6. In cell G10, change Huy's broadcast sales to **100000**.

7. Display the PivotTable by Salesperson worksheet.
Notice that Huy's broadcast sales still display as 200,000. Changes to the source data do not automatically update in the PivotTables.

Refresh PivotTables

8. Choose Options→Data→Refresh menu ▼→Refresh All from the Ribbon.
Huy's broadcast sales now display as 100,000.

9. Display the PivotTable by Region worksheet.
Notice that the value was refreshed in this PivotTable also.

10. Save 💾 the changes to your workbook.

Creating PivotCharts

A PivotChart presents data from a PivotTable. There are two ways to create a Pivot Chart.

1. You may chart an existing PivotTable using the same command from the Insert Ribbon as for a normal Excel chart.

2. You may use the PivotChart command to create a PivotTable and chart from the source data at the same time. The chart builds as you choose fields in the PivotTable Field List task pane.

The field(s) in the Values area of the PivotTable display as column data series in the chart. The fields in the Row Labels are the category axis labels, and the Column Labels become the data series labels in the chart legend.

PivotChart Filter Pane

After you create the chart, the PivotChart Filter Pane appears. If you prefer to use it for filtering, you may move the pane or dock it next to the PivotTable Field List task pane. Any changes you make using this pane also are reflected in the PivotTable. You may, however, choose or move fields in the PivotTable Field List task pane as usual. Changes to the PivotTable update the chart automatically.

This button toggles the PivotTable Field List task pane display on/off.

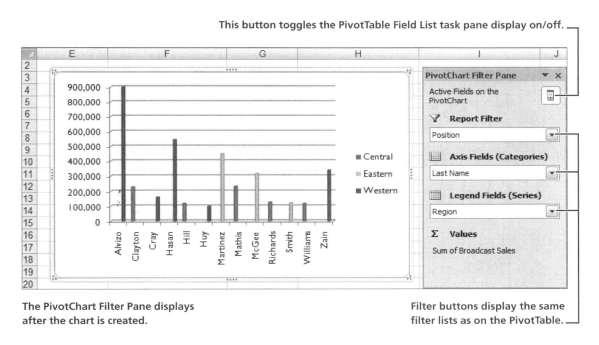

The PivotChart Filter Pane displays after the chart is created.

Filter buttons display the same filter lists as on the PivotTable.

TIP! *Copy a PivotTable before creating a PivotChart. Any changes to the chart update in the table copy. Data in the original PivotTable is preserved.*

Formatting PivotCharts

You format PivotCharts using the same Ribbon commands as for normal Excel charts. You choose from the same variety of chart styles, including column, line, and cone. You format chart objects just as you would on a normal Excel chart.

QUICK REFERENCE: CREATING A PIVOTCHART

Task	Procedure
Create a PivotChart from an existing PivotTable	■ Select any cell within the PivotTable. ■ Choose Insert→Charts and choose a chart type from the Ribbon. The chart is created next to the PivotTable.
Create a PivotTable and PivotChart concurrently from a worksheet range or table	■ Select any cell in the worksheet range or table. ■ Choose Insert→Tables→PivotTable menu ▼→PivotChart from the Ribbon. ■ Verify the worksheet range or table name in the Create PivotTable with PivotChart dialog box and click OK to place the PivotTable and PivotChart placeholders on a new worksheet. ■ Choose options for the PivotTable in the PivotTable Field List task pane. These options also create a bar PivotChart automatically.
Modify PivotChart format	■ Select the chart and choose from the Design, Layout, and Format Ribbons as for a normal Excel chart.
Collapse or expand detail in a PivotChart	■ Click the expand (+) and collapse (–) buttons on the related PivotTable. *or* ■ Click the axis labels in the chart and choose Analyze→Active Field→Expand Entire Field or Collapse Entire Field.

 Hands-On 12.5   Create a PivotChart

In this exercise, you will create a PivotChart from a PivotTable.

1. Display the PivotTable by Salesperson worksheet of the Media Sales workbook.

Create a PivotChart

2. Select any cell within the PivotTable and choose Insert→Charts→Column. Below Cylinder in the chart types menu, choose Clustered Cylinder.
A new column chart is created immediately from the PivotTable data, and the PivotChart Filter Pane displays.

Position the Chart

3. Point to the chart frame and drag the chart to the right of the PivotTable.

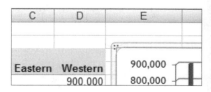

Explore Panes

4. On the PivotChart Filter Pane, click the filter button next to Last Name. (If the pane isn't visible, make certain the chart is selected.)

   The filter list is identical to the Row Labels filter list on the PivotTable. You could use this pane to filter the PivotTable and PivotChart.

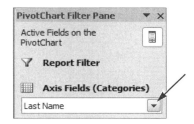

5. Cancel the filter list and close the PivotChart Filter Pane to make more room in the window.

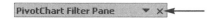

   Notice that while the PivotChart is selected, the Column Labels area of the PivotTable Field List task pane is labeled Legend Fields. The Row Labels area is labeled Axis Fields.

6. Close the PivotTable Field List task pane so that you can view the PivotChart.

   Notice that the chart data is arranged by Last Name, just as it is in the PivotTable. Once you have created the PivotChart, you may add, delete, and move fields just as you did with the PivotTable.

Filter the PivotTable and PivotChart

7. In the PivotTable, display the Row Labels filter list and choose Values Filters→Greater Than or Equal To, type **300000** in the Value Filter (Last Name) dialog box, and click OK.

   Both the PivotTable and PivotChart display five salespeople who meet the criterion.

8. Display the Row Labels filter list and choose Clear Filter from "Last Name."

Format the PivotChart

9. Select the chart.

10. Choose Design→Type→Change Chart Type→Column→Clustered Cone from the Ribbon and click OK.

    The chart is reconfigured to the new chart type. You may use chart formatting commands on any PivotChart.

11. Choose Layout→Labels→Chart Title→Centered Overlay Title from the Ribbon, type **By Salesperson** (your text appears in the Formula Bar), and tap Enter.

12. Feel free to add other formatting to the chart. For example, the last names used as the horizontal axis labels could be rotated to −55 degrees, as shown here.

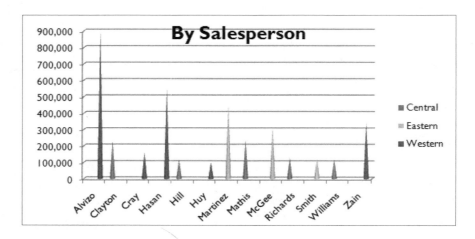

13. Save  the changes.

14. Use `Ctrl` + `W` or the Close button shown to close the workbook but leave Excel open.

Changing Macro Security

A macro is a recorded set of mouse and keyboard actions that can be played back at any time. Macros are useful for automating routine tasks, especially if those tasks are lengthy. Though macros are a huge timesaver for your frequently used procedures, they also are a prime way to pass viruses to computers. Therefore, be cautious about opening workbooks containing macros that you receive from others.

Security Levels

You change macro security in the Trust Center section within Excel Options. Your setting there is in effect for all Excel workbooks that you open on your computer. The setting is not embedded in any workbooks that you save and share with others. You may choose among four different levels of security in Excel that control whether macros in an opened workbook are available or disabled:

■ **Enable all macros:** You are not protected from potentially unsafe macros. This option is not recommended for general use.

■ **Disable all macros except digitally signed macros:** This option automatically disables unsigned macros and enables macros from publishers you previously added to the trusted publishers list in the Trust Center. Digital signatures were introduced in Lesson 9, Using Templates and Protecting Workbooks.

- **Disable all macros with notification:** This is the default option, and it displays a message allowing you to enable macros in the specified workbook if you wish or use the workbook without enabling the macros.

- **Disable all macros without notification:** Only macros in workbooks that you placed in a trusted location of the Trust Center are allowed to run. All other digitally signed and unsigned macros are disabled.

If you have antivirus software installed, the file will be scanned for viruses before it is opened regardless of the security level you set.

 NOTE! *Your network system administrator may set macro security and prevent users from changing it.*

 QUICK REFERENCE: CHANGING MACRO SECURITY

Task	Procedure
Change macro security	Choose Office→Excel Options→Trust Center→Trust Center Settings button→Macro Settings and choose a macro security option.

Hands-On 12.6   Verify Macro Security

In this exercise, you will verify the macro security setting on your computer. Then you will open a workbook and enable its macros.

1. Choose Office→Excel Options→Trust Center. Click the Trust Center Settings button and choose the Macro Settings category from the left side of the window. Choose Disable All Macros with Notification if not already selected.

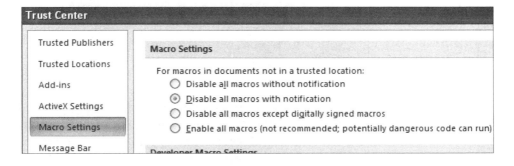

2. Choose the Message Bar category from the left side of the window. Verify that the following option is selected: Show the Message Bar in All Applications When Content Has Been Blocked.

3. Click OK twice to exit the Excel Options window.

4. Open the Macro Test workbook from the Lesson 12 folder of your file storage location.
   A Security Warning message displays below the Ribbon to alert you that macros are disabled. If you do not respond, the message will disappear after you begin working in the workbook.

5. Click the Options button next to the Security Warning.
   Read the information in the Microsoft Office Security Options dialog box.

6. Choose Enable This Content and click OK.
   The Security Warning message disappears, and the macros are enabled.

7. Click the Sort by Student button.
   The worksheet list should sort in order by student name, indicating that the macro worked successfully.

8. Close the workbook without saving changes.

Recording Macros

Excel's macro recording feature saves your keystrokes and the commands you issue for a task. For example, you may record steps to choose page setup options and print a document. You then may play back a recorded macro at a later time. This is similar to using a video camera. You turn it on, press the record button, and stop recording when finished. You may replay the recording as many times as you want. Similarly, macros play back recorded keystrokes and mouse actions.

 After the Record Macro button is clicked, the Stop Recording button appears.

Naming a Macro

You should name your macros. If you do not, Excel names them Macro1, Macro2, and so on. Name your macros following the same rules that you used for defined names in Lesson 10, Managing Multiple-Sheet Workbooks. Macro names may not contain spaces but may include capital letters or underscores to separate words. For example, you may name a macro Format-Title or Format_Title.

Recording Macro Steps

Most actions you perform are recorded in the macro. These include mouse actions, choosing Ribbon commands, selecting options in dialog boxes, using cursor keys to navigate the worksheet, and typing text. Any mistakes and corrections you make during recording also are saved in the macro. You may decide not to rerecord the macro, however, if the final result is correct.

 TIP! *You should practice the procedure you wish to automate before you actually record the macro. This will help you avoid mistakes during the recording process.*

Storing Macros

Macros are available only in the workbook in which you create them unless you assign them to the Personal Macro Workbook.

Current Workbook

Some macros are useful only in a particular workbook. For example, you may develop a macro to sort worksheet rows in a specific manner. The macro is useful only in the workbook in which it is created, so you would choose the storage option This Workbook.

Personal Macro Workbook

The Personal.xlsb file is a hidden file that makes its macros available in all open workbooks on your computer system. For example, you may create a macro to format headings with a consistent style to be used in various workbooks. You will assign a macro to the Personal Macro Workbook and delete macros from it in a Skill Builder exercise of this lesson.

Saving a Workbook Containing Macros

If you attempt to save a workbook containing macros using the normal Excel Workbook file format, Excel displays the message "The following features cannot be saved in macro-free workbooks: VB Project." Clicking No in the message box displays the Save As dialog box, where you should choose the Excel Macro-Enabled Workbook file format. The file is saved with the extension .xlsm in the file name to indicate that it contains a macro.

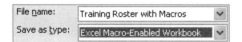

QUICK REFERENCE: RECORDING A MACRO	
Task	**Procedure**
Record a macro	■ Develop the worksheet and prepare to record the macro.
	■ Click the Record Macro 🔲 button on the status bar in the lower-left corner of the window.
	■ Type a descriptive name in the Macro Name box (spaces are not allowed) and fill in other options as desired.
	■ Click OK to begin recording.
	■ Execute the commands and actions you want the macro to record.
	■ Click the Stop Recording 🔲 button on the status bar when you have finished recording.
Delete a macro	■ Choose View→Macros→Macros 🔲 from the Ribbon or use [Alt]+[F8].
	■ Choose the desired macro name and click Delete.
Save a workbook containing macros	■ Choose Save 🔲 and click No in the message box or choose Save As.
	■ Choose Excel Macro-Enabled Workbook from the Save as Type list in the Save As dialog box.

Hands-On 12.7 Record a Macro

In this exercise, you will create a name for the range that contains student and instructor information. Assigning a defined name is important because it allows Excel to sort all rows properly after new student records are inserted. You will then record a macro to sort the list by the instructor column.

Before You Begin: Macro security should be set to Disable All Macros with Notification from Hands-On 12.6.

Open the Workbook

1. Open the Training Roster workbook.

   Take a moment to review the worksheet. Notice that it contains a list of students and that each student has been assigned to an instructor. Also notice that the list isn't sorted in any particular order. The goal of the next few exercises is to add new students to the list and to sort the list. You will record macros to automate the sorting process.

Assign a Defined Name to the List

2. Select the range A3:D21.

3. Follow these steps to assign a defined name:

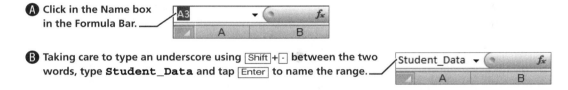

A Click in the Name box in the Formula Bar.

B Taking care to type an underscore using Shift + - between the two words, type **Student_Data** and tap Enter to name the range.

Practice Selecting the Range

4. Click cell A1 to deselect the range and position the highlight in cell A1.

5. Follow these steps to select the range using its name:

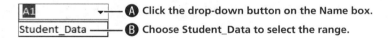

A Click the drop-down button on the Name box.

B Choose Student_Data to select the range.

In the next part of this exercise, you will use this technique as the first step of the macro. You will then sort the rows in the selected range. The macro recorder will record all of your actions.

6. Click in cell A1 again to deselect the range.

Record the Sort_by_Instructor Macro

7. Click the Record Macro ![icon] button on the status bar at the bottom-left corner of the window. (Right-click the status bar and choose Macro Recording in the context menu if the button does not display. Press Esc to hide the context menu.)
The Record Macro dialog box appears.

8. Follow these steps to name the macro and begin the recording process:

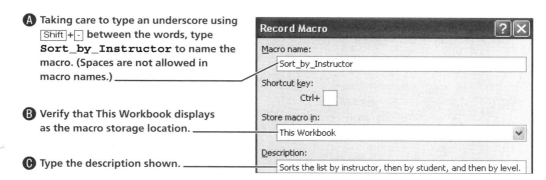

Ⓐ Taking care to type an underscore using Shift + - between the words, type **Sort_by_Instructor** to name the macro. (Spaces are not allowed in macro names.)

Ⓑ Verify that This Workbook displays as the macro storage location.

Ⓒ Type the description shown.

9. Click OK, and the macro will begin recording your actions.
If you make any mistakes, just correct the errors as you would normally. Major errors may be fixed either by stopping the recording and starting over or by editing the macro in the Visual Basic Editor (not covered in this lesson).

10. Choose the Student_Data defined name from the Name list on the Formula Bar.
This step ensures that the proper data is selected prior to sorting whenever the macro is run.

11. Choose Data→Sort & Filter→Sort from the Ribbon.

12. Follow these steps to set the Sort parameters and initiate the Sort:

Ⓐ Click the drop-down button on the Sort By list and choose Instructor.

Ⓑ Click the Add Level button.

Ⓒ Choose Student from the list and click Add Level.

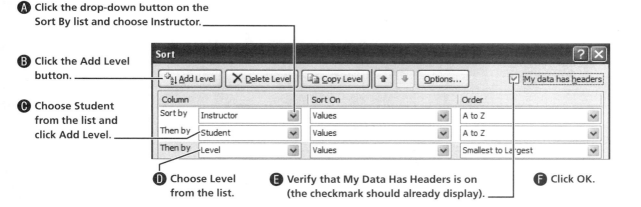

Ⓓ Choose Level from the list.

Ⓔ Verify that My Data Has Headers is on (the checkmark should already display).

Ⓕ Click OK.

13. Click cell A1 to deselect the range.

14. Click the Stop Recording  button on the status bar at the bottom-left corner of the window.

Your actions have been saved in the macro. The list is sorted as shown in the following illustration. Keep in mind that the macro recorded this sort sequence.

	A	B	C	D
1	Excel Training Student Roster			
2				
3	**Instructor**	**Student**	**Level**	**Score**
4	Allison	Ames, Alice	2	86
5	Allison	Ames, Donna	1	68
6	Allison	Ames, Jason	1	88
7	Allison	Williams, Cora-Lee	1	90
8	Allison	Williams, Cora-Lee	2	94
9	Allison	Yee, Donese	3	100
10	Dawes	Brown, Lisa	1	99
11	Dawes	Davis, Ted	2	92
12	Dawes	Jackson, Mary	1	87
13	Dawes	Jones, Al	1	85
14	Dawes	Jones, Al	2	79
15	Smith	Ames, Donald	2	94

Save the Workbook as Macro-Enabled

15. Click Save 💾.

A message displays as shown. The VB Project indicated is a Visual Basic Project module containing your macro.

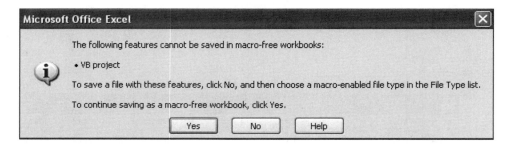

16. Click No to display the Save As dialog box.

17. Edit the File Name to **Training Roster with Macros**.

18. Drop down the Save As type list, choose Excel Macro-Enabled Workbook, and click Save.

The macro is saved as part of the workbook named Training Roster with Macros.xlsm. If you were to close the workbook, the macro would be available the next time you opened the workbook. The Disable All Macros with Notification security setting is in effect, so you still can control whether macros actually are enabled in an opened workbook.

Running Macros

 You may run macros in a variety of ways. The method you use depends on how the macro was assigned. You may create a macro and assign it to a shortcut key, graphic, or Quick Access toolbar button. An unassigned macro must be run by using the Macros command on the Ribbon and selecting a macro. This procedure may be used to run any macro recorded in the current workbook, even if the macro was assigned. The keyboard shortcut ⌈Alt⌉+⌈F8⌉ may be used to display the Macro dialog box.

FROM THE KEYBOARD

⌈Alt⌉+⌈F8⌉ to view macros

QR QUICK REFERENCE: RUNNING A MACRO

Task	Procedure
Run an unassigned or assigned macro from the Ribbon	■ Choose View→Macros→Macros from the Ribbon or use ⌈Alt⌉+⌈F8⌉. ■ Choose the desired macro name and click Run.
Run an assigned macro	■ Use the shortcut key or click the assigned graphic, worksheet button, or Quick Access toolbar button.

 ## Hands-On 12.8 Run an Unassigned Macro

In this exercise, you will sort the student list manually in a different order and then run the Sort_by_Instructor macro.

Before You Begin: Macro security should be set to Disable All Macros with Notification from Hands-On 12.6. If you reopened the Training Roster with Macros workbook and the Security Warning message appears under the Ribbon, choose Options and enable macros.

1. Select cell B4 and choose Data→Sort & Filter→Sort A to Z ⌈A↓Z⌉ from the Ribbon.
   The student list is sorted alphabetically by student name. Now you will run the macro you created in the previous exercise.

2. Choose View→Macros→Macros from the Ribbon.

3. Choose the Sort_by_Instructor macro and click Run in the Macro dialog box.
   The list is sorted by instructor, then by student, then by level. The macro saves you time because you did not need to choose the Sort command and set options manually.

4. Save the changes to the workbook.

Assigning Macros

You may run a macro from within the Macro dialog box. However, macros are more accessible if you assign them to shortcut keys, custom buttons or graphics on a worksheet, or buttons on the Quick Access toolbar. You then run the macro by issuing the shortcut key or clicking the object to which the macro is assigned.

Assigning Macros to Shortcut Keys

Excel lets you assign a macro to a shortcut key as you name the macro. You may run the macro simply by using the shortcut key combination. You must use Ctrl or Ctrl+Shift as part of the shortcut key combination. Any shortcut you assign will override an existing Excel command shortcut. For example, you may assign Ctrl+B to a macro, but that combination would no longer choose Bold from the Ribbon.

 TIP! *If you are in the habit of using Microsoft's command shortcuts, use Ctrl+Shift for your macro shortcuts.*

 Hands-On 12.9   Assign a Macro to a Shortcut Key

In this exercise, you will create a macro to add a new student to the list and assign the macro to a shortcut key. You will run the macro to add a student. Then you will assign a shortcut key to the macro you created in the previous exercise and use its shortcut key to sort the list.

Before You Begin: Macro security should be set to Disable All Macros with Notification from Hands-On 12.6. If you reopened the Training Roster with Macros workbook and the Security Warning message now appears under the Ribbon, choose Options and enable macros.

Assign a Shortcut Key and Record the Insert_Student Macro

You will record a new macro that automates the process of inserting new student records just below the header row.

1. Click the Record Macro ▦ button on the status bar.
   The Record Macro dialog box appears.

2. Follow these steps to name a new macro:

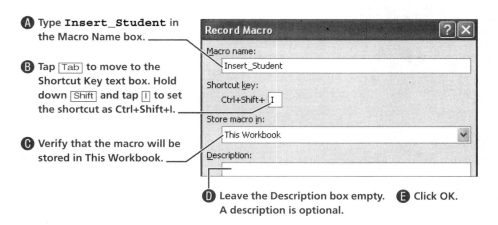

Ⓐ Type **Insert_Student** in the Macro Name box.

Ⓑ Tap Tab to move to the Shortcut Key text box. Hold down Shift and tap I to set the shortcut as Ctrl+Shift+I.

Ⓒ Verify that the macro will be stored in This Workbook.

Ⓓ Leave the Description box empty. A description is optional.   Ⓔ Click OK.

In the next few steps, you will perform the actions to be recorded in the macro. You will copy blank cells A2:D2, which have the correct formatting already applied, and insert those cells below the column headings.

3. Select cells A2:D2.

4. Choose Home→Clipboard→Copy from the Ribbon to copy the cells.

5. Select cell A4 to position the pointer below the column headings.

6. Choose Home→Cells→Insert from the Ribbon to insert blank cells at A4:D4.

7. Choose Home→Clipboard→Paste from the Ribbon to paste the copied cells.

8. Tap [Esc] to remove the marquee around cells A2:D2.

9. Select cell A4 to position the pointer for data entry.

10. Click the Stop Recording ◼ button on the status bar.

Run the Macro to Add New Students

11. Delete the blank row 4 that you inserted while creating the macro.

12. Use [Ctrl]+[Shift]+[I] to run the Insert_Student macro. (Hold down [Ctrl], then also hold down [Shift], and then tap [I]. Release [Ctrl] and [Shift].)
    The pointer moves to cell A4 and blank cells are inserted. New students always will be added to a new row below the header row.

    If your macro did not work correctly, choose View→Macros→Macros→Insert_Student, and then click Delete. Then repeat steps 1–6.

13. Add this student to the list:

4	Dawes	Almore, Brian	3	97

14. Run the Insert_Student macro again and add this student to the list:

4	Allison	Zobe, Wayne	1	85

Assign a Shortcut Key to the Sort_by_Instructor Macro

15. Choose View→Macros→Macros  from the Ribbon.

16. Choose the Sort_by_Instructor macro and click Options in the Macro dialog box.

17. Click in the Shortcut Key text box, press [Shift], and tap [S] to set the shortcut key to Ctrl+Shift+S. Click OK.

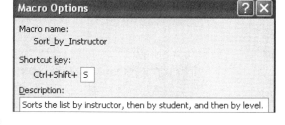

18. Click Cancel to exit the Macro dialog box.

19. Use [Ctrl]+[Shift]+[S] to run the macro.
    The list is sorted by instructor, then student, and then level. The Zobe, Wayne student record moves to row 10 and becomes the last of Allison's students. The Almore, Brian student record moves to row 11.

20. Save 🖫 the changes to the workbook.

Assigning Macros to Custom Buttons

A macro assigned to a custom button is run whenever the button is clicked. The easiest way to create a custom button is to add a shape, such as a rectangle, to the worksheet. You then assign a macro to the button. You may position custom buttons anywhere in a worksheet. To avoid deleting buttons in error, do not place them in rows or columns that could be deleted in the future. A custom button may also contain a descriptive label to help identify its function or the macro that is assigned to it.

 TIP! *You may create custom buttons using the Button (Form Control) tool on the Developer tab. To display this tab, choose Office→Excel Options→Popular→Show Developer Tab in the Ribbon. The Developer tab contains other commands for working with macros.*

QR **QUICK REFERENCE: ASSIGNING A MACRO**

Task	Procedure
Assign a macro to a shortcut key as the macro is created	■ Click the Record Macro button on the status bar. ■ While filling in options in the Macro dialog box, click in the Shortcut Key text box and key a single letter, or hold Shift and key the letter.
Assign a macro to a shortcut key after the macro is created	■ Choose View→Macros→Macros from the Ribbon. ■ Choose the macro name and click Options in the Macro dialog box. ■ In the Macro Options dialog box, click in the Shortcut Key text box and key a single letter, or hold Shift and key the letter.
Assign a macro to a custom button or graphic on the worksheet	■ Record the macro. ■ Insert a shape, picture, or clip art image on the worksheet. Right-click the object and choose Assign Macro from the context menu. Choose the desired macro from the Assign Macro dialog box. ■ To display a text label in a shape used as a custom button, select the button in the worksheet and type the desired text in the button. ■ If necessary, resize the button or graphic, drag it to the desired worksheet location, and align multiple buttons.

Hands-On 12.10 Assign Macros to Custom Buttons

In this exercise, you will create buttons and assign the Insert_Student and Sort_by_Instructor macros to them.

Before You Begin: Macro security should be set to Disable All Macros with Notification from Hands-On 12.6. If you reopened the Training Roster with Macros workbook and the Security Warning message appears under the Ribbon, choose Options and enable macros.

Create Buttons

1. Choose Insert→Illustrations→Shapes→Rectangles→Rectangle ☐ shape tool from the Ribbon.

2. Drag the mouse to draw a button on cells F11:G11.

	A	B	C	D	E	F	G
10	Allison	Zobe, Wayne	1	85			
11	Dawes	Almore, Brian	3	97			

3. Copy and paste the button to cell F13.

Name Buttons

4. Select the first button and type **Insert Student**; do *not* tap Enter.

5. Select the second button and type **Sort by Instructor**.
Button text may contain spaces because it is only a label.

6. Click outside the button to deselect it.

7. If necessary, align the buttons: Select the first button, use Shift+click to select the second button, and choose Format→Arrange→Align→ Align Left from the Ribbon.
Formatting the buttons is easier if completed before you assign macros to the buttons. If you wish, you may change the colors and outline in custom buttons.

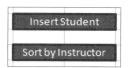

Assign Macros to Buttons

8. Deselect the two buttons.

9. Right-click the Insert Student button and choose Assign Macro from the context menu.

10. In the Assign Macro dialog box, choose Insert_Student from the list and click OK.

11. Use the preceding steps to assign the Sort_by_Instructor macro to its button.

Run Macros Using the Buttons

12. Deselect the button.

13. Click the Insert Student button to run the Insert_Student macro. (Deselect the button and select again if the pointer does not display as a hand as you select the button.)
A new row appears just below the header row.

14. Add this student to the new row:

4	Dawes	Carlson, Michael	2	82

15. Click the Sort by Instructor button to run the Sort_by_Instructor macro.
The new row is sorted into the worksheet.

16. Save 🖫 the changes and close the workbook.
Now you have learned to create simple macros to automate routine tasks. You ran macros using the Ribbon, shortcut keys, and custom buttons on the worksheet.

Concepts Review

True/False Questions

T 1. A PivotTable field corresponds to a column in the worksheet range or table on which the PivotTable is based.   TRUE   FALSE

T 2. Changing the order of the fields in the Row Labels or Column Labels area affects how the data displays in a PivotTable.   TRUE   FALSE

F 3. All fields from the source worksheet range or table must be included in a PivotTable.   TRUE   FALSE

F 4. To filter data for a PivotTable, you must filter the source worksheet data before creating the PivotTable.   TRUE   FALSE

F 5. PivotTables automatically update whenever the source worksheet range or table is changed.   TRUE   FALSE

F 6. Fields used in a PivotChart may be rearranged separately from those in a related PivotTable.   TRUE   FALSE

F 7. The Enable All Macros security setting is recommended for most Excel users.   TRUE   FALSE

T 8. Ribbon commands are recorded in a macro by clicking on them with the mouse.   TRUE   FALSE

T 9. Workbooks containing macros must be saved using a different type of file format than that of normal workbooks in order for the macros to be available.   TRUE   FALSE

T 10. Errors and corrections made while a macro was recorded also will be performed when the macro is run.   TRUE   FALSE

Multiple Choice Questions

1. What happens in a PivotTable when you add a text field, such as employee names, to the Row Labels area?
   a. Nothing happens; only numeric data fields can be placed in the Row Labels area.
   b. The field exchanges positions with a field already positioned in the Column Labels area.
   c. The employee names display in the Pivot-Table, one name per row.
   d. The employee names display in the Pivot-Table, but they cannot be filtered.

2. How do you change the chart type of a Pivot-Chart?
   a. You may only use the chart types designed specifically for PivotCharts.
   b. You use the same chart type commands that you use for normal charts.
   c. You create a normal chart and then issue the PivotChart command.
   d. You cannot change the chart type of a PivotChart; you must use the default format.

3. Which of the following may be used in a macro name?
   a. Underscores and capital letters
   b. Underscores and spaces
   c. Spaces only
   d. Capital letters only

4. Which of the following can run a macro?
   a. The Macro dialog box
   b. A shape on the worksheet
   c. A shortcut key combination
   d. All of the above

# Skill Builders

Skill Builder 12.1 Create a PivotTable and a PivotChart

In this exercise, you will create a PivotTable and PivotChart simultaneously from a worksheet table. You will practice placing and pivoting fields to change your view of the data.

1. Start Excel and open the sb-Jan Sales PivotTable workbook from the Lesson 12 folder.
   The January Sales worksheet displays one month's activity at Avery Auto Sales. Before you create a PivotTable, take a moment to look over the layout of the data fields and records. For example, notice that there is just one field for numeric data in this table.

Create the PivotTable and PivotChart

2. Select cell A4.
   This tells Excel to use the table data when you create the PivotTable.

3. Choose Insert→Tables→PivotTable menu ▾→PivotChart from the Ribbon, verify JanSales as the table data to be used, and click OK to create a PivotTable and PivotChart in a new worksheet.

4. Rename the Sheet1 sheet tab to **PivotTable**.
   Both the PivotTable Field List task pane and the PivotChart Filter Pane display. If they do not and you made certain the chart is selected, choose Analyze→Show/Hide→Field List or choose PivotChart Filter. You may turn on/off the panes as needed.

5. Close the PivotChart Filter Pane.
   You may choose all settings from the PivotTable Field List task pane.

6. In the PivotTable Field List task pane, place a checkmark in the Sold By and Price checkboxes.
   The PivotTable displays the total sales for each salesperson. The chart is selected, so the task pane displays Axis Fields (Categories) and Legend Field areas.

7. Select a cell in the PivotTable, and the same areas now are titled Row Labels and Column Labels to reflect those items in the PivotTable.

Add a Field

Since you might want to know which types of cars each salesperson sold this month, you will place a new field in the row field's area.

8. Place a checkmark in the Type box on the task pane to add the field to the Row Labels area.

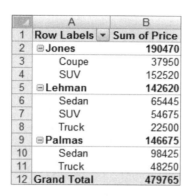

	A	B
1	Row Labels ▼	Sum of Price
2	⊟ Jones	**190470**
3	Coupe	37950
4	SUV	152520
5	⊟ Lehman	**142620**
6	Sedan	65445
7	SUV	54675
8	Truck	22500
9	⊟ Palmas	**146675**
10	Sedan	98425
11	Truck	48250
12	**Grand Total**	**479765**

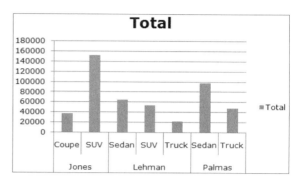

The PivotTable and PivotChart expand to display the sales of the various types of vehicles sold by each salesperson. It might also be interesting to summarize how the revenue at the dealership breaks down by vehicle type, so in the next step you will pivot the Type field from the row area to the column area.

Arrange Items in the Window

You may not see the entire PivotTable and PivotChart as items change in the window.

9. Follow these steps to maximize space:

A Undock the task pane by dragging its title bar down and to the left. The task pane now is smaller, and you may move it at any time.

B Resize the PivotTable Field List by dragging its bottom border up or down to keep desired options visible.

C To prevent the PivotChart from covering the PivotTable, move the PivotChart to the right by dragging the chart frame.

Pivot the View

10. Drag the Type field to the Column Labels area.

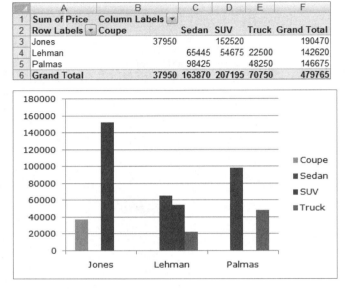

The Grand Total line at the bottom of the PivotTable displays the revenue for each type of car. The chart displays bars for each car type.

Add a Field and Pivot the View

11. Place a checkmark in the New/Preowned box on the task pane to add the field to the Row Labels area and observe the effect in the PivotTable and the PivotChart.

12. Drag the New/Preowned field above Sold By in the Row Labels area of the task pane as shown.

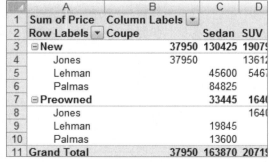

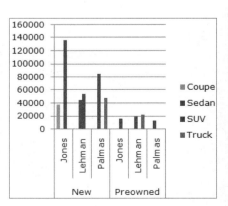

This view clearly shows that revenue is much greater for new cars than preowned, as might be expected.

13. Move the PivotChart to below the PivotTable so both fit on one printed page.

14. Drag the PivotTable Field List task pane to the right edge of the screen, until the task pane is docked.

15. Save ![save icon] the changes and close the workbook.

As you have seen, PivotTables and PivotCharts help you display and analyze data in various ways with a minimum of setup steps.

Skill Builder 12.2 Filter a PivotTable

In this exercise, you will filter to exclude data items from a PivotTable. You also will filter by a field not displayed in the PivotTable.

1. Open the sb-Feb Sales PivotTable workbook.
Look at the table data in the February Sales worksheet. A PivotTable and a PivotChart were created using this data.

2. Display the PivotTable worksheet.

3. Select a cell within the PivotTable to display the PivotTable Field List task pane.

Filter the Display of Data Items in the PivotTable

4. Follow these steps in the PivotTable to suppress the display of data for Walk-In sales:

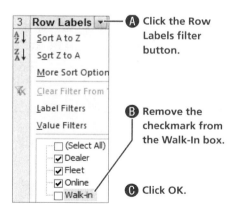

Ⓐ Click the Row Labels filter button.

Ⓑ Remove the checkmark from the Walk-In box.

Ⓒ Click OK.

Notice that no data is displayed for Walk-In sales, and the Row Headers filter button displays a filter icon. You may use this method to switch the display of individual data items on and off for any field in the Row Labels or Column Labels.

5. Display the Row Labels filter list again and choose Clear Filter from "Source."

Delete and Add Fields in the PivotTable

6. In the PivotTable Field List task pane, remove the checkmark from the Source box.

7. Place a checkmark in the Financing box to add the field to the PivotTable.
The pie chart displays bank/credit union financing as 46 percent and dealer financing as 42 percent for all vehicles sold.

Use a Report Filter

8. Notice the New/Preowned report filter in cells A1:B1, which currently displays (All).
This filter list was created by dragging the New/Preowned field to the Report Filter area of the Pivot-Table Field List task pane.

9. Follow these steps to filter the PivotTable for preowned vehicles:

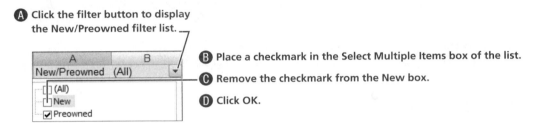

Ⓐ Click the filter button to display the New/Preowned filter list.

Ⓑ Place a checkmark in the Select Multiple Items box of the list.

Ⓒ Remove the checkmark from the New box.

Ⓓ Click OK.

The filter button displays a filter icon, and cell B1 displays Preowned to indicate the filter type. The New/Preowned field also displays a filter icon in the PivotTable Field List task pane.

10. Review the chart to see that dealer financing is only 21 percent and a majority of preowned vehicle purchases were paid in cash.

11. Change the page orientation and resize the chart, if necessary, to fit the PivotTable and PivotChart on one printed page.

12. Save 🖫 the changes and close the workbook.

Skill Builder 12.3   Create a Macro for the Personal Macro Workbook

In this exercise, you will create a macro that selects an entire worksheet, formats all cells with bold, and widens the columns. You will assign the macro to the personal macro workbook.

Begin Recording the Macro

1. Start a new workbook.

2. Click the Record Macro button on the status bar.

3. Type the macro name **FormatSheet** in the Record Macro dialog box.

4. Set the Store Macro In option to Personal Macro Workbook.

⚠NOTE!   *Choose This Workbook instead if you cannot save a macro to the Personal Macro Workbook on your computer system.*

5. Click OK (and replace the macro if it already exists) to begin the recording process.

Set Worksheet Formats

6. Use Ctrl + A to select the entire worksheet.

7. Use Ctrl + B to bold all cells.

8. Choose Home→Cells→Format→Column Width to display the Column Width dialog box, type **12**, and tap Enter to choose OK.

9. Select cell A1 to deselect the highlighted cells.

10. Click the Stop Recording button on the Run the Macro status bar.

11. Choose Office→Close and choose No when Excel asks if you want to save the workbook.

Run the Macro

12. Start a new workbook and choose View→Macros→Macros to display the Macro dialog box.
    Any macro with PERSONAL.XLSB! in its name has been saved to the Personal Macro Workbook and is available to all open workbooks.

13. Choose the PERSONAL.XLSB!FormatSheet macro and click the Run button. (Choose FormatSheet rather than PERSONAL.XLSB!FormatSheet if you saved the macro to This Worksheet.)
    The column and text formats are set. Keep in mind that you may apply virtually any formatting to cells, columns, rows, text, or numbers with a macro.

Delete the Macro from the Personal Macro Workbook

Macros stored in the Personal Macro Workbook cannot be removed with the Delete button in the Macro dialog box. Just read the next steps and complete step 20 if you saved the macro to This Workbook rather than Personal Macro Workbook.

14. Choose View→Macros→Macros from the Ribbon.

15. Follow these steps to delete the FormatSheet macro from the Personal Macro Workbook:

A If you don't see the macro name, change the Macros In setting to All Open Workbooks.

B Click the PERSONAL.XLSB!FormatSheet macro from the list box (not from the first box under Macro Name).

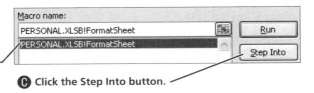

C Click the Step Into button.

The macro code displays in the Visual Basic Editor window.

16. In the Visual Basic Editor, choose Tools→Macros.

17. In the Macro dialog box, set the Macros In option to VBA Project (PERSONAL.XLSB).

18. Choose the FormatSheet macro, click Delete, and click OK to confirm.

19. Close ☒ the Visual Basic Editor window to reveal the Excel workbook window.
In this exercise, you deleted the macro to keep the computer system "clean." Normally, you would leave macros stored in the personal macro workbook so they could be used in all workbooks.

20. Close the empty workbook without saving it.

Assessments

Assessment 12.1 Create a PivotTable

In this exercise, you will create a PivotTable to calculate the cost of care and shelter for healthy and sick animals at Capital City Animal Shelter.

1. Open the as-April Expenses workbook from the Lesson 12 folder.

2. Examine the April Expense Report worksheet. Identify the fields you will use in the PivotTable.

Create the PivotTable

3. Create a PivotTable on a new worksheet.

4. Rename the new sheet with a descriptive name of your choice.

5. Rename the PivotTable as April Expenses.

6. Set up fields for the PivotTable so that the rows summarize the data by cats/dogs and then by age.

7. Set up fields so that the columns compare the cost of caring for healthy and sick animals.

8. Set up fields to total the cost of care and shelter.

Format the PivotTable

9. Apply a PivotTable style.

10. Format all numbers with Comma Style and two decimal places.
When you finish, your PivotTable should match the following figure, except for field labels.

	A	B	C	D
3	Sum of Total Costs			
4		Healthy	Sick	Grand Total
5	⊟Cat	320.25	267.75	588.00
6	Adult	320.25	167.50	487.75
7	Kitten		100.25	100.25
8	⊟Dog	840.50	422.00	1,262.50
9	Adult	516.00	63.00	579.00
10	Pup	324.50	359.00	683.50
11	Grand Total	1,160.75	689.75	1,850.50

Your PivotTable displays some additional labels. They were removed from this figure because they would display a significant part of the exercise solution.

Change Worksheet Data and Update the PivotTable

11. In the April Expenses worksheet, change the cost per day in cell F1 to **$5.25**.

12. Do whatever is necessary to update the PivotTable to reflect the change you just made.

13. Save the changes and close the workbook.

Assessment 12.2   Create a PivotTable and PivotChart

In this exercise, you will create a PivotTable and PivotChart that display the cost of care and shelter for sick and healthy animals summarized by animal type and health. The chart will be a stacked column chart.

1. Open the as-May Expenses workbook.

2. Examine the May Expense Report worksheet. Identify the fields you will use to create the PivotTable and its accompanying PivotChart.

Create the PivotTable and PivotChart

3. Create a PivotTable and PivotChart together on a new worksheet.

4. Rename the new sheet with a descriptive name of your choice.

5. Rename the PivotTable as **May Expenses**.

6. Set up fields for the PivotTable and PivotChart so that the table and chart summarize the data by cats/dogs and then by health.

7. Set up fields so that the shelter cost and veterinary cost are calculated separately.

8. Format all numbers in the PivotTable with Comma Style and no decimal places.

Format the PivotChart

9. Change the chart type to Stacked Column.

10. Apply a PivotChart style of your choice.
    When you finish, your PivotTable and PivotChart should match the following figure, except for field labels.

Your PivotChart style may differ from that shown.

Your PivotTable displays some additional labels. They were removed from this figure because they would display a significant part of the exercise solution.

	A	B	C
1		Sum of Shelter Cost	Sum of Veterinary Cost
2	⊟ Cat	594	75
3	Healthy	325	40
4	Sick	270	35
5	⊟ Dog	1,155	265
6	Healthy	869	90
7	Sick	286	175
8	Grand Total	1,749	340

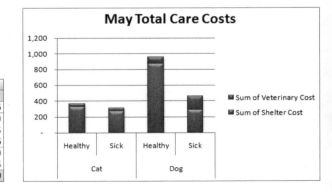

11. Change the page orientation and make any other adjustments necessary to fit the Pivot-Table and PivotChart on one printed page.

12. Save 💾 the changes and close the workbook.

Assessment 12.3   Create a Macro that Inserts the Date

*In this exercise, you will create a macro that inserts the phrase **Today's Date** in cell A1 and the TODAY() function in cell A2. The macro also will format the two cells. You will assign the macro to the current workbook only.*

1. Start a new workbook containing three blank worksheets.

2. Select cell A10.

Record the Macro

3. Begin recording a new macro.

4. Name the macro **TodaysDate**, assign the shortcut keystroke Ctrl+Shift+D to the macro, and store it in This Workbook. Your macro should record all of the actions in steps 5–11.

5. Select cell A1.

6. Type **Today's Date** into cell A1.

7. Enter the formula **=TODAY()** in cell B1.
   This function displays the current date in the cell.

8. Left-align the date in cell B1.

9. Format cells A1:B1 with size 12, bold, and a blue color for text.

10. Set the width of column A to **20**.

11. Select cell B1.

12. Stop the macro recording.

13. Save 💾 as a Macro-Enabled Workbook with the name **as-Today's Date** in the Lesson 12 folder in your file storage location.

Test the Macro Using the Ribbon Command

14. Display the Sheet2 worksheet.

15. Run the macro using the Run command in the Macro dialog box.
    If your macro does not insert text, format the text, and widen column A as specified in steps 5–11, then delete the macro and rerecord it.

Test the Macro Shortcut Key

16. Display the Sheet3 worksheet.

17. Test the macro using the Ctrl + Shift + D keystroke combination.

18. Have your instructor or a teaching assistant initial that you have successfully run the macro. _____

19. Save as **as-Today's Date** again and close the workbook.

Assessment 12.4   Create Macros and Assign Buttons

In this exercise, you will create a defined name for a list, create two macros, assign buttons to them, and finally run the macros using the buttons.

1. Open the as-Holiday Donations workbook.

2. In the November Donations worksheet, assign the defined name **Patron_List** to the range A6:D16.

3. Create two macros for use in this workbook only and assign them to buttons as shown in the following table. The table describes the button text, macro names, and macro functions for each button. Position the buttons above the list in rows 3:4.

Button Text	Macro Name	Macro Function
Sort by Patron	Sort_by_Patron	Sort Patron_List in A to Z order based on the patron last names and first names in columns A:B.
Sort by Details	Sort_by_Details	Sort the Patron_List from highest to lowest based on the donation details in column D.

4. Save 💾 as a Macro-Enabled Workbook in the Lesson 12 folder in your file storage location.

Test the Macros

5. Manually sort the list in A to Z order by the type of donation in column C.

6. Test the Sort_by_Patron macro.

7. Test the Sort_by_Details macro.

8. Have your instructor or a teaching assistant initial that you have successfully run the macros. _____

9. Save 💾 again and close the workbook.

Critical Thinking

Critical Thinking 12.1   Create a PivotTable and PivotChart

Linda Ochoa, owner of Ochoa Nursery, asks you to design a PivotTable and a PivotChart from a table containing data for wholesale supplies received by the nursery.

Task A: Create a PivotTable

You have 15 minutes to complete Task A.

- Open the ct-Wholesale PivotTable workbook from the Lesson 12 folder.

- Create a PivotTable on a new worksheet from the Deliveries table.

- Add fields to the PivotTable to summarize the wholesale value, first by supplier and then by product.

- Remove the Product field from the PivotTable and add the Category ID field.

- Edit the PivotTable to exclude the Building category from the summary.

- Format the number column. When you are finished, your PivotTable should look similar to the following example.

	A	B
3		Sum of Wholesale Value
4	⊟ Harbor Garden Tools	2,551.40
5	Plants	36.00
6	Supplies	21.60
7	Tools	2,493.80
8	⊟ Nursery Warehouse	401.28
9	Indoor	166.08
10	Supplies	127.20
11	Tools	108.00
12	⊟ Wholesale Flower Supply	446.34
13	Indoor	83.70
14	Plants	145.44
15	Supplies	179.40
16	Tools	37.80
17	Grand Total	3,399.02

- Take a few minutes to try other configurations of the PivotTable. See if there are any other useful ways to display the data.

- When you are finished, save 🖫 the workbook and go on to Task B.

Task B: Create a PivotChart

You have 15 minutes to complete Task B.

■ On a new worksheet, create a new PivotTable and PivotChart from the data on the Table worksheet. (Leave the PivotTable that you created in Task A as is.)

■ Add fields to display a summary of the wholesale value organized by supplier and then by product.

■ The high wholesale value of the rototiller and planter products causes the other bars to be barely visible on the chart. Filter Rototiller and Planter out of the chart.

■ Add a chart title, remove the legend, and apply attractive formatting.

■ Move the PivotChart to a new worksheet. When you are finished, your PivotChart should look similar to the following example.

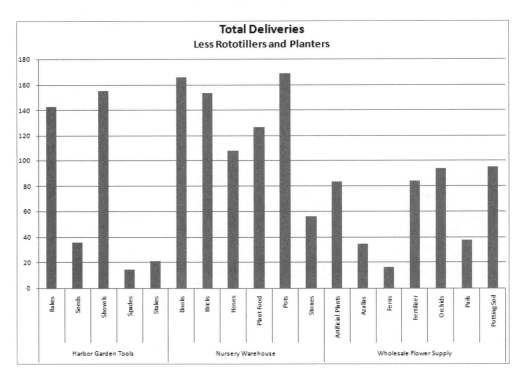

■ When you are finished, save [save icon] and close the workbook.

Sk – 12.1, 12.2
Ass – 12.2, 12.4
Test.

Critical Thinking 12.2   Create Sorting Macros in a Contact List

In this exercise, you will set up a contact list and create macros that sort the list.

1. Set up a contact list in a new workbook. Make up at least six contacts. Include the first name, last name, company, street address, city, state, ZIP code, and phone number in separate columns. Format the contact list as desired.

2. Create three sorting macros in the current workbook: one to sort by last name, one by company, and one by ZIP code.

3. Create buttons to assign to each macro, and take care to position them in a worksheet area where they will be easily accessible and not likely to be deleted. Add descriptive names to each button.

4. Test all buttons.

5. Save 💾 your completed macro-enabled workbook as **ct-Contact List** in the Lesson 12 folder.

Critical Thinking 12.3   Create Macros to Format Cells

Amy Lynn is a student intern in the human resources department of a food and beverage distribution company. Most of the managers are interested primarily in the subtotal and total rows within worksheets. They want those cells to have a consistent format for use throughout the department. Help Amy set up two macros.

- Open the ct-Human Resources Budget workbook. You will save macros to that workbook. The network system administrator would transfer macros to the personal macro workbook once the macros were approved.

- Use the Sample Data worksheet to create macros.

- The first macro will be used to format cells selected in subtotal rows so they stand out in worksheets. You may use a cell style, bold type, colors, or fill patterns.

- The second macro will be used to format cells selected in total rows in the same fashion. Create consistency between the formats you use for the subtotal and total rows. The formats and macros should be designed so that they may be used in a wide range of worksheets.

- Assign the macros to shortcut keys that are easy to remember for running the macros.

- Test the macros using the three subtotal rows and one total row in the HR Budget worksheet.

- Save 💾 your completed macro-enabled workbook and close Excel.

LESSON 13

Using Financial Functions and Data Analysis

Several Excel tools allow you to perform a *what-if analysis* on worksheet data. For example, you might ask, "What if our company obtained a loan for 9 percent rather than 8 percent?" By changing the interest rate used in a formula to various rates, you could see the effect on the monthly loan payment. Excel's built-in financial functions may be used for various types of calculations. In this lesson, you will use the PMT (Payment) function to determine the monthly payment for a new car. You also will use the FV (Future Value) function to determine the future value of investments. Excel provides other tools to help you find solutions to what-if questions. In this lesson, you will use Goal Seek, Solver, and the Analysis ToolPak to answer a variety of questions. Excel also provides the Scenario Manager to view alternative scenarios with up to 32 input variables for advanced data analysis.

LESSON OBJECTIVES

After studying this lesson, you will be able to:

- Use the PMT and FV functions to analyze loans and investments
- Adjust one or more variables using the Goal Seek and Solver tools
- Create what-if models in the Scenario Manager
- Choose tools in the Analysis ToolPak

Case Study: Planning Personal Finances

Ashley Diehl recently was promoted in her job and received a significant pay raise. She has also profited handsomely from some wise investments. Ashley decides it is time to explore the idea of making her dream of owning a shiny new coupe-model car come true. Ashley sets up an Excel worksheet that calculates the monthly payment for a car loan using a variety of input variables. She uses the PMT (Payment) function to calculate the monthly payment and the FV (Future Value) function to forecast a savings plan. Then she will use Excel's Goal Seek and Solver tools to explore various financing scenarios. In her job, she will use the Scenario Manager to view various models for income and expenses. The following illustrations show a car loan worksheet and a report from the Scenario Manager.

	A	B
1	Car Loan Analysis	
2		
3	Purchase Price	$ 37,000.00
4		
5	Loan	
6	Loan Amount	$ 27,000.00
7	Interest Rate	8.20%
8	Number of Months	60
9	Monthly Payment	$ 550.00
10	Total Interest	$ 5,999.99
11		
12	Total Cost	
13	Down Payment	$ 10,000.00
14	Total Loan Payments	$ 32,999.99
15	Total Vehicle Cost	$42,999.99

Ashley used this worksheet and the Goal Seek and Solver tools to determine the auto loan that she can afford.

Scenario Summary

	Current Values:	Scenario 1	Scenario 2	Scenario 3
Changing Cells:				
Net_Sales	2,000,000	1,000,000	1,000,000	2,000,000
Sample_Costs	17,000	10,000	10,000	17,000
Trade_Shows	35,000	10,000	20,000	35,000
Vehicle	28,000	10,000	7,000	28,000
Cell_Phones	15,000	10,000	4,000	15,000
Entertainment	35,000	10,000	10,000	35,000
Result Cells:				
Expenses_vs._Net_Sales	6.50%	5.00%	5.10%	6.50%
Projected_Bonus	$7,000	$5,000	$4,900	$7,000

Scenario Manager compiles a report to compare the results of several scenarios.

Creating Financial Functions

Excel provides more than 50 financial functions that calculate important financial numbers. For example, Excel has basic financial functions for determining monthly payments on loans, the total interest paid on loans, the future value of investments, and other such questions. Excel also has advanced financial functions for calculating depreciation of assets, internal rates of return, and other more advanced business topics.

PMT and FV Functions

The PMT (Payment) and FV (Future Value) functions are the most useful financial functions for the average Excel user. The PMT function calculates the required payment for a loan when you specify the loan amount, interest rate, and number of payments you will make. The FV function calculates the total amount you will have in an investment when you specify the deposit amount, interest rate, and number of deposits.

Financial Function Syntax

You may enter financial functions using the Insert Function dialog box or by typing them. You may use the actual values or cell references in the formulas. Keep in mind that using the cell reference offers more flexibility. For example, you may easily change the number of deposits in an FV function without having to edit the formula. Like all other functions, financial functions have a specific syntax you must follow. The generic format of the PMT and FV functions are shown in the following table.

Function	Syntax
PMT (Payment)	PMT (rate, periods, loan amount)
FV (Future Value)	FV (rate, periods, payment)

Most car loans and fixed-rate mortgages have payment amounts that remain constant throughout the term of the loan. The PMT and FV functions can be used when the payment amount remains constant. The various arguments in the PMT and FV functions are outlined in the following table.

Argument	Description
Periods	This is the number of payments made for a loan or deposits for an investment. Most loans have a monthly payment period, so you should specify the number of months instead of the number of years. For example, use 60 as the number of periods for a five-year auto loan (5 years*12 months per year).
Rate	This is the interest rate for each period of the loan or investment. Although loans are quoted as annual rates, payments usually are made monthly. Therefore, you will need to divide the interest rate by 12 in the formula. For example, a 7 percent annual rate would be expressed as 7%/12.
Payment	This is the amount invested in each period. The payment must be the same for each period.
Loan amount	This is the amount borrowed.

Converting Negative Numbers to Positive

Excel treats payments as debits (money you owe), so the PMT and FV functions display the result as a negative number. This is a convention that bankers and other financial professionals use. Placing a minus (–) sign before the cell reference for the loan amount or payment in the formula changes the result to a positive number, which may be more easily understood.

 TIP! *A minus (–) sign may be entered before the loan amount or payment in a PMT or FV formula. As an alternative, the minus sign may be entered just before the function name, as in =–PMT or =–FV. Placing the minus sign in either location converts the result to a positive number.*

Hands-On 13.1   Use the PMT and FV Functions

In this exercise, you will set up a loan worksheet that will calculate the monthly payment on a car loan using the PMT function. You also will use the FV function to calculate the monthly deposit required to save the $10,000 down payment.

Create a PMT Function

1. Start Excel and open the Car Loan workbook from the Lesson 13 folder in your file storage location.

2. Maximize ⬜ the window.
   The $37,000 purchase price and $10,000 down payment are already entered in the Car Loan worksheet.

3. In the Loan worksheet, select cell B6 and enter the formula **=B3-B13**.
   The result is $27,000. The loan amount is the purchase price minus the down payment. The PMT function will use the loan amount as one of its arguments.

4. Select cell B7 and enter **6%** as the interest rate.

5. Select cell B8 and enter **60** as the number of months.

6. Select cell B9 and enter the formula **=PMT(B7,B8,B6)**.
   The result equals ($1,670.64). Remember that the generic PMT function syntax is =PMT(rate, periods, loan amount). Notice that the B7, B8, and B6 references in the function refer to the interest rate, number of months, and loan amount in the worksheet.

   Excel formats the payment in Currency Style, red, and in parentheses. The red color and parentheses indicate that this is a negative number. You will convert this number to a positive number in the following steps.

   Finally, notice that $1,670.64 seems a very large payment because the interest rate in cell B7 is an annual rate of 6 percent. Ashley would not pay 6 percent interest per month. The interest rate must be divided by 12 (the number of months in a year) to calculate a monthly interest rate in the function. You will do this in the following steps.

7. Select cell B9.

8. Click in the Formula Bar, position the cursor between the comma and B6 in the formula, and type a minus (–) sign.

9. Position the cursor after B7 in the formula and type **/12** to divide the B7 rate by 12, and complete the entry.

   The completed formula is =PMT(B7/12,B8,-B6). The new payment equals $521.99. This payment certainly will be more affordable. The minus sign converts the number to a positive, and the B7/12 argument establishes a 0.5 percent per month rate.

10. Format cell B9 in Accounting format with two decimal places.

11. Select cell B14 and enter the formula **=B9*B8**.

    Total loan payments equal $31,319.14.

12. Select cell B10 and enter the formula **=B14-B6**.

    Total loan interest equals $4,319.14. The loan amount in cell B6 is subtracted from the total payments to determine the total interest.

13. Select cell B15 and enter the formula **=B13+B14**.

    The total vehicle cost equals $41,319.14 for a car with a $37,000 purchase price. Your worksheet should match the following illustration.

	A	B
1	**Car Loan Analysis**	
2		
3	Purchase Price	$ 37,000.00
4		
5	**Loan**	
6	Loan Amount	$ 27,000.00
7	Interest Rate	6.00%
8	Number of Months	60
9	Monthly Payment	$ 521.99
10	Total Interest	$ 4,319.14
11		
12	**Total Cost**	
13	Down Payment	$ 10,000.00
14	Total Loan Payments	$ 31,319.14
15	Total Vehicle Cost	**$41,319.14**

14. Save 🖫 the changes to your workbook.

Create the FV Function

15. Display the Savings worksheet and enter the following values in the range B3:B5:

	A	B
1	**Saving for Down Payment**	
2		
3	Amount Saved Each Month	$225.00
4	Interest Rate	2.5%
5	Number of Months	60
6	**Total Saved**	

16. Select cell B6.

17. Follow these steps to choose the FV (Future Value) function:

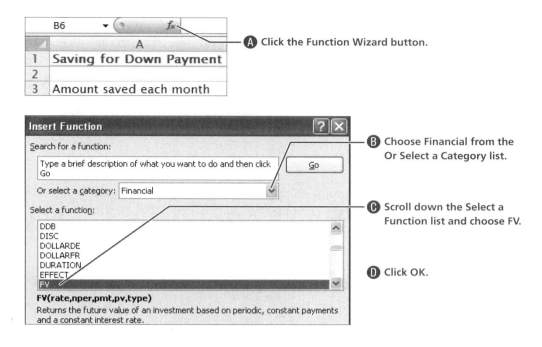

A Click the Function Wizard button.

B Choose Financial from the Or Select a Category list.

C Scroll down the Select a Function list and choose FV.

D Click OK.

18. Follow these steps to specify the function arguments:

A If necessary, drag the Function Arguments dialog box aside so that the range A1:B6 is visible.

B Click in the Rate box, select cell B4 in the worksheet, and type **/12**. This divides the annual interest rate by 12 months.

C Click in the Nper box and select cell B5 in the worksheet to set the number of payment periods.

D Click in the Pmt box. Type a minus (–) sign and click cell B3 to set the payment amount to a negative value.

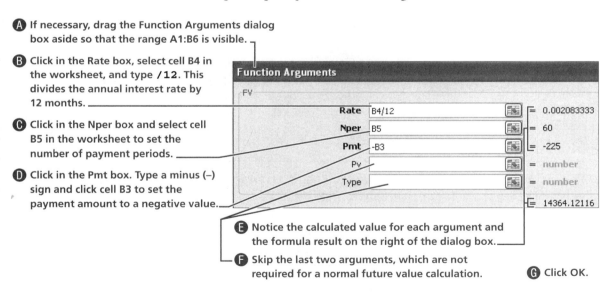

E Notice the calculated value for each argument and the formula result on the right of the dialog box.

F Skip the last two arguments, which are not required for a normal future value calculation.

G Click OK.

The completed formula is =FV(B4/12,B5,-B3), and the result $14,364.12 appears in cell B7. By depositing $225 per month in her savings account, Ashley would save this amount in five years.

19. Change the number of months in cell B5 until the total saved is slightly more than $10,000, the amount Ashley needs for her car down payment.
By experimenting with the values for rate, number of periods, and payment used in the FV function, you may create various plans for saving the desired amount. In the next exercises, you will use Excel's tools to automate this analysis.

20. Save 📄 the changes to your workbook.

Using Data Analysis Tools

Excel provides several tools to perform advanced what-if analyses. Goal Seek is best used when you know the formula answer you want but not the specific value in one cell that would achieve the answer. The Solver sets the values of multiple cells to produce the desired result that you specify for a target cell. You also may set minimum and maximum values for Solver to use in calculations. Scenario Manager saves a model worksheet with various changes to values so that you may compare the scenarios side by side. Other tools for statistical and engineering analyses, such as the Rank and Percentile tool, are included in the Data Analysis ToolPak.

Using Goal Seek

With Goal Seek you set a goal for a specific formula result. For example, you will set a monthly payment goal of $500 in the Car Loan worksheet. The goal cell must contain a formula, which is a PMT function in this example. You will instruct Goal Seek to adjust the down payment to achieve the $500 monthly payment.

QUICK REFERENCE: USING GOAL SEEK	
Task	**Procedure**
Set up a Goal Seek solution	■ Test the worksheet with sample data to make sure formulas are functioning properly.
	■ Select the cell for which you want to set a goal. The cell must contain a formula.
	■ Choose Data→Data Tools→What-If Analysis Tools→Goal Seek from the Ribbon.
	■ Type the desired goal value in the To Value box.
	■ Click in the By Changing Cell box and choose the worksheet cell for which Goal Seek will adjust the value.

 ## Hands-On 13.2   Use Goal Seek

In this exercise, you will use Goal Seek to adjust the down payment based on a specific monthly payment that you enter. Then you will adjust the interest rate.

Use Goal Seek to Adjust the Down Payment

Ashley wants to see the effect on the down payment she would be required to pay if her monthly payment were $500 rather than $521.99 as previously calculated.

1. Display the Loan worksheet of the Car Loan workbook.

2. Select cell B9.
   Clicking the cell for which you want to set a goal prior to starting Goal Seek will ensure that you set the goal for the correct cell. The currently selected cell reference displays in the Set Cell box when you open Goal Seek.

3. Choose Data→Data Tools→What-If Analysis→Goal Seek from the Ribbon.

4. Follow these steps to set the Goal Seek parameters:
You may either type cell references or use point mode in the Goal Seek dialog box.

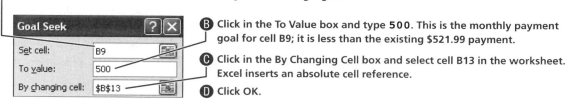

Ⓐ Notice that the **Set Cell** option displays **B9**, the cell you selected prior to launching Goal Seek. This is the formula cell for which you are setting a goal.

Ⓑ Click in the **To Value** box and type **500**. This is the monthly payment goal for cell B9; it is less than the existing $521.99 payment.

Ⓒ Click in the **By Changing Cell** box and select cell B13 in the worksheet. Excel inserts an absolute cell reference.

Ⓓ Click OK.

5. Click OK in the Goal Seek Status dialog box.
Goal Seek found a solution for the goal. The down payment in the worksheet has been adjusted to $11,137.22. As you can see, a higher down payment is required with a $500 monthly payment.

6. Undo 🔄 the change to the down payment.

Use Goal Seek to Adjust the Interest Rate

Ashley wants to know what her loan interest would have to be if her monthly payment were $550.

7. Make certain cell B9 is still selected and choose Data→Data Tools→What-If Analysis→Goal Seek from the Ribbon.

8. Type **550** in the To Value box to set the monthly payment goal.

9. Click in the By Changing Cell box, and then select cell B7 (the Interest Rate cell) in the worksheet.

10. Click OK, and the interest rate is changed to 8.20 percent.

11. Move the Goal Seek Status dialog box, if necessary, to see cell B7.

12. Click OK again to confirm the change to the interest rate.

13. Save 💾 the changes.

Change Values in a What-If Analysis

After seeking a goal, you also may experiment with the what-if analysis by changing the purchase price or other values directly in the worksheet. The cells you change should contain values and not formulas.

14. Select cell B3 and change the purchase price to **$20,000**.
What impact does this change have on the other amounts?

15. Feel free to experiment with Goal Seek. When you are finished, close the workbook without saving the changes.

Using Solver

Goal Seek is easy to use but is somewhat limited. Goal Seek adjusts only one variable at a time. Excel's Solver tool can solve problems when more than one variable requires adjustment. In fact, you may specify up to two hundred variables, but all variables must appear in a formula related to the target cell. You may specify a precise target cell value, as with Goal Seek, or you may specify a Max (maximum) or Min (minimum) value. For example, you may specify a maximum monthly payment of $300. In addition, Solver lets you specify one or more constraints. Constraints give you extra control by limiting a cell's possible range of values in the suggested solution.

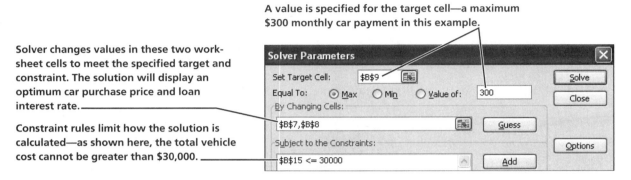

A value is specified for the target cell—a maximum $300 monthly car payment in this example.

Solver changes values in these two worksheet cells to meet the specified target and constraint. The solution will display an optimum car purchase price and loan interest rate.

Constraint rules limit how the solution is calculated—as shown here, the total vehicle cost cannot be greater than $30,000.

Changing values in two cells based on a target cell value and a constraint rule

Installing Solver

Solver is not part of the typical Office 2007 installation but is an add-in program. The Solver command displays in an Analysis group on the Data Ribbon after installation.

!NOTE! *Your network administrator may not grant permission to install add-in programs.*

QUICK REFERENCE: INSTALLING ADD-INS AND USING SOLVER

Task	Procedure
Install or remove an add-in tool	■ Choose Office→Excel Options→Add-Ins.
	■ Choose Excel Add-Ins to the right of Manage and click Go.
	■ In the Add-Ins dialog box, place a checkmark in the box for each desired add-in. Removing checkmarks uninstalls add-ins that are currently installed.
	■ Answer Yes to proceed with installation.
Set up a Solver solution	■ Test the worksheet with sample data to make sure formulas are functioning properly.
	■ Choose Data→Analysis→Solver from the Ribbon.
	■ If desired, click the Reset All button to clear previously set options in the Solver Parameters dialog box.
	■ Click in the Set Target Cell box and choose the worksheet cell for which you want to set a goal.
	■ Choose Max, Min, or Value Of and type a desired goal value for the target cell in the text box.
	■ Click in the By Changing Cells box and choose one or more worksheet cells whose values you want Solver to adjust. Type a comma between cell references. Or, to allow Solver to enter all possible cell references, click the Guess button.
	■ If desired, click the Add button and set one or more constraint rules in the Add Constraint dialog box.
	■ Click Solve in the Solver Parameters dialog box.
	■ Read the message in the Solver Results dialog box, choosing Keep Solver Solution or Restore Original Values.
Save Solver results as a scenario to view again later	■ Click Save Scenario in the Solver Results dialog box.
	■ Type a scenario name.

Hands-On 13.3   Use Solver

In this exercise, you will use Solver to determine the purchase price and interest rate required to achieve the total vehicle cost that you specify.

Before You Begin: Solver must be installed using the procedure given in the preceding Quick Reference table.

Reset to Original Values

1. Open the Car Loan workbook from the Lesson 13 folder.

2. In the Loan worksheet, reenter the original values of **$37,000** in cell B3 and **6%** in cell B7. *All worksheet cells should contain the values or formulas you created in Hands-On 13.1.*

Use Solver to Adjust the Purchase Price and Interest Rate

3. Choose Data→Analysis→Solver 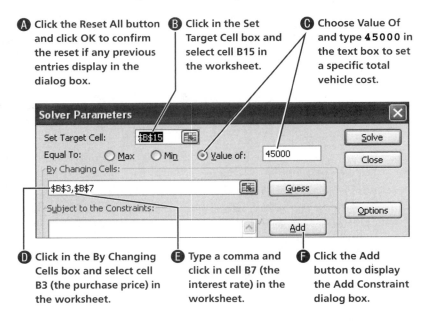 from the Ribbon.

4. Follow these steps to set the target cell value and specify the variable cells:

Ⓐ Click the Reset All button and click OK to confirm the reset if any previous entries display in the dialog box.

Ⓑ Click in the Set Target Cell box and select cell B15 in the worksheet.

Ⓒ Choose Value Of and type **45000** in the text box to set a specific total vehicle cost.

Ⓓ Click in the By Changing Cells box and select cell B3 (the purchase price) in the worksheet.

Ⓔ Type a comma and click in cell B7 (the interest rate) in the worksheet.

Ⓕ Click the Add button to display the Add Constraint dialog box.

Excel converts the target cell and variable cells to absolute cell references as you entered them in the Solver Parameters dialog box.

5. Follow these steps to specify a constraint:

Ⓐ Click cell B10 (total interest) in the worksheet to enter an absolute cell reference in this box.

Ⓑ Make certain the operator is set to <= (less than or equal to).

Ⓒ Type **7500** in the Constraint box to limit the total interest to $7,500 or less.

Ⓓ Click OK to complete the constraint.

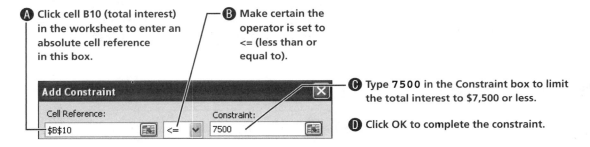

The constraint rule appears in the Subject to the Constraints box of the Solver Parameters dialog box.

6. Take a moment to review the options you have set in the Solver Parameters dialog box.

7. Click the Solve button, and the Solver will go to work.
When the Solver has completed its calculations, the Solver Results dialog box should report that a solution has been found that meets all conditions.

8. Make certain the Keep Solver Solution option is chosen and click OK.
The completed solution should match the following example.

	A	B	
1	Car Loan Analysis		
2			
3	Purchase Price	$ 37,500.00	→ Solver suggested a $37,500 purchase price and 9.93 percent interest rate for the two variables you specified.
4			
5	Loan		
6	Loan Amount	$ 27,500.00	
7	Interest Rate	9.93%	
8	Number of Months	60	
9	Monthly Payment	$ 583.33	→ The monthly payment rate recalculates as $583.33. No constraint was placed on this formula.
10	Total Interest	$ 7,500.00	
11			
12	Total Cost		
13	Down Payment	$ 10,000.00	→ The total vehicle cost is $45,000, and total interest is $7,500, the limits you set.
14	Total Loan Payments	$ 35,000.00	
15	Total Vehicle Cost	$ 45,000.00	

Use Solver to Adjust the Purchase Price

Ashley determines that she can afford a maximum $450 monthly payment, and her credit union offers a discounted 6 percent auto loan. She wants to know the maximum purchase price that she can negotiate, but her research shows that $33,000 is the lowest offer she is likely to receive.

9. Choose Data→Analysis→Solver 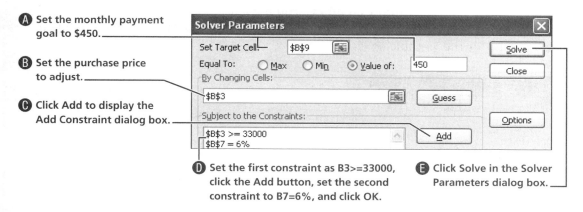 from the Ribbon.

10. Click Reset All to clear the previous options.

11. Follow these guidelines to set options in the Solver Parameters dialog box:

Ⓐ Set the monthly payment goal to $450.

Ⓑ Set the purchase price to adjust.

Ⓒ Click Add to display the Add Constraint dialog box.

Solver Parameters

Set Target Cell: $B$9

Equal To: ○ Max ○ Min ● Value of: 450

By Changing Cells: $B$3

Subject to the Constraints:
$B$3 >= 33000
$B$7 = 6%

Solve · Close · Guess · Options · Add

Ⓓ Set the first constraint as B3>=33000, click the Add button, set the second constraint to B7=6%, and click OK.

Ⓔ Click Solve in the Solver Parameters dialog box.

Solver reports it could not find a solution. Although one is available, the existing interest rate is hindering Solver.

12. Choose Restore Original Values and click OK.

13. In cell B7, change the interest rate to 6 percent.

14. Choose Data→Analysis→Solver and click Solve to use the options you previously set.
This time a solution was found. The purchase price equals $33,276.50. This is the maximum price Ashley may negotiate to meet her $450 monthly payment goal.

15. Save the changes to your workbook.

Experiment with Solver

16. Take a few minutes to experiment with Solver.
Depending on the variables and constraints you create, Solver may report that no solution was found or suggest a 0 (zero) or negative amount in one or more cells. If this occurs, choose Restore Original Values and solve again after editing the options.

17. When you have finished, close the workbook without saving changes.

Scenario Manager

Excel provides the Scenario Manager to create and save what-if models with up to 32 variables. This allows you to model virtually any what-if scenario. Scenario Manager does not solve for a specific variable value to achieve a formula result as Goal Seek and Solver do. You may, however, save a Solver solution as a scenario.

What Is a Scenario?

A scenario is a group of values assigned to cells in a what-if model. The model calculates formula results based on the values you enter in the scenario. Scenarios are given names to identify them, and they are saved and organized using the Scenario Manager.

Managing Scenarios

You may create and manage a large number of scenarios in the Scenario Manager. This way, you may compare various scenarios and the results they achieve. The Scenario Manager also lets you display and print a summary of all scenarios.

Adding Scenarios

You use the Manage Scenarios command to display the Scenario Manager dialog box. The Scenario Manager has an Add button that allows you to create new scenarios. Each scenario may contain different values. The following illustration shows the Scenario Values dialog box with values entered for the variable cells.

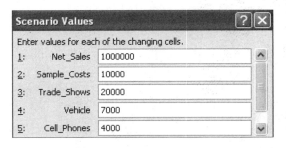

The entered values are applied to cells in the worksheet, thus forming a scenario.

QUICK REFERENCE: USING SCENARIO MANAGER

Task	Procedure
Create a scenario	■ Create defined names for all worksheet cells containing variables or result formulas affected by the variables.
	■ Select the worksheet cells containing the desired variables but do not select any cells containing result formulas.
	■ Choose Data→Data Tools→What-If Analysis→Scenario Manager from the Ribbon.
	■ Click the Add button in the Scenario Manager dialog box.
	■ In the Add Scenario dialog box, type a scenario name.
	■ In the Scenario Values dialog box, edit values as desired.
	■ In the Scenario Manager dialog box, click Show to view results.
Edit a scenario	■ Choose the desired scenario name in the Scenario Manager dialog box.
	■ Click the Edit button.
	■ In the Scenario Values dialog box, edit values as desired.
Display and print a summary of all scenarios	■ Click the Summary button in the Scenario Manager dialog box.
	■ Choose Scenario Summary or Scenario PivotTable Report.
	■ Click in the Result Cells box and choose one or more worksheet cells containing result formulas based on the scenario values. Type a comma between cell references. Excel places the report on a new worksheet.
	■ Print the scenario report worksheet, if desired.

 ## Hands-On 13.4   Use the Scenario Manager

In this exercise, you will help Ashley Diehl set up a model to analyze her department's expenses. Ashley understands that reducing expenses will increase the bonus she receives from her employer. Therefore, she wants to take a closer look at each component of the expenses. You will create a model and use Scenario Manager to set up and manage multiple scenarios.

Set Up the Model

1. Open the Net Sales workbook from the Lesson 13 folder.

2. In the Bonus Analysis worksheet, enter the model values in the range B3:B8 as shown.

	A	B
1	Expenses vs. Net Sales Model	
2		
3	Net Sales	1,000,000
4	Sample Costs	10,000
5	Trade Shows	10,000
6	Vehicle	10,000
7	Cell Phones	10,000
8	Entertainment	10,000
9	**Expenses vs. Net Sales**	

3. In cell B9, enter the formula **=SUM(B4:B8)/B3**.
   The result equals 0.05. Notice that this formula sums the expenses and divides by the Net Sales.

4. Format cell B9 as Percent Style with two decimal places.
   Expenses are 5.00 percent of net sales. This model is the starting point from which you will create scenarios to see the effect on the Expenses vs. Net Sales percentage.

5. Review the results of the formula in cell B11.
   Ashley's projected bonus is $5,000. The formula bases the bonus partly on her efficiency in achieving a low Expenses vs. Net Sales percentage.

Name the Variable Cells and Results Cells

In the next few steps, you will name the variable cells in the model using the Create from Selection command that was introduced in Lesson 10, Managing Multiple-Sheet Workbooks. Naming the variable cells is beneficial because the names, rather than cell references, will appear in the Scenario Manager dialog box. You also will name the results cells containing formulas because they will appear in a summary report.

6. Select the range A3:B11, which includes labels and the cell values to which they refer.

7. Choose Formulas→Defined Names→Create From Selection ⊞ from the Ribbon.

8. Place a checkmark in the Left Column box (if not already checked) and click OK.

9. Choose Formulas→Defined Names→Name Manager 🗐 to view all defined names and their Refers To entries.

10. Widen the Name column and Refers To column, if necessary, to view entire entries in the Name Manager dialog box.

11. Close the Name Manager dialog box.

Create the First Scenario

12. Taking care not to select cell B9, select the range B3:B8 as shown to the right.
    Only the variables will be adjusted in the Scenario Manager. Usually it is best to preselect the cells as you did here, though you may always select the cells once the Add Scenario dialog box is displayed.

	A	B
1	Expenses vs. Net Sales Model	
2		
3	Net Sales	1,000,000
4	Sample Costs	10,000
5	Trade Shows	10,000
6	Vehicle	10,000
7	Cell Phones	10,000
8	Entertainment	10,000
9	**Expenses vs. Net Sales**	5.00%

13. Choose Data→Data Tools→What-If Analysis→ Scenario Manager from the Ribbon.
    The dialog box should indicate that no scenarios are currently defined.

14. Click the Add button to add a new scenario.

15. Follow these steps to set scenario options in the Add Scenario dialog box:

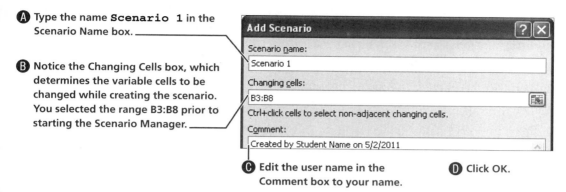

Ⓐ Type the name **Scenario 1** in the Scenario Name box.

Ⓑ Notice the Changing Cells box, which determines the variable cells to be changed while creating the scenario. You selected the range B3:B8 prior to starting the Scenario Manager.

Ⓒ Edit the user name in the Comment box to your name.

Ⓓ Click OK.

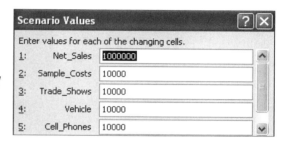

The Scenario Values dialog box appears as shown; do not make any changes in the dialog box. Review the defined names displayed to the left of the variable boxes. Notice that Excel filled in the variable boxes with the values from the range B3:B8 that you selected in the worksheet. You also may create scenarios by entering values or formulas in these boxes.

16. Scroll down until the Entertainment variable is visible.
A scenario may contain up to 32 variables.

17. Click OK to complete the scenario.
The Scenario Manager dialog box displays the scenario name you just created. This scenario will serve as a starting point and a comparison for other scenarios.

Add Another Scenario

18. Click the Add button in the Scenario Manager dialog box.

19. Enter the name **Scenario 2** in the Add Scenario dialog box, make certain the Changing Cells are B3:B8, edit the Comment to include your name, and click OK.

20. Change the variables for Trade_Shows, Vehicle, and Cell_Phones, as shown to the right.

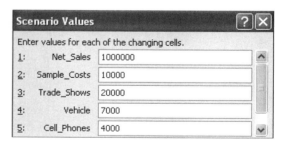

21. Click OK in the Scenario Values box.
Scenario 1 and Scenario 2 now appear in the Scenario Manager dialog box.

Show the Results

22. Make certain Scenario 2 is chosen, and click the Show button in the Scenario Manager dialog box. (Move the dialog box to view the worksheet values, if necessary.)
Excel substitutes the scenario values into the model. The formula in cell B9 calculates the Expenses vs. Net Sales result, which equals 5.10 percent. Ashley's bonus in B11 would be $4,900.

23. Choose Scenario 1 and click the Show button.
As you can see, the Scenario Manager rapidly lets you see the results of various scenarios.

24. Now add two new scenarios using the data in the following table:

Variable	Scenario 3 Scenario Value	Scenario 4 Scenario Value
Net Sales	2,000,000	2,000,000
Sample Costs	17,000	20,000
Trade Shows	35,000	20,000
Vehicle	28,000	10,000
Cell Phones	15,000	7,500
Entertainment	85,000	35,000

25. Use the Show button to display the results of each scenario.

Edit a Scenario

26. Choose Scenario 3 in the Scenario Manager dialog box and click the Show button.
The Expenses vs. Net Sales equals 9 percent. The projected bonus would be $2,000 for this scenario. Ashley will not be happy with this! Fortunately, the Scenario Manager lets you adjust scenario values until a desired result is achieved.

27. With Scenario 3 still chosen, click the Edit button.

28. Click OK in the Edit Scenario box.

29. Change the Entertainment value to **35000** in the Scenario Values dialog box and click OK.

30. Click the Show button again, and the results equal 6.50 percent and $7,000.
Ashley can use these scenarios to determine which expense items to trim.

Display a Summary of All Scenarios

31. Click the Summary button in the Scenario Manager dialog box.
Notice that you may display a scenario summary or a scenario PivotTable report.

32. Follow these steps to select Scenario Summary report options:

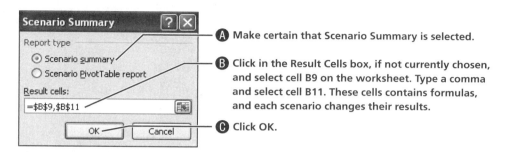

Ⓐ Make certain that Scenario Summary is selected.

Ⓑ Click in the Result Cells box, if not currently chosen, and select cell B9 on the worksheet. Type a comma and select cell B11. These cells contains formulas, and each scenario changes their results.

Ⓒ Click OK.

Excel inserts the summary on a new worksheet named Scenario Summary. Review the summary carefully. You may print a summary as you would print any other worksheet. You also may remove a summary by deleting its worksheet.

33. Save and close the workbook.

Using the Analysis ToolPak

The Analysis ToolPak contains a set of data analysis tools. You display a dialog box that contains all the tools. After you choose a tool, Excel runs the appropriate statistical or engineering macro and then displays the results either on the same sheet as the data or on a separate worksheet. You will use the Rank and Percentile analysis tool in this course.

Installing Analysis ToolPak

Like Solver, the Analysis ToolPak is an add-in program. The Data Analysis ⊞ command displays in the Analysis group on the Data Ribbon after installation. Depending on the desired tools, you may need to install both Analysis ToolPak and Analysis ToolPak VBA.

QR▶

QUICK REFERENCE: USING THE ANALYSIS TOOLPAK	
Task	**Procedure**
Install or remove an add-in tool	▪ Choose Office→Excel Options→Add-Ins.
	▪ Choose Excel Add-Ins to the right of Manage and click Go.
	▪ In the Add-Ins dialog box, place a checkmark in the box for each desired add-in. Removing checkmarks uninstalls add-ins that are currently installed.
	▪ Answer Yes to proceed with installation.
Use a tool in the Analysis ToolPak	▪ Install the Analysis ToolPak add-in, if not installed.
	▪ Choose Data→Analysis→Data Analysis ⊞ from the Ribbon.
	▪ Choose the desired tool in the Data Analysis dialog box.
	▪ Choose options in the tool's dialog box.

Hands-On 13.5   Use the Rank and Percentile Analysis Tool

In this exercise, you will use the Rank and Percentile Analysis Tool to produce a table in the same worksheet as the data. The table contains the rank and percentile of each test score.

Before You Begin: *The Analysis ToolPak must be installed using the procedure given in the preceding Quick Reference table.*

1. Open the Evaluations workbook from the Lesson 13 folder.
   The worksheet includes student scores for Test 1 and Test 2.

2. Choose Data→Analysis→Data Analysis 📊 from the Ribbon.
   Notice the Help button in the Data Analysis dialog box. You could use this to get a description of each tool in the list.

3. Scroll through the Analysis Tools list, choose Rank and Percentile, and click OK.
   The Rank and Percentile dialog box appears. You must specify the cell range to be analyzed in the Input Range box and the location to display the results in the Output Range box.

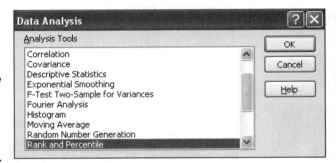

4. Follow these steps to specify the rank and percentile settings for Test 1 scores:

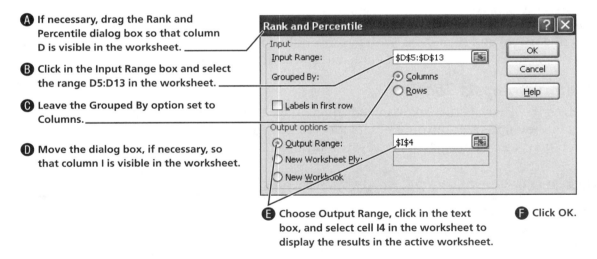

Ⓐ If necessary, drag the Rank and Percentile dialog box so that column D is visible in the worksheet.

Ⓑ Click in the Input Range box and select the range D5:D13 in the worksheet.

Ⓒ Leave the Grouped By option set to Columns.

Ⓓ Move the dialog box, if necessary, so that column I is visible in the worksheet.

Ⓔ Choose Output Range, click in the text box, and select cell I4 in the worksheet to display the results in the active worksheet.

Ⓕ Click OK.

Four columns of results display beginning at cell I4. (Some worksheet columns are hidden in the following illustration.) The data are sorted and do not match the student name in each row. For this reason, the results may be analyzed easily for high and low statistics but not matched to specific students as easily unless you sort the results.

The scores are sorted in Column1 from highest to lowest.

	A	B	C	D	I	J	K	L
3		Student		Test 1		Test 1 Ranking		
4	Last Name	First Name	Mid	Score	Point	Column1	Rank	Percent
5	Evanov	Lisa	A.	78	1	78	1	100.00%
6	Franklin	Ross	G.	77	2	77	2	87.50%
7	Kim	Anne	Y.	65	9	76	3	75.00%
8	McLeod	Marshall	B.	64	8	73	4	62.50%
9	Nguyen	Diep	T.	68	6	72	5	50.00%
10	Preston	Dorothy	H.	72	7	70	6	37.50%
11	Santoyo	Marta	A.	70	5	68	7	25.00%
12	Thompson	Greta	I.	73	3	65	8	12.50%
13	Yunkers	Gavin	O.	76	4	64	9	0.00%
14	Average Increase							

The Point column indicates the original location of each score; that is, the score 76 in cell J7 is ranked 3 but actually belongs to Gavin Yunkers, the ninth student listed.

The scores are ranked 1 through 9.

The scores are divided into equal percentile groups. The highest score, 78, falls in the 100% percentile group. The lowest score, 64, falls in the 0% percentile group.

5. Deselect the highlighted cells in columns I–L of the worksheet.

6. Scroll to the right until columns E–N are visible.

7. Using the technique described in steps 2–4, analyze the Test 2 scores in column E. Take care to highlight the entire entry in the Input Range box before selecting the new range. Display the results beginning in cell N4.

   Take a few minutes to look at the data in the analysis tables and understand how they correlate to the data in columns D and E. Rankings and percentile groups are even more helpful in analyzing long statistical lists.

8. When finished, save the changes and close the workbook.

Concepts Review

True/False Questions

T 1. The PMT function may be used only if the payment amount is the same for each payment period.   **TRUE**   FALSE

T 2. You must insert a minus (–) sign in the PMT formula to have the result display as a positive value.   **TRUE**   FALSE

T 3. The FV function is used to calculate the amount of an investment after periodic payments (deposits) are made.   **TRUE**   FALSE

F 4. The rate argument should be entered as a yearly payment period, such as 7%, in financial functions.   TRUE   **FALSE**

T 5. The target cell for which you are seeking a goal using Goal Seek must contain a formula.   **TRUE**   FALSE

F 6. Goal Seek can adjust more than one variable to solve for a specific formula result.   TRUE   **FALSE**

T 7. Solver can adjust more than one variable to solve for a specific formula result.   **TRUE**   FALSE

F 8. Scenario Manager can adjust more than one variable to solve for a specific formula result.   TRUE   **FALSE**

F 9. Solver is installed in a normal Office 2007 installation.   TRUE   **FALSE**

F 10. The Analysis ToolPak tools help you to record macros.   TRUE   **FALSE**

Multiple Choice Questions

1. Which term means "changing values in a worksheet to try out different solutions"?
   a. What-if analysis
   b. Analysis tools
   c. Data validation
   d. Setting goals

2. Which of the following PMT functions has the correct arguments?
   a. =PMT(rate, loan amount)
   b. =PMT(rate, periods, loan amount)
   c. =PMT(rate, payment, loan amount)
   d. =PMT(periods, rate, payment)

3. Which tool allows you to set constraints on values?
   a. Solver
   b. Goal Seek
   c. Analysis ToolPak
   d. Scenario Manager

4. Which tool allows you to save and compare different model versions side by side?
   a. Solver
   b. Goal Seek
   c. Analysis ToolPak
   d. Scenario Manager

Skill Builders

Skill Builder 13.1 Use the PMT Function and Solver

In this exercise, you will use the PMT function to calculate mortgage payments for a 30-year fixed mortgage. The generic syntax of the PMT function is repeated below for your convenience. You also will use Solver to determine the purchase price and interest rate required for a specified total cost.

Payment Function Syntax =PMT(rate, periods, loan amount)

Before You Begin: The Solver add-in must be installed on your computer system to complete the last steps of this exercise.

Create a PMT Function

1. Start a new workbook and set up the worksheet shown to the right using a formula in cell B5 to calculate the loan amount as Purchase Price – Down Payment.

	A	B
1	**30-Year Mortgage Analysis**	
2		
3	Purchase Price	260,000.00
4	Down Payment	25,000.00
5	Loan Amount	235,000.00
6	Interest Rate	9.00%
7	Number of Years	30
8	Monthly Payment	
9	Total Interest	
10	Total Cost of Home	

2. Select cell B8 and enter the formula **=PMT(B6/12,B7*12,-B5)**.
   The result equals $1,890.86. Notice that the formula has a minus (–) sign between the comma and B5. Also, the first argument divides the interest rate in cell B6 by 12 because payments will be made monthly. Likewise, the second argument multiplies the number of years in cell B7 by 12 months in a year. Excel formats the result with the Currency Style because you used the PMT function.

3. Select cell B9 and enter **=B8*B7*12-B5** to calculate the total interest.
   The result equals $445,710.73. Take a few moments to study the formula and notice that it calculates the total payments over the term of the loan and subtracts the loan amount. Also notice that the number of months is determined by multiplying the number of years in cell B7 by 12.

4. Select cell B10 and enter **=B9+B3** to calculate the total cost of the home.

5. Format all dollar amounts in Comma Style with two decimal places. Format the percentage with two decimal places.

Create a Pie Chart

You will create a pie chart that compares the two costs—purchase price and total interest.

6. Select the noncontiguous ranges A3:B3 and A9:B9, as shown.

	A	B
1	**30-Year Mortgage Analysis**	
2		
3	Purchase Price	260,000.00
4	Down Payment	25,000.00
5	Loan Amount	235,000.00
6	Interest Rate	9.00%
7	Number of Years	30
8	Monthly Payment	1,890.86
9	Total Interest	445,710.73
10	Total Cost of Home	705,710.73

This selection allows the pie chart to compare the Purchase Price to the Total Interest.

7. Choose Insert→Charts→Pie→3-D Pie and create the following embedded pie chart.

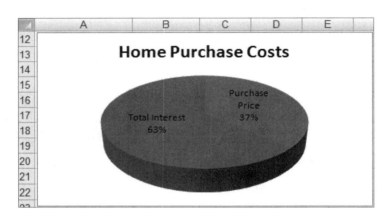

8. Resize the chart smaller and position it in row 12 below the data.

Use a What-If Analysis

Notice that the monthly payment in cell B8 is approximately $1,891.

9. Select cell B6.

10. Change the Interest Rate to **6%** and notice the impact on the monthly payment and the chart slices.

11. Experiment with various interest rates. Also, try changing the down payment and note the impact on the monthly payment.

12. When you are finished, make certain that the purchase price is 260,000 and change the down payment back to **25000** and the interest rate to **6%**.

Use Solver

What interest rate and purchase price are needed to achieve a monthly payment of $1,500, an interest rate not to exceed 7 percent, and total interest not to exceed $300,000? You will use Solver to find these values.

13. Select cell B8 and choose Data→Analysis→Solver from the Ribbon.
The Solver Parameters dialog box displays.

14. Verify that the Set Target Cell box displays cell $B$8.

15. Choose the Value Of option and type **1500** for the monthly payment.

16. Click in the By Changing Cells text box, select cell B3 in the worksheet for the purchase price, type a comma, and select cell B6 for the interest rate.

17. Click the Add button and create a constraint for the interest rate not to exceed **7%**.

18. Add a constraint for the total interest not to exceed **300000**.

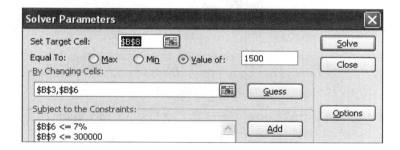

19. Click Solve and OK to accept Solver's suggested solution.
The new purchase price should be $265,000 with an interest rate of 6.39 percent. Solver may suggest a different solution, but the variables should meet all the requirements that you set in the dialog box.

20. Save 💾 as **sb-Home Mortgage** in the Lesson 13 folder, and then close the workbook.

Skill Builder 13.2   Use the FV Function

In this exercise, you will use the Future Value (FV) function to determine the future value of a college fund. This is important if you are saving for a college education, but the worksheet also may be used to determine the future value of nearly any investment that has consistent contributions. The generic syntax of the FV function is repeated below for your convenience.

Future Value Function Syntax =FV(rate, periods, payment)

1. Start a new workbook.

2. Use the Column Width command to set the width of column A to 19 and column B to 14.

3. Enter the data shown to the right:

4. Format the interest rate in cell B3 as a percentage with two decimal places.

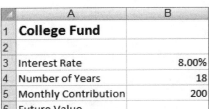

	A	B
1	**College Fund**	
2		
3	Interest Rate	8.00%
4	Number of Years	18
5	Monthly Contribution	200
6	Future Value	

5. Select cell B6 and enter the function **=FV(B3/ 12,B4*12,-B5)**.
   The result equals $96,017.23. Notice that the formula has a minus (–) sign between the comma and B5. Otherwise, the FV function would return a negative number. Also, notice that the interest rate in cell B3 is divided by 12 to produce a monthly rate. The number of years in cell B4 is multiplied by 12 to produce the total number of monthly payments.

6. Save 💾 as **sb-Original College Fund** in the Lesson 13 folder.
   You will continue to use this workbook in the next exercise.

Skill Builder 13.3   Use Goal Seek

In this exercise, you will use Goal Seek to determine the interest rate required to save $200,000 by contributing $300 monthly for 18 years.

Before You Begin: You must have completed Skill Builder 13.2, and the sb-Original College Fund workbook should be open.

Use Goal Seek

1. Choose Office→Save As ![save icon], name the new workbook **sb-College Fund Goal**, and save it in the Lesson 13 folder.

2. Select cell B5 and change the monthly contribution to **300**.
    Notice that this increases the future value of the investment to approximately $144,000. In the next few steps, you will use Goal Seek to determine the interest rate necessary to achieve a future value of $200,000 with a monthly contribution of $300 for 18 years.

3. Select cell B6 and choose Data→Data Tools→What-If Analysis→Goal Seek from the Ribbon.

4. Set the To Value option to **200000**.

5. Set the By Changing Cell option to **B3** (the Interest Rate cell).

6. Click OK and notice that a 10.91 percent interest rate is required.

7. Click OK in the Goal Seek Results dialog box to accept the change to the interest rate.

8. Use Goal Seek to determine the interest rate required to achieve a $275,000 future value with a $325 monthly contribution.

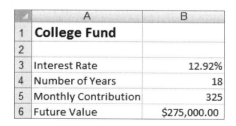

	A	B
1	**College Fund**	
2		
3	Interest Rate	12.92%
4	Number of Years	18
5	Monthly Contribution	325
6	Future Value	$275,000.00

9. Save ![save icon] and close the workbook.

Skill Builder 13.4 Use the Scenario Manager

In this exercise, you will use the Scenario Manager to project the profit for a new toy manufacturer named KidCraft. Donna Williams, the founder of KidCraft, needs to set up the model as part of her business plan. She is trying to raise funds, and a business plan and financial model are a crucial part of this process.

Create the Worksheet

1. Start a new workbook.
   In the next steps, you will create the worksheet shown to the right.

2. Enter the labels in column A and the values in the range B3:B8.

3. Use the SUM function in cell B9 to calculate the expenses in the range B5:B8.

4. Calculate the Gross Profit in cell B11 as the Forecasted Revenue – Total Costs.

5. Calculate the Net Profit in cell B12 as the Gross Profit*70%.

▲	A	B
1	KidCraft FY 5 Projected Income	
2		
3	Forecasted Revenue	$ 345,000
4		
5	Employee Costs	62,000
6	Capital Expenditures	75,900
7	Manufacturing	58,650
8	Marketing and Sales	55,200
9	Total Costs	$ 251,750
10		
11	Gross Profit	$ 93,250
12	Net Profit	$ 65,275

6. Format the values with the Comma Style and Accounting formats shown.

7. Rename the worksheet tab as Projected Income.

Name the Cells

8. Select the range A3:B12.

9. Choose Formulas→Defined Names→Create from Selection ▦ from the Ribbon.

10. Make certain that the Left Column box is checked, and click OK.
    The names are defined for the cells in column B. This will be helpful when you use the Scenario Manager.

Create the First Scenario

The first scenario will be based on existing values in the worksheet.

11. Press and hold Ctrl while you click each cell to select cells B3, B5, B6, B7, and B8.
    The blank cell B4 should not be included in the selection. You will create scenarios by changing the selected cells.

12. Choose Data→Data Tools→What-If Analysis→Scenario Manager from the Ribbon.
    The dialog box should indicate that no scenarios are currently defined.

13. Click the Add button to add a new scenario.

14. Type the name **Scenario 1**, edit the Comment box to include your name, and click OK.
    The Scenario Values dialog box displays.

15. Click the Add button to complete Scenario 1 and display the Add Scenario dialog box.
    You may create additional scenarios without returning to the initial Scenario Manager dialog box.

Add Scenario

Scenario name:

Scenario 1

Changing cells:

B3,B5,B6,B7,B8

Ctrl+click cells to select non-adjacent changing cells.

Comment:

Created by Student Name on 5/2/2011

Add Other Scenarios

16. Type the name **Scenario 2** and click OK.

17. Change only the Forecasted Revenue number to **500000** and click Add.

18. Now add two new scenarios using the data in the following table, making certain that you click OK after entering values for Scenario 4 rather than using Add as you will do for Scenario 3.

Variable	Scenario 3 Scenario Value	Scenario 4 Scenario Value
Forecasted Revenue	700,000	700,000
Employee Costs	80,000	80,000
Capital Expenditures	35,000	42,000
Manufacturing	98,000	85,000
Marketing and Sales	85,000	70,000

19. Use the Show button in the Scenario Manager dialog box to show the results of each scenario.

Display a Summary of All Scenarios

20. Click the Summary button in the Scenario Manager dialog box.

21. Choose the Scenario Summary option; set results cells for the Total Costs, Gross Profit, and Net Profit; and click OK.

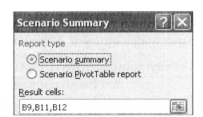

Excel inserts the summary on a new worksheet, shown here:

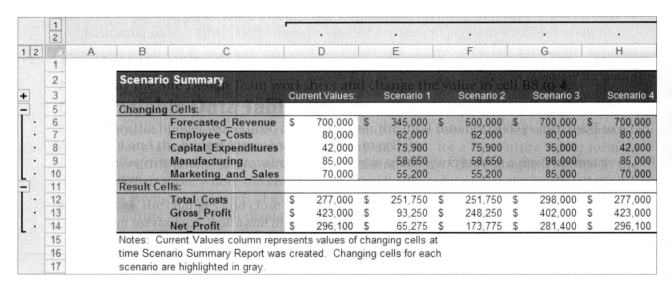

		Current Values:	Scenario 1	Scenario 2	Scenario 3	Scenario 4
Changing Cells:						
	Forecasted_Revenue	$ 700,000	$ 345,000	$ 500,000	$ 700,000	$ 700,000
	Employee_Costs	80,000	62,000	62,000	80,000	80,000
	Capital_Expenditures	42,000	75,900	75,900	35,000	42,000
	Manufacturing	85,000	58,650	58,650	98,000	85,000
	Marketing_and_Sales	70,000	55,200	55,200	85,000	70,000
Result Cells:						
	Total_Costs	$ 277,000	$ 251,750	$ 251,750	$ 298,000	$ 277,000
	Gross_Profit	$ 423,000	$ 93,250	$ 248,250	$ 402,000	$ 423,000
	Net_Profit	$ 296,100	$ 65,275	$ 173,775	$ 281,400	$ 296,100

Notes: Current Values column represents values of changing cells at time Scenario Summary Report was created. Changing cells for each scenario are highlighted in gray.

22. Save 💾 as **sb-Financial Scenarios** in the Lesson 13 folder and close the workbook.

Assessments

Assessment 13.1   Use the FV Function and Solver

In this exercise, you will calculate the future value of a mutual fund investment. Then you will use Solver to determine the rate of return needed to achieve a specific future value.

Before You Begin: The Solver add-in must be installed on your computer system to complete this exercise.

1. Create the worksheet shown at right.

2. Taking care to display the answer as a positive number, use the FV function to calculate the future value in cell B6.

3. Format all cells as shown and adjust the column widths.

	A	B
1	Investment Projections	
2		**Utilities Mutual Fund**
3	Projected Annual Rate of Return	11.00%
4	Number of Years	20
5	Monthly Contribution	$ 800
6	Future Value	$

4. Use Solver to determine the annual rate of return needed to achieve a future value of $300,000 with a monthly contribution of $400 or less. Accept Solver's suggested answer.

5. Save 🖫 with the name **as-Mutual Fund** in the Lesson 13 folder of your storage location and close the workbook.

Assessment 13.2   Use the PMT Function and Goal Seek

In this exercise, you will calculate the monthly payment for a home equity loan. Then you will use Goal Seek to determine the amount you could borrow with a monthly payment of $200.

1. Create the worksheet shown at right.

2. Taking care to display the answer as a positive number, use the PMT function to calculate the monthly payment in cell B7.

3. Format all cells as shown and adjust the column widths.

	A	B
1	Home Equity Loan Analysis	
2		
3		Credit Union
4	Interest Rate	6.00%
5	Number of Years	10
6	Loan Amount	$15,000.00
7	Monthly Payment	

4. Use Goal Seek to determine what the loan amount could be if the monthly payment were $200, and accept Goal Seek's suggested answer.

5. Save 🖫 with the name **as-Home Equity Loan** in the Lesson 13 folder and close the workbook.

Assessment 13.3   Use Scenario Manager

In this exercise, you will use Scenario Manager to project salaries and expenses by creating three scenarios for a budget worksheet.

1. Open the as-Budget Scenarios workbook from the Lesson 13 folder of your storage location.

2. Create Scenario 1 using the existing model data in the Budget worksheet. Use only the Sales and Customer Support costs as variables.

3. Create Scenarios 2 and 3 using the data in the following table:

Variable	Scenario 2	Scenario 3
Sales	2,500,000	2,000,000
Customer Support	100,000	85,000

4. Show Scenario 3 in the worksheet.

5. Display a scenario summary report to include the following results: Salaries and Wages Total, Staffing Expenses Total, Sales Staffing Ratio, and Customer Support Staffing Ratio.

6. Save 🖫 and close the workbook.

Scenario Summary		Current Values:	Scenario 1	Scenario 2	Scenario 3
Changing Cells:					
Sales		2,000,000	2,316,780	2,500,000	2,000,000
Customer_Support		85,000	93,450	100,000	85,000
Result Cells:					
Salaries_and_Wages_Total		$15,751,900	$16,077,130	$16,266,900	$15,751,900
Staffing_Expenses_Total		$4,000,983	$4,083,591	$4,131,793	$4,000,983
Sales_Staffing_Ratio		12.70%	14.41%	15.37%	12.70%
Customer_Support_Staffing_Ratio		0.54%	0.58%	0.61%	0.54%

Critical Thinking

Critical Thinking 13.1   Use the FV Function

Steve Hayashi is an independent investor who manages his own investment portfolio. Steve recently discovered a bond fund in which he feels his investment will be quite safe. Steve makes every investment decision with retirement in mind.

■ Set up a worksheet that uses the Future Value function to determine the projected total in Steve's bond fund investment when he retires.

■ Steve wants to contribute $350 per month, and he plans to retire in 10 years. The fund currently pays a 4 percent annual return.

■ Save 🖫 the workbook as **ct-Retirement Planning** in the Lesson 13 folder in your storage location.

You will continue to use this workbook in the next exercise.

Critical Thinking 13.2   Use Goal Seek

Before You Begin: You must have completed Critical Thinking 13.1, and the ct-Retirement Planning workbook should be open.

After analyzing the future value of his potential bond fund investment, Steve Hayashi realizes that his investment just won't be large enough after 10 years to give him the income he will need at retirement. Steve has other investments in stocks and real estate; however, he expects a significant part of his retirement income to come from the bond fund. Steve decides to explore other funds and considers increasing his monthly contribution.

■ Copy the FV worksheet that you set up in Critical Thinking 13.1 and rename the new worksheet **Goal Seek** in the ct-Retirement Planning workbook.

■ Use the Goal Seek command to answer the following questions (write your answers in the spaces provided):

◆ If the annual rate of return is 5 percent and the number of years is 10, what must be the monthly contribution to result in a future value of $100,000?

_____

◆ If the rate of return is 3 percent and the monthly contribution is $800, what must be the number of years to result in a future value of $200,000?

_____

◆ If the number of years is 15 and the monthly contribution is $600, what must be the rate of return to result in a future value of $150,000?

_____

■ Save 🖫 the changes.

You will continue to use this workbook in the next exercise.

Critical Thinking 13.3   Use the PMT Function

Before You Begin: You must have completed Critical Thinking 13.1 and Critical Thinking 13.2, and the ct-Retirement Planning workbook should be open. Start a new workbook if your instructor did not assign those exercises.

Steve Hayashi purchased his home 25 years ago. Since that time, he has built up more than $100,000 of equity in the house. Steve is considering taking out a home equity loan to pay off some bills and consolidate the rest of his debts.

■ Set up another worksheet in the ct-Retirement Planning workbook that uses the PMT function to determine monthly payments on a home equity loan. Assume an annual interest rate of 8 percent, a 10-year term, and a loan amount of $15,000.

■ Save 💾 the changes.

You will continue to use this workbook in the next exercise.

Critical Thinking 13.4   Use Scenario Manager

Before You Begin: You must have completed Critical Thinking 13.3, and the ct-Retirement Planning workbook should be open.

Steve Hayashi wants to see how the monthly payment for a home equity loan would change based on various loan rates, loan periods, and total payments.

■ Display the payment worksheet that you set up in Critical Thinking 13.3.

■ Keeping in mind that loan payments occur monthly, create a formula that calculates the total of the loan payments over the life of the loan.

■ Create another formula that calculates the total interest paid.

■ Use Scenario Manager to create scenarios for the following variables:

Variable	Scenario 1	Scenario 2	Scenario 3
Interest Rate	9%	8%	7%
Number of Years	15	10	12
Loan Amount	$15,000	$15,000	$20,000

■ Show Scenario 3 in the worksheet.

■ Display a scenario summary report to include the following results: Monthly Payment, Total Payments, and Total Interest.

■ Save 💾 the workbook.

LESSON 14

Auditing and Additional Functions

Complex worksheets for decision making often require advanced functions based on the values in other cells. You may set up detailed worksheets with an identical design for various categories or time periods of a project and summarize the data on a separate worksheet. In this lesson, you will use 3-D cell references in formulas to create the summary calculations. The HLOOKUP and VLOOKUP functions help to use one piece of information to find another in a list. You will use the VLOOKUP function to locate commission rates for each salesperson. With an IF function, you may flag a cell with a text label, display a value, or perform a calculation when specific criteria are satisfied. For example, you may display "Over Budget" in a cell if the value in another cell is greater than your budget estimate. In addition, you will learn how to work with formula auditing tools, which are particularly useful in locating errors in complex formulas that are dependent on other formulas.

LESSON OBJECTIVES

After studying this lesson, you will be able to:

- Use 3-D cell references in formulas to summarize workbook data
- Create a lookup formula to locate a value or text in a list
- Build formulas with IF functions to perform actions based on criteria
- Correct formula errors using the auditing tools

Case Study: Tracking Sales

Wanda Richardson is the sales manager at a wholesale paper distributor named Paper Plus. To track the performance of her salespeople, Wanda uses an Excel workbook with a worksheet for each month. To combine the data from the monthly worksheets into a quarterly summary worksheet, Wanda uses 3-D cell references in SUM formulas.

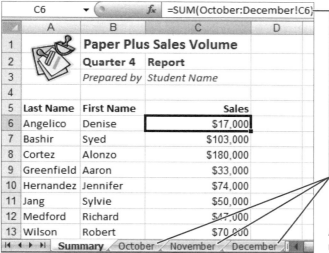

A worksheet formula containing a 3-D cell reference to cell C6 on three worksheets

Wanda also needs to calculate monthly commissions for the Paper Plus sales force. The commission rate depends on a salesperson's total monthly sales. Wanda uses the VLOOKUP function and a lookup table to determine the commission rate for each salesperson. She creates a formula containing an IF function to display *Yes* in the Award? column for salespeople who are over their sales goals and are eligible for an award.

A worksheet using VLOOKUP and a lookup table to find the commission percentage and the IF function to display the sales quota status

Using 3-D Cell References in Formulas

You used a workbook containing detail worksheets and a summary worksheet in Lesson 10, Managing Multiple-Sheet Workbooks. You created a linking formula in the summary worksheet to refer to the contents of a cell in a single detail worksheet. Excel also allows you to perform calculations using the contents of the same cell address in multiple worksheets, which is called a 3-D cell reference. Contrast the following linking formula and normal summing formula with a formula containing a 3-D cell reference.

Type of Formula	Example	What It Does
Linking	=Supplies!C6	Gets the contents from cell C6 in the Supplies worksheet
Normal	=Supplies!C6 + Utilities!C6	Sums cell C6 from the Supplies and Utilities worksheets only
3-D	=SUM(Supplies:Equipment!C6)	Sums cell C6 in all worksheets from Supplies through Equipment in the workbook

Why Use a 3-D Reference?

Using a 3-D reference provides two advantages over normal cell references in a multisheet formula. First, you do not have to click the cell in each worksheet to build the formula. Also, the formula automatically includes the specified cell from additional worksheets that you insert within the worksheet range.

 WARNING! *Deleting a worksheet or moving a worksheet tab to outside the range in the 3-D reference removes that worksheet's values from the formula result.*

Creating a 3-D Reference

Functions that you may use to create 3-D references include SUM, AVERAGE, COUNT, MAX, MIN, and some statistical functions. A formula may contain a single cell or a cell range as a 3-D reference. Remember that the cells being referenced must be the identical cell addresses in all detail worksheets. You cannot, for example, use cell B2 from one worksheet and cell C3 from another. But, you may, for example, use the range B2:E2 from all the worksheets. The cell or range must also contain the same type of data, such as values.

QR

QUICK REFERENCE: CREATING 3-D CELL REFERENCES IN FORMULAS

Task	Procedure
Create a 3-D reference	■ Design all worksheets so that the cell contents to be calculated are in the identical cell addresses. ■ Select the cell to contain the formula in the summary worksheet. ■ Type the function beginning, such as =SUM(. ■ Click the first sheet tab and hold down [Shift] while clicking the last sheet tab to be referenced. ■ In the sheet currently displayed, select the cell or range to be referenced, and complete the formula.

In this exercise, you will create 3-D cell references to one cell in several worksheets. You will also create a 3-D reference to a cell range.

1. Start Excel and open the Sales Volume workbook from the Lesson 14 folder in your file storage location.

2. Maximize ⬜ the window.
   You will create 3-D references on the Summary worksheet to sum values from the other three worksheets.

3. Display the October worksheet to see that the worksheet design for rows 1 through 13 is identical to that of the Summary worksheet. Display the November worksheet, and then display December to see that they contain an identical structure.

4. Display the Summary worksheet.

5. In cell C3, replace *Student Name* with your name.

Create a 3-D Cell Reference Formula for Employee Sales

6. Follow these steps to create a formula that adds the values in cell C6 from each of the monthly sales worksheets:

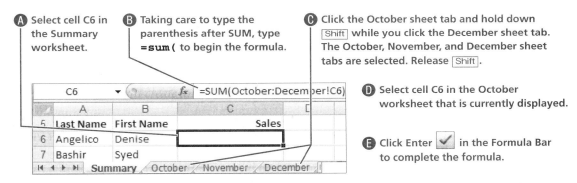

Ⓐ Select cell C6 in the Summary worksheet.

Ⓑ Taking care to type the parenthesis after SUM, type **=sum(** to begin the formula.

Ⓒ Click the October sheet tab and hold down Shift while you click the December sheet tab. The October, November, and December sheet tabs are selected. Release Shift.

Ⓓ Select cell C6 in the October worksheet that is currently displayed.

Ⓔ Click Enter ✓ in the Formula Bar to complete the formula.

The Formula Bar displays =SUM(October:December!C6). Notice that an exclamation (!) point separates the worksheet names from the cell address. The formula result is $17,000, which is Denise Angelico's total sales from cell C6 in the October, November, and December worksheets.

7. Use Autofill to copy the formula in cell C6 to the range C7:C13.

8. Deselect the highlighted range.

9. Select cell C10 and look in the Formula Bar to see that the 3-D reference is included in the formula that you copied.

Create a 3-D Cell Range Formula for Total Sales Expenses

Now you will calculate the total direct sales expenses. You will use the SUM function for the same cell range across the three monthly worksheets.

10. Display the October worksheet.
    Review the expense data in rows 16–18. The other monthly worksheets are designed identically with values in the range C16:C18.

11. Display the Summary worksheet.

12. Select cell C16.

13. Choose Home→AutoSum Σ from the Ribbon.

14. Click the October sheet tab.

15. Hold down [Shift] while you click the December sheet tab to select all monthly sales worksheets, and then release the [Shift] key.

16. Drag to select cells C16:C18 in the October worksheet.
    Although the October worksheet is displayed, you are specifying the cells to be summed in all the detail sheets that you selected.

17. Click Enter ✔ in the Formula Bar to complete the formula.
    The Formula Bar displays =SUM(October:December!C16:C18). The formula result is $160,000.

	A	B	C
5	Last Name	First Name	Sales
6	Angelico	Denise	$17,000
7	Bashir	Syed	$103,000
8	Cortez	Alonzo	$180,000
9	Greenfield	Aaron	$33,000
10	Hernandez	Jennifer	$74,000
11	Jang	Sylvie	$50,000
12	Medford	Richard	$47,000
13	Wilson	Robert	$70,000
14	Total Sales		$574,000
15			
16	Total Direct Expenses		$160,000

18. Save 💾 the changes and close the workbook.

Introducing Lookup Functions

The VLOOKUP (Vertical Lookup) and HLOOKUP (Horizontal Lookup) functions are used to retrieve a piece of data from a lookup table located somewhere in the same worksheet, a separate worksheet, or a different workbook. In this lesson, you will look up the sales commission rate, which depends on the salesperson's sales volume. The sales volume increment values display down the first column of a vertical lookup table or across the first row of a horizontal lookup table. You may use either format and its matching function.

⚠ **WARNING!** *Take care to place a lookup table outside rows or columns that might be deleted in the future.*

	D	E
16	**Sales**	**Rate**
17	0	0%
18	10,000	3%
19	20,000	5%
20	30,000	7%
21	50,000	10%

A vertical lookup table containing sales volume amounts and their corresponding commission rates

The same data arranged in a horizontal lookup table

	C	D	E	F	G	H
16	**Sales**	0	10,000	20,000	30,000	50,000
17	**Rate**	0%	3%	5%	7%	10%

Lookup Function Syntax

The generic parts of the HLOOKUP and VLOOKUP functions are identical, as shown in the following table.

Function	Syntax
HLOOKUP (Horizontal Lookup)	HLOOKUP(lookup value, table array, column index number, range lookup)
VLOOKUP (Vertical Lookup)	VLOOKUP(lookup value, table array, column index number, range lookup)

The following table outlines the arguments of the VLOOKUP function.

Argument	Description
Lookup value	The value in the worksheet to be looked up in the first column of the table array
Table array	The cell range containing the lookup table, which may be expressed as absolute cell references or a defined name
Column index number	The column number in the table array that contains the corresponding data to be retrieved
Range lookup (optional; the default is TRUE)	A logical value that specifies a search for an exact or approximate value in the table array (TRUE) or an exact match only (FALSE)

How the VLOOKUP Function Works

The formula =VLOOKUP(C6,Comm_Rate,2) is used as an example to explain how the search takes place in the lookup table. Cell C6 contains the lookup value 14,000. The defined name Comm_Rate indicates that the search takes place in the table array located in the range $D$17:$E$21. The search is conducted down the first column of the table array until the highest value not greater than the lookup value is located. The number 2, the column index number in the formula, indicates that the corresponding commission rate will be retrieved from the second column of the lookup table.

Cell D6 contains the VLOOKUP formula to find Denise's commission rate based on $14,000 in sales.

	A	B	C	D
5	Last Name	First Name	Sales	Rate
6	Angelico	Denise	14,000	3%
7	Bashir	Syed	38,000	7%
8	Cortez	Alonzo	59,000	10%

Excel searches for the lookup value 14,000 down the first column of the lookup table. The search stops at 10,000 on row 18 because the lookup value is at least 10,000 but not 20,000.

	D	E
16	Sales	Rate
17	0	0%
18	10,000	3%
19	20,000	5%
20	30,000	7%
21	50,000	10%

Traveling along row 18, the search moves to column 2 of the lookup table, as specified by the column index number in the function.

The commission rate 3 percent is returned to cell D6.

Sorting a Table Array

The rows in the table array must be sorted in lowest to highest (A to Z) order in the first column. This way, you can be assured that VLOOKUP will stop at the proper row and return the correct value.

 ## Hands-On 14.2   Use VLOOKUP

In this exercise, you will set up a three-column table array and then use the VLOOKUP function to calculate commissions and display messages.

Create a Table Array

1. Open the Commissions workbook from the Lesson 14 folder.
   You will create the table array in the range D17:E21 and assign a defined name to that range. The labels in row 16 are optional and not part of the table array.

2. Complete the table array by entering the numbers and text shown in the following illustration.
   The number formatting is already applied to the blank cells.

	D	E	F
16	Sales	Rate	Message
17	0	0%	Under Achiever
18	10,000	3%	Below Quota
19	20,000	5%	Above Quota
20	30,000	7%	Above Quota
21	50,000	10%	Over Achiever

Assign a Range Name to the Table Array

In the next few steps, you will assign a defined name to the table array. Naming a range for a table array is optional. You would use absolute cell references in the lookup formula if you did not use a defined name.

3. Follow these steps to create the range name:

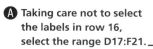

A Taking care not to select the labels in row 16, select the range D17:F21.

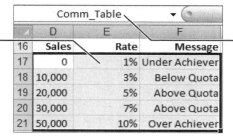

	D	E	F
16	**Sales**	**Rate**	**Message**
17	0	1%	Under Achiever
18	10,000	3%	Below Quota
19	20,000	5%	Above Quota
20	30,000	7%	Above Quota
21	50,000	10%	Over Achiever

Comm_Table

B Click in the Name box to the left of the Formula Bar and type **Comm_Table** to give the range a name.

C Tap Enter to complete the defined name.

4. Deselect the table array.

Create a VLOOKUP Formula for the Commission Rate

You will use the VLOOKUP function to calculate the commission rate for each salesperson in column D.

5. Enter the formula **=VLOOKUP(C6,Comm_Table,2)** in cell D6.
The 3 percent commission rate is returned from the lookup table to cell D6.

6. Take a few moments to study the three arguments in the function you just entered and understand how the lookup works.

7. Use Autofill to copy the formula from cell D6 down to the range D7:D13.

8. Select cell D7 and review the formula in the Formula Bar.
The commission rate returned from the lookup table is 7 percent. Notice that all arguments are the same for this function, except that the relative cell reference tells VLOOKUP to look up the value from cell C7.

Calculate the Commissions

The formula Sales*Commission Rate calculates the salesperson's commission.

9. Enter the formula **=C6*D6** in cell E6.
The result equals 420.

10. Use AutoFill to copy the commission formula in cell E6 down for the other salespeople.

	A	B	C	D	E	F
5	**Last Name**	**First Name**	**Sales**	**Rate**	**Commission**	**Above or Below Quota?**
6	Angelico	Denise	14,000	3%	420	
7	Bashir	Syed	38,000	7%	2,660	
8	Cortez	Alonzo	59,000	10%	5,900	
9	Greenfield	Aaron	8,000	0%	0	
10	Hernandez	Jennifer	26,000	5%	1,300	
11	Jang	Sylvie	18,500	3%	555	
12	Medford	Richard	15,000	3%	450	
13	Wilson	Robert	27,000	5%	1,350	

Create a VLOOKUP Formula for the Quota Messages

11. Select cell F6 and enter the function **=VLOOKUP(C6,Comm_Table,3)**.

    The message Below Quota is returned. Notice that you used the same arguments for this function that you did in cell D6 except that the last argument is 3 instead of 2. This instructs VLOOKUP to return the message text from column 3 of the table array.

12. Use AutoFill to copy the quota message formula in cell F6 down for the other salespeople.

13. Right-align cells F6:F13 (the cells with the Above or Below Quota results).

    Rows 5–21 should match the following illustration.

	A	B	C	D	E	F
5	Last Name	First Name	Sales	Rate	Commission	Above or Below Quota?
6	Angelico	Denise	14,000	3%	420	Below Quota
7	Bashir	Syed	38,000	7%	2,660	Above Quota
8	Cortez	Alonzo	59,000	10%	5,900	Over Achiever
9	Greenfield	Aaron	8,000	0%	0	Under Achiever
10	Hernandez	Jennifer	26,000	5%	1,300	Above Quota
11	Jang	Sylvie	18,500	3%	555	Below Quota
12	Medford	Richard	15,000	3%	450	Below Quota
13	Wilson	Robert	27,000	5%	1,350	Above Quota
14						
15						
16				Sales	Rate	Message
17				0	0%	Under Achiever
18				10,000	3%	Below Quota
19				20,000	5%	Above Quota
20				30,000	7%	Above Quota
21				50,000	10%	Over Achiever

14. Select cell E17 and change the rate to **1%**.

    The rate in cell D9 changed to 1 percent, and the corresponding commission in cell E9 now is 80.

15. Select cell F17 and change the message to **Counsel**.

    Notice that the result in cell F9 changed to Counsel because you changed the message in the lookup table.

16. Click Undo ↺ to change the entry back to *Under Achiever*.

17. Save 💾 the changes and leave the workbook open.

Creating Formulas with the IF Function

Excel's IF function displays a value or message based on a logical test that you design. Depending on the result of the logical test, the IF function displays whatever you choose for a true or false result. For example, you may check to see whether the purchase amount is greater than $200. If true, a discount is calculated; if false, the text *No discount* is displayed.

IF Function Syntax

The generic parts of the IF function are shown in the following table.

Function	Syntax
IF	IF(logical test, value if true, value if false)

The following table outlines the arguments of the IF function.

Argument	Description
Logical test	The condition being checked using a comparison operator, such as =, >, <, >=, <=, or <> (not equal to)
Value if true	The value, text in quotation (") marks, or calculation returned if the logical test result is found to be true
Value if false	The value, text in quotation (") marks, or calculation returned if the logical test result is found to be false

How the IF Function Works

The formula =IF(C6>=200,C6*D6,0) is used as an example to explain the function result. Excel performs the logical test to determine if the value in C6 is greater than or equal to 200. A value of 200 or more would evaluate as true. Any of the following would evaluate as false: the value 50, a blank cell, or text entered in cell C6. If the logical test proves true, the calculation C6*D6 is performed and the result displays in the formula cell. If the calculation proves false, the value 0 (zero) displays instead.

You may specify various actions to be performed for the Value if True and Value if False arguments. You may display a text message or leave the cell blank. You may create complex calculations and even use other functions in arguments within an IF function, called nesting. Two examples that display text are shown in the following table.

 NOTE! *If you type the IF formula directly in its cell, you must add quotation (") marks around text arguments. If you use the Insert Function command, Excel will add the quotation marks for you.*

Formula	Action if True	Action if False
IF(F3>150000, "Over Budget", "Within Budget")	The text *Over Budget* displays	The text *Within Budget* displays
IF(D6<=30," ","Late")	The cell displays blank	The text *Late* displays

 TIP! *If you type* **" "** *(quotation marks without a space between) as the Value if True or Value if False argument, Excel leaves the cell blank.*

 Hands-On 14.3 **Create an IF Function**

In this exercise, you will use the IF function to displays a text message when a salesperson achieves at least $30,000 in monthly sales.

Create an IF Formula to Display a Message

1. Center the blank cells in the range G5:G13 in the December worksheet of the Commissions workbook.

2. Enter the column heading **Award?** in cell G5.

3. Bold the heading in cell G5.
   You will create a formula that compares the value in the Sales cell with an Over Quota value in the lookup table. If sales are equal or greater, a message displays. Otherwise, the cell displays no message.

4. Select cell G6 and click the Insert Function *fx* button in the Formula Bar.

5. Follow these steps to find the IF function:

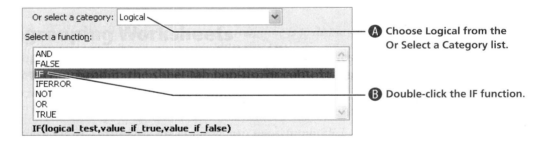

The Function Arguments dialog box appears for the IF function.

6. If necessary, move the Function Arguments dialog box out of the way by dragging its title bar until you can see column G.

7. Follow these steps to specify the IF function arguments:

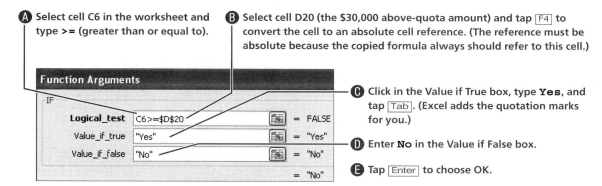

Ⓐ Select cell C6 in the worksheet and type **>=** (greater than or equal to).

Ⓑ Select cell D20 (the $30,000 above-quota amount) and tap F4 to convert the cell to an absolute cell reference. (The reference must be absolute because the copied formula always should refer to this cell.)

Ⓒ Click in the Value if True box, type **Yes**, and tap Tab. (Excel adds the quotation marks for you.)

Ⓓ Enter **No** in the Value if False box.

Ⓔ Tap Enter to choose OK.

8. Review the completed formula in the Formula Bar.
The formula is =IF(C6>=$D$20,"Yes","No"). The message No *appears in cell G6 because Denise Angelico's sales are not at least $30,000, the value in cell D20. The Value if False argument applies.*

9. Use AutoFill to copy the formula in cell G6 down to the range G7:G13.
The cells for Bashir and Cortez display Yes *as specified by your Value if True argument. The cells for all other salespeople display* No.

Edit the IF Function

Now you will edit the Value if False argument to **" "** *to display no message.*

10. Select cell G6.

11. In the Formula Bar, click between the quotation (") mark and the N, and tap Delete twice to delete *No*.

f_x =IF(C6>=$D$20,"Yes","")

12. Click Enter ✓ in the Formula Bar to complete the formula.
Now cell G6 does not display any message because the Value if False argument contains no text.

13. Use AutoFill to copy the formula in cell G6 down to the range G7:G13.
Notice that the cells that previously displayed No in column G now display no message, as shown in the illustration below. The salespeople who will receive an award are easier to identify.

	A	B	C	D	E	F	G
5	**Last Name**	**First Name**	**Sales**	**Rate**	**Commission**	**Above or Below Quota?**	**Award?**
6	Angelico	Denise	14,000	3%	420	Below Quota	
7	Bashir	Syed	38,000	7%	2,660	Above Quota	Yes
8	Cortez	Alonzo	59,000	10%	5,900	Over Achiever	Yes
9	Greenfield	Aaron	8,000	1%	80	Under Achiever	
10	Hernandez	Jennifer	26,000	5%	1,300	Above Quota	
11	Jang	Sylvie	18,500	3%	555	Below Quota	
12	Medford	Richard	15,000	3%	450	Below Quota	
13	Wilson	Robert	27,000	5%	1,350	Above Quota	

14. Save 💾 the changes.

Creating Formulas Using Criteria IF Functions

Excel also provides functions that average, count, or sum cells that meet one or more criteria. The AVERAGEIF, COUNTIF, and SUMIF functions calculate using one criterion. The AVERAGEIFS, COUNTIFS, and SUMIFS functions calculate using multiple criteria that you specify. Only cells meeting all the criteria are averaged, counted, or summed.

Function Syntax

The generic parts of the two types of functions are shown in the following table.

Function	Syntax
AVERAGEIF	AVERAGEIF(range, criteria)
COUNTIF	COUNTIF(range, criteria)
SUMIF	SUMIF(range, criteria, sum range)
AVERAGEIFS	AVERAGEIFS(range1, criteria1, range2, criteria2)
COUNTIFS	COUNTIFS(range1, criteria1, range2, criteria2)
SUMIFS	SUMIFS(sum range, range1, criteria1, range2, criteria2)

 TIP! *The AVERAGEIFS, COUNTIFS, and SUMIFS functions may include up to 127 ranges and corresponding criteria.*

The following table outlines the arguments of these functions.

Argument	Description
Range	The cells to be compared with the criteria
Criteria	Enclosed in quotation (") marks, the comparison value, text, or expression using a comparison operator, such as =, >, <, >=, <=, or <> (not equal to)
Sum range	The potential cells to be summed

How the SUMIF Function Works

The formula =SUMIF(C6:C13,">=30000",C6:C13) is used as an example to explain the function result. The range to be evaluated is C6:C13. The criterion is greater than or equal to 30,000. The sum range C6:C13 contains the potential cells to be summed. Excel performs the logical test C6:C13>=30000. Only the values of cells containing at least 30,000 in the range C6:C13 are summed. The formula also could be entered as =SUMIF(C6:C13,">=30000") without the last argument because the range and sum range are the same.

 NOTE! *The range will be used both to evaluate for criteria and to calculate the result if the sum range is not specified in a SUMIF formula.*

How the COUNTIFS Function Works

The formula =COUNTIFS(D6:D13,"Yes",E6:E13,"Yes") is used as an example to explain the function result. The range D6:D13 is evaluated for cells containing the text *Yes*. Also, the range E6:E13 is evaluated for *Yes*. Only records meeting both criteria are counted.

	A	B	C	D	E
4				Seminars	
5	Last Name	First Name	Sales	Cust Svc	Leader
6	Angelico	Denise	$6,000		
7	Bashir	Syed	$38,000	Yes	Yes
8	Cortez	Alonzo	$59,000	Yes	Yes
9	Greenfield	Aaron	$12,000	Yes	
10	Hernandez	Jennifer	$26,000		
11	Jang	Sylvie	$18,000		Yes
12	Medford	Richard	$15,000	Yes	
13	Wilson	Robert	$27,000		Yes
14				Count:	2

The COUNTIFS function finds two employees who meet both criteria of *Yes* in columns D and E.

Hands-On 14.4 Create a SUMIF Function

In this exercise, you will use the SUMIF function to add cells containing more than $30,000 in monthly sales.

1. Enter **Sales Over $30,000** in cell A14 in the December worksheet of the Commissions workbook.

2. Use Format Painter to copy the number format from cell C13 to C14.

3. Format the range A14:C14 as bold.
   Next you will create a formula that adds the values in cells where sales are at least $30,000.

4. Select cell C14 and click the Insert Function 𝑓ₓ button in the Formula Bar.

5. Follow these steps to find the SUMIF function:

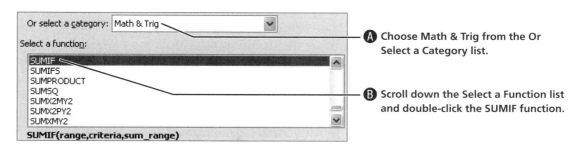

Ⓐ Choose Math & Trig from the Or Select a Category list.

Ⓑ Scroll down the Select a Function list and double-click the SUMIF function.

The Function Arguments dialog box appears for the SUMIF function.

6. If necessary, move the Function Arguments dialog box out of the way of column C by dragging its title bar.

7. Follow these steps to specify the SUMIF function arguments:

Ⓐ Select the range C6:C13 in the worksheet as the range to be evaluated. ⎯⎯

Ⓑ Click in the Criteria box and type **>30000**. ⎯⎯

Ⓒ Leave the Sum_Range box empty because the cells are the same as for the range. ⎯⎯

Ⓓ Click OK.

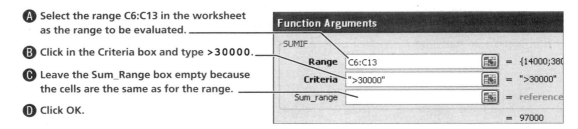

8. Review the completed formula in the Formula Bar:
The formula is =SUMIF(C6:C13, ">30000"). The result is 97,000.

9. Save 🖫 the changes.

	A	B	C	D	E
13	Wilson	Robert	27,000	5%	1,35
14	Sales Over $30,000		97,000		

C14 ▾ *fx* =SUMIF(C6:C13,">30000")

Tracing Formulas

Excel's auditing tools are useful for analyzing complex formulas that are dependent on other formulas. The auditing tools are also quite helpful for locating errors in formulas.

The Formula Auditing Tools

The Formula Auditing tools are used primarily for displaying and hiding cell tracers. Cell tracers are arrows that identify precedent and dependent cells of formulas. The Formula Auditing group of the Formulas Ribbon is shown at right.

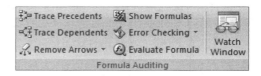

The Formula Auditing tools on the Formulas Ribbon

Tracing Precedents

The Trace Precedents 📇 command displays arrows that point from the cells referenced by a formula to the cell containing the formula. A formula may reference cells containing values and/or cells that contain other formulas. Thus, a formula may have several levels of precedents. Repeating the Trace Precedents command adds the next level to the display. The following illustrations show the Commissions workbook with the precedent cell tracers (arrows) displayed for the commission formula in cell E6. The first level includes cells C6 and D6, referenced in the formula. Cell D6 contains its own formula for the commission rate. The second level displays the precedent for that formula, which depends on a lookup table.

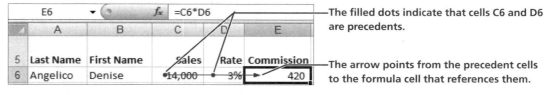

The first level of precedents for the formula C6*D6

—The filled dots indicate that cells C6 and D6 are precedents.

—The arrow points from the precedent cells to the formula cell that references them.

	A	B	C	D	E	F
5	Last Name	First Name	Sales	Rate	Commission	Above or Below Quota?
6	Angelico	Denise	14,000	3%	420	Below Quota
7	Bashir	Syed	38,000	7%	2,660	Above Quota
8	Cortez	Alonzo	59,000	10%	5,900	Over Achiever
9	Greenfield	Aaron	8,000	1%	80	Under Achiever
10	Hernandez	Jennifer	26,000	5%	1,300	Above Quota
11	Jang	Sylvie	18,500	3%	555	Below Quota
12	Medford	Richard	15,000	3%	450	Below Quota
13	Wilson	Robert	27,000	5%	1,350	Above Quota
14	Sales Over $30,000		97,000			
15						
16				Sales	Rate	Message
17				0	1%	Under Achiever
18				10,000	3%	Below Quota
19				20,000	5%	Above Quota
20				30,000	7%	Above Quota
21				50,000	10%	Over Achiever

The second level showing the lookup table as a precedent for the VLOOKUP formula in cell D6

Hands-On 14.5 Trace and Clear Precedent Arrows

In this exercise, you will trace to cells that make up the formula in cell E6 and then trace precedents for cell G6.

1. Select cell E6 in the December worksheet of the Commissions workbook.

2. Choose Formulas→Formula Auditing→Trace Precedents 🔲 from the Ribbon.
   Tracer arrows appear, indicating that the formula in cell E6 is dependent on cells C6 and D6. Next you will look for any precedents to those two cells.

3. Choose Formulas→Formula Auditing→Trace Precedents 🔲 again in the Ribbon.
   A tracer arrow from the table array in rows 17–21 to cell D6 appears. This shows that the formula in cell D6 depends on the table array. Cell C6 has no precedents because it does not contain a formula.

4. Choose Formulas→Formula Auditing→Remove Arrows menu ▾→Remove Precedent Arrows from the Ribbon to hide the second level of tracer arrows.
   Now only the first precedent level displays.

5. Choose Formulas→Formula Auditing→Remove Arrows 🔲 to hide all tracer arrows.
   This command removes all levels at one time.

6. Select cell G6 and choose Formulas→Formula Auditing→Trace Precedents 🔲 from the Ribbon.
   The formula in cell G6 clearly is dependent on cell C6 and cell D20 in the table array.

7. Choose Formulas→Formula Auditing→Remove Arrows 🔲 to hide all tracer arrows.

8. You made no changes, so just leave the workbook open.

Tracing Dependents

The Trace Dependents command shows you the dependents for a selected cell. Dependents are formula cells that reference the selected cell. Repeating the Trace Dependents command displays an additional set of arrows that trace the next level of dependents until all dependent cells are identified.

 ## Hands-On 14.6   Trace Dependents

In this exercise, you will trace to cells that are dependent on the value in cell C6.

1. Select cell C6 in the December worksheet of the Commissions workbook.

2. Choose Formulas→Formula Auditing→Trace Dependents from the Ribbon.
   As indicated by the five arrow heads shown here, five cells include a reference to cell C6 in their formulas. You will trace the dependents for those five cells in the next step.

	C	D	E	F	G
	Sales	**Rate**	**Commission**	**Above or Below Quota?**	**Award?**
5					
6	14,000	3%	420	Below Quota	
7	38,000	7%	2,660	Above Quota	Yes
8	59,000	10%	5,900	Over Achiever	Yes
9	8,000	1%	80	Under Achiever	
10	26,000	5%	1,300	Above Quota	
11	18,500	3%	555	Below Quota	
12	15,000	3%	450	Below Quota	
13	27,000	5%	1,350	Above Quota	
14	97,000				

3. Repeat the Trace Dependents command.
   An additional tracer arrow points from cell D6 to cell E6. The filled dot in cell D6 indicates that the cell is a precedent for cell E6, which has a formula dependent on cell D6.

4. Choose Formulas→Formula Auditing→Remove Arrows to remove the tracer arrows.

5. Select cell F17 in the table array and choose the Trace Dependents command.
   A number of tracer arrows are drawn from cell F17 to cells with formulas dependent on the data in that cell.

6. Repeat the Trace Dependents command until all dependent cells are revealed.

7. Use the Remove Arrows command to remove the tracer arrows.

8. Close the workbook and leave Excel open.

Auditing Formula Errors

Cells with formulas sometimes display error messages such as #VALUE!, #NAME!, or #DIV/0!. A formula may display an incorrect result rather than a message. Errors may be caused by incorrect cell entries in precedent cells, empty cells, incorrect or missing defined names, or incorrect formulas. Excel can help you identify cells that contain errors that prevent the display of correct formula results.

 TIP! *If error checking does not appear to be working, ensure that Enable Background Error Checking and the desired Error Checking Rules have a checkmark in the Formulas category of the Excel Options dialog box.*

Auditing Single Cells

Excel continuously checks for common errors as you work, depending on the error checking options selected in the Excel Options dialog box. Excel alerts you to inconsistent formulas and other potential errors by displaying a small triangle icon in the upper left of a cell. You may handle marked cells one cell at a time. An error checking menu is available while the cell is selected to get help, show calculation steps, edit the formula, or ignore the error. The menu commands vary depending on the error type. Excel marks a SUM formula when it determines that adjacent cells are not included in the sum range. If the range is correct, you would choose the Ignore Error command from the menu.

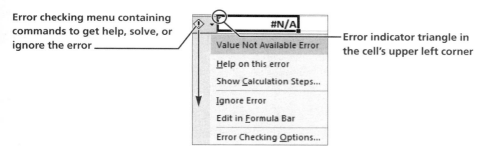

Error checking menu containing commands to get help, solve, or ignore the error

Error indicator triangle in the cell's upper left corner

Error Checking in Multiple Cells

The Error Checking command on the Formulas Ribbon allows you to navigate and respond to error messages throughout the worksheet, similar to the spell checker. The Error Checking dialog box summarizes each error and provides the same commands as the error checking menu available on a single cell.

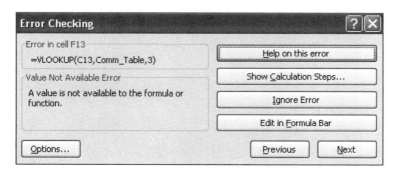

Tracing Errors

The Trace Error command on the Formulas Ribbon draws arrows that point from any precedent cells to the selected cell containing the error message.

> **QUICK REFERENCE: AUDITING FORMULAS**
>
> | Task | Procedure |
> |------|-----------|
> | Audit a single cell marked as containing an error | ■ Select the cell containing a triangle icon in its upper-left corner.
■ Click the error checking button to the left of the cell and choose a command from the menu. |
> | Audit all cells marked as containing an error | ■ Choose Formulas→Formula Auditing→Error Checking from the Ribbon.
■ Choose a command in the Error Checking dialog box.
■ Click Resume after editing a formula to view the next error. |
> | Trace precedents for a cell displaying an error message | ■ Select the cell displaying the error message.
■ Choose Formulas→Formula Auditing→Error Checking→Trace Error from the Ribbon to display tracer arrows. |
> | Restore triangle icons for ignored errors | ■ Choose Office→Excel Options→Formulas category.
■ Under Error Checking, click Reset Ignored Errors. |
> | Show calculation steps in any formula | ■ Select a cell containing a formula.
■ Choose Formulas→Formula Auditing→Evaluate Formula from the Ribbon.
■ In the Evaluate Formula dialog box, click Step In to view more information about an underlined expression, if desired, and then click Step Out to display the result.
■ Click Evaluate to display the result of the next underlined expression.
■ Continue clicking Evaluate until all expressions are evaluated and the formula result displays. |

Hands-On 14.7 Check Errors in Formulas

In this exercise, you will respond to formula error messages using Excel's error checking commands.

Enable Error Checking

1. Open the Error Check workbook from the Lesson 14 folder.

2. Choose Office→Excel Options→Formulas category.

3. Follow these steps to review the error checking options, but do not make any changes unless your instructor directs:

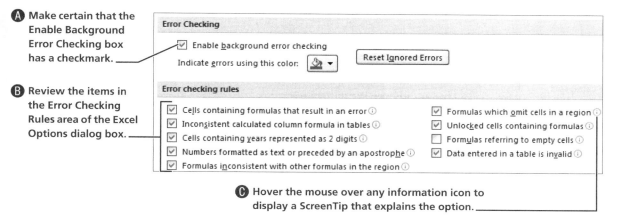

A Make certain that the Enable Background Error Checking box has a checkmark.

B Review the items in the Error Checking Rules area of the Excel Options dialog box.

C Hover the mouse over any information icon to display a ScreenTip that explains the option.

4. Click Cancel (or OK if your instructor directs you to change any options).

Edit a Formula to Correct an Error

5. Notice that a #REF! error message displays in cell F9.

6. Select cell F9.
   The Formula Bar displays =VLOOKUP(C9,Comm_Table,4). The formula in cell F9 is dependent on the value in cell C9 and the table array in rows 17–21.

7. Point to the error checking menu button to the left of the selected cell.

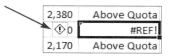

A ScreenTip displays possible causes of the error, including a reference error in the function. Cell C9 and the defined name Comm_Table appear to be correct in the formula. The column index number, however, refers to a nonexisting column 4 in the table array. The column index number should refer to column 3.

8. Click the error checking menu button to the left of cell F9 and choose Edit in Formula Bar from the menu.

9. Replace 4 with **3** in the formula and tap Enter to complete the entry.
   Cell F9 now correctly displays Below Quota.

Check for Errors

The Error Checking command is useful for responding to multiple error messages in a worksheet.

10. Choose Formulas→Formula Auditing→Error Checking from the Ribbon.
    The Error Checking dialog box displays, and cell D13 is selected in the worksheet.

11. Move the dialog box, if necessary, to view row 13 in the worksheet.

12. Click the Help on This Error button in the Error Checking dialog box.

13. Take a few moments to explore the help information, and then close the Help window.

14. Read the left side of the Error Checking dialog box.
    The dialog box displays the cell D13 formula and analyzes the problem as a Value Not Available Error. Notice that the a28000 entry in cell C13 is not a value.

15. Select cell C13 in the worksheet, delete the letter "a" in the Formula Bar, and complete the entry.

16. Click Resume in the Error Checking dialog box.
    Correcting the error in cell C13 allowed the other formulas in row 13 to display correct results. No error messages now exist in any cells.

17. Click OK to respond to the message that error checking is complete.

18. Save the changes, close the workbook, and leave Excel open.

Evaluating Formulas

The Evaluate Formula command allows you to see what each part of a formula includes. You may evaluate any formula, but this tool is particularly helpful with multiple-operator formulas. For example, in the formula =B13*(1-$F$18), the Evaluate Formula dialog box would show you the actual value of B13. The formula is easier to analyze than just looking at the cell reference. As you step through the evaluation process, you will see the actual values and calculations that make up the complete formula.

Hands-On 14.8   Evaluate a Formula

In this exercise, you will evaluate the Manufacturing Costs formula in the Calculations worksheet of a financial report.

1. Open the Financial Report workbook from the Lesson 14 folder.
   This workbook contains two worksheets. The Factors worksheet contains values that are used in formulas on the Calculations worksheet.

2. Select cell B5 in the Calculations worksheet.
   *This cell contains the manufacturing costs formula =Factors!$B$3+B3*Factors!$B$4*0.8. Notice that the cell references include the Factors worksheet name because they are on a different worksheet.*

3. Choose Formulas→Formula Auditing→Evaluate Formula from the Ribbon.
   The Evaluate Formula dialog box displays the formula with the first expression underlined to indicate cell B3 in the Factors worksheet.

4. Click the Evaluate button in the Evaluate Formula dialog box.

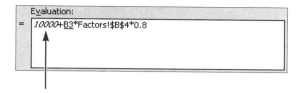

The first part of the formula, Factors!B3, is evaluated, and the cell's actual value of 10000 is displayed in the dialog box.

5. Click the Evaluate button to evaluate the next part of the formula.

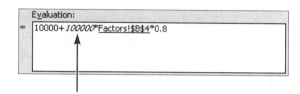

The second expression of the formula evaluates as 100000, the actual value of cell B3 in the Calculations worksheet.

6. Click Evaluate.

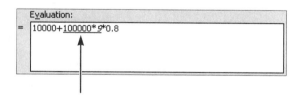

The underlined evaluation shows that the 100000 in cell B3 is being multiplied by 9, the value of cell B4 in the Factors worksheet.

7. Continue to click the Evaluate button until the final answer of 730,000 is displayed in the Evaluate Formula dialog box.
With every click of the Evaluate button, each part of the formula is displayed, showing you step by step how the final result of 730,000 is calculated.

8. Click Restart in the Evaluate Formula dialog box to repeat the evaluation process.

9. This time click Step In to preview the upcoming evaluation, and then click Step Out to complete the evaluation.

10. Continue using Step In and Step Out when the expression includes a cell reference, and then use Evaluate for the final steps of the formula evaluation.

11. When finished, close the Evaluate Formula dialog box.

12. Leave the workbook open.

Keeping Tabs in the Watch Window

The Watch Window lets you keep an eye on formula results even if the formula is out of view, in a separate worksheet, or in a different workbook. The Watch Window is actually a toolbar and, as such, can remain displayed anywhere on the worksheet or be docked on any side of the window.

QUICK REFERENCE: USING THE WATCH WINDOW	
Task	**Procedure**
Display or hide the Watch Window	■ Choose Formulas→Formula Auditing→Watch Window  from the Ribbon. (The same command toggles the window display on and off.)
Add a formula cell to the Watch Window	■ Click the Add Watch button in the Watch Window. ■ Select a worksheet cell containing a formula. ■ Click the Add button in the Add Watch dialog box.
Delete a formula cell from the Watch Window	■ Display the Watch Window, if hidden. ■ Select the desired cell in the Watch Window. ■ Click the Delete Watch button.

 ## Hands-On 14.9   Watch a Formula

In this exercise, you will add a watch to the Revenue formula in the Calculations worksheet of a financial report.

Add a Cell to the Watch Window

1. Select cell B4 in the Calculations worksheet of the Financial Report workbook.
   The formula =B3*Factors!\$B\$2*80% displays in the Formula Bar. You can see that this formula uses a value from the Factors worksheet. If you were experimenting with different values in the Factors worksheet, switching back and forth between the Calculations and Factors worksheets to view the formula results would be quite time-consuming.

2. Choose Formulas→Formula Auditing→Watch Window  from the Ribbon.

3. Click Add Watch on the Watch Window toolbar.

Add Watch

Select the cells that you would like to watch the value of:

=Calculations!\$B\$4

[Add]   [Cancel]

Notice the linking formula in the Add Watch window, indicating that the cell in the Calculations sheet will be watched.

4. Click the Add button.
   All information about the cell is displayed: workbook name, worksheet name, cell, value, and formula.

5. Follow these steps to AutoFit column contents in the Watch window:

A Double-click the border before the Sheet heading and the border before the Name heading.

B Drag the right window border to the right to widen the window until the entire Formula column is visible.

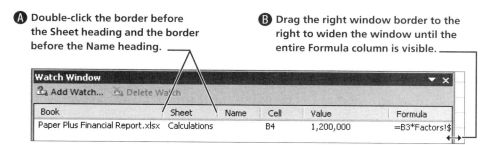

6. Display the Factors worksheet.
   The Watch Window is visible on any worksheet in the workbook.

7. Change the value of cell B2 to **22**.
   Notice the change to cell B4 in the Watch Window. The formula result now is 1,760,000.

8. Feel free to add other formulas to the Watch Window and experiment by changing values in the Factors worksheet.

9. When finished, close the Watch Window.

10. Save 💾 the changes.

Concepts Review

True/False Questions

1. A 3-D cell reference may refer to different cell addresses across multiple worksheets. TRUE **FALSE**

2. The VLOOKUP function searches down the first column of the table array (lookup table). **TRUE** FALSE

3. The data in the first column or row of a table array may be arranged in any order. TRUE **FALSE**

4. The SUMIFS function adds values of cells that meet any one of the multiple criteria specified in the formula. TRUE **FALSE**

5. The Trace Dependents command may be repeated to display additional levels of dependents. **TRUE** FALSE

6. A small triangle icon in a worksheet cell indicates that a formula may contain an error. **TRUE** FALSE

7. The Error Checking command is used to display the result of a logical test, such as *True* or *False*. TRUE **FALSE**

8. The Evaluate Formula command helps you to understand each calculation step of a formula. **TRUE** FALSE

9. In the Evaluate Formula dialog box, cell references are converted to the values contained in those cells. **TRUE** FALSE

10. The Watch Window is used to keep track of formula errors and their error messages. TRUE **FALSE**

Multiple Choice Questions

1. When is the cell of an inserted worksheet automatically included in a 3-D cell reference?
   a. Always
   b. When the inserted worksheet is within the 3-D reference's worksheet range
   c. When the formula containing the 3-D reference uses the IF function
   d. Never

2. Where may a table array (lookup table) be located?
   a. In the same worksheet as the lookup formula
   b. In a different worksheet of the same workbook
   c. In a worksheet of a different workbook
   d. Any of the above

3. What is the significance of the two quotation (") marks in the formula that follows?
   =IF(B3=20, B4*B5,"")
   a. Quotation marks display if B3 equals 20.
   b. Quotation marks display if B3 is not equal to 20.
   c. A table array will be searched for two quotation marks.
   d. Nothing will display if B3 is not equal to 20.

4. What is the purpose of the Tracing Precedents command?
   a. To display arrows from cells referenced by a formula
   b. To count cell references in a formula
   c. To display an error message
   d. To calculate the formula step by step

Skill Builders

Skill Builder 14.1   Create 3-D Cell References

In this exercise, you will add a new worksheet to the workbook and use a 3-D cell reference to add values from several worksheets.

Copy a Worksheet

1. Open the sb-Project Budget workbook from the Lesson 14 folder.

2. Display each worksheet in the workbook to see that they have an identical design.
   Cell B9 of each worksheet contains the total number of days to complete a task.

3. Copy the Site Design Team worksheet and position the copy first in the worksheet order.

4. Rename the new worksheet as **Budget**.

5. Change the label in cell A1 to **Website Development Budget**.

6. Change cell A3 to **Estimated Cost Per Day** and center the label.

7. Delete the labels and values in the range A4:B9.

8. Type and align the entries in cells A4 and A6 as shown in the following illustration.

	A	B
1	Website Development Budget	
2		
3	Estimated Cost Per Day	Days to Complete
4	$700	
5		
6	**Budget**	

Enter a 3-D Cell Reference

You will use a 3-D cell reference to cell B9 in the four task worksheets to calculate the total number of worker-days for the entire project.

9. Select cell B4.

10. Tap ⌨=.

11. Type **s** to display functions beginning with the letter *s* in the Formula AutoComplete function list. (Choose Office→Excel Options→Formulas→Working with Formulas→ Formula AutoComplete to turn the option on if the function list does not appear.)

12. Type **u** to display the SUM function in the AutoComplete list.

13. Tap ⌨↓ twice to highlight SUM, and then tap ⌨Tab to select SUM.
    The function =SUM(displays in the cell and the Formula Bar.

14. Click the Site Design Team sheet tab.

15. Hold down ⌨Shift while you click the Shopping Cart sheet tab.

16. Select cell B9 in the currently displayed worksheet.

17. Click Enter ✔ in the Formula Bar to complete the formula.
The result equals 63 total days. The formula totaled cell B9 from all four worksheets.

18. Examine the 3-D cell reference in the Formula Bar.
The formula displays as =SUM('Site Design Team:Shopping Cart Team'!B9). A colon (:) indicates the range of worksheet names, and an exclamation (!) point separates the worksheet reference from the cell reference. Single quotation marks (') surround the sheet name because they contain spaces.

The 3-D reference must refer to the same cell in each of the detail worksheets, but you may create the formula in any cell.

Create the Cost Formula

19. In cell B6 of the Budget worksheet, enter the formula **=A4*B4** to calculate the budget needed to complete the website development project.

20. Format the budget amount as Currency format with no decimal places, if not already formatted so.

Test the 3-D Cell Reference

21. Display the Site Design Team worksheet and change the value in cell B8 to **4**.
Take note of the new sum in cell B9.

22. Display the Budget worksheet, and verify that the total number of days increased to 65 in cell B4 and the budget increased to $45,500 in cell B6.
3-D cell references allow you to calculate the values in several worksheets on a single summary worksheet.

23. Save 🖫 the changes and close the workbook.
You will use this workbook again in Skill Builder 14.4.

Skill Builder 14.2 Create a Table Array and HLOOKUP Function

In this exercise, you will use a table array and the VLOOKUP function to assign the letter grades A–F to students based on their test scores. Then you will learn to use the Transpose command to convert the table array for use with the HLOOKUP function. You also will review how to edit properties for a defined name (introduced in Lesson 10, Managing Multiple-Sheet Workbooks.)

Create a Table Array

1. Open the sb-Test 1 Grades workbook from the Lesson 14 folder.

2. Enter the table array data in the range F5:G9 as shown to the right:
   Notice that you listed the test score values in ascending (lowest to highest) order so that the VLOOKUP function will assign the proper grade. In a moment, you will create a formula to determine the letter grades in column D.

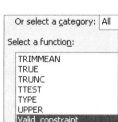

	F	G
3	**Grade Table**	
4	Test Scores	Letter Grade
5	0	F
6	60	D
7	70	C
8	80	B
9	90	A

3. Taking care not to select the labels in rows 3 and 4, select the range F5:G9.

4. Click in the Name box on the left of the Formula Bar, and type **Grade_Table**.

5. Tap [Enter] to assign Grade_Table as the defined name for the table array.
   You may always use the absolute cell range for a table array and reference that range in the lookup formula. A defined name, however, usually is clearer.

Use the VLOOKUP Function

6. Select cell D4 and click the Insert Function f_x button in the Formula Bar.

7. Choose All from the Select a Category list in the Insert Function dialog box.

8. Tab $\boxed{V}$ to jump to the functions beginning with the letter *V* in the Select a Function list.

9. Continue tapping $\boxed{V}$ until VLOOKUP is highlighted, and then tap [Enter] to choose VLOOKUP.

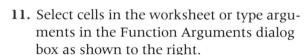

Or select a category: All

Select a function:
TRIMMEAN
TRUE
TRUNC
TTEST
TYPE
UPPER
Valid_constraint

10. Move the Function Arguments dialog box aside until you can see columns D–G.

11. Select cells in the worksheet or type arguments in the Function Arguments dialog box as shown to the right.

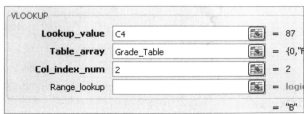

VLOOKUP

Lookup_value	C4		= 87
Table_array	Grade_Table		= {0,"F
Col_index_num	2		= 2
Range_lookup			= logi

= "B"

12. Click OK.
   The grade result should be B. Take a few moments to understand how this formula works. VLOOKUP searched down the left column of the table array for the lookup value 87 (the value in cell C4). It stopped at 80 because the lookup value is at least 80 but not 90. Traveling along row 8, the lookup proceeded to the second column in the table array and returned the letter grade B from cell G8.

13. Use AutoFill to copy the formula down the column for the other students.
The worksheet should match the following illustration.

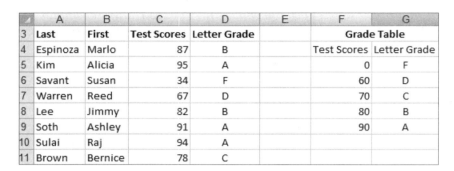

	A	B	C	D	E	F	G
3	**Last**	**First**	**Test Scores**	**Letter Grade**		**Grade Table**	
4	Espinoza	Marlo	87	B		**Test Scores**	**Letter Grade**
5	Kim	Alicia	95	A		0	F
6	Savant	Susan	34	F		60	D
7	Warren	Reed	67	D		70	C
8	Lee	Jimmy	82	B		80	B
9	Soth	Ashley	91	A		90	A
10	Sulai	Raj	94	A			
11	Brown	Bernice	78	C			

14. Save 💾 the changes.

Sort the List and Delete a Record

Notice that the lookup table is located in the same rows as the student data. In the next steps, you will see how this may cause a problem.

15. Select cell A4 and choose Data→Sort & Filter→Sort A to Z ↕ from the Ribbon.
The student records are sorted in alphabetical order by last name, and Excel protected the table array from being included in the sort. Notice that two students have a B grade.

16. Right-click row 8 and choose Delete from the context menu to remove Susan Savant's record.

As you can see, row 8 included the table array data for the B grade. The formula now returns a C grade instead of B for two students.

17. Click Undo ↩ to restore row 8.

Convert the Table Array from Vertical to Horizontal

Rows 1 and 2 would not likely be deleted, so they are a safer location for the lookup table. You will convert the vertical array to horizontal to fit in these two rows.

18. Select the range F4:G9 (including the labels) and use ⎹Ctrl⎸+⎹C⎸ to copy.

19. Select cell E1 and choose Home→Paste menu ▾→Transpose.
The copied cells are pasted in a horizontal orientation rather than vertical. Transpose means "to switch or reverse." The command is available if you copy cells but not if you cut them.

20. Center the test scores in the range F1:J1 so that they align with their matching grades.

21. Widen column E so that the labels display completely.

22. Select the range F4:G9 and tap ⌐Delete⌐.

The grade formulas in column D display the #N/A error message because cells F5:G9 now are empty. You will rebuild the formula using the HLOOKUP function.

Edit the Defined Name

Next you will display the Name Manager dialog box and update the Refers To range for one of the defined names.

23. Choose Formulas→Defined Names→Name Manager 🖼 from the Ribbon.

24. Select Grade_Table.

25. Click the Collapse 🖼 button next to Refers To in the bottom right of the dialog box.

26. Taking care not to select the labels in column E, select the range F1:J2.

27. Click the Expand 🖼 button to display Name Manager.

28. Click Close, and then click Yes to confirm.

The grade formulas currently return the value 60.

Use the HLOOKUP Function

29. Select cell D4, edit the first letter to **H** so the function name reads *HLOOKUP*, and complete the formula.

The formula now is =HLOOKUP(C4,Grade_Table,2). The only difference between VLOOKUP and HLOOKUP is the orientation of the table array. Occasionally you may decide to use a horizontal table array for a better worksheet design.

30. Use AutoFill to copy the D4 formula down for the other students.

	A	B	C	D	E	F	G	H	I	J
1	Final Grade Calculations				Test Scores	0	60	70	80	90
2					Letter Grade	F	D	C	B	A
3	Last	First	Test Scores	Letter Grade			Grade Table			
4	Brown	Bernice	78	C						
5	Espinoza	Marlo	87	B						
6	Kim	Alicia	95	A						
7	Lee	Jimmy	82	B						

31. Save 🖼 the changes and close the workbook.

Skill Builder 14.3   Use the VLOOKUP Function and Error Checking

In this exercise, you will create a simple financial worksheet that uses tax rates from a table array to calculate the Net Profit. The tax rate calculations have been simplified to make the data easy to understand. You will use Error Checking to locate the source of a formula error.

Calculate the Five-Year Growth Using Percentages

1. Open the sb-Financial Projections workbook from the Lesson 14 folder.
   The owner of King's Bakery is projecting sales growth of 27 percent for each of the next five years. These calculations appear in rows 4–9.

Use Error Checking and Create a Formula

The gross profit is equal to the projected sales in row 4 minus the expenses in rows 5–9. You will calculate the gross profit with a formula that uses the SUM function to sum the expenses and then subtracts the result from the projected sales.

2. In cell B10, enter **=B4-(B5:B9)**.
   Cell B10 should display an error.

3. Choose Formulas→Formula Auditing→Error Checking 🔷 from the Ribbon.
   Take a moment to read the information on the left side of the Error Checking dialog box, which cannot pinpoint the exact location of the error.

4. Click the Show Calculation Steps button in the dialog box.
   Cell B4 is evaluated as 400000, which is correct.

5. Click the Evaluate button in the Evaluate Formula dialog box.
   The next formula expression –(B5:B9) evaluates as a #VALUE! error. Evaluating the formula helped to locate the problem area in the formula. The function SUM is missing.

6. Click Close in the Evaluate Formula dialog box.

7. Click the Edit in Formula Bar button in the Error Checking dialog box.

8. Click in the Formula Bar between the minus (–) sign and the parenthesis, type **SUM,** and tap Enter.
   The result equals $15,000. You may nest functions like SUM inside a formula.

9. Click Resume in the Error Checking dialog box, and then click OK.

Calculate the Total Taxes Using the VLOOKUP Function

10. Drop down the Name list to the left of the Formula Bar and choose Tax_Table.
    The tax table at the bottom of the worksheet is selected. This table array was assigned the defined name Tax_Table when the worksheet was first created.

11. In cell B11, enter **=B10*VLOOKUP(B10,Tax_Table,2)**.
    The result equals $1,500. In this example, the total taxes are calculated as the gross profit in cell B10 multiplied by the tax rate returned by the VLOOKUP function.

Calculate the Net Profit and Format All Cells

12. In cell B12, enter a formula to calculate the net profit as Gross Profit–Total Taxes.
    The result equals $13,500.

13. Use AutoFill to copy the formulas in the range B10:B12 across the rows.
    Rows 10–12 should match the following illustration.

10	Gross Profit	$ 15,000	$ 61,850	$ 127,530	$ 218,041	$ 341,148
11	Total Taxes	$ 1,500	$ 15,463	$ 47,186	$ 85,036	$ 133,048
12	Net Profit	$ 13,500	$ 46,388	$ 80,344	$ 133,005	$ 208,100

14. Save 🖫 the changes and close the workbook.

Skill Builder 14.4   Use the IF Function

In this exercise, you will use the IF function to display a message if the project is going over budget.

Before You Begin: *You must have completed Skill Builder 14.1, and the sb-Project Budget workbook should be open.*

Add Budget Data to the Worksheet

1. Display the Budget worksheet in the sb-Project Budget workbook.

Create an IF Function

Now you will use an IF function to indicate whether the project is over budget as compared with the budget objective.

2. Enter **Budget Objective** in cell A7 and **50000** in cell B7.

3. Format cells A7 and B7 to match the format of cells A6 and B6.

4. Select cell C6 and click the Insert Function 𝑓𝑥 button in the Formula Bar.

5. Select the IF function from the Most Recently Used or Logical category and click OK.
   The Function Arguments dialog box displays.

6. For the Logical Test entry, select cell B7 in the worksheet and use [Shift]+[>] for greater than.

7. Select cell B6 and tap [Tab] to complete the entry.

8. Type **Within Budget** in the Value if True box and tap [Tab].

9. Type **Exceeds Budget** in the Value if False box and tap [Enter].
   The result displays as Within Budget.

10. Change the value in cell B7 from $50,000 to **40000**.
    Now the IF function displays that the project exceeds its budget objective.

11. Save 🖫 the changes and close the workbook.

Skill Builder 14.5   Use the COUNTIF and COUNTIFS Functions

In this exercise, you will use the COUNTIF function to count students who achieved a minimum test score on one test and COUNTIFS for multiple tests.

Create a COUNTIF Formula

1. Open the sb-Test 3 Grades workbook from the Lesson 14 folder.
   In the next steps, you will create a formula to count students who earned at least 70 points on Test 1.

2. Select cell C13 and click the Insert Function f_x button in the Formula Bar.

3. Choose the Statistical category and double-click the COUNTIF function in the list.
   The Function Arguments dialog box displays.

4. Select cells C4:C11 in the worksheet for Range.

5. Type **>=70** in the Criteria box and click OK.
   The result is 6. Excel added quotation (") marks around the criteria in the formula =COUNTIF(C4:C11,">=70").

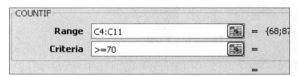

6. Copy the formula in cell C13 to the range D13:E13.

Create a COUNTIFS Formula

In the next steps, you will create a formula to count students who earned at least 70 points on every test. Only records meeting all the criteria in the COUNTIFS formula are counted.

7. Select cell E14 and click the Insert Function f_x button in the Formula Bar.

8. Choose the Statistical category and double-click the COUNTIFS (not COUNTIF) function in the list.
   The Function Arguments dialog box displays.

9. Select the range C4:C11 in the worksheet for Criteria Range1.

10. Type **>=70** in the Criteria1 box.
    Excel will add quotation (") marks around the criteria when you click the next text box.

11. Click in the Criteria Range2 box and select the range D4:D11 in the worksheet.

12. Copy ">=70" from the Criteria1 box and paste it in the Criteria2 box.

13. Click in the Criteria Range3 box and select the range E4:E11 in the worksheet.

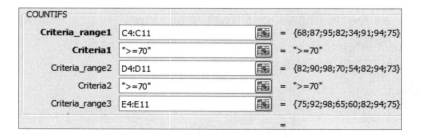

14. Tap ⌈Tab⌉ to display the Criteria3 box.

Only five text boxes display in the dialog box at one time.

15. Paste ">=70" in the Criteria3 box.

16. Click OK.

The result is 5, indicating that five students earned a minimum score of 70 on each of the three tests. The COUNTIFS function may have up to 127 sets of criteria ranges and criteria.

Your worksheet should look like the following illustration.

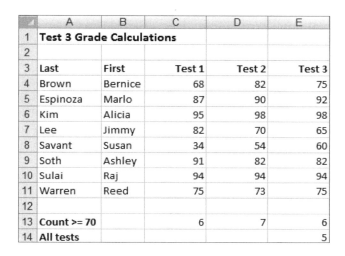

	A	B	C	D	E
1	**Test 3 Grade Calculations**				
2					
3	**Last**	**First**	**Test 1**	**Test 2**	**Test 3**
4	Brown	Bernice	68	82	75
5	Espinoza	Marlo	87	90	92
6	Kim	Alicia	95	98	98
7	Lee	Jimmy	82	70	65
8	Savant	Susan	34	54	60
9	Soth	Ashley	91	82	82
10	Sulai	Raj	94	94	94
11	Warren	Reed	75	73	75
12					
13	**Count >= 70**		6	7	6
14	**All tests**				5

17. Save 🖫 the changes and close the workbook.

Assessments

Assessment 14.1 Use Auditing Tools

In this exercise, you will respond to messages about possible formula errors.

1. Open the as-Vehicle Sales workbook in the Lesson 14 folder.

2. Display the Robert's Sales worksheet.
   Cell E15 displays a triangle icon in the upper-left corner of the cell.

3. Trace precedents for the formula in cell E15 and determine whether the formula includes the appropriate cell range. Leave the tracer arrow displayed.

4. Use the error checking menu on cell E15 to review possible causes for the triangle icon alert. Determine whether the formula is correct or needs to be changed. Choose an appropriate command in the menu to remove the triangle icon from the cell.

5. Display the Sales Summary worksheet.

6. Use the Error Checking dialog box to find and repair formulas containing errors. Each linking formula should point to the grand total sales in a salesperson's worksheet.
   The formula results are shown in the following illustration.

	A	B	C
1	Avery Auto Sales		
2	**Sales for January**		
3			
4	**Sales**		
5	New		
6	Used		
7	**Grand Total**		
8			
9			
10			
11			
12	**Salesperson**		**Total Sales**
13	Robert	Bendel	$ 251,190
14	David	Johnson	$ 122,620
15	Gwen	Wenski	$ 193,160

7. Save 🖫 the changes.
   You will continue to use this workbook in the next exercise.

Assessment 14.2 Create 3-D Cell References

In this exercise, you will use 3-D cell references in formulas.

Before You Begin: You must have completed Assessment 14.1, and the as-Vehicle Sales workbook should be open.

1. Display the Sales Summary worksheet in the as-Vehicle Sales workbook.

2. In the appropriate cell, create a formula with a 3-D cell reference that sums new vehicle sales for the three sales-people.

3. Create similar formulas for sales of used vehicles and the grand totals.
   The formula results are shown in the illustration to the right.

4. Save 🖫 the changes.
   You will continue to use this workbook in the next exercise.

	A	B
1	Avery Auto Sales	
2	**Sales for January**	
3		
4	**Sales**	
5	New	$ 452,780
6	Used	$ 114,190
7	**Grand Total**	$ 566,970

Assessment 14.3 Use the IF Function

In this exercise, you will create an IF function to indicate whether a salesperson met his or her monthly sales quota.

Before You Begin: You must have completed Assessment 14.1 and Assessment 14.2, and the as-Vehicle Sales workbook should be open.

1. Display the Gwen's Sales worksheet in the as-Vehicle Sales workbook.

2. In cell F17, create an IF function that indicates whether Gwen met her sales quota. Display **Quota Met** if the grand total sales is greater than or equal to the quota amount in cell B17. Display **Quota Not Met** if the grand total sales is less than the quota amount in cell B17.

Grand Total	193,160	Quota Met

3. Create the same IF function on the Robert's Sales and David's Sales worksheets.

4. Save 🖫 the changes and close the workbook.

Assessment 14.4   Create a Table Array and VLOOKUP Function

In this exercise, you will use the VLOOKUP function to determine how many free rentals the customer receives.

1. Open the as-Frequent Renters workbook from the Lesson 14 folder.

2. Set up the table array under the worksheet data as shown here:

	A	B	C	D	E
1	**Julie's Equipment Rentals - Frequent Renter Awards**				
2					
3		**Customer**		**Frequent Renter Points Earned**	**Number of Free Rentals**
4	Hansen	Leslie	A	6	
5	Liu	Shen		17	
6	Ortiz	Maria	D	3	
7	Park	Young	Min	22	
8	Randall	Lynn	G	11	
9	Salcedo	Nicolas		4	
10	Tate	Deborah	M	14	
11					
12				**Free Rentals Table**	
13				**Frequent Renter Points**	**Free Rentals**
14				0	0
15				5	1
16				10	2
17				15	3
18				20	4
19				25	5

3. Assign the defined name **Free_Rentals_Table** to the table array.

4. Use the VLOOKUP function in column E to determine the number of free rentals each customer should receive. The function should use the frequent renter points earned in column D as the lookup value and search the Free_Rentals_Table for the correct number of free rentals.

5. Save 🖫 the changes and close the workbook.

Critical Thinking

Critical Thinking 14.1 Use VLOOKUP to Calculate Late Fees

Leonard James has asked you to complete a worksheet that allows him to easily determine the late charges for customers returning overdue equipment. Leonard charges late fees as shown in the following table.

Days Late	Late Fee
1	$5
2	$10
3	$15
4 or more	$20

- Open the ct-Late Fees workbook from the Lesson 14 folder.
- Insert a new worksheet and create a table array for the late fees.
- In the Late Fee Charges worksheet, use a VLOOKUP function to calculate the late fee for each customer.
- Save the changes and close the workbook.

Critical Thinking 14.2 Create a Simple IF Formula

You are responsible for preparing the payroll for a small business firm. Employees receive an hourly wage 1.5 times their regular hourly wage for all hours worked over 40. Although simply looking at the Hours Worked column for any numbers over 40 would help you conclude that hours at the overtime rate should be included in the gross pay, using the IF function would tell you this in plain language.

- Open the ct-Weekly Payroll workbook from the Lesson 14 folder. This payroll workbook contains a worksheet for each week in January and a summary of all weeks.
- In cell G3 of the Week1 worksheet, create a formula using the IF function for the first employee (Aberdeen). The formula should check for over 40 hours worked and display the text **YES** to indicate that overtime hours are included in the gross pay or the text **NO** that overtime hours are not included.
- Copy this formula to the cells of the remaining employees in the Week1 worksheet.
- Copy this formula to the other worksheets.
- Save the changes.

You will continue to use this workbook in the next exercise.

Critical Thinking 14.3   Create a Complex IF Formula

Before You Begin: You must have completed Critical Thinking 14.2, and the ct-Weekly Payroll workbook should be open.

After adding the IF function to indicate when an employee must be paid overtime in the previous exercise, you consider ways to make your worksheet more efficient. When an employee works a regular work week, a single calculation of hours*hourly rate determines his or her gross pay. When an employee works overtime, however, two separate calculations are required:

■ Pay for the first 40 hours at the regular hourly rate.

■ Pay for hours above 40 at the overtime rate (hourly rate*1.5).

An IF function can determine if an overtime pay calculation is required and then calculate both regular pay and overtime pay. Otherwise, you would need a separate worksheet column for the overtime pay calculation.

■ In the Week1 worksheet of the Weekly Payroll workbook, create a formula in cell H3 using the IF function to calculate the gross pay for Aberdeen. The formula calculates gross pay using the appropriate hourly rate for 40 or fewer hours and the rate for more than 40 hours. Your Value if True argument may contain several expressions requiring multiple parentheses. Take a few moments to think about the logical sequence of each calculation.

Regular Hourly Rate	Overtime Hourly Rate	Hours Worked	Gross Pay Includes Overtime	Gross Pay
$ 12.00	$ 18.00	42	YES	$ 516.00
$ 12.00	$ 18.00	40	NO	$ 480.00
$ 11.50	$ 17.25	35	NO	$ 402.50

■ Copy the gross pay formula to the other employees listed on the Week 1 worksheet. Do the same for the Week 2 through Week 5 worksheets.

■ Save 🖫 the changes.

You will continue to use this workbook in the next exercise.

Critical Thinking 14.4   Create a Summary Formula

Before You Begin: You must have completed Critical Thinking 14.2 and Critical Thinking 14.3, and the ct-Weekly Payroll workbook should be open.

You already keep records of the gross pay for each employee on a weekly basis. Now you want to total the gross pay for all weeks for each employee.

■ In the Summary worksheet of the Weekly Payroll workbook, create a formula using a 3-D cell reference that totals the gross pay for all five work weeks of the month for each employee.

■ Save ![save icon] the changes and close the workbook.

Critical Thinking 14.5   Present Car Pricing Research

Use Internet Explorer and a search engine of your choice to visit a car shopping website and locate prices for six to eight new Toyota vehicles in the following categories: compact sedan, midsize sedan, minivan, pickup truck, and SUV.

■ Use the VLOOKUP function and a table array to display the words **Inexpensive**, **Average**, or **Expensive** in a cell depending upon the price of each vehicle as follows:

Inexpensive	Up to $20,000
Average	Between $20,001 and $30,000
Expensive	$30,001 or more

■ Save ![save icon] the workbook as **ct-New Vehicle Prices**.

LESSON 15

Using Advanced Formatting and Analysis Tools

You have learned to summarize data in previous lessons using such features as linking formulas and 3-D cell references in formulas. In this lesson, you will consolidate data from detail worksheets by position and category. Occasionally, you may need to set up multiple worksheets before data common to all of them are available. You will group worksheets to enter the data into multiple worksheets simultaneously. Many Excel workbooks are designed by experienced users but used by individuals with little Excel experience. Excel's Data Validation tool can assist users of all levels with data entry by forcing values to fall within a specified range. Excel's Conditional Formatting tool may be used to format values that fall within an acceptable range, thus drawing attention to those values. Data tables assist with what-if analyses by adjusting variables in a formula. Trendlines are another aid to analysis, helping you perceive and forecast trends in chart data.

LESSON OBJECTIVES

After studying this lesson, you will be able to:

- Group worksheets for efficient data entry
- Consolidate data from multiple worksheets by position and category
- Set data validation rules to restrict data entry
- Apply conditional formatting to flag positive or negative trends
- Create data tables to perform what-if analyses
- Develop trendlines to analyze chart data

Case Study: Consolidating Sales Performance Data

John Adams is the sales manager for Seminar Solutions. Part of John's compensation package is a quarterly bonus based on the sales and expenditures of the regions he manages. John needs a workbook to store detailed information in separate sheets. He will use Excel's consolidation feature to summarize the data into a summary sheet. In addition, he will use data validation, conditional formatting, and other tools to format the workbook and analyze the data. The following illustrations show the summary worksheet and a data table.

	A	B	C	D	E
4	Sales	Q1	Q2	Q3	Q4
5	Gross Sales	$3,320,000	$3,310,000	$4,380,000	$4,590,000
6	Returns	$ 166,000	$ 94,000	$ 185,000	$ 124,000
7	Net Sales	$3,154,000	$3,216,000	$4,195,000	$4,466,000
8					
9	Expenses	Q1	Q2	Q3	Q4
10	Sample Costs	$ 50,700	$ 24,000	$ 97,890	$ 44,450
11	Trade Shows	$ 107,490	$ 6,700	$ 122,000	$ 96,000
12	Automobile	$ 18,000	$ 18,500	$ 15,000	$ 14,600
13	Cell Phones	$ 10,800	$ 12,900	$ 11,140	$ 11,100
14	Entertainment	$ 17,900	$ 20,100	$ 11,700	$ 10,200
15	Total Expenses	$ 204,890	$ 82,200	$ 257,730	$ 176,350
16					
17	Expenses vs Net Sales	6.50%	2.56%	6.14%	3.95%

Summary / Region1 / Region2 / Region3

Conditional formatting uses criteria to flag certain formula results in red.

A consolidated summary worksheet with conditional formatting

B2 f_x =A2*1%*(1-10*B1)

	A	B	C	D	E	F	G
1			Expenses vs. Net Sales				
2		0	1%	2%	4%	6%	8%
3	Net Sales	$ 1,000,000	9000	8000	6000	4000	2000
4		$ 2,000,000	18000	16000	12000	8000	4000
5		$ 3,000,000	27000	24000	18000	12000	6000
6		$ 4,000,000	36000	32000	24000	16000	8000
7		$ 5,000,000	45000	40000	30000	20000	10000

A data table showing the various results when two variables are adjusted in a formula

Working with Grouped Worksheets

You may temporarily group two or more worksheets to save time when entering data, creating formulas, and formatting worksheets. When worksheets are grouped, whatever you type is entered on all sheets simultaneously. The same is true of formatting. For example, changing the column width on one worksheet also affects the same column on the other grouped worksheets. You may copy data from an ungrouped worksheet and paste to all worksheets in a group.

Grouping Worksheets

deselect

By grouping worksheets, you work with them as a set. For example, imagine that you used a budget template to create a workbook with 12 monthly worksheets. Rather than typing or pasting the same row labels multiple times, you may group the sheets and type the labels just once. You may group contiguous or noncontiguous worksheets using the Shift and Ctrl keys, just as you do when selecting multiple cells. In this lesson, you will work with contiguous worksheets. When worksheets are grouped, their sheet tabs change color, and *[Group]* displays in the window's title bar.

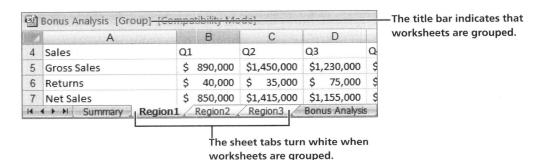

The title bar indicates that worksheets are grouped.

The sheet tabs turn white when worksheets are grouped.

Ungrouping Worksheets

Grouping and ungrouping actually are selecting and deselecting procedures. The Ungroup Sheets command in the sheet tab pop-up, or context, menu removes the grouping so that you may work in one worksheet at a time.

!TIP! *If all sheets in a workbook are grouped, you may simply click on any sheet tab, other than the first one, to ungroup them.*

QUICK REFERENCE: GROUPING AND UNGROUPING WORKSHEETS

Task	Procedure
Group contiguous worksheets	■ Click the first sheet tab to be grouped. ■ Hold down Shift and click the last sheet tab to be grouped.
Group noncontiguous worksheets	■ Click the first sheet tab to be grouped. ■ Hold down Ctrl and click the individual sheet tabs to be grouped with the first.
Copy and paste cells to grouped worksheets	■ Select cells to be copied and use Ctrl+C to copy. ■ Select the destination cell in one of the grouped sheets. ■ Group the sheets to receive the copied cells. ■ Use Ctrl+P to paste.
Ungroup worksheets	■ Right-click a sheet tab and choose Ungroup Sheets from the context menu.

Hands-On 15.1 Group Worksheets

In this exercise, you will explore the structure of summary and detail worksheets. You will group four worksheets, enter new data, copy existing data, and apply formatting to all sheets simultaneously.

Explore the Workbook

1. Start Excel and open the Bonus Analysis workbook from the Lesson 15 folder in your file storage location.

2. Take a few moments to study the Summary and three region worksheets.
   The number cells are empty in the Summary sheet. Later in this lesson, these cells will receive data from the Region1–Region3 sheets through the Consolidation command. Some row and column headings are missing from the four worksheets. You will group the worksheets and type the labels once.

Group Worksheets

3. Follow these steps to group the four worksheets:

Ⓐ Click the Summary sheet tab.

Ⓑ Hold down Shift and click the Region3 sheet tab. Release Shift.

The four sheets are now grouped. Notice [Group] in the title bar and that the grouped sheet tabs are white.

Enter Data in Grouped Worksheets

The ranges A10:A15 and B9:E9 are empty in all four worksheets. You will enter data once into these cells for all grouped worksheets.

4. In cell A10, type **Sample Costs** and tap ⌐Enter¬.

5. Continue entering the following labels in cells A11:A15: **Trade Shows**, **Vehicle**, **Cell Phones**, **Entertainment**, and **Total Expenses**.

6. In cell B9, type **Q1** and center the label.

7. Use AutoFill to extend the series through cell E9.
   The range B9:E9 should display Q1, Q2, Q3, and Q4.

8. Deselect the highlighted cells.

Ungroup the Worksheets

9. Right-click the Summary sheet tab and choose Ungroup Sheets from the context menu.

10. Display each of the region worksheets.
    Notice that the labels you entered in the ranges A10:15 and B9:E9 are now on all of the worksheets.

Copy and Paste Cells to Grouped Worksheets

Some row headings on the Summary worksheet should be included on the region worksheets.

11. Display the Summary worksheet.

12. Select the range A5:A7 and use ⌐Ctrl¬+⌐C¬ to copy.

13. Display the Region1 worksheet and select cell A5, the destination cell.

14. Hold down ⌐Shift¬ and click the Region3 sheet tab to select all region sheets.

15. Use ⌐Ctrl¬+⌐V¬ to paste.
    The labels were pasted to cells A5:A7 in the three region worksheets.

16. Deselect the cells.

Format Grouped Worksheets

Now you will apply formatting to cells in a worksheet group.

17. Display the Summary worksheet.

18. Tap ⌐Esc¬ to clear the marquee surrounding the range A5:A7.

19. Group the four worksheets again.

20. Follow these steps to select the desired cells to format:

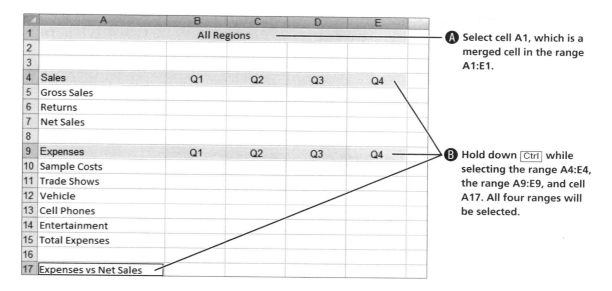

The spreadsheet shows:

	A	B	C	D	E
1	All Regions				
2					
3					
4	Sales	Q1	Q2	Q3	Q4
5	Gross Sales				
6	Returns				
7	Net Sales				
8					
9	Expenses	Q1	Q2	Q3	Q4
10	Sample Costs				
11	Trade Shows				
12	Vehicle				
13	Cell Phones				
14	Entertainment				
15	Total Expenses				
16					
17	Expenses vs Net Sales				

A Select cell A1, which is a merged cell in the range A1:E1.

B Hold down Ctrl while selecting the range A4:E4, the range A9:E9, and cell A17. All four ranges will be selected.

21. Choose Home→Styles→Cell Styles→Themed Cell Styles→Accent4.
The selected cells display a purple fill and white text.

22. Deselect the cells.

23. Use Ctrl to select the ranges A5:A7 and A10:A15.

24. Choose Home→Styles→Themed Cell Styles→20% – Accent4.
The row labels display a light purple fill.

25. Deselect the cells.

26. Take a few moments to view the changes that were made to each worksheet.
All the worksheets should have the same formatting as the Summary sheet.

27. Experiment with grouping and ungrouping contiguous and noncontiguous sheets.
Remember, use the Shift key to group contiguous sheets and the Ctrl key to group noncontiguous sheets.

28. When finished, make certain to ungroup the worksheets.

29. Save 🖫 the changes and leave the workbook open.

Consolidating Worksheet Data

Excel's Consolidate command combines values from source worksheets into a destination worksheet. You select an entire range, and all its value and formula cells (but not text cells) are consolidated simultaneously to the destination worksheet. The calculation results are values rather than formulas unless you select the Create Links to Source Data option. When the results are values, you must repeat the Consolidate command if values change later in the source worksheets. You may redisplay the Consolidate dialog box to add a reference range for any worksheet added to the workbook, and you may delete any reference range.

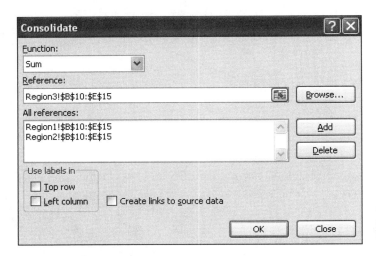

A consolidation reference being created to the Region3 worksheet in the Consolidate dialog box

!TIP! *The Browse button in the Consolidate dialog box allows you to navigate to other workbooks and consolidate data from them.*

Consolidation Functions

The SUM function is the most commonly used consolidation function. You also may use AVERAGE, MIN, MAX, and some other statistical functions when consolidating. You choose the desired function in the Consolidate dialog box when you set up the consolidation.

Types of Consolidation

You may consolidate data using either of the following methods:

- **By Position:** This method is useful when all worksheets have the same layout. To consolidate by position, specify the same range in all worksheets. Excel uses the function you choose to consolidate values in the same cell of each of the specified worksheets.

- **By Category:** This method is used when the supporting worksheets have different layouts but identical row or column labels. Excel uses the row and column headings to determine which rows or columns to consolidate with the other consolidation ranges you specify. The consolidation produces one row or column in the summary sheet for each unique row or column encountered in the supporting sheets.

Creating Links to Source Data

By default, consolidated data is not linked to the source cells. The Create Links to Source Data option does create linking formulas on the summary worksheet. (Lesson 10, Managing Multiple-Sheet Workbooks, describes linking formulas.) The consolidated data is formatted as an outline that may be expanded to view the source data or collapsed to view the totals. Any changes to source data on the original worksheets will update in the summary sheet.

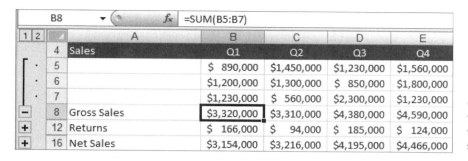

Consolidated data in outline format in the summary worksheet with links to source data

QUICK REFERENCE: CONSOLIDATING DATA

Task	Procedure
Consolidate by position or category	■ Select a cell in the destination worksheet to be used as the starting point for the consolidation. *By category:* This range will include column and/or row labels.
	■ Choose Data→Data Tools→Consolidate from the Ribbon.
	■ Choose a consolidation function (usually SUM) in the Consolidate dialog box.
	■ Click in the Reference box.
	■ Click the sheet tab of the first source worksheet and select the data range. *By category:* The range must include either row or column labels.
	■ Click the Add button to add the range to the All References list.
	■ Click the next source sheet tab, and click Add to add the same range to the All References list. *By category:* Select a different range, if necessary.
	■ Continue adding the remaining source sheet ranges. *By category:* Place a checkmark in the Top Row box in the Use Labels In area if you included column labels or in the Left Column box if you included row labels.
	■ Place a checkmark in the Create Links to Source Data box, if desired. Using this option avoids updating the consolidation manually after changes are made to the source data.
Update the consolidation manually after changing values in source worksheets	■ Choose Data→Data Tools→Consolidate from the Ribbon and click OK.

Hands-On 15.2   Consolidate Data

In this exercise, you will use the Consolidate command to consolidate the gross sales, returns, and net sales from the region worksheets by position. This is possible because all worksheets have the same layout. You will also use 3-D formulas as an alternative to consolidating data in the same workbook.

Consolidate Sales by Position

1. Display the Summary worksheet in the Bonus Analysis workbook.

2. Select cell B5 as the starting point for the consolidated data.

3. Choose Data→Data Tools→Consolidate ![icon] from the Ribbon.

4. If necessary, move the Consolidate dialog box until the range B5:E7 in the Summary sheet and the sheet tabs at the bottom of the Excel window are visible.

5. Follow these steps to set consolidation options in the Consolidate dialog box:

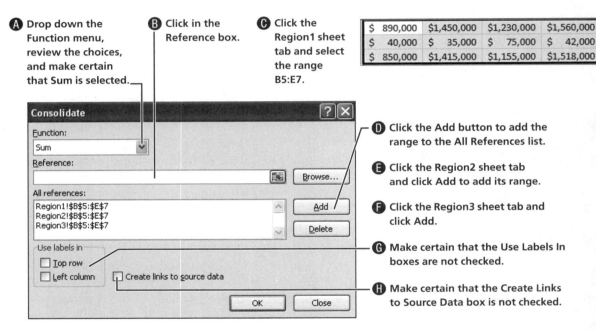

Ⓐ Drop down the Function menu, review the choices, and make certain that Sum is selected.

Ⓑ Click in the Reference box.

Ⓒ Click the Region1 sheet tab and select the range B5:E7.

$ 890,000	$1,450,000	$1,230,000	$1,560,000
$ 40,000	$ 35,000	$ 75,000	$ 42,000
$ 850,000	$1,415,000	$1,155,000	$1,518,000

Ⓓ Click the Add button to add the range to the All References list.

Ⓔ Click the Region2 sheet tab and click Add to add its range.

Ⓕ Click the Region3 sheet tab and click Add.

Ⓖ Make certain that the Use Labels In boxes are not checked.

Ⓗ Make certain that the Create Links to Source Data box is not checked.

Review the references in the All References list. You build a consolidation range by adding references to this list.

6. Click OK.
   Excel consolidates the data into the Summary sheet. The Summary worksheet should display the consolidated numbers shown in the following illustration.

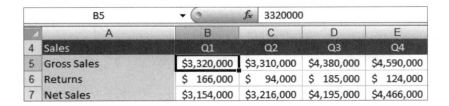

	A	B	C	D	E
	B5		$\mathit{f_x}$ 3320000		
4	Sales	Q1	Q2	Q3	Q4
5	Gross Sales	$3,320,000	$3,310,000	$4,380,000	$4,590,000
6	Returns	$ 166,000	$ 94,000	$ 185,000	$ 124,000
7	Net Sales	$3,154,000	$3,216,000	$4,195,000	$4,466,000

Examine the Results

7. Select any cell in the range B5:E7 in the Summary worksheet.
   The Formula Bar displays a value rather than a formula. The Consolidate command sums the values in the specified ranges and enters the results as values in the Summary sheet. You would need to give the Consolidate command again if the numbers in the detail worksheets were updated. Assume that you did not switch on Create Links to Source Data in the Consolidate dialog box because you will not update the data.

8. Save 🖫 the changes.

Create 3-D Formulas

Now you will create a SUM formula containing a 3-D cell reference to consolidate the expenses in rows 10–15.

9. Display the Summary sheet, if not already displayed.

10. In cell B10, type **=SUM(** and make certain to type the parenthesis.

11. Group the Region1–Region 3 sheet tabs.

12. Select cell B10 in the currently active sheet.

13. Click Enter ✔ in the Formula Bar to complete the formula.
    The value 50700 displays in cell B10.

14. Format cell B10 as Accounting number format with 0 decimal places.

15. Use [Ctrl]+[C] to copy cell B10, select the range B10:E15, and use [Ctrl]+[V] to paste. (Do not use the fill handle, which would paste 50700 in all cells.)
    The pasted formulas sum their respective cells using a 3-D cell reference.

    If data you want to consolidate resides in the same cell or range on contiguous worksheets, you may use 3-D formulas. Use the Consolidate command when data resides in different ranges, noncontiguous worksheets, or multiple workbooks.

Create the Expenses vs. Net Sales Formula

16. Group the four worksheets.

17. Select cell B17 in the Summary worksheet.

18. Enter the formula **=B15/B7** to calculate the percentage that Total Expenses is of Net Sales.
    The result equals .06496195. Your result may contain a different number of decimal places.

19. Format cell B17 as Percent Style with two decimal places.

20. Copy the cell B17 formula to the range C17:E17.

21. Ungroup the worksheets.

22. Save 🖫 the changes.

Working with Data Validation

Excel's data validation tool lets you restrict data entry in cells. The default validation setting for a cell is Any Value, meaning that until you specify a validation setting and criteria, any value may be entered in the cell. You may restrict both the type and range of acceptable values. For example, you may want to restrict data entry to whole numbers between 0 and 100,000. You may also create input messages to guide the user in entering acceptable data and error alert messages. An input message displays whenever the restricted cell is selected. An error message displays whenever data entry is attempted and the data is not of the correct type or within the accepted range. Data validation cannot be applied while worksheets are grouped; it must be set one worksheet at a time.

 NOTE! *Data validation operates only when the user attempts to type directly in a cell. No alert occurs when cell contents result from using the fill handle, Paste command, or an incorrect cell reference in a formula.*

The following table describes the available validation criteria.

Type	Entries Must Be
Any Value	No restrictions; may display an input message without checking for valid entries
Custom	A formula, expression, or reference to a calculation in another cell
Dates	Dates
Decimal	Numbers or fractions
List	Only those in a specified list
Text Length	A specific number of characters
Time	Times
Whole Number	Integers without decimal places

 TIP! *If the values in the worksheet are formatted with decimal places, use Decimal rather than Whole Number.*

 QR **QUICK REFERENCE: VALIDATING DATA ENTRIES**

Task	Procedure
Set validation criteria and messages	■ Select the cells to be validated. ■ Choose Data→Data Tools→Data Validation ⊞ from the Ribbon. ■ Choose the criteria for data to be entered in the cells. ■ If desired, set an input message and/or error alert message using the tabs in the Data Validation dialog box.

Hands-On 15.3   Set Up Data Validation

In this exercise, you will assign names to ranges, set up data validation, and create an error alert message for the named ranges.

Assign Range Names

In the first few steps, you will assign names to the ranges B5:E6 and B10:E14 in all four worksheets. These names will be useful as you develop the workbook.

1. Display the Summary worksheet of the Bonus Analysis workbook, if not already displayed.

2. Follow these steps to select multiple ranges:

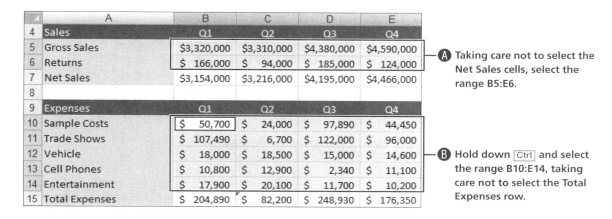

Ⓐ Taking care not to select the Net Sales cells, select the range B5:E6.

Ⓑ Hold down Ctrl and select the range B10:E14, taking care not to select the Total Expenses row.

3. Click in the Name box to the left of the Formula Bar.

4. Type the name **Consolidation_Data** and tap Enter to assign the name to the range.

5. Display the Region1 worksheet.

6. Select the ranges B5:E6 and B10:E14 using the Ctrl key technique, as you did in step 2.

7. Assign the name **Region1_Data** to the range.

8. Assign the names **Region2_Data** and **Region3_Data** to the same ranges in the Region2 and Region3 worksheets.

9. Display each worksheet and deselect the highlighted cells.
Make it a habit to deselect cells to avoid accidental deletions or changes.

Set Data Validation

10. Drop down the Name box menu to the left of the Formula Bar and choose Region1_Data.
The range B5:E6 and B10:E14 is selected in the Region1 worksheet.

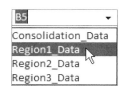

11. Choose Data→Data Tools→Data Validation 📋 from the Ribbon.

12. Follow these steps to set the data entry restrictions:

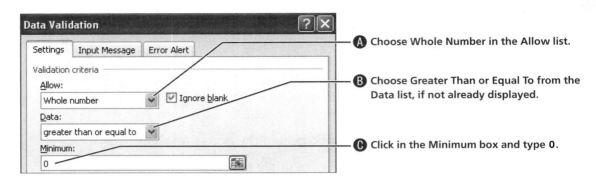

A Choose Whole Number in the Allow list.

B Choose Greater Than or Equal To from the Data list, if not already displayed.

C Click in the Minimum box and type **0**.

13. Display the Input Message tab in the dialog box.
Notice that you may create an input message that appears whenever a restricted cell is selected. You will not use this option in this exercise. You will use an error alert message instead.

14. Display the Error Alert tab.

15. Follow these steps to set an error alert message:

A Drop down the Style list to view the available actions, and make certain that Stop is chosen.

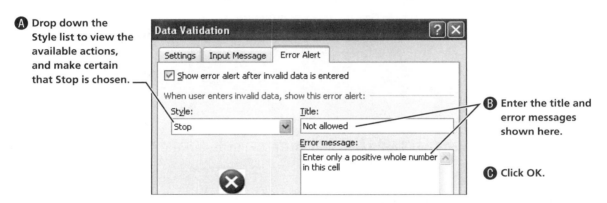

B Enter the title and error messages shown here.

C Click OK.

Test the Data Validation

16. Select cell B5 in the Region1 sheet.

17. Type the number **−1000** and tap [Enter].
The error alert message appears. The data validation restriction allows you to enter only a positive whole number in this cell.

18. Click the Retry button in the message box.
Retry lets you edit an incorrect entry, while Cancel deletes the entry.

19. Type **1000.50** and tap [Enter].
Once again, the entry is not accepted because it is not a whole number.

20. Click the Retry button and enter the original number **890000**.

21. Now repeat steps 10–15 to apply the same data validation restriction and error alert message to the ranges named Region2_Data and Region3_Data.
You may select the desired range easily by choosing the defined name from the Name box to the left of the Formula Bar.

22. Save 💾 the changes.

Circling Invalid Data

At times, data may already be entered in worksheet cells before data validation rules are created. Some cells then may contain invalid data, so you should use the Circle Invalid Data command to find them. The command does just what the name implies: it places circles around any data that does not conform to the validation rules set for the cells. Once the data is circled, you may ignore or correct an entry. The red circles are easy to spot and do not print.

 WARNING! *Circles around invalid data are temporary. Even if you don't clear the circles before you close the file, they will be gone when you reopen the file. You may, however, choose the Circle Invalid Data command again.*

QR > **QUICK REFERENCE: CIRCLING INVALID DATA**

Task	Procedure
Circle invalid data entered prior to creation of validation rules	■ Choose Data→Data Tools→Data Validation menu ▼→ Circle Invalid Data from the Ribbon. ■ Edit or ignore circled cells, as desired.
Remove validation circles	■ Enter valid data in the cells. *or* ■ Choose Data→Data Tools→Data Validation menu ▼→ Clear Validation Circles from the Ribbon. ■ Close the workbook.

 ## Hands-On 15.4   Circle Invalid Data

In this exercise, you will reset data validation for a range of cells and then circle invalid data.

Change Data Validation for a Range

In the first steps, you will set a data validation rule only for the expense values in the Region1 worksheet.

1. Display the Region1 worksheet of the Bonus Analysis workbook, if not already displayed.

2. Taking care not to select the totals in row 15, select the expense values in the range B10:E14.

3. Choose Data→Data Tools→Data Validation 🖾 from the Ribbon.

4. Display the Settings tab in the Data Validation dialog box.

5. Follow these steps to restrict expense values to a maximum of $32,000:

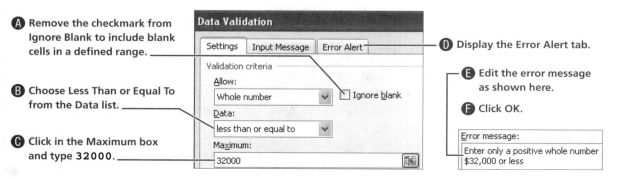

A Remove the checkmark from Ignore Blank to include blank cells in a defined range.

B Choose Less Than or Equal To from the Data list.

C Click in the Maximum box and type **32000**.

D Display the Error Alert tab.

E Edit the error message as shown here.

F Click OK.

Test Data Validation

6. Enter **41500** in cell D13.

7. Read the error message, click Retry, and enter **4500**.

Circle Invalid Data

8. Choose Data→Data Tools→Data Validation menu ▼→Circle Invalid Data ⊞ from the Ribbon.
   Red circles appear around the cells that do not meet the validation set for those cells.

Expenses	Q1	Q2	Q3
Sample Costs	$ 12,300	$ 5,000	$ 32,890
Trade Shows	$ 35,000	$ 2,300	$ 42,000
Vehicle	$ 6,000	$ 4,500	$ 6,000

9. Select cell B11 and enter **31000**.
   Notice that the red circle disappeared after you completed a valid entry.

10. Select cell D10 and enter **30000**.
    The red circle disappeared because you entered a valid entry.

Clear Validation Circles

11. Leave the value in cell D11 as is.
    At times you may want to keep previous values in the worksheet even if they do not meet the validation rules.

12. Choose Data→Data Tools→Data Validation menu ▼→Clear Validation Circles ⊞ from the Ribbon.
    The remaining validation circle disappears.

13. Save ⊞ the changes.

Working with Conditional Formatting

The Conditional Formatting ⊞ command applies formatting to cells that meet criteria that you set. Conditional formats are activated only when the criteria are met. For example, you may assign a yellow fill to a cell when its value is greater than 12. You may apply conditional formatting to cells containing values, text, dates, blanks, or errors. Conditional formats are often used as alerts. They draw attention to better-than-expected results or values that fall outside an acceptable range. Conditional formatting cannot be applied while worksheets are grouped and must be set in one worksheet at a time.

Using Presets and Multiple Conditions

Excel 2007 includes conditional formatting presets on a menu for frequently used criteria, such as Greater Than, Equal To, Above Average, and Top 10 Items. Unlike with prior Excel versions, now you may set any number of conditional formats and create multiple rules to check for more than one condition in a cell.

Creating a Conditional Formatting Rule

If no preset item on the Conditional Formatting menu has your desired criteria or formatting, you may create a new conditional formatting rule. The following illustration defines the parts of the New Formatting Rule dialog box.

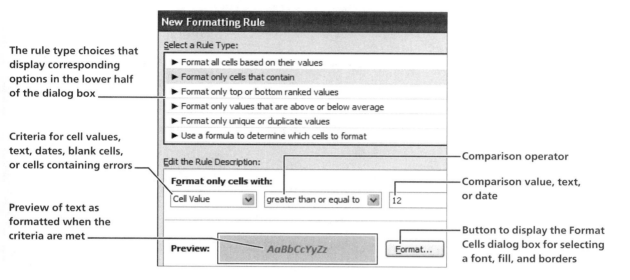

The rule type choices that display corresponding options in the lower half of the dialog box

Criteria for cell values, text, dates, blank cells, or cells containing errors

Preview of text as formatted when the criteria are met

Comparison operator

Comparison value, text, or date

Button to display the Format Cells dialog box for selecting a font, fill, and borders

Formatting and Filtering with Graphics

New to Excel 2007 is the capability to format cells with data bars, a color scale, or an icon set. These graphics identify values that are average, above average, and below average in the selected cell range. You may select a menu preset or create a custom conditional formatting rule using any of these visual aids. After bars, colors, or icons are applied with conditional formatting, you may filter by color or icon. For example, you may filter a column in a table for cells containing a down-pointing arrow to view only the cells with below-average results. (For information about filtering, review Lesson 11, Creating Tables and Outlines).

$ 24,000	$ 95,000	⇨ $44,450
$ 6,700	$ 122,000	⬆ $96,000
$ 18,500	$ 15,000	⬇ $14,600
$ 12,900	$ 11,340	⬇ $11,100
$ 20,100	$ 11,700	⬇ $10,200

Conditional formatting with data bars, a color scale, or icons helps you to categorize data, identify trends, and highlight trouble areas.

 TIP! *Use consistent formatting and limit the use of data bars, color scales, and icon sets on one worksheet. Using multiple styles in adjacent columns, as in the preceding figure, could confuse the reader.*

QUICK REFERENCE: APPLYING CONDITIONAL FORMATTING

Task	Procedure
Apply preset conditional formatting	■ Select the cells to receive formatting. ■ Choose Home→Styles→Conditional Formatting ▦ from the Ribbon, display a preset menu, and choose a command.
Create a conditional formatting rule	■ Select the cells to receive formatting. ■ Choose Home→Styles→Conditional Formatting→New Rule from the Ribbon. ■ Choose a rule type and formatting options in the New Formatting Rule dialog box.
Apply conditional formatting with data bars, a color scale, or an icon set	■ Select the cells to receive formatting. (All cells in the selection will display formatting.) ■ Choose Home→Styles→Conditional Formatting→Data Bars or Color Scales or Icon Sets from the Ribbon. ■ Choose a preset item on the command's submenu or New Rule to create a custom rule.
Clear conditional formatting from specific cells	■ Select specific cells to remove formatting. ■ Choose Home→Styles→Conditional Formatting→Clear Rules→Clear Rules from Selected Cells from the Ribbon.
Clear all conditional formatting from a worksheet	■ Display the desired worksheet. ■ Choose Home→Styles→Conditional Formatting→Clear Rules→Clear Rules from Entire Sheet from the Ribbon.
Manage conditional formatting rules	■ Choose Home→Styles→Conditional Formatting→ Manage Rules from the Ribbon to display the Conditional Formatting Rules Manager window. ■ Choose Current Selection or a different worksheet from the Show Formatting Rules For list. ■ Use buttons in the dialog box to create a new rule or select an existing rule and edit, delete, or change its order.

 Hands-On 15.5   Apply Conditional Formatting

In this exercise, you will specify various types of conditional formatting for cell ranges.

Use a Preset

1. Select the range B17:E17 in the Summary worksheet of the Bonus Analysis workbook.

2. Choose Home→Styles→Conditional Formatting ▦→Highlight Cells Rules→Greater Than from the Ribbon.
   The Greater Than dialog box appears with the suggested value 4.46 percent.

3. Change 4.46% to **5%** in the Format Cells that Are Greater Than box.

4. Drop down the With list to view the choices, and then make certain that Light Red Fill with Dark Red Text is selected.
   The color red often is used to highlight "bad" results. Yellow is used to indicate "average," and green means "good."

5. Click OK.

Cells B17 and D17 display the red formatting because they are more than 5 percent. The expenses for those quarters are higher in relation to net sales.

Create a Conditional Formatting Rule

6. Display the Region1 worksheet.

7. Select cell B13 and tap [Delete] to erase its contents.

8. Taking care not to select the totals in row 15, select the range B10:E14.
You selected the Quarter 1–Quarter 4 expenses.

9. Choose Home→Conditional Formatting→Highlight Cells Rules→More Rules from the Ribbon.
The New Formatting Rule dialog box appears. Format Only Cells That Contain is the selected rule type.

10. Follow these steps to create a custom conditional formatting rule:

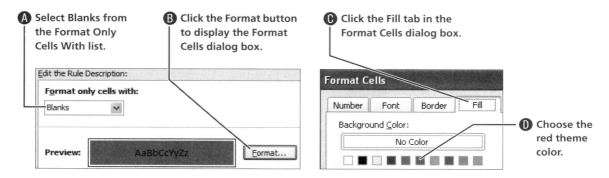

A Select Blanks from the Format Only Cells With list.

B Click the Format button to display the Format Cells dialog box.

C Click the Fill tab in the Format Cells dialog box.

D Choose the red theme color.

Notice the red fill in the Preview box.

11. Click OK to exit the Format Cells dialog box.

12. Click OK to exit the New Formatting Rule dialog box.
The conditional formatting is applied to cell B13, the blank cell, to draw attention to a potential error.

Format with Data Bars and Icons

You will select the expense values in one column at a time and apply conditional formatting. Selecting all the Q1–Q4 cells at once would compare each value with the Q1–Q4 grand total, which is not the result you need.

13. Display the Summary worksheet.

14. Select the range B10:B14 and choose Home→Conditional Formatting→Data Bars→Blue Data Bar from the Ribbon.
The data bars display each part of the Q1 total expenses like a bar chart inside the cells.

15. Select the range C10:C14 and apply green data bars.
By comparing the bars, you can easily spot high and low amounts.

16. Select the range D10:D14 and choose Home→Conditional Formatting→Icon Sets→5 Quarters (black and white circles) from the Ribbon.

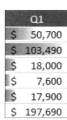

17. Widen column D to display all cell contents.

18. Select the range E10:E14 and choose Home→Conditional Formatting→Icon Sets and choose any other icon set that would categorize the values well. *Mixing data bars, color scales, and icon sets on one worksheet could make the data look confusing. Normally you would limit the styles for consistency.*

Q3	
◖	$ 95,000
●	$122,000
○	$ 15,000
○	$ 11,340
○	$ 11,700
	$ 255,040

Remove Conditional Formatting

19. Select the range D10:D14 and choose Home→Conditional Formatting→Clear Rules→Clear Rules from Selected Cells from the Ribbon.
The icons disappeared from the range. Conditional formats may be removed from a selected range or from the entire worksheet.

20. Save 💾 the changes.

Using Data Tables

Data tables are different from the tables that you produced in Lesson 11, Creating Tables and Outlines. Data tables preview the effect that changing some values would have on a formula's result. A data table is structured around a specific formula to perform a what-if analysis. Various values from a list are substituted for either one or two cell references in the formula. The Data Table command calculates the formula result for each value listed.

One-Variable Data Tables

One-variable data tables compute results for various values substituted for a cell reference in a formula. For example, the data table may display the result for a FV (Future Value) formula with the monthly payment as a variable in increments of $20. This example is shown in the following illustration, where the empty Payment cell (B5) is known as the input cell. Each value from Payment column C of the data table is substituted in the input cell, and its corresponding Future Value result displays in column D.

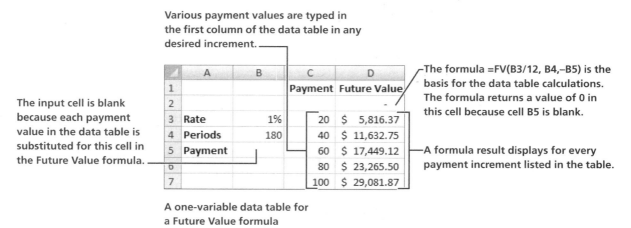

A one-variable data table for a Future Value formula

Two-Variable Data Tables

You will work with two-variable data tables in this lesson. While a one-variable data table has one input cell, this type has two input cells. Values are substituted for two cell references in the formula. The following illustration shows the layout of a two-variable data table using the same Future Value formula as in the previous example. Take a few moments to review this illustration carefully.

The formula =FV(B3/12, B4,–B5) is the basis for the data table calculations. The formula returns a value of 0 in this cell because cells B3 and B5 are blank.

Various payment values are typed into the first column of the data table, and rates are entered into the first row.

The input cells are blank because each rate and payment value in the data table are substituted for these cells in the Future Value formula.

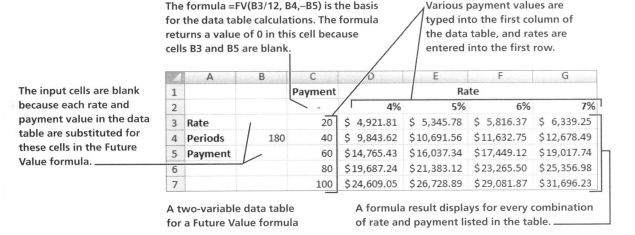

	A	B	C	D	E	F	G
1			Payment		Rate		
2			-	4%	5%	6%	7%
3	Rate		20	$ 4,921.81	$ 5,345.78	$ 5,816.37	$ 6,339.25
4	Periods	180	40	$ 9,843.62	$10,691.56	$11,632.75	$12,678.49
5	Payment		60	$14,765.43	$16,037.34	$17,449.12	$19,017.74
6			80	$19,687.24	$21,383.12	$23,265.50	$25,356.98
7			100	$24,609.05	$26,728.89	$29,081.87	$31,696.23

A two-variable data table for a Future Value formula

A formula result displays for every combination of rate and payment listed in the table.

QUICK REFERENCE: CREATING DATA TABLES

Task	Procedure
Create a one-variable data table	■ Enter a formula in the worksheet. The formula must include a reference to one input cell outside the data table. ■ Enter input variable values down the column (under the formula cell) to substitute for one cell address in the formula. ■ Select the data table, including the formula cell, all input variable values, and the cells that will hold the calculated results. ■ Choose Data→Data Tools→What-If Analysis→Data Table from the Ribbon. ■ In the Data Table dialog box, specify the column input cell that is outside the data table and used in the formula.
Create a two-variable data table	■ Enter a formula as the upper-left cell in the data table. The formula must include references to two input cells outside the data table. ■ Enter input variable values across the first row (to the right of the formula cell) to substitute for one cell address in the formula. ■ Enter input variable values down the first column (under the formula cell) to substitute for one cell address in the formula. ■ Select the data table, including the formula cell, all input variable values, and the cells that will hold the calculated results. ■ Choose Data→Data Tools→What-If Analysis→Data Table from the Ribbon. ■ In the Data Table dialog box, specify the row input cell and column input cell that are outside the data table and used in the formula.

Hands-On 15.6 Create a Two-Variable Data Table

John Adams wants to estimate his next quarter's bonus compensation. The bonus is based on two factors: the net sales and the expenses vs. net sales percentage achieved by his team. In this exercise, you will create a data table with two variables and add conditional formatting.

Set Up the Data Table

1. In the Bonus Analysis workbook, insert a new worksheet named Bonus Analysis at the end of the worksheet order.

2. Enter the following data into the new sheet, formatting the numbers as shown.

	A	B	C	D	E	F	G
1				Expenses vs. Net Sales			
2			1%	2%	4%	6%	8%
3	Net Sales	$ 1,000,000					
4		$ 2,000,000					
5		$ 3,000,000					
6		$ 4,000,000					
7		$ 5,000,000					

A two-variable data table is always set up this way. One set of variables is placed immediately to the right of the formula (the percentages in this exercise). The other set of variables is placed immediately below the formula (the dollar amounts). The Net Sales and Expenses vs. Net Sales labels may be placed anywhere as long as they do not interfere with the table.

3. Select cell B2.

   You will create a formula with references to two input cells. Any two blank cells may be used as the input cells as long as they are outside the data table range. You will use cell A1 as the Expenses vs. Net Sales (row) variable and cell A2 as the Net Sales (column) variable.

4. Enter the formula **=(1-10*A1)*0.5%*A2** in cell B2.

   The result equals 0 because cells A1 and A2 are blank. This formula calculates John's quarterly bonus. The (1–10*A1) part of the formula calculates a percentage factor. This component penalizes John as the Expenses vs. Net Sales ratio increases. In other words, if his regions spend too much compared with what they sell, John earns a smaller bonus. The percentage factor is multiplied by 0.5 percent of the net sales for all regions. As net sales increase, so does John's bonus.

Complete the Data Table

The final steps in creating the data table are selecting the table range and issuing the Data Table command.

5. Select the range B2:G7 as shown.

	A	B	C	D	E	F	G
1				**Expenses vs. Net Sales**			
2		0	1%	2%	4%	6%	8%
3	Net Sales	$ 1,000,000					
4		$ 2,000,000					
5		$ 3,000,000					
6		$ 4,000,000					
7		$ 5,000,000					

When selecting the range for a data table, you must include the formula, variables, and cells that will hold the calculated results in the selection. Notice that the text labels and input cells are not included.

6. Choose Data→Data Tools→What-If Analysis→Data Table from the Ribbon.

7. Follow these steps to choose the input cells:

Ⓐ Select cell A1 in the worksheet for the Row Input Cell.

Ⓑ Click in the Column Input Cell box and select cell A2 in the worksheet.

The Row Input Cell is the cell in which you want the row variables (Expenses vs. Net Sales) to be substituted. Likewise, the Column Input Cell substitutes the column variables (Net Sales). If you look at the formula in cell B2, you will see that these substitutions make sense.

8. Click OK in the Data Table dialog box.
The data table is completed as shown in the following illustration.

	A	B	C	D	E	F	G
1				**Expenses vs. Net Sales**			
2		0	1%	2%	4%	6%	8%
3	Net Sales	$ 1,000,000	4500	4000	3000	2000	1000
4		$ 2,000,000	9000	8000	6000	4000	2000
5		$ 3,000,000	13500	12000	9000	6000	3000
6		$ 4,000,000	18000	16000	12000	8000	4000
7		$ 5,000,000	22500	20000	15000	10000	5000

9. Save ▢ the changes.

Apply Conditional Formatting to the Table

John has a bottom line when it comes to his quarterly bonus. He is unwilling to accept a bonus that is less than $10,000. For this reason, you will format the cells in the data table using a conditional format. Cells in which the bonus is at least $10,000 will be formatted with a blue color. John will quickly see which combinations of Net Sales and Expenses vs. Net Sales are acceptable.

10. Select the range C3:G7.

11. Choose Home→Styles→Conditional Formatting→New Rule from the Ribbon.

12. In the New Formatting Rule dialog box, choose the rule type Format Only Cells that Contain.

13. Follow these steps to set the condition:

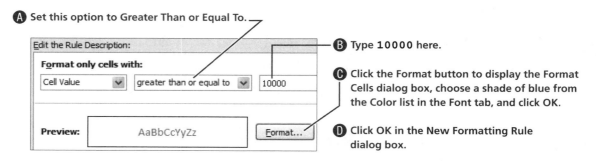

Ⓐ Set this option to Greater Than or Equal To.

Ⓑ Type **10000** here.

Ⓒ Click the Format button to display the Format Cells dialog box, choose a shade of blue from the Color list in the Font tab, and click OK.

Ⓓ Click OK in the New Formatting Rule dialog box.

Only values greater than or equal to 10000 should appear in blue. As you can see, this data table and conditional formatting clearly show which Net Sales and Expenses vs. Net Sales ratio combinations are required to achieve a $10,000 (or greater) bonus.

14. Feel free to experiment with your data table. For example, try changing the Net Sales variables in column B and the Expenses vs. Net Sales variables in row 2.
The data table will be recalculated each time you change a variable.

15. Save ▯ the changes when you have finished, and close the workbook.

Creating Trendlines

Trendlines are used on charts for data analysis and prediction. A trendline visually displays the trend (increasing or decreasing) of one data series in a chart. There are several types of trendlines available, each suited to the display of particular types of data. For example, a linear trendline works well with data that follow a fairly straight path. A moving average trendline smoothes out fluctuations in data by averaging two or more adjacent data points for each trendline data point.

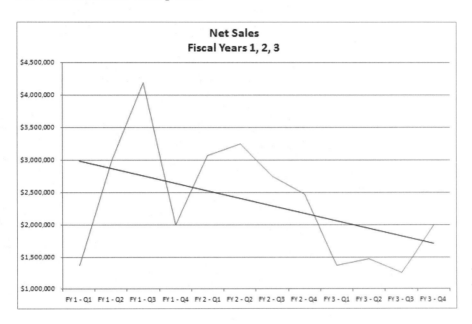

This linear trendline depicts the downward trend for Net Sales over three years.

!NOTE! *You cannot add a trendline to certain types of charts, such as 3-D, pie, and area charts.*

QUICK REFERENCE: CREATING A TRENDLINE

Task	Procedure
Add a trendline to a chart	■ Display the chart to which you wish to add a trendline. ■ Choose Layout→Analysis→Trendline ⬚ from the Ribbon. ■ Choose a trendline type. ■ Select a data series in the Add a Trendline Based on Series dialog box, if more than one exists in the chart.
Change the trendline type	■ Select the trendline. ■ Choose Layout→Analysis→Trendline ⬚ from the Ribbon. ■ Choose a trendline type.
Format the trendline	■ Right-click the trendline and choose Format Trendline from the context menu. ■ Choose the desired options in the Format Trendline dialog box.
Add objects specific to the chart type and trendline type	■ Select the trendline. ■ Display the Layout Ribbon and choose options from those displayed in the Analysis group.

Hands-On 15.7   Add a Trendline

In this exercise, you will add a trendline to an existing chart.

Insert a Trendline

1. Open the Net Sales Trend workbook from the Lesson 15 folder.
   The Summary worksheet and trend chart summarize net sales for four quarters of a year.

2. Display the Trend Chart worksheet.

3. Select the chart.

4. Choose Layout→Analysis→Trendline [icon] →Linear Trendline from the Ribbon.
   The new trendline appears. This best-fit line indicates that net sales are increasing at an excellent rate.

Edit the Trendline

5. Taking care to position the tip of the pointer arrow against the trendline as shown below, select the trendline (not the data series line).

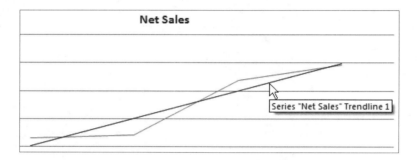

6. Choose Layout→Analysis→Trendline→Linear Forecast Trendline.
   The trendline lengthens to forecast net sales in the next two quarters.

7. Right-click the trendline and choose Format Trendline from the context menu. (Reposition the mouse pointer and right-click again if the context menu displays Format Plot Area rather than Format Trendline.)

8. In the Forecast area of the Format Trendline dialog box, change Forward from 2.0 periods to **1**.

9. Take a few moments to view the other options in the dialog box.

10. Click Close.
    The trendline now forecasts only one quarter in the future, a more conservative analysis.

11. Right-click the trendline and choose Format Trendline from the context menu.

12. Move the Format Trendline dialog box so that you may view the trendline.

13. Under Trendline Options in the dialog box, choose Moving Average.
    This type of trendline follows data fluctuations. In the next step, you will set more data points to be averaged, which will smooth out this trendline.

14. Change the Period box from 2 to **3** as shown and click Close.

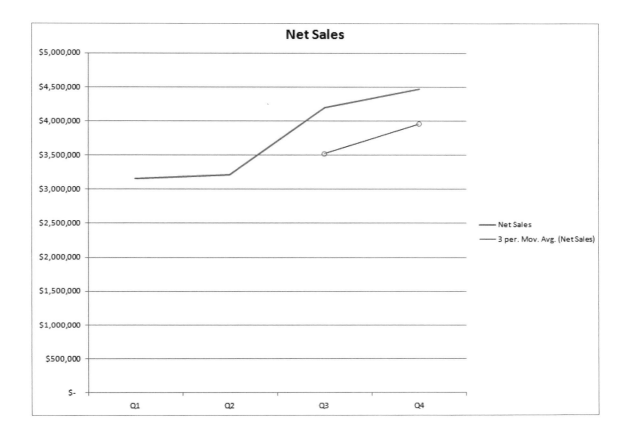

The trendline shortens and smooths out to reflect the greater number of data points being averaged for each point on the trendline. To use trendlines options effectively, an understanding of statistics in math is helpful.

15. Save ![save icon] the workbook.

Concepts Review

True/False Questions

1. Data is entered to all grouped worksheets at the same time.   TRUE FALSE
2. Functions other than SUM may be used when consolidating worksheets.   TRUE FALSE
3. Consolidation may be used only in worksheets that have identical layouts.   TRUE FALSE
4. Data validation may be used only in cells that contain numbers.   TRUE FALSE
5. Data validation helps to prevent a user from entering unacceptable data.   TRUE FALSE
6. Red circles around cells mean that the cells contain important data.   TRUE FALSE
7. Conditional formatting can apply colors to cells.   TRUE FALSE
8. Conditional formatting may be a applied to grouped worksheets.   TRUE FALSE
9. A data table may use up to four variables.   TRUE FALSE
10. A trendline indicates the general direction of a data series.   TRUE FALSE

Multiple Choice Questions

1. Which of the following may be accomplished while grouping worksheets?
   a. Group adjacent worksheets
   b. Group nonadjacent worksheets
   c. Change the width of a column in all grouped worksheets.
   d. All of the above

2. Which of the following may appear in cells as a result of conditional formatting?
   a. Trendlines
   b. Data tables
   c. Icons
   d. Macros

3. For what purpose is a data table used?
   a. To display all formulas in the worksheet
   b. To display all data in the worksheet
   c. To display error messages about formulas
   d. To display various results of a formula

4. Where would you find a trendline?
   a. Grouped worksheet
   b. Chart
   c. Data table
   d. Conditional format

# Skill Builders

Skill Builder 15.1   Group Worksheets and Consolidate Data by Category

In this exercise, you will complete a workbook that tracks compensation paid to independent contractors. The employer issues 1099 statements (similar to W-2 forms) to independent contractors at the end of the year for their income tax returns. The workbook contains a Year-to-Date worksheet as well as worksheets for each month. You will group the worksheets and enter the headings for all the sheets. In addition, you will use the Consolidate by Category option to consolidate the monthly data in the Year-to-Date worksheet.

Browse the Workbook

1. Open the sb-Consolidated Compensation workbook from the Lesson 15 folder.
   Notice that the Year-to-Date worksheet has column headings in row 3 but no data. The Consolidation command will insert the data.

2. Display the January worksheet.
   Six 1099 recipients are listed with their respective number of hours and compensation. This recipient list is different for each month because these temporary contractors come and go on a regular basis.

3. Select cell C4.
   Notice that the compensation is calculated as the hours multiplied by $21.35. The Consolidate command will combine the hours and compensation from the monthly worksheets. You can consolidate cells with both values and formulas, as in this exercise.

4. Display the February worksheet.
   Seven recipients are listed for February. Several of these recipients differ from those in the January worksheet.

5. Display the March worksheet and notice that, again, the recipient list has changed.
   In a later step, you will use the Consolidate command for the Year-to-Date worksheet. You cannot consolidate by position, as you did in the Bonus Analysis workbook, because the monthly sheets have different layouts. The list of independent contractors varies.

Group Multiple Worksheets

Next you will group the worksheets to prepare for data entry and formatting.

6. Display the Year-to-Date worksheet.

7. Hold down ⟨Shift⟩ and click the March sheet tab.
   Notice that the sheets are now grouped so that whatever you do on one worksheet occurs simultaneously on all worksheets in the group.

Enter and Format Labels Across Worksheets

8. Select cell A1 in the Year-to-Date worksheet and enter **Compensation**.

9. Merge and center the label in cell A1 across cells A1:C1.

10. With cells A1:C1 still selected, choose Home→Styles→Cell Styles→Themed Cell Styles→Accent1 (white text with dark blue fill) from the Ribbon.

11. Select cells A3:C3 and choose Home→Styles→Cell Styles→Themed Cell Styles→ 20% - Accent1 (black text with light blue fill) from the Ribbon.

12. Deselect the highlighted cells.

13. Right-click the Year-to-Date sheet tab and choose Ungroup Sheets from the context menu.

14. Edit cell A1 in the Year-to-Date worksheet to **1099 Recipient Compensation**.

15. Display each of the monthly worksheets.
    Notice that the formatting you applied while the worksheets were grouped appears on every worksheet. You edited the title in cell A1 while the worksheets were ungrouped, so only the Year-to-Date worksheet reflects that change.

Select Data to Consolidate

16. Display the Year-to-Date worksheet and select cell A4 as the starting point for the consolidated data.
    When consolidating by category, it is best to select the starting point of the consolidated data prior to issuing the Consolidate command.

17. Choose Data→Data Tools→Consolidate ▦ from the Ribbon.

18. Move the Consolidate dialog box until the range A4:C12 and the sheet tabs at the bottom of the Excel window are visible, if necessary.
    In the next few steps, you will specify the range references you wish to consolidate. You will do this by selecting the ranges in the various sheets and adding them to the All References list.

19. Follow these steps to set consolidation options in the Consolidate dialog box:

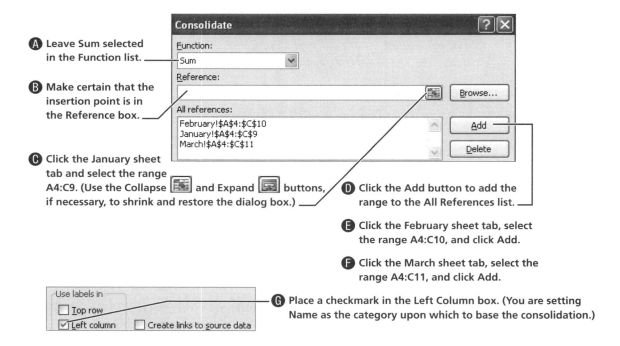

Ⓐ Leave Sum selected in the Function list.

Ⓑ Make certain that the insertion point is in the Reference box.

Ⓒ Click the January sheet tab and select the range A4:C9. (Use the Collapse ▦ and Expand ▦ buttons, if necessary, to shrink and restore the dialog box.)

Ⓓ Click the Add button to add the range to the All References list.

Ⓔ Click the February sheet tab, select the range A4:C10, and click Add.

Ⓕ Click the March sheet tab, select the range A4:C11, and click Add.

Ⓖ Place a checkmark in the Left Column box. (You are setting Name as the category upon which to base the consolidation.)

Review the references in the All References list. You build a consolidation by adding references to this list. Notice that the row labels in column A are included in the references. The Consolidate command uses the labels in the left column (column A) to determine which rows to consolidate from the monthly sheets. Excel will create one consolidated row in the Year-to-Date worksheet for each name. For example, the name Dennis Johnson appears in two worksheets. Excel will create one Dennis Johnson row in the Year-to-Date sheet summing his numbers.

20. Click OK in the Consolidate dialog box.

The Year-to-Date worksheet displays the consolidated numbers shown in the following illustration.

	A	B	C
1	1099 Recipient Compensation		
2			
3	Name	Hours	Compensation
4	Johnson, Dennis E.	27	576.45
5	Lake, Cheryl Y.	77	1,643.95
6	Parson, Robin J.	67	1,430.45
7	Williams, Scott G.	35	747.25
8	Richardson, Eddie	46	982.10
9	Jones, William T.	51	1,088.85
10	Thomas, Wanda M.	65	1,387.75
11	Wilson, Leslie A. Jr.	38	811.30
12	Simpson, Lakisha D.	12	256.20
13	Ellis, Ellen E.	10	213.50
14	Williams, Stewart M.	8	170.80

Notice that each name appears just once in the consolidated list. Feel free to browse through the monthly sheets. You will notice that the consolidated numbers are sums of the numbers for the individual months.

21. Deselect the highlighted range.

Add Another Worksheet

You can easily consolidate the data again by adding a consolidation range for any monthly worksheet added later. In the next few steps, you will add an April worksheet and reconsolidate the data.

22. Copy the March worksheet and name the new sheet **April**.

23. In the April worksheet, select rows 6 and 7 and use the Delete command to remove them.

Scott Williams and Eddie Richardson did not receive compensation in April.

24. Add the recipients and hours shown to rows 10 and 11.

10	Sanchez, Pedro	23	491.05
11	Yee, Doness U.	21	448.35

Excel will automatically calculate the compensation in cells C10 and C11 when you Tab *through the cells during data entry.*

Consolidate Again

25. Display the Year-to-Date worksheet.

26. Select all consolidated data in the range A4:C14 and tap the [Delete] key.
It is best to delete the existing data before reconsolidating because the new consolidation will overwrite the existing data. If the new consolidation has fewer rows than the original consolidation, there will be leftover (and incorrect) rows at the bottom of the consolidated data.

27. Select cell A4 and choose Data→Data Tools→Consolidate ▦ from the Ribbon.
Notice that the consolidation ranges you chose are still in the All References list. Now you need only add the April range.

28. Make certain that the insertion point is in the Reference box.

29. Click the April sheet tab and select the range A4:C11 in the worksheet.

30. Click the Add button in the dialog box.

31. Click OK to complete the consolidation.
The updated consolidation includes 13 unique names in rows 4–16.

32. Deselect the highlighted range.

33. Save ▦ the changes and close the workbook.

Skill Builder 15.2   Construct a Loan Payment Data Table with Conditional Formatting

In this exercise, you will create a two-variable data table. The data table will calculate monthly payments on a car loan using various interest rates and payment periods.

Set Up the Data Table

1. Start a new workbook and enter the data shown. Make certain that the numbers in column B are formatted with percent symbols.

	A	B	C	D	E	F	G
1	Car Loan Analysis						
2							
3	Opening Balance		$ 22,000				
4							
5			Months				
6			36	42	48	54	60
7	Rate	8%					
8		9%					
9		10%					
10		11%					
11		12%					
12		13%					
13		14%					
14		15%					

2. Select cell B6, the upper-left corner cell of the data table.
   In the next step, you will enter a formula that uses the PMT function. The PMT function calculates payments using a monthly interest rate, number of payments, and opening balance as arguments.

3. Enter the function **=PMT(B5/12,A6,-C3)** and complete the entry.
   The result displays as #DIV/0! because cells B5 and A6 (the input cells for the data table) are empty. The formula is interpreted as follows.

   The B5/12 reference is the interest rate argument. The B5 reference is divided by 12 because the payments will be made monthly, and the rates in column B are annual rates. The interest rates in column B will be substituted into input cell B5 when the Data Table command is issued.

   The A6 reference is the second input cell. The months in row 6 will be substituted into this cell when the Data Table command is issued.

   Cell C3 contains the loan amount. The PMT function always returns a negative number, so you added a minus (–) sign to reverse it to a positive number.

Complete the Data Table

4. Select the range B6:G14 and choose Data→Data Tools→What-If Analysis→Data Table from the Ribbon.

5. Enter **A6** as the row input cell and **B5** as the column input cell.

6. Click OK and the table is calculated.

7. Taking care not to select the months in row 6 or rates in column B, select the range C7:G14.

8. Format the selected cells as Comma Style with two decimal places.
Assume that your budget allows a maximum payment of $550.

9. Apply a conditional format that changes the font color to green when the value is less than or equal to 550.

Use the Conditional Formatting Rules Manager

The green values may not be easy to differentiate from the other values. You will edit the rule in the Conditional Formatting Rules Manager window.

10. With the range C7:G14 still selected, choose Home→Styles→Conditional Formatting→ Manage Rules from the Ribbon.
Close the dialog box and select the correct range if the rule that you created is not displayed in the Conditional Formatting Rules Manager dialog box.

11. Follow these steps to edit the rule:

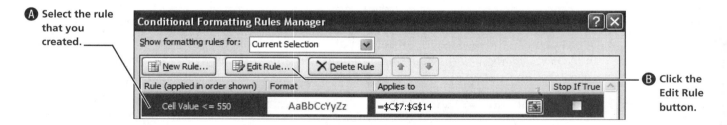

Ⓐ **Select the rule that you created.**

Ⓑ **Click the Edit Rule button.**

12. Click the Format button in the Edit Formatting Rule dialog box.

13. Change the font to white, choose a green fill, and click OK.

14. Click OK in the Edit Formatting Rule dialog box.
Your worksheet should match this example.

		Months				
5						
6		#DIV/0!	36	42	48	54	60
7	Rate	8%	689.40	602.29	537.08	486.47	446.08
8		9%	699.59	612.58	547.47	496.97	456.68
9		10%	709.88	622.97	557.98	507.59	467.43
10		11%	720.25	633.46	568.60	518.35	478.33
11		12%	730.71	644.06	579.34	529.24	489.38
12		13%	741.27	654.77	590.20	540.27	500.57
13		14%	751.91	665.57	601.18	551.42	511.90
14		15%	762.64	676.48	612.28	562.71	523.38

Adjust the Loan Amount

Now imagine that you want to see the same analysis for a different loan amount. This is easily accomplished by changing the loan amount in cell C3.

15. Select cell C3 and change 22000 to **25000**.

16. Complete the entry, and the data table will recalculate.
The conditional formatting also adjusts to highlight only cells with a monthly payment of $550 or less.

#DIV/0!	36	42	48	54	60
8%	783.41	684.42	610.32	552.81	506.91
9%	794.99	696.11	622.13	564.73	518.96
10%	806.68	707.92	634.06	576.81	531.18
11%	818.47	719.85	646.14	589.04	543.56
12%	830.36	731.89	658.35	601.41	556.11
13%	842.35	744.05	670.69	613.94	568.83
14%	854.44	756.33	683.16	626.62	581.71
15%	866.63	768.73	695.77	639.44	594.75

Respond to an Alert

The PMT formula cell displays a small triangle icon in the upper left of the cell to alert you to the #DIV/0! error. For the purpose of the data table, this is not actually an error.

17. Select cell B6, click the alert button displayed to the left of the cell, and choose Ignore Error from the context menu.

If you were to determine that #DIV/0! would confuse other workbook users, you could format the cell with a white font to "hide" the message, or you could hide the cell and turn on worksheet protection.

18. Save as **sb-Loan Data Table** in the Lesson 15 folder then close the workbook.

Skill Builder 15.3　Work with Trendlines

In this exercise, you will add a trendline to the data on an existing chart.

1. Open the sb-Trendline workbook from the Lesson 15 folder and take a moment to review the data.
   The Net Sales worksheet depicts the quarterly net sales over the course of four years.

2. Display the Trend Chart worksheet.
   This chart displays the four years of data. Notice that the data pattern fluctuates up and down. A linear trendline would not provide much help in analyzing the trends.

3. Select the chart and choose Layout→Analysis→Trendline→More Trendline Options from the Ribbon.

4. Move the Format Trendline dialog box to one side of the workbook window as you work so that you can view the trendline.

5. Under Trend/Regression Type in the Format Trendline dialog box, choose Polynomial.
   This trendline type is useful for tracking fluctuations in data. Inspecting the columns in the chart indicates several significant changes over the four-year period.

6. Use the spinner button to set the Order option to 4 as shown.
   Each click displays an additional rise or dip in the trendline.

   One way to compare the accuracy of a trendline is to display its R-squared value. The closer a trendline's R-squared value is to 1, the better it fits the data.

7. Place a checkmark in the Display R-squared Value on Chart option near the bottom of the dialog box.
   The R-squared value displays near the end of the trendline as $R^2 = 0.531$.

8. Change the Order option to **6** next to Polynomial and click Close.
   The trendline displays $R^2 = 0.628$. Since its value is closer to 1, this trendline represents a more accurate forecast. An ideal trendline would have an R^2 value very close to 1.

9. Save ![save icon] the changes and close the workbook.

Assessments

Assessment 15.1   Consolidate Data by Category

In this exercise, you will consolidate the shares bought and sold each month into a summary investment portfolio worksheet.

1. Open **as-Consolidated Portfolio** from the Lesson 15 folder.
   The workbook contains a Beginning Balance worksheet showing the number of shares owned at the beginning of the year. The January and February worksheets include the shares purchased, reinvested, and sold.

2. Copy a worksheet to create the March worksheet and Portfolio Activity worksheet shown in the illustrations below. (Copying will ensure that the column widths and cell formats are the same as in the other worksheets.) Make certain to enter the data in the correct cells as shown because you will consolidate the data by position later in this exercise.

	A	B	C	D	E
1	March				
2					
3	Investment Name	Shares Purchased	Shares Reinvested	Shares Sold	Net Shares
4	Prigem			12.39	(12.39)
5	American Fund	40.52	1.23		41.75
6	Guardian Balanced Fund	12.31	4.70		17.01

	A	B	C	D	E
1	Portfolio Activity				
2					
3	Investment Name	Shares Purchased	Shares Reinvested	Shares Sold	Net Shares

3. Rename the sheet tabs using the entries from cell A1.

4. Use the Consolidate command to combine the Beginning Balance and three monthly worksheets into the Portfolio Activity worksheet.
   The names of eight investments and their consolidated numbers should result.

5. Sort the investments into alphabetical order on the Portfolio Activity worksheet.

6. Save 🖫 the changes and close the workbook.

Assessment 15.2　Construct a Mortgage Payment Data Table with Conditional Formatting

In this exercise, you will create a data table to calculate monthly payments for a home mortgage using various interest rates and periods.

1. Start a new workbook.

2. Begin creating the data table by typing labels in cells as needed.

3. Enter the loan amount **$200,000** in cell C3.

4. Enter interest rates from **6%**, **6.5%**, and up through **8.5%** in column B.

5. Enter the number of *months* for loan periods of 15, 20, 25, and 30 years in row 6.

6. Use the PMT function to create a formula in the appropriate cell. You used the PMT function in Skill Builder 15.2.

7. Issue the Data Table command.

8. Format the values in the data table as Comma Style with two decimal places.

9. Apply a conditional format that changes the font and fill color when a data table value is less than 1,550.01.

10. Clear any alert or error message that appears in a cell.

11. Save 💾 with the name **as-Mortgage Data Table** in the Lesson 15 folder then close the workbook.

Assessment 15.3　Create a Trendline

In this exercise, you will add a trendline to a column chart.

1. Open the as-Projected Revenue workbook.

2. Display the Chart worksheet.

3. Add a linear trendline for the Revenue series in the chart.

4. Save 💾 the changes and close the workbook.

Critical Thinking

Critical Thinking 15.1 Create an Investment Data Table

Rosa Richardson is considering investing in an IRA (Individual Retirement Account). Rosa is 35 years old and wants to retire by the time she turns 60. For this reason, she plans on making uniform, monthly IRA contributions for the next 25 years.

- Use Internet Explorer and a search engine of your choice to locate the maximum allowable IRA contribution per year for a person of Rosa's age.

- Based on the annual maximum contribution, determine the maximum monthly amount that Rosa could contribute.

- Start a new workbook and set up a data table that uses the FV (Future Value) function to calculate the future value of Rosa's IRA contributions assuming that she makes uniform monthly contributions for 25 years. Use interest rates as one of the variables in the data table. Use the rates 5 percent, 7 percent, 9 percent, 12 percent, and 15 percent to represent the potential returns Rosa could realize from various investment products. Use several monthly contributions from $100 to the maximum allowable amount as the other variable in the data table.

- Generate the data table results.

- Save as **ct-IRA Data Table** and close the workbook.

Critical Thinking 15.2   Consolidate a Personal Budget

In this exercise, you will create a monthly budget and enter estimated and actual expenses for a three-month period. Conditional formatting will help you spot actual expenses that are higher than estimated.

- Start a new workbook.

- Create a monthly budget worksheet for one person or a family for the month of January. Type labels in one or more rows in column A for the sources of income (paycheck, savings, support from a family member, and so on). Also include row labels for typical expenses (rent or mortgage payment, groceries, transportation, utilities, phone, books and supplies, entertainment, and so on). Add the label **Income Less Expenses** as the last row label in column A.

- Label column B as **Estimated**, column C as **Actual**, and column D as **Difference**.

- Enter values for the estimated income and expenses in column B. Also enter amounts for actual income and expenses in column C, including some values that are higher or lower than the estimated values. Use amounts that would be typical for one person or a family. To preserve privacy, do not use your actual personal data. Format values using an appropriate number format.

- Create formulas for the total income and total expenses in the Estimated, Actual, and Difference columns. Create the Net Income Less Expenses formulas.

- Create formulas in column D to calculate the difference between estimated and actual amounts for all data rows. Make certain that the formula results display positive and negative numbers correctly.

- Create a conditional formatting rule for the difference amounts in column C. Flag the difference amount when income is less than the estimate and expenses are over the estimate.

- Copy the January worksheet to create the February and March worksheets. Change a few values in the February and March worksheets.

- Create a summary worksheet and consolidate the monthly data.

- Save ![save icon] as **ct-Monthly Budget**.

LESSON 16

Collaborating in Exce

ollaborating on projects is a typical business activity. The Internet simplifies exchanging documents and other types of information to coordinate geographically diverse activities. However, the lack of face-to-face contact also places a premium on sharing information efficiently. In this lesson, you will learn how to participate in workbook collaboration. You will set up folders for project files, place comments into an Excel workbook, and prepare to send the workbook as an email attachment. The ability to create shared workbooks is one of Excel's most powerful collaboration features. You can set up a workbook that several other users can access simultaneously on a network server. Excel's change history tracking feature can help you avoid and resolve potential conflicts when data is edited by multiple users. You will learn how to merge all of the users' changes automatically into one workbook.

LESSON OBJECTIVES

After studying this lesson, you will be able to:

- Create folders to organize project documents
- Insert, view, and print comments in workbooks
- Track and consolidate changes made by multiple authors
- Share workbooks for simultaneous collaboration
- Merge multiple versions of a shared workbook
- Send workbooks by email

Case Study: Collaborating on Grant Reports

Grace Vargas is the director for the Connections Grant at Columbia State College. She administers grant funds awarded to the college to support various educational activities and uses Excel for several of the project activities. Grace administers a consortium project that involves another college as well as her own. She must assemble financial data from both colleges each quarter and submit it by email to the granting agency to show how the funds were spent. Grace and her colleagues use email to transmit information back and forth in the form of messages and Excel workbooks.

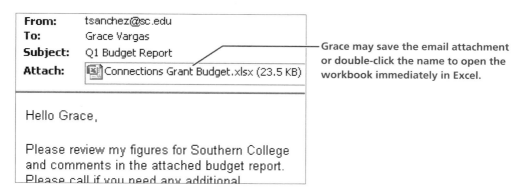

From:	tsanchez@sc.edu
To:	Grace Vargas
Subject:	Q1 Budget Report
Attach:	Connections Grant Budget.xlsx (23.5 KB)

Grace may save the email attachment or double-click the name to open the workbook immediately in Excel.

Hello Grace,

Please review my figures for Southern College and comments in the attached budget report. Please call if you need any additional

Grace and her colleagues use comments to ask questions and make suggestions. Comments can also help everyone involved in the project understand special formulas and values contained in worksheet cells.

When Grace points at the cell containing the comment marker, the comment pops up with Terry's question about a formula in the draft budget report.

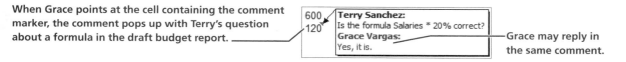

Terry Sanchez:
Is the formula Salaries * 20% correct?
Grace Vargas:
Yes, it is.

Grace may reply in the same comment.

Grace may also share a workbook with others working on the project. As they return revisions to the workbook, Grace uses Excel's Compare and Merge Workbooks command. Excel automatically enters all revisions from the other workbooks and marks them to be accepted or rejected. This allows Grace to review everyone's revisions in a single workbook.

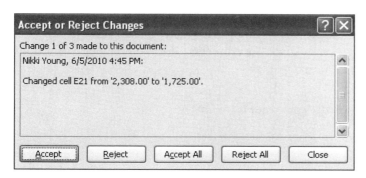

Accept or Reject Changes

Change 1 of 3 made to this document:

Nikki Young, 6/5/2010 4:45 PM:

Changed cell E21 from '2,308.00' to '1,725.00'.

[Accept] [Reject] [Accept All] [Reject All] [Close]

Grace may accept or reject each change that other collaborators made to the workbook.

Creating Folders in Excel

When you work on a project, you usually will create one or more folders on your computer to store the documents and other types of files with which you will work. This topic will give you practice in creating folders and teach you techniques to access the new folders quickly.

Working with Project Folders

Depending on the size of the project and the number of files you must organize, you may need to create more than one folder. You may create a main folder for the project as well as subfolders inside of it for major types of documents or major sections of the project. The following diagram displays an example of project folders.

This folder window displays the Grant Project main folder that Grace created for the project.

Grace created subfolders to hold documents for each quarterly report.

Various files that apply to the entire grant project are kept in the main folder.

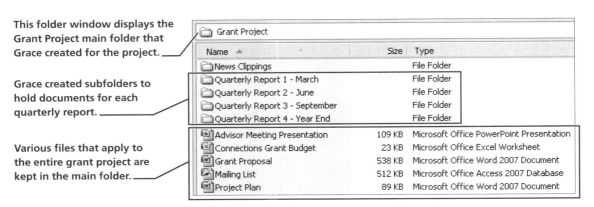

Creating Folders

You don't need to leave Excel to create a new folder. Simply choose the Open or Save As command, and then click the Create New Folder button on the dialog box toolbar. You may create a single folder or several. If desired, you may also create folders inside other folders.

The Create New Folder button

Renaming Folders

You may rename folders from within Excel by right-clicking the folder and choosing Rename from the context menu. Or you may click once on the folder, pause one second, and click again to select the folder name for renaming.

 **The folder name ready for renaming**

Hands-On 16.1 Create and Rename a Project Folder

In this exercise, you will create a folder from within the Excel program.

1. Start Excel and choose Office→Open from the Ribbon.

Uni

2. Follow these steps to begin creating the new folder:

 NOTE! *The dialog box may appear slightly different depending on your Windows version.*

Ⓐ **Navigate to the Lesson 16 folder in your file storage location.**   Ⓑ **Click the Create New Folder button.**

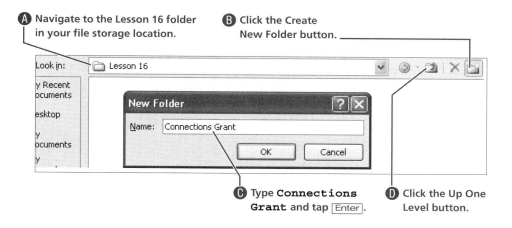

Ⓒ **Type** **Connections Grant** **and tap** Enter.   Ⓓ **Click the Up One Level button.**

The new folder appears at the top of the file list. It is now ready to store files.

3. Right-click the Connections Grant folder and choose Rename from the bottom of the context menu.
   The folder name is selected for renaming.

4. Type **Grant Project** and tap Enter.

5. Click the Cancel button in the Open dialog box.
   This cancels the Open command, not the creation of the new folder.

6. Leave the Excel window open.

Organizing Workbooks in Folders

Many computer users store their files in the Documents or My Documents folder found on most Windows systems. Sometimes you will store files in a separate folder such as the one you just created. This allows you to place your project on a portable drive to use at another computer. Excel's Open and Save As dialog boxes allow you to move or copy files to different folders and to delete files from within Excel.

QUICK REFERENCE: ORGANIZING WORKBOOKS IN FOLDERS

Task	Procedure
Create a new folder	■ Choose Office→Open from the Ribbon.
	■ Navigate to the folder that will contain the new folder.
	■ Click the Create New Folder ![button] button in the dialog box toolbar.
	■ Type the folder name and tap Enter.
Rename a folder	■ Choose Office→Open from the Ribbon.
	■ Navigate to the folder containing the folder to be renamed.
	■ Right-click the desired folder, type the new name, and tap Enter.
Copy or move files	■ Choose Office→Open from the Ribbon.
	■ Navigate to the folder containing the files to be copied or moved.
	■ Select the desired file. Use Ctrl or Shift to select multiple files.
	■ Use Ctrl+C to copy or Ctrl+X to cut the files.
	■ Navigate to the destination folder.
	■ Use Ctrl+V to paste the files.

Hands-On 16.2   Copy Files to a Folder

In this exercise, you will copy some files into the folder you created in the previous exercise and then open a workbook from that folder.

Copy Four Files to a Folder

1. Choose Office→Open from the Ribbon and navigate to the Lesson 16 folder in your file storage location.

2. Follow these steps to copy the files:

 NOTE! *The display of files will appear slightly different depending on your Windows version and the type of view that is selected.*

A Scroll down the list, if necessary, until the Connections files are visible.

B Select the Connections Grant Budget file.

C Hold down Ctrl and click both the Connections Grant Budget Merged 1 file and the Connections Grant, Southern College Budget file; then release Ctrl.

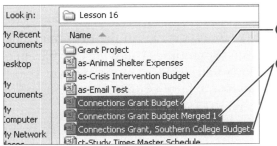

The Ctrl key allows you to select multiple contiguous or noncontiguous files.

3. Use Ctrl+C from the keyboard to copy the files to the Clipboard.
   The files' appearance does not change, but the files have been copied.

4. Scroll up, if necessary, until the Grant Project folder is visible at the top of the file list, and then double-click the folder to open it.

5. Use Ctrl + V from the keyboard to paste the files.
The files are copied into the Grant Project folder.

6. Click Cancel to exit the Open dialog box.

Open a File in the Folder

7. Choose Office→Open from the Ribbon.

8. Navigate to the Grant Project folder, if necessary.
Navigating to a folder and opening files from it is easy as long as you keep track of the locations of your folders.

9. Open the Connections Grant, Southern College Budget workbook file. (Do not open Connections Grant Project.)

Inserting and Viewing Comments

Excel's Comment feature is a great tool for online collaboration. A comment is a text note that you can embed inside a workbook cell without cluttering the normal view of the workbook. You may display all comments on a worksheet and even print them.

When to Use a Comment

Comments are an excellent way to handle many situations. You may want to insert a comment:

- To document the formula or value in a cell.

- To record a question about the worksheet data to be followed up later.

- To ask a question of an online collaborator without placing it into the normally printed page of the workbook.

Viewing Comments

When someone inserts a comment, Excel places a small red triangle at the top-right corner of the cell. When you point at the cell containing the red triangle, Excel displays the name of the author and the text of the comment. You also may display or hide one or all comments using commands in the Comments group on the Review Ribbon. The following illustration shows a cell and its associated comment.

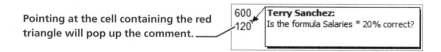

Pointing at the cell containing the red triangle will pop up the comment.

600
120

Terry Sanchez:
Is the formula Salaries * 20% correct?

Navigating Through Comments

You may jump from one comment to the next with the Next and Previous commands in the Ribbon. Using these commands is especially useful in large worksheets. When you reach the last comment in the workbook, the Next command starts over with the first comment in the workbook. The following figure displays the Comments group commands on the Ribbon.

These buttons navigate backward and forward through the comments.

 ## Hands-On 16.3   Review Comments

In this exercise, you will review comments inserted into the workbook by Terry Sanchez.

1. Follow these steps to display some comments on the Southern College worksheet of the Connection Grant, Southern College Budget workbook:

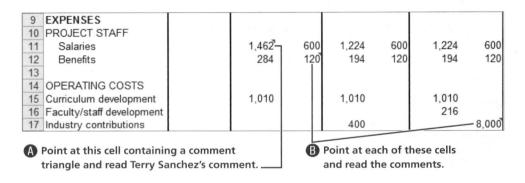

A Point at this cell containing a comment triangle and read Terry Sanchez's comment.

B Point at each of these cells and read the comments.

2. Choose Review→Comments→Show All Comments 🔲 from the Ribbon.
   All comments on the worksheet are displayed when you choose this command.

3. Choose Review→Comments→Show All Comments 🔲 from the Ribbon again to toggle off the display of the comments.

4. Choose Review→Comments→Next 🔲 from the Ribbon

5. Repeat the Next command to view the second comment.

6. Choose Review→Comments→Previous 🔲 from the Ribbon.
   The Next and Previous commands are useful for navigating through comments one by one.

7. Issue the Next command three times until prompted that you are at the end of the workbook.

8. Click OK in the Microsoft Office Excel dialog box to start over at the first comment.

9. Leave the workbook open.

Setting the Username

Before you insert comments, you should set the username to identify that the comment came from you. You make this setting in the Excel Options window in the Popular category. Once you set the username, Excel will keep this setting until the username is changed to something else.

 NOTE! *You may not have permission rights to change the username on a classroom computer. The computer number may display as the username on a network of computers, or all computers may have the same username.*

Inserting Comments

You may insert a comment into any cell with the New Comment command on the Ribbon or by right-clicking a cell and choosing Insert Comment from the context menu. A comment is specific to a cell; you cannot assign a comment to a range of cells. You cannot insert more than one comment box in a cell, but you may add to an existing comment. After you give the command, a comment box appears in which you may type the text of the comment. Clicking outside the comment box hides it when Show All Comments is turned off.

FROM THE KEYBOARD
Shift + F2 to insert comment

 TIP! *Tap Enter after typing a comment. If another user adds to your comment later, that person's username will start on a separate line rather than the same line as your comment.*

Adding to Comments

You may add to comments made by other authors by clicking in the comment box and typing. If the comment is not displayed, you may select the cell and choose Edit Comment from the Ribbon or context menu. When you click to add to a comment made by another author, that author's username and text remain in the comment box and cannot be deleted or edited. Your username appears after the previous author's text followed by your typed addition. To remove the previous author's comment, you must delete the entire comment box and then may insert a new comment in the cell.

TIP! *The New Comment command on the Ribbon changes to Edit Comment when a comment box is selected.*

Example of an Edited Comment

As she reads comments inserted by her counterpart at the other college, Grace notices one that asks a question. Rather than insert a new comment, Grace decides to add her answer by editing the existing comment. Grace also applies a different text color to this edit so that the other readers can readily distinguish her addition from the original comment.

Formatting Comment Text

You may change most text attributes for your comment using commands on the Home Ribbon, but the Font Color command is not available on the Ribbon. Instead, you should use the Format Comment command to display the Font dialog box, where you may change the font color.

Positioning and Sizing a Comment

A comment box may be moved by dragging its border or using the cursor keys to nudge the box. You may resize a comment box by dragging any of the eight resizing handles that appear around its edge. A comment box does not expand automatically to display all the text of a lengthy comment. You may use cursor keys to scroll through text in a comment, but resizing the comment box will ensure that everyone can read the entire comment.

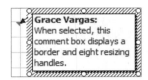

Grace Vargas:
When selected, this comment box displays a border and eight resizing handles.

QUICK REFERENCE: WORKING WITH COMMENTS

Task	Procedure
Associate your name with new comments	■ Choose Office→Excel Options→Popular from the Ribbon. ■ Under Personalize Your Copy of Microsoft Office, enter your name in the User Name box.
Insert a comment in a worksheet cell	■ Select the desired cell. ■ Choose Review→Comments→New Comment ⬚ from the Ribbon (or right-click on the desired cell and choose Insert Comment from the context menu). ■ Type the desired text in the comment box. ■ Click outside the comment box to complete the comment.
Make a comment pop up and then hide it	■ Point at the cell containing the comment triangle for about one second to make the comment box pop up. ■ Point at any other cell to hide the comment.
Show or hide a comment	■ Select the cell containing the comment triangle. ■ Choose Review→Comments→Show/Hide Comment ⬚ from the Ribbon (or right-click the cell and choose Show/Hide Comments from the context menu).
Show or hide all comments in a workbook	■ Choose Review→Comments→Show All Comments ⬚ from the Ribbon.

QUICK REFERENCE: WORKING WITH COMMENTS (CONTINUED)

Task	Procedure
Navigate through comments	■ Choose Review→Comments→Next from the Ribbon to find the next comment. ■ Choose Review→Comments→Previous from the Ribbon to go back one comment.
Add to a comment	■ Select the cell containing the comment. ■ Choose Review→Comments→Edit Comment from the Ribbon (or right-click on the cell with the comment and choose Edit Comment from the context menu) if the comment box is not visible. ■ Edit the comment text normally. You may change the text color of your addition if you like. ■ Click outside the comment box to complete the comment.
Format comment text	■ Select the desired comment cell and choose Review→Comments→Insert Comment or Edit Comment from the Ribbon, as needed (or right-click the cell and choose the command from the context menu). ■ Select existing text or position the insertion point for new next. ■ Choose Home→Cells→Format→Format Comment from the Ribbon (or right-click inside the comment box and choose Format Comment from the context menu). ■ Change the font, size, and color, as desired.
Move and resize a comment	■ Display the comment. ■ Drag its border to move the comment box. ■ Drag one of the eight resizing handles to resize.
Delete a comment	■ Select the desired comment cell and choose Review→Comments→Delete Comment from the Ribbon (or right-click on the cell and choose Delete Comment from the context menu).

 ## Hands-On 16.4   Insert and Add to Comments

In this exercise, you will insert a new comment into a cell and edit an existing comment with Grace's answer to a question. Then you will move comments so that the underlying cells are visible.

Before You Begin: Verify with your instructor, staff, or class notes whether you have permission to change the username on your computer. Verify the procedure for restoring the original username if you do have permission.

Set the Username

1. Choose Office→Excel Options from the Ribbon. Display the Popular category, if not already displayed.

2. Under Personalize Your Copy of Microsoft Office, notice the current User Name.

 NOTE! *Click Cancel and skip to step 5 if you do not have permission to change the username on your computer.*

3. As directed by your instructor, write the current username *exactly as shown* so that you may restore that name at the end of this exercise, or write the restoration procedure in the space provided:

_____

4. Change the existing username in the User Name box to your first name and last name, and click OK to save the change.

Insert a Comment

5. Verify that the Connections Grant, Southern College Budget workbook is open.

6. Right-click cell G20 and choose Insert Comment from the context menu.
   A comment box appears. Notice that the username is exactly as entered in the User Name box.

7. Type the following comment in the comment box:

   Participation in the League for Innovation conference.

8. Tap Enter, and then select cell G20 to close the Edit Comment box and hide your comment.

9. Point at cell G20 to pop up your comment.

Add to a Comment

10. Right-click cell D12 and choose Edit Comment from the context menu.
    The comment box appears and displays Terry Sanchez's question. Your computer's username appears next, followed by the insertion point (text cursor). Drag down the center-bottom handle of the comment box to enlarge the box, if necessary.

11. Right-click anywhere in the comment text and choose Format Comment from the context menu.

12. In the Font dialog box, drop down the Color list, choose a new text color, such as Blue, and then click OK.

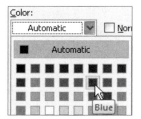

13. Type the following: **Yes, it is.**

14. Select cell D12 to close the Edit Comment box.

15. Right-click cell D12 and choose Show/Hide Comments from the context menu.
    Only your comment text changes color to help other readers notice that the comment has been edited. Terry Sanchez's comment is not affected. You could also drag to select your username and change its color using the Format Comment command.

Move a Comment

16. Choose Review→Comments→Show All Comments 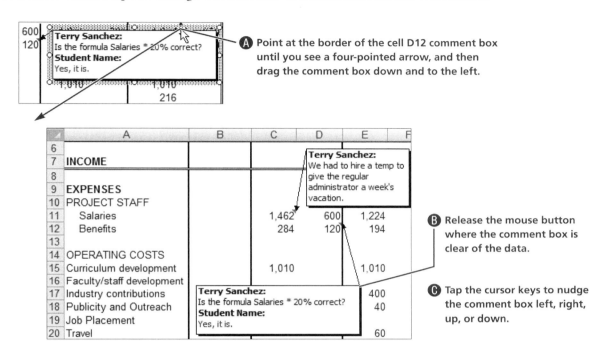 from the Ribbon to display all comments.

Notice that some comments cover worksheet data or overlap another comment. You will move a comment off the data portion of the workbook.

17. Follow these steps to change the location of a comment on the worksheet:

Ⓐ Point at the border of the cell D12 comment box until you see a four-pointed arrow, and then drag the comment box down and to the left.

Ⓑ Release the mouse button where the comment box is clear of the data.

Ⓒ Tap the cursor keys to nudge the comment box left, right, up, or down.

A line still connects the comment to its cell. You may move a comment box to any location on the worksheet so it is out of the way of important data. This may be necessary before you print the comments on the worksheet, as you will learn to do in the next topic.

Delete a Comment and Save the Workbook

18. Right-click cell H17 and choose Delete Comment from the context menu.

19. Save the changes.

20. Leave the workbook open for the next exercise.

Printing Comments

Excel's default setting is to suppress the printing of comments. To print the comments in a workbook, you choose a comments printing mode in the Page Setup dialog box. You may print each currently displayed comment where it appears on the worksheet or print all comments (whether displayed or not) on a separate sheet.

QUICK REFERENCE: PRINTING COMMENTS

Task	Procedure
Print the comments in a workbook	■ If you are going to print comments as they appear on the worksheets, display all comments that you want printed. ■ Choose Page Layout→Page Setup dialog box launcher from the Ribbon. 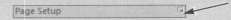 ■ Display the Sheet tab in the Page Setup dialog box. ■ Under Print, choose a print mode from the Comments list.
Switch off printing comments	■ Choose Page Layout→Page Setup dialog box launcher from the Ribbon. ■ Under Print, choose (None) from the Comments list.

 ## Hands-On 16.5   Print Comments

In this exercise, you will make settings to control the printing of comments. Then you will print the worksheet with comments printed on a separate sheet. Finally, you will switch off the printing of comments.

***Before You Begin:** The Connections Grant, Southern College Budget workbook should be open. The username should be set to your name if you have permission to do so (see steps 1–4 in Hands-On 16.4).*

1. Choose Review→Comments→Show All Comments 🔲 from the Ribbon to display all comments, if not already displayed.
   Notice that all of the comments on the worksheet are displayed. One of the page setup options prints comments as they are currently displayed on the worksheet.

2. Choose Page Layout→Page Setup dialog box launcher 🔲 from the Ribbon.

3. Display the Sheet tab in the Page Setup dialog box.

4. Under Print, drop down the Comments list and choose As Displayed on Sheet.

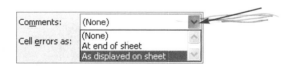

5. Click the Print Preview button near the bottom of the Sheet tab.
   Excel displays the Print Preview window. Click near a comment in the Print Preview window to zoom in to a closer view. The comments will print exactly as shown. You moved a comment in Hands-On 16.4 to avoid covering important worksheet data.

6. Click the Close Print Preview ❌ button.

7. Choose Page Layout→Page Setup dialog box launcher 🔲 from the Ribbon.

8. Display the Sheet tab in the Page Setup dialog box.

9. Choose At End of Sheet from the Comments list.

10. Display Print Preview and choose Next Page in the Print Preview Ribbon.
    A second sheet has been added to the printout. This prints the comments along with their cell references. Since the comments print on a separate sheet, they will not cover any of the data as they did with the As Displayed on Sheet option.

11. Click the Print button on the Print Preview toolbar, and then click OK to print the worksheet with a separate comments page.

12. Retrieve the printout from the printer.

Switch Off Printing Comments

13. Choose Page Layout→Page Setup dialog box launcher 🔲 from the Ribbon.

14. Display the Sheet tab in the Page Setup dialog box.

15. Choose (None) from the Comments list and click OK.
    Now the printing of comments is suppressed until you switch on this option again.

16. Save 🔲 the changes and close the workbook. Leave Excel open.

!NOTE! *Skip steps 17–18 if you did not change the username in Hands-On 16.4. If you did change the username, refer to the procedure that you wrote in step 3 of that exercise to restore the original username, which may vary from the following steps.*

Restore the Username

17. Choose Office→Excel Options from the Ribbon. Display the Popular category, if not already displayed.

18. Under Personalize Your Copy of Microsoft Office, carefully type the original username that you wrote down during Hands-On 16.4 in the User Name box and click OK.

Sharing Workbooks

In a workgroup environment, several team members may need to access the same workbook simultaneously. For example, they may be independently checking data, entering data into areas of a project workbook assigned to them, or updating rapidly changing data. You may set up a shared workbook for other users to edit. You may distribute the shared workbook using any of the following three methods:

1. Sending one copy to the first team member to make changes and then routing the same file to the next user

2. Placing one copy on a network server for all users to access

3. Giving each user his/her own copy in which to make changes

For all distribution methods, you will set the workbook as shared, track changes made by the various users, and review the changes. The Excel commands that you use will vary depending on the method.

Tracking Changes to Workbooks

When several people make changes to the same workbook, one person usually is assigned to review and approve each change. Excel can maintain a change history that tracks each change to the workbook. The change history displays the username of the person who made each change along with the original and new contents of each cell. The change history lets you review each change and accept or reject it. A changed cell may be identified by its border and a triangle in the upper-left corner. Each user's changes are marked in a different color.

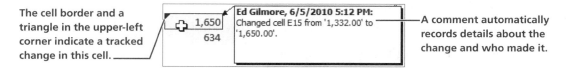

The cell border and a triangle in the upper-left corner indicate a tracked change in this cell.

Ed Gilmore, 6/5/2010 5:12 PM:
Changed cell E15 from '1,332.00' to '1,650.00'.

A comment automatically records details about the change and who made it.

Example of Tracked Changes at Work

Grace gives a workbook file to her assistant and asks him to contact several faculty members and then input any expenditures not yet included in the workbook. Grace turns on the Track Changes feature so that she can quickly see and review all changes her assistant made. When used alone, the Track Changes feature is employed for one workbook copy that travels from one person to another for changes and then back to the project manager to approve the changes. Switching on Track Changes also sets that workbook to be shared. In this case, Grace need not also use the Share Workbook command, which is described later in this lesson.

QUICK REFERENCE: TRACKING CHANGES TO A WORKBOOK	
Task	**Procedure**
Switch on tracking changes for a workbook	■ Choose Review→Changes→Track Changes→Highlight Changes from the Ribbon. ■ Make certain that the box next to Track Changes While Editing has a checkmark. This option also sets the workbook to be shared. ■ Under When, Who, and Where in the Highlight Changes dialog box, choose the options for the changes that should be highlighted. ■ Set whether you wish the changed cells to be highlighted on the screen and click OK. ■ Choose Yes when prompted to save the workbook. You must save the workbook to activate tracking changes.
Switch off tracking changes	■ Choose Review→Changes→Track Changes→Highlight Changes from the Ribbon. ■ Remove the checkmark from the box next to Track Changes While Editing. Note that the change history will be erased.

Hands-On 16.6 Track Changes to the Workbook

In this exercise, you will switch on the Track Changes feature and then edit several workbook cells. As you work, your edits will be recorded for later review.

1. Open the Connections Grant Budget workbook from the Grant Project folder, which is within the Lesson 16 folder in your file storage location. (Do not open Connections Grant, Southern College Budget.)

Check the Username

Because Track Changes records the name of each user who edits the workbook, you will check the username and change it to your own name, if necessary.

2. Choose Office→Excel Options from the Ribbon. Display the Popular category, if not already displayed.

3. Under Personalize Your Copy of Microsoft Office, notice the name in the User Name box.

 Click Cancel and skip to step 5 if you do not have permission rights to change the username on your computer.

4. Change the existing name in the User Name box to your first name and last name, if necessary, and click OK.

Switch On Track Changes

5. Choose Review→Changes→Track Changes→Highlight Changes from the Ribbon.

6. Follow these steps to set up tracking changes:

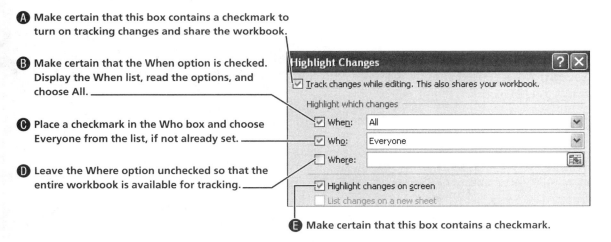

A Make certain that this box contains a checkmark to turn on tracking changes and share the workbook.

B Make certain that the When option is checked. Display the When list, read the options, and choose All.

C Place a checkmark in the Who box and choose Everyone from the list, if not already set.

D Leave the Where option unchecked so that the entire workbook is available for tracking.

E Make certain that this box contains a checkmark.

7. Click OK to close the dialog box, and then click OK when prompted to save the workbook. *You must save the file to activate the tracking changes feature. Now Excel is set up to record every change made to the workbook. Notice that* [Shared] *appears after the filename in the title bar at the top of the window, as shown in the following illustration. You will learn more about sharing workbooks later in this lesson.*

Connections Grant Budget [Shared] - Microsoft Excel

Edit the Workbook

8. Display the Columbia State College worksheet.

9. Select cell E21, which currently has a value of 2,308, and enter **1725**.
   Notice the border around the cell and the small triangle in the upper-left corner. This mark tells you that the cell has been edited since Track Changes was activated.

10. Right-click cell E21 and choose Insert Comment from the context menu. Type the comment **Network server was repaired.**

11. Click outside the comment box.

12. Read the change history and your comment for cell E21. (If necessary, point at cell E21 but do not click to display the comment box.)

13. If the comment box remains visible when you point to a different cell, choose Review→Comments→Show All Comments from the Ribbon to turn off the display of comments.

14. Select cell G16 and enter a value of **725**.

15. Select cell G11 and change the value to **5844**.

16. Save 💾 the changes.
    You are finished editing the workbook. Now read on to see how Grace reviews the edits.

Reviewing Tracked Changes

You may review changes to a workbook that has the Track Changes feature switched on. When you review changes, Excel can jump from one change to the next, giving you the opportunity to accept or reject each change. After you have reviewed a change, Excel keeps a record of the change until you deactivate the Track Changes feature. The following list describes your review options.

- **Accept:** An accepted change is kept in the cell. The change history records the old value that was replaced.

- **Reject:** A rejected change restores the old value in the cell. The change history records the new value that was rejected.

- **Accept All or Reject All:** All changes that have not yet been reviewed may be rejected or accepted with a single command.

The Change History

After you have reviewed changes to a worksheet, the change history retains a copy of the reviewed cells, including their old and new values and any rejected values. Thus, even after you accept a change, you may refer to the change history and manually reinstate an old or rejected value. You may view the change history by displaying a separate History worksheet. This worksheet is deleted automatically when you save the workbook, but you may give the command again.

⚠️**WARNING!** *When you switch off track changes, the change history is erased.*

QUICK REFERENCE: REVIEWING TRACKED CHANGES

Task	Procedure
Review and approve changes to a workbook	■ Choose Review→Changes→Track Changes→Accept/Reject Changes from the Ribbon. ■ Choose the categories of changes you wish to review in the Select Changes to Accept or Reject dialog box and click OK. ■ Use the buttons in the Accept or Reject Changes dialog box to navigate through the changes and accept or reject them as desired.
View the change history for a workbook	■ Choose Review→Changes→Track Changes→Accept/Reject Changes from the Ribbon. ■ Place a checkmark in the box next to List Changes on a New Sheet and click OK. The new History worksheet will remain visible until you give the Save command.

 Hands-On 16.7   Review the Changes

In this exercise, you will take on the role of Grace reviewing the changes.

Before You Begin: You may not have permission rights to change the username on your computer. If directed by your instructor, close the Connections Grant Budget workbook and open it on a different computer. That way, you may still use a different username while reviewing the changes.

Set the Username

1. Choose Office→Excel Options from the Ribbon. Display the Popular category, if not already displayed.

2. Under Personalize Your Copy of Microsoft Office, notice the current User Name.

 Click Cancel and skip to step 4 if you do not have permission rights to change the username on your computer.

3. Enter **Grace Vargas** in the User Name box and click OK to save the change.
   Notice that the borders around the changed cells have changed color. This alerts you that the cells were changed by someone other than Grace Vargas, the current user.

Accept or Reject Changes

4. Choose Review→Changes→Track Changes→Accept/Reject Changes from the Ribbon.
A dialog box appears in which you can select the changes to accept or reject.

5. Follow these steps to examine your choices:

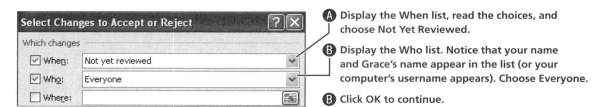

A Display the When list, read the choices, and choose Not Yet Reviewed.

B Display the Who list. Notice that your name and Grace's name appear in the list (or your computer's username appears). Choose Everyone.

B Click OK to continue.

The Accept or Reject Changes dialog box appears so that you may navigate from one changed cell to the next, as shown in the following illustration.

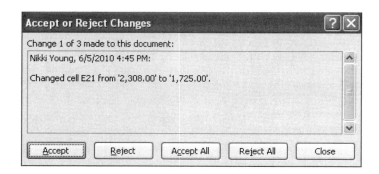

6. If necessary, drag the title bar to move the Accept or Reject Changes dialog box so that cell E21 is visible.
Notice that the first cell that you changed already has a marquee around it.

7. Point at cell E21, but do not click.
Notice that you cannot view the comment. Before reviewing a changed worksheet, you may want to display or review any comments first.

8. Click the Accept button to accept this change to the workbook.
Notice that cell E21 no longer has a change box around it. The change has been reviewed. The marquee moves on to the next changed cell, G16. You recognize this figure as advance payment for travel by a faculty member to a training seminar. You decide to reject this change because you know that this expense should not be recorded until next quarter, when the training actually takes place.

9. Click the Reject button.
Cell G16 reverts to its old value, which is blank.

10. Click the Accept button for cell G11.
Notice that the change boxes have returned to cells E21 and G11, where you accepted the change. These cells will remain marked until you switch off Track Changes.

11. Scroll down so that row 16 is at the top of the window.
This allows enough space to view the comment in cell E21, which you will do next.

12. Point at cell E21.

Notice that the entry from the change history appears for this cell. It tells you the name of the person who changed the cell, the old and new values, and the name of the person who entered the comment.

13. Scroll up until row 1 is visible.

14. Save 💾 the workbook.

The change history is not complete unless you save the workbook. Next you will create a change history worksheet.

View the Change History

15. Choose Review→Changes→Track Changes→Highlight Changes from the Ribbon.

16. Place a checkmark in the box next to List Changes on a New Sheet near the bottom of the dialog box and click OK.

	A	B	C	D	E	F	G	H	I	J	K
1	Action Number	Date	Time	Who	Change	Sheet	Range	New Value	Old Value	Action Type	Losing Action
2	1	6/5/2010	4:45 PM	Nikki Young	Cell Change	Columbia State College	E21	1,725.00	2,308.00		
3	2	6/5/2010	4:45 PM	Nikki Young	Cell Change	Columbia State College	G16	725	<blank>		
4	3	6/5/2010	4:45 PM	Nikki Young	Cell Change	Columbia State College	G11	5,844.00	1,063.00		
5	4	6/5/2010	4:53 PM	Grace Vargas	Cell Change	Columbia State College	G16	<blank>		Result of rejected action	2
6											
7	The history ends with the changes saved on 6/5/2010 at 4:53 PM.										

The History worksheet appears. (Your Date, Time, and Who entries will vary from the illustration.) The change history maintains a complete record of every change to the workbook. Notice that the last action line even describes how cell G16 reverted to blank as a result of a rejected change.

17. Save 💾 the workbook.

The temporary History worksheet disappears after you save the workbook, and the first worksheet in the workbook is displayed.

Switch Off Track Changes

Now that Grace has reviewed the changes, she no longer needs to track them.

18. Choose Review→Changes→Track Changes→Highlight Changes from the Ribbon.

19. Remove the checkmark from the Track Changes While Editing box and click OK.

20. Click Yes when asked to confirm removal of the change history and workbook sharing.

Wait briefly as Excel deletes the hidden change history data from the workbook.

21. Display the Columbia State College worksheet.

Notice that the changed cells contain the accepted values but no longer display borders.

22. Leave the workbook open for the next exercise.

You will use Track Changes again later in this lesson to consolidate changes made by multiple users.

Sharing Workbooks on a Network

Excel's Share Workbook command lets you set up a workbook for sharing and choose options for recording a history of changes to the workbook. Then you can review the change history for any conflicts between entries to the same cells and see how they were resolved. When the shared workbook is stored on a network drive and you have the file open, you may have Excel give you automatic updates of all user changes. When sharing files, you should give users clear instructions about the data that they should and should not change.

Characteristics of Shared Workbooks

When you set up a workbook for sharing on a network, several features work together to coordinate the use of the workbook.

- **Shared Access:** Multiple users can access the same file at once and see which other users currently have the file open.

- **User Settings:** Users may save their own printing and filtering settings as a custom view with the file.

- **Change History:** The change history is activated automatically whenever you create a shared workbook. This feature must be active as long as the workbook is shared.

- **Resolving Conflicts:** When changes are saved to a shared workbook, Excel displays a dialog box to help you review and resolve any conflicts between what you and another user have entered.

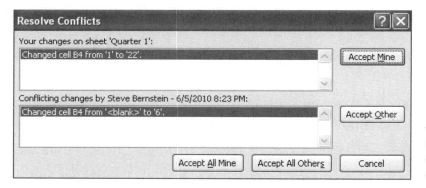

The Resolve Conflicts dialog box appears after two users change the same cell and save a shared workbook.

Simultaneous Access to Shared Workbooks

When you share a workbook on a network drive, several users can open and change the workbook simultaneously. Changes saved by multiple users are recorded in the change history for later review. When two users change the same cell and the second user gives the Save command, Excel analyzes the change history and alerts the second user to review both changes and choose one. Excel cannot keep both changes in one cell.

!NOTE! *If more than one person tries to open a standard (unshared) Excel workbook, the second person to open the workbook will receive a warning message and must open a read-only copy in order to view the file.*

Disabled Features in Shared Workbooks

Several Excel features are disabled when a workbook is shared, whether on a network drive or distributed to individual users. For example, you cannot delete rows and columns from a worksheet, insert a new worksheet, or add tables and charts in a shared workbook. Nor can you change passwords to protect worksheets—although password protection applied before the workbook is shared remains in effect. For a complete list of disabled features, see the Use a Shared Workbook to Collaborate topic in Excel Help.

QUICK REFERENCE: SHARING A WORKBOOK

Task	Procedure
Set up a workbook to be shared	■ Choose Review→Changes→Share Workbook <img> from the Ribbon.
	■ In the Editing tab of the Share Workbook dialog box, place a checkmark in the box next to Allow Changes by More Than One User at the Same Time.
	■ Display the Advanced tab in the dialog box, choose any desired options, and click OK.
	■ Click OK to confirm saving the workbook.
	■ Copy the workbook to a network drive or other location where the entire workgroup has access to it, or make multiple copies of the original file and distribute a copy to each user.

 ## Hands-On 16.8   Set Up and Edit a Shared Workbook

In this exercise, you will set up the Connections Grant Budget workbook to be shared. Then you will open the workbook in two different Excel windows simultaneously to simulate multiple users working in a shared workbook on a network drive.

Before You Begin: *The Microsoft Excel username should still be Grace Vargas from Hands-On 16.7 if you were allowed to change the username.*

Set Up the Shared Workbook

1. Verify that the Connections Grant Budget workbook is still open.

2. Choose Review→Changes→Share Workbook <img> from the Ribbon.

3. On the Editing tab, place a checkmark in the box next to Allow Changes by More than One User at the Same Time.

4. Display the Advanced tab and read the various options.

5. Make certain that the Ask Me Which Changes Win option is chosen near the bottom of the dialog box, as shown at right. *This option ensures that you can review and accept or reject any conflicting changes to cells whenever you save the workbook.*

> Conflicting changes between users
> ⦿ Ask me which changes win
> ○ The changes being saved win

6. Click OK, and then click OK again to confirm saving the workbook. *Notice that* [Shared] *appears on the title bar next to the filename. This tells you that sharing has been enabled for this workbook.*

> Connections Grant Budget [Shared] - Microsoft Excel

7. Choose Review→Changes→Track Changes→Highlight Changes from the Ribbon.
   Notice that the Track Changes While Editing option is checked. Track Changes was switched on automatically when you gave the command to share the workbook.

8. Make certain that When is set to Since I Last Saved.

9. Place a checkmark in the box next to Who and make certain that Everyone is chosen in the Who list.
   This sets the change history to display change boxes around the changes that everyone makes in the workbook. Remember that Grace Vargas (or your computer's username) is still the username set in the Excel Options dialog box from Hands-On 16.7, so Excel considers her to have created this shared workbook.

10. Click OK to close the dialog box. Click OK again in the dialog box with the message No Changes Were Found with the Specified Properties.
    Initially, Excel finds that no changes have yet been made.

Edit the Shared Workbook

Now you will play the role of Grace editing some data in the workbook.

11. Display the Columbia State College worksheet, if not already displayed.

12. Select cell C15 and enter **2000** as the new value for the cell.

13. Select cell H18, a blank cell, and enter **700**.

14. Select cell G15, a blank cell, and enter **1450**.

15. Do *not* save yet.
    You set the When option to track changes from the last save. Saving now would not track the changes you just made.

Start a Second Copy of Excel

Now you will work as if you are accessing the workbook simultaneously with Grace.

 NOTE! *This new window will be referred to as the second Excel window for the remainder of this exercise and the following Hands-On exercise.*

16. Display the Start menu in Windows and navigate to Excel to open a second Excel program window.

Change the Username

 NOTE! *Skip to step 19 if you do not have permission rights to change the username on your computer.*

17. Choose Office→Excel Options from the Ribbon. Display the Popular category, if not already displayed.

18. Under Personalize Your Copy of Microsoft Office, enter your first name and last name in the User Name box and click OK to save the change.
    Now when you open the workbook, Excel will recognize you as a different user making changes to the workbook.

Open a Second Copy of the Workbook

19. Open the Connections Grant Budget workbook from the Grant Project folder, which is within the Lesson 16 folder in your file storage location.

Notice that [Shared] appears just to the right of the filename on the title bar. You now have this file open in two Excel program windows at once. This is possible only with a shared workbook, not a standard Excel workbook.

20. Choose Review→Changes→Share Workbook  from the Ribbon and notice that two users are listed under Who Has This Workbook Open Now (if you were allowed to change the username).

21. Click Cancel to exit the dialog box without making any changes.

22. Display the Columbia State College worksheet, select cell C15, and enter **3250** as the new value for the cell.

This new value will conflict with the 2000 entry Grace made in step 12. However, as you will see later, Excel will help you catch conflicts like this. Notice also that, unlike the first copy, this second copy of the shared workbook does not display change boxes. The changes are being saved to the change history, though, and will be displayed later in the exercise when you review the changes.

23. Select cell G16 and enter **350**.

This value does not conflict with any value entered by Grace.

24. Save  the changes and leave the second Excel window open.

Excel saves the changes to this second copy of the shared workbook in the change history. Later, Excel will use the change history to enter the data into Grace's copy of the workbook in the first Excel window and to resolve the conflict in cell C15.

Switch to the First Workbook and Resolve Conflicts

25. Click the first Microsoft Excel button in the Windows taskbar to switch to Grace's copy of the workbook. (Your buttons may look slightly different.)

The first Excel window becomes the active window, and you are back to viewing Grace's work in this copy of the shared workbook. Notice that the changes you made in the second Excel window are not yet visible. They are in the change history. The changes won't be visible until Grace gives the Save command on her copy of the shared workbook.

26. Save  the workbook in the first Excel window.

A Resolve Conflicts dialog box appears. This alerts Grace that her change conflicts with a change you made and saved in the second Excel window a few moments ago. Notice that Excel displays the name, time, and other details of the conflicting change. Based on her knowledge of the project, Grace recognizes that the higher figure is correct.

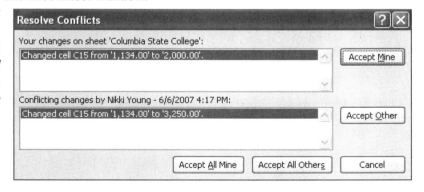

27. Click the Accept Other button on the right side of the dialog box.

28. Click OK to acknowledge the message that the workbook has been updated with the various changes.
Notice that the 350 in cell G16 of the second Excel window was entered automatically because it did not conflict with any other edits to the workbook.

Review Changes to the Shared Workbook

Now you will look over the change boxes on the worksheet and review the change history worksheet.

29. Choose Review→Changes→Track Changes→Highlight Changes from the Ribbon.

30. Follow these steps to review the change history:

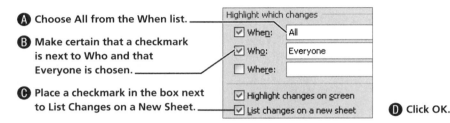

Ⓐ Choose All from the When list.

Ⓑ Make certain that a checkmark is next to Who and that Everyone is chosen.

Ⓒ Place a checkmark in the box next to List Changes on a New Sheet.

Ⓓ Click OK.

The History worksheet appears. Your Date, Time, and Who columns will differ from the illustration.

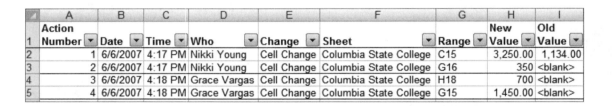

	A	B	C	D	E	F	G	H	I
1	Action Number	Date	Time	Who	Change	Sheet	Range	New Value	Old Value
2	1	6/6/2007	4:17 PM	Nikki Young	Cell Change	Columbia State College	C15	3,250.00	1,134.00
3	2	6/6/2007	4:17 PM	Nikki Young	Cell Change	Columbia State College	G16	350	<blank>
4	3	6/6/2007	4:18 PM	Grace Vargas	Cell Change	Columbia State College	H18	700	<blank>
5	4	6/6/2007	4:18 PM	Grace Vargas	Cell Change	Columbia State College	G15	1,450.00	<blank>

As you may expect, all changes are recorded here. Notice, however, that the 2000 entry made in cell C15 of the first Excel window is not recorded. That was the cell with the conflicting changes. Since you dismissed the 2000 value for the 3250 value, the change history does not record the conflict, just the resolution.

31. Display the Columbia State College worksheet.
Notice that change boxes have appeared around all four of the cells that were changed earlier in this exercise.

32. Save 🖫 the workbook in the first Excel window.
Notice that the History worksheet disappears after the save. However, you may still see the change boxes.

33. Leave both Excel windows open for the next exercise.

Switching Off Sharing

You may want to switch off sharing only temporarily or after a project is completed. When you switch off sharing, the change history is erased and any unsaved changes by other users are lost. You should not turn off sharing to a workbook unless you are satisfied that everyone's data have been saved and that any conflicts have been resolved satisfactorily. Once you disable the sharing feature for a workbook, there is no turning back.

 WARNING! *Before you turn off sharing, make certain that all other network users have saved their changes and closed the workbook. Otherwise, their changes will be lost.*

QUICK REFERENCE: DISABLING WORKBOOK SHARING

Task	Procedure
Disable workbook sharing	■ Print or copy the History worksheet to another workbook, if desired.
	■ Make certain that all other users have saved their work. Otherwise, any unsaved changes are lost.
	■ Choose Review→Changes→Share Workbook ⊞ from the Ribbon.
	■ In the Editing tab of the Share Workbook dialog box, remove the checkmark in the box next to Allow Changes by More than One User at the Same Time.
	■ Click Yes when you are warned that the change history will be erased and that other users will not be able to save their work.

 Hands-On 16.9 Stop Sharing the Workbook

In this exercise, you will disable sharing for the workbook. This command will also erase the change history and deactivate the Track Changes feature.

1. Verify that the first Excel window with Grace's work is the active window.

2. Choose Review→Changes→Share Workbook ⊞ from the Ribbon.
   Notice that the Who Has This Workbook Open Now list on the dialog box displays both Excel users. You should see your own name (or computer username) on the second line along with the time you opened the workbook in the second window. Although you could use the Remove User button near the bottom of the dialog box to close the other window, it is much more polite to contact the user and provide an opportunity to save the workbook. Otherwise, the unsaved changes will be lost.

3. Click Cancel to close the dialog box.

4. Make the second Excel window active by clicking its button on the Windows taskbar, and then close that Excel window.

5. Choose Review→Changes→Share Workbook ⊞ from the Ribbon.
   The Who Has This Workbook Open Now list now shows just one open copy of the shared workbook. Now it is safe for Grace to turn off sharing for this workbook.

6. Uncheck the Allow Changes by More than One User at the Same Time option and click OK.

7. Click Yes to confirm removing the workbook from shared use.
   Now this workbook may be opened by only one user at a time.

8. Close the workbook and click Yes if prompted to save the changes.

Merging Multiple Workbooks

 You may choose to share a workbook by distributing a copy to each user rather than placing it on a network server. The Compare and Merge Workbooks command gives you the capability to merge the multiple copies of the workbook containing all user changes into a single workbook. This saves you the tedium of opening each workbook individually and then selecting, copying, and pasting the necessary cells into the primary workbook. The files to be merged must all be copies of the *original* workbook, and the copies must have unique file-names. For example, users may add their initials to the filename, such as mw-Budget and tg-Budget.

!TIP! *You may only merge the edited copies of the workbook when it has been set up as a shared workbook with Track Changes. The Compare and Merge Workbooks command is dimmed for normal (unshared) Excel workbooks.*

Example of a Merge

Grace creates a shared workbook. She sends the workbook to several people by email as an attachment. Grace requests that the recipients fill in data on specific sections. After the work-book copies are returned, Grace uses the Compare and Merge Workbooks command to merge them into her original shared workbook. Grace will not have to look for, copy, and paste the data. Then she uses the Accept/Reject Changes command to resolve any changes that multiple users made to the same cell.

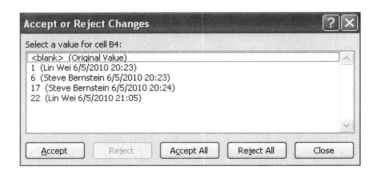

The Compare and Merge Workbooks command displays all changes made to a cell.

!NOTE! *The Compare and Merge Workbooks command does not appear on the Ribbon. You must add it to the Quick Access toolbar.*

What Happens When Workbooks Are Merged

Excel performs several operations when you merge workbooks. The details are described in the following table.

Change	Description
Data is merged into the currently active workbook	Whichever copy of the shared workbook you have open when you give the Compare and Merge Workbooks command is the one that receives the merged data. The copies of the workbook you are merging from do not receive merged data.
Merged data replaces original data	Data merged from other workbook(s) will replace any data already existing in the same cells of the workbook into which you are merging.
A change history is recorded	Excel records all changes that occur during the merge, including where the data came from and who made the change. You may review the changes and accept any one change to a cell.

Merged Cells Compared to Merged Workbooks

Do not confuse the Compare and Merge Workbooks command with merged cells. Merged cells allow you to combine a range of cells and center a label across the cells. You cannot merge cells in a shared workbook. You must either merge cells before sharing the workbook or turn off sharing.

QUICK REFERENCE: MERGING MULTIPLE VERSIONS OF A SHARED WORKBOOK

Task	Procedure
Add the Compare and Merge Workbooks command to the Quick Access toolbar	■ Choose Office→Excel Options→Customize from the Ribbon. ■ Choose Commands Not in the Ribbon from the Choose Commands From list. ■ Scroll down the list, select Compare and Merge Workbooks, and click the Add button.
Merge multiple copies of a shared workbook	■ Set up the workbook to be shared. Distribute copies of the original shared workbook to others who will contribute data. The files must have unique filenames. ■ After the workbook copies are edited and returned, open the one file into which all others will be merged. ■ Make certain that all other workbooks to be merged are closed. ■ Choose Compare and Merge Workbooks from the Quick Access toolbar. ■ In the dialog box, select the workbook to be merged or use Ctrl or Shift to select multiple files.
Review merged changes to a workbook	■ Choose Review→Changes→Track Changes→Accept/Reject Changes from the Ribbon. ■ Choose the types of changes you wish to review and click OK. ■ Use the buttons in the dialog box to navigate through the changes and accept or reject changes as desired.

Protecting Elements in a Shared Workbook

You may protect worksheet elements before setting the workbook to be shared. For example, you may lock or unlock cells and then turn on worksheet protection. The Protect and Share Workbook command sets the workbook to be shared and provides two additional protection levels. The share and track changes features are dimmed in dialog boxes to prevent users from switching them off in an individual copy of a shared workbook. You may also set a password to ensure that only designated users may alter this protection. This password is distinct from any passwords set to protect cells or worksheets.

 TIP! *When you use the Protect and Share Workbook command, the shared workbook is automatically created and the Track Changes feature activated. Thus, you do not have to execute the Share Workbook command separately.*

 QUICK REFERENCE: SETTING PASSWORD PROTECTION FOR WORKBOOK SHARING

Task	Procedure
Share a workbook and protect the change history from being disabled	■ Choose Review→Changes→Protect and Share Workbook 🖥 from the Ribbon. ■ In the Protect Shared Workbook dialog box, place a checkmark in the box next to Sharing with Track Changes. ■ Enter a password, if desired, and reenter the password when prompted to confirm. Users must enter the password to alter protection. ■ If desired, choose Review→Changes→Share Workbook 🖥 from the Ribbon and set options in the Advanced tab of the Share Workbook dialog box.
Switch off workbook sharing and password protection for the change history	■ Choose Review→Changes→Unprotect Shared Workbook 🖥 from the Ribbon. ■ Enter the password. ■ Click Yes to confirm removing the workbook from shared use.

 ## Hands-On 16.10 Merge Two Workbooks

In this exercise, you will merge changes from a copy of a shared workbook into the original shared workbook.

Before You Begin: *The Compare and Merge Workbooks ⊙ command should be available on the Quick Access toolbar, or you must have permission rights to add the command.*

Create a Shared Workbook with Track Changes Protection

In this section of the exercise, you will create a protected shared workbook. You will then create a second copy of the workbook with a different name.

1. Open the Connections Grant Budget Merged 1 workbook.

2. Choose Review→Changes→Protect and Share Workbook 🖥 from the Ribbon.

3. Place a checkmark in the box next to Sharing with Track Changes and click OK.
   You just turned on workbook sharing and track changes, and you protected both features. Excel warns you that the workbook will now be saved.

4. Click OK to confirm saving the shared workbook.

5. Choose Review→Changes→Share Workbook from the Ribbon.
   Notice that the Allow Changes by More than One User option is dimmed. Users cannot switch off workbook sharing, nor can they switch off change tracking in the Highlight Changes dialog box.

6. Click Cancel to exit the dialog box without making any changes.

Copy the Shared Workbook

You will save a second copy with a different name. You can do this to create as many copies of the shared workbook as you need. Excel will still recognize these variously named workbooks as being shared with the original workbook.

7. Choose Office→Save As from the Ribbon. Change the number from 1 to **2** in the filename and click Save.
   The new filename is Connections Grant Budget Merged 2. Notice that the title bar displays [Shared] after the filename.

Enter Data in the Workbook Copy

8. Display the Southern College worksheet.
   When you merge data into a workbook, the new data in a cell being merged always replaces any data already in the cell. You will place a new value in one of the cells and see how Excel helps us catch any potential problems during the merge.

9. Select cell H17 and enter **6000** as the new value.

10. Enter **600** in cell H11.

11. Enter **120** in cell H12.

12. Close the workbook and choose Yes when you are asked to save the changes.
    You cannot merge from an open workbook.

Merge the Workbooks

Now that the Southern College worksheet is edited, you will merge the changes into the original workbook.

13. Verify that the Compare and Merge Workbooks ⬤ command is installed on the Quick Access toolbar. If it is not, follow these steps to install the command:

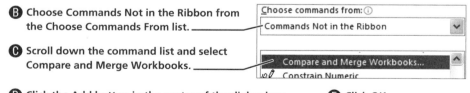

Ⓐ Choose Office→Excel Options→Customize category from the Ribbon.

Ⓑ Choose Commands Not in the Ribbon from the Choose Commands From list.

Ⓒ Scroll down the command list and select Compare and Merge Workbooks.

Ⓓ Click the Add button in the center of the dialog box. Ⓔ Click OK.

14. Open the Connections Grant Budget Merged 1 workbook.

15. Display the Southern College worksheet
    Notice that no data values are entered into cells H11 and H12 of this worksheet.

16. Choose Compare and Merge Workbooks 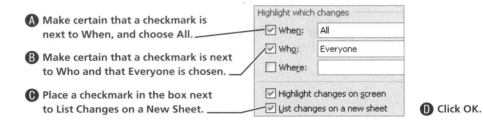 from the Quick Access toolbar.

    A dialog box opens from which you can select one or more files to merge. To select more than one file from the list, you would hold down the Ctrl *key as you make your selections. In this exercise, you will merge just one file.*

17. Double-click the Connections Grant Budget Merged 2 workbook to merge it into your open workbook.

    Excel saves the workbook as it processes the merge. All data for the Southern College worksheet have been merged into place. Notice that the newly merged number 6000 in cell H17 that you entered into the Southern College workbook has replaced the old figure of 8000. However, you still have the opportunity to review the changes and reject incorrect merge results.

Visually Review the Changes

You will use two methods to survey the results. First, you will perform a visual review of highlighted changes. Then you will use the Accept/Reject Changes command to review them.

18. Choose Review→Changes→Track Changes→Highlight Changes from the Ribbon.

19. Follow these steps to display the change history worksheet:

A Make certain that a checkmark is next to When, and choose All.

B Make certain that a checkmark is next to Who and that Everyone is chosen.

C Place a checkmark in the box next to List Changes on a New Sheet.

Highlight which changes
☑ When: All
☑ Who: Everyone
☐ Where:
☑ Highlight changes on screen
☑ List changes on a new sheet

D Click OK.

20. Examine columns H and I of the History worksheet. These columns display a new and an old value for cell H17.

21. Display the Southern College worksheet.

    Notice the change box around the changed cell, another visual indication that a change you might not want has taken place. You could manually change this cell if necessary. However, you will use the Accept/Reject Changes command instead.

Accept and Reject Changes

22. Choose Review→Changes→Track Changes→Accept/Reject Changes from the Ribbon.

23. Make certain that the dialog box is set as shown at right, and click OK.

    The first change is displayed. In fact, it's the only one we need to worry about.

    Which changes
    ☑ When: Not yet reviewed
    ☑ Who: Everyone
    ☐ Where:

24. Click Reject to replace 6000 with the old value.

    Now you see the next change on the Southern College worksheet. You know that this and the next change values are good. Rather than click Accept for changes one by one, you can simply accept them all.

25. Click Accept All to accept all remaining changes.

    That saved some time! Now let's turn off sharing on this workbook.

Disable Sharing for the Workbook

26. Choose Review→Changes→Unprotect Shared Workbook 🖳 from the Ribbon.

Although protection has been removed, the workbook is still shared. You must use the Share Workbook command to switch off sharing.

27. Choose Review→Changes→Share Workbook 🖳 from the Ribbon.

28. On the Editing tab, uncheck the box next to Allow Changes by More than One User at the Same Time, and click OK.

29. Click Yes to confirm removing the workbook from shared use.

Now that the workbook is no longer shared, you cannot perform any additional merge commands. You would need to share the workbook again and then create additional copies to merge with this workbook. Notice that the change boxes are no longer visible because the change history has also been deactivated.

30. Save 🖬 the changes and leave the workbook open.

Restore the Username

!NOTE! *Skip steps 31 and 32 if you did not change the username. If you did change the username, refer to the procedure that you wrote in step 3 in Hands-On 16.4 to restore the original username, which may vary from the following steps.*

31. Choose Office→Excel Options from the Ribbon. Display the Popular category, if not already displayed.

32. Under Personalize Your Copy of Microsoft Office, carefully type the original username that you wrote down during Hands-On 16.4 in the User Name box and click OK.

Emailing a Workbook

When you want to send an Excel workbook to someone by email, you have two choices. You may send the entire workbook as an attachment, or you may send a single worksheet as the body of the email message. Each method has its uses. Sending a worksheet as an email message may cause some formatting to be lost. However, if you just need to transmit a single worksheet, sending it as the body of an email message may be more convenient for the recipient to quickly view and print.

 TIP! *If you need to send a multisheet workbook, you must use the attachment method.*

Attaching a Workbook

You may send email from within Excel if you previously set up a Microsoft Outlook or Windows Mail email account. After you give the Email command, an email message window appears with the workbook file already attached. You simply enter the recipient's email address and type your message. You may edit the subject line and attach more files, if desired. You may attach Excel workbooks from within most other email programs if you do not have an Outlook or Windows Mail account.

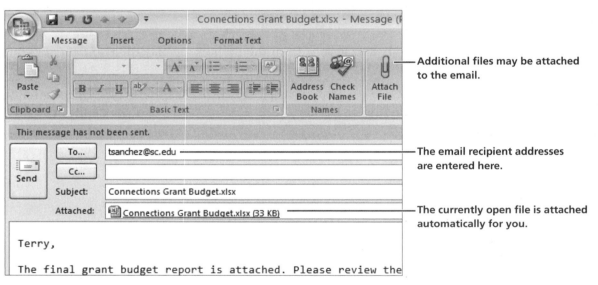

A Microsoft Outlook email message window

Inserting a Worksheet in an Email Message

The Send to Mail Recipient command places the currently displayed worksheet in the email message area. You fill in the email address, a subject for the message, and a short introduction to the worksheet before sending the message. The Introduction box will not be available in an email program other than Outlook.

 NOTE! *The Send to Mail Recipient command does not appear on the Ribbon. You must add it to the Quick Access toolbar.*

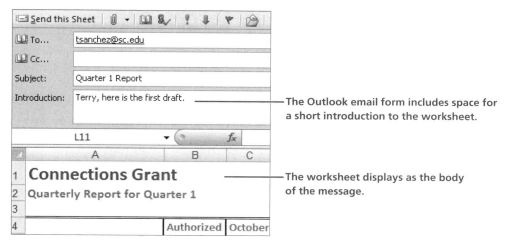

The Outlook email form includes space for a short introduction to the worksheet.

The worksheet displays as the body of the message.

Sending one worksheet as the message body

QUICK REFERENCE: SENDING A WORKBOOK VIA EMAIL

Task	Procedure
Add the Send to Mail Recipient command to the Quick Access toolbar	■ Choose Office→Excel Options→Customize from the Ribbon. ■ Choose Commands Not in the Ribbon from the Choose Commands From list. ■ Scroll down the list, select Send to Mail Recipient, and click the Add button.
Send an entire workbook as an attachment to an Outlook email message	■ Open the workbook file you wish to send by email. ■ Choose Office→Send→Email from the Ribbon (or click the Send to Mail Recipient button on the Quick Access toolbar and choose Send the Entire Workbook as an Attachment). ■ Address the message, and revise the default subject (the document name) for the message, if desired. ■ Click the Send button on the message window. ■ Close the message window.
Send a single worksheet as an Outlook email message	■ Display the worksheet you wish to send by email. ■ Click the Send to Mail Recipient button on the Quick Access toolbar. ■ Enter the email recipient(s), subject, and a brief introduction. ■ Click the Send This Sheet button on the email form toolbar. ■ Click the Send to Mail Recipient button on the Quick Access toolbar to hide the email window.

Hands-On 16.11 Send a Workbook via Email

In this exercise, you will set up the Connections Grant Budget Merged 1 workbook to be emailed as an attachment. Because an email account may not be available on your computer, you will not actually send the message.

1. Choose Office→Send→Email from the Ribbon.
   A new message is created in an Outlook message window (or another program set as the default email program for your computer). Notice that the Excel workbook is already attached. Its filename is visible in the Attached box.

2. Address the message to **tsanchez@sc.edu** (for a fictitious email correspondent named Terry Sanchez).

3. Change the message subject to **Quarterly Report**.

4. Click in the body of the message and type the following text:

   Hello Terry,

   Attached is the Quarterly Budget Report for our consortium. For your convenience, some figures have explanatory comments.

   Regards, Grace

   A Send button may not be available in the email form. Because many computer classrooms are not equipped with email accounts, at this point you will close the message rather than send it.

5. Close the email program window.

6. Close the workbook. Choose No when asked if you wish to save.

Concepts Review

Unit III – (3)
428 – Chap 17.
60 mts final.
1 attempt.

True/False Questions

1. You may create a new folder from within Excel to store files. **TRUE** FALSE

2. To view comments on a worksheet, you must point at each cell individually. **TRUE** FALSE

3. Once a comment has been created, you may add text to it. **TRUE** FALSE

4. Excel automatically prints the comments in any workbook. TRUE **FALSE**

5. When you review tracked changes, Excel displays a change box around each cell that has been changed since the Track Changes feature was activated. **TRUE** FALSE

6. You may create a new worksheet that lists a workbook's change history. **TRUE** FALSE

7. If a workbook is set up for sharing on a computer network, several users can open it simultaneously. **TRUE** FALSE

8. When you switch off workbook sharing, Excel automatically closes and saves any open copies of the shared workbook. TRUE **FALSE**

9. You can perform the Merge command with standard (unshared) Excel workbooks. TRUE **FALSE**

10. A workbook may be attached to an email message. **TRUE** FALSE

Multiple Choice Questions

1. Which of the following statements about usernames in comments is true?
   a. The name is set up in the Comments window.
   b. You must reinstall Excel to change the name.
   c. The name is set up in the Excel Options window.
   d. Excel uses the same name as is used for logging on to your computer.

2. Which of the following statements about shared workbooks is true?
   a. Only one user at a time may open a shared workbook.
   b. Copies of a shared workbook must have the same filename.
   c. Passwords are not allowed in a shared workbook.
   d. Some Excel features do not work in a shared workbook.

3. Which features must be active to merge workbooks?
   a. Shared workbooks and Track Changes
   b. 3-D cell references and Track Changes
   c. Shared workbooks and comments
   d. Email and comments

4. When you merge data into a workbook, what happens when the new data being merged conflicts with old data already in a cell?
   a. The conflicting new data is excluded from the merge, and all other new data merges into empty cells.
   b. The new data replaces the existing data.
   c. Excel immediately displays a Conflict Resolution dialog box so that you can review the conflicts.
   d. The merge is canceled.

Skill Builders

Skill Builder 16.1   Create a New Folder

In this exercise, you will create a new folder for a project from within Excel's Save As dialog box.

1. Launch Excel and open the sb-Expense Report workbook from the Lesson 16 folder in your file storage location.

2. Choose Office→Save As from the Ribbon.

3. Follow these steps to create a new folder:
   Your dialog box may appear slightly different from what is shown here, depending on your version of Windows.

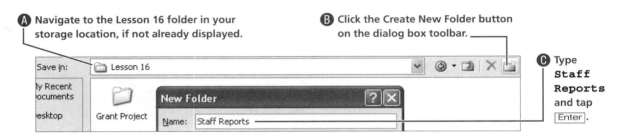

Ⓐ Navigate to the Lesson 16 folder in your storage location, if not already displayed.

Ⓑ Click the Create New Folder button on the dialog box toolbar.

Ⓒ Type **Staff Reports** and tap Enter.

Notice the new folder name in the Save In box. Excel immediately opened the new folder after you named it.

4. Save the workbook in the folder you just created, and leave the workbook open.
   Now you have two copies of this workbook file in your file storage location: one where you opened the file originally and one in the new folder. You will use the copy in the Staff Reports folder in the next exercise.

Skill Builder 16.2   Work with Comments

In this exercise, you will add comments to a workbook. You will also edit, move, delete, and print comments.

Before You Begin: You must have completed Skill Builder 16.1, and the sb-Expense Report workbook should be open. The Microsoft Office username should be set to your name if you have permission to do so (see steps 1–4 in Hands-On 16.4).

Insert Comments

1. Select cell B11 and then choose Review→Comments→New Comment [image] from the Ribbon. Enter the following comment: **Presentation binders and blank DVDs**

2. Right-click cell B12 and choose Insert Comment from the context menu. Enter the following comment: **Photocopying, including 10 color pages**

3. Enter the following comment in cell I19: **Travel to/from airport at 50 cents per mile**

4. Enter the following comment in cell E22: **Find receipt**

5. Save ![save icon] the changes.

Display and Hide the Comments

6. Choose Review→Comments→Show All Comments ![icon] from the Ribbon.
   Notice that the comments for cells B11 and B12 overlap. You need to move them to new positions.

7. Follow these steps to move a comment:

Ⓐ Click in the comment box for cell B11.

Ⓑ Point at the comment box border until the pointer displays four arrows, and then drag the comment up so that it no longer overlaps the other comment.

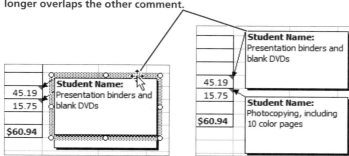

8. Move the comment for cell B12 down.

9. Move the comment for cell I19 up so it is above row 18 and no longer overlaps the data in cells J19 and K19.

Delete and Edit Comments

10. Right-click cell E22 and choose Delete Comment from the context menu.

11. Click in the comment box for cell B12, type **and color paper** at the end of the comment, and click outside the comment box.

Print the Comments

12. Choose Page Layout→Page Setup dialog box launcher ![Page Setup] from the Ribbon.

13. Display the Sheet tab in the Page Setup dialog box.

14. Under Print, drop down the Comments list and choose As Displayed on Sheet. Click OK.

15. Print ![print icon] the workbook and retrieve your printout from the printer.

16. Save ![save icon] the changes and close the workbook.

Skill Builder 16.3 Share a Workbook and Review Changes

In this exercise, you will set up a workbook to be routed to Corey Owens, a coworker. Then you will review the changes in a workbook that Corey returns to you. Finally, you will create the History worksheet to display the change history.

Before you Begin: The Microsoft Office username should be set to your name if you have permission to do so (see steps 1–4 in Hands-On 16.4).

Turn On Workbook Sharing and Track Changes

1. Open the sb-Workforce Grant Budget workbook from the Lesson 16 folder.

2. Choose Review→Changes→Protect and Share Workbook 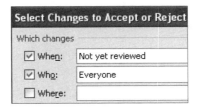 from the Ribbon.

3. Switch on Sharing with Track Changes but do not set a password.

4. Click OK, and then click OK again to confirm saving the workbook.
   The word [Shared] *appears after the filename in the title bar. Any changes that users make will be highlighted in the workbook.*

5. Close the workbook.
   Now the workbook is ready to distribute so that coworkers can input their data.

Review Changes in a Workbook

Assume that your coworker Corey Owens edited and returned the shared workbook to you.

6. Open the sb-Corey's Grant Budget workbook from the Lesson 16 folder.

7. Choose Review→Changes→Track Changes→Highlight Changes from the Ribbon.
   Notice that the Track Changes While Editing option is checked. Track Changes was switched on automatically when the command was given to share the workbook.

8. In the Highlight Changes dialog box, choose options to highlight all changes from everyone and click OK.

9. Choose Review→Changes→Track Changes→Accept/Reject Changes from the Ribbon.

10. Set options as shown in the following illustration.

11. Click OK in the Select Changes to Accept or Reject dialog box.

12. Click Accept to accept the first edit in cell C15.

13. Read the details of the next change and notice that Corey entered a formula.

Users may enter values, text, or formulas in cells.

Accept or Reject Changes

Change 2 of 4 made to this document:

Corey Owens, 6/10/2007 11:04 PM:

Changed cell E15 from '<blank>' to '=C15'.

14. Accept this edit in cell E15 and the next change for cell G15.

Notice that now the Q2 Budget worksheet is displayed.
Excel jumps you to the next change on the second worksheet in the workbook.

15. Click Reject to restore cell E21 to blank.

After you have reviewed all of the changes, the dialog box disappears. Notice that the change boxes are still displayed, however. They remain until you switch off Track Changes.

16. Save 💾 the workbook.

Display and Print the Change History

Excel can display the change history of the workbook. This can be useful for reviewing edits.

17. Choose Review→Changes→Track Changes→Highlight Changes from the Ribbon.

18. Place a checkmark in the box next to List Changes on a New Sheet and click OK.

A History worksheet appears, listing all Corey's changes to the workbook that you accepted. Notice that the change to cell E21 of the Q2 Budget worksheet does not appear because you rejected it. Therefore, the original value was restored. Your Who, Date, and Time entries will vary from the following illustration.

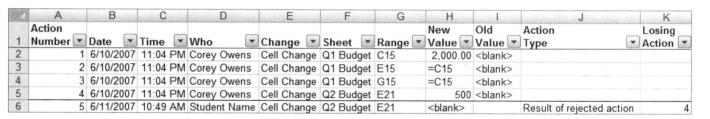

	A	B	C	D	E	F	G	H	I	J	K
1	Action Number	Date	Time	Who	Change	Sheet	Range	New Value	Old Value	Action Type	Losing Action
2	1	6/10/2007	11:04 PM	Corey Owens	Cell Change	Q1 Budget	C15	2,000.00	<blank>		
3	2	6/10/2007	11:04 PM	Corey Owens	Cell Change	Q1 Budget	E15	=C15	<blank>		
4	3	6/10/2007	11:04 PM	Corey Owens	Cell Change	Q1 Budget	G15	=C15	<blank>		
5	4	6/10/2007	11:04 PM	Corey Owens	Cell Change	Q2 Budget	E21	500	<blank>		
6	5	6/11/2007	10:49 AM	Student Name	Cell Change	Q2 Budget	E21	<blank>		Result of rejected action	4

19. Print 🖨 the History worksheet and retrieve your printout from the printer.

20. Close the workbook.

Skill Builder 16.4   Set Up a Workbook for a Network Share

In this exercise, you will create a shared workbook for access by other users on a network.

1. Open the sb-Network Share Budget workbook from the Lesson 16 folder.

2. Choose Review→Changes→Share Workbook ⊞ from the Ribbon.

3. Place a checkmark in the box next to Allow Changes by More than One User at the Same Time.

4. Display the Advanced tab and follow these steps to set options in the dialog box.

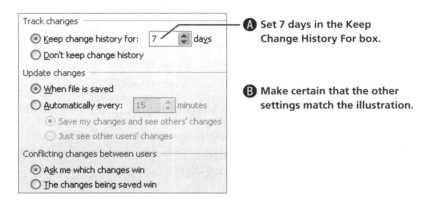

Ⓐ Set 7 days in the Keep Change History For box.

Ⓑ Make certain that the other settings match the illustration.

Saving the change history for seven days rather than 30 days reduces the potential size of the file. The longer changes are kept and the more changes that are tracked, the larger the workbook file will become.

5. Click OK, and then click OK again to approve saving the workbook.
Notice the word [Shared] *to the right of the filename in the title bar.*

6. Choose Review→Changes→Track Changes→Highlight Changes from the Ribbon.
Notice that the Track Changes feature has been switched on. This was done automatically when you set the workbook for sharing. Notice also that the When setting is Since I Last Saved. This causes the highlight around changes to disappear each time you save the workbook. However, all changes will still be listed in the Change History.

7. Click Cancel in the dialog box.

8. Have your instructor or a teaching assistant initial that you have successfully shared the workbook. _____

9. Close the workbook.
The workbook is now ready to be placed on a network drive for multiple users to open and work on the file simultaneously.

Skill Builder 16.5   Merge Workbooks

In this exercise, you will merge data from three copies of a shared workbook. Each copy was created from the original shared workbook and then changed by various coworkers.

Before You Begin: The Compare and Merge Workbooks 🔵 *command should be available on the Quick Access toolbar, or you must have permission rights to add the command.*

Merge Data into the Shared Workbook

1. Verify that the Compare and Merge Workbooks 🔵 command is installed on the Quick Access toolbar. If it is not, follow these steps to install the command:

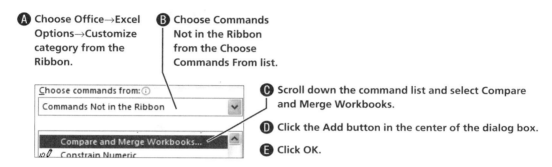

Ⓐ Choose Office→Excel Options→Customize category from the Ribbon.

Ⓑ Choose Commands Not in the Ribbon from the Choose Commands From list.

Ⓒ Scroll down the command list and select Compare and Merge Workbooks.

Ⓓ Click the Add button in the center of the dialog box.

Ⓔ Click OK.

2. Open the sb-Merged Budget 1 workbook.
   Look at the title bar at the top of the Excel window. Notice that this is a shared workbook.

3. Choose Compare and Merge Workbooks 🔵 from the Quick Access toolbar.
   The Select Files to Merge into Current Workbook dialog box appears. Remember that you may merge only copies of workbooks made from the original shared workbook. The files on your file storage location have already been created and edited from the sb-Merged Budget 1 file you are sharing.

   Next you will choose the three edited copies of the workbook that were returned by your coworkers.

4. Navigate to the Lesson 16 folder and click sb-Merged Budget 2.

5. Hold down ⎡Shift⎤ and select sb-Merged Budget 4.
   Three files should appear selected for merging, including sb-Merged Budget 3. Using ⎡Shift⎤ includes all files between the first and last in the selection. During the next step, watch the status bar at the bottom of the Excel window to monitor the progress of the command. You also will see the values update in the Curriculum Development and Faculty/Staff Professional Development rows.

6. Click OK to start the merge.
   After a few moments, all data is merged into the Q1 Budget worksheet and Q2 Budget worksheet. Excel automatically saved the sb-Merged Budget 1 file after the merge.

Accept and Reject Changes

7. Choose Review→Changes→Track Changes→Accept/Reject Changes from the Ribbon.

8. Make certain that the Accept or Reject Changes dialog box is set as shown at right, and click OK.
The dialog box displays a conflict for cell C15.

Select Changes to Accept or Reject

Which changes

☑ When: Not yet reviewed

☑ Who: Everyone

☐ Where:

9. Resolve the conflict by choosing Oscar Valencia's change of 1,000 and then click Accept.
Another conflict for cell E21 of the Q2 Budget worksheet is displayed. Lawrence Harris changed your original value of 1,000 to 5,000. You know that is not correct.

10. Click Reject to restore the cell E21 value to 1,000. (Do not click Accept.)

11. Click Accept All to accept the remaining changes.

12. Save 💾 the workbook.

Display the Change History

13. Choose Review→Changes→Track Changes→Highlight Changes from the Ribbon.

14. Choose All from the When list. Make certain that Who has a checkmark and Everyone is chosen.

15. Place a checkmark in the box next to List Changes on a New Sheet, and click OK.
A History worksheet appears, listing all changes to the workbook that you accepted. Compare Action Numbers 2 and 10. You rejected Lawrence Harris's change to cell E21 of the Q2 Budget worksheet. Both changes to cell C15 are listed; the second change "won" because you accepted Oscar Valencia's number. The last change listed for a cell is the one that appears in the merged worksheet. Your Who, Date, and Time entries will vary from the illustration below.

	A	B	C	D	E	F	G	H	I	J	K
1	Action Number	Date	Time	Who	Change	Sheet	Range	New Value	Old Value	Action Type	Losing Action
2	1	7/28/2007	11:26 AM	Lawrence Harris	Cell Change	Q1 Budget	C15	4,500.00	<blank>		
3	2	7/28/2007	11:26 AM	Lawrence Harris	Cell Change	Q2 Budget	E21	5,000.00	1,000.00		
4	3	7/28/2007	11:26 AM	Iridza Paloma	Cell Change	Q1 Budget	C16	500	<blank>		
5	4	7/28/2007	11:26 AM	Iridza Paloma	Cell Change	Q1 Budget	E16	500	<blank>		
6	5	7/28/2007	11:26 AM	Iridza Paloma	Cell Change	Q1 Budget	G16	500	<blank>		
7	6	7/28/2007	11:26 AM	Iridza Paloma	Cell Change	Q2 Budget	G20	500	<blank>		
8	7	7/28/2007	11:27 AM	Oscar Valencia	Cell Change	Q1 Budget	C15	1,000.00	<blank>		
9	8	7/28/2007	11:27 AM	Oscar Valencia	Cell Change	Q1 Budget	E15	1,500.00	<blank>		
10	9	7/28/2007	11:27 AM	Oscar Valencia	Cell Change	Q1 Budget	G15	2,000.00	<blank>		
11	10	7/28/2007	11:45 AM	Student Name	Cell Change	Q2 Budget	E21	1000		Result of rejected action	2

16. Print 🖨 the History worksheet and retrieve your printout from the printer.
Normally you would remove workbook sharing after approving changes. In this exercise, however, you will leave the change history available to re-create the History worksheet, if necessary.

17. Save 💾 and close the workbook.

Skill Builder 16.6   Email a Worksheet

In this exercise, you will place a worksheet into the body of an email message.

Before You Begin: The Send to Mail Recipient 🖼 *command should be available on the Quick Access toolbar, or you must have permission rights to add the command.*

1. Open the sb-Expense Report workbook from the Lesson 16 folder in your file storage location.

2. Verify that the Send to Mail Recipient command is installed on the Quick Access toolbar. If it is not, follow these steps to install the command:

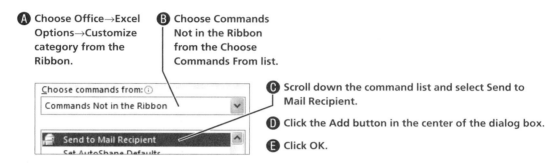

A Choose Office→Excel Options→Customize category from the Ribbon.

B Choose Commands Not in the Ribbon from the Choose Commands From list.

C Scroll down the command list and select Send to Mail Recipient.

D Click the Add button in the center of the dialog box.

E Click OK.

3. Click the Send to Mail Recipient 🖼 button on the Quick Access toolbar.
    A prompt appears, telling you about the two options for sending the entire workbook or a single worksheet.

4. Choose the Send the Current Sheet as the Message Body option and click OK.
    An Outlook (or other default email program) message window appears, in which you can address the message.

5. Follow these steps to set up the email message:

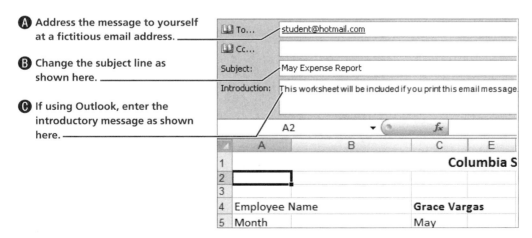

A Address the message to yourself at a fictitious email address.

B Change the subject line as shown here.

C If using Outlook, enter the introductory message as shown here.

A Send button may not be available in the email form. Because many computer classrooms are not equipped with email accounts, at this point you will close the message rather than send it.

6. Click the Send to Mail Recipient 🖃 button on the Quick Access toolbar.
The button toggles between the email message window and the Excel workbook window when a worksheet is in the message body.

7. Close the workbook. Choose No when asked if you wish to save.
An email message cannot be saved in a workbook.

Assessments

Assessment 16.1   Add Comments to a Workbook

In this exercise, you will insert a new comment and edit an existing comment on a worksheet.

Before You Begin: The Microsoft Office username should be set to your name if you have permission to do so (see steps 1–4 in Hands-On 16.4).

1. Open the as-Crisis Intervention Budget workbook from the Lesson 16 folder in your file storage location.

2. Add the following comment in cell C6: **Added an evening volunteer coordinator to the hotline staff.**

3. Edit the comment in cell D7 by adding the following text below the existing comment text: **Repairs completed by November 18 within the originally estimated cost.**

4. Display all comments.

5. Move comments below the data area so that all data is visible while the comments are displayed.

6. Resize comments as necessary to display all text in a comment.

7. Make certain that the worksheet and comments fit on one page.

8. Print 🖨 the workbook with comments on the same sheet (not on a separate sheet).

9. Save 💾 and close the workbook.

Assessment 16.2 Track Changes to a Workbook

In this exercise, you will set the workbook to track changes and make several edits in a worksheet. You will then review the edits and turn off the Track Changes feature.

1. Open the as-Animal Shelter Expenses workbook from the Lesson 16 folder.
   This workbook does not have data in it yet. You will enter data during the various Assessment exercises.

2. Set the workbook to highlight and track changes and use the appropriate options.

3. In cell B5 of the Expense Report worksheet, create a linking formula to cell E9 on the Cats worksheet.

4. In cell B6, create a linking formula to cell E9 on the Dogs worksheet.

5. Create a formula in cell B7 that sums the range B5:B6.

6. Save 💾 the workbook.

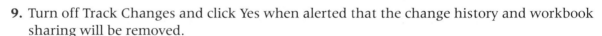

7. Display and print the change history for the workbook.

8. Give the command to accept or reject changes and approve all changes you made to the workbook.

9. Turn off Track Changes and click Yes when alerted that the change history and workbook sharing will be removed.

10. Save 💾 the workbook and leave it open for the next exercise.

	A	B
4	Animal	Total Costs
5	Cats	$ -
6	Dogs	$ -
7	Total Costs	$ -

Assessment 16.3 Share a Workbook

In this exercise, you will share a workbook file and then create two copies of it to merge in the next exercise.

Before You Begin: *You must have completed Assessment 16.2, and the as-Animal Shelter Expenses workbook should be open.*

1. Share the workbook.

2. Create two copies of the shared workbook, one named **as-Animal Shelter Cats** and the other named **as-Animal Shelter Dogs**.
   Remember that each must be a copy of the original workbook. You cannot copy the Cats workbook to create the Dogs workbook.

3. Close any workbook still open.

Assessment 16.4   Merge Workbooks

In this exercise, you will edit the two copies of the shared workbook you created in Assessment 16.3. Then you will merge the contents of the edited workbooks into the as-Animal Shelter Expenses workbook.

Before You Begin: You must have completed Assessment 16.2 and Assessment 16.3, and the as-Animal Shelter Expenses workbook should be open. The Compare and Merge Workbooks command should be available on the Quick Access toolbar.

1. Open the as-Animal Shelter Cats workbook from the Lesson 16 folder.

2. Type new data into the Cats worksheet to match the data items shaded in gray in the following illustration.

Animal	Age	Health	Date Arrived	Shelter Cost
Cat	Adult	Healthy	1-May	$ 82.50
Cat	Adult	Healthy	9-May	$ 60.50
Cat	Kitten	Healthy	10-May	$ 57.75
Cat	Adult	Healthy	30-May	$ 2.75

3. Save and close the as-Animal Shelter Cats workbook.

4. Open the as-Animal Shelter Dogs workbook.

5. Type new data into the Dogs worksheet to match the data items shaded in gray in the following illustration.

Animal	Age	Health	Date Arrived	Shelter Cost
Dog	Adult	Healthy	2-May	$ 79.75
Dog	Adult	Healthy	8-May	$ 63.25
Dog	Pup	Sick	15-May	$ 44.00
Dog	Adult	Healthy	20-May	$ 30.25

6. Save and close the as-Animal Shelter Dogs workbook.

7. Open the as-Animal Shelter Expenses workbook.

8. Merge the contents of the as-Animal Shelter Cats and as-Animal Shelter Dogs workbooks into the as-Animal Shelter Expenses workbook.
   Your data should appear in the Cats and Dogs worksheets. The Expense Report worksheet should display totals as shown on the right.

	A	B
4	Animal	Total Costs
5	Cats	$ 203.50
6	Dogs	$ 217.25
7	Total Costs	$ 420.75

9. Save and close the as-Animal Shelter Expenses workbook.

Restore the Username

 NOTE! *Skip steps 10–11 if you did not change the username. If you did change the username, refer to the procedure that you wrote in step 3 in Hands-On 16.4 to restore the original username, which may vary from the following steps.*

10. Choose Office→Excel Options from the Ribbon. Display the Popular category, if not already displayed.

11. Under Personalize Your Copy of Microsoft Office, carefully type the original username that you wrote down during Hands-On 16.4 in the User Name box and click OK.

Assessment 16.5   Send a Workbook via Email

In this exercise, you will email a workbook to yourself.

 NOTE! *You should not perform this exercise if your computer cannot send and receive email.*

1. Open the as-Email Test workbook from the Lesson 16 folder.

2. Attach the entire workbook to an email message to yourself at your own email address.

3. Change the subject line to **Sending a Workbook via Email**.

4. In the message area, enter a greeting, a line describing the file, and a closing with your name.

5. Send the message.

6. Display your Inbox in Outlook (or other email program you used) and click the Send/Receive button every 30 seconds until the message that you sent arrives.

7. Print 🖨 the message after it appears in your Inbox. (It is not necessary to print the attachment).

8. Close the Outlook (or other) program window.

9. Close the workbook. Choose No when asked if you wish to save.

Critical Thinking

Critical Thinking 16.1   Set Up Folders for a Project

The organization of files into folders is an important key to managing complex projects with many collaborators and files. In this exercise, you are a project manager getting ready to launch a new project. The project will last two years and involve several people and reports.

In Task A, you will define the project. In Task B, you will create folders in your file storage location in which to store project files. In Task C, you will review the folder structure and consider their completeness and utility.

Task A: Define the Project

■ Based on your past experience, or envisioning the sort of project in which you might participate in the future, define a project according to the following items. Enter the details into a Word document or Excel workbook.

■ Give the project a title.

■ Identify three to five fictitious people who will collaborate on the project.

■ Identify the sorts of quarterly and annual reports to be filed by the project participants.

■ Identify any data that might be tracked in the project.

■ When you are finished, print the basic project definition.

Task B: Create Project Folders

■ Use the project definition and the Excel Open dialog box to create a set of folders in the Lesson 16 folder in your file storage location according to the following guidelines.

■ Create folders to manage the information over the expected two-year term of the project.

■ Create folders you think might be useful to store files related to the project but not specifically required for project reporting. For example, you might create folders to store documents with meeting minutes or travel reports.

■ After creating the folders, use [Alt]+[Print Screen] to capture a picture of the Open dialog box and automatically copy it to the Clipboard. Use [Ctrl]+[V] to paste the picture into a Word or Excel document.

■ Print the document containing the picture, and then close the document without saving.

Task C: Review the Folders

■ Review the folder printout or view the folders on the computer. Write comments on the completeness and utility of the folders you created. Are there too many folders? Too few? Will it be easy to find project-related files in these folders? Could someone not very familiar with the project find the files he or she needs?

Critical Thinking 16.2   Document Formulas with Comments

An important feature of a mission-critical workbook used in business is the careful documentation of formulas and its other features. While the formulas in a workbook can be intuitive to the person who created them, this may not be the case for others who must maintain the workbook in the future. Thus, any complex formulas in a workbook should be documented with comments that explain their structure and function.

Imagine that you are responsible for preparing the payroll for a small business firm. You have created a useful workbook with several formulas that make your job easier. Now that this work is done, you will document the formulas and any other workbook features that will help others use the workbook effectively. The illustration at right displays an example of a comment that documents a formula used in a column.

Total Monthly Gross Pay to Date		Judy Roberts: The formula in this column sums the...
$	3,036.52	
$	3,783.19	
$	3,122.25	
$	3,661.84	

- Open the ct-Weekly Payroll workbook, which you created in Lesson 14, Auditing and Additional Functions. Rename the workbook **ct-Weekly Payroll Comments**.

- Use comments to describe the formulas on the two types of worksheets in the workbook. You may place most of the comments in the cells of the heading row above the columns where the formulas are used. Use the list below to get started. However, all formulas used in the workbook should be documented—not just these that follow: Summary worksheet column D, Week1 worksheet column E.

   ◆ Do not document formulas on the Week 2–Week 5 worksheets.
   ◆ Display all comments so that they do not overlap any data.
   ◆ Print just the worksheets containing comments.
   ◆ Save 🖫 and close the workbook.

Critical Thinking 16.3   Combine Several Schedules

Graciela is a member of a study group for her biology class. The members want to set up a schedule for weekly meetings. Graciela creates a workbook with a worksheet for herself, Mary, Richard, and Rose. She emails the copies and suggests that they each submit a weekly schedule. The schedules can be compared to see what time slots are open for everyone. After all schedules are entered, Graciela merges them into one of the shared workbook files and creates a formula to calculate which hours of time each week will be free for the study group members to meet.

Task A: Create a Shared Workbook

■ Open the ct-Study Times Master Schedule workbook.

■ In the Master Schedule worksheet, create a formula in the 8 AM Monday cell. Use a 3-D cell reference to sum the values in cell B4 of all the student schedule worksheets. The formula result is zero until data is entered into the worksheets.

■ Copy the formula you just created to all of the other time schedule cells in the Master Schedule worksheet.

■ Set the workbook to be shared. Create a copy of the shared workbook for each student in the group.

Task B: Mark the Schedules

Next, you will play the role of the four students and enter one student's schedule in each of the four workbook copies.

■ Open one student's workbook copy and make up a schedule in that student's worksheet. Place a **1** in each cell that the student is available for a group meeting.

■ Enter a schedule for each of the remaining students in their workbook copies. Each workbook copy will contain a schedule for one student.

■ Make certain to save 💾 the changes in each workbook copy.

	A	B	C	D	E	F	G
1	Rose						
2							
3		Mon	Tue	Wed	Thu	Fri	Sat
4	8:00 AM			1		1	
5	9:00 AM	1		1		1	
6	10:00 AM			1			
7	11:00 AM			1			
8	12:00 PM			1			
9	1:00 PM	1	1	1	1	1	1
10	2:00 PM	1	1	1	1	1	1
11	3:00 PM	1	1	1	1	1	1
12	4:00 PM	1	1	1	1	1	1
13	5:00 PM						
14	6:00 PM						
15	7:00 PM						
16	8:00 PM	1	1	1	1	1	
17	9:00 PM	1	1	1	1	1	
18	10:00 PM						

Example of one student's availability for group meetings.

Task C: Merge the Shared Workbooks

■ After you have created schedules for all students in their copies of the shared workbook, merge their changes into the ct-Study Times Master Schedule workbook.

■ Review each worksheet to confirm that the merge was successful.

Task D: Analyze the Schedules

■ Remember that some features are not available in shared workbooks. You must give a command before you may apply conditional formatting in the next step.

■ Create a conditional format in the cells containing formulas in the Master Schedule worksheet. The conditional format should display a background color whenever the value in the cell's formula is equal to 4. This makes it easy to see which hours are available for the study group to meet.

After you complete Task D, the format of your Master Schedule worksheet will look similar to the following illustration. In the following example, 8–10 AM on Wednesdays and Fridays are good times to meet.

3		Mon	Tue	Wed	Thu	Fri	Sat
4	8:00 AM	2	0	4	0	4	0
5	9:00 AM	3	1	4	1	4	0
6	10:00 AM	0	1	1	1	0	0

■ Save 💾 and close any open workbooks.

LESSON 17

Integrating Excel with Other Programs

Information is shared electronically in many ways. In this lesson, you will learn how to make Excel 2007 workbooks compatible with prior Excel versions so that all project collaborators may share data. You will learn how to convert workbooks to other file formats, including PDF and XPS for document sharing. A program other than Excel may be the basis for a project. For example, you often will create reports using Word and make presentations using PowerPoint. Through the power of application integration, you may link or embed Excel data, tables, and charts in those documents. You also will bring data into Excel from external sources such as a plain-text file or Word document.

LESSON OBJECTIVES

After studying this lesson, you will be able to:

- Save workbooks for use with prior Excel versions
- Convert workbooks to text, PDF, and XPS file formats
- Share Excel data with Word, PowerPoint, and Access
- Import text and data from external sources into Excel workbooks

Case Study: Producing an Annual Report

Deion Jenett is a print production manager in Los Angeles with the Acme Trading Company, an import-export firm. His primary role is to coordinate the efforts of his production team to get various publications ready for print. The production team members are scattered geographically. For example, one copy editor lives in Oregon, and a graphic artist lives in Boston. Each team member is an expert, and they can all work smoothly together over the Internet. Deion is about halfway through a project to produce Acme's annual report. He wants all of the production team members to know the status of the project. So, he decides to assemble information about the production tasks and the schedule into an Excel workbook and then publish the workbook in a universal file format so that everyone can review it.

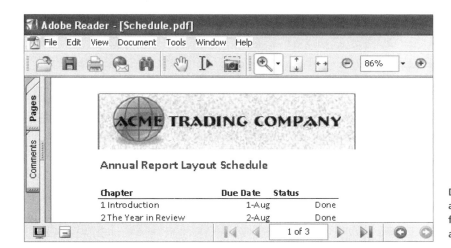

Deion saves the Excel workbook as a PDF file, a universal file format that may be viewed by anyone in a PDF reader.

Employee Name:	«First» «Last»
Employee ID:	«Employee_ID»
Job Title:	«Position»

Employee Name:	Millie Aberdeen
Employee ID:	064-55
Job Title:	Senior Designer

Chris, the administrative manager, inserts merge fields and uses Word's mail merge feature to assemble personalized forms.

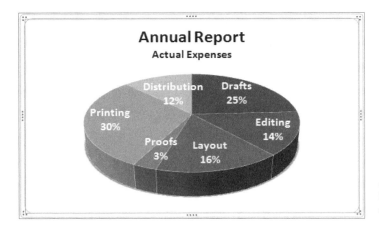

Jenna, a project editor, uses the Copy and Paste commands to import a linked Excel chart into a PowerPoint slide.

Maintaining Compatibility with Previous Versions of Excel

You can open and work with Excel workbooks saved in Excel 2007 or earlier versions such as Excel 97, 2000, and 2003. At times, you will need to share your workbooks and templates with others who have one of the earlier Excel versions or may not have Excel installed. You must ensure that files are saved in a format that those users can open.

About File Formats

A file format is a structure for storing data in a computer file. An application program uses specific file formats to save anything that you create in that program. The format that an application program normally uses to save files is called its *native* file format. For example, Word saves files using the format Word Document (.docx), and a web page editor may use the HTML file format.

Identifying a File's Format

When you give Excel's Save As command, you may choose from a number of file formats in the Save As Type list in the Save As dialog box. The default is Excel Workbook. While browsing filenames in Excel or Windows Explorer, you may identify files that are compatible with Excel by viewing the icons next to the filenames. You may also read the extension at the end of the filename, if extensions are displayed. For example, the extension .xls indicates a spreadsheet workbook saved for use with a previous Excel version.

 TIP! *Can't view any filename extensions? See the Working with File Formats Quick Reference table on page 646 for the procedure to switch on their display.*

The file's icon and extension in the filename identify the file type.

The following table shows the file formats that you may use to save workbooks for various Excel versions along with their file extensions.

 TIP! *All Excel filename extensions begin with the letters xl and contain additional letters that have special meanings. In Excel 2007, the third letter is s for spreadsheet (workbook), t for template, or a for add-in. The fourth letter x indicates that the file is without macros, and m indicates that it does have macros.*

File Type	Excel Version	Description	File Extension
Excel Workbook	2007	Workbooks without macros	.xlsx
Excel Macro-Enabled Workbook	2007	Workbooks with macros	.xlsm
Excel Template	2007	Template workbooks without macros	.xltx
Excel Macro-Enabled Template	2007	Template workbooks with macros	.xltm
Excel 97-2003 Workbook	97–2003	Workbooks with or without macros	.xls
Excel 97-2003 Template	97–2003	Template workbooks with or without macros	.xlt
Excel Binary Workbook	97–2007	Non-XML workbooks	.xlsb
Microsoft Excel 5.0/95 Workbook	95	Early-version workbooks	.xls

Excel 2007 Open XML File Formats

As you can see from the preceding table, Excel 2007 has more file formats than previous versions to help identify files containing macros and reduce the file size, which is beneficial when you share files. The file structure, called Open XML, is based on the Extensible Markup Language (XML) used by software developers. XML is a growing standard for the exchange of structured data on the Internet.

Earlier Excel File Formats

Versions prior to Excel 2007 use different file formats than XML. For this reason, some Excel 2007 features are not viewable in the earlier versions. Files saved in these formats display the words *[Compatibility Mode]* in the Excel 2007 title bar as shown in the following illustration.

Schedule [Compatibility Mode] - Microsoft Excel

You have the following two options to enable users of earlier versions to open and work with your Excel 2007 file:

- **Save in a Non-XML File Format:** You may save your workbook in a file format that removes the incompatible features.

- **Use the Compatibility Pack:** Users may download and install a file converter that hides the incompatible features.

QUICK REFERENCE: WORKING WITH FILE FORMATS

Task	Procedure
Save a workbook in an Excel 97-2003 file format	■ Choose Office→Save As→Excel 97-2003 Workbook from the Ribbon. (Two files will now exist if you previously saved the file in Excel Workbook format.) ■ Correct any issues reported by the Compatibility Checker.
Display filename extensions	■ Open Windows Explorer. ■ Choose (Win XP) Tools→Folder Options or (Win Vista) Organize→Folder and Search Options. ■ Display the View tab, and under Advanced Settings remove the checkmark next to Hide Extensions for Known File Types.
Identify the format of files	■ Choose Office→Open 🗁 from the Ribbon or open Windows Explorer. ■ Navigate to the folder containing the file(s) in your file storage location. ■ Display the Files of Type list and choose All Files if working in Excel's Open dialog box. ■ Click the Views ▦ ▾ menu button on the dialog box or Explorer toolbar and choose Details. ■ Look at the icon next to the filename, read the filename extension (if displayed), and read the file type.

 Hands-On 17.1 Save a Workbook for an Earlier Excel Version

In this exercise, you will save an Excel 2007 workbook in a file format compatible with an earlier version of Excel. You will view file details to identify file formats.

Save the Workbook

1. Start Excel and open the Schedule workbook from the Lesson 17 folder in your file storage location.

2. Maximize ⬜ the window.
   This workbook contains three worksheets. Notice that the words [Compatibility Mode] do not appear after the filename in the title bar. This workbook was saved in Excel 2007, and all its features are visible.

3. Choose Office→Save As→Excel 97-2003 Workbook from the Ribbon.

4. In the Save As dialog box, notice that the filename remains the same and that the Save As Type is changed to the file format you chose.

File name:	Schedule
Save as type:	Excel 97-2003 Workbook

   No other filenames display because you are currently filtering for only this Excel 97-2003 type. Other files do exist in the folder, but they are not in this file format.

5. Click Save.
   No alerts appeared because Excel found no compatibility issues in this workbook. This file could be opened and edited in Excel versions 97 through 2003.

Identify the Format of Files

Next you will display the filenames in the Lesson 17 folder and review their file formats.

6. Choose Office→Open from the Ribbon and navigate to the Lesson 17 folder, if not already displayed.

7. Follow these steps to display details about the files in the folder:
   Your dialog box displays more files than shown here.

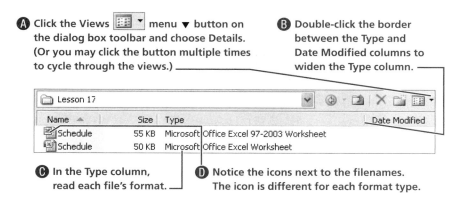

A Click the Views ▦ ▾ menu ▾ button on the dialog box toolbar and choose Details. (Or you may click the button multiple times to cycle through the views.)

B Double-click the border between the Type and Date Modified columns to widen the Type column.

Name ▲	Size	Type	Date Modified
Schedule	55 KB	Microsoft Office Excel 97-2003 Worksheet	
Schedule	50 KB	Microsoft Office Excel Worksheet	

C In the Type column, read each file's format.

D Notice the icons next to the filenames. The icon is different for each format type.

Also, each filename displays a filename extension, such as .xlsx, if the display option is switched on in Windows.

8. Click Cancel to exit the Open dialog box.

9. Close the workbook and leave Excel open.

Checking for Excel Version Compatibility

The Compatibility Checker scans your workbook and identifies any features that would not be included if you were to save the workbook in a non-XML (nonnative) file format. The report summarizes various incompatibilities as significant or minor, and it provides a Find button to help you locate each occurrence in the workbook. You may decide to proceed if the compatibility check reports only a minor loss of fidelity, such as table formatting. Significant issues usually must be resolved. The dialog box contains an option that, when switched on, will check for compatibility every time the workbook is saved.

 !TIP! *The Compatibility Checker automatically scans any file that you save in a non-XML format even if you did not run the Checker before giving the Save As command.*

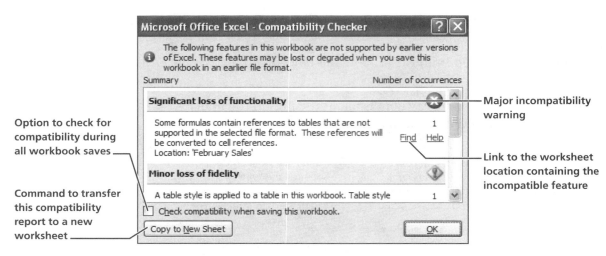

Option to check for compatibility during all workbook saves

Command to transfer this compatibility report to a new worksheet

Major incompatibility warning

Link to the worksheet location containing the incompatible feature

A report displayed by the Compatibility Checker before or while a file is saved

---

 ## Hands-On 17.2   Check Excel Version Compatibility

In this exercise, you will run the Compatibility Checker to check for compatibility issues before attempting to save a file in the Excel 97-2003 file format.

1. Open the Compatibility Check workbook from the Lesson 17 folder.
   Notice that the Editing Schedule worksheet contains a table, which is not supported in previous Excel versions.

Run the Compatibility Checker

If you accidentally close the Compatibility Checker window in the following steps, just give the command again.

2. Choose Office→Prepare→Run Compatibility Checker from the Ribbon.
   After a few moments, the Microsoft Office Excel – Compatibility Checker window appears with its report of two issues related to the table in the workbook.

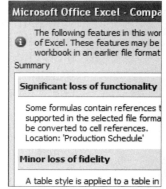

3. Scroll through the window and read both messages.

4. Click the Help link under Minor Loss of Fidelity.
   Excel Help displays information to help resolve table compatibility issues.

5. Browse the Help topic, and then close the Help window.

6. In the Compatibility Checker window, scroll up and click the Find link under Significant Loss of Functionality.
   The pointer jumps to cell C15 on the Production Schedule worksheet. This cell contains a formula with a structured reference to table cells on the Editing Schedule worksheet. You would edit the workbook to correct this significant compatibility issue before saving. However, you are not required to make any corrections in this exercise.

7. Notice that the Compatibility Checker window is closed because you used the Find link.
   You may run the Compatibility Checker again as needed, and any resolved issues will no longer display.

Use Save As

Next, you will give the Save As command to save the file for an earlier Excel version. Remember that two compatibility issues still exist in the workbook.

8. Choose Office→Save As from the Ribbon.

9. In the Save As dialog box, drop down the Save As Type list, and choose Excel 97-2003 Workbook.
   You may choose the file format in the dialog box rather than in the Office→Save As menu.

File name:	Compatibility Check
Save as type:	Excel 97-2003 Workbook

10. Click Save.
    The Compatibility Checker window appears. Excel automatically runs the checker whenever you attempt to save a workbook in a non-XML file format. Notice the buttons at the bottom of the dialog box. The Continue button would save the file with the issues unresolved. That might be appropriate for minor compatibility issues but is not the action that you want to take now.

11. Click Copy to New Sheet.
    The compatibility issues report, including cell locations, is transferred to a separate worksheet for documentation and printing. You could use this information to continue resolving any compatibility issues until the workbook would be ready for saving.

12. Close the workbook without saving.

Using the Compatibility Pack

A free compatibility download from Microsoft allows users of previous Excel 2000, XP (2002), and 2003 versions to open and work with Excel 2007 files. Users are prompted to download and install the Microsoft Office Compatibility Pack the first time they attempt to open an Excel 2007 file. Thereafter, any opened Excel 2007 files will be converted automatically. Any formatting or other features specific to Excel 2007 do not display when the file is opened in the previous version but are preserved when the file is reopened in Excel 2007. Having that capability may be worth asking other users to take the time to install the Compatibility Pack.

TIP! *If asking others to install the Compatibility Pack could cause a problem—perhaps inconveniencing your best customers—you may opt to save files in the Excel 97-2003 file format as previously described in this lesson. Just remember that some Excel 2007 features may be removed permanently from those files.*

Converters

A converter is a small program that allows an application program such as Excel to open files that are not in the program's native file format. For example, you may need to import data from a Word document into a worksheet. Excel features a variety of converters that are installed automatically. You also may download and install additional converters that may become available as new file formats are introduced. For example, when a new version of an application program is released, it often introduces a new native file format.

Example of Using a Converter

You send a workbook saved in an Excel 2007 file format to another user who uses Excel 2003. The other user installs the Compatibility Pack, which includes converter programs. When she opens your Excel 2007 file, it is converted to a format that is compatible with her Excel version. Any incompatible features will be hidden.

Task	Procedure
Check a workbook for features incompatible with earlier Excel versions	■ With the workbook open, choose Office→Prepare→Run Compatibility Checker from the Ribbon.
	■ Click the Find link in the Compatibility Checker dialog box to locate the first incompatible cell, if any issues are reported.
	■ Edit the worksheet to correct a major incompatibility.
	■ Run Compatibility Checker again to verify that the previous issue is no longer reported. Find and, if necessary, correct any additional major issues. Correct minor issues as necessary.
Install the Microsoft Office Compatibility Pack	■ Start Internet Explorer, navigate to the Office 2007 Downloads web page, enter *Compatibility Pack* in the Search box, and initiate the search.
	■ Follow instructions to download and install the Microsoft Office Compatibility Pack for Word, Excel, and PowerPoint 2007 file formats.

Converting Workbooks to Other File Formats

At times, you may need to save worksheet data to use in a program other than Excel or upload a worksheet onto a web page. You may choose from several file formats in the Save As dialog box, such as XML Data or Web Page. This topic explains two common methods of sharing data between incompatible programs or with users who do not have the original program.

Text File Formats

Text file formats are commonly used to export data to or from another program that is incompatible with Excel. All worksheet formatting, such as fonts, colors, and graphics, is removed. Two types of text files are used most often in conjunction with Excel: comma delimited and tab delimited.

Comma Delimited

A comma delimited text file uses a comma to separate two columns of data. The following illustration shows an example of Excel data converted in a comma delimited file. When saving a workbook in this file format, you would choose CSV (Comma Delimited) from the Save As Type list. The filename extension .csv is added to the filename.

```
First,Last,Phone,City
Deion,Jenett,310-555-7823,Los Angeles
Jacqueline,Chan,541-555-8989,Ashland
Terry,Sanchez,617-555-2220,Boston
```

Excel column data converted to the comma delimited format

Tab Delimited

A tab delimited file uses a tab character to separate two columns of data. In the following example of a tab delimited file, each small arrow represents a non-printing tab code. When saving a workbook in this file format, you would choose Text (Tab Delimited) from the Save As Type list. The filename extension .txt is added to the filename.

Excel column data converted
to the tab delimited format

Limitations of File Formats

Some file formats will not save all information in the workbook file. For example, a tab delimited file won't save data on multiple worksheets or any cell formatting. Excel will warn you about features, formatting, or data you might lose in the new file format. When you save a workbook to a non-Excel file format, a second file is created. The original workbook file is not changed.

Icons and filenames for an original Excel workbook
and a version saved in tab delimited format

Example of a File Format Limitation

You decide to convert a workbook to tab delimited format. Excel warns you that only the currently selected worksheet can be saved to the new file. So, you perform a save command for each worksheet in the workbook. Now each worksheet is contained in a separate file. You also notice that comments on the worksheets are not saved in the tab delimited format.

QR> | **QUICK REFERENCE: CONVERTING WORKSHEET DATA TO A TEXT FORMAT**

Task

Save workbook data in comma delimited or tab delimited format

Procedure

- Choose Office→Save As ⊟ from the Ribbon.
- In the Save As dialog box, choose CSV (Comma Delimited) or Text (Tab Delimited) from the Save As Type list.
- Enter the name in the File Name box and click Save.

Hands-On 17.3   Convert Excel Data to Text

In this exercise, you will use the Save As command to save a copy of a worksheet in a different file format. You will then use the Notepad application to view the workbook in its new file format.

Convert a Worksheet to Text

1. Open the original Schedule workbook that is in the Excel Workbook file format. Its icon is shown to the right.

2. Display the Editing Schedule worksheet, if not already displayed.

3. Choose Office→Save As from the Ribbon.

4. Follow these steps to save the workbook in the tab delimited file format:

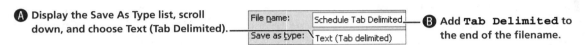

Ⓐ Display the Save As Type list, scroll down, and choose Text (Tab Delimited).

File name: Schedule Tab Delimited

Save as type: Text (Tab delimited)

Ⓑ Add **Tab Delimited** to the end of the filename.

5. Click the Save button and read the warning box.
   Excel warns you that the selected file type cannot save a file containing multiple worksheets. It will save only the active worksheet.

6. Click OK to acknowledge the warning, and then review the next warning box that appears.
   Excel now warns you that the tab delimited file format may not be compatible with features in your workbook file. Features other than the text in cells, such as cell formatting, will be removed in the resulting file.

7. Choose Yes to continue the conversion to the tab delimited format.
   Excel completes the conversion. Notice that the worksheet tab has been renamed to the new filename. Although the name of the new file appears in the Excel title bar, you are not really viewing the converted file. You must open the newly converted file to see the changes.

8. Use ⌈Ctrl⌉+⌈W⌉ to close the workbook. Choose No when you are asked if you wish to save the workbook.

View the Converted Data

9. Choose Office→Open from the Ribbon and navigate to the Lesson 17 folder, if necessary.
   Notice that the newly converted file is not listed. That's because Excel is displaying only workbook files. A tab delimited file is saved in text format. In the next step, you will tell Excel to display all text format files.

10. Choose Text Files from the Files of Type list, as shown at right.
    Three files with this file format display. You used the Open dialog box only to navigate to a file. In the next step, you will open the file using a different program. The Notepad applet is a simple text editor that comes with Windows. It allows you to view exactly what the data in your converted file looks like.

File name:

Files of type: Text Files

11. Follow these steps to open the text file in Notepad:

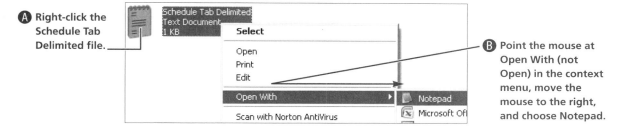

Ⓐ Right-click the Schedule Tab Delimited file.

Ⓑ Point the mouse at Open With (not Open) in the context menu, move the mouse to the right, and choose Notepad.

The file opens in Notepad, the Windows text editor program. Notice that the file contains only plain text separated by tabs. The original worksheet's cell formatting and the logo graphic were removed. This file format, however, may be the only means of bringing the data into certain programs that are not compatible with Excel.

12. Close the Notepad window. Choose No if you are asked to save changes to the file.

13. Cancel Excel's Open dialog box.

PDF and XPS File Formats

The PDF (Portable Document Format) and XPS (XML Paper Specification) file formats may be applied to Excel workbooks and many other types of documents. This file format allows colleagues to view and print a workbook with all formatting intact even if they don't have any Excel version, and it also prevents them from making any changes or accessing any hidden information. For example, a user who installs the free Adobe Acrobat Reader may view a PDF document. After you install a free download from Microsoft, the Save As submenu displays an additional command, Save As PDF or XPS. You may publish a selected range, a worksheet, or the entire workbook.

 TIP! *Personal information from the document's properties, such as your Microsoft Office user name, are saved with the PDF or XPS document unless you choose Options and uncheck Document Properties.*

 QR **QUICK REFERENCE: PUBLISHING A WORKBOOK IN PDF OR XPS FORMAT**

Task	Procedure
Install the PDF or XPS converter	■ Choose Office→Save As→Find Add-Ins for Other File Formats from the Ribbon.
	■ In the Enable Support for Other File Formats, Such as PDF and XPS topic in Microsoft Excel Help, click the hyperlink to the download section and follow the instructions to download and install the converter.
Publish a PDF or XPS document	■ To save part of a workbook, display the desired worksheet. Select a range, if desired.
	■ Choose Office→Save As→PDF or XPS.
	■ Enter the workbook name in the File Name box.
	■ Choose PDF (or choose XPS) from the Save As Type list.
	■ Choose an Optimize option, and then choose other options as desired.
	■ Click Publish.

Hands-On 17.4 Publish Excel Data as a PDF Document

In this exercise, you will convert a workbook to the PDF file format, and then you will view the file in a PDF reader program.

Before You Begin: *Your computer must have Excel's PDF or XPS publisher installed, as well as a PDF reader such as Adobe Acrobat Reader.*

1. Open the original Schedule workbook. Its icon is shown to the right. If necessary, change Files of Type to Excel Files to see the filename.

2. Choose Office→Save As→PDF or XPS from the Ribbon.

 If necessary, use the steps in Publishing a Workbook in PDF or XPS Format Quick Reference table on page 653 to install the command. Skip the remainder of this exercise if you do not have permission to install the PDF or XPS command.

The Publish as PDF or XPS dialog box displays. The file-name Schedule should already be entered, and the default file type is PDF. Notice that the Open File After Publishing option is switched on.

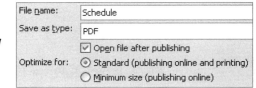

3. Click the Options button at the lower-right corner of the dialog box.

4. Under Publish What in the Options dialog box, choose Entire Workbook.
   Notice that you may publish a selected range, the active worksheet, the entire workbook, or a table (available when a table range is selected). The Ignore Print Areas option is used to disregard any print area set in Excel.

5. Click OK.

6. Click the Publish button in the Publish as PDF or XPS dialog box.
   After a few moments, the published workbook displays in an Adobe Acrobat (or other PDF reader) window. This occurs because the Open File After Publishing option was switched on. Depending on the PDF reader you use, the filename Schedule.pdf usually appears in the window's title bar.

7. Maximize the PDF reader window.

8. Use the following tools to browse through the document (your reader window may differ from the one shown):

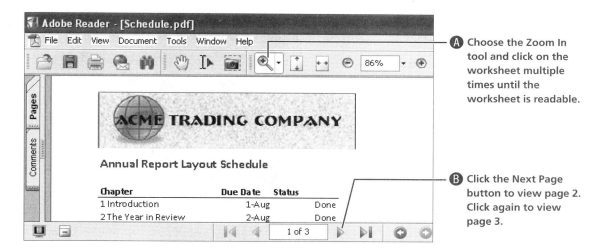

Ⓐ Choose the Zoom In tool and click on the worksheet multiple times until the worksheet is readable.

Ⓑ Click the Next Page button to view page 2. Click again to view page 3.

The toolbar buttons allow you to print or select and copy text and objects, but you cannot alter anything in this document.

9. Close the reader window.

10. Close the Schedule workbook and leave Excel open.

Using Excel Tables with Word Mail Merge

Chris Smith, the administrative manager at Acme Trading Company, periodically sends multiple customers a letter or an envelope containing sales materials. Word's mail merge feature helps Chris prepare a standard message (called the main document) and personalize each copy with the customer's name, address, most recent order date, and other data unique to that customer. You may use a list or table from an Excel worksheet as a data source for these and other documents in Word. In this lesson, you will work with tables. A table should be set up with each field (column) containing one type of data, such as the order date. You insert various field names in the main document to personalize the message. When the mail merge is completed, data from each record (row) of the data source replace the field names, and you have a personalized document copy for each record.

 TIP! *For a successful mail merge, break up data into its smallest segments. For example, each of the following segments in an address list should be in a separate column: title, first name, middle initial, last name, street, city, state, and ZIP code.*

QUICK REFERENCE: USING EXCEL TABLES WITH WORD MAIL MERGE

Task	Procedure
Create the table and name the worksheet in Excel	■ Create the table in an Excel workbook. For best results, enter the table column headings in row 1 of the worksheet. ■ Double-click the sheet tab, type the sheet name, and tap [Enter]. ■ Save the workbook.
Start the mail merge in Word	Do one of the following: ■ Open the desired main document. ■ Start a new, blank document in Word. ■ Choose Mailings→Start Mail Merge→Start Mail Merge ▣ and choose the document type from the Ribbon.
Choose an Excel worksheet as the data source	■ Choose Mailings→Start Mail Merge→Use an Existing List from the Ribbon. ■ In the Select Data Source dialog box, select the Excel file containing the table and click Open. ■ In the Select Table dialog box, choose the desired worksheet, place a checkmark in the box next to First Row of Data Contains Column Headers, and click OK.
Select records	■ Choose Mailings→Start Mail Merge→Edit Recipient List ▣ from the Ribbon. ■ Use options to sort, filter, find, and deselect records, as desired.
Complete the main document	■ Type text and use Mailings→Write & Insert Fields→Insert Merge Field from the Ribbon.
Preview the merged copies	■ Choose Mailings→Preview Results→Preview Results ▣ from the Ribbon. ■ Use navigation buttons in the Preview Results group on the Ribbon to view the document for any one record.
Print or email the completed document copies	■ Choose Mailings→Finish→Finish & Merge→Print Documents (or Send E-mail Messages) from the Ribbon.

 TIP! *After starting the mail merge, you use commands in sequence on the Mailings Ribbon from left to right. The next command usually is dimmed until you complete the preceding step.*

Hands-On 17.5   Mail Merge Excel Table Data in Word

Chris needs to send a reservation form to each employee in the Graphics Department. In this exercise, you will merge a form document with employee data from an Excel table to fill in the form with each employee's name, identification number, and so on.

View the Table Data

1. Open the Employee List workbook from the Lesson 17 folder in your file storage location.

2. Display the Graphics worksheet.
   Notice that the table's column headings are in row 1 of the worksheet. This helps you work with the data more easily during the merge. Each column (field) contains a specific category of data, such as Last Name. Each row (record) contains the data for one employee.

3. Close the workbook.

Start the Merge

4. Start Word and open Seminar Form from the Lesson 17 folder.
   This is the main document that you will merge with employee data from the Excel table. You may also start with a new, blank document and enter the necessary information for the main document.

   Next you will use commands on the Mailings Ribbon. After using a Ribbon command, you will use the command to its right until you complete the merge.

5. Choose Mailings→Start Mail Merge→Start Mail Merge 🖹 from the Ribbon.
   Notice that the formatting choices on the menu include letters, envelopes, labels, an address directory, and a normal document. You would select one of these to start the main document if one were not already created.

6. Press ⎋Esc to cancel the menu.

Connect to the Data Source

7. Choose Mailings→Start Mail Merge→Select Recipients→Use Existing List from the Ribbon.

8. In the Select Data Source dialog box, navigate to the Lesson 17 folder, choose the Employee List workbook, and click Open.

9. Follow these steps to select the Graphics worksheet:

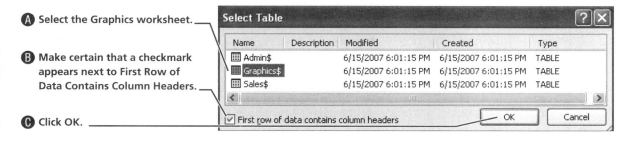

Ⓐ Select the Graphics worksheet.

Ⓑ Make certain that a checkmark appears next to First Row of Data Contains Column Headers.

Ⓒ Click OK.

10. Choose Mailings→Start Mail Merge→Edit Recipient List 📝 from the Ribbon.

11. In the Mail Merge Recipients dialog box, click in the checkbox next to employees Eng and Sullivan to deselect the department's editors.

Data Source	☑	Last ▼	First ▼	Position ▼	Email ▼	Employee ID
Employee List.xlsx	☑	Aberdeen	Millie	Senior Designer	maberdeen@acme.com	064-55
Employee List.xlsx	☑	Brown	Jennifer	Graphic Artist	jbrown@acme.com	142-84
Employee List.xlsx	☐	Eng	David	Editor	deng@acme.com	467-22
Employee List.xlsx	☑	Fox	Barbara	Proofreader	bfox@acme.com	656-01
Employee List.xlsx	☑	Garcia	Joe	Compositor	jgarcia@acme.com	987-65
Employee List.xlsx	☑	Milano	Michael	Graphic Artist	mmilano@acme.com	555-01
Employee List.xlsx	☑	Rodriguez	Maria	Compositor	mrodriguez@acme.com	550-65
Employee List.xlsx	☑	Scorr	Lawrence	Compositor	lscorr@acme.com	098-69
Employee List.xlsx	☐	Sullivan	Jenna	Editor	jsullivan@acme.com	798-34
Employee List.xlsx	☑	Zack	Glenn	Photographer	gzack@acme.com	985-67

Notice the commands to sort, filter, and find records in the lower half of the dialog box. You may also perform these tasks by clicking the triangle next to a column heading, which displays a menu. You may edit the worksheet and refresh the list from within this dialog box.

12. Click OK in the Mail Merge Recipients dialog box.

Insert Merge Fields

You will insert field names in the form. Word will substitute one employee's data in those locations on each copy of the form.

13. Click in the blank to the right of Employee Name in the form.

14. Choose Mailings→Write & Insert Fields→Insert Merge Field→First from the Ribbon, and then tap [Spacebar].

15. Choose Mailings→Write & Insert Fields→Insert Merge Field→Last from the Ribbon.

16. Use the preceding step to add the Employee ID and Position fields as shown in the following illustration.

Employee Name:	«First» «Last»
Employee ID:	«Employee_ID»
Job Title:	«Position»

You may insert field names within a paragraph or in a mailing address to create a business letter, envelope, or labels. You type punctuation and spaces between words as necessary.

17. Click in the blank to the right of Manager and type **Tyrone Washington**.

Manager:	Tyrone Washington

You typed directly in the form because all employees have the same manager. All text typed in the main document appears in every individualized copy.

18. Click in the blank to the right of Department and type **Graphics**.

19. Choose Mailings→Write & Insert Fields→Highlight Merge Fields 📄 from the Ribbon.
The field names are identified with a gray background to show you the location of inserted fields in the entire document.

20. Choose Mailings→Write & Insert Fields→Highlight Merge Fields 📄 from the Ribbon again to toggle off the highlighting.
If displayed, the highlighting would appear in printed copies, which is not desirable.

Preview the Form Copies

21. Choose Mailings→Preview Results→Preview Results  from the Ribbon.

The view switches to the form for the first employee in the table. (If the tenth record displays, click the First Record button on the Ribbon.)

22. Choose Mailings→Preview Results→Next Record in the Ribbon. Click the button again to view the next few records.

Record 3 (Eng) and record 9 (Sullivan) do not display because you unchecked them in step 11 of this exercise.

Print a Copy

23. Choose Mailings→Finish→Finish and Merge→Print Documents from the Ribbon.

24. In the Merge to Printer dialog box, choose Current Record and click OK.

25. Click OK in the Print dialog box to print one copy of the form.

26. Retrieve the printout from the printer.

27. Save 💾 the changes and exit Word.

Sharing Excel Data with Access

Access, a software application in Microsoft Office, stores data in tables that look similar to Excel worksheets. While you usually may format data and create calculations more easily in Excel, the database capabilities of Access allow you to filter large amounts of data using queries and to combine data from multiple sources to create various reports. When you import an Excel worksheet into a new Access table, you have the option to link the data. Then, any updates made to the original worksheet data in Excel are shown when you reopen the database and the related Access table. Without linking, the data is not updated in Access. Linked data cannot be edited in Access.

⚠ WARNING! *If the original linked Excel workbook is moved or deleted, its link is broken and the data is not available in Access. The Linked Table Manager command in Access allows you to give the new location if the file was moved. Make frequent backups of linked workbooks in case a file is deleted inadvertently.*

QUICK REFERENCE: IMPORTING EXCEL DATA INTO ACCESS

Task	Procedure
Import worksheet data as a new Access table or into an existing table	■ Open the Access database. ■ Choose External Data→Import→Excel 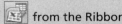 from the Ribbon. ■ In the Get External Data – Excel Spreadsheet dialog box, click Browse and choose the desired workbook. ■ Choose an import option and click OK. ■ In the Import Spreadsheet Wizard dialog box, place a checkmark in the box next to First Row Contains Column Headings. ■ Continue choosing options and clicking Next in the wizard. ■ Enter the name for the new or existing Access table and click Finish. ■ Respond to any message box that appears. ■ Display All Tables in the Navigation Pane and double-click the table to open it.

Hands-On 17.6 Import Worksheet Data into Access

Chris has partially completed an Access database to track tasks and projects assigned to various company employees. In this exercise, you will import employee data from an Excel worksheet as a new table in the database. Then you will import the same worksheet but set a link to observe the difference.

1. Start Access.

2. Click the More link at the right of the Getting Started with Microsoft Office Access window, navigate to the Lesson 17 folder, and open the Acme Employees database.
   The design of this database is not yet complete. The Navigation Pane on the left contains the names of various tables, forms, and reports that make up the database.

Open Recent Database
📂 More...

Import a Worksheet as a New Table

3. Choose External Data→Import→Excel 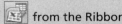 from the Ribbon.

4. In the Get External Data – Excel Spreadsheet dialog box, click Browse and choose the Acme Staff workbook from the Lesson 17 folder.
   Read the three options for importing worksheet data in the dialog box.

5. Make certain that the Import the Source Data into a New Table in the Current Database option is selected, and then click OK.
   The Import Spreadsheet Wizard dialog box appears and displays a preview of the All Staff worksheet. (If the workbook contained multiple worksheets, you would be prompted to select one.) Notice that the column headings display as the first data row as shown to the right. They should be above row 1, and you will correct this in the next step.

1	Employee ID	Last Name	First Name
2	779-54	Olivier	Jillian

6. Place a checkmark in the box next to First Row Contains Column Headings.
   The column headings display above the first row of data. Remember to choose this option, or the worksheet data will not import correctly.

7. Click Next and review the options.
   The wizard displays options to format the worksheet columns as fields in the database. You will not change any options.

8. Click Next, review the options, and click Next again.

9. In the Import to Table box, change the existing name to **Employees**.
   You are naming the new Access table. You need not use the worksheet name.

10. Click Finish, and click Close in the next window. (Do not select the Save Import Steps option.)
    The new Employees table name displays under the Employees group in the Navigation Pane on the left.

11. Double-click Employees: Table to open the table.
    Notice that Access added ID as the first field in the table and automatically numbered the records. Depending on the database design, you may want to delete this field in the Import Spreadsheet Wizard dialog box while importing the data.

Import as a Linked Worksheet

Now you will import the same data by linking to the original worksheet to observe the difference.

12. Choose External Data→Import→Excel from the Ribbon.

13. In the Get External Data – Excel Spreadsheet dialog box, click Browse and choose the Acme Staff workbook.

14. Choose Link to the Data Source by Creating a Linked Table and click OK.

15. Place a checkmark in the box next to First Row Contains Column Headings.

16. Click Next.
    This time no field options appear because you are linking to the worksheet.

17. Leave the Linked Table Name as All Staff, and then click Finish. Click OK when alerted that the link has been completed.
    Notice that the icon next to All Staff in the Navigation Pane indicates a linked Excel worksheet.

18. Double-click All Staff in the Navigation Pane to open the table.

19. Click in any cell and try to type a different entry.
    You cannot edit the data from within Access. You may only edit the original worksheet in Excel.

20. Close Access. Click Yes if prompted to save the table design.

Inserting Excel Charts in PowerPoint

Using the Paste command is usually the best method for inserting an existing Excel chart in PowerPoint. If no chart yet exists, you may create one entirely in PowerPoint using the same commands and options as in Excel, as long as Excel is installed on the same computer.

 NOTE! *PivotCharts are converted to normal charts when pasted in a presentation. You may adjust formatting but cannot adjust fields and calculations.*

Linking Compared to Embedding

By default, a pasted chart is linked to its original Excel workbook. This means that if the worksheet data is updated and saved, the chart automatically updates in the PowerPoint presentation. Take care not to delete the original worksheet data or the workbook file because the link would be broken. Immediately after a chart is pasted, a Paste Options SmartTag appears in the lower-right corner. You may use the options in the SmartTag menu, shown in the following illustration, to embed the chart or paste it as a picture. Embedding places an editable copy of the chart in the destination document. The user does not need the original workbook file, which simplifies sharing the presentation, but any changes to the workbook are not updated in the document holding the embedded copy.

The Paste Options default is to link the chart, or you may use the SmartTag menu to embed the chart or paste it as a picture.

 WARNING! *Embedding a chart in another document gives users access to the entire workbook upon which the chart is based. If that is not desirable, you should copy a worksheet and its chart to a separate workbook.*

 QUICK REFERENCE: LINKING AND EMBEDDING EXCEL CHARTS IN A POWERPOINT SLIDE

Task	Procedure
Link an Excel chart on a slide	■ Create and save the worksheet and chart in Excel. ■ Right-click in a blank area of the chart and choose Copy from the context menu. ■ Close the workbook. ■ Open the desired presentation in PowerPoint and create a slide using a layout containing a content placeholder. ■ Right-click the content placeholder and choose Paste from the context menu.
Update a linked chart in PowerPoint	■ Right-click on the chart and choose Edit Data from the context menu. ■ Edit the worksheet upon which the chart is based. ■ Close the workbook and click Yes to save.
Embed an Excel chart on a slide	■ Perform the preceding steps for linking a chart. ■ Immediately after pasting the chart, click the Paste Options SmartTag button at the lower-right of the chart and choose Excel Chart (Entire Workbook) from the menu.

In this exercise, you will copy a chart from an Excel workbook and paste the chart onto a PowerPoint slide. Then you will change a value on the linked worksheet from within PowerPoint to update the chart.

1. Open the AR Project Expenses workbook.

2. Right-click in a blank area of the chart and choose Copy from the context menu.

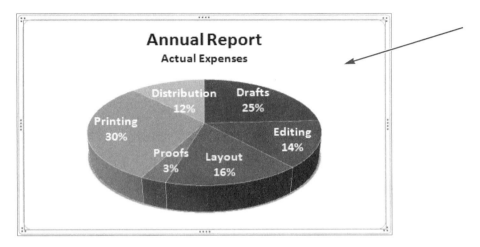

3. Close the workbook.
   The chart remains on the Clipboard even though you closed the source document.

4. Start PowerPoint and open the Project Budget presentation from the Lesson 17 folder.

5. Select slide 2 in the Slides tab at the left of the window.
   This slide has the Title and Content layout.

6. In the Slide Pane, right-click in a blank area within the content place-holder and select Paste from the context menu. (If the placeholder is not visible, click in the center of the slide.)

Because you selected the placeholder prior to pasting, the chart fills the placeholder and you need not resize or center the chart on the slide.

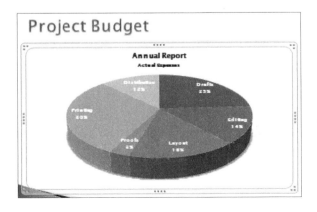

Update the Linked Chart

Next you will change a worksheet value and the chart from within PowerPoint.

7. Right-click anywhere on the chart and choose Edit Data from the context menu.
   Excel opens and displays the original worksheet next to the PowerPoint window.

8. In cell D14, notice that Distribution is 12 percent of the total expenses. Scroll to the right, if necessary, to see that 12 percent is also shown in the Distribution pie slice.

9. Change cell C14 to **1000**.
   The percentage changes to 26 percent.

10. Close the workbook and click Yes when asked if you want to save.
    Saving the changes will update the linked chart in PowerPoint. Notice that Distribution is now 26 percent in the PowerPoint chart.

11. Close PowerPoint and click Yes when asked if you want to save.

Importing External Data

You can bring data from other application programs into Excel. This is called *importing*. For example, if a coworker types some information in Word, you may import this data directly into an Excel worksheet. Excel can import a variety of data into your workbooks. You may import data from as many sources as needed to complete a document. Converters are installed in Excel to import data from many popular applications.

 TIP! *If Excel can't import a specific type of data, check in the source application to see if you can save the data in another file format that is compatible with Excel. Some loss of formatting may occur.*

The three methods that you may use to import data into an Excel worksheet are the following:

■ **Copy and Paste:** You may use standard copy and paste commands to bring text, images, and charts into a worksheet.

■ **Drag and Drop:** You may select data in another application program, use the mouse to drag the selection into an Excel worksheet, and release the mouse button.

■ **Import a File:** The Get External Data command on the Data Ribbon is used to import an entire text file, Access table, web page table, or data from other sources such as a network server.

Using Copy and Paste

You may copy and paste data between another application and an Excel workbook. For example, you may copy and paste a table or text from a Word document into an Excel worksheet. You simply select the data in the other document window, cut or copy the selection, and paste it into the desired cell in the Excel window. You may also use the Paste Special command to paste data, such as images, into Excel in a specific format.

Importing Data with Drag and Drop

You may drag and drop data between another application window and an Excel workbook. For example, you may drag and drop a table or text from a Word document into an Excel worksheet. You select the data to be imported and then drag and drop it onto the desired worksheet. When you use this technique, the data is cut from the source file. However, if you close the source file without saving, the original data will be retained.

QUICK REFERENCE: IMPORTING DATA BETWEEN DOCUMENTS

Task	Procedure
Import text data with Copy and Paste	■ Open the application window. ■ Select the text in the source document and choose Home→Clipboard→Copy (or use ⟨Ctrl⟩+⟨C⟩). ■ Select the desired cell of the worksheet and choose Home→Clipboard→Paste (or use ⟨Ctrl⟩+⟨V⟩). ■ Format the pasted text as desired.
Import text data with Drag and Drop	■ Display the Excel worksheet window and an application window containing the text data side by side. ■ Drag to select the text data in the other program. Point to the selection, drag toward the Excel window, point to a cell in the worksheet, and release the mouse button.

Hands-On 17.8 Import Data between Documents

Deion is compiling several schedules for producing the Acme Trading Company's annual report into one workbook. In this exercise, you will insert the Acme Trading Company logo at the top of a worksheet and then use the Copy and Paste commands to add the logo to other worksheets. You will drag and drop text from a Word document into the workbook. Finally, you will copy a table and text from Word and paste it in the workbook.

Insert and Duplicate the Logo

1. Open the AR Production Schedule workbook and maximize the window.

2. Select cell A1 on the Editing Schedule worksheet, if not already selected, and then choose Insert→Illustrations→Picture from the Ribbon.

3. Navigate to the Lesson 17 folder in your file storage location, if not already displayed.
   Excel displays only one picture file in the Insert Picture dialog box. Notice that Files of Type near the bottom of the dialog box is set to All Pictures.

4. Double-click Acme Logo to insert the image in cell A1.

5. With the image still selected, right-click the image and choose Copy from the context menu.

6. Display the Layout Schedule worksheet.

7. Right-click cell A1 and choose Paste from the context menu.
   As you may recall from Lesson 2, Editing, Viewing, and Printing Worksheets, the Clipboard retains the most recently copied or cut items. Thus, you can paste the logo multiple times after you give the Copy command.

8. Display the Production Schedule worksheet and paste the logo into cell A1.

Drag and Drop Text

Another staff member used Word to compose her status list. You will use drag and drop to copy a heading from her Word document into Excel.

9. Display the Layout Schedule worksheet.

10. Start Word and open the AR Layout Schedule document.

11. Right-click in a blank area of the Windows taskbar at the bottom of the screen and choose Tile Windows Vertically (or Show Windows Side by Side) from the context menu.
The Excel and Word windows display side by side. This will make it easy for you to drag and drop from one window to the other. If any other window also displays, minimize it and repeat the Tile Windows Vertically (or Show Windows Side by Side) command.

12. Click the AR Layout Schedule button in the Windows taskbar to activate the Word document.

13. Follow these steps to drag and drop text into the worksheet:

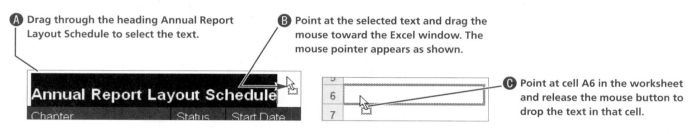

A Drag through the heading Annual Report Layout Schedule to select the text.

B Point at the selected text and drag the mouse toward the Excel window. The mouse pointer appears as shown.

C Point at cell A6 in the worksheet and release the mouse button to drop the text in that cell.

Notice that the heading text disappeared from the Word document. A drag and drop cuts the selection from the source document.

14. Click the first navigation button on the toolbar at the lower left of the window to display the Editing Schedule tab, as shown to the right.

15. Use the Format Painter on the Ribbon to copy the formatting from cell A6 in the Editing Schedule worksheet to cell A6 that you just added in the Layout Schedule worksheet.

Copy and Paste a Word Table and Text

Now you will transfer the remainder of the Word document. You could use drag and drop, but you may find copying and pasting to be easier for a longer selection.

16. Maximize the Word window.

17. Follow these steps to copy the Word table and legend text:

Ⓐ Point to the left of the word *Chapter* outside the table and drag straight down to select the table and the Key legend text.

Ⓑ Use `Ctrl`+`C` to copy the selection.

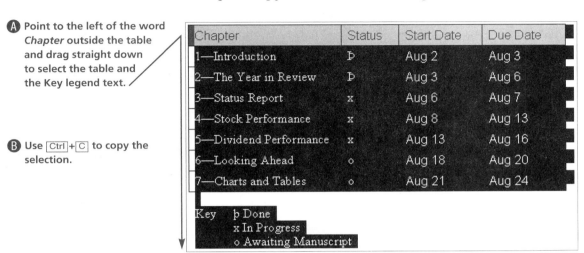

18. Switch to the Excel window in the Windows taskbar.

19. Maximize the Excel window.

20. Select cell A7 in the Layout Schedule worksheet, and then use `Ctrl`+`V` to paste.
Thanks to Excel's Word converter, the formatting carried over into the Excel worksheet. The table cells from Word display in separate cells of the worksheet. The tab codes in the Key legend text caused that text to be placed into two columns. Notice that Excel reformatted the dates in Custom format, such as 2-Aug.

21. Format the range A7 through D18 in Calibri font and a font size of 11.
You may format imported text just like any other text in the worksheet.

22. Deselect the range.

23. Right-align the Start Date and Due Date labels over their numbers.
Your worksheet should look similar to the illustration at right.

24. Close Word and click No when asked if you want to save.
This prevents the loss of the text that you dragged and dropped. If you were to reopen this document, all of the content would reappear.

25. Save 💾 the changes in Excel and leave the workbook open.

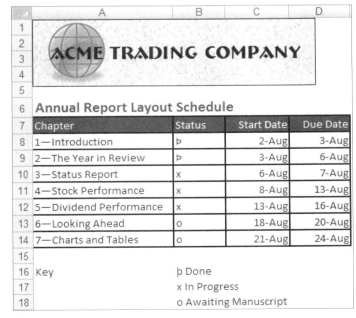

Importing a Text File

The From Text command imports an entire text file into an Excel worksheet as data. The source file format may be either tab delimited (.txt) or comma delimited (.csv). When another program is not compatible with Excel, you may need to save its data as text in one of those two formats. When you import a text file, Excel examines the file to determine whether the formatting in the file will help lay out the data neatly into rows and columns. For example, if the text file is comma delimited, Excel will place each data item following a comma in a separate column. The From Text command can also help you deal with certain formatting problems that you may encounter with tab delimited or comma delimited text files.

QR⟩ QUICK REFERENCE: IMPORTING A TEXT FILE INTO EXCEL

Task	Procedure
Import a tab delimited or comma delimited text file into an Excel worksheet	■ Display the worksheet in which you wish to import the text file data. ■ Choose Data→Get External Data→From Text from the Ribbon. ■ Navigate to the folder containing the text data file, select the file, and click Import. ■ Follow the instructions in the Text Import Wizard, and then click Finish. ■ In the Import Data dialog box, choose the cell where you wish to begin the data import (or choose New Worksheet). ■ Click Properties and change any desired options to refresh or format data.

Hands-On 17.9   Import Data from a Text File

Jenna, a project editor, uses a program that is not compatible with Excel to create schedule documents. She saved her data as a tab delimited text file and sent it to Deion. In this exercise, you will import Jenna's text file into a worksheet.

Before You Begin: You must have completed Hands-On 17.3 to create the Schedule Tab Delimited file, and the AR Production Schedule workbook should be open.

Import a Text File

1. Display the Editing Schedule worksheet of the AR Production Schedule workbook.

2. If a warning displays, read the warning in the Microsoft Office Excel Security Notice dialog box and click OK to confirm that you trust the website source.

3. Choose Data→Get External Data→From Text from the Ribbon.

4. Navigate to the Lesson 17 folder, if necessary.
   Notice that Files of Type is set to Text Files near the bottom of the dialog box. The Schedule Tab Delimited filename is displayed, but not the Word file that you used previously because its file format is Word Document (.docx).

5. Select the Schedule Tab Delimited text file and click Import.
   The Text Import Wizard dialog box appears. This wizard will guide you through the steps of importing the text file data. In the upper half of the dialog box, notice that Delimited is selected. The wizard always analyzes text files to determine whether they are a specific type of file that can aid the import process.

6. In the preview of the text file in the lower portion of the dialog box, scroll until row 8 is visible.

The preview shows the tab codes between columns of data as small boxes rather than arrows. You want to leave out the blank rows and headings in rows 1 through 7, so you will start the import process with row 8.

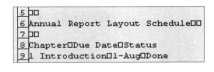

7. In the Start Import at Row box, enter **8** as shown to the right.

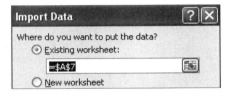

8. Click the Next button.

Step 2 of the wizard displays the next set of options. Since the file to be imported is recognized as tab delimited, Tab has already been chosen for you under Delimiters.

9. Scroll in the Data Preview section to see that text displays correctly in columns.

The text converter places the text following a tab code into the next column.

10. Click Next to continue with step 3 of the wizard.

This step lets you select one or more columns and change their format to text or adjust the date format. You may even exclude selected columns from being imported.

11. Read the description of General format in the upper-right area of the dialog box.

The three columns are formatted in General format. You need not make any changes to the options.

12. Click Finish to display the Import Data dialog box.

The wizard asks you where you want to put the data. You can specify the top-left cell of the range to receive the data.

Specify the Location for the Imported Text

13. Select cell A7 in the Editing Schedule worksheet, and click OK.

The text data appear on the worksheet. Notice that the dates are listed in day/month format, but the year is not displayed. Jenna did not type the year in her original file, so the Import command did not include the year in the conversion.

Format the Text

14. Select the range A7:C7 and add bold and a bottom border.

Your worksheet should look similar to the following illustration.

	A	B	C
6	**Annual Report Editing Schedule**		
7	**Chapter**	**Due Date**	**Status**
8	1 Introduction	1-Aug	Done
9	2 The Year in Review	2-Aug	Done
10	3 Status Report	3-Aug	Done
11	4 Stock Performance	7-Aug	On schedule
12	5 Dividend Performand	8-Aug	On schedule
13	6 Looking Ahead	16-Aug	Late 1 day
14	7 Charts and Tables	17-Aug	Late 2 days

15. Add any other formatting that you think will make the text easier to read.

16. Save 💾 the changes and leave the workbook open.

Importing Data from a Web Page

Many web pages are created using a table structure. The From Web command imports data from a table on a web page. Text and some graphics may be imported from the web page, and you usually must format the text once it is on a worksheet. When you point at a yellow arrow on the web page, a border appears around the table data. Clicking the yellow arrow selects that table area, and you may select more than one area. You may select the entire web page by clicking the arrow at the top-left corner of the web page. A green checkmark identifies a selected area.

Pointing at or clicking an arrow marker... 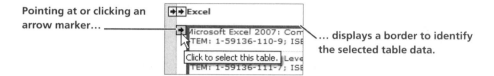 ... displays a border to identify the selected table data.

 TIP! *When importing data, make certain that there are enough blank rows and columns to accommodate the data without interfering with other data already on the worksheet.*

Working with Connections

You may set the data to refresh automatically as you import data using a command from the Get External Data group on the Ribbon. Excel establishes a connection to the external data source, such as a text file or web page. If the source data is updated, you may refresh the connection. It is usually best to refresh one text source at a time rather than use Refresh All because you must identify the file connected to specific text. You may break the link to the external data if you do not need to update to more recent data. The existing data remains in the workbook even though the link is broken.

QR▶

QUICK REFERENCE: IMPORTING WEB PAGE TEXT INTO EXCEL

Task	Procedure
Import some or all text from a web page into an Excel worksheet	■ Display the worksheet in which you wish to import the text file data. ■ Choose Data→Get External Data→From Web 📇 from the Ribbon. ■ Navigate to the web page, click one or more yellow arrows to select text areas on the web page, and click Import. ■ Format the imported text, as needed.
View the current connections to external data	■ Choose Data→Connections→Connections 📇 from the Ribbon. ■ Select the connection name and view properties or change connection options, as desired.
Refresh the connection to external data	■ Choose Data→Connections→Connections 📇 from the Ribbon. ■ Choose the connection name and choose Refresh menu ▼→Refresh.
Remove a connection to external data	■ Choose Data→Connections→Connections 📇 from the Ribbon. ■ Choose the connection name and click Remove. (The link to the data is broken, but the data remains in the worksheet.)

Hands-On 17.10 Import Data from a Web Page

In this exercise, you will add Deion's production schedule to the workbook. Deion had already saved his production schedule worksheet as a web page.

Before You Begin: Your Internet connection should be active.

Import Data

1. Select cell A7 in the Production Schedule worksheet of the AR Production Schedule workbook.

2. Choose Data→Get External Data→From Web 🔲 from the Ribbon.
   In the New Web Query dialog box, Internet Explorer connects with the web.

3. Enter **labpub.com/learn/excel07/** into the address bar and tap ⏎Enter⏎.
   Internet Explorer displays the homepage for your textbook.

4. Click the Production Schedule link on the web page.
   This page displays an Excel worksheet that was saved as a web page without any interactive features.

5. Follow these steps to select the data on the web page:

Ⓐ **Point at the yellow arrow next to the logo image. (The selection border previews only one cell, so do not click to select this item.)**

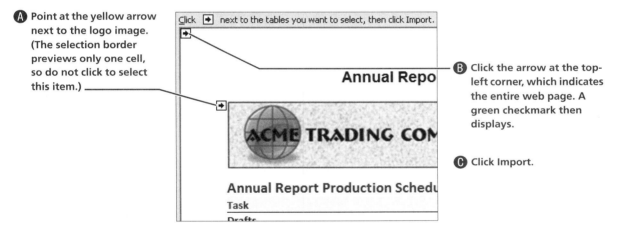

Ⓑ **Click the arrow at the top-left corner, which indicates the entire web page. A green checkmark then displays.**

Ⓒ **Click Import.**

6. If a warning displays, read the warning in the Microsoft Office Excel Security Notice dialog box and click OK to confirm that you trust the web site source.

7. In the Import Data dialog box, verify that cell A7 is selected and click OK.
   Notice that the logo graphic and the text imported from the web page. Some formatting, such as font color and shading, did not transfer with the text.

Clean Up Data

8. Right-click the logo image and choose Size and Properties from the context menu.

9. Under Scale (not Size and Rotate), change the Width to 100% as shown.

10. Close the Size and Properties dialog box.
The original proportion is restored to the logo image.

11. Delete rows 7–14 in the worksheet to remove the duplicate headings and blank rows.

12. Adjust the column widths until the table is similar to the following example. Adjust the formatting of the labels. Add shading if you like.

	A	B	C
6	**Annual Report Production Schedule**		
7	**Task**	**Start Date**	**Due Date**
8	Drafts	16-Jul	27-Jul
9	Editing	30-Jul	17-Aug
10	Layout	2-Aug	24-Aug
11	Proofs	27-Aug	31-Aug
12	Printing	5-Sep	12-Sep
13	Distribution	13-Sep	21-Sep

Check Data Connections

13. Choose Data→Connections→Connections from the Ribbon.

14. Follow these steps to check the connection for the web data:

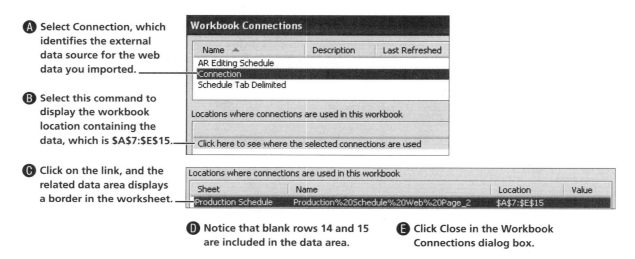

Ⓐ Select Connection, which identifies the external data source for the web data you imported.

Ⓑ Select this command to display the workbook location containing the data, which is $A$7:$E$15.

Ⓒ Click on the link, and the related data area displays a border in the worksheet.

Ⓓ Notice that blank rows 14 and 15 are included in the data area.

Ⓔ Click Close in the Workbook Connections dialog box.

15. Delete rows 14 and 15 in the worksheet.
Checking the connection allowed you to identify the additional blank rows imported from the web page. It is a good idea to remove the blank rows so that they are not in the way of any data you may want to add to the worksheet later.

16. Save the changes and close the workbook.

Concepts Review

True/False Questions

1. You may identify the file format of a workbook by viewing the icon next to the filename.   **TRUE**   FALSE

2. A file saved in Excel 2007 retains all features when the file is opened in an earlier Excel version.   TRUE   **FALSE**

3. You may save Excel workbooks in non-Excel (nonnative) file formats.   **TRUE**   FALSE

4. The tab delimited file format preserves the cell formatting of the Excel worksheet from which it was saved.   TRUE   **FALSE**

5. Users may edit and print PDF documents using a reader program such as Adobe Acrobat Reader.   TRUE   **FALSE**

6. A Word mail merge can produce a set of documents, each containing unique data for one customer listed in an Excel table.   **TRUE**   FALSE

7. An Excel chart embedded in a PowerPoint slide automatically updates when the original Excel workbook is updated.   **TRUE**   FALSE

8. The Copy and Paste commands may be used to import images and charts into a workbook from other programs.   **TRUE**   FALSE

9. Data from a tab delimited text file may be imported into an Excel workbook.   **TRUE**   FALSE

10. Data from a web page may be imported into an Excel workbook.   **TRUE**   FALSE

Multiple Choice Questions

1. Which of the following commands is used in Excel to convert a workbook to another file format?
   a. Convert
   b. Get External Data
   c. Connections
   d. Save As

2. Which file format matches the following data?
   Mr.,Tyrone,Washington,14 Main Street
   a. Tab delimited (.txt)
   b. Comma delimited (.csv)
   c. Portable Document Format (.pdf)
   d. XML Paper Specification (.xps)

3. Which file format includes all formatting in the workbook from which it was saved?
   a. Tab delimited (.txt)
   b. Comma delimited (.csv)
   c. Portable Document Format (.pdf)
   d. All of the above

4. What happens in an Access table when a linked Excel workbook is deleted?
   a. The workbook data still displays and may be edited.
   b. The workbook data still displays but may not be edited.
   c. The workbook data reappears after you reopen the Access database.
   d. The workbook data no longer displays.

 **Skill Builders**

Skill Builder 17.1   Save a Worksheet in Comma Delimited Format

In this exercise, you will save a workbook in a nonnative file format. Then you will open the newly converted file in Excel and Notepad.

Save the Worksheet

1. Open the sb-TyncoLabs Q1 Sales workbook from the Lesson 17 workbook in your file storage location.

2. Choose Office→Save As from the Ribbon.

3. Display the Save As Type list and choose CSV (Comma Delimited).

4. Change the filename to **sb-TyncoLabs Comma Delimited**.

5. Click Save.
   Excel warns you that you may lose some features if you convert the data to this new file format.

6. Choose Yes to continue saving in the new file format.
   Excel saves the worksheet to the new file but continues displaying the normal Excel workbook file. To see the file in its newly converted format, you must open it.

7. Use Ctrl + W to close the workbook and leave Excel open. Choose No when you are asked to save any changes to the file.

Open the Converted File in Excel

8. Choose Office→Open from the Ribbon.
   Notice that the newly converted file is not listed. That's because the conversion changed it from an Excel file to a text file.

9. Display the Files of Type list and choose Text Files.
   Now the converted filename should be visible.

10. Open the sb-TyncoLabs Comma Delimited file.
    Although the layout of data in specific cells is preserved, the table formatting and cell border formatting have been lost.

11. Select cell D5, and then read its data in the Formula Bar.
    Since the entire date is entered, Excel determined that this data should be displayed in Date format.

12. Use Ctrl + W to close the workbook and leave Excel open. Choose No if you are asked to save any changes.

Open the Converted File in Notepad

Now you will open the converted file in a different program. The Notepad applet is a simple text editor program that comes with Windows. It will allow you to view exactly what the data in your converted file looks like.

13. Choose Office→Open from the Ribbon.

14. Right-click the sb-TyncoLabs Comma Delimited filename and choose Open With→Notepad from the context menu.
    You also can use the Start menu to navigate to Notepad and then use the File→Open command.

    Notepad displays the data in the file. Notice the commas that separate data items. Each comma represents a column when you open the file in Excel.

15. Exit Notepad. Choose No if you are asked to save any changes.

16. Cancel Excel's Open dialog box.

Skill Builder 17.2   Import Data from Access

In this exercise, you will bring data into Excel from an Access database table.

Import an Access Database

1. Start a new workbook in Excel and save it as **sb-Shelter Summary** in the Lesson 17 folder.

2. Rename the Sheet1 tab as **Occupancy**.

3. Choose Data→Get External Data→From Access 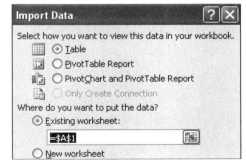 from the Ribbon.

4. In the Select Data Source dialog box, navigate to the Lesson 17 folder in your file storage location.
   Excel displays only Access files in the folder.

5. Choose the sb-Shelter Occupancy database file and click Open.
   Excel displays the three tables in the database file and asks you to select the one to be imported. In this case, you want to import the Year 1 occupancy data.

6. In the Select Table dialog box, choose Shelter Occupancy – Year 1 and click OK.

7. In the Import Data dialog box, make certain that the options appear as shown in the illustration at right and click OK.
   You may view data as a table, PivotTable, or PivotTable with PivotChart. You may place the imported data on the existing worksheet or a new worksheet.

   Your imported database table should look like the following illustration. You set the data to start in cell A1 on the currently displayed worksheet.

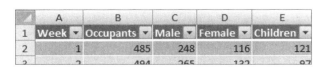

8. Save the changes and leave the workbook open for the next exercise.

Skill Builder 17.3   Import Data from Word

In this exercise, you will bring data into Excel from a Word table.

Before You Begin: The sb-Shelter Summary workbook should be open from Skill Builder 17.2. If your instructor directed you to skip that exercise, start a new workbook and save as sb-Shelter Summary in the Lesson 17 folder.

Import from a Word Document

1. Rename the Sheet2 tab as **Q1 Budget Summary**.

2. Start Word and then open the sb-Quarter 1 Budget document from the Lesson 17 folder.
   You will use the Copy and Paste commands to import data from a Word table.

3. If necessary, scroll down the document and then select the Q1 Budget Summary heading row and all the other rows of the budget table as shown. (Do not include the title Cypress Shelter in the selection.)

Q1 Budget Summary				
	January	February	March	Totals
Mortgage & Insurance	$ 3,779	$ 3,779	$ 3,779	$11,337
Utilities	720	678	623	2,021
Food	1,860	1,900	1,720	5,480
Staff Salaries	5,895	5,895	5,895	17,685
Maintenance & Repairs	325	370	1,493	2,188
Outreach & Fundraising	280	280	260	820
Grand Total	$12,859	$12,902	$13,770	$39,531

4. Choose Home→Clipboard→Copy 📋 from the Ribbon.

5. Close Word. Click No if asked to save any changes.
   The data you copied to the Clipboard remains there even after you close the application from which you made the copy.

6. Select cell A1 in the Q1 Budget Summary worksheet and choose Home→Clipboard→Paste from the Ribbon.
   Excel pastes the heading and table, including the text formatting that was set in the Word document.

Clean Up the Pasted Data

The column widths and row heights may need to be adjusted.

7. Adjust column widths as necessary.

8. Reset the row 1 height to 18.75.

9. Select rows 2 through 11 and reset the row height to 15.00.

10. Select the range B4:E4. Hold down ⌃Ctrl and select the range B11:E11.
    Both ranges are highlighted.

11. Format the selected cells as Accounting format with no decimal places.
Your worksheet should look like the following illustration.

	A	B	C	D	E
1	Q1 Budget Summary				
2					
3		January	February	March	Totals
4	**Mortgage & Insurance**	$ 3,779	$ 3,779	$ 3,779	$ 11,337
5	**Utilities**	720	678	623	2,021
6	**Food**	1,860	1,900	1,720	5,480
7	**Staff Salaries**	5,895	5,895	5,895	17,685
8	**Maintenance & Repairs**	325	370	1,493	2,188
9	**Outreach & Fundraising**	280	280	260	820
10					
11	**Grand Total**	$ 12,859	$ 12,902	$ 13,770	$ 39,531

As you can see, some formatting was necessary after pasting the table from Word. Also, the numbers in the Grand Total row pasted as values, not formulas.

12. Select cell B11 and create a formula that sums the range B4:B9.

13. Copy the formula in cell B11 to the other grand total cells.

14. Save 🖫 the changes and leave the workbook open for the next exercise.

Skill Builder 17.4   Import Data from the Web

In this exercise, you will bring data into Excel from a web page.

Before You Begin: You must have completed Skill Builder 17.3, and the sb-Shelter Summary workbook should be open. Your Internet connection should be active.

Import Data from a Web Page

1. Rename the Sheet3 tab as **Q2 Budget Summary**.

2. Select cell A1 on the Q2 Budget Summary worksheet.

3. Choose Data→Get External Data→From Web 📑 from the Ribbon.
In the New Web Query dialog box, Internet Explorer connects with the web.

4. Enter **labpub.com/learn/excel07/** into the address bar and tap ⌷Enter⌷.
Internet Explorer displays the homepage for this book.

5. Click the Shelter Budget link on the web page.
This page displays a Word document that was saved as a web page.

6. Follow these steps to select the data on the web page:

A Scroll down until the Q2 Budget Summary heading in the table is visible.

B Click the yellow arrow at the upper-left corner of the table to select the table. _____

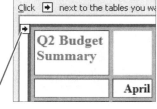

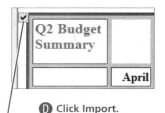

C Notice that the arrow changes to a checkmark, a selection border surrounds the table, and the cell borders change color to indicate that they are selected. _____

D Click Import.

7. Click OK in the Import Data dialog box to place the data at cell A1.

8. If a warning displays, read the warning in the Microsoft Office Excel Security Notice dialog box and click OK to confirm that you trust the website source.
The web data is pasted. Notice that the formatting was not retained from the original source. However, it will be easy to insert blank rows to match the Q1 Budget Summary worksheet and then use the Format Painter to copy its formatting.

Clean Up the Web Data

In the next steps, you will format the Q2 Budget Summary worksheet to match the Q1 Budget Summary worksheet.

9. Right-click the row selector for row 2 at the left of the worksheet and choose Insert from the Ribbon to insert a blank row after row 1.

10. Insert a blank row at row 10 (before the Grand Total row).

11. Select cell B11 and create a formula that sums the range B4:B9.

12. Copy the formula in cell B11 to the other grand total cells.

Copy Worksheet Formatting

13. Display the Q1 Budget Summary worksheet.

14. Click the Select All ▨ button above the upper-left corner of the worksheet and choose Home→Clipboard→Format Painter from the Ribbon.
The Format Painter copies the format from all cells of the worksheet.

15. Display the Q2 Budget Summary worksheet and click the Select All ▨ button.
The formatting is pasted to all cells of the worksheet. Now the two budget worksheets match.

16. Deselect the cells in both worksheets you just used.
It is a good idea to deselect cells to avoid accidental changes and deletions.

17. Save ▨ the changes and leave the workbook open for the next exercise.

Skill Builder 17.5   Check Compatibility and Save a Workbook

In this exercise, you will check a workbook's compatibility with prior Excel versions and then save for a prior version.

Before You Begin: *You must have completed Skill Builder 17.1–Skill Builder 17.4, and the sb-Shelter Summary workbook should be open.*

Run the Compatibility Checker

1. Choose Office→Prepare→Run Compatibility Checker from the Ribbon.
   After a few moments, the Microsoft Office Excel – Compatibility Checker window appears with its report of three issues causing a minor loss of fidelity.

2. Click the Copy to New Sheet button in the lower-right area of the dialog box.

3. Read the report in the new worksheet that appears.
   Two issues relate to the table in the first worksheet, and another general formatting issue is reported with three occurrences. Because these issues are reported as minor, you will not correct them.

4. Save  the workbook with the Compatibility Report worksheet included.

Use Save As

Next you will give the Save As command to save the file for an earlier Excel version.

5. Choose Office→Save As→Excel 97-2003 Workbook from the Ribbon.
   The filename and Save As Type are already filled in.

File name:	sb-Shelter Summary
Save as type:	Excel 97-2003 Workbook

6. Click Save.
   The Compatibility Checker window reappears to report the same issues as it did previously.

7. Click the Continue button to save the file with the issues unresolved.
   This save creates a separate workbook with the Excel 97-2003 file format. If that workbook is opened in Excel 2003, the table in the first worksheet is converted to a normal list and loses its font colors and shading, but the data is not altered.

8. Close the workbook.

 **Assessments**

Assessment 17.1   Save a Worksheet in Tab Delimited File Format

In this exercise, you will save a workbook in a different (nonnative) file format. Then you will open the converted file in Excel and print it.

1. Open the as-Cypress Budget workbook from the Lesson 17 folder in your file storage location.

2. Save the Budget worksheet in a tab delimited file format with the name **as-Cypress Budget Tab Delimited**.
   This step saves the data to a separate file, but the original workbook still appears.

3. Close the workbook and choose No when asked if you want to save changes.
   Remember that the newly converted workbook is a text file.

4. Start a new workbook.

5. Import the as-Cypress Budget Tab Delimited file. Start the import with row 3 of the data (the column headings Q1, Q2 and so on). Use the General column data format for all columns. Import to cell A1 of the worksheet.

6. After completing the import command, adjust column widths, if necessary, to make all text visible.

7. Print the worksheet.
   Your tab delimited data should look like the following illustration.

	A	B	C	D	E	F
1		Q1	Q2	Q3	Q4	Totals
2	Mortgage & Insurance	11,337	11,337	11,337	11,337	45,348
3	Utilities	2,021	1,464	1,504	1,809	6,798
4	Staff Salaries	13,093	17,685	17,685	17,685	66,148
5	Maintenance and Repairs	845	951	3,113	724	5,633
6	Outreach & Fundraising	820	2,006	576	712	4,114
7	Grand Totals	28,116	33,443	34,215	32,267	128,041

8. Save 💾 the workbook with the name **as-Delimited Import** and close the workbook.

Assessment 17.2   Import Data from Another File Format

In this exercise, you will import data into Excel from a comma delimited file and then format the data.

1. Start a new workbook and save it with the name **as-Data Import** in the Lesson 17 folder.

2. Rename the Sheet1 tab as **Imported Data**.

3. Import all the data (including titles) from the as-Comma Delimited Data file in the Lesson 17 folder. In the wizard, choose Comma as the delimiter type and make certain to preview the data. Place the imported data at cell A1 on the Imported Data worksheet.

4. After you complete the import command, set the column widths and add other formatting so that the data is easy to read.

5. Make certain that the totals in the bottom row are formulas.
   Your worksheet may vary slightly from the following illustration.

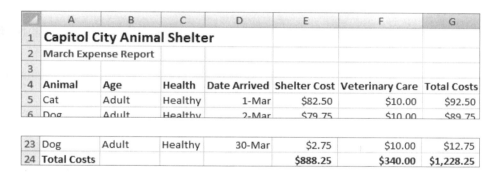

	A	B	C	D	E	F	G
1	**Capitol City Animal Shelter**						
2	March Expense Report						
3							
4	**Animal**	**Age**	**Health**	**Date Arrived**	**Shelter Cost**	**Veterinary Care**	**Total Costs**
5	Cat	Adult	Healthy	1-Mar	$82.50	$10.00	$92.50
6	Dog	Adult	Healthy	2-Mar	$79.75	$10.00	$89.75
23	Dog	Adult	Healthy	30-Mar	$2.75	$10.00	$12.75
24	**Total Costs**				**$888.25**	**$340.00**	**$1,228.25**

6. Save 💾 the changes and close the workbook.

Assessment 17.3 Import Data from Word

In this exercise, you will copy and paste text and an image into Excel from a Word document and then format the data.

1. Start a new workbook and save it with the name **as-Cypress Fiscal Summary** in the Lesson 17 folder.

2. Rename the Sheet1 tab as **Year-End Budget**.

3. Start Word and then open the as-Cypress Year-End Report document from the Lesson 17 folder.

4. Drag and drop the text Year-End Report from the Word document to cell A1 of the Year-End Budget worksheet.

5. Copy the Q1 through Q4 headings, data rows, and the Total row from the Word document. Paste them into an appropriate row of the Excel worksheet.

6. Close the Word document without saving.

7. Format the data in the worksheet, such as column widths and row heights, as necessary to make the data easy to read.

8. Do whatever is necessary to have the Total row contain formulas, not values.
   Your worksheet may vary slightly from the following illustration.

	A	B	C	D	E
1	Year-End Report				
2					
3		Q1	Q2	Q3	Q4
4	Mortgage and Insurance	$6,779	$6,750	$6,750	$6,846
5	Utilities	2,120	1,678	1,728	1,893
6	Food	4,860	4,900	4,720	5,720
7	Staff Salaries	8,695	8,695	8,895	8,895
8	Maintenance and Repairs	3,325	1,370	1,493	1,493
9	Outreach and Fundraising	1,280	1,280	1,260	1,260
10					
11	Total	$27,059	$24,673	$24,846	$26,107

9. Save the changes and close the workbook.

Critical Thinking

Critical Thinking 17.1   Transfer Excel Data to Word

On a Friday afternoon, you get a frantic call from an administrative assistant in the Marketing Department. She is going to use Microsoft Word to perform a mail merge to generate form letters. However, she cannot open the Excel data file containing key client mailing addresses that you sent earlier in the week. Without this data, she cannot enter the names and addresses of clients into the mail merge. Apparently, Word's converter, which interprets Excel data, has become corrupted on her computer. She does not have permission rights to reinstall the necessary converter on her computer. The administrative assistant says that the mailing must go out today and that she needs you to send her the data again via email as soon as possible.

You have 15 minutes to figure out how to get her the data in some other format that she can open in Word.

- Open the ct-Contact Information workbook from the Lesson 17 folder in your file storage location.

- This workbook contains a number of worksheets: ContactInfo, SalesSumm, and a worksheet to be used for each month of the year. ContactInfo contains the data that the marketing department needs (name of the company, address, city, and so on).

- Convert the data to some other format, saving only the Contact Info worksheet with the name **ct-Contact Information – Converted Data**.

- Start Microsoft Word. In a new document, type step-by-step instructions that tell the administrative assistant how to open the file in Word so that she can proceed with the mail merge. Name the Word document **ct-Contact Information - Instructions**. Print the document.

- Using your printed instructions, open the ct-Contact Information – Converted Data file in Word and save it as a Word document with the name **ct-Contact Information - Word**.

When you finish this exercise, you will have four Contact Information files, including two Word files as shown in the following illustration. Evaluate how easy it was to follow your written instructions and how well structured the converted data appeared when you opened it in Word.

- If necessary, edit your procedure in the ct-Contact Information – Instructions file in Word and save again.

- Close any open files.

Critical Thinking 17.2   Import Data from a Word Document

You have created a travel itinerary in Word and saved it as a text file. You decide to import the data from Word into Excel. There are several ways to do so. You will perform the three methods for importing the data from Word into Excel––each on an appropriately named worksheet.

■ Start a new workbook in Excel.

■ Save the workbook as **ct-Data Import Practice (Completed)** in the Lesson 17 folder. This is the destination file.

■ Start Word and open the ct-Travel Itinerary document.

■ Convert the Word document to Plain Text file format. Use the Save As command in Word to make this conversion and name the file **ct-Travel Itinerary Plain Text**. In the File Conversion dialog box, accept the defaults and click OK.

■ Close the ct-Travel Itinerary Plain Text file and leave Word open.

■ Import the plain text file you just created as an external data file into the first worksheet. Adjust column widths, if necessary, and leave the other formatting as is. Rename the worksheet with a descriptive name.

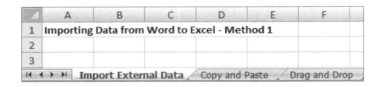

■ Open the original ct-Travel Itinerary document in Word. (Do not open the ct-Travel Itinerary Plain Text file that you converted.)

■ Drag and drop the itinerary from Word into the second worksheet. Adjust the formatting so that all data displays. Rename the worksheet.

■ Notice that dragging and dropping cut the text from the Word document.

■ Use Undo to restore the itinerary in Word.

■ Copy and paste the itinerary from Word into the third worksheet. Adjust the formatting so that all data displays. Rename the worksheet.

■ Save ▣ the changes and close the workbook.

■ At the end of the ct-Travel Itinerary document, write a short paragraph stating which method you found most efficient for the data import task and why.

■ Save ▣ your edited Word document as **ct-Travel Itinerary (Method)**.

Storing Your Exercise Files

This appendix contains an overview for using this book with various file storage media, such as a USB flash drive or hard drive. Detailed instructions for downloading and unzipping the exercise files used with this book appear in exercies for each type of media.

The following topics are addressed in this appendix:

Topic	Description	See Page
Downloading the Student Exercise Files	Retrieving the exercise files and copying them to your file storage location.	686
Using a USB Flash Drive	Storing your work on a USB flash memory drive.	687
Using the Documents Folder	Storing your work in the My Documents folder.	691
Using a Network Folder	Storing your work in a custom folder on a network.	693
Using a Floppy Disk with This Book	Using a floppy disk with this book is not recommended. This topic covers how you can use a floppy with most of the lessons.	694

Downloading the Student Exercise Files

The files needed to complete certain Hands-On, Skill Builder, Assessment, and Critical Thinking exercises are available for download at the Labyrinth website. At the end of each media type topic is an exercise with instructions to copy the files to your computer and prepare them for use with this book.

 NOTE! *It is not possible to store all of the unzipped student exercise files on a floppy disk. See the Using a Floppy Disk with This Book section in this appendix for instructions on using a floppy disk to work with student exercise files.*

Using a USB Flash Drive

NOTE!

Most students using this book store their files on a USB flash drive.

A USB flash drive stores your data on a flash memory chip. You simply plug it in to a USB port on any computer and Windows immediately recognizes it as an additional disk drive. USB flash drives typically can store 256 megabytes (MB) or more. Large capacity USB flash drives can store 1 gigabyte (GB) or more. Flash drive versatility, capacity, and reliability have made them a popular replacement for the role once filled by the ancient (in computer terms) floppy disk.

Win XP

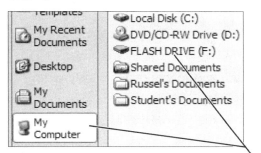

The Word 2007 Open dialog box displays a flash drive in the My Computer view in Windows XP.

Win Vista

The Word 2007 Open dialog box displays a flash drive in the Computer view in Windows Vista.

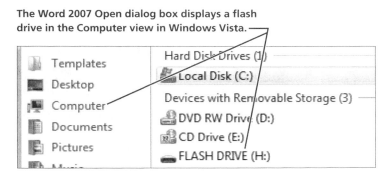

USB Flash Drive Letter

When you plug in a USB flash drive to a Windows computer, Windows automatically assigns it the next available drive letter. Windows uses drive letters to identify each drive connected to the computer. For example, the primary part of the hard drive is always identified as the C drive. A CD/DVD drive is typically the D or E drive. Windows assigns a drive letter to your flash drive when you plug it in. The drive may receive a different drive letter on each computer you use it with.

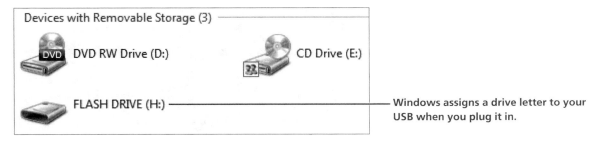

Windows assigns a drive letter to your USB when you plug it in.

Windows lists a USB flash drive as a removable storage device.

TIP! *Your USB flash drive may receive a different drive letter on different computers. This does not affect any files stored on the drive.*

Hands-On A.1   Download and Unzip the Exercise Files— USB Flash Drive

Follow these steps to download a copy of the student files necessary for this book.

1. Launch Internet Explorer.

2. Enter **labpub.com/learn/excel07** in the browser's address bar and tap ⌷Enter⌷.

3. Click the Student Exercise Files link below the Downloads heading.
   A prompt to run or save the student exercise files appears.

4. Click the Save button.
   Internet Explorer asks where you wish to save the downloaded file.

5. Carefully plug your USB flash drive into a USB port on the computer.

6. Click the Close ⌷x⌷ (Win XP) / ⌷x⌷ (Win Vista) button if a window appears asking what you want to do with the plugged-in flash drive.

7. Follow these steps for your version of Windows to choose the flash drive as the save destination:

Win XP

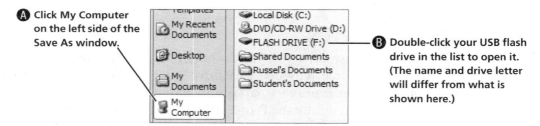

A Click My Computer on the left side of the Save As window.

B Double-click your USB flash drive in the list to open it. (The name and drive letter will differ from what is shown here.)

Win Vista

A Click the Browse Folders button on the lower-left side of the dialog box if it does not display the computer option like the figure for steps B and C.

B Click Computer on the left side of the Save As window.

C If necessary, scroll down the drive list until the flash drive is visible, and then double-click your USB flash drive in the list to open it. (The name and drive letter will differ from what is shown here.)

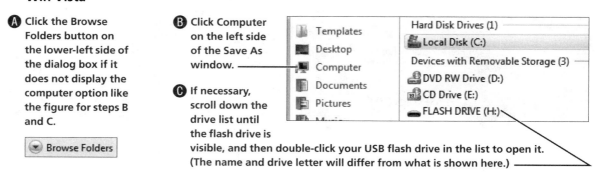

Now that you've shown Windows where to save the file, you are ready to download it.

The rest of the instructions for this exercise apply to both Win XP and Vista.

8. Click the Save button.
After a pause, the exercise file will begin downloading to your computer. Continue with the next step after the download is complete.

NOTE! *If you are downloading the files via a dial-up modem connection, it will take several minutes or more for the download to be completed.*

Unzip the Files

9. Click the Open Folder button on the Download Complete dialog box.

If the Download Complete dialog box closes after the download is completed, you will need to open a folder window to the USB flash drive you used in step 7:

- **Win XP**: Choose Start→My Computer. Double-click to open your USB flash drive.
- **Win Vista**: Choose Start→Computer. Double-click to open your USB flash drive.

10. Double-click the ex07_student_files icon, as shown at right.
Windows may ask if you wish to run the software. This confirmation helps protect your computer from viruses. In this case, you know the file is safe.

11. Choose Run if Windows asks you if you are sure you want to run this software, otherwise continue with step 14.
A prompt appears, telling you where the student exercise files will be unzipped.

12. Click the Unzip button.
The self-extracting archive unzips all of the student exercise files for this book into the new folder. This should take less than one minute to complete.

13. Click OK to acknowledge the successful unzip process.

14. Click the Close button to close the self-extractor window.
All of the files necessary to use this book are now unzipped to your file storage location. They are located in a new folder named Excel 2007 Comprehensive.

Since the zip file is no longer needed, you will delete it in the next step. (You can always download it again if you need fresh copies of the exercise files in the future.)

15. (Optional) Make sure that the ex07_student_files zip file is chosen, and then tap the ⌈Delete⌋ key on the keyboard. Click OK if you are asked to confirm the deletion.

Renaming Your Flash Drive

It may be easier to identify your flash drive on various computer systems if you give it a custom name. For example, you can use your first name, or a generic name such as Flash Drive or Pen Drive. The next exercise shows how you can rename your flash drive on most computer systems.

 NOTE! *Some Windows systems may not give you renaming privileges for drives. This depends on privileges associated with your login name.*

Hands-On A.2   Rename Your USB Flash Drive

You may find it convenient to rename your USB flash drive to make it easier to recognize when you save or open files.

 TIP! *Some Windows systems may not give you renaming privileges for drives.*

1. Plug in the USB flash drive to an available USB port.

2. Click the Close ⌧ / ⌧ button if a window appears asking what you want to do with the plugged-in flash drive.

3. Follow the step for your version of Windows:
   - **Win XP**: Choose Start→My Computer.
   - **Win Vista**: Choose Start→Computer.

4. Right-click your USB flash drive and choose Rename from the context menu.

 NOTE! *In the next step, Windows may display a prompt indicating that you cannot rename this flash drive. You have not done anything wrong! You can use the drive with its current name. You may also want to try renaming it later using a different login.*

If you have renaming rights, Windows highlights the existing name.

5. Type **Flash Drive** (or any other custom name you wish to use) as the new drive name and tap Enter, or click OK if you receive a prompt that you do not have sufficient rights to perform this operation.
   If you were unable to rename the flash drive, don't worry. Renaming the flash drive is a convenience for recognition and has no other effect.

■

Using the Documents Folder

NOTE!

Many computer labs do not allow students to use this folder.

Windows creates a unique Documents folder for each login ID. This folder resides on the main system drive (usually the C drive). The Office 2007 application programs provide a Documents navigation link in their Open and Save As dialog boxes for quick navigation to this folder.

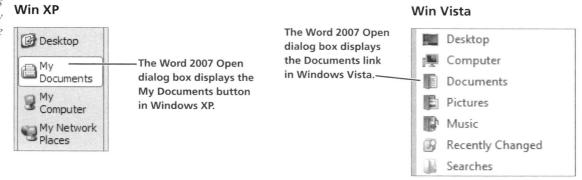

Win XP

The Word 2007 Open dialog box displays the My Documents button in Windows XP.

Win Vista

The Word 2007 Open dialog box displays the Documents link in Windows Vista.

Hands-On A.3   Download and Unzip the Exercise Files— Documents Folder

Follow these steps to download a copy of the student files necessary for this book.

1. Launch Internet Explorer.

2. Enter **labpub.com/learn/excel07** in the browser's address bar and tap [Enter].

3. Click the Student Exercise Files link below the Downloads heading.
   A prompt to run or save the student exercise files appears.

4. Click the Save button.

5. Follow the steps for your version of Windows:
   - **Win XP:** Choose My Documents on the left side of the Save As window.
   - **Win Vista:** If necessary, click the [Browse Folders] button, and then choose Documents on the left side of the Save As window.

   Now that you've shown Windows where to save the file, you are ready to download it.

6. Click the Save button.
   After a pause, the exercise file will begin downloading to your computer. Continue with the next step after the download is complete.

NOTE!   *If you are downloading the files via a dial-up modem connection, it will take several minutes or more for the download to be completed.*

7. Click the Open Folder button on the Download Complete dialog box.

If the Download Complete dialog box closes after the download is completed, follow the step for your version of Windows to open a folder window to the Documents folder you used in step 5.

- **Win XP**: Choose Start→My Documents.
- **Win Vista**: Choose Start→Documents.

8. Double-click the ex07_student_files icon, as shown at right. *Windows may ask if you wish to run the software. This confirmation helps protect your computer from viruses. In this case, you know the file is safe.*

9. Choose Run if Windows asks you if you are sure you want to run this software, otherwise continue with step 10.
A prompt appears, telling you where the student exercise files will be unzipped.

10. Click the Unzip button.
The self-extracting archive unzips all of the student exercise files for this book into the new folder. This should take less than one minute to complete.

11. Click OK to acknowledge the successful unzip process.

12. Click the Close button to close the self-extractor window.
All of the files necessary to use this book are now unzipped to your file storage location. They are located in a new folder named Excel 2007 Comprehensive.

Since the zip file is no longer needed, you will delete it in the next step. (You can always download it again if you need fresh copies of the exercise files in the future.)

13. (Optional) Make sure that the ex07_student_files zip file is chosen, and then tap the Delete key on the keyboard. Click OK if you are asked to confirm the deletion.

Using a Network Folder

You may use a system connected to a network. There may be a folder on a network server computer in another location that is dedicated to storing your work. Usually, you will find this folder within the (Win XP) *My Network Places* or (Win Vista) *Network* folder of your computer. The Office 2007 application programs provide a Network link in their Open and Save As dialog boxes for quick navigation to this folder. You may have to navigate deeper into the folder to locate your personal network drive folder.

Win XP

In Windows XP, the Word 2007 Open dialog box displays the My Network Places button.

Win Vista

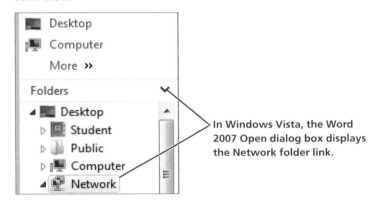

In Windows Vista, the Word 2007 Open dialog box displays the Network folder link.

Hands-On A.4   Download and Unzip the Exercise Files— Network Drive Folder

Follow these steps to download a copy of the student files necessary for this book.

1. Launch Internet Explorer.

2. Enter **labpub.com/learn/excel07** in the browser's address bar and tap ⌨Enter.

3. Click the Student Exercise Files link below the Downloads heading.
   A prompt to run or save the student exercise files appears.

4. Click the Save button.

5. Follow the steps for your version of Windows:

   - **Win XP:** Choose My Network Places on the left side of the Save As window, and then navigate to your network folder.

   - **Win Vista**: Click the menu button as shown at right, and then choose Network. Navigate to your network folder.

   Now that you've shown Windows where to save the file, you are ready to download it.

6. Click the Save button.
   The download begins. Continue with the next step after it is complete.

> **NOTE!** *Downloading the files via a dial-up modem connection will take several minutes.*

7. Click the Open Folder button on the Download Complete dialog box.
   If the Download Complete dialog box closes after the download is completed, you will need to open a folder window to the file storage location you used in step 5.

8. Double-click the ex07_student_files icon, as shown at right. *Windows may ask if you wish to run the software. This confirmation helps protect your computer from viruses. In this case, you know the file is safe.*

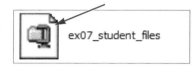

9. Choose Run if Windows asks you if you are sure you want to run this software, otherwise continue with step 10.
   A prompt appears, telling you where the student exercise files will be unzipped.

10. Click the Unzip button.
    The self-extracting archive unzips all of the student exercise files for this book into the new folder. This should take less than one minute to complete.

11. Click OK to acknowledge the successful unzip process.

12. Click the Close button to close the self-extractor window.
    All of the files necessary to use this book are now unzipped to your file storage location. They are located in a new folder named Excel 2007 Comprehensive.

    Since the zip file is no longer needed, you will delete it in the next step. (You can always download it again if you need fresh copies of the exercise files in the future.)

13. (Optional) Make sure that the ex07_student_files zip file is chosen, and then tap the ⌨️Delete key on the keyboard. Click OK if you are asked to confirm the deletion.

Using a Floppy Disk with This Book

It is not recommended that students use floppy disks with this textbook. There are two primary reasons for this:

■ Due to the increasing sophistication of files you can create with programs in the Microsoft Office 2007 Suite, it is no longer practical to store all of the exercise files for this book on a floppy disk.

■ Many computers no longer feature a floppy drive, and this trend should continue as USB flash drives take over the portable file storage role once filled by floppies.

This section describes how to work around the space limitations of floppy disks for most of the lessons in this book.

Storage Limitations of Floppy Disks

As you work through the exercises in this book, you will create numerous new files that must be saved. A floppy disk will not have enough storage capacity to hold all files created during the course. Thus, you must store your exercise files on a hard drive, and then copy and paste (copy) individual lesson folders between this hard drive and the floppy disk. Use the following instructions to work with this book using a floppy disk.

Hands-On A.5   Using a Floppy Disk with This Book

If you have no choice to use the recommended USB flash drive or other file storage location with this book, use the following procedure to work with the lessons using a floppy disk.

1. Following the instructions in Hands-On A.3, download and unzip the student exercise files for this book to a folder on a computer hard drive or other storage location.

2. Open a folder window to the location where you unzipped the files.

3. Select the folder for the next lesson you will study, and then give the Copy command.

4. Open a window to your floppy disk, and then use the Paste command to paste (move) the folder and its files to the floppy disk.

5. Study the lesson, choosing the $3\frac{1}{2}$ Floppy (A) drive then the lesson folder to open and save files as directed in the exercises.

6. After you complete the lesson, *cut* and paste (do not copy and paste) the lesson folder from the floppy disk back to the same location from which you copied it originally.

   Choose Yes to All if Windows asks if you wish to replace any files with the same name in the destination folder.

7. Repeat steps 2–6 for each lesson.

   If Windows tells you the floppy disk is full, check to make sure that you moved (cut and pasted) the folder in step 6. (The previous folder should no longer be on the floppy disk.)

Glossary

3-D cell reference   Address in a formula that refers to the same single cell in adjacent worksheets of the workbook; may be used to sum or average the contents of those cells

Example: *Sheet1:Sheet4!C6*

Adjacent   Arrangement of cells, objects, or files that are next to each other; often may be selected as a group by using Shift; also known as *contiguous*

See also Nonadjacent

Alignment   Horizontal placement of text relative to the left and right margins of a cell or a page, where text is left-, right-, or center-aligned; or, vertical placement of text relative to the top and bottom margins of a cell or page, where text is top-, middle-, or bottom-aligned

Ascending   Sort order in which cells in a column are arranged alphabetically from A to Z, numerically from smallest to largest, or chronologically from earliest to most recent

See also Descending and Sort

Auditing   Reviewing formulas to locate errors

Calculated Field   Column in a worksheet table or PivotTable containing one formula that applies to all cells in the table

Callout   Box or bubble containing an explanation of the item to which it points; used in charts and illustrations

Cells   Rectangles that make up a worksheet; the intersection of a column and row

Change history   Record of changes that were accepted and rejected in a workbook; the Track Changes feature must be switched on to create the change history

Clip art   Images, photographs, sounds, and animated GIFs that can be easily searched and inserted from the Clip Art task pane

Color scheme   Each Document Theme has 12 colors that are applied to text, backgrounds, hyperlinks, and so forth

See also Document theme

Comma delimited   Text file that uses a comma to separate two columns of data; all other text formatting is removed so that data may be imported from an incompatible application

Comments   Notes that can be attached to cells by reviewers

Compatibility Checker   When an Excel 2007 workbook is saved for an earlier Excel version, the Compatibility Checker notifies the user how features specific to Excel 2007 will be handled in the earlier version

Compatibility Pack   Free download from Microsoft which, when installed on a system running an older version of Office, allows the user to open and edit files created in the newer Office 2007 format

Conditional formatting   Formatting applied to cell contents when user-specified criteria are met

Consolidation   Combining values from source worksheets into a destination worksheet by position in the worksheets or by category

Context menu   Menu that appears when you right-click; also known as pop-up menu

Contextual tab   Ribbon tab that appears only when a certain object on the worksheet is selected; for example, the Table→Design contextual tab appears only when a table is selected

See also Tab

Converter   Small program that allows an application program such as Excel to open files that are not in its native file format

Crop   Hiding parts of a picture to make certain other elements stand out or to remove unwanted elements

Data source   In mail merge, the variable data that merges with the main document; controlled by merge fields

Data table   Analysis tool that substitutes various values from a list for either one or two cell references in a formula; the table displays results for each combination of values

Data validation   Procedure that checks the data being entered in a cell against a criterion; a message displays if the data is outside the criterion boundaries

Default   Setting that a computer program assumes you will use unless you specify a different setting

Defined name   Name given to a single cell or range of cells; may be used to navigate the workbook or create formulas

Demote bullet   Demoted bullets are indented to the right; increases the list level

See also Promote bullet

Dependents   Cells containing formulas that refer to the selected cell; the Trace Dependents command draws an arrow from the selected cell to the dependent cells

Descending   Sort order in which cells in a column are arranged alphabetically from Z to A, numerically from largest to smallest, or chronologically from most recent to earliest

See also Ascending and Sort

Dialog box launcher   Appears in some Ribbon groups; opens a dialog box or task pane that contains commands related to the group

Digital certificate   Electronic credential from a trusted source that allows the user to create a digital signature in a document

Digital signature   Means of authenticating the identity of a document's originator; a signed document cannot be modified

Document inspector   Reviews documents for hidden data or personal information that might be stored in the document

Document theme   Preset design consisting of color scheme, text formatting, and placeholder positions

See also Color scheme

Drag and drop   Method for copying and moving text or objects; most useful when copying or moving a short distance within a worksheet or between two documents displayed side by side

Embedded object   Object, such as an Excel chart, inserted or pasted as embedded within a destination document; changes to an embedded object have no effect on the original object

See also Linked object

Field   Column that contains a specific type of data

Example: *First name, last name, city, hourly wage*

File format   Technique for storing information in a computer file; application programs normally have a special file format that they use by default

See also Native file format and Nonnative file format

Filter   Process that hides records that do not meet user-specified criteria

Filter by Selection   Command that displays only the records containing the same data as in the active cell

Footer   Text located within the bottom margin of a worksheet that repeats on all printed pages

See also Header

Format Painter   A tool that allows you to copy formats from a cell or range and apply them to another cell or range

Freezing   Setting rows at the top and/or columns at the left of a worksheet to remain displayed as the worksheet is scrolled

Function   Predefined formula that performs calculations on table cells

Example: *SUM, AVERAGE*

See also Lookup function

Goal Seek   Analysis tool in Excel that calculates the value of one variable cell that is necessary to achieve a specific formula result

Header   Text located within the top margin of a worksheet that repeats on all printed pages

See also Footer

Header row   First row in a table or external data source that contains text labels to describe the data in the columns below those labels

HTML   Hypertext Markup Language; programming language used to create web pages

Hyperlink   Block of text or a graphic that jumps you to another location in a workbook, to another document, or to a web page when clicked

Import   Retrieve data from another file saved in a file format compatible with the destination application

Input message   Message that instructs the user to enter data consistent with the validation rule set for a cell; also known as *validation text*

Intranet   Internal computer network in a company or organization in which users may access shared files and resources, such as printers

Linked object   Object, such as an Excel chart, created in a source file and inserted or pasted in a destination file; the object retains a link to the source file; the destination file can be updated when the source file is modified

See also Embedded object

Linking formula   Cell content beginning with an equals (=) sign that connects to a cell in another area of the same worksheet, a different worksheet, or a different workbook

Live Preview   When pointing at formatting commands on the Ribbon, Live Preview displays how the format would appear on selected text and objects without actually applying the format

Lookup function   Formula component that retrieves a piece of data from a lookup table located somewhere in the same worksheet, a separate worksheet, or a different workbook

See also Function

Macro   Series of frequently used commands that can be grouped together as a single command; used to speed up repetitive tasks

Mail Merge   Feature in Word used to personalize standard letters, envelopes, mailing labels, and other documents by combining a main document with a data source such as an Excel worksheet

See also Merging

Main document   In a mail merge, document that contains the content that remains constant for each recipient; controls the merge with merge fields

Example: *letters, envelopes, mailing labels, forms*

Merge fields   Placeholders in a mail merge main document that instruct Word to insert information from a data source, such as an Excel table or list

Merging   Combining multiple copies of a workbook containing all user changes into a single workbook

See also Mail Merge

Mini toolbar   Contains frequently used formatting commands; appears when you select cells, select text in a cell, or when you right-click on these

Native file format   Default file format used by a program

See also File format and Nonnative file format

Nonadjacent   Arrangement of cells, objects, or files that are not next to each other; often may be selected as a group by using Ctrl; also known as *noncontiguous*

See also Adjacent

Nonnative file format   File format that can be used by a program, but is not the default (native) file format

See also File format

Object   Element shared between documents, such as an Excel spreadsheet or chart

See also Embedded object and Linked object

Office button   Expands to a menu containing commands to open, save, and print files; includes commands to prepare and distribute documents

Open XML   File format used by Office 2007 programs to save documents

Orientation   Direction in which the page is turned for viewing and printing, either portrait (short edge on top) or landscape (long edge on top)

Outline pane   Attached to a SmartArt frame; displays the text content of each graphic element

PDF   Portable Document Format; file format that allows others to view and print a document with all formatting intact even if they do not have the application that created the document

PivotChart   Chart view based on a PivotTable

PivotTable   Table view of row and column data that allows the data to be summarized and compared in multiple ways

Precedents   Cell addresses referenced in a formula; the Trace Precedents command draws arrows from these cells to the formula cell

Print Preview   Feature that allow you to see how a document will look when it is printed

Promote bullet   Promoted bullets are outdented to the left; decreases the list level

See also Demote bullet

Quick Access toolbar   Graphical User Interface (GUI) that contains buttons for frequently used commands; can be customized according to your preference

Record   Collection of data in one row for one person, item, or category

Ribbon   Contains commands that help you perform tasks; organized in tabs that relate to a particular type of activity and groups that contain related commands

Scaling   Enlarging or reducing an object's overall size to a percentage of its original size

Scenario Manager   Analysis tool that creates and saves what-if models with up to 32 variables

Select text   Highlight text by dragging it with the mouse pointer or other techniques; used in preparation for certain tasks, such as formatting or copying text

Shapes   Graphic tools for drawing images in your documents

Example: *arrow, callout, oval, rectangle*

Shared workbook   Workbook set up to track changes that multiple users make; may be distributed to users one at a time or placed on a network server for multiple users to access simultaneously

Smart Tags   Buttons that automatically pop up to provide menus of options that are in context with the task being performed at the time

SmartArt   Predesigned graphic images you can add to a document; categories include List, Hierarchy, Pyramid, and so forth

Solver   Analysis tool in Excel that sets the values of multiple cells used in a formula to produce the desired result that is specified for a target cell

Sort   To arrange data in alphabetic, numeric, or date order

See also Ascending and Descending

Structured reference   Method of indicating the location of a cell or other component within a table; allows formulas to adjust results automatically as rows and columns are added to the table

Example: *JanSales[#This Row]*

Style   Group of formats that allows you to quickly apply multiple formats at once; when a style is modified, all text with the style applied is updated with the modification

Tab   Area on the Ribbon that contains groups of commands, with seven default tabs displayed on the Excel Ribbon; also, a code that sets a specific amount of space between two text items

See also Contextual tab

Tab delimited   Text file that uses a tab code to separate two columns of data; all other text formatting is removed so that data may be imported from an incompatible application

Table   Grouping of worksheet cells that may be sorted, filtered, formatted with a table style, and calculated with structured references

Table styles   Predesigned colors and formatting that can be applied to a table

Template   Preformatted document that acts as a master document that can be used over and over again; can also contain text, graphics, and other objects

Theme   Set of formatting selections that can be applied to a document; includes colors, graphic elements, and fonts all designed to work well together

Title bar   Appears across the top of the Excel window; contains the name of the application (Excel) and the name of the current document

Toggle   Button or setting that switches on when clicked and switches off when clicked again

Track Changes   Feature that, when activated, marks each change to a document; changes can then be reviewed and either accepted or rejected

Trendline   Line that illustrates the direction (increasing or decreasing) of one data series in a chart

Validation rule   Criterion used to limit the type of data or specific value entered into a cell

Views   Varying ways you can look at a document; optimized for specific types of work
Example: *Normal, Page Layout, Page Break Preview*

What-if analysis   Changing the value in one or more cells that are used in a formula to see the various results of the changes

Wizard   Sequence of steps, usually presented in a dialog box, to guide the user in completing a task

XPS   XML Paper Specification; file format that allows others to view and print a document with all formatting intact even if they do not have the application that created the document

Zoom   Command that allows you to view a document in varying levels of magnification

Index

text
   adding to SmartArt, 282
   indenting, 104–105
   line breaks, 107
   long entries in Excel, 17
   rotating in cells, 141–143
   wrapping within cells, 107, 108–109
text boxes, 277, 278
text file formats, 650–653, 668–669
themes, 117–118
thesaurus tool, 155, 156–157
thumb (USB flash) drives, 687–690
time functions, 119
title rows and columns, 240, 241–242, 353, 357
TODAY( ) function, 119
totals
   and linking worksheets, 341, 342
   total row in tables, 388, 390
tracing
   dependents, 524
   errors, 526
   formulas, 522–524
   precedents, 522–523, 526
tracked changes feature, 602–607
translation tool, 155, 157
trendlines, 571–573
two-variable data tables, 567–570

U

Undo and Redo buttons, 46–47
ungrouping worksheets, 550, 551
USB (universal serial bus) flash drives, 687–690
username for comments, 595

V

value axis, charts, 178
values, field, 439, 441
vertical alignment in cells, 141, 142, 143
VLOOKUP function, 513–516

W

Watch Window, 530–531
web pages, importing data from, 670–672
what-if analyses, 78
Windows protection settings, 310
Word, Microsoft, and Excel data in Mail Merge,
   655–659
workbooks/worksheets

(*see also* multiple-sheet workbooks)
3-D references, 510
change history, 604
closing, 24
converting files, 650–655
definition, 8
deleting data, 37
digital certificates, 318–324
disabled features, 609
editing entries, 17, 37, 42–49
emailing, 620–622
entering data, 16–20
grouping, 550–553
managing, 174–176
merging, 614–619, 655–659
navigating in, 8, 10
New Workbook dialog box, 302–303
opening, 36
organizing, 591–592
outlining, 408–410
PivotTables from, 432
printing, 56–58
protecting, 309–317, 616
renaming, 174
saving, 22–24, 449, 452, 644–650
sharing, 601, 608–613, 659–664
Sheet options, 240–243
sheet tabs, 7, 8, 174–176
storing macros, 449
ungrouping, 550
views, 221–226
wrapping text option, 107, 108–109

X

XML (Extensible Markup Language), 645
XPS file format, 653

Z

Zoom feature, 7, 53, 54–55